中国廊桥

CHINA'S COVERED BRIDGES

中国公路学会　主编

人民交通出版社股份有限公司
北　京

图书在版编目（CIP）数据

中国廊桥 / 中国公路学会主编. — 北京：人民交通出版社股份有限公司，2019.12
ISBN 978-7-114-15754-7

Ⅰ.①中… Ⅱ.①中… Ⅲ.①古建筑—桥—介绍—中国 Ⅳ.①K928.78

中国版本图书馆 CIP 数据核字（2019）第 157993 号

书　　名：	中国廊桥
著　作　者：	中国公路学会
责任编辑：	韩亚楠　陈　鹏　郭晓旭　齐黄柏盈
责任校对：	张　贺　赵媛媛
责任印制：	张　凯
出版发行：	人民交通出版社股份有限公司
地　　址：	（100011）北京市朝阳区安定门外外馆斜街 3 号
网　　址：	http://www.ccpress.com.cn
销售电话：	（010）59757973
总 经 销：	人民交通出版社股份有限公司发行部
经　　销：	各地新华书店
印　　刷：	北京印匠彩色印刷有限公司
开　　本：	787×1092　1/6
印　　张：	100
字　　数：	2208 千
版　　次：	2019 年 12 月　第 1 版
印　　次：	2019 年 12 月　第 1 次印刷
书　　号：	ISBN 978-7-114-15754-7
定　　价：	680.00 元

（有印刷、装订质量问题的图书由本公司负责调换）

诗与远方的尽头，有一座美丽的廊桥。

An amazing bridge spanning the river of poems.

《中国廊桥》编委会

主　　　任：翁孟勇
副　主　任：刘文杰　谭　鸿
编　　　委：巨荣云　乔　云　梅　君　王　娜　张征宇　韩亚楠
主　　　编：刘文杰
执行主编：梅　君　王　娜
主创/摄影：吴卫平
总　撰　稿：刘　杰
英文翻译：东　鸿　莫佳玲　屈天舒　葛淏钰　宇　菲　蒋音成
英文校译：沈姗姗　李焕阳　卢晓红
图表制作：曹　晨　贾　非　钟晓波

China's Covered Bridges Committee

Director: Weng Mengyong

Deputy director: Liu Wenjie Tan Hong

Editorial board member: Ju Rongyun Qiao Yun Mei Jun Wang Na Zhang Zhengyu Han Ya'nan

Chief editor: Liu Wenjie

Executive chief editor: Mei Jun Wang Na

Chief creator/photographer: Wu Weiping

Chief writer: Liu Jie

Translator: Abraham Moses Zamcheck Mo Jialing Qu Tianshu Amber Ge Arina Tokareva Jiang Yincheng

Proofreading: Shen Shanshan Li Huanyang Lu Xiaohong

Graphic: Cao Chen Jia Fei Zhong Xiaobo

序言

廊桥是中华民族宝贵的物质文化遗产,具有人文、历史、建筑、科学以及美学艺术价值,也是交通文化和技术瑰宝。

廊桥是中国除寺庙、祠堂、戏台等设施之外,最为重要并常用的公共工程,备受广大百姓的重视和关注。廊桥的结构造型具有鲜明的独创性特点,建筑工艺奇妙、文化内涵丰富、民族和地方特色浓郁,承载了人们审美怀古的精神需求,是人类实现时空跨越最具智慧、最为精彩的创造之一,在世界桥梁发展史上具有重大影响。

中国是廊桥的发源地。据考证,最早的廊桥始建于秦代,汉代有廊桥构件出土,完整廊桥实体为隋代遗存,宋元时期廊桥数量较少,明清两代是中国廊桥大量建造、创新升华、经典定型的黄金时期,遗存量较大。

梳理中国廊桥发展脉络,研究和传承廊桥文化,具有深远的历史和现实意义。中国公路学会非常重视公路文化研究与传承,近年来陆续编辑出版了《中国桥谱》《中国路谱》《桥文化》《路文化》等典籍,积累了丰富的大型文献类图书出版经验。

本书的主创吴卫平先生,是交通运输行业知名摄影家。他从 21 世纪初开始对廊桥进行保护性研究与拍摄,经过近 20 年实地调研考察,拍摄纪录 520 余座廊桥,涵盖全国不同风格的桥型,形成图片资料 5 万余幅,积累了丰富的廊桥研究资料,并依据地域关联性、风格连贯性、民族相融性,梳理出既相互区别又相互影响的六大廊桥遗存带,廊桥研究取得丰硕成果。

在中国公路学会的倡导和组织下,将吴卫平先生拍摄的资料、廊桥研究专家刘杰教授撰写的文字稿,凝聚成这部具有史料价值和艺术价值的专著,作为献给新中国成立 70 周年的礼物,并被列为"新中国成立 70 周年交通运输行业主题出版物",得到国家出版基金资助。

希望更多的有识之士积极投身于廊桥的研究与保护,为世界交通文化发展作出积极的贡献。

全国人大常委会委员、中国公路学会理事长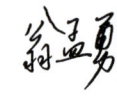

2019 年 9 月

Preface

The covered bridge is a tangible cultural heritage of China with human, historical, architectural, scientific and aesthetic values, as well as a treasure of transportation culture and technology.

The covered bridge is one of the most commonly used public facilities apart from the temple, the ancestral temple and the drama stage. The structure of the covered bridge has distinct features of originality. The ingenious craft, the rich cultural implication and the strong regional characteristics of the covered bridge which has a profound significance in the Bridge's history are the carrier of people's nostalgia and one of the most intelligent and wonderful inventions.

China is the cradle of the covered bridge. According to research, the first covered bridge was built in Qing Dynasty. Some components of the covered bridge in Han Dynasty was found. A complete covered bridge site in Sui Dynasty has been preserved. There were not many in Song and Yuan Dynasty. However, there are a large number which were built, innovated and evolved in Ming and Qing Dynasty and have been well preserved.

The study of the development process and the culture of the covered bridge has a profound historical and practical significance. China Highway and Transportation Society pays special attention to the culture and inheritance of the highway and transportation. We have published *A Guide to Chinese Bridges*, *A Guide to Chinese Roads*, *Bridge Culture*, *Road Culture* and have accumulated experiences publishing literature books.

Mr. Wu Wiping, the chief editor of this book, is a well-known photographer in transportation. He has started the protection and photography for the covered bridge since the beginning of the 21st century. He has taken over 50,000 photos of over 520 covered bridge of various styles in the past twenty years and gathered an abundance of materials for research. He defined the six areas of the covered bridge remains which have distinctions and connections between one another, according to the relevance, the style consistence and the people integration.

With the support and organization from China Highway and Transportation Society, we made the book a gift for the 70th anniversary of the People's Republic of China incorporating the photos taken by Mr. Wu Weiping and the text written by Prof. Liu Jie specialized in the covered bridge study, condensed into this monograph with great historical and artistic value. It is sponsored by the national publication fund.

We hope that more friends with insight will devote to the study and protection of the covered bridge and contribute to the development of the global transportation.

Member of the standing committee of the National People's Congress, President of China Highway and Transportation Society.

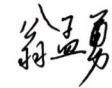

September 2019

概述　六大廊桥遗存带	003

Brief Description: Six Remaining Covered Bridge Belts

第一章　绪论	005

Chapter I　Introduction

第一节・廊桥的起源、类型及分布	007
第二节・简支梁廊桥	010
第三节・伸臂梁廊桥	011
第四节・撑架廊桥	015
第五节・木拱廊桥	018

Section Ⅰ　Origin of Covered Bridges: Types and Geographic Distribution ……… 031

Section Ⅱ　Simply Supported Beam Covered Bridges ……… 036

Section Ⅲ　Cantilever Beam Covered Bridges ……… 038

Section Ⅳ　Bracing Covered Bridges ……… 044

Section Ⅴ　Timber Arch Covered Bridges ……… 048

第二章　华北廊桥遗存带 …… 067

Chapter II　Covered Bridge Belt in North China

第一节・皇家苑囿中的亭桥与廊桥 …… 068

Section I　Pavilion Bridges and Covered Bridges in Royal Gardens

01. 柳桥 …… 068
    Liuqiao Bridge
02. 练桥 …… 070
    Lianqiao Bridge
03. 镜桥 …… 070
    Jingqiao Bridge
04. 豳风桥 …… 071
    Binfeng Bridge
05. 荇桥 …… 073
    Xingqiao Bridge
06. 水榭廊桥 …… 075
    Shuixie Covered Bridge

第二节・庙宇祠观中的飞阁与楼殿桥 …… 076

Section II　Covered Bridges in Temples and Shrines

01. 桥楼殿 …… 076
    Qiaolou Temple

02. 天桥 …… 078
    Tianqiao Bridge
03. 二仙观廊桥 …… 079
    Erxianguan Covered Bridge
04. 峦桥 …… 080
    Luanqiao Bridge
05. 龙王庙桥 …… 082
    Longwangmiao Bridge
06. 仙桥 …… 083
    Xianqiao Bridge

第三节・源泉景观和水利工程中的廊桥 …… 084

Section III　Covered Bridges in Water Projects and Spring Landscapes

01. 分水廊桥 …… 084
    Fenshui Covered Bridge
02. 方亭桥 …… 086
    Fangting Bridge
03. 洪济桥 …… 087
    Hongji Bridge

第三章　西北廊桥遗存带 …… 089

Chapter III　Covered Bridge Belt in Northwest China

第一节・渭水流域的廊桥 …… 090

Section I　Covered Bridges in Weihe River Basin

01. 灞陵桥 …… 090
    Baling Bridge
02. 云龙桥 …… 092
    Yunlong Bridge
03. 小山门桥 …… 093
    Xiaoshanmen Bridge
04. 断涧仙桥 …… 095
    04.Duanjianxian Bridge
05. 鹿仁廊桥 …… 096
    Luren Covered Bridge

第二节・白龙江流域的廊桥 …… 097

Section II　Covered Bridges in Bailong River Basin

01. 中山桥 …… 097
    Zhongshan Bridge
02. 康庄桥 …… 097
    Kangzhuang Bridge
03. 合作化桥 …… 098
    Hezuohua Bridge

第三节·茶马古道上的廊桥 ········· 100
Section III　Covered Bridges along the Ancient Tea Horse Road

01. 窑坪桥 ········· 100
　　Yaoping Bridge
02. 三功桥 ········· 101
　　Sangong Bridge
03. 龙凤桥 ········· 102
　　Longfeng Bridge
04. 古松桥 ········· 103
　　Gusong Bridge
05. 映月桥 ········· 104
　　Yingyue Bridge

第四节·陕南廊桥 ········· 106
Section IV　Covered Bridges in South Shaanxi Province

01. 东河桥 ········· 106
　　Donghe Bridge
02. 西河桥 ········· 107
　　Xihe Bridge

第四章　西南廊桥遗存带 ········· 109
Chapter IV　Covered Bridge Belt in Southwest China

第一节·渝北渝西廊桥 ········· 111
Section I　Covered Bridges in North and West Chongqing

01. 五星桥 ········· 111
　　Wuxing Bridge
02. 锡福桥 ········· 112
　　Xifu Bridge

第二节·渝东南阿蓬江、酉水流域的廊桥 ········· 113
Section II　Covered Bridges in Apeng River and Youshui River Basins in Southeast Chongqing

01. 客寨桥 ········· 113
　　Kezhai Bridge
02. 天生桥 ········· 114
　　Tiansheng Bridge
03. 濯江桥 ········· 116
　　Zhuojiang Bridge
04. 迴龙桥 ········· 117
　　Huilong Bridge
05. 两河风雨桥 ········· 119
　　Lianghefengyu Bridge

第三节·四川省域内的廊桥 ········· 121
Section III　Covered Bridges in Sichuan Province

一、江河纵横　紫色盆地　夺目繁星 ········· 121
I. The Purple Basin with Crossing Rivers Shines under the Twinkling Stars

01. 姊妹桥 ········· 121
　　Zimei Bridges
02. 合益桥 ········· 122
　　Heyi Bridge
03. 太平桥 ········· 123
　　Taiping Bridge
04. 南桥 ········· 124
　　Nanqiao Bridge
05. 安顺廊桥 ········· 126
　　Anshun Covered Bridge
06. 遍能桥 ········· 127
　　Bianneng Bridge

二、山泉终日伴佛灯——峨眉山伏虎寺 ········· 128
II. Fuhu Temple in Emei Mountain, Springs Murmur by the Buddha All Day Long

01. 虎溪桥 ········· 128
　　Huxi Bridge
02. 虎啸桥 ········· 130
　　Huxiao Bridge
03. 虎浴桥 ········· 131
　　Huyu Bridge

三、龙溪畅流——宜宾龙华镇 ········· 133
III. Longxi River at Longhua Town, Yibin

龙华凉桥 ········· 133
Longhualiang Bridge

四、青衣江畔茶马古道东起点——雅安 ········· 135
IV. Ya'an by Qingyi River, the East Starting Point of the Ancient Tea Horse Road

雅州廊桥 ········· 135
Yazhou Covered Bridge

第四节·云南省域内的廊桥 ········· 137
Section IV　Covered Bridges in Yunnan Province

一、大理白族自治州云龙县廊桥 ········· 137
I. Covered Bridges in Yunlong County, Dali Bai Autonomous Prefecture

01. 通京桥 ········· 137
　　Tongjing Bridge
02. 检槽桥 ········· 138
　　Jiancao Bridge

03. 双龙桥 ··· 139
　　Shuanglong Bridge
04. 彩凤桥 ··· 141
　　Caifeng Bridge
05. 永镇桥 ··· 142
　　Yongzhen Bridge
06. 龙潭桥 ··· 143
　　Longtan Bridge

二、龙川江流域的廊桥 ····································· 144
II. Covered Bridges in Longchuan River Basin
01. 高桥 ··· 144
　　Gaoqiao Bridge
02. 太极桥 ··· 145
　　Taiji Bridge
03. 成德桥 ··· 146
　　Chengde Bridge

三、滇东南廊桥 ··· 149
III. Covered Bridges in Southeast Yunnan Province
01. 双龙桥 ··· 149
　　Shuanglong Bridge
02. 保兴桥 ··· 150
　　Baoxing Bridge
03. 乡会桥 ··· 151
　　Xianghui Bridge
04. 天缘桥 ··· 153
　　Tianyuan Bridge

第五章　中南廊桥遗存带 ································· 155
Chapter V　Covered Bridge Belt in South Central China

第一节・鄂东南廊桥 ······································ 156
Section I　Covered Bridges in Southeast Hubei Province

一、鄂南淦河流域廊桥 ····································· 156
I. Covered Bridges in Ganhe River Basin, South Hubei Province
01. 万寿桥 ··· 156
　　Wanshou Bridge
02. 刘家桥 ··· 158
　　Liujia Bridge
03. 白沙桥 ··· 159
　　Baisha Bridge

二、长江中游北岸鄂东门户——黄梅县 ······················ 160
II. Huangmei County, a Portal to East Hubei Province on the North Bank of the Middle Reach of the Yangtze River
01. 灵润桥 ··· 160
　　Lingrun Bridge

02. 飞虹桥 ··· 161
　　Feihong Bridge

第二节・鄂西廊桥 ·· 163
Section II　Covered Bridges in West Hubei Province

鄂西南、湘北——山连水缠 ································· 163
Southwest Hubei Province and North Hunan Province, Rolling Mountains and Intertwined Rivers
01. 永顺桥 ··· 163
　　Yongshun Bridge
02. 深溪河桥 ··· 165
　　Shenxihe Bridge
03. 龙家桥 ··· 166
　　Longjia Bridge
04. 龙山口桥 ··· 167
　　Longshankou Bridge
05. 凉亭桥 ··· 169
　　Liangting Bridge

第三节・黔北黔东廊桥 ··································· 170
Section III　Covered Bridges in North and East Guizhou Province

长寿桥 ··· 170
Changshou Bridge

第四节・黔东南廊桥 ····································· 173
Section IV　Covered Bridges in Southeast Guizhou Province

01. 地坪风雨桥 ·· 173
　　Dipingfengyu Bridge
02. 六约风雨桥 ·· 174
　　Liuyuefengyu Bridge
03. 仁团桥 ··· 175
　　Rentuan Bridge
04. 孟猫花桥 ··· 176
　　Mengmaohua Bridge
05. 牙双花桥 ··· 177
　　Yashuanghua Bridge
06. 守寨桥 ··· 178
　　Shouzhai Bridge
07. 翠谷桥 ··· 180
　　Cuigu Bridge
08. 岑管花桥 ··· 181
　　Cenguanhua Bridge
09. 增盈桥 ··· 182
　　Zengying Bridge
10. 村尾花桥 ··· 183
　　Cunweihua Bridge

11. 金勾风雨桥 ································· 185
　　Jingoufengyu Bridge

第五节·湖南省域内的廊桥 ··············· 186
Section V　Covered Bridges in Hunan Province

一、芷江县㵲水河——三楚第一桥 ·········· 186
I. The Number One Bridge of Hunan Province over Wushui River at Zhijiang County
　　龙津桥 ································· 186
　　Longjin Bridge

二、湘西沱江凤凰城 ······················ 189
II. Fenghuang Ancient Town by the Tuojiang River, West Hunan Province
　　虹桥 ··································· 189
　　Hongqiao Bridge

三、湘西通道侗族自治县坪坦河风雨桥群 ···· 191
III. Fengyu Bridges at Pingtan River, Tongdao Dong Autonomous County, West Hunan Province
　　01. 普修桥 ······························· 191
　　　　Puxiu Bridge
　　02. 迴龙桥 ······························· 192
　　　　Huilong Bridge
　　03. 通坪桥 ······························· 193
　　　　Tongping Bridge
　　04. 普济桥 ······························· 195
　　　　Puji Bridge
　　05. 迴福桥 ······························· 196
　　　　Huifu Bridge
　　06. 永福桥 ······························· 197
　　　　Yongfu Bridge
　　07. 大路桥 ······························· 198
　　　　Dalu Bridge
　　08. 过路桥 ······························· 199
　　　　Guolu Bridge
　　09. 黄土桥 ······························· 199
　　　　Huangtu Bridge

四、湘江、资水、沅水流域的廊桥 ·········· 201
IV. Covered Bridges in Xiangjiang River, Zishui River, Yuanshui River Basins
　　01. 马渡桥 ······························· 201
　　　　Madu Bridge
　　02. 红岩塘桥 ····························· 202
　　　　Hongyantang Bridge
　　03. 永锡桥 ······························· 203
　　　　Yongxi Bridge
　　04. 思贤桥 ······························· 204
　　　　Sixian Bridge

　　05. 燕子桥 ······························· 205
　　　　Yanzi Bridge
　　06. 复古双桥 ····························· 207
　　　　Fugushuang Bridge
　　07. 福星桥 ······························· 208
　　　　Fuxing Bridge
　　08. 晏家桥 ······························· 209
　　　　Yanjia Bridge
　　09. 肖家桥 ······························· 210
　　　　Xiaojia Bridge

五、"入溆浦余儃佪兮，迷不知吾所如"——《涉江》 ···· 212
V. "I Hesitated on Arriving at Xupu River, and not Know Where to Go."—*Shejiang*
　　01. 万寿桥 ······························· 212
　　　　Wanshou Bridge
　　02. 壶圆桥 ······························· 213
　　　　Huyuan Bridge
　　03. 回龙桥 ······························· 215
　　　　Huilong Bridge

六、资江中游　湘中宝地 ·················· 217
VI. The Middle Reaches of Zijiang River, Treasured Land of Hunan Province
　　01. 余庆桥 ······························· 217
　　　　Yuqing Bridge
　　02. 长丰桥 ······························· 218
　　　　Changfeng Bridge
　　03. 广利桥 ······························· 219
　　　　Guangli Bridge
　　04. 木瓜桥 ······························· 221
　　　　Mugua Bridge

七、莽山长乐河——盐铁古道上的廊桥 ······ 222
VII. Changle River and Mangshan Mountain, Covered Bridges along the Ancient Salt Iron Road
　　01. 观音阁桥 ····························· 222
　　　　Guanyinge Bridge
　　02. 广济桥 ······························· 225
　　　　Guangji Bridge

第六节·湘黔桂交界地及广西桂林的廊桥 ····· 226
Section VI　Covered Bridges on the Hunan, Guizhou and Guangxi Borders and in Guilin, Guangxi

一、大江三条——榕江、浔江、苗江廊桥群 ·· 226
I. Three Rivers, Covered Bridges on Rongjiang, Xunjiang and Miaojiang Rivers
　　01. 程阳桥 ······························· 226
　　　　Chengyang Bridge

02. 安济桥 ·········· 228
　　Anji Bridge
03. 赐福桥 ·········· 229
　　Cifu Bridge
04. 华练培风桥 ·········· 230
　　Hualianpeifeng Bridge
05. 巩福桥 ·········· 231
　　Gongfu Bridge

二、中国罕见的立交式风雨桥 ·········· 232
II. The Rare Flyover-Type Fengyu Bridge
　　岜团桥 ·········· 232
　　Batuan Bridge

三、万山环峙　五水分流——龙胜县 ·········· 234
III. Longsheng County, Encompassed by Mountains with Five Rivers Flowing in It
　　孟滩桥 ·········· 234
　　Mengtan Bridge

四、湘江上游　湘桂走廊——全州县 ·········· 236
IV. Quanzhou County, in the Upstream of the Xiangjiang River along the Hunan-Guangxi Corridor
　　01. 广福桥 ·········· 236
　　　　Guangfu Bridge
　　02. 虹饮桥 ·········· 237
　　　　Hongyin Bridge

五、桂林山水甲天下 ·········· 239
V. Guilin, the Most Excellent Landscape under the Heaven
　　花桥 ·········· 239
　　Huaqiao Bridge

六、三省、自治区交界处的潇贺廊桥群 ·········· 241
VI. The Group of Xiaohe Covered Bridges, along Three Provinces or Autonomous Regions' Borders
　　01. 青龙桥 ·········· 241
　　　　Qinglong Bridge
　　02. 迴澜桥 ·········· 242
　　　　Huilan Bridge
　　03. 集贤桥 ·········· 243
　　　　Jixian Bridge
　　04. 钟灵桥 ·········· 245
　　　　04.Zhongling Bridge
　　05. 东辕桥 ·········· 246
　　　　Dongyuan Bridge
　　06. 西门桥 ·········· 247
　　　　Ximen Bridge
　　07. 双溪桥 ·········· 247
　　　　Shuangxi Bridge
　　08. 环涧桥 ·········· 249
　　　　Huanjian Bridge

第六章　东南廊桥遗存带 ·········· 251
Chapter VI　Covered Bridge Belt in Southeast China

第一节·瓯江流域的廊桥 ·········· 252
Section I　Covered Bridges in Oujiang River Basin
　　01. 回龙桥 ·········· 252
　　　　Huilong Bridge
　　02. 熟溪桥 ·········· 254
　　　　Shuxi Bridge
　　03. 西津桥 ·········· 255
　　　　Xijin Bridge
　　04. 仁安桥 ·········· 256
　　　　Ren'an Bridge
　　05. 红军桥 ·········· 258
　　　　Hongjun Bridge
　　06. 宏济桥 ·········· 259
　　　　Hongji Bridge
　　07. 永和桥 ·········· 261
　　　　Yonghe Bridge
　　08. 双溪桥 ·········· 262
　　　　Shuangxi Bridge
　　09. 古溪桥 ·········· 264
　　　　Guxi Bridge
　　10. 林坑桥 ·········· 265
　　　　Linkeng Bridge
　　11. 慕义桥 ·········· 267
　　　　Muyi Bridge

第二节·钱塘江流域的廊桥 ·········· 268
Section II　Covered Bridges in Qiantang River Basin
　　01. 通州桥 ·········· 268
　　　　Tongzhou Bridge
　　02. 席场桥 ·········· 270
　　　　Xichang Bridge
　　03. 湖南亭桥 ·········· 271
　　　　Hunanting Bridge

第三节·甬江流域的廊桥 ·········· 273
Section III　Covered Bridges in Yongjiang River Basin
　　01. 戈场桥 ·········· 273
　　　　Gechang Bridge
　　02. 镇东桥 ·········· 274
　　　　Zhendong Bridge
　　03. 中山桥 ·········· 275
　　　　Zhongshan Bridge

04. 金朱桥 …… 277
　　Jinzhu Bridge
05. 老人桥 …… 278
　　Laoren Bridge
06. 多亭桥 …… 279
　　Duoting Bridge

第四节·长溪流域及其边缘地区的廊桥 …… 280
Section IV　Covered Bridges in Changxi River Basin and Surrounding Areas

一、瓯江发源地庆元县廊桥 …… 280
I. Covered Bridges in Qingyuan County, the Origin of Oujiang River
　　01. 兰溪桥 …… 280
　　　　Lanxi Bridge
　　02. 白云桥 …… 282
　　　　Baiyun Bridge
　　03. 步蟾桥 …… 283
　　　　Buchan Bridge
　　04. 如龙桥 …… 284
　　　　Rulong Bridge
　　05. 五步桥 …… 286
　　　　Wubu Bridge
　　06. 来凤桥 …… 287
　　　　Laifeng Bridge
　　07. 护龙桥 …… 289
　　　　Hulong Bridge
　　08. 查洋桥 …… 290
　　　　Zhayang Bridge
　　09. 双门桥 …… 291
　　　　09.Shuangmen Bridge
　　10. 垄桥 …… 292
　　　　Longqiao Bridge
　　11. 后坑桥 …… 294
　　　　Houkeng Bridge
　　12. 包果桥 …… 295
　　　　Baoguo Bridge
　　13. 黄水长桥 …… 296
　　　　Huangshuichang Bridge

二、众壑闹飞流——景宁县廊桥 …… 299
II. Covered Bridges in Jingning County, Stream Fallen Down in the Valley of the Mountains
　　01. 大赤坑桥 …… 299
　　　　Dachikeng Bridge
　　02. 清风桥 …… 300
　　　　Qingfeng Bridge
　　03. 回龙桥 …… 301
　　　　Huilong Bridge
　　04. 环胜桥 …… 302
　　　　Huansheng Bridge
　　05. 怀胜桥 …… 304
　　　　Huaisheng Bridge
　　06. 护关桥 …… 305
　　　　Huguan Bridge
　　07. 畲桥 …… 307
　　　　Sheqiao Bridge
　　08. 芎岱上桥 …… 308
　　　　Xiongdaishang Bridge
　　09. 芎岱下桥 …… 309
　　　　Xiongdaixia Bridge
　　10. 接龙桥 …… 310
　　　　Jielong Bridge

三、浙江屋脊——泰顺县廊桥 …… 312
III. Covered Bridges in Taishun County, Roof Ridge of Zhejiang Province
　　01. 仙居桥 …… 312
　　　　Xianju Bridge
　　02. 永庆桥 …… 313
　　　　Yongqing Bridge
　　03. 薛宅桥 …… 315
　　　　Xuezhai Bridge
　　04. 北涧桥 …… 317
　　　　Beijian Bridge
　　05. 溪东桥 …… 318
　　　　Xidong Bridge
　　06. 南阳桥 …… 319
　　　　Nanyang Bridge
　　07. 文兴桥 …… 320
　　　　Wenxing Bridge
　　08. 文重桥 …… 322
　　　　Wenchong Bridge
　　09. 登云桥 …… 323
　　　　Dengyun Bridge
　　10. 三条桥 …… 324
　　　　Santiao Bridge
　　11. 刘宅桥 …… 327
　　　　Liuzhai Bridge
　　12. 泰福桥 …… 328
　　　　Taifu Bridge
　　13. 霞光桥 …… 329
　　　　Xiaguang Bridge
　　14. 毓文桥 …… 330
　　　　Yuwen Bridge
　　15. 旗峰桥 …… 333
　　　　Qifeng Bridge

16. 普宾桥 ································· 334
    Pubin Bridge
17. 道均洋桥 ······························· 335
    Daojunyang Bridge
18. 城水桥 ································· 337
    Chengshui Bridge

第五节 · 闽江流域的廊桥 ······················· 338
Section V Covered Bridges in Minjiang River Basin

一、山深溪流十八曲——寿宁县廊桥 ············· 338
I. Covered Bridges in Shouning County, Eighteen Bends of Hills and Streams
01. 飞云桥 ································· 338
    Feiyun Bridge
02. 仙宫桥 ································· 339
    Xiangong Bridge
03. 升平桥 ································· 339
    Shengping Bridge
04. 小东下桥 ······························· 340
    Xiaodongxia Bridge
05. 小东上桥 ······························· 342
    Xiaodongshang Bridge
06. 福寿桥 ································· 343
    Fushou Bridge
07. 大宝桥 ································· 344
    Dabao Bridge
08. 鸾峰桥 ································· 346
    Luanfeng Bridge
09. 杨溪头桥 ······························· 347
    Yangxitou Bridge
10. 升仙桥 ································· 348
    Shengxian Bridge
11. 岭兜桥 ································· 351
    Lingdou Bridge

二、山涧清泉鲤鱼溪——周宁县廊桥 ············· 352
II. Covered Bridges in Zhouning County, Liyu Brook Flowed in the Mountains
01. 观音桥 ································· 352
    Guanyin Bridge
02. 赤岩虹桥 ······························· 354
    Chiyanhong Bridge
03. 金凤桥 ································· 355
    Jinfeng Bridge
04. 三仙桥 ································· 356
    Sanxian Bridge
05. 观音桥 ································· 358
    Guanyin Bridge
06. 院林桥 ································· 359
    Yuanlin Bridge
07. 登龙桥 ································· 361
    Denglong Bridge

三、溪涧纵横交错——柘荣县廊桥 ··············· 362
III. Covered Bridges in Zherong County, Stream Flowed between the Hills Crisscrossing
01. 东源桥 ································· 362
    Dongyuan Bridge
02. 登云桥 ································· 363
    Dengyun Bridge

四、丘陵溪流交汇——政和县廊桥 ··············· 365
IV. Covered Bridges in Zhenghe County, intersection of Hills and Streams
01. 花桥 ··································· 365
    Huaqiao Bridge
02. 水尾桥 ································· 366
    Shuiwei Bridge
03. 雾中桥 ································· 367
    Wuzhong Bridge
04. 矮殿桥 ································· 368
    Aidian Bridge
05. 文泰桥 ································· 370
    Wentai Bridge
06. 洋后桥 ································· 371
    Yanghou Bridge

五、白水洋鸳鸯溪——屏南县廊桥 ··············· 372
V. Covered Bridges in Pingnan County, with Baishui River and Yuanyang Brook
01. 百祥桥 ································· 372
    Baixiang Bridge
02. 千乘桥 ································· 374
    Qiansheng Bridge
03. 金造桥 ································· 375
    Jinzao Bridge
04. 万安桥 ································· 376
    Wan'an Bridge
05. 庵前桥 ································· 378
    Anqian Bridge
06. 龙井桥 ································· 378
    Longjing Bridge
07. 迎风桥 ································· 379
    Yingfeng Bridge
08. 龙津桥 ································· 381
    Longjin Bridge

六、岩茶故乡——武夷山九曲溪廊桥 ············· 383
VI. Covered Bridges on Jiuqu Stream in Wuyi Mountain, Home of the Rock Tea

01. 扣冰桥 ……………………………………… 383
   Koubing Bridge
02. 遇仙桥 ……………………………………… 384
   Yuxian Bridge
03. 馀庆桥 ……………………………………… 385
   Yuqing Bridge

七、钱塘江水系与闽江分水岭——浦城县廊桥 …… 387
VII. Covered Bridges in Pucheng County, the Divide between Qiantang River System and Minjiang River
01. 镇安桥 ……………………………………… 387
   Zhen'an Bridge
02. 乐丰桥 ……………………………………… 388
   Lefeng Bridge
03. 青龙桥 ……………………………………… 389
   Qinglong Bridge
04. 观音桥 ……………………………………… 391
   Guanyin Bridge

八、百里松荫碧长溪——松溪县廊桥 …………… 392
VIII. Covered Bridges in Songxi County, Green Streams with the Shadow of Pine-trees on Bath Sides
01. 花桥 ………………………………………… 392
   Huaqiao Bridge
02. 马登桥 ……………………………………… 394
   Madeng Bridge
03. 家坛桥 ……………………………………… 395
   Jiatan Bridge
04. 五福桥 ……………………………………… 397
   Wufu Bridge

九、武夷山北段、富屯溪上游——光泽县廊桥 …… 398
IX. Covered Bridges in Guangze County, North of Wuyi Mountain, Upstream of Futun stream
   承安桥 ……………………………………… 398
   Cheng'an Bridge

十、闽北—闽江建溪水系全域发育——建瓯市廊桥 … 400
X. Covered Bridges in Jian'ou, along Jianxi River System of Minjiang River Basin in North Fujian Province
01. 腾云桥 ……………………………………… 400
   Tengyun Bridge
02. 普通桥 ……………………………………… 401
   Putong Bridge
03. 后建桥 ……………………………………… 402
   Houjian Bridge
04. 上桥 ………………………………………… 404
   Shangqiao Bridge
05. 登云桥 ……………………………………… 405
   Dengyun Bridge
06. 钱仓桥 ……………………………………… 405
   Qiancang Bridge
07. 值庆桥 ……………………………………… 406
   Zhiqing Bridge
08. 接龙桥 ……………………………………… 407
   Jielong Bridge
09. 德胜桥 ……………………………………… 408
   Desheng Bridge
10. 仙恩桥 ……………………………………… 409
   Xian'en Bridge
11. 集瑞桥 ……………………………………… 410
   Jirui Bridge
12. 兴龙桥 ……………………………………… 411
   Xinglong Bridge
13. 步月桥 ……………………………………… 413
   Buyue Bridge

十一、源短流急暴涨暴落——南平市廊桥 ………… 414
XI. Covered Bridges in Nanping, Turbulent River with Rising and Falling
01. 种善桥 ……………………………………… 414
   Zhongshan Bridge
02. 高地桥 ……………………………………… 416
   Gaodi Bridge
03. 瑞龙桥 ……………………………………… 417
   Ruilong Bridge

十二、鳌江不犯闽江——古田县廊桥 ……………… 418
XII. Covered Bridges in Gutian County, Where Aojiang River doesn't Inflooded into Minjiang River
01. 沉字桥 ……………………………………… 418
   Chenzi Bridge
02. 田地桥 ……………………………………… 419
   Tiandi Bridge

十三、降雨分四季——闽东闽侯县廊桥 …………… 421
XIII. Covered Bridges in Minhou County, East Fujian Province, Rain Fallen in Four Seasons
01. 塘里桥 ……………………………………… 421
   Tangli Bridge
02. 坑坪桥 ……………………………………… 422
   Kengping Bridge
03. 岭下桥 ……………………………………… 423
   Lingxia Bridge
04. 三溪桥 ……………………………………… 425
   Sanxi Bridge
05. 泰山桥 ……………………………………… 427
   Taishan Bridge

十四、串珠状河谷盆地——连城县廊桥 …………… 428
XIV. Covered Bridges in Liancheng County, Where Basin Valleys Linked like a String of Beads
01. 玉沙桥 ……………………………………… 428
   Yusha Bridge

02. 永隆桥 ··· 429
　　Yonglong Bridge
03. 云龙桥 ··· 431
　　Yunlong Bridge

十五、源溪流呈树枝状分布——上杭县廊桥 ··· 433
XV. Covered Bridges in Shanghang County, Where Streams Distribute as Branches
01. 振兴桥 ··· 433
　　Zhenxing Bridge
02. 天后宫桥 ··· 434
　　Tianhougong Bridge
03. 镇隆桥 ··· 435
　　Zhenlong Bridge

十六、溪河短小湍急——宁化县廊桥 ··· 436
XVI. Covered Bridges in Ninghua County, with Short and Turbulent Streams
01. 神仙桥 ··· 436
　　Shenxian Bridge
02. 万荷桥 ··· 437
　　Wanhe Bridge
03. 蛟潭桥 ··· 438
　　Jiaotan Bridge

十七、山地切割强烈——永安市廊桥 ··· 441
XVII. Covered Bridges in Yong'an, with Intensely Cutting Mountain Area
01. 安仁桥 ··· 441
　　An'ren Bridge
02. 福兴桥 ··· 442
　　Fuxing Bridge
03. 永宁桥 ··· 443
　　Yongning Bridge
04. 会清桥 ··· 444
　　Huiqing Bridge

十八、闽江支流沙溪贯穿——沙县、大田县、泰宁县廊桥 ··· 446
XVIII. Covered Bridges in Shaxian County, Datian County and Taining County, with Shaxi Brook, Tributaries of Minjiang River Flowing through
01. 进谷桥 ··· 446
　　Jingu Bridge
02. 流泗桥 ··· 447
　　Liusi Bridge
03. 仁寿桥 ··· 449
　　Renshou Bridge

十九、山多水足，闽中宝库——德化、安溪、仙游、永定、永春县廊桥 ··· 450
XIX. Covered Bridges in Dehua County, Anxi County, Xianyou County, Yongding County and Yongchun County, Fujian's Treasury with Abundant Mountains and Water

01. 铭新桥 ··· 450
　　Mingxin Bridge
02. 济美桥 ··· 452
　　Jimei Bridge
03. 湖山桥 ··· 453
　　Hushan Bridge
04. 广济桥 ··· 455
　　Guangji Bridge
05. 登龙桥 ··· 456
　　Denglong Bridge
06. 宴林口桥 ··· 457
　　Yanlinkou Bridge
07. 天竺桥 ··· 458
　　Tianzhu Bridge
08. 瑞云桥 ··· 459
　　Ruiyun Bridge
09. 济行桥 ··· 460
　　Jixing Bridge
10. 通仙桥 ··· 462
　　Tongxian Bridge

二十、闽江源头——尤溪县廊桥 ··· 465
XX. Covered Bridges in Youxi County, the Origin of Minjiang River
01. 新坑桥 ··· 465
　　Xinkeng Bridge
02. 水尾桥 ··· 466
　　Shuiwei Bridge
03. 岐坑桥 ··· 467
　　Qikeng Bridge
04. 见龙桥 ··· 469
　　Jianlong Bridge

第七章　江南廊桥遗存带 ··· 471
Chapter VII　Covered Bridges in Jiangnan

第一节·皖赣廊桥 ··· 473
Section I　Covered Bridges in Anhui Province and Jiangxi Province

一、新安江水系徽派廊桥群 ··· 473
I. Anhui-style Covered Bridges in Xin'an River System
01. 北岸桥 ··· 473
　　Bei'an Bridge
02. 拱北桥 ··· 474
　　Gongbei Bridge
03. 三棵树桥 ··· 475
　　Sankeshu Bridge
04. 高阳桥 ··· 476
　　Gaoyang Bridge

05. 桃源桥 ························· 478
Taoyuan Bridge
06. 乐寿桥 ························· 479
Leshou Bridge
07. 唐模高阳桥 ··················· 480
Tangmogaoyang Bridge
08. 环秀桥 ························· 480
Huanxiu Bridge
09. 虹桥 ···························· 481
Hongqiao Bridge
10. 云溪桥 ························· 483
Yunxi Bridge

二、龙山湖水之侧——太湖县廊桥 ········· 484
II. Covered Bridge in Taihu County by Longshan Mountain and Taihu Lake
龙门桥 ···························· 484
Longmen Bridge

三、婺江之源——泛徽派廊桥群 ·········· 486
III. The Group of Anhui-style Covered Bridges at the Origin of Wujiang River
01. 通济桥 ························· 486
Tongji Bridge
02. 韩家庄桥 ······················ 488
Hanjiazhuang Bridge
03. 上庙桥 ························· 489
Shangmiao Bridge
04. 上大夫桥 ······················ 490
Shangdafu Bridge
05. 水口虹桥 ······················ 492
Shuikouhong Bridge
06. 题注桥 ························· 493
Tizhu Bridge
07. 霞港桥 ························· 495
Xiagang Bridge
08. 贾耕桥 ························· 496
Gugeng Bridge
09. 麟清桥 ························· 497
Linqing Bridge
10. 彩虹桥 ························· 498
Caihong Bridge
11. 庆远桥 ························· 500
Qingyuan Bridge
12. 龙岗桥 ························· 500
Longgang Bridge
13. 罗溪桥 ························· 501
Luoxi Bridge

14. 护禾桥 ························· 501
Huhe Bridge
15. 梅岭桥 ························· 502
Meiling Bridge
16. 登云桥 ························· 504
Dengyun Bridge
17. 富春桥 ························· 505
Fuchun Bridge

四、赣江水系廊桥群 ·························· 506
IV. Covered Bridges in Ganjiang River System
01. 花桥 ···························· 506
Huaqiao Bridge
02. 善述桥 ························· 507
Shanshu Bridge
03. 三川桥 ························· 509
Sanchuan Bridge
04. 横港桥 ························· 510
Henggang Bridge
05. 新丰桥 ························· 511
Xinfeng Bridge
06. 澄波桥 ························· 513
Chengbo Bridge
07. 登仙桥 ························· 514
Dengxian Bridge
08. 永宁桥 ························· 515
Yongning Bridge
09. 万寿桥 ························· 517
Wanshou Bridge
10. 玉带桥 ························· 519
Yudai Bridge
11. 永镇桥 ························· 520
Yongzhen Bridge
12. 永安桥 ························· 521
Yong'an Bridge
13. 初石桥 ························· 523
Chushi Bridge
14. 太平桥 ························· 524
Taiping Bridge

第二节·江苏省、上海市、浙江省北部 ········ 527
Section II Covered Bridges in Jiangsu Province, Shanghai, and North Zhejiang Province

一、大运河水系廊桥群 ···················· 527
I. Covered Bridges in Grand Canal River System
01. 五亭桥 ························· 527
Wuting Bridge

02. 小飞虹桥 ······ 528
　　Xiaofeihong Bridge
03. 永丰桥 ······ 528
　　Yongfeng Bridge
04. 三亭桥 ······ 529
　　Santing Bridge
05. 古荷桥 ······ 530
　　Guhe Bridge
06. 怀古桥 ······ 532
　　Huaigu Bridge
07. 镇东桥 ······ 533
　　Zhendong Bridge
08. 镇西桥 ······ 535
　　Zhenxi Bridge
09. 惠民桥 ······ 537
　　Huimin Bridge
10. 坝子桥 ······ 538
　　Bazi Bridge
11. 晴雨亭桥 ······ 539
　　Qingyuting Bridge
12. 玉带桥 ······ 541
　　Yudai Bridge
13. 云溪桥 ······ 542
　　Yunxi Bridge
14. 逢源双桥 ······ 543
　　Fengyuanshuang Bridge
15. 送子来凤桥 ······ 544
　　Songzilaifeng Bridge
16. 雨读桥 ······ 545
　　Yudu Bridge

二、甬江水系廊桥群 ······ 546
II. Covered Bridges in Yongjiang River System
01. 普济桥 ······ 546
　　Puji Bridge
02. 洞桥 ······ 547
　　Dongqiao Bridge
03. 百梁桥 ······ 548
　　Bailiang Bridge
04. 万安桥 ······ 550
　　Wan'an Bridge
05. 广济桥 ······ 551
　　Guangji Bridge
06. 毓秀桥 ······ 552
　　Yuxiu Bridge

07. 长安桥 ······ 554
　　Chang'an Bridge
08. 关爷殿桥 ······ 555
　　Guanyedian Bridge
09. 卧波桥 ······ 557
　　Wobo Bridge

第八章　其他地区遗存的廊桥 ······ 559
Chapter VIII　Covered Bridges in Other Areas

第一节·雪域高原廊桥遗存 ······ 561
Section I　Covered Bridges on the Tibetan Plateau

01. 波日桥 ······ 561
　　Bori Bridge
02. 琉璃桥 ······ 563
　　Liuli Bridge

第二节·岭南地区廊桥遗存 ······ 564
Section II　Covered Bridges in the Lingnan Region

一、潮州市母亲河，韩江上的巨星——世界首座开合式、国内最长廊桥 ······ 564
I. The First Folding Bridge in the World and the Longest Covered Bridge in China, as the Superstar across Hanjiang River, the Mother River of Chaozhou
　　广济桥 ······ 564
　　Guangji Bridge
二、余荫山房廊桥 ······ 566
II. Covered Bridge in Yuyin Ancestral Garden
　　余荫桥 ······ 566
　　Yuyin Bridge
三、"石头、木头、水头"资源大县——封开 ······ 567
III. Covered Bridge in Fengkai County, with Rich Stone, Wood and Water Resources
　　泰新桥 ······ 567
　　Taixin Bridge

附录　中英文词汇对照表 ······ 568
Appendix　Comparison Table of Chinese and English Vocabulary

后记 ······ 570
Postscript

中国
廊桥

Brief Description: Six Remaining Covered Bridge Belts

This book is mainly focused on distinguishing different covered bridges belts by the cultural differences. In the same architectural culture, there is a considerable amount of similarities in the structure and appearance of the bridges. The core factors to form the architectural style of the covered bridge are not only the geographical connection of river systems or mountain barriers, but also the common characteristics of the formation of the living areas of the specific ethnic groups.

The drainage area has a great influence on the technology of the bridge construction. In ancient times, people lived along the river. Within the one river system, it is easy to form similar architectural culture. Different river systems are often blocked by high watersheds, which form communication barriers or even uninhabited regions.

However, there are some cross-basin phenomena occurring in some covered bridge areas, such as Dongzu (Dong Nationality) Covered Bridge, which belongs to the Yangtze and the Zhujiang River Basins at the junction of Hunan, Guangxi and Guizhou provinces in the Dong minority region. Yaozu (Yao Nationality) Covered Bridge also has the same phenomenon. The watershed of the Yangtze River and the Zhujiang River Basin is low and gentle in Xiaohe area, and the living area of Yao nationality distributes across the mountains. The Yaozu Covered Bridge on both sides of the watershed has the similar features.

According to the regional architectural culture, we divide Chinese covered bridges into six main bridge belts: Southeast Covered Bridge belt, Jiangnan Covered Bridge belt (the territory to the south from Yangtze River), South-central Covered Bridge belt, Northwest Covered Bridge belt, Southwest Covered Bridge belt and North China Covered Bridge belt.

中国廊桥

概述

六大廊桥遗存带

本书主要以廊桥建筑文化差异来区分不同的廊桥带。在一建筑文化带内,廊桥的结构和外观仍然有许多共性,形成廊桥建筑文化的核心因素。既有地理上的水系连通或山脉阻隔,也有特定族群生活区域或其同传统流域对廊桥来影响巨大,古时百姓沿河而居;在水系之间,容易形成相近的建筑文化,不同水系之间往往被高大的分水岭阻隔,形成交流障碍得其奏若无人区,但有些廊桥跨越分水岭出现跨流域现象,比如侗族廊桥,在湘桂黔交界的三省坡两侧的侗族地区(分别属上长江流域和珠江流域)瑶族廊桥也有同样现象,长江和珠江流域的分水岭往满贺地区,两侧的瑶族廊桥广为流行。我们对中国廊桥划分为六个主要廊桥带:东南廊桥带、江南廊桥带、中南廊桥带、西南廊桥带和华北廊桥带。

Chapter I Introduction

China's territory is vast. Its history ancient, and architectural heritage and culture are rich and spectacular. So to the country's bridge architecture. China's bridge construction is highly diverse with amazing structural forms. Up to now many famous bridges exist in the country that have earned praise in past and present and in China and abroad. And out of all the sorts of ancient bridges created in China's past, covered bridges (*langqiao*), come closest to the architectural form represented by the set of architecture that includes common dwelling, temples and palaces. Covered bridges are also referred to as house bridges (*wuqiao*) and woven beam arch bridges (*cuoqiao*). In minority areas in the southwest, they are also referred to as Wind and rain bridges (*fengyuqiao*) and flower pridges (*huaqiao*). Simply, covered bridges are a type of bridge architecture that support a covered house. The architecture of Chinese covered bridges is not less advanced than that of common dwellings. Their forms are rich and diverse, their spatial combinations complex and mutable. It's no doubt that, compared with other forms of bridges, the architectural space of China's covered bridges is richer, their structure more complicated, and their artistic qualities greater.

中国廊桥

第一章 绪论

我国幅员辽阔，历史悠久，建筑文化遗存非常丰富和精彩，桥梁建筑亦是如此。桥梁建筑不但类型多样，且构造巧妙，至今留下不少为古今中外所推崇的名桥。如果以建筑形式而论，在中国古代创造出的各式桥梁中，有一类与普通的房屋建筑甚至宫殿和庙宇形式最为接近的，那便是廊桥。廊桥，亦称屋桥、厝桥，在西南地区也叫风雨桥或花桥。简言之，廊桥就是桥上架设了廊屋的一种桥梁建筑类型。由于廊屋实际上与普通的房屋并无二致，因此其建筑造型就更加丰富多彩，空间组合亦是复杂多变。毋庸置疑的是，与其他类型的桥梁形式相比，廊桥的建筑空间更丰富，结构更复杂，也更具艺术性。

本项研究受国家重点研发计划"绿色生态木竹结构体系研究及示范应用"项目资助,课题名称:大跨木结构体系研究及工程示范,课题编号:2017YFC0703506。

本项研究受国家自然科学基金面上项目资助,项目名称:中国古代木构桥梁的发展与演变研究,项目编号:51478259。

第一节　廊桥的起源、类型及分布

一、廊桥的起源

廊桥起源很早，先秦时期宫殿或苑囿中出现的阁道或复道，就是运用廊桥建筑技术营造而成的。十多年来，笔者就在不同的场合与出版物中反复强调，廊桥、阁道或称复道，都是干阑建筑的一个类型或一种形式[1]。从本质上讲，在中国上古时代以来广泛分布的干阑建筑中，就孕育着廊桥这一建筑类型。换句话说，它与普通房屋建筑同出一脉、同宗同源。但有趣的是，廊桥这个复合名词在历史上的出现，却是很晚的事。

20世纪40年代，著名建筑史学家刘敦桢先生在考察其家乡湖南新宁江口木桥后撰写的一篇文章《中国之廊桥》中，才首次将这种桥上架设廊屋的建筑形式称之为"廊桥"。当然，把它命名为廊桥——这一非常具有文学性的名字，又与中国唐代大诗人白居易的文章《修香山寺记》有关。刘敦桢先生正是根据白文中"登寺桥一所，联桥廊七间"之词句，"今秉斯旨，暂以'廊桥'二字撰述此文，或与桥之外形结构较为接近"，故名之为"廊桥"[2]。

有学者将廊桥和先秦到两汉时期流行的阁道相联系，认为廊桥的技术源于阁道。其实，根据对中国南方地区古代木作技术源流的研究，廊桥建造技术与阁道技术并不存在发展的先后顺序问题，它们都源于史前南方地区广泛存在的干阑（也有学者写为"干栏"）建筑技术。阁道一词也极有可能源自干阑。因为"干阑"只是一注音符号，是表音文字，并无任何意义，在南方少数民族地区大多称之为"阁阑""葛栏""麻栏"等。因此，笔者认为廊桥与阁道这两种建造技术应当是并行发展起来的，它们都应源于新石器晚期江南地区颇为流行的干阑长屋[3]。

廊桥与阁道，在古代有的文献中习惯称之为"桥阁"。如《宋史·五行志》载有南宋绍熙二年（1191年）四川嘉陵江洪水一事："七月癸亥，嘉陵江爆溢，兴州圯城门、郡狱、官舍凡十七所，漂民居三千四百九十余，潼川、崇庆府、绵、果、合、金、龙、汉州、怀安、石泉、大安军、鱼关皆水。时上流西蕃界古松州江水爆溢，龙州败桥阁五百余区，江油县溺死者众。"[4]

事实上，刘敦桢先生也早就注意到这一点。他不仅注意到阁道与廊桥存在着内在联系，甚至认定，阁道与廊桥是同时产生的。为此，他在《中国之廊桥》一文中说：

"惟木梁之上加构廊屋，则不知始于何时。以义度之，殆与阁道之产生，前后同时。……西汉长安诸殿，著录于李好问《长安图志》者，胥截山为基，渺若仙居，台殿之间，则联以阁道，窈窕相通；其巨者，且自未央，跨逾长安西墉，以达建章。而阁道咸以木构，有室有窗，方之廊桥，名谓虽殊，而用途结构，似无二致。故廊桥之诞生，或在西汉以前，春秋战国之际。"[2]这段文字的主要意思有三层：其一，阁道与廊桥都有廊道；其二，两者结构相近；其三，二者都具有作为交通联系的相同用途。因此，刘先生讲阁道与廊桥"名谓虽殊"，实质上"似无二致"。

先秦至两汉的古籍文献中，虽无"廊桥"一词，仔细研读，从中多少可以搜寻到一些反映廊桥的文字。比如，在古文献中汉代的桥与阁道，都以"间"作为唯一的计量单位。换句话说，这一时期几乎所有文献都是以"间"为单位，计量桥梁规模。这里的"间"，极可能指的是桥面上廊屋的间数。时至今日，浙西南、闽东北等有廊桥遗存的地区，仍然以廊屋的"间数"为单位来计量桥梁规模，可做民俗学的佐证。

西汉长安灞桥建成之初，就是一座标准的廊桥。据《水经注·渭水》记载："霸水又北经枳道，在长安县东十三里。王莽九庙在其南。……自东都门过枳道……水上有桥，谓之霸桥。"[5] 由此得知，灞桥是通往长安枳道上的桥梁。从当时重要阁道"周行数里，仰不见日"[6]看，该桥设有廊屋。灞桥于王莽时期失火被焚，据《汉书·王莽传下》："二月癸巳之夜，甲午之辰，火烧霸桥，从东方西行，直至甲午夕，桥尽火灭。……或云寒民会居桥下，疑以火自燎，为此灾也。"[7] 刘敦桢先生在《石轴柱桥述要》一文中谈及灞桥火灾，也认为："（灞桥）石构桥身之上，必更有木造之桥屋，故焚烧尽一昼夜，史籍以灾称也。"[8]

桥上架设廊屋，表面上看是一个建筑形式（或"艺术形象"）的问题，但实际上对于早期的木构桥梁而言，还有一个加强结构与维护耐久的问题。后者在生产力和科学技术都不甚发达的古代于桥梁而言更为紧要。"廊屋"之于木构桥梁至少有三重功能：

第一，可供路人避风雨、行休憩之用；

第二，还具有保护木构桥身之需；

第三，更为重要的是增加了木结构桥梁的自重，"利用桥屋重量，抵抗洪涛之冲击，如《闽部疏》谓：'闽中桥梁甲天下，虽山坳细涧，皆以巨石梁之，上施楹栋，都极壮丽，初谓山间木石易办，乃已知非得已，盖闽水怒而善奔，故以数十重重木压之。'"[2]

二、廊桥的类型

受社会生产力发展的局限，在相当长时期内，古代中国都是以木构桥梁为主。在北方地区，石拱桥技术至迟出现在东汉，有明确文献记载的石拱桥出现于晋朝，现存最早的石拱桥是建于隋代的河北赵县安济桥（又名"赵州桥"）。而在南方地区，木构桥梁也曾是主流的桥梁类型，但约在宋元时期发生过一次木、石材质的大更替。促成这次材质变换的主要原因，应归于整个社会生产力的发展。当时产生了新的运输、起重装备以及建造方法。正是由于这些技术的革新和发展，才使得传统的造桥材料从完全木材转换为木材、石材、砖混合或者完全石材。此后，除少数林木资源丰富的山区之外，南方地区绝大多数的城市与村镇的桥梁都更替为石构桥梁。时至今日，笔者仍能在宋元时期的桥梁遗构中发现木、石、砖混合结构的桥梁，如上海市青浦区金泽镇的迎祥桥就是例证。

迎祥桥在金泽镇之南栅，为一木石结构混合结构，挺秀简洁，具有现代桥梁的风姿，不论形制、结构和运用之材料，都具有独特的地方。此桥为梁式石桥，长34.25米，宽2.41米，共五跨，中间最大跨度为5.86米。构造是在石柱上置木梁——密铺圆形檩木，桥面铺厌砖，每间隔约1米处，复有一列砖。桥面两侧木梁外贴水磨砖，用以保护木梁，兼增美观，整个桥的细部手法非常工整。据《金泽志》记载，这座桥是金泽八景之一，有"月印川流，水天一色"的描写。据《金泽志》及《青浦县志》的记载，此桥建于元代，明天顺六年（1462年）重建，清乾隆五十六年（1791年）重修。明清重建重修当指桥之上部，其石柱形式等犹存旧制。

为什么会出现这种木石混合的梁式桥梁形式呢？其实，从今天结构科学的视角来看极易理解。木材尽管在露天情况下并不耐久，实际上它是一种抗弯能力极好的天然材料。砖或石材，尤其是花岗岩虽然经久耐用，抗压能力极强，但是它的抗弯能力并不如木材。作为梁式桥，其主梁是受弯的构件。因此，石墩作为桥梁的受压构件，木材作为主梁结构承受弯矩，桥面铺砌的砖块只是作为铺装，保护桥梁整体不受风雨侵蚀和通行人畜、行车的磨损。三种材料，将其各自的力学性能发挥到极致，物尽其用——可说是中国古代工匠最具智慧的桥梁建筑案例了。

中国古代创造的廊桥式样中，若按材料分，大致有木廊桥，木石结合廊桥两大类；若按结构形式分，又有梁式廊桥、撑架式廊桥和拱式廊桥等三类。再具体一些，梁式廊桥又可以有简支梁式廊桥和伸臂梁式廊桥之分；撑架式廊桥又可分为八字撑架式廊桥和双八字撑架式廊桥；拱式廊桥可分为石拱与木拱两大类，其中木拱桥梁也可再细分为编木拱式廊桥和编木拱式廊桥。一般而论，简支梁式廊桥的结构最为简单，制作方便，技术成熟且易于建造，它可以是单跨梁也可是多跨连续梁的形式，因此其分布最为广泛，其足迹遍布中国内陆各地；伸臂梁式木廊桥是在伸臂梁式木桥的基础上发展起来，有一定的技术含量，且对材料要求较高，其规模和造价也相对高些，其主要分布在中国长江流域及以南地区的浙江省、福建省、江西省、安徽省、湖南省、湖北省、广西壮族自治区、重庆市、四川省等地。此外，在西北地区历史上也有这种伸臂梁式廊桥的身影。比如早期的西安灞桥、石轴桥等都是这类形式。拱式廊桥又有石拱廊桥和木拱廊桥之分。石拱廊桥分布的地区主要也在长江流域及其以南的广袤地区。木拱廊桥主要分布在闽、浙两省和西南地区（云南、重庆）和甘肃等地。

通常情况下，为了简洁、完整地描述所研究对象，我们会将材料和结构形式结合在一起，将中国古代廊桥分为：木平廊桥（即简支木梁式木廊桥）、石平廊桥（即简支石梁式木廊桥）、木伸臂廊桥、木撑架廊桥、石拱廊桥和木拱廊桥等。

前文已述，木质廊桥的特点是造型与房屋建筑非常相似，建筑艺术性较强，但缺点是费工费材，不耐久。自从石质材料开始应用于桥梁建造之后，廊桥这一特别的桥梁形式就逐渐减少。近二十年来，由于中国建筑史界、桥梁史界众多学者的努力，闽、浙地区的木拱廊桥已于2012年列入世界文化遗产中国国家申报后备名单，其造桥技艺也已于2009年进入世界非物质文化遗产名录。出于非物质文化遗产的传承与保护需要，浙、闽两省以及中国其他各地，甚至欧美等国，都在模仿或邀请中国传统木拱廊桥建造工艺的传承人奔赴各地建造中国特色的木拱廊桥。

本节中以结构形式分类，具体讨论梁式廊桥、撑架式廊桥和拱式廊桥的结构特点、实例及分布。

（一）梁式廊桥

梁式廊桥是指下部桥跨结构为梁式结构的廊桥。古代桥梁桥跨结构中的梁，多数是简支梁和伸臂梁两种形式。由于材料差异，木梁廊桥的数量还是远远多于石梁廊桥，且分布广泛，如今的石梁廊桥比较多见于皇家和私家园林之中，或江南地区狭窄的河道之上。

伸臂梁桥作为梁式桥的一种衍生类型，是在简支梁桥的基础上发展起来的先进桥型。其构造是通过在两端桥堍或桥墩处逐层向外出挑木梁或石梁，其上再支承木梁或石梁，这样通过两端向河心出挑的伸臂梁与简支梁，形成桥跨结构，伸臂梁桥的跨度往往要大于简支梁桥，并且更加耐久。

根据其结构特征，伸臂梁结构有单向伸臂梁、双向伸臂梁以及斜撑伸臂梁等三类（图1）。常见的单跨伸臂梁桥通常是由位于两端桥堍之上的两组单向或斜撑伸臂梁组合而成，而多跨伸臂梁桥则是由位于两端桥堍之上的两组单向伸臂梁与位于桥墩之上的双向伸臂梁组合而成。

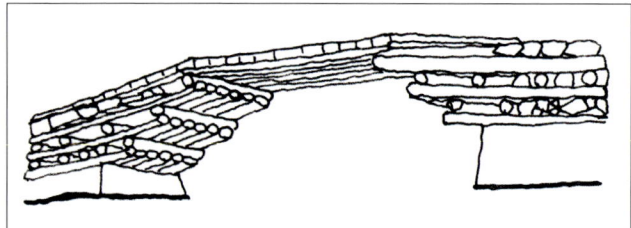

a) 单向伸臂梁

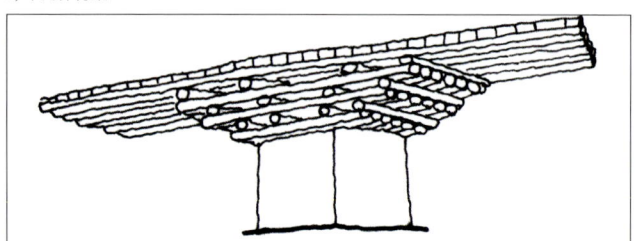

b) 双向伸臂梁

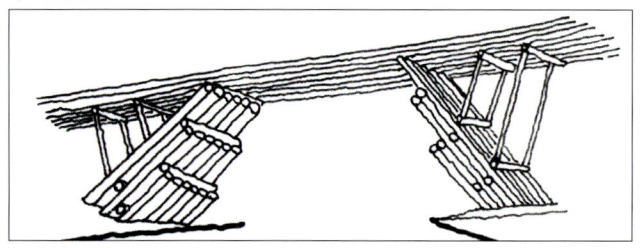

c) 斜撑伸臂梁

■ 图1　伸臂梁结构（引自茅以升《中国古桥技术史》）

伸臂梁廊桥以木伸臂梁廊桥为多见，石伸臂梁廊桥比较少见，恐是因为石梁的受弯性能不及木梁所致。如位于浙江省泰顺县泗溪镇的南阳桥，就是一座比较特殊的木石混合伸臂廊桥（图2）。该桥建于清末，一墩两孔，桥堍与桥墩均为条石砌筑且其上各出2～3层的石伸臂梁，上承数根木梁，其上再架设10余间廊屋，这种石伸臂梁与简支木梁的组合方式在已知廊桥结构中比较少见。

伸臂木廊桥在中国各个廊桥分布区都普遍存在，包括

■ 图2　浙江泰顺泗溪南阳桥（吴卫平　摄）

浙江、福建、湖南、湖北、四川、重庆、云南等地，构造特征大同小异，形式风格也多是结合地方营造特色而略有变化。

（二）撑架式廊桥

撑架式廊桥是指桥跨结构为撑架结构的廊桥。桥梁结构中的撑架，是介于梁与拱之间的桥跨结构类型，是由数根斜向和水平杆件组合而成的支撑结构。撑架结构起源于简支梁桥结构中用以加固或增强简支木梁用的斜撑构架，当木梁下的多个斜撑协同工作、共同形成支撑构架时，我们就把这类组合形成的桥跨结构称为撑架结构。闽浙地区至今保存着目前已知的几乎所有类型撑架式廊桥。

与伸臂梁式结构一样，撑架式结构的产生源于对桥梁结构大跨度的追求，也是另外一种大跨解决方案。撑架式结构以木撑架为主，石撑架比较少见，仅浙江、福建等地偶见。这可能是由材料性能决定的，木材比石材更适合应用于撑架结构，更加方便与经济。所以，现存的撑架式廊桥基本上都是木撑架式廊桥，且多分布于东南地区等。

（三）拱式廊桥

拱式廊桥是指桥跨结构是结构学意义上"拱"的廊桥。拱式结构起源很早，尤其是在西欧各国，拱券和穹顶结构有着两千多年辉煌灿烂的历史。在我国，拱式结构在桥梁中的应用至迟于汉代，魏晋南北朝也有文献和考古材料印证。

而木拱结构并非一般意义上的拱结构，中外的木拱结构构造原则迥然不同。国内学术界对木拱结构的认识肇始于宋代名画《清明上河图》中的"汴水虹桥"（图3），以及后来对闽浙山区木拱廊桥的研究。中国历史上的木拱技术起源的确切时间尚待进一步探究，但从目前的文献资料、考古发掘以及实物遗存等来看，木拱桥在中原地区曾广泛存在过，并且是中国古代桥梁技术最重要成就之一。

从目前的廊桥遗存看，木拱廊桥的分布比较集中于东南地区，而石拱廊桥则相对广泛，除东南地区外，中南、西南等地都普遍保存。

三、廊桥的分布

廊桥在中国古代的分布是非常普遍的，可以说基本上覆盖了中国内陆的全境。它作为一种建筑文化的特殊形式

■ 图3　（宋）张择端《清明上河图》中"虹桥"段

■ 图4　西藏拉萨琉璃桥（吴卫平　摄）

■ 图5　不丹王国境内的廊桥（Cris Haring 提供）

传播到了雪域高原——拉萨（图4），也拓展到了今天的朝鲜半岛、日本以及越南等东亚和东南亚国家。喜马拉雅山区的尼泊尔、不丹等国以及印度洋岛国斯里兰卡，甚至土耳其等国，也保存有古代沿袭下来的廊桥（图5），其营造技术与中国的渊源，尚待进一步研究梳理。

时光流转，廊桥这一曾经普遍存在的桥梁建筑，在中国的东南、西南、西北以及中南等地区带仍有较多遗存。若以省（自治区、直辖市）为行政单位来比较，则又以东南地区的福建、浙江两省为最。西南地区的云南、四川、重庆等省、直辖市，历史上也拥有丰富的廊桥建筑资源。贵州、湖南和广西交界的侗族、苗族聚居区，廊桥则以风雨桥的形式从古代一直保存到今天。江南地区也有一定数量的遗存。总之，在中国，如果某地的民居是从干阑演变而来的、以诸如穿斗架为主的建筑构架，那么在当地就存在木构廊桥的可能。实际上，在东亚的绝大多数地区，这个推论也是成立的。这也从另外的角度证明了廊桥与穿斗架等建筑构架，都是以干阑为共同祖源发展起来的。

与其他类型的桥梁比较起来，廊桥是一种更具文化特色与建筑艺术性的桥梁建筑形式。它的分布是与当地营造传统和社会经济相关联的。它的出现往往是在政府主导建

造的官道，或者是政府与民间都积极参与建设的重要商道之上，以及一些地方乡绅或豪门聚居的村落水尾，作为庇护整个宗族或家族的风水桥而存在。廊桥在中国上古至中古时代的江南地区分布非常广泛，比如江苏省历史上就曾有许多廊桥。在古代文献中时常见到如下文字：

《建苑拾英》第二辑（下册）记"饮虹桥"："一名新桥，旧名万岁桥，在古凤台坊。按《建康实录》：南临淮有新桥，本名万岁桥，后改名饮虹新桥，今俗呼为新桥，袭其旧也。宋乾道五年，留守史正志重建，覆大屋数十楹，甚壮丽，丘崇记之。开禧元年，丘崇重建，刘叔向记之。宝祐四年，马光祖重建，梁椅记之。明正德中重修。"

《建苑拾英》第二辑（下册）记"冶浦桥"："在六合县东五里冶浦河。五代时，避杨浦讳，人呼之冶清桥。唐天宝中建，宋嘉定中改造。明宣德中，知县史思古大其制，用木桩万余，叠石为五空，铺以板木，覆以瓦屋十七间，长三十余丈，伟然为邑巨观，后倾颓。嘉靖十六年，知县周薇重建。按冶浦桥于丁丑之变，寇自西来，桥东居民思楚桥据水可守，寇果不能渡，获保，而仅杨一带俱得免。后邑贡生历振岳就石为基，横木作址，旁营二阁，中屋二楹，比旧制更加轩豁。"

而今天的江苏省境内依然保存有相当数量的古桥，但大多数已不是廊桥的形式，而是石梁或石拱桥了。虽然在一些园林或古镇还有极少数廊桥的遗存，与之前相比却是九牛一毛。同属江南的浙江省，北部和东部的经济状况最好，因而其廊桥遗存也较少，但在西南部欠发达地区，还有不少的廊桥被较好地保存下来。为什么会出现这种情况呢？

这种情况与当地当时的经济发展水平相关。经济发展较快、水平较高的地区，比较容易利用新技术替代旧技术。从这个角度来看，木质廊桥被耐久性更佳的石质拱、梁桥替代，在当时就是一种进化，或言一种进步，这是好的方面；不过从建筑文化遗产传承的角度来看，廊桥的快速消失，又不能不说是一种无可奈何的遗憾。

一个不能忽略的事实是，古代中国曾司空见惯的廊桥，经历了漫长的时间到了今天，却因为种种原因，正以数十倍甚至数百倍于建造的速度被毁灭着。以浙江省的泰顺县为例，到1949年，据有关部门统计当时尚有数百座的各式廊桥，到半个世纪后尚余26座（不包括2000年后新建的廊桥），这个数字还包括与福建省寿宁县共享的一座木拱廊桥。鲜为人知的另一个事实是，泰顺县的木拱廊桥却曾经拥有中国保存着的木拱桥的两项桂冠：其一，有确凿纪年历史的木拱桥——建于明朝景泰五年（1454年）的叶树阳桥；其二，木拱结构跨度最大的木拱桥——拱跨为42米的三滩桥。可惜的是，前者已于1965年因修建公路被拆除，后者于1950年毁于洪水[9]。同样的厄运也降临在了另外两座木拱廊桥身上，它们分别是清朝道光二十八年（1848年）始建的漈下桥（也称福庆桥）、始建于中华民国二十六年（1937年）的双神桥。前者于1990年毁于山洪，后者在1989年因建电站而被拆除[10]。

总体上来看，中国廊桥遗存分布状况并不均衡，这跟廊桥建造的地理资源、社会经济、功能需求、技术能力等方面差异有关，在一定程度决定了中国廊桥的类型与分布的多样性。

从已掌握的资料来看，目前中国遗存的古代廊桥尚有一千余座。总体上看，古代廊桥无论从数量还是从类型上，南方地区要多于北方地区，这跟南北地区的地理、气候、资源等方面差异有密切关系。从中国地理分区上看，北方地区的廊桥集中分布于华北、西北地区，南方地区的廊桥则普遍分布于华东、华中、华南、西南地区。当然在各个地理分区内，廊桥数量与类型分布，也存在不均衡的现象。

总结中国廊桥分布特征，如果要做一个地域上的划分，我们大致可以归纳出六大廊桥遗存带，亦即分别是华北、西北、西南、中南、东南、江南等廊桥遗存带以及其他零星分布区域。

（一）华北廊桥遗存带

华北地区的廊桥主要保存在北京、河北、山西等地的园林苑囿、庙宇祠观内，以石梁、石拱廊桥为主，数量不多，但各具特色。如著名的北京颐和园，作为清代皇家园林的代表，汲取了江南园林的造园艺术手法又结合当地的自然条件建成的大型山水园林。园内就有众多的亭（廊）桥，如柳桥、练桥、镜桥、廓风桥、荇桥等，形态各异，桥上或亭、或廊，作为园中的景观桥，无论远观还是近览，或是进入桥亭之内凭栏眺望园内的湖光山色，都是旖旎的风景。

当然，还有一些散落于寺院祠观中的廊桥，也别有特色。如位于河北井陉苍岩山的楼殿桥，就是中国为数不多的桥殿合一的石拱廊桥，石拱横跨于苍岩山两峰对峙的峡谷之上，桥上建五开间重檐歇山顶的殿堂，远观如空中楼阁，巧夺天工。

（二）西北廊桥遗存带

西北地区的廊桥现主要保存在甘肃中南部、陕西南部以及四川西北部等地，有木梁、木拱、石拱等多种廊桥类型。西北地区历史上曾有不少的廊桥，但遗存至今的并不多。过去，甘肃兰州八景之一"虹桥春涨"所在的雷坛河上的"握桥"就是当时远近闻名的廊桥，可惜该桥在20世纪50年代因交通建设而被拆除。而在定西渭源县清源河上现有一座于中华民国时期仿握桥而建的灞凌桥得以保留，这是座木伸臂梁与木拱混合结构的廊桥，这种桥型至今也是绝无仅有。甘肃东南部地区的廊桥也多建于峡谷、河谷之上，多是古代陕甘"茶马古道"上重要的交通咽喉之地。而甘肃西南部以及四川西部藏族、羌族等少数民族聚居区，也遗存不少富有地域与民族特色的木伸臂梁廊桥。

（三）西南廊桥遗存带

西南地区的廊桥现主要保存在四川中东部、重庆西部、云南西部等地，有木梁、石梁、石拱等廊桥类型，数量不少。四川中东部、重庆西部地处四川盆地、长江上游流域北部，居民以汉族人为主。云南西部则地处横断山脉南侧、怒江与澜沧江流域，主要是白族、彝族、回族等少数民族的聚居地。境内的廊桥具有鲜明的少数民族和地方特色，并与滇藏"茶马古道"有着密切的关联。

（四）中南廊桥遗存带

中南地区的廊桥现主要保存在湖北西南部、重庆东南部、湖南西部、贵州东部以及广西东北部等地，这一地区位于云贵高原以东，地形以山地、丘陵为主。该地区自古以来就是少数民族聚居区，如湘、鄂、渝、黔交界地带的武陵山区，是土家族、苗族、侗族等少数民族的聚居地；而湘、黔、桂交界地带，则是侗族、苗族等少数民族的聚居地。境内廊桥主要有木梁、石梁、石拱等多种类型，数量众多。这一遗存带所保存的廊桥，也极富地方与民族特色。

（五）东南廊桥遗存带

东南地区的廊桥现主要保存在浙江南部、福建北部、江西东部等地，地处浙闽丘陵地带，地形以山地、丘陵为主，是汉族、畲族以及汉族的客家民系世居地。东南沿海地区又有如瓯江、飞云江、长溪、闽江等诸多小流域。这里廊桥遗存丰富，数量众多，几乎囊括所有廊桥类型，且以保留有最具中国特色的木拱廊桥而举世闻名。

（六）江南廊桥遗存带

江南地区的廊桥现主要保存在江苏南部、浙江北部、安徽东南部以及上海西部等，地处长江三角洲平原、宁绍平原以及徽州盆地，地形以平原、盆地为主，属太湖流域、新安江流域范围。境内水网纵横，廊桥众多，有木梁、石梁、石拱等廊桥类型，或位于村镇之中，或藏于园林之内，大都精巧别致。江南地区自隋唐得到开发以来，商贸繁盛、人文荟萃，一直以来都是后世历朝的经济重镇，其廊桥营造技术相较于其他地区也更加先进与突出。

（七）其他地区遗存

除上述地区外，在西藏自治区以及岭南地区尚能见到数座独特的廊桥。如位于青藏高原之上的"日光城"——拉萨的城关就有座"琉璃桥"，是一座石梁廊桥，相传始建于唐贞观年间，重修于清代，原为拉萨古城内外的交通要道，但现在河流已干涸。

而岭南地区的如广东潮州的广济桥，又名"湘子桥"，是中国"四大名桥"之一，也是国内集梁桥、浮桥、拱桥于一体的古桥"孤例"，该桥始建于南宋乾道七年（1171年），元、明、清三代均有重修。广济桥由东、西梁桥段与中间浮桥段组合而成，东、西桥段分别为十二孔、七孔石墩石梁桥，中桥段为十八木木船连接而成的浮桥。梁桥段的石墩多为细条石纵横交错叠砌而成的船形墩，大小不一、形态各异，多是因桥墩多次损毁修复所致。每个桥墩上都修建有潮汕地域风格的亭或阁，或单个或组合，形态各异，极富特色。

第二节 简支梁廊桥

一、简支梁廊桥的起源及特征

简支梁桥是最原始、也是最简单的梁桥结构类型。《说文解字注》中注"桥，水梁也。水梁者，水中之梁也。梁者，宫室所以关举南北者也。然其字本从水。则桥梁其本义而栋梁其假借也。凡独木者曰杠。骈木者曰桥。大而为陂陀者曰桥。古者挈皋曰井桥。……"[11] 由此可知，"桥"是水上之"梁"，"梁"的本义来自"桥"，后来演义为建筑之上的"梁"。古时，数木并列用以跨越河流或壕沟等障碍，即为桥，也就形成最简单的简支梁桥。

据考古发掘资料，新石器时期人类聚落遗址中，居住区周边就环有2～6米宽的壕沟，作用是防止其他部落或野兽侵入。而日常生产生活时，壕沟之上必然有类似桥的活动装置或者可移动构件可供通行，而多地的考古发掘也印证这种观点，壕沟上的桥多是简单的骈木桥，即早期的简支梁桥多数为木构桥梁（图6）。

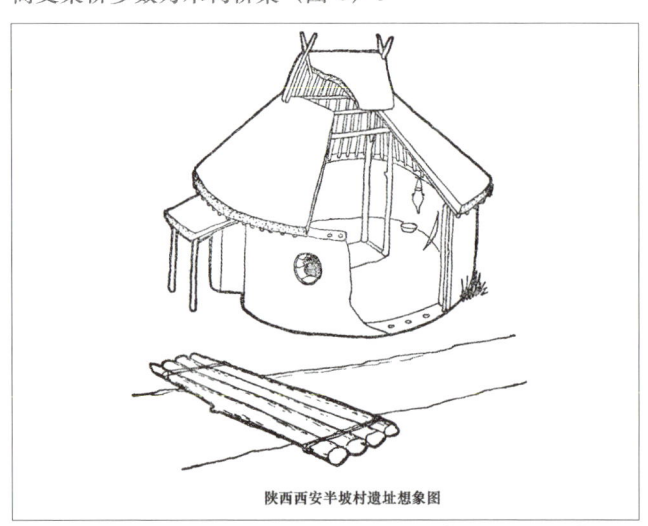

■ 图6 陕西西安半坡村遗址复原想象图（引自茅以升《中国古桥技术史》）

简支梁桥即指木或石梁的两端搁置在桥堍或桥墩之上的桥，这类桥型的单孔跨度通常受限于单根木梁或石梁的长度，多数不超过10米。除临时性桥梁外，现存的木简支梁桥上，通常架设有若干间廊屋，而形成木简支梁廊桥（以下简称"简支木廊桥"），其在平面上多呈水平形态，也被称为木平廊桥。由于构造简单，建造相对容易，这类廊桥在国内众多廊桥分布带中随处可见。单跨的简支木廊桥通常架设在狭窄的河道或溪流之上，而多跨的简支木廊桥则架设在宽阔的河道或溪流之上，即在河中设置桥墩或桥柱形成"长桥"。

二、简支梁廊桥的类型及分布

单跨简支木廊桥构造比较简单，也比较常见，南方地区各廊桥分布带内都能很容易见到。由于石梁在抗弯性能上的劣势，限制了简支石梁桥上架设廊屋技术的推广，所以简支石廊桥的遗存较少，目前多见于园林或江南地区狭窄的河道之上的小型廊桥或亭桥。

多跨简支梁廊桥，即设有桥墩或桥柱的简支梁廊桥，根据桥墩或桥柱与跨梁的材料组合不同，常见的有石柱木梁廊桥、石墩木梁廊桥、木柱木梁廊桥、石柱石梁廊桥等。

（一）石柱木梁廊桥

由于木柱作为桥柱，长期受水流、微生物侵蚀，容易腐朽损坏，后来人们逐渐将林立于水中的木柱替换为石柱，就形成了石柱木梁的廊桥结构。

石柱木梁桥比较著名的要数上海青浦迎祥桥（图7）。

■ 图7 上海青浦迎祥桥（刘杰 摄）

（二）石墩木梁廊桥

石墩，顾名思义，是指石砌的桥墩。石墩通常由条石规则砌筑而成，相比较石柱或木柱，更加坚固稳定耐久，更抗水流侵蚀、洪水冲击、船舶或河面漂流物撞击。所以，石墩成为多跨桥中支承桥跨结构的主要形式。石墩在平面上有矩形（含圆端形与圆角形等）、船形等，其选型通常与河流的流量、流速以及流向有关。矩形墩常设置在水量少、流速缓的河流中，船形墩常设置在水量大、流速急的河流中。船形墩的迎水侧通常做成尖端面，称为"分水尖"，起到分散水流，减少水流对桥墩直接冲击与冲蚀的作用。

由于上述优点，石墩木梁廊桥成为古代多跨简支梁廊桥的主要类型，其分布也比较广泛，几乎在各个廊桥分布带都能见到。比较著名的如江西婺源彩虹桥，该桥始建于宋代，后又重建，桥名取自"两水夹明镜，双桥落彩虹"的诗句。彩虹桥是一座四墩五孔的石墩木梁廊桥，船形桥墩硕大，其上置木梁，并架立数十间的廊屋。又如浙江宁波百梁桥（图8），该桥也始建于宋代，元明清三代均有重修，桥系五墩六孔的石墩木梁廊桥，桥墩细窄，并有收分，迎水面带分水尖，两墩之间架设14～16根木梁，合计约100根，号称"百梁"，桥名因此而来，桥上也架立有数十间的廊屋。同样，在中国东南、西南、中南等地区，也随处可见这种类型的廊桥。

■ 图8 浙江宁波百梁桥（贾非 摄）

（三）木柱木梁廊桥

早期的木柱木梁桥形象，可从汉画像砖石或者墓室壁画中发现，如四川省成都市跳蹬河街道出土的东汉时期"车马过桥"画像砖（图9），每排桥柱上置横枋，枋上顺桥身方向搭梁，其上铺设三角楔形与矩形交替排列的桥板，桥上可以行驶车马。内蒙古自治区和林格尔县出土的东汉时期墓室壁画描绘的"渭水桥"（图10），也是座木柱木梁桥，相关的考古发掘也得以证实，并与壁画中形象相参照。实物遗存至今尚可见于山西省太原市晋祠内圣母殿前的鱼沼飞梁（图11）。当然，还有一些形式上更加简单的木柱木梁桥，如古徽州地区比较常见的"板凳桥"。

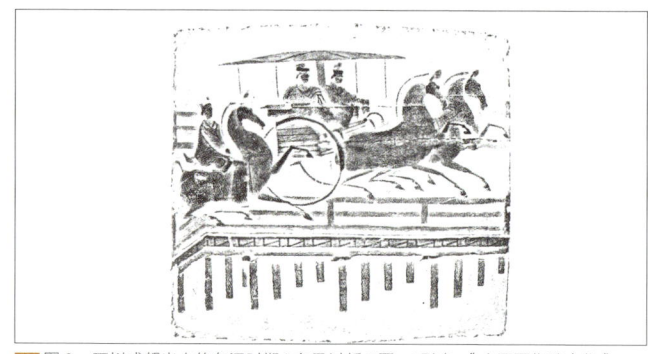

■ 图9 四川成都出土的东汉时期"车马过桥"图（引自《中国画像砖全集》编辑委员会《中国画像砖全集·四川汉画像砖》）

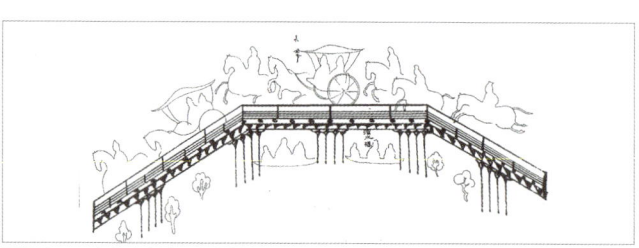

■ 图10 内蒙古自治区和林格尔县出土的东汉时期墓室壁画描绘的"渭水桥"（引自傅熹年《中国科学技术史·建筑卷》）

■ 图11 山西省太原市晋祠内圣母殿前的鱼沼飞梁（刘杰 摄）

而现藏于北京故宫博物院的宋代名画《千里江山图》中就有两座木柱木梁廊桥（图12）：一座为三十余孔的长桥，长桥中间有座组合式廊亭；另一座为三孔的廊（亭）桥。当然，相似的案例在古画中还很多，木柱木梁廊桥曾是廊桥的一种主要存在类型，案例不胜枚举。

■ 图12

■ 图12 《千里江山图》中的廊桥

如今的木柱木梁廊桥，在中南地区特别是在山区普遍存在，如在桂北的侗寨、黔东南的侗寨、苗寨内抑或林野乡间，都可见这种木梁木柱廊桥。究其构造，与传统侗族、苗族建筑营造无异，造型也大抵相近，与南方地区常见的干阑式建筑形式以及穿斗架建筑同根同源。

（四）石柱石梁廊桥

古代的石柱石梁桥遗存颇多，特别是江南或东南地区，至今仍留存有相当数量的宋代以来建成的石柱石梁，桥短者仅两三跨，长者多达九跨，或是平桥，或是弧桥。值得一提的是，江南地区的石柱石梁桥与东南地区在构造上尚存有差异，具体地讲，江南地区桥梁每排桥柱中的立柱通常是竖直紧密排列，而东南地区则通常是中间竖直，两侧倾斜松散排列，类似于"爪"形。究其原因，一方面，"爪"形的桥柱形式，使得桥柱的基石、立柱、帽梁石三部分形成的支撑框架更加稳定。同时也可能考虑到东南地区山多河窄，并时常受山洪威胁，为保证河水湍急时不至于冲毁石桥，通过斜向石柱提供支撑抵御河水冲击（图13）。

■ 图13 福建寿宁永安桥（引自刘杰、林蔚虹《乡土寿宁》）

前文已述，如今简支石廊桥的遗存并不多见，其中多跨的石柱石梁廊桥更是凤毛麟角，目前所知仅存江苏苏州拙政园内的"小飞虹"廊桥（图14）。该桥是苏州园林中少见的廊桥，桥系两柱三孔，桥面微折呈八字，桥柱由2根立柱上承帽梁石组成，每跨系5根石梁组成桥面，桥上架3间廊屋与周围廊榭相连，十分美观雅致。

第三节　伸臂梁廊桥

一、伸臂梁桥的起源及历史分布

英国著名科学技术史家李约瑟（Joseph T. M. Needham）博士曾在其著《中华科学文明史》（Science

■ 图14 江苏苏州拙政园内的"小飞虹"（吴卫平 摄）

and Civilisation in China）中针对伸臂梁桥还表达了以下几个观点：

其一，他认为这种桥梁（伸臂梁桥）可能起源于喜马拉雅地区，在中国很早就被熟知并广泛使用；

其二，他认为伸臂梁桥的起源还可能与汉代的"梯桥"有关；

其三，他也认为中国木伸臂梁桥与中国古代建筑屋顶的托臂支撑体系——斗拱体系有关；

其四，他还认为中国木伸臂梁桥的技术传到了国外；

其五，在中国也有可能建造了石质的伸臂梁式桥。

以上观点中，除了"梯桥"需要做些解释外，其余几点比较容易理解。在这里，简单介绍一下"梯桥"。在中国汉代画像石中，有一幅出土于山东两城山的画像石内容就是一座"梯桥"（图15）。

■ 图15 汉画像砖上的"梯桥"图案（引自《中国画像石全集》，山东曲阜孔庙 藏）

李约瑟博士解释说，在中国汉代，为修建湖上亭阁，常需将亭阁置于托臂之上，而这和伸臂非常相似，这种结构被称为"梯桥"。问题是这种梯桥是当时已出现的建筑，还仅仅是汉代艺术家们的凭空想象？1971年，越南河内发现了一座建于1049年的与梯桥相似的楼阁——烟雨寺（现称独柱寺）。此阁坐落在立于水中的石柱之上，顶部由悬臂木梁托和横梁支撑。其实，在中国汉画像石中，类似于此的"楼阁"、或被李约瑟称的"梯桥"形象并不止一处。诸如山东微山、枣庄出土的"楼阁观鱼图"和"钓鱼图"等。

实际上，笔者认同李约瑟博士关于木伸臂梁桥与中国古代建筑中斗拱体系的结构相似性的观点。从构造角度来看，两者显然有非常相似之处，其间必然有密切的渊源关系。不过，李约瑟将北宋名画《清明上河图》中"虹桥"结构也纳入伸臂梁桥类型，今天看来显然是个错误。

到目前为止，已知记载木伸臂梁桥的历史文献最早在4世纪初。北魏地理学者郦道元在《水经注》引段国《沙洲记》："吐谷浑于河上作桥，谓之河厉，长一百五十丈（疑记载有误，恐单位为尺）。两岸累石作基陛，节节相次，大木更镇压，两边俱来，相去三丈。"《水经注》还有类似的桥梁记载，如秦州乞佛所作的飞桥皆有可能都是木伸臂梁桥。有学者认为，木伸臂梁桥可能始创于西北地区青海、甘肃诸省，而遍布西藏、陕西、四川、重庆、宁夏、云南、贵州、广西、湖南、湖北、浙江、安徽、江西、福建等地。这些地区因木材比较丰富，因而使得这种比较消耗木材的桥梁形式得以保存。

陕西省西安市的灞河桥、石轴桥等都曾为木伸臂梁桥，可以知道这类梁桥曾在北方被广泛使用过。但是，随着桥梁建造技术的发展和北方森林的逐渐消失，导致北方古代木桥遗存逐渐减少，今天已很难在广袤的北方大地看到更多的此类桥梁，仅能从在20世纪30年代左右的一些旧照片中，发现这一地区木伸臂梁桥的寥寥身影（图16）。当然，这一地区也有运用了伸臂梁技术的木构廊桥，如甘肃渭源灞陵桥、兰州握桥等。

■ 图16 青海—甘肃交界峡谷上的木伸臂梁廊桥（Samuel M. Zwemer 摄）

二、木伸臂梁式廊桥的地域分布及其特征

总体而言，从中国现存的木伸臂梁式廊桥（以下简称"伸臂木廊桥"）分布状况来看，中国南方地区更为普遍。据目前学术界的看法，伸臂木廊桥可根据其坐落的地域或流域，将这个广大的范围划为闽浙赣、沅水和资水上游地区、湘桂黔、滇西四个分布区域。从建筑结构形式来论，沅水和资水上游地区和湘桂黔的伸臂木廊桥结构较为接近。在这四个区域内的伸臂木廊桥，存在着早晚年代的渊源关系和发展变化趋势。

（一）闽浙赣地区的伸臂木廊桥

闽浙赣地区的伸臂木廊桥主要分布在以福建为中心的地区。江西境内的伸臂木廊桥则分布在与福建接壤的南部和东部地区，浙江境内的伸臂木廊桥主要分布在浙江省的西南地区，福建地区的伸臂木廊桥则散布在福建省的西部地区。闽浙赣三地伸臂木廊桥的分布基本都在崇山峻岭的山地。在此区域的伸臂木廊桥的共同特点是：桥梁结构的伸臂部分都是用杉木，纵横相间，层层挑出，承托桥梁上建筑。桥墩均用石块或条石砌筑的船形墩为主，如江西安远永镇桥、江西南康永安桥和福建建瓯步月桥（图17）等。也有个别廊桥采用两头尖的六边形墩，如始建于南宋绍兴十五年（1145年）的福建永春东关桥。从桥墩的体积大小来看，在此区域内的伸臂木廊桥的桥墩，无论是众多的船形墩还是个别的六边形桥墩，体积都非常大，这是它们所共有的，也是比较突出的外部形态特征。

■ 图17　福建建瓯步月桥　（吴卫平 摄）

闽浙赣地区的伸臂木廊桥间的不同之处，主要表现在廊屋的形式上。如赣地的廊屋多为简单的悬山屋顶或两端设山墙的硬山山墙，墙上再设置出入廊桥的门洞，造型普通且建筑等级较低，类似简易的民居，比如江西铅山澄波桥的桥屋。而闽浙两地的廊屋的造型则比较丰富，多用歇山顶或组合屋顶，建筑等级较高，类似寺庙的殿堂，如福建建瓯值庆桥、步月桥和福建连城云龙桥等。此外，赣地的廊桥廊屋均不设风雨挡板，有的仅在桥栏上方有一道浅浅的批檐，如始建于清顺治九年（1652年）、重建于乾隆十四年（1749年）的安远县永镇桥；而闽浙两地的伸臂木廊桥则采用一种斜挂式的挡雨板，如云龙桥、步月桥和东关桥等，都把挡雨板斜挂于屋檐下。根据年代早晚情况判断，赣地的伸臂木廊桥从唐贞观四年（627年）到顺治年间（1644－1661年）都有建设，桥梁的建造时代都比较早；闽浙两地的古代各类桥梁也比较多，现存宋明时期的桥梁资料极其丰富，其伸臂木廊桥的建设年代也至迟至宋代。有的重建年代比较早，如福建连城云龙桥，始建年代为明末，重建年代为清代早期。尽管江西与浙江、福建两地的伸臂木廊桥的廊屋样式有些不同，但木伸臂梁的结构和硕大的船形墩却表现出区域一致性，建筑形式比较接近，况且，闽浙赣伸木臂梁廊桥又都在三地接壤的范围以内[12]。

在此区域，伸臂木廊桥的建造年代相对较早、规模也较大、廊屋的造型主要以寺庙和民居的建筑形式为主。

（二）湘南沅水、资水上游地区的伸臂木廊桥

湖南省的伸臂木廊桥主要分布在湖南省内洞庭湖流域及沅水、资水等上游地区，具体而言，主要在益阳、邵阳等地。

其桥梁建筑形态主要是由条石砌筑成的船形墩、木伸臂梁以及通常情况下的单檐廊屋构成，悬山式屋顶下常常有一道浅浅的披檐。尽管当地也有不少在桥首两端设置了华丽桥楼的廊桥，但桥的中心很少像闽浙赣地区那样出重楼或阁的样式，也不像闽浙赣桥那样用风雨板将桥身保护得严实，一般仅在伸臂梁部位使用风雨板遮挡，桥头两端的入口处，多用砖石砌筑类似牌楼来强调廊桥的入口，即桥门。益阳、邵阳两地的廊桥伸臂梁结构与闽浙赣地区的基本相同，其出挑部位的圆木纵横叠置构造与斗拱出挑原理一致。湖南省内将构成伸臂梁的圆木称作"鹊木"，大概是因为其纵横叠置的形状仿若喜鹊所构筑的鹊巢的缘故。比如湖南省益阳市安化县洞市乡锡潭村的永锡桥（图18），横跨于麻溪之上，三墩四孔，长83米，高12.8米，宽4.2米，上设廊屋34间，为清光绪二年（1876年）四月邑人陈五芝等捐资修建，光绪七年（1881年）十月落成。其船形桥墩上搭建纵横叠置的杉树圆木，出挑三层，承托桥梁，桥面铺木板，桥两侧施木栏，桥栏上方出檐，伸臂梁用风雨板遮蔽，两端桥首建有牌楼式的桥门。

■ 图18　湖南安化永锡桥　（吴卫平 摄）

湖南省益阳、邵阳两市的伸臂木廊桥的梁架部分和桥墩形式与闽浙地区相类似，区别在于前者廊屋上较少用风雨板而代之以桥身一侧的浅披檐，两端桥首入口处普遍建有牌楼式桥门，或木构或砖石砌筑，较为气派。闽、浙两省桥首设置山墙的廊桥也有不少，从绝对数量来说不如湖南。据统计，该地区大约有20座伸臂木廊桥施建有砖石砌筑或木牌楼的桥门，形成该地区廊桥桥屋独特的建筑风格。

邵阳、益阳两市现存的少数伸臂木廊桥始建年代为明代或清代中期，其中重建年代较早的有江东桥、龙潭桥、栗山桥等，现存桥梁绝大多数都属清代晚期建造。从存量廊桥来看，该区域内伸臂廊桥建造年代整体上晚于闽浙地区的同类桥梁。因此，有观点认为伸臂廊桥有可能是从闽浙由南向北、从东往西传播，在沅水、资水的上游地区被当地的工匠对桥屋的建筑形式稍稍做了些修改，从而形成了该区域廊桥特有的桥屋样式。

处在邵阳、益阳两市之西北的湘西地区，其伸臂廊桥在梁架结构上发生了一些新的变化，显示出此类桥桥在其传播过程中，越往北、往西其变化就越明显的特征。比如湘西土家族苗族自治州龙山县洗车河镇新建村的凉亭桥。该桥始建于乾隆四十五年（1780年），重建于光绪十三年（1887年），两墩三跨伸臂廊桥，全长43.3米，宽4.9米，六边形砌石桥墩高11.5米，桥墩略显单薄，桥屋共设12间，单檐悬山顶，桥栏下出一道浅檐，桥首用砖砌筑牌楼式桥门。该桥的伸臂梁部分安放在桥墩里。这种构造方式与浙江泰顺的南阳桥、文重桥相似。泰顺南阳桥始建于同治九年（1870年），文重桥重建于中华民国十年（1921年），洗车河镇凉亭桥重建于光绪十三年（1887年），因此，将伸臂木梁安放在桥墩里的构造方法显然属于晚期做法。此外，该廊桥的伸臂梁部分只有纵木，不设横木，与湖南南部地区鹊木纵横叠置、呈井字形构架的伸臂梁做法已有不同，而与重庆、云南等更加西部的地区却颇为相似。诸多迹象显示湘西地区的伸臂木廊桥已呈现出晚期特征和简化趋势。

据相关学者研究，历史上的沅水、资水上游地区和湘西地区都是土家族苗族等少数民族的聚居地，也是古代五溪蛮活动的重要地区，就年代和区域来看，这些建造于明清时期的伸臂廊桥应该是土家族、苗族等南方少数民族干阑建筑的遗存。有意思的是，与黔桂湘交界山区一样，邵阳、益阳等地把廊桥叫作风雨桥[12]。湘西地区则与黔东北、鄂西、渝东南都叫凉桥，这些都是土家族为主地区。毗邻的巴蜀地区也叫凉桥或凉亭桥。

（三）黔桂湘交界地区的伸臂木廊桥

有学者认为，在黔桂湘交界地区，从闽浙地区传入的伸臂木廊桥受到当地侗族建筑样式的影响，转而形成了一种风格迥异的廊桥样式和较为独立的分布区域。这种风格别致的伸臂木廊桥，主要分布在广西三江、贵州黎平和湖南通道等县市，其桥墩多呈六边形平面，即带有分水尖和金刚墙的桥墩，外形比船形墩显得高而薄。桥墩上纵横叠置、呈井字形构架的伸臂木梁用材粗大，因而上下两层圆木之间的空隙比闽浙地区和湘南地区等地的更大，从而增加了桥梁结构自身的高度，使得桥梁刚度更佳。与湖南南部的廊桥一样，为保护桥梁结构和桥栏，多在桥栏下方设一道浅披檐，有的桥栏上方也有出檐。该区域的廊桥常常在桥屋中部或桥头建造诸如侗寨鼓楼似的楼阁，多为重檐攒尖顶，或三层，或五层，或七层不等。湖南省通道侗族自治县伸臂木廊桥的桥墩却多采用船形墩，显示出它们与湖南南部沅水和资水流域同类桥梁存有渊源。与此同时，其桥面廊屋的建筑形式却与三江侗族地区的伸臂廊桥相一致，建造像侗寨鼓楼一样的楼阁。比如通道县观月桥的楼阁建筑规模，约占桥屋总面积的三分之二，其中间桥墩上建有五重檐四角攒尖顶的楼阁，两端是三重檐的歇山顶桥亭。

广西壮族自治区柳州市三江侗族自治县程阳马安寨风雨桥是此区域伸臂木廊桥的典型代表（图19），它集桥、廊、亭三者于一身，在中国各地廊桥式样中别具一格。程阳桥又叫永济桥、盘龙桥，建于清末民初，前后修建12年，于1916年才告完成。它横跨于林溪河之上，是一座三墩四孔木廊桥。桥面上总共建有5座楼式桥亭和19间廊屋间隔相连，十分壮观。桥面架杉木，铺木板，桥长77.76米，托架梁分2层，上层伸出4米，下层伸出2.5米，各以7根直径为40厘米的杉木密排而成，其上再竖柱立梁构筑桥面廊屋。廊屋宽4米，高10.6米，桥的两旁设木桥栏。中央为六角攒尖三重檐楼亭，顶距桥面高7.3米，其两侧

为正方形攒尖三重檐楼亭，高7米。两端桥楼成正方形，歇山三重檐屋顶，高6.5米。远远望去，犹如一组空中楼阁临空架在林溪河上，恍如琼楼玉宇。

图19　广西三江程阳风雨桥（贾非 摄）

三江县境内还有一座人畜分道行走的岜团风雨桥，其规模比程阳桥稍小，坐落在独峒乡岜团寨旁的苗江上。两桥堍之间距离30.4米，下设一石砌桥墩，桥面廊桥长50米，上设三座楼亭，建于清宣统二年（1910年）。它的特别之处，是在人行廊道旁边另设畜生行走小桥，成为双层桥，两层高差为1.5米。人畜分行，能使行人更安全，桥梁更清洁，是桥梁建筑空间运用上的创造[13]。

（四）滇西地区的伸臂木廊桥

云南省现存的伸臂木廊桥，主要分布在滇西地区大理州的云龙县和保山市的腾冲，以单跨梁桥为主。云南伸臂木廊桥有以下几个显著特点：一是其伸臂式结构一般都附加有斜撑；二是其廊屋多为单檐，桥梁结构部分大都用风雨板遮蔽；三是两端桥首一般都建有四方形土墙或砖砌的桥门；四是伸臂部分从外观上很难见到纵横相间的井字形构架，伸出的纵木比较显著而很难发现横木，这显然是因为横木尺寸偏小或隐藏较深的特殊构造。如果去除桥头建筑，云南廊桥外观与闽浙的木拱廊桥极其相似。

典型桥梁以大理州云龙县大包罗村的通京桥和保山市腾冲的通济桥为代表。通京桥是云南省单跨跨度最大的一座伸臂木廊桥，净跨约30米（图20）。通济桥单跨跨度约27.5米，仅次于前者（图21）。

图20　云南大理云龙通京桥（吴卫平 摄）

在云龙县还有类似结构的伸臂廊桥，诸如位于检槽镇的检槽桥和位于白石乡顺荡村的彩凤桥。检槽桥全长约18米，净跨约10米，廊屋宽约2.5米。彩凤桥横跨于沘江之上，全长约33.3米，净跨约27米，廊屋宽约4.7米。在腾冲除通济桥外，还有位于界头乡石桥村的永顺桥和曲石乡箐桥村的成德桥。腾冲的伸臂木廊桥都建在龙川江上。永顺桥始建于明嘉靖年间（1522—1566年），曾多次重修，长约20米，宽约3米，高约10米。成德桥，因地处深山密林，常有野猪出没，故又名"野猪箐桥"（图22）。该桥始建年代不详，清光绪八年（1882年）由同知陈宗海倡捐重修。此次重修时，在原桥面底部增添四条铁链牵拉。1942年为阻击日寇过江而毁，中华民国三十六年（1947年）李根源按原样重建，重建时采用了天然防腐的楸木。成德桥全长约29米，净跨约18.2米，宽约2.2米，高约10米。成德桥维系着的是一条古老驿道，那些从高黎贡山东面怒江峡谷翻越而来的马帮商旅们，穿过桥后，就抵达腾冲北部的曲石乡。

图21　云南腾冲保山通济桥（吴卫平 摄）

图22　云南保山腾冲成德桥（吴卫平 摄）

通济桥横卧在腾冲界头乡顺河村的龙川江面上，始建于明成化年间（1465—1487年），中华民国三十五年（1946年）重建，是一座美丽的伸臂木廊桥，桥身四周被雨水浸蚀的围栏仍清晰地透露着木材质感。桥长约37.5米，桥面宽约4.5米，桥面设廊屋9间，净跨约27.5米，高约9.3米。据《腾冲县志》载："桥身用木材构成，最下层建筑于两岸石墩或桥亭上；第二层用榫卯接在第一层上；第三层、第四层……依次建造；最上一层铺上长厚的梁木，两边固定，构成整座大桥。桥身如弓形梯，以两端相向递升。两岸有亭，桥身上有厦，两侧有凳，凳外有护栏护板。桥厦可避雨遮日，利人歇息，又可延长桥梁寿命。该桥构思精巧，结构独特，重力由各层梁架传向两端桥墩，增加了坚固性，颇合力学原理……"[14]

在通济桥朴素的外表下，隐藏的内部结构却相当复杂。桥面采用悬挑结构的方式，由各层梁架组合搭构而成。如第一层建筑设于河岸两边的石墩和桥亭上，之后逐层向上叠置、向前出挑，再用榫卯固定，并根据桥身的长度，依次向前伸出。跨度越大，桥出挑的"层数"就越多，桥面也随之不断上升，俟桥面合龙之后，再铺上长而结实的"梁木"和面板，将两边固定，一座类似拱形的廊桥就诞生了[15]。

滇西地区伸臂木廊桥的始建年代较早，以明代和清代早期为主。根据木伸臂梁桥结构及构造特征的异同，暂可把甘肃、西藏东北部、四川西北部和云南大理的划为同一区域，该区域遗留下来的伸臂木廊桥，大都具有以单跨为主、伸臂梁出挑仰角较大（比南方其他地区的都大）、桥头多建屋宇等建筑特征[12]。

三、伸臂木廊桥技术在中国古代历史上迁徙的道路

对于伸臂木廊桥技术的传播路径，重庆市三峡博物馆研究员王玉女士有如下观点：伸臂木廊桥的建造技术是从中国东南部的闽浙地区逐渐向西、向北传至湖南南部、江西的北部等地，然后再传播到黔桂湘交界侗族、苗族等少数民族聚居的山区，与当地建筑风格相融合，形成风雨桥，再往西、往北传至云南西部、重庆南部、四川北部以及甘青藏等地区。这一传播路线，差不多将中国长江以南和上游地区全部覆盖。亦即是说，中国南方木构建筑是以江南干阑建筑技术为基础，在融合北方文明和各地土著文明之后逐步发展、演变形成的。干阑建筑技术的传播路线基本上与王玉女士发现的伸臂木廊桥迁徙路线保持一致。这些观点及其详细的论述内容详见《江南木构》一书。[1]

不过，从王玉论述伸臂廊桥的基本材料来看，大都集中在明清时期。实际上，伸臂廊桥在古代的发展及演变，并不局限于明清。王玉揭示的这一传播路径，只能是伸臂梁桥若干轮技术发展过程中的最后一个轮次。从本书前文讨论的内容来看，诚如李约瑟在《中华科学文明史》一书中所言，伸臂梁桥的起源至迟于汉代。从北魏地理学者郦道元在《水经注》中引段国《沙洲记》记录吐谷浑于黄河上作飞桥的事迹亦可表明，这一桥式在北魏时期已得到广泛应用。缘何现存伸臂木廊桥大多数始建于明清时期？除了木构建筑保存时间不够长久的因素之外，还与桥梁建造技术处在不断革新的历史轮回之中有关，后者恐怕是更为重要的原因。

为了阐明历史上建筑技术传播路线的复杂性问题，笔者曾借用物理学中波的传播原理打过比方：如果将先进技术发生、发展和传播的过程，比喻成由石头投入平静的湖面所形成的由中心向四周传播的水波形式，大致可以说明这个问题。先进技术发明地当然是水波的中心，中心扩散四周的波纹则是代表技术传播的路径和过程。如果湖面上并不都是水，也有突出的岛屿或其他物体，水波的扩散必然会受到影响，其传播的路径必然会绕开这些障碍。当旧的一轮技术传播即将结束时，新一轮的技术传播中心也可能会挪动位置。这个位置与前次的中心位置或远或近，但新旧两种技术的交流与传播就如同水波荡漾，一般会发生干涉或称重叠的现象。

这一理论也可解释为什么越边远的地区所保存的技术越古老的现象。由于边远地区距离文明中心较远，再加上先进技术的传播并不都是同等能量。因此，每一次的技术

传播并不都能覆盖到边远的地区，边远地区所保存的技术很有可能是在早期传播过来的。因此，它们所保存的技术往往会比较古老。孔子在春秋时期就发现了这个道理，所以他说"礼失而求诸野"。笔者曾引用杨鸿勋观点，即江南文明是属于古东夷族海洋文明的一个范畴。古代山东所属海岱地区是东夷文化的发祥地，东夷族后被黄帝所属的炎黄联盟击溃后，往东南沿海分布以及溯长江而上，在长江以南地区形成了后来的百越民族。这一区域大致就是今天稻作文化分布地带，也是干栏建筑分布地带。这一文化的根本发祥地在海岱地区，即今日之山东半岛。因此，李约瑟发现反映有伸臂梁桥结构的"梯桥"图案的汉画像石，大都出土于山东一地。当然，这一结构早就随干栏建筑传遍了百越地区，甚至再往西、往北传至甘青等西北地区，才有后来郦道元在《水经注》中记录段国沙洲的飞桥故事。

四、中国著名的伸臂木廊桥

在本小节中，笔者选择部分省市较为著名的伸臂木廊桥，略作介绍，让读者对中国古代遗存至今的伸臂木廊桥稍加了解。

（一）浙江龙泉永和桥

永和桥横跨于浙江省龙泉市安仁镇安仁溪上，长125.7米，宽7.5米，高13米，是1座三墩四孔伸臂木廊桥。永和桥建于明代成化元年（1465年），原名永宁桥，清顺治年间毁于火，清康熙五十七年（1718年）募费3000余两白银重建，始称"永和桥"（图23）。

图23　浙江龙泉永和桥　（吴卫平摄）

桥身下3个石砌桥墩平面皆为船形，迎水面砌成雁翅金刚墙，桥墩之上设数层双向伸臂式木梁，承托桥身。上设廊屋42间，桥首两端设置3间四柱五层式牌楼，形成非常壮观的桥门。4根柱前后皆设有木质抱鼓石，以加强柱子的稳定性。明间一根枋梁做成月梁形制，其上用斗子蜀柱承托伸出屋面的五间楼屋。桥身下不仅设有一道浅披檐，桥梁结构部分还用风雨板遮蔽。东西两端皆设有石台阶与两边道路相连。廊屋内设有桥栏和条凳，以供行人休憩小坐。清人有诗赞叹此桥："风帆叶叶漾中流，两岸疏林绘晚秋。横锁彩虹分玉镜，钟灵不亚古槎洲。"[16]

（二）福建建瓯值庆桥

值庆桥位于福建省建瓯市迪口镇黄村自然村内，南北走向，明弘治三年（1490年）建。廊桥北半部架于碎石砌筑的石墩台上，南半部横跨溪流之上。悬山顶，上施小青瓦，中三间屋顶略高于两侧，形成重檐，檐下设披檐。

桥跨结构系伸臂木梁结构，分别由9根、7根杉木圆条组成的上、下两层伸臂木梁构成。木梁上再横铺窄木条龙骨，其上再顺桥铺设木板。廊屋架设于木梁之上，共设9间，四柱九檩构架，廊内两侧设栏杆、坐凳，桥内中间与两端都设有神龛，中间顶施藻井。藻井系由斗拱出四跳形成的四方藻井，顺桥身方向两跳斗拱上承1根月梁，梁下墨书"昔大明弘治叁年岁次庚戌建己丑朔日戊申越初五旦壬子大吉良晨募众鼎新建上祝"的字样，详细记录了该桥的建桥时间。桥内梁架用斗拱，柱、梁等构件用材颇大，月梁与柱连接处用重拱；剳牵、楮头、驼峰等构件雕刻精美；主要梁架、藻井上均施彩绘，但现已斑驳；梁架特征颇显福建地区宋元时期地域建筑风格。该桥屋面用扁椽，其上再垂直铺设相同尺寸的木条，形成类似于今天的"挂瓦条"，其上再干铺小青瓦，且无明显屋脊与脊饰，显得既朴素又特别。

（三）福建建瓯步月桥

步月桥位于福建省建瓯市吉阳镇玉溪村，横跨于玉溪河上，长127.5米，宽5米，是1座两墩三孔伸臂木廊桥。步月桥始建于元至正十年（1350年），明正德十四年（1519年）重建，于清乾隆、道光、光绪年间先后经历3次修缮，1998年再次大修，并在木构伸臂梁体系中加入了钢桁架梁，在外观上维持了古貌，可惜的是，此桥于2019年被焚毁。

桥身下两个石砌桥墩的平面呈船形，迎水面砌筑雁翅金刚墙。桥墩上设置3组纵横叠置的圆木形成井字形伸臂梁构架，构架之上再设置3组纵横叠置的圆木构成桥梁的主体结构。桥面上加建了廊屋42间，正面为三间四柱，共设43排柱架，共172根柱，抬梁式构庑殿顶，梁架与槛柱全都做成红漆。两端桥首都起庑殿重楼伸出屋面，檐下为层层叠叠的如意斗拱，形成飞檐翘角、巍峨壮观的门楼。桥廊内两边都设长条凳，供行人休憩小坐。屋檐下设木质风雨板。桥中央间设置神龛，奉祀观世音菩萨。桥梁东端门楼左侧墙体上竖刻"步月古桥"4个隶书大字，廊屋内梁架上悬挂着数十面捐资芳名匾和功德榜，重檐梁架下施八角形藻井，上施"八仙图"和"创业图"的彩画。桥梁西端门楼的墙上也镌刻有"步月桥"三字匾额，以及槛联一副："桥连夜堨发祥光，地对屏峰浮瑞气。"[17]

（四）福建连城云龙桥

云龙桥坐落在福建省连城县罗坊乡下罗村，呈东西走向横跨于青岩河上，长81米，宽5米，高6米，是一座四墩五孔伸臂木廊桥。云龙桥始建于明崇祯七年（1634年），清乾隆三十七年（1772年）重建，后历经多次维修，最近一次维修时间是1984年[18]。

桥身下设4个平面呈船形的花岗岩石砌桥墩，迎水面砌筑雁翅金刚墙。桥墩上设置3组纵横叠置的圆木形成井字形伸臂梁构架，构架之上再设置3组纵横叠置的圆木形成桥梁的主体结构。桥梁之上铺筑鹅卵石为桥面，上覆廊屋26间，桥身两侧檐下设红漆披檐两层，四柱九檩抬梁构架，廊屋内共设槛柱108根。廊屋之上再建了2座建筑，1座为六角攒尖双重檐的楼阁式建筑，伸出屋面的六面桥身皆设壶门形方窗，上施直棂栏杆；另1座为单檐歇山屋顶的楼亭，山面顺着桥身朝东西向。六角形楼阁为"文昌阁"，奉祀文昌帝君。桥梁的两端各设置1个三间四柱木牌楼为桥门，主楼为庑殿顶，檐下层层叠叠的斗拱拼出象鼻昂，在中间的额枋上方悬挂着"云龙桥"的匾额。

有关"云龙桥"桥名的来历，有人认为是构成桥梁伸臂梁系统的圆木皆已氧化成褐色，河面常有云雾缭绕，水天相映，似在云间，桥如腾空蛟龙而得名。实际上，被冠以云龙桥一名的南北廊桥并不在少数。本书前文已述的甘肃省兴隆山脚下也有一座云龙桥。恐怕也都有"长桥卧波，未云何龙"的历史文化内涵。

（五）福建浦城镇安桥

镇安桥位于福建省浦城县临江镇临江村，横跨于南浦溪支流临江溪，长79米，宽3.5米，是1座两墩三孔伸臂木廊桥。据明代《八闽通志》和清代《建宁府志》记载：镇安桥初名临江桥，宋时建，明洪武元年（1368年）、嘉靖八年（1529年）重建，清代又经多次修缮。中华民国十四年（1925年）毁于火灾，中华民国二十二年（1933年）再建[19]。桥身下设2个花岗岩条石砌筑的船形桥墩，迎水面砌筑雁翅金刚墙。桥墩上设置3组纵横叠置的圆木形成井字形伸臂梁构架，构架之上再设置1组纵横叠置的圆木构成桥梁的主体结构。除此之外，每面桥墩又向桥跨中心伸出4根木斜梁支撑桥体。斜梁的一端支撑在石砌桥墩或桥块的岩石之上，另一端伸进桥面上的廊屋梁架结构之中。如此一来，桥梁除了伸臂梁结构之外，又增加了几组斜梁支撑的结构体系。这种做法在早期的伸臂梁桥之中甚为罕见，极可能是后来重修时加建。

（六）福建宁化宜生桥

宜生桥位于福建省宁化县曹坊乡滑石村，长58米，宽4.6米，是1座四墩五孔的伸臂木廊桥。宜生桥所连接的是古代宁化通往长汀、连城的交通要道，原名"滑桥"。明正德十六年（1521年），由通判陈龙、毛公毅及主簿陈瓒措置官钱建成。明嘉靖二十一年（1542年）桥毁，嘉靖二十三年（1544年）由知县潘时宜与义民卢瑞银、张亨驯为首倡建修复，明万历三十九年（1611年），由知县唐世济再次修复，并易名"济川桥"。明崇祯九年（1636年）再次损毁，由郡守唐世涵、檄署县丞黄色中第三次修复，并改名"唐公桥"。清光绪年间（1875—1908年），有义民曹煜费资万计重建石墩木伸臂梁廊桥，被称"神仙桥"。1953年由宁化县人民政府拨款重修，遂改名为"解放桥"。[20]

桥身下设有4个花岗岩条石砌筑的船形桥墩，迎水面砌筑雁翅金刚墙。桥墩上设置3组纵横叠置的圆木形成井字形伸臂梁构架，构架之上再设置1组纵横叠置的圆木构成桥梁的主体结构。重建后的宜生桥，共建有梁架26榀，廊屋25间，廊屋内中间为行人道，两旁设置休憩用的长条凳，中间廊屋内设置神龛，檐下设有1道浅披檐。两端桥首构建三间四柱木牌楼为桥门，桥门额坊之上悬挂匾额。

第四节 撑架廊桥*

一、撑架桥的起源及特征

撑架桥是介于梁桥与拱桥之间的结构类型，其也可大致分为两类，一是简单撑架，二是组合撑架。早期撑架桥，也称之为斜撑桥，多是在简支梁桥基础上发展而来。一般来说，有以下三种情形时会考虑使用撑架桥：其一，简支梁桥的跨度需求接近或超过木梁的极限跨度；其二，桥梁横跨水流湍急的河流、溪涧以及深堑的峡谷等不具备架设桥墩、桥柱等条件；其三，为加强桥梁结构的整体刚度、可靠度以及耐久性。

撑架桥发展历史悠久，其发展演变来源于古代人民在实践中的创造，用材简单。虽然历史上的撑架桥实物难存，但可从历代图画资料中窥见一斑。

最早在汉代，就出现各种类型的桥梁，汉画像砖石上描绘有拱桥、梁桥等大量的桥梁形象。如1984年出土于四川彭州，现藏于四川省博物馆的东汉时期的"骖车过桥"画像砖（图24），其上刻画有一座弧形桥梁，桥面下无立柱支撑，却用点、线描绘成人字撑架的形式，并在撑架与桥面形成的空格内左刻青龙、右刻白虎，桥上设栏杆，桥面正通过一辆两人乘坐的骖驾。此种桥型虽无实物例证，也难排除是画师的臆想之作，但其画面直接反映了撑架结构特征。

图24 骖车过桥图（引自《中国画像砖全集》编辑委员会《中国画像砖全集·四川汉画像砖》）

北宋著名画家范宽《秋林飞瀑图》（现藏台北故宫博物院）中绘有一座撑架拱桥（图25），此桥可代表早期的撑架拱桥桥式。由于范宽绘画注重写生，对其居所终南太华山地区的自然和人文景观非常熟悉[21]，因此其绘画中虽然经过艺术的提炼，但对人造物——桥梁结构的把握与描摹非常准确的栩栩如生。画中描绘有一耸峙的高峰，峰峦下密布丛林，漫山红遍的秋叶作为画面的大背景；画面中部有茅舍隐约其中，飞瀑逐级而下，背后远景中还有隐现的城楼；近景是陡岸和飞湍的激流，画面下部的中心就是那座连通山路与栈道的撑架式木拱桥。至关重要的是，画面非常写实地反映出这类拱桥适宜的建造环境。

图25 《秋林飞瀑图》撑架桥（摹本）（引自唐寰澄《中国科学技术史·桥梁卷》）

在位于山西省临汾市洪洞县水神庙明应王殿内，留存有中国为数不多的戏曲题材的元代壁画，其中南壁"太宗千里行径图"中有这样一段：一座拱桥横跨溪涧，桥上老翁拄杖持牒、回首呈惊讶状，身后桥头文官执笏、武官横钺拱手，似为送别。从画面上看，桥系梁柱与人字撑架组合结构，跨中立两排石柱，通过水平木梁联系，中跨梁上架斗子蜀柱支承桥面横梁，同时还有人字形撑架，撑杆穿过两根木梁，杆端支撑中跨桥面横梁。该桥规模虽小，但结构简单明确，构造精巧，画面也描绘细致，推测可能为原物摹画（图26）。

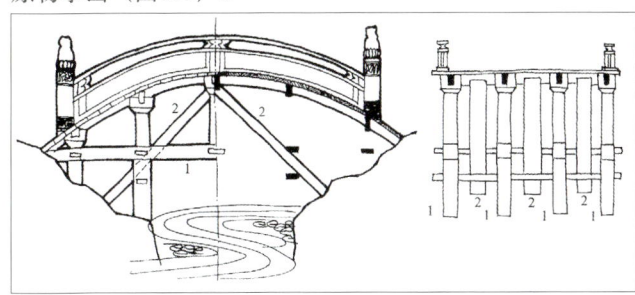

图26 山西洪洞水神庙元代壁画木桥结构图（引自唐寰澄《中国科学技术史·桥梁卷》）

同样的，在清代画家石涛的山水画作《荷塘游艇图》中，也有一座撑架桥（图27），桥横跨河流，连接乡间道路。桥下近桥台两端分别立两排桥柱，斜撑一端支承桥面横梁，一端固定在桥柱上，形成八字撑架结构。桥面横铺桥板，桥上两侧立4间廊架。该画虽是山水画技法绘制，但大体反映了该桥的构造特征。

二、撑架廊桥的类型及分布

撑架结构与"叠木为梁"的伸臂梁结构一样，都是限于木材的力学性能，提高桥梁跨越空间能力的不同解决方案。两种类型都是在简支梁结构基础上改进或增强，但却属不同技术方向演化出的两种结构类型，并在各自的系统内都有发展完备的结构体系，后期也有相互融合的类型，这一点也反映了桥梁技术实践过程中的多样性特征。

考察现存的木撑架式廊桥（简称：撑架木廊桥），数量不多但类型繁多，分布也相对分散。除传统的廊桥遗存最为集中的浙闽地区外，在云南、湖北、重庆、四川等省市内均有少数遗存，基于各地木构廊桥技术发展起来的撑架木廊桥呈现出多样化的特征。

图27 （清）石涛《荷塘游艇图》中的木桥（引自吴宪生、王经春《中国历代名家技法集萃·山水卷·树法》）

（一）简单撑架木廊桥

撑架结构从早期的斜撑结构发展而来，即在原有简支梁下两侧增设各一组斜撑，以达到减小木梁净跨与变形的目的。典型的案例是位于福建省屏南县棠口乡漈头村水尾的聚宝桥（图28），该桥下设两组斜撑，每组斜撑由垫木、横木、系杆及4根撑杆组成，撑杆倾角约60°，有效地减少了桥面木梁的净跨。当然，从材料力学以及构造措施上来看，聚宝桥的斜撑方案有以下两个特点：（1）斜撑支撑位置距支座较短，即桥面木梁的净跨仍然较大；（2）斜撑倾度较大，尚能独立支撑，无需辅助支撑。

图28 福建屏南聚宝桥（引自刘杰、周芬芳《乡土屏南》）

一般来讲，斜撑结构在发生之初，往往是独立于桥梁主体结构之外。但随着桥梁技术的不断发展，独立的斜撑也逐步进化成为完整的支撑框架，即撑体系，产生了八字形撑架（简称"八字撑架"）、人字形撑架（简称"人字撑架"）等多种类型。撑架木廊桥分布广泛，下面就几种类型分别举例：

1. 八字形撑架木廊桥

八字形撑架即由左右两组斜杆、一组水平杆以及两根横木组成，呈"八"字形，因此得名（图29）。

八字形撑架木廊桥遗存较多，中国各廊桥分布区均有发现，八字形撑架的亚类也较多，下面举例分别论述：

八字形撑架木廊桥通常是在原有简支梁桥的基础上，

下部增设数组八字形撑架构成，撑架数量至少是两组，如福建省尤溪县梅仙镇玉石村的玉麟桥。多数是由两组以上的八字形撑架组成，如浙江省庆元县白云桥、泰顺县池源桥，福建省寿宁县奖禄村上桥、下桥、宫桥等。

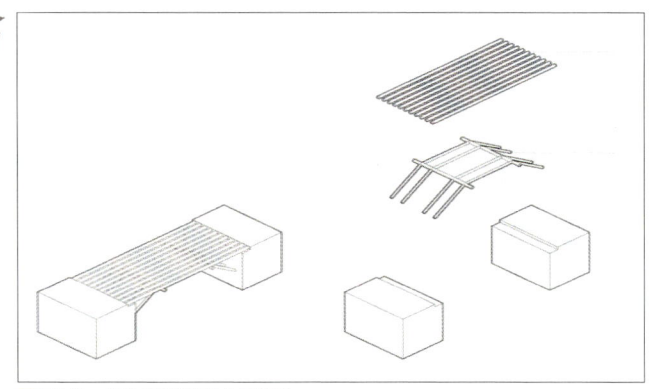

▉ 图29　简单八字撑架结构示意图

福建省内尚遗存数座体系更加完善的八字形撑架木廊桥，它们是通过增设垫木、剪刀撑、排架等构件与八字形撑架组合而成的结构体系（图30）。据此可以判断出，此类八字形组合撑架与更为复杂的编木拱梁式，在营造技艺上极有可能存在着渊源。例如福建省寿宁县下党乡碑坑村的观音桥，卵石垒砌的桥台上架设八字形撑架，共计7组，两端架立排架，用于架设桥面木梁，尚有左右两组剪刀撑支撑八字撑架中的横木。这样的构造方式增加了撑架的结构强度与刚度，保证了撑架结构的耐久性。同样的案例还有同省寿宁县犀溪镇仙峰村升仙桥、周宁县纯池镇院林桥等。

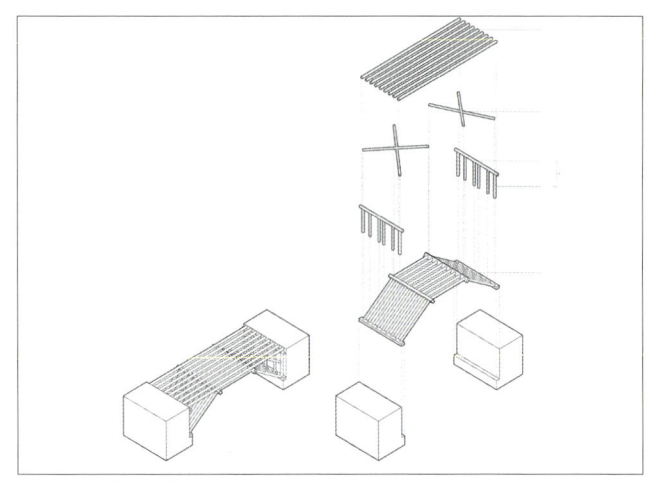

▉ 图30　八字撑架结构示意图

上述两类均是通长木梁与八字形撑架的组合，还有个别比较特殊的形式是八字撑架与两根短木梁的组合（图31），如位于福建省南平市建阳区漳墩镇龙安村的龙凤桥，该桥桥拱由十一组八字撑架与两根横木组成，比较特殊的是桥面两端的水平短木梁也与横木相连，拱架的水平杆即作为桥面梁的一部分。这样的构造方式，看似比较简洁合理，实则桥梁的结构冗余度不够，桥体也易变形。

同样的在福建建阳，位于水吉镇安口村也有一座特殊的八字形撑架木廊桥（图32）。有别于前面几例榫卯连接方式，安口桥特殊在于其独特的穿插别压的连接方式，其八字形撑架由两边各8根斜杆、9根水平杆、4根横木组成，杆件均为圆木，斜杆与水平杆交叉连接，外侧两根水平杆件稍低于其他7根，上部架设1根垫木

支承中间2根横木，外2根横木通过外两侧的2根水平杆穿插连接。

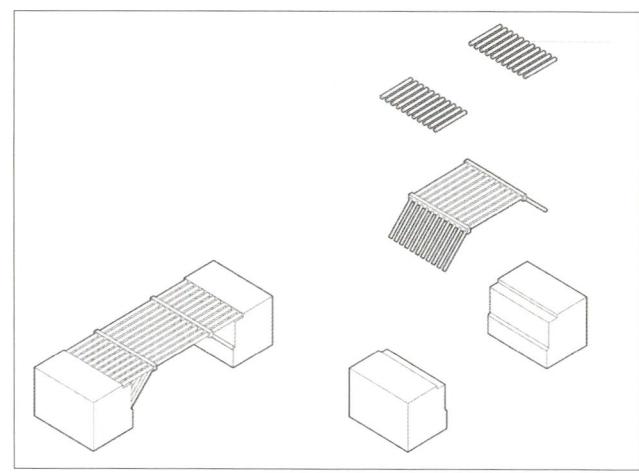

▉ 图31　福建建阳龙凤桥撑架结构示意图

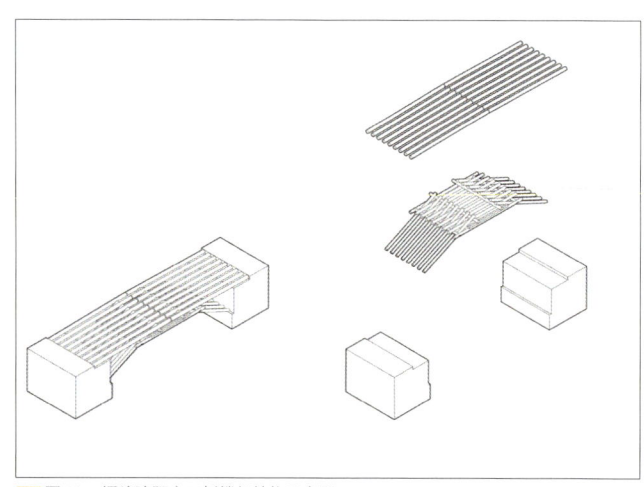

▉ 图32　福建建阳安口桥撑架结构示意图

2. 人字形撑架木廊桥

人字形撑架即由两组斜向撑杆与横梁组成，呈"人"字形，因而得名。人字形撑架木廊桥遗存较少，目前实例仅发现1座。此桥是位于福建省莆田市仙游县菜溪乡溪边村的象溪廊桥（图33），廊桥系由三组两层人字形撑架组成。其中，下层斜杆较粗，后尾部压入桥台，其上置条石，形成悬臂梁；下层斜杆较细，与下层斜杆近似平行，其间横木穿插。2层斜杆尽端共同支撑横梁，构成人字形撑架。严格地讲，象溪木构廊桥并不是纯粹意义上的人字形撑架木廊桥，其组合式结构中存有伸臂梁结构成分，但其明显的人字形撑架构造方式，可暂且归为人字形撑架类型。

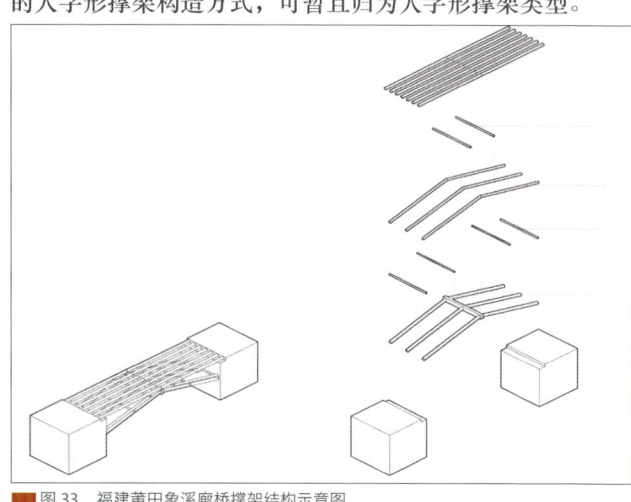

▉ 图33　福建莆田象溪廊桥撑架结构示意图

另外，笔者在历史照片中也发现了一座人字形撑架廊桥。该照片是由来华传教的美国基督教传教士萨穆埃尔 M. 茨维默（Samuel Marinus Zwemer，1867－1952年）在1932－1933年间考察中国期间拍摄，拍摄地点位于青海省循化县，是其考察离开循化县时途经的一座木构廊桥（图34）。该桥横跨峡谷，系人字形撑架木廊桥，桥上廊屋五间，两端接悬山顶单开间牌楼式桥门，廊屋结构上可见八字形撑架、两柱间都设有斜撑加强，形成类似于现在的桁架结构形式。卵石与土混合砌筑桥台，两侧桥台出2层伸臂梁支承桥面木梁，跨中由2组人字形撑架支撑，斜杆倾角40°左右。这座廊桥结构合理，造型优美，是位于西北地区的一座非常精致典雅的木拱廊桥。

▉ 图34　青海省循化县的撑架木廊桥（Samuel M. Zwemer 摄）

3. 其他简单撑架木廊桥

除前述及的闽浙地区的人字、八字撑架木廊桥外，在云南省内尚存在一类特殊的撑架木廊桥。现代桥梁结构中根据桥梁桥面与桥跨结构（包含拱架、桁架等）的相对位置关系，将拱桥或桁架桥分为上承式、下承式、中承式3类。顾名思义，上承式即桥面系位于拱架或桁架上部，下承式即桥面系位于拱架或桁架下部，中承式即位于中部。

考察中国古代桥梁，不论是石拱桥，还是木撑架桥，多数桥梁为上承式类型，仅有少数的竹拱桥或"弓弓桥"为中承式。从撑架木廊桥来看，多数也是上承式结构，桥面位于撑架之上。而在云南地区，撑架木廊桥却多是中承式或下承式，下面分别举例：

位于云南省巍山彝族回族自治县永建乡巡检村的永济桥（图35），系单孔撑架木廊桥，桥体以5根圆木横跨河道，梁下两端还设2组短斜撑，短斜撑之下各出2根长斜杆，倾角约45°，由下至上穿出桥面约1米，2根斜杆之间系横梁，榫卯连接，横梁中点悬吊垂直竖杆并与桥面梁联系。全桥共2组八字形撑架，分居两侧。这种中承式的撑架桥在云南省内还有数座，构造方法大同小异，主要变化在于八字形撑架的联系横梁的长度、设置高度以及垂直吊杆的数量等方面，在此不一一列举。

位于云南省洱源县炼铁乡茄叶村的茄叶桥（图36），同样系单孔撑架木廊桥，但不同的是此桥的八字形撑架落脚点与水平木梁支承点一样，都位于桥台顶部，八字形撑架联系横梁的位置较高，上下并无垂直吊杆，横梁直接承托在屋架的单步梁下。这样的结构组合形态类似于现代桥

梁结构中的下承式桁架结构，结构合理可靠。

图35　云南巍山永济桥（Terry E. Miller 提供）

图36　云南大理洱源茄叶桥（贾非 摄）

同样地，在云南地区尚存在几座多跨撑架木廊桥，也均为下承式八字形撑架式或"桁架式"结构。如大理白族自治州宾川县力角乡大会村的岩涧桥（图37），系三孔八字形撑架木廊桥；同位于大理鹤庆县松桂镇龙珠村的河头风雨桥（图38），系两孔八字形撑架木廊桥。

图37　云南宾川岩涧桥（贾非 摄）

图38　云南鹤庆河头桥（贾非 摄）

值得注意的是，云南省境内的撑架木廊桥多数以中承式或者下承式为主，在云南省外屡见不鲜的上承式撑架木拱廊桥却在云南保存不多；而云南省内独特的中承式或下承式撑架木拱廊桥，在省外却也是寥寥无几。从撑架桥梁技术演化的角度来看，上承式应当是早期撑架桥的主要形式，后逐步演化为中承式、下承式，最终形成桁架式。唐寰澄先生在《中国木拱桥》一书中也认为，"撑架桥是木拱与木桁架之源"[22]。

从近现代桥梁发展历程来看，中承式、下承式桥梁是后期桥梁结构发展的主流，笔者认为产生这种现象的主要原因：一是近现代大型船舶的出现，需要更高更大的航行空间，中承式与下承式的桥梁结构恰恰满足此要求，这也对桥梁与船舶安全都有益；二是中承式与下承式的桥梁建设减少了水上施工，改为更加便利的陆上施工，提高了施工的便捷性与安全性。

从以上视角来看，如前文举例的位于青海省循化县的撑架木廊桥，其上部结构即是桁架式结构，但该桥的建设年代无考；又如位于重庆市丰都县的包鸾桥，建于1951年，系下承式八字形撑架木拱廊桥。

（二）组合撑架木廊桥

组合撑架通常由两类撑架结构组合而成，比较典型的有：八字形与斜撑组合撑架，人字形与八字形组合撑架以及双八字形组合撑架三类。组合撑架都是在八字形撑架结构基础上的发展与演变，组合形式提高了拱架结构的整体性能。下面就几类组合撑架木廊桥分别举例：

1. 八字形与斜撑组合撑架

八字形撑架与斜撑组合的拱架结构并不多见，现仅发现1例，即位于浙江省宁波市奉化区萧王街道袁家岙村内的卧渡桥（图39）。该桥拱架结构由4组八字形撑架、8根斜撑杆、2组斜撑架组成，斜撑杆倾角较小，分别压在八字撑架的2根横木之间，斜撑架上顶横木，由八字撑架中的斜杆与斜撑杆夹持，形成类似于剪刀撑的结构，结构精巧妙绝。

图39　浙江奉化卧渡桥（吴卫平 摄）

2. 人字形与八字形组合撑架式

人字形撑架与八字形撑架均为独立的撑架结构体系，两者组合的实例也比较少见。目前仅发现的两例，浙江、福建两省各一例，下面分别说明。

一例是位于浙江省新昌县巧英乡上三坑村的风雨桥，又名梅树坂桥（图40）。该桥拱架系由八字形撑架、人字形撑架以及2根横木构成，八字形撑架由左右各4根斜杆、中间5根水平杆组成，人字形撑架由左右各3根斜杆与横木组成。值得注意的是，人字形撑架的横木并不连续，即3组人字形撑架并不是支撑同一根横木，而是夹紧三小段木块，各自形成人字形撑架。另外，尚有2根通长横木别压在人字形撑架与八字形撑架的斜撑杆之间。

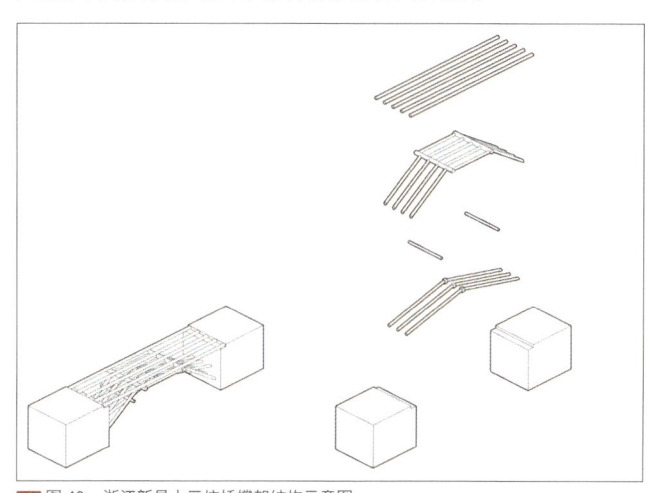
图40　浙江新昌上三坑桥撑架结构示意图

另一例则是位于福建省周宁县玛坑乡上坑村的上坑桥（图41）。该桥拱架系由八字形撑架、人字形撑架以及剪刀撑组成，人字形撑架由左右各4根斜杆以及1根通长横木组成，八字形撑架由左右各9根斜杆、9根水平杆以及2根通长横木组成，左右各1组剪刀撑支撑八字形撑架中的横木。

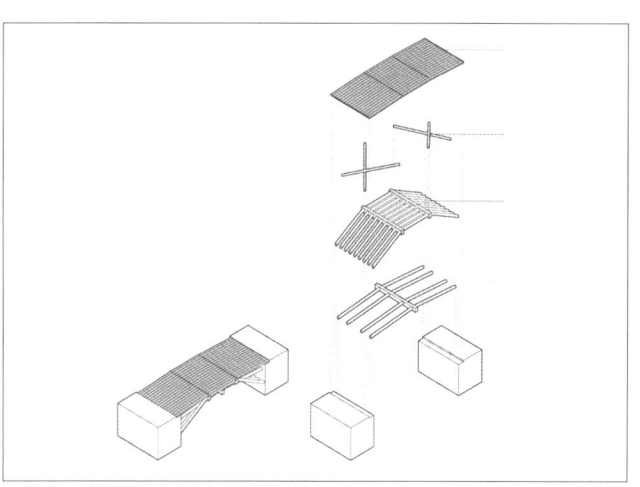
图41　福建周宁上坑桥撑架结构示意图

3. 双八字形组合撑架

双八字形组合撑架结构即由2套八字形撑架组合而成，可有相互叠合以及交叉组合方式，下面各举几例加以说明。

双八字形撑架叠合的案例仅见于兴龙桥（图42）。该桥位于福建省建瓯市迪口镇可建村，桥体结构综合运用了梁柱、八字形撑架、叠梁等结构类型。其中，横跨河流的主体结构是上、下2层八字形撑架，上层撑架斜杆倾角约60°，共五组；下层撑架斜杆倾角约45°，共四组。八字形撑杆均立于垫木上，架立在卵石砌桥台上。

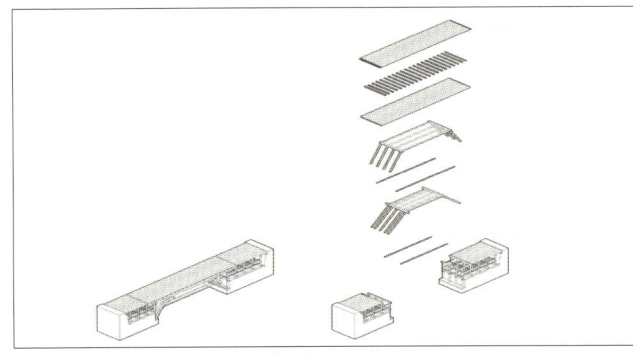
图42 福建建瓯兴龙桥拱架结构示意图

另外一类双八字形组合撑架则是八字形撑架交叉组合的形式（图43）。这一类撑架结构有典型的编木拱梁式结构特征。近年来，有地方学者在闽北南平地区发现了多座双八字形组合撑架木廊桥，其中南平市延平区峡阳镇八字桥是同时运用了3组八字形组合撑架结构。实际上，最下层的八字形撑架，是为了要加强桥梁的结构强度，于1979年附加上去的[23]。简单而言，南平地区的双八字形组合撑架木廊桥，其拱架基本式由两副八字形撑架交叉组合而成，辅助设置剪刀撑、排架等构件，结构体系比较完整，撑架净跨在15～20米。

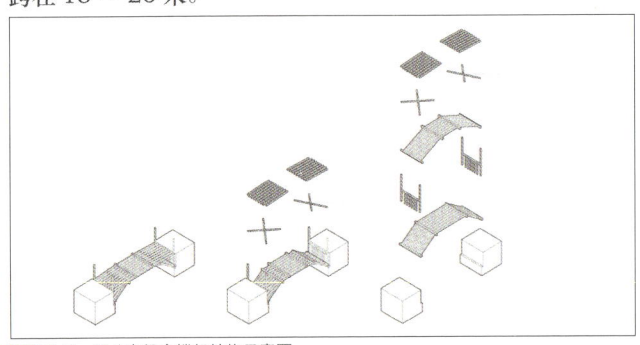
图43 双八字组合撑架结构示意图

（三）几种特殊撑架木廊桥

除上文提及的简单与组合撑架式外，还存在着一类特殊的撑架形式，其特殊之处在于桥体主要承重结构是由八字形撑架与伸臂梁结构的结合。下面举例分别说明。

1. 重庆市酉阳县龙凼沟回龙桥（图44）

该桥原于横跨峡谷之上，现已迁建。原桥系水平伸臂梁与八字形撑架组合式木拱廊桥，单孔，上承式结构。伸臂梁系3层6组，逐层出挑，梁下设有八字撑架与斜撑以及众多辅助支撑构件，构件之间联系复杂，却也合理。

图44 重庆酉阳龙凼沟回龙桥（吴卫平 摄）

2. 湖北省利川市毛坝乡永顺桥

该桥又名群策凉桥，系斜伸臂与八字撑架组合式廊桥，单孔，上承式结构。伸臂梁系3层6组，端部卵石压置。与一般的伸臂梁逐层出挑不同，该桥的3层伸臂仅2挑，上2层出挑一致。更为特别的是，两端伸臂梁之间通过两层水平系杆连接，每层5根，系杆与伸臂梁之间用横木穿插，相互夹持，形成整体。拱架上设水平桥面木梁，通过竖向立柱与拱架相互联系。

3. 云南省云龙县通京桥

通京桥是古代盐马古道以及运银通道上的重要桥梁，该桥跨度近30米，为斜伸臂与八字撑架组合式木拱桥，单孔，中承式结构。伸臂系5组7层，逐层出挑，梁端压入桥台，上砌桥屋。左右2组八字撑架自伸臂梁下穿过桥面，并通过水平方向的方木榫卯连接。方木与桥面梁通过竖向系杆连接，使得两组结构形成整体。

通京桥的桥体结构并非孤例，同样的案例还有同样地处云龙县的永镇桥、彩凤桥以及保山市腾冲的野猪箐桥等等。稍有不同的是，野猪箐桥桥体结构除伸臂梁、撑架结构外，尚有斜拉索作为加强措施，但并不影响对其桥梁主体是伸臂梁与撑架组合结构的判断。

当然，特殊形式的撑架廊桥尚不止上述几例。现存此类廊桥还有福建省浦城县镇安桥，系水平伸臂梁与八字形撑架组合式木拱廊桥，中承式结构。特殊的是，该桥系两墩三孔，每孔均设八字形撑架，且两边各两组平行的撑架，一高一低，低处撑架与栏杆结合一体，高处撑架与廊屋梁架结合，大大地提高了桥体结构的整体性。撑架式廊桥类型分布见表1。

撑架式廊桥的类型分布表（不完全统计） 表1

类型	特征		实例	备注
	撑架形式与组合方式	桥面系与撑架的相对位置		
简单撑架式	八字形	上承式	浙江省丽水市莲都区观音桥、京花桥、普济桥、龙泉市双溪桥、庆元县白云桥、包果桥、景宁县怀胜桥、松阳县八仙桥、温州市泰顺县城水桥、霞庄桥、南庆桥、宁波市奉化区外岙桥 福建省宁德市寿宁县外洋垟桥、碑坑桥、建瓯市观音桥、奖禄上桥、葫芦门桥、奖禄村下桥、升仙桥、奶殿桥、周宁县林蛤桥、古田县韦端桥、建安市金山村水尾桥、南平市建阳区龙凤桥、安口桥、建瓯市小桔村水尾桥、政和县澄源村观音桥；三明市尤溪县玉鳞桥 四川省绵阳市平武县红军桥	
		中承式	云南省大理州云龙县五里桥、检槽桥、小岭桥、炼登桥、下地登桥、巍山县永济桥；普洱市镇沅县邦海桥、景东县文俄桥、沽牛桥；文山州广南县大牡蕗桥	
		下承式	云南省大理州洱源县茄叶桥、宾川县岩涧桥、鹤庆县河头桥、丽江市永胜县仁和桥；青海省循化县廊桥△	桁架式
	人字形	上承式	福建省莆田市仙游县象溪廊桥、青海省循化县廊桥△	
		中承式	云南省普洱市景东县文献桥	
组合撑架式	斜撑与八字形		浙江省宁波市奉化区卧洲桥	
	人字形与八字形		浙江省新昌县上三坑桥、福建省周宁县上坑桥	

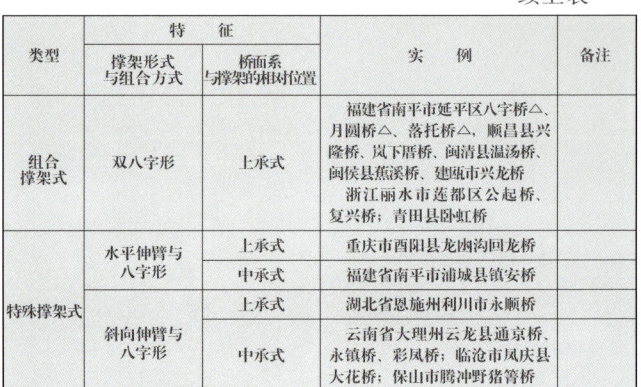

续上表

类型	特征		实例	备注
	撑架形式与组合方式	桥面系与撑架的相对位置		
组合撑架式	双八字形	上承式	福建省南平市延平区八字桥△、月圆桥△、落托桥△、顺昌县兴隆桥、岚下厝桥、闽清县温汤桥、闽侯县蕉溪桥、建瓯市兴龙桥、浙江丽水市莲都区公起桥、复兴县卧虹桥	
特殊撑架式	水平伸臂与八字形	上承式	重庆市酉阳县龙凼沟回龙桥	
		中承式	福建省南平市浦城县镇安桥	
	斜向伸臂与八字形	上承式	湖北省恩施州利川市永顺桥	
		中承式	云南省大理州云龙县通京桥、永镇、彩凤桥、临沧市凤庆县大花桥、保山市腾冲野猪箐桥	

注："△"表示已毁或改建为其他结构形式。

第五节　木拱廊桥**

一、木拱廊桥的命名、分类与分布

在浙江省的西南、福建省的东北以及福州地区，至今还保存着古代遗存的百余座木拱廊桥，笔者将之命名为"编木拱梁廊桥"。这种廊桥的下部结构是"编木拱梁"与简支梁相组合形成的亦拱亦梁结构。与北宋著名画家张择端所绘的《清明上河图》中虹桥结构略有不同，虹桥结构被笔者命名为"编木拱"。在浙闽交界的山区，有一小部分木拱桥的结构就非常接近于虹桥结构的"编木拱"。

中国木拱桥的发现，在学术界是比较晚的一件事。李约瑟博士在其巨著《中华科学文明史》一书中将虹桥结构错误地归类在伸臂式木梁桥的范畴。后来在1986年出版由茅以升主编的《中国古桥技术史》一书中，"竹木拱桥"一节的作者之一唐寰澄先生，才在学术界第一次将虹桥结构归为木拱桥，并且对新发现的浙闽木拱桥也作了考察和描述，对二者分别命名为"拱式木桥"和"虹桥式木拱桥"。这是中国现代学者在权威著作中第一次对虹桥结构进行系统研究，并初步对其进行概括归类。

唐寰澄先生在后来的著述中，力图进一步规范虹桥及浙闽木拱桥结构的命名。他在随后编著的《中国古桥》一书中，将两种桥梁结构笼统称为"叠梁拱"，应用"叠梁拱"结构的桥梁自然称作"叠梁拱桥"，英文译作 Combined Beam-arch Bridges。他在书中还解释说："介于梁与拱之间的木桥，笔者姑且名之为叠梁拱桥，可以宋代《清明上河图》上的汴水虹桥为代表。"这是中国现代学者第一次将虹桥桥式的下部结构，明确地给予命名，代表着中国学者对虹桥研究的一个阶段性成果。

然而，唐寰澄先生是一位资深的桥梁专家，他可能并不了解，"叠梁"二字在中国古代木构建筑中有约定俗成的意义：即是指木梁纵横交错、层层相叠，房屋或桥梁结构中较多运用叠梁的方式层层出挑，以求更多更大的空间或跨度。这种叠梁结构在建筑上运用较早，在先秦时期的青铜器上就有所刻画。用"叠梁拱"来称呼虹桥的下部结构，极易与上文提到的"伸臂式梁桥"的结构相混淆，因为后者的"伸臂"正是通过叠梁的方式来形成的。其实，唐先生自己当时也觉得并不妥，故在书中用了"姑且名之为叠梁拱桥"的叙述。北京大学的方拥教授在1995年11月发表在《建筑学报》上的《虹桥考》一文中，也引用了唐寰澄先生命名的"叠梁拱"一词。

在2000年1月由科学出版社出版，唐寰澄著的《中国科学技术史·桥梁卷》一书中，汴水虹桥的结构又被命名为"贯木拱桥"。由此看来，唐先生依然对虹桥结构以"叠梁拱"的命名并不满意。据作者称，"贯木"取自《渑水燕谈录》中"取巨木数十相贯"一句描述虹桥的建造的文字。客观地讲，用"贯木"二字要比"叠梁"要准确，并有古文献为据，但是"贯木拱"在结构上仍然存在较多的模糊性，它没能明确描绘出，如何形成虹桥的拱式结构。

最初，提议用"编梁木拱桥"来命名汴水虹桥的下部结构。用"编织"的方式形成一种结构，小到日常生活用的器皿，比如竹篓、竹筐等，大到一种建筑结构（如编竹墙），在中国历史上都出现较早。事实上，后一名称用"编梁木拱"四个字作桥的定语，比较完整地描述了该结构的三大特征：

(1) 构造特征："编梁"，如果笔者分别把第一系统4根拱骨和第二系统3根拱骨视为连续的经线，把横木视作纬线、则虹桥拱骨和横木上下穿插则压的交叠构造，正好与用经纬线编成织物的技术相同。而且两者都同样利用了经纬之间的摩擦力，保持结构和织物的整体稳定性；

(2) 材料特征："木"，表示采用圆木；

(3) 结构力学特征："拱"，表示是构件主要受压的结构。采用有限元法对其结构进行计算机模拟，证实该结构构件主要内力为纵向压力，是结构力学严格意义上的拱结构。因而具有优越的承载能力。

2004年6月14日，笔者团队应邀在芬兰拉赫蒂市举行的"第八届世界木工程大会（World Conference on Timber Engineering, WCTE2004）"上做了题为《中国虹桥》(Chinese Rainbow Bridges) 的报告，重点介绍了汴水虹桥和浙闽木拱廊桥的结构特点，并在大会上首次使用了"编梁木拱桥"，作为汴水虹桥结构的名称。但笔者团队对浙闽木拱廊桥进行的结构力学分析和计算机模拟证实，由于第一系统采用5根而不是虹桥的4根拱骨，这一差别使第二系统中央拱骨主要受弯，因而该桥结构兼具拱桥和梁桥特征，参照上述名称，应称为"编梁木拱梁桥"。这一名称中出现了两个"梁"字，乃修辞之大忌。而且这两个"梁"有不同含义：第一个"梁"指用来编织的"圆木"，第二个"梁"指结构力学上受弯的构件。

因此，建议对上述名称略作改动，为"编木拱桥"，这一名称仍准确完整描述了虹桥结构三大特征。《续资治通鉴长编》中亦曾以"编木为之"来描述虹桥结构。相应的浙闽木拱廊桥的下部结构名称，应为"编木拱梁桥"，两个名称反映了两类桥梁结构的大同和小异。在WCTE2004报告英文稿中，上述两个名称分别被译为"Woven Timber Arch Bridge"和"Woven Timber Arch-Beam Bridge"。

因此，将汴水虹桥和现存的浙闽木拱廊桥的下部结构命名分别规范为："编木拱桥"（英文译作"Woven Timber Arch Bridge"）和"编木拱梁桥"（英文译作 Woven Timber Arch-Beam Bridge）。而将目前国内的"廊桥"一词英文译名规范为"Covered Bridge"，浙闽一带尚存的"木拱廊桥"一词的英文译名规范为"Timber Arch Covered Bridge"[24]。

就在2004年的暑期，笔者应邀赴福建省宁德市屏南县，出席当地一年一度的"白水洋旅游节"系列活动的廊桥文化论坛。主办方也邀请了唐寰澄先生莅临发言。在研讨会上，笔者也曾就木拱桥的命名问题与唐先生商讨。当时，唐先生表示他已完成了一部中国木拱桥的专著，即将出版，在这一著作中，他将对木拱桥的命名问题仔细斟酌后再做确定。果然，笔者见到了2010年由唐寰澄著、中国建筑工业出版社出版的《中国木拱桥》一书。在书中第20页唐先生写道："世界上唯独中国有的特殊木拱桥，发明于11世纪，画在一幅有名的长卷画上。作者在发表第一篇文章时名之为'叠梁拱'。之后经过深入调查和研究，改名为'贯木拱'或'编木拱'，因历史记载上说桥是'以巨木相贯'。实际上桥像织成的竹或藤篮子的一段。"中国现代最早进行木拱桥研究的唐寰澄先生经过了几乎半个世纪的研究历程，在其耄耋之年，最后将木拱桥的研究报告正式出版，且接受笔者的建议将近年来众说纷纭的中国木拱桥结构学名正式定为"贯木拱"和"编木拱"。可以说，这是他作为中国最资深古桥研究学者的杰出贡献之一。

诚如唐寰澄先生以及笔者的著述，编木拱桥曾广泛分布于以北宋东京汴梁古城为核心的黄河流域。在今之西北的甘肃尚能见到类似木构造的遗存。而编木拱梁桥则更多以廊桥的形式保存在长江以南的区域，尤其是聚集在浙西南、闽东北的山区里。笔者及其团队在这一区域里经过了长达20余年的调查和研究，大致可以将这一区域确定在如下的县市里：浙江省丽水市景宁县、青田县、庆元县、龙泉市，温州市的泰顺县；福建省宁德市寿宁县、屏南县、周宁县、古田县、福安市、柘荣县、福鼎市、霞浦县，南平市的政和县、武夷山市、建瓯市，福州市的晋安区、闽清县、闽侯县等县市。总的说来，从数量上看，闽多于浙；从保存的质量上看，是浙优于闽，尤其是庆元县和泰顺县的木拱廊桥。

除去近年来因廊桥热而新造的木拱廊桥外，这一地区的古代木拱桥大致保存着100余座，且大都为编木拱梁结构的木拱廊桥。表2为现存的古代编木拱梁廊桥数量统计。

闽浙地区现存的古代编木拱梁廊桥数量统计 表2

省份	地市	区县	名称	数量
福建省	宁德市	寿宁县	鸾峰桥、杨梅州桥、飞云桥、升平桥、仙宫桥、登云桥、杨溪头桥、张坑桥、长濑桥、里仁桥、文明桥、小东上桥、大宝桥、福寿桥、单桥、寿春桥、红军桥、回澜桥、普济桥	19
		屏南县	万安桥、千乘桥、百祥桥、广利桥、广福桥、龙井桥、龙津桥、金造桥、清晏桥、惠风桥、锦溪桥、樟口桥、迎风桥	13
		周宁县	登龙桥、后垅桥、三仙桥、七仙桥、楼下桥、竹岭桥、长峰桥	7
		古田县	公心桥、徐州桥、亭下桥、兰溪桥、树荫桥	5
		福安市	登稔桥、玉拏桥、积谷桥、洋坑桥、柘头桥	5
		柘荣县	东源桥、归驷桥	2
		福鼎市	老人桥	1
		霞浦县	临清桥	1
	南平市	政和县	后山厝桥、洋后厝桥、赤溪桥、龙滩桥、大梨溪桥、落岭桥、下坂桥	7
		建瓯市	接龙桥、后建桥、德胜桥、仙恩桥	4
		武夷山市	余庆桥	1
	福州市	闽侯县	远济桥、坑坪桥、泰山桥、塘里桥	4
		晋安区	店坂桥	1
		闽清县	合龙桥	1
浙江省	丽水市	景宁畲族自治县	接龙桥、东坑下桥、东坑上桥、大赤坑桥、梅岐桥、连813大地桥、永镇桥、苎岭岭脚桥、北溪桥、长濂桥、永平桥、石梗坑桥	12
		庆元县	如龙桥、兰溪桥、后坑桥、咏归桥、路亭桥、袅桥、半路涨大桥、甫田桥、竹坪桥、双门桥	10
		龙泉市	顺德桥、合porte桥	2
		青田县	怀仁桥	1
	温州市	泰顺县	三条桥、北涧桥、溪东桥、薛宅桥、文兴桥、仙居桥	6

注：本表统计范围为截至2019年5月，闽浙各地现存的古代编木拱梁廊桥。

二、木拱廊桥的发展与演变

笔者在20多年前旧作中，已经比较过汴水虹桥和浙闽木拱廊桥的建筑和结构特点，并作过详细的分析。这是笔者最初所持的一种观点。在本书中也简单叙述如下：

汴水虹桥与浙闽木拱廊桥都是全木构体系的桥梁，有相似的编木拱结构，这是它们最大的共同点，也是能够被称为"虹桥"的必备特征。然而，两者之间也存有较多的差异。

第一，汴水虹桥为纯粹的编木拱结构，而后者却是编木拱与木梁相结合的拱梁结构；

第二，汴水虹桥的编木拱在节点上使用北方常用的棕绳绑扎技术，而后者使用的是南方惯用的榫卯技术；

第三，汴水虹桥的木拱之上并不设廊屋，而后者的拱梁之上均设置翘角飞檐的青瓦木屋顶；

第四，汴水虹桥的拱形结构外形呈完整的弧形，而后者的拱梁结构外形却略似"八"字形；

第五，汴水虹桥的结构跨度在18米左右，而后者单跨跨越河道的宽度从9米一直到42米的范围均可，比较而言，后者适应河道的能力更强，跨越空间的能力更甚；

第六，汴水虹桥因为使用于地势平坦的中原地区，只用了编木拱一种结构体系，而后者是运用在浙闽山区的大山密林之中，深沟高涧之上，除了拱梁体系外，还常常在靠近两岸的下部结构中运用了门式刚架，增强桥梁结构的受力性能，也能增大拱梁结构的跨度。如果仔细比较两种结构，当会寻找到更多差异来。面对两种木拱结构的众多差异，我们能否结合对历史文献的研究和浙闽山区百余计的木拱廊桥的实地考察，从中寻找出二者的渊源关系？按建筑进化论的观点分析，如果它们真有亲缘关系，那么，哪些基因是共同遗传下来的，哪些又是发生了变异的呢？

唐寰澄先生认为：浙闽木拱廊桥是汴水虹桥的改进型桥式，是随着宋室南渡，士工农商将造桥技术带到了浙闽山区，再结合当地的木构技术逐步发展起来的。这种观点在其主编和著述的《中国科学技术史·桥梁卷》和《中国古桥》两书中都有体现，在稍早出版的茅以升主编的《中国古桥技术史》一书中，木拱桥一章的撰作也主要是出自唐先生之手，故观点一致。后来桥梁和建筑专家也多持此观点。不过，也有专家有不同意见，其中包括浙闽山区的文物工作者，可惜拿不出更多、更可靠的证据[25]。

通过多年的考察研究，笔者认为浙闽山区保存的木拱廊桥在拱梁结构上基本是一致的，由于不同地区，尤其是出于不同木匠师傅（工匠家系）之手，在桥梁结构的建造过程中或多或少有些差别。但是，这些细微的差别都改变不了浙闽木拱廊桥的拱梁结构特征。

笔者以前过多地把考察和研究的注意力集中在木拱桥一种桥式上，并且研究的着眼点一直局限在建筑学和建筑史学的狭窄范畴，经过几年的研究积累，仍然没能从中找到这些木拱桥的技术来源。从2001年起，随着研究队伍的扩大，尤其是有着深厚工程以及结构力学背景的专家加盟，笔者将研究视野扩展到浙闽地区所有的以木构为主的桥梁，并运用了工程技术学和其他学科的思维方法进行综合研究。由于这一地区地域辽阔，山高水长，木构桥梁的总数不下千余。

以浙江省泰顺县为例，对所有的以木构为主的桥梁进行了对比考察、研究和总结，发现这些形形色色的木桥从其主体结构来看，大致呈现出有简有繁的状况。并且这种从简到繁有许多中间层次，可能是这一地区木构桥梁在发展过程中各类桥式的一种孑遗现象。

木桥的营造自古以来都属于工程技术的范畴，于是，笔者联想到工程技术由发生、发展到成熟的过程，遵循类似生物通过遗传和变异实现进化的规律（图45）。

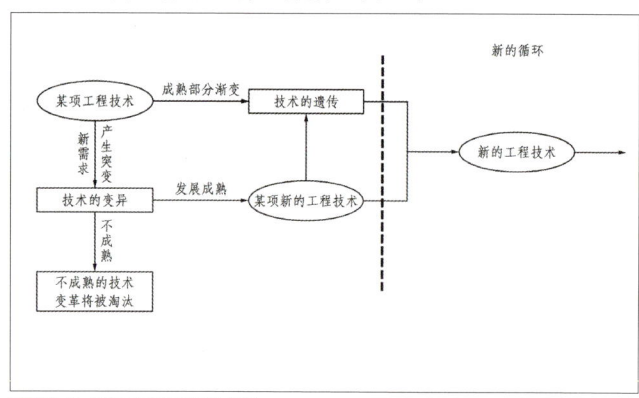

■ 图45 工程技术进化理论框图

其原理简述如下：某种技术在尚能满足需要时，将会"遗传"，即基本稳定地复制；当有新需求出现，原技术不能满足时，将会引发技术变革，产生"变异"；推动技术进步的是创新性的变革，即"突变"；"突变"一般发生于局部，其余大部分仍是"遗传"，即全局"渐变"，局部"突变"；"突变"初生时会有多种形式，在一定时期内并存，且不稳定；一段时期后，不同形式的"突变"会"优胜劣汰"，即淘汰较差的，保留完善较好的；最终保留的一种或少数种"突变"形式会趋于完善稳定进入"遗传"阶段。上述过程周而复始，多次发生，形成某一种技术发展的历史过程[26]。

遵循上述原理，笔者将泰顺县的木构桥梁进行了分类整理，基本上勾勒出了如下的桥梁发展谱系（图46）：
（1）简支木梁桥→（2）中间有支撑的木平梁桥→（3）两端设斜撑的木平梁桥→（4）向编木拱梁结构过渡的木拱桥→（5）浙闽编木拱梁桥→（6）由编木拱梁结构向编木拱过渡的木桥→（7）编木拱桥（汴水虹桥），要完成此谱系，需要经历七个桥式的发展过程。在这七个过程中，笔者通过实地考察，先是掌握了（1）（2）（3）（5）（7）5个桥式的实例，根据上述原理推断出应该有（4）（6）2种中间过程的桥式。在此科学假象之下，笔者又经过2年多的实地考察，最终在浙闽山区寻找到了这两个中间过程的桥式实例。

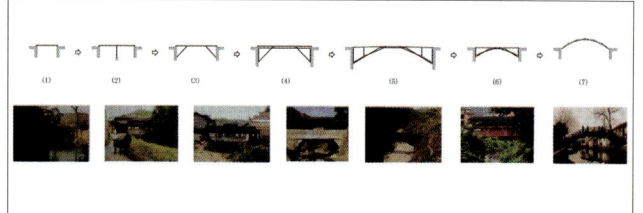

■ 图46 浙闽山区木构桥梁发展谱系示意图

除第（6）种桥式的实例在泰顺相邻的庆元县发现外，其余六个实例全部是泰顺一地所有。如果这一木桥向木拱桥发展演变过程的假想成立，那么，在浙闽山区独立发展编木拱梁桥的观点就有可能成立。反观汴水虹桥所在的北宋东京，即使将整个中原地区算在内，恐怕要找到上千座的木构桥梁也非易事。因为，当时经济文化发达的中原，可以有石桥乃至石拱桥等先进桥式的更多选择。没有了广泛的木桥建造基础，从技术上讲就失去了在当地产生高水平的先进木拱桥式的可能，何况是汴水虹桥如此完美的编木拱式结构呢？

再看看浙闽山区木拱廊桥的实地营造情况。

谈到虹桥营造的历史，研究者们都会共同关注到一座特殊的桥梁，那就是浙江泰顺县的三条桥。现存的三条桥位于洲岭乡通往垟溪乡的横溪上，临近福建省寿宁县。三条桥远离喧嚣的公路以及现代文明下的城乡环境，置身于幽溪深涧之中，山道曲折，风景优美而古雅。登临三条桥，极易让人忘却了历史，展开无限遐想。但正是这座三条桥，承载了太多中国虹桥营造的秘密。

据清光绪年间泰顺《分疆录》记载："三条桥在七都。此桥最古，长数十丈，上架屋如虹，俯瞰溪水。旧渐就圮。道光二十三年，里人苏某独力重建，拆旧瓦有'贞观'年号。"1982年，泰顺县文博馆专门调查，又在此桥的屋面上发现一块刻有"丁巳绍兴七年九月十三日开工作瓦其年米谷直价每斛五十文"字样的旧瓦（图47），经考证为宋绍兴七年（1137年）。桥上发现唐宋的旧瓦似乎并不能证明在同一时期的桥身就是木拱结构，但是，木桥结构的存在应该是没有多大问题的。

■ 图47 浙江泰顺三条桥上发现的宋瓦（刘杰 摄）

另据泰顺县交通局编，1991年由海洋出版社出版的《泰顺交通志》记载："距现桥上游十余米的西岸巨石上，尚有旧桥址的柱孔遗迹，四个方孔向东岸倾斜，两个圆孔朝天。"唐寰澄和泰顺文博馆馆长张俊都曾根据这些桥洞遗迹做过木桥的复原图。由于二人的观点不同，所复原

的木桥形式也有所差别。唐所复原之桥式更像笔者上面提及的第（3）（4）过程之间，而张复原的桥式更趋向第（4）（5）过程之间。但不管怎样，三条桥上游的旧桥肯定是上述七个中间过程桥式之一。也许，众多的桥洞遗迹根本就不是一座木桥所有，更可能是多座不同桥式桥梁建造后的遗迹之总和。同样根据《分疆录》记载，最初的三条桥就是由三根巨木跨溪而成的简支桥，亦即上述的第（1）过程桥式，因而命名为"三条桥"。

笔者根据对三条桥的研究认为，三条桥及其周边桥洞遗迹上的原有桥梁组合在一起，极有可能完成了上述桥梁发展历程中的七个步骤中的第（1）（2）（3）（4）（5）五种桥式的演进。当然，最终桥梁结构的演进止步于第（5）种桥式，即编木拱梁桥。

同样，在庆元县调查时，笔者发现大济村的"双门桥"在丽水地区创建年代最早（虽于1992年底曾重建，但桥式和梁架基本无大变化）。其廊屋明间梁下，有墨书"大宋天圣三年甲子（1025年）吴毂、吴榖兄弟二公仝建双门桥"字样。清光绪三年（1877年）编修的《庆元县志·建置》也记载："双门桥，吴毂、吴榖兄弟联登，竖双门于桥侧，故名。"如果双门桥果真是北宋天圣三年（1025年）建成，那其建造的时间要早于夏竦于明道年间（1032－1033年）建造的虹桥至少7年，正好晚于天禧元年（1017年）魏化基罢修无脚桥8年。

这里，还得提及一下魏化基及其建造无脚桥的故事。北宋初期，京城汴水上有许多座有柱梁桥，但一遇洪水或船运繁忙之时，就经常发生船撞桥事件。《续资治通鉴长编》记载："内殿承制魏化基言，汴水悍激，多因桥柱坏舟，遂献无脚桥式，编木为之，钉贯其中。诏化基与八作司营造。至是，三司度所费工逾三倍，乃诏罢之。"《宋会要》中也有记载："天禧元年（1017年）正月，罢修汴河无脚桥。"这种无脚桥到底是何种桥式？方拥先生认为："这种因耗工太多而未建造成功的无脚桥可能为伸臂木梁式。"[27]根据对"编木为之，钉贯其中"等文字理解，笔者认为这种无脚桥也有可能就是编木拱梁桥。因为"编木为之，钉贯其中"描述的极有可能就是编木结构的南方榫卯做法。2001年11月，笔者曾参与了中央电视台拍摄《虹桥寻踪》的电视纪录片，节目为了真实再现浙闽木拱桥的建造实景，曾在福建省寿宁县的小东村请造桥世家的传人郑多金师傅主持建造了一座规模较小的木拱桥的主体结构模型。在美籍华人余敏的帮助下，笔者得到了美国NOVA电视台拍摄的《虹桥》电视纪录片，片中记录了唐寰澄以及汤姆·彼得斯（Tom F. Peters）教授主持在上海市青浦区金泽镇恢复汴水虹桥的建造全过程。对比而言，编木拱梁结构适合建造跨度较大的桥梁，建造时两岸的石砌岸基非常重要。编木拱梁结构的两端断面都很粗大，并运用了门式刚架，所有节点几乎都是榫接，做法要比汴水虹桥的编木拱结构要复杂费事得多，故云"三司度所费工逾三倍"。

再说说吴毂、吴榖两兄弟及其双门桥。据清光绪三年（1877年）编修的《庆元县志·选举志》记载："天圣（仁宗）二年甲子科（宋郊榜）：吴毂：官至太子赞善改殿中丞，

有传。景祐（仁宗）元年甲戌科：吴毂：濠州知府特授守秘丞，有传。"吴毂是宋朝第一位通过科举入仕的庆元籍人士，并且官至殿中丞。据上海辞书出版社1992年版的《中国历代职官词典》载："殿中丞：官名。唐改殿内省为殿中省，殿中丞为其属官。"又"殿中省：官署名。唐武德元年（618年），改殿内省为殿中省，掌皇帝生活诸事，所属有尚食、尚药、尚衣、尚舍、尚乘、尚辇六局。……宋沿置，仅为寄禄官，六尚局职掌分由他署担任……"根据以上信息可知，吴毂建议甚至参与皇城内的桥梁营造也不是没有可能。现存之双门桥，单孔净跨11.2米，宽4.6米，其桥身结构非常接近于上述所提及的第（6）种桥式。由于第二系统的五节苗变为四根，中间一根被省略，亦即形成了编木拱桥式，其跨度与汴水虹桥（跨度估计是16～18米）也比较接近。因此，在汴水虹桥之前的一种桥式，由吴毂这样背景的官员带到北宋东京城也是极有可能的。编木拱梁桥的技术再与北方京城的固有木构技术融合，最终形成了千古奇观的编木拱桥——汴水虹桥。

除却上述二例，浙闽山区营造木拱廊桥的历史至少可以追溯到明代。据《中国古桥技术史》一书记载，浙闽山区最古老的当数泰顺叶树阳桥，建于明景泰五年（1454年），可惜于1965年修建公路遭拆除。至今保存完好的庆元县如龙桥建于明天启五年（1625年）。据泰顺文博馆研究人员的考证，当地还有几座木拱桥的初建年代，大多是在明代，如泗溪镇的溪东桥（亦名东溪桥）始建于明隆庆四年（1570年）。此外，笔者亲自考察过的庆元县咏归桥始建于元大德十年（1306年），明天顺年间（1457－1464年）重建，福安市康厝乡积谷桥也是建于明崇祯年间（1628－1644年）。屏南金造桥也有可能始建于明代（1368－1644年）[28]。由此可见，浙闽山区木拱廊桥营造的历史极有可能是上迄宋代，往下一直延续至今，没有间断的迹象。

后来笔者在福建省还发现了多座始建年代在两宋时期的木桥。其中屏南县就有两座有可能在宋代始建的编木拱梁廊桥——千乘桥和万安桥，另一座是福州市闽清县的合龙桥。合龙桥位于省璜乡省璜村，始建于南宋乾道年间（1165－1173年），元延祐年间（1314－1320年）毁，明万历年间（1573－1619年）、清康熙三十八年（1699年）两度重建，后再毁，中华民国十六年（1927年）再次重建。千乘桥位于福建省宁德市屏南县棠口村，《屏南古代桥梁》（2003年，政协屏南县文史委编印）记载："（千乘桥）始建于南宋理宗年间（1201－1264年），明末毁于火患，清康熙五十四年（1715年）重建，雍正十年（1729年）落成。嘉庆十四年（1809年）被大水冲毁，嘉庆二十五年（1821年），周大权等人再次募建"。万安桥，当地人俗称长桥，位于长桥镇长桥村东面，为一座五墩六孔的编木拱梁廊桥，也是中国现存最长的木拱桥。据清光绪三十四年版《屏南县志》载："长桥《玉田志略》称：两溪相接，亘如长虹，俗云仙人所建。古志，一名龙江公济桥，宋时建，垒石为墩五，构亭于上，戌子（当为戊子）被盗焚毁，仅存一板。乾隆七年重建。"后文博人员又在中间墩离水面约三米处发现一块石刻，上

有文字曰："弟子江稹舍钱一拾三贯又谷三十四石，结石墩一，造为考妣二亲。承此良因，又为合家男女乃自身各乞保平安。元祐五年庚午九月谨题。"这块石刻嵌在石砌桥墩内，镌刻文字共计54字，全部分9行竖书，每行6字（图48）。

图48 福建屏南万安桥桥墩上的石刻（引自刘杰、周芬芳《乡土屏南》）

元祐为北宋哲宗赵煦的年号，元祐五年亦即1090年。如果此桥在修建之初即为编木拱梁桥，那么它将是已知的仅晚于浙江省庆元县大济村双门桥的一座古老的木拱桥。唐寰澄先生显然也注意到这条线索，他在最近出版的《中国木拱桥》一书中解释说："假如当初的万安桥便是贯木拱，此记无疑打破了第一假定（即先前著作中所说的由士工农商在南宋时期由北方将木拱桥技术带到南方的假定），即桥式自南宋后南传。但1090年已在贯木拱最晚的发明期1041-1048后又50年，此时汴京虹桥已建成。"如此一来，唐先生还是坚持木拱桥技术是由汴京传来浙闽地区的。但为了在逻辑上能够说通，他认为或有人如北宋名臣周邦彦等可能成为此类桥式的传播者。周邦彦（1056－1121年），钱塘人，《宋史》载其"元丰初（约1080年）游京师，献《汴都赋》万余言，神宗异之"。《汴都赋》中对汴河上繁忙的水上运输有深入细致的刻画描写，因此，唐先生推测他不可能不关注到汴河上的编木拱桥。况且，《宋史》还记载周邦彦先在京师做官，后"知龙德府，从明州（今宁波）……未几知顺昌府（今福建顺昌），徙处州（今浙江丽水），卒年六十六"。周邦彦或者类似经历者，极有可能在北宋年间就已将这编木拱技术从汴京带到了浙闽地区。无论如何，唐先生都不赞成这一先进的木拱技术会是浙闽独立发展起来的。因此，在《中国木拱桥》一书中，唐寰澄先生也从反面提出一个疑问："如果北宋闽浙已独立发明了贯木拱，为什么不能像夏竦、陈希亮一样的闽浙地方官上报中央，解决汴京船撞桥毁的问题？"

当然，笔者从技术进化论角度，推导出浙闽地区有可能独立发展编木拱梁桥技术的。但并没有肯定这一技术一定是从浙闽地区率先发展起来的。以笔者考量，在没有寻找到足够的证据之前，至少以下三种可能都还是存在的。即：

第一种可能是如唐寰澄先生所推测，木拱技术是由北宋东京汴梁城传播而来；

第二种是浙闽地区率先发展起编木拱梁以及编木拱技术，然后再由地方官员将之带到了中央；

第三种可能是编木拱梁技术是由浙闽地区独立发展起来的，与北宋东京的编木拱没有必然的渊源关系。

从各方面的材料看来，前二种的可能性更大。唐寰澄先生的推测也不是没有道理。如果历史确实如唐先生的观点，那么笔者首先要确认的关键问题是：这一种先进的木拱技术为何独存于浙闽地区的崇山峻岭之中，且都是经济并不发达的地区？再进一步提问，这一经济整体欠发达区域，有何种迫切的实际需求采用这一国家最先进、尖端的桥梁营造技术？这将是笔者以后需要继续弄清楚的重要问题。

三、木拱廊桥的类型与特征

编木拱结构是近代学者对《清明上河图》中"虹桥"的桥拱结构的称谓，其桥拱结构主要是由两类不同拱架系统排列组合而成（图49）。一类是由3根长杆组成，一平两斜，称为系统Ⅰ；另一类是由2根长杆2根短杆组成，均为斜杆，称为系统Ⅱ。两类拱架系统横向交替排列，其中系统Ⅰ拱架10榀，系统Ⅱ拱骨11榀，4根横木穿插别压，并通过棕绳绑扎连接，形成整体的拱架[29]。时至今日，汴河上的"虹桥"早已无存，与之相同的桥梁结构也难寻踪迹。编木拱桥也仅"虹桥"这一孤例。

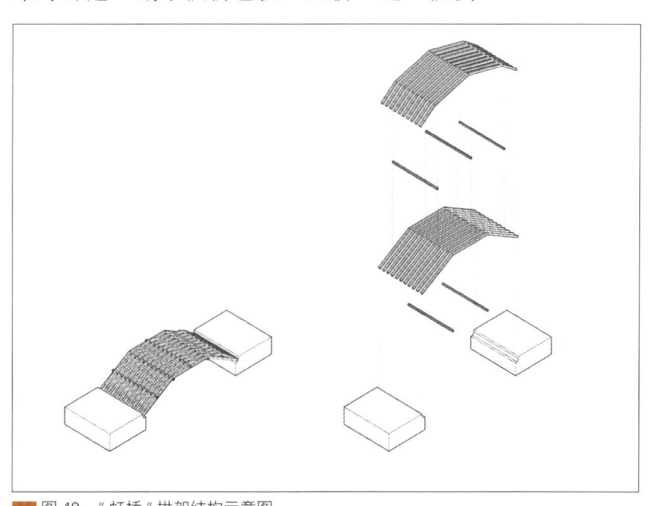
图49 "虹桥"拱架结构示意图

而闽浙地区的编木拱梁廊桥，现存数量可观、分布广泛、类型丰富。其中以单孔为主，个别为两孔、三孔、六孔等。以典型的单孔编木拱梁廊桥为例，其桥拱结构主要也是由两类不同拱架系统排列组合而成。一类是由3根长杆组成，一平两斜，称为系统Ⅰ；另一类是由5根长短不一的杆件组成，一平四斜，称为系统Ⅱ。两类拱架系统横向交替排列，其中系统Ⅰ拱架数量通常为9榀，系统Ⅱ拱架数量通常为8榀，也有8榀与7榀、7榀与6榀的组合，一般来讲系统Ⅰ拱架的数量较系统Ⅱ数量多1根。同系统拱架内的杆件通过榫卯连接横木，拱脚垫木块或石块，紧贴桥台立竖向排架，拱架上部增设剪刀撑。系统Ⅱ下横木上架小排架，支撑桥面木梁，通常还有撑杆支撑小排架。两系统拱架组合之后，协同剪刀撑、撑杆、排架、桥面梁等辅助构件，构成了完整的编木拱梁桥的主体承重结构（图50）。当然作为地方的营造技术，闽浙地区的木拱廊桥造桥匠师们对构件也有独特的称谓。

闽浙地区的编木拱梁廊桥的类型大同小异，这里不一一列举，举比较特殊的两例，一是位于浙江省庆元县松源镇大济村的甫田桥，系单孔编木拱梁廊桥，该桥孔跨9余米，系统Ⅰ拱架9榀、系统Ⅱ拱架8榀，特别的是其系统

Ⅱ拱架的水平杆件长度极短，近与横木宽度相同。同样的，同村的双门桥结构也如出一辙，仅仅不同的是双门桥孔跨稍大，达11余米，系统Ⅰ拱架7榀、系统Ⅱ拱架6榀（图51）。

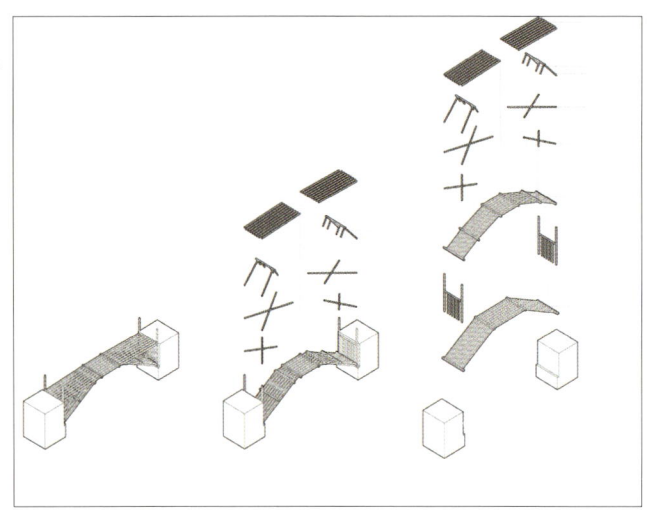

▇ 图50　典型的编木拱梁廊桥拱架结构示意图

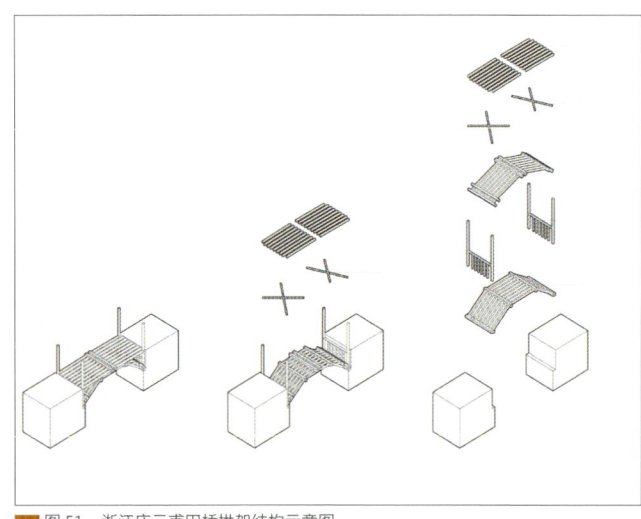

▇ 图51　浙江庆元甫田桥拱架结构示意图

二是位于福建省福州市闽清县省璜乡省璜村的合龙桥，前文已述相关历史背景，在此不赘述。桥系两孔编木拱梁廊桥，两孔跨度长短不一，短跨约为12米，长跨约为14米。两跨均由系统Ⅰ拱架8榀、系统Ⅱ拱架7榀组成。不同的是短跨桥拱结构中系统Ⅱ拱架是由4根斜杆组成，并与系统Ⅰ拱架组合，形成类似于"虹桥"的结构体系，为闽浙地区罕见（图52）。

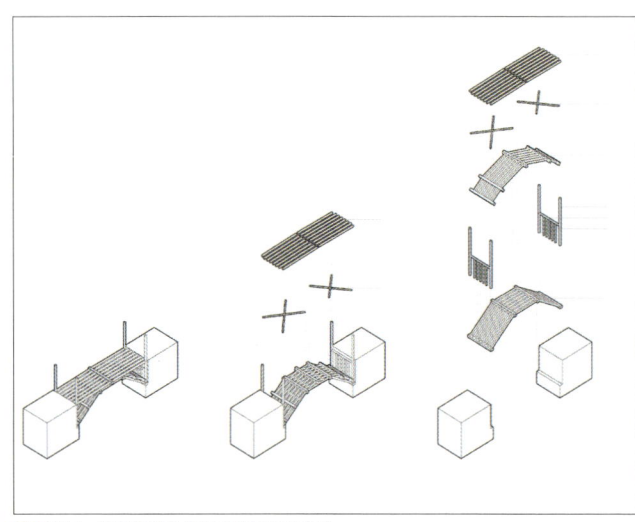

▇ 图52　福建闽清合龙桥拱架结构示意图

编木拱梁结构的发展渊源迄今尚无定论，但其在闽浙地区却是普遍应用。作为一种先进的木构桥梁结构技术，编木拱梁廊桥的矢高较大，桥跨短至约9米、长至约30米，易于取材，有着较好的适应性与灵活性，适合在市镇河道、郊野峡谷等不同地质环境建设。从桥梁技术发展历程来看，编木拱梁结构技术的成熟与发展，代表了中国古代木构桥梁技术的高峰。

四、木拱廊桥的营造技艺与习俗

在传统的中国社会里，几乎所有的建筑工程活动，都始终会伴随着一些重要的宗教仪式与民间的信仰行为，作为重要的土木工程内容之一的造桥也不例外。建桥礼仪只是中国传统建筑礼仪中的一个重要组成部分。架桥铺路，自古以来就是中国乡村社会里重要的公共事业活动，其牵涉面广，投资巨大，对乡民们的生活影响极其深远。传统的风水学说，总会对造桥铺路做出许多的解释，其中多数虽然是牵强附会，比如"关锁水口"之类。但作为在过去相当漫长的历史长河中占据了重要规划建设理论地位的风水术，毕竟对传统的营造活动起着指导性的作用。

建桥礼仪的发生与存在，至少部分地是由于它伴随着自然空间之境界的打破和全新的文化或人为空间境界的生成。比如，在德国，人们认为河里住着神或精灵，而架桥就会冒犯河流自然形成的境界。因此必须通过各种供品以安慰河里的神或精灵。其实，中国古代也有类似记载，西门豹治邺的故事中就有祭河伯之事。"隋人建石桥，凡二百八十祀"，这是从河北赵州桥下河床里发现的八角石柱上所刻刘超然《新修石桥记》里的说法。中国古代建桥活动中祭祀活动之频繁，由此可见一斑。

闽浙交界山区已有1000年的建桥历史，木拱廊桥的营造也至少有500～600年。造桥工匠们在长期的劳动中，形成了各式各样的造桥习俗。由于政治、经济和文化等方面的原因，建造木拱桥从1949年后逐渐减少，到了1980年后再也没有人建造木拱桥了。现尚健在的中老年桥工越来越少，主墨工匠更是屈指可数，几百年来形成的造桥习俗已逐步走向鲜为人知。这些习俗既有它合理的因子，也有迷信和蒙昧的东西。但它们是在漫长的劳作岁月中逐渐形成的，对了解中国传统的造桥文化，仍有很高的历史价值和学术价值。

木拱廊桥的营造过程中有较多的仪式和仪礼，这是因为造桥而产生的。造桥过程顺利结束以后，也即是新桥使用的开始。一座新桥从投入使用到最后被废弃，是一个漫长的过程，往往达上百年乃至几百年。在桥使用期间，为桥或乡民们自己祈福的仪式仪礼在桥屋里进行，都是非常普遍而隆重的。这些仪礼相对建桥仪礼而言，更加自由和多样，形式也不如前者固定。这一类仪式仪礼的发生、发展同样也非常有意义，但不纳入此节论述之列。

笔者在包括泰顺县的浙闽山区现存的众多木拱廊桥的详细考察和研究基础上，通过对老桥匠们的调查访问，以及对木拱桥建造和修理现场的观摩和体验，将木拱桥营造过程中的传统仪礼归纳总结如下：

（一）建桥首事与立约"桥批"

中国传统的乡土社会中，修桥铺路从来都是造福一方的善举，更是公益性的工程活动，极易受到无论是官方还是民众的支持。闽浙廊桥不但有官府出钱组织修造，诸如泰顺县城南门的登云桥和仙稔乡的仙居桥；更多的廊桥却是宗族或家族合力修建的，比如三魁镇的薛宅桥、洲岭乡的三条桥、筱村镇的文兴桥以及戬州村的永庆桥和南阳桥等。从建造的数量来看，私建的廊桥在泰顺县占多数。

由家族或宗族组织建造的廊桥，在募集到足够或相当的资金后，便要"求大木，择工师"。募集资金和寻求造桥"工师"都是责任重大而异常艰难的事情，需要杰出的人才，这就有了"建桥首事"一职的产生。一般来说，建造廊桥的首事会有好几位，但其中只有一位是主要首事者。官府修桥自然是由官府中人出任首事，私建的桥梁一般由组织建造廊桥的宗族或家族中德高望重又有旺盛精力的人出任，因为主事造桥是一件需要付出太多智慧和精力的苦差事。在筱村镇流传着这样一个关于造桥首事的感人故事[30]：

泰顺县筱村镇文兴桥的建造首事之一——王光奕，为了建造文兴桥，变卖了十八亩良田与全部家产。廊桥落成后，完成了历史重任的王光奕已经身无分文，只有靠乞讨度日。王家山村的同宗族人得知他的情况后，立即凑足了三担白米送给他。可惜的是，王光奕在建造廊桥期间废寝忘食，以致积劳成疾，还没能吃完族人所送的白米就悄然过世了。由于既无家产，又无田地，王光奕留下的8个儿子都过着非常艰难的生活，更别提娶妻生子。最后，无路可走的兄弟几人学着畲族乡民，在山上垦荒为生，有一个入赘做了倒插门女婿。多亏了那个做上门女婿的儿子，尚替王光奕生得2个孙子，其中一个随父姓王，倒为王家延续了一脉香火。

历史悠悠而过，昔日王家山村的繁华与荣辱早就没入了黄土，只剩下那斜晖脉脉的夕阳仍然还天天照耀在文兴桥头的几块石碑上，其中也包括镌刻着"造桥首事王光奕"的那块，熠熠生辉……

虽然，造桥首事的工作比较艰辛和困难，但是造桥的事业在大多时候总会得到众人的拥戴。因为造桥是善举，不仅本族人，邻近村落的乡民也乐于捐助。族人们更是有钱出钱，有力出力，也有到自家山上伐木捐赠，"或一家一支，或二三家（一支），或八九十家（一支）不等"（见三魁镇薛氏宗谱《重修锦溪桥记略》）。

"建桥首事"选出后，建造廊桥的工作就可以正式开始，第一步就是要"择工师"。"择工师"并不只是选择造桥工匠，还要编制预算，并且将这些内容都写进特定的条约。这种条约有些类似当今的委托合同书，而签订这种合同就叫立约。在包括泰顺县在内的浙闽山区，建桥董事、缘首等与造桥工匠签订的建桥合同书，称为"桥批""桥约""请约"，到晚些时代就直称合同了。

桥批一般为毛边纸或宣纸，用毛笔竖式书写。书写的内容主要是董事、缘首为建造或重修某地某桥，今在某邑某某村请得木匠某某某造桥之类。其具体内容主要有：一是建桥方提出所建桥的长度、高度、宽度，桥面上立几根柱子,桥内是否架设板凳和设置神龛等;二是若为拆旧桥重建,则提出要拆换何处桥苗(作拱骨用的梁木)、桥面板、枋檩木若干等;三是两端桥台的高度、宽度、厚度及砌法、用石规格尺寸;四是材料的供给,如桥苗(作拱骨用的梁木)运送何处,毛竹搭架木料、蔑绳、铁钉,有的连工匠墨斗用的墨斗线是自备或建桥方供给也写得清清楚楚;五是除木匠外,建桥台的石匠、盖桥屋的泥水匠等由建桥方或是承建方谁来负责;六是总造价多少,如何兑付;七是每月初一、十五以及敬神福仪的开支,上梁的花红(给主墨工匠的红包)开支数额;八是双方中有一方违约的罚款情况等。而后书写签约时间、签约人姓名(盖章或画押)、见证人、代笔者。在时间后还要慎重书上骑缝字(多为吉祥词),最后常在左上角书上"□□大吉"等字。若有添补遗漏约定,也还要再由书写人签字画押,以示慎重(图53)。

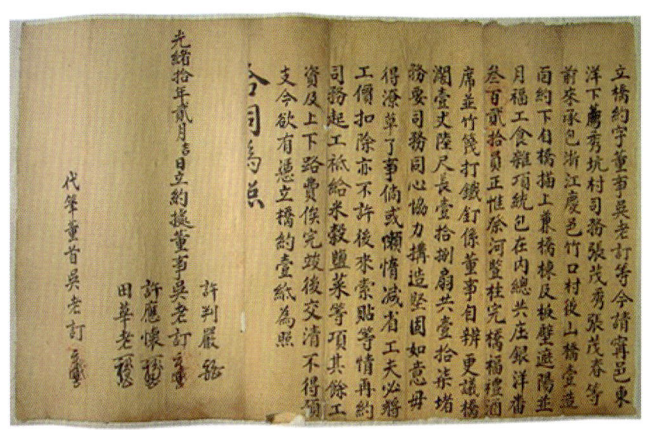

■图53 浙江庆元后坑桥桥约(引自刘杰、胡刚《乡土庆元》)

桥约签订之后,即可择日起工。择日也需要严格的程序和特定的仪式,对整个造桥工程进行详细日程的安排。这些时间的排定,需专门的择日先生根据传统历书上的黄道吉日选取。

(二) 择日先生与择日起工

在筹建桥的董事们与首事在正式聘请了造桥工匠之后,就要开始正式谋划桥梁的建造事宜。在泰顺、寿宁、屏南等县,建造廊桥首先要做的就是确定桥墩的具体位置。桥梁具体位置、桥身的朝向对于建成后之桥梁安全非常关键,建造木拱廊桥尤其如此。要选址造桥,得请地理先生(即风水师)出马。

地理先生在测定了两端桥台的坐向方位后,就得再请择日先生选取架马上梁等黄道吉日。择日吉课(择吉的文本)要送给造桥工匠鉴定是否可用。仍以现存的福建省文物资料为例:清同治四年(1865年)龙岩市竹森后村要建造双广桥,延请张茂秀(周宁县礼门乡秀坑村人,大概生活在1850-1920年之间)、张茂巢二位工匠主其事,当时送给造桥匠师鉴定的择日吉课现在还保存了下来,其内容如下:

一择六月廿四辛亥日宜午时木匠起马大吉;
一择七月十二日戊辰宜辰时定磉大吉;
一择七月二十日丙子日宜卯时拆旧桥大吉;
一择十月初十乙未日宜卯时搭桥架或铺下层桥板;
一择十月十五庚子日宜辰时平桥板大吉;
一择十月二十一丙午日宜卯时聘架,未时入山迎梁;
一择十月廿二丁未日宜辰时竖柱,未时上梁大吉。

在泰顺县泗溪镇也流传着一个建桥首事林正绪和择日先生的故事:

位于泗溪镇的溪东桥和北涧桥是泰顺县境内形态最漂亮的两座木拱廊桥,因为两桥相距不远,其下溪水相连,故当地人又分别称它们为上桥和下桥,也称姊妹桥。林正绪是溪东桥的建造首事,廊桥正式竣工后,按当地习俗要举行"圆桥"仪式。在选出良辰吉日后,择日先生却对林正绪说:"择此良辰吉日,日子上佳,惟此日会损一方,不损首事,亦损师傅,二者何从,汝自定夺。"林正绪为了尽快让桥梁通行,当即决定按既定良辰吉日开始圆桥。但为了不损师傅,他毅然决定阖家迁离泗溪。首事顾大局舍小家的无私精神,以及择日先生的"金口",在这则故事中都表现得淋漓尽致。

择日吉课一般书有"大士阁坐巽正桥基坐未本年两得其利查十月节二龙俱配利月用同课构造乃属上吉"等语,也有较为简单的,如"择十月初六乙未日卯时架马及起工修造吉,十八丁未日卯时换柱升梁钉椽并吉"等语。有的桥还把地理先生、择日先生姓名书于桥内梁上。

择日吉课虽说带有迷信的色彩,但是它对与整个造桥工程的日程和施工内容安排,对控制整个工程的工期等都起到了非常重要的作用。

(三) 风水先生与桥埠选址

风水先生,也就是前文说到的地理先生,对他们的作用,社会评价向来都是褒贬不一。堪舆风水之说带有太多的迷信色彩,连古代的有识之士也曾不屑。据光绪《永嘉县志》记载,明代温州知府文林、何文渊等和地方上比较有学识的乡绅,曾经对巫风淫祠、卜巫堪舆等做过批判且明令禁止,把这些迷信的风行看作是人心浇漓的一种现象。不过,清代泰顺人董永孚在《重修登云桥记》一文中记录了一段关于风水说的话,也很耐人寻味:"桥梁之设,原以利行人也。形家(即堪舆风水师的一种)以水口紧关为利,似不可信,而有可信者。邑城南里许,两山分峙,瀑布悬崖。故明万历丁巳,乡士大夫建桥于其间,不过资利涉耳。碳而棣萼联辉,后先继美,邑人利之,似不尽形家臆说也。"

地理先生凭借手中的罗盘,口中念念有词,手中指指点点,却就如此将偌大的廊桥之桥埠、桥台以及桥梁的走向和方位都一一确定了下来。位于泰顺县龟湖镇的城水桥桥屋大梁上就留有风水先生王石玉的名字。据说,在建城水桥之前,已经多次在此处建桥,可惜均毁于洪水。桥毁期间,乡民们一边用巨木搭起临时梁桥,权宜两岸交通;一边延请县内知名的风水大师王石玉到实地勘察选址。王石玉从风向、水害等方面考虑,最终确定桥址。经王石玉选址建成的城水桥一直安全地使用到了今天。

当然,确定廊桥建造的地点并不一定非要地理先生来确定不可,只要拥有比较丰富的水文、地质以及工程经验的人都可担当。比如,泰顺县三魁镇薛宅桥的重建就是由新上任的县令杨炳春确定的。据薛氏宗谱《重修锦溪桥记略》中记载,他亲身履勘,一路博询,认为如果建在大溪处,则"上面当风易坏,下面水势湍急,下桩不固。"如果建在小溪下,"则上面易于存风,下面水亦平稳,于此建桥,自可经久,且众议皆然"。

(四) 挑选栋梁

在中国传统的房屋结构中,称正房正中屋脊下的一根檩木(宋代称桁木)为栋梁。在浙江省泰顺山区的木拱廊桥的廊屋中,同样位置的檩木也被当地人称为"栋梁",福建省的宁德地区则称之为"喜梁"。因为栋梁所在的屋架结构中位置所处最高,故地位最高,所受的待遇也最高(图54)。

■图54 南山伐梁(姚家飞摄)

建造廊桥将使用很多数量的木材,除栋梁外,其他材木可由乡民捐助得来,只要树种、规格和强度符合要求即可,其他则不太讲究。栋梁就不一样了,其用材以及选材则要严格得多,并且有一个专门挑选栋梁的仪式。必须是建桥首事亲自组织人员到山林中去选择栋梁之材。能被选为栋梁之材的树木必须满足下列条件:比如必须是长在"洁净"之处,所谓"洁净之地"是指这棵树的周围没有坟墓、茅厕,树木的上方没有道路;被选中的树木必须是高大挺拔的杉树。在福建省的宁德地区则要选择三株或两株同根、枝叶茂盛的杉木,俗称"双胞柴"。在泰顺县,被选中做栋梁之树木要维持原貌,不能去皮(通常伐树后,都会剥下树皮再才扛下山),被砍倒后树木不能着地,须用木马支撑着,等待村里的有功名或是有身份的人来象征性地抬一抬，做起抬仪式，然后再由壮汉抬下山。谁家山林里有树木被挑中做栋梁，主人不但不懊恼，反而会高兴，更愿意多捐些木材。理由很简单：因为自家山林里出了栋梁之材，不就意味着家族中的子弟成为栋梁之材已为时不远了，能不开心吗？

在毗邻的福建省宁德地区，伐木时要择吉日，须备"山礼"一担，"山礼"有公鸡一只、猪肉一块、素菜五碗、茶和酒。并选择乡村中父母双全，三代同堂的"好命仔"4人去砍伐（4人意为东西南北四方）。砍伐前要在山上祭山神，将一担"山礼"的物品摆在要伐杉木旁边山地，并点烛焚香。所伐杉木要选择向山上方向放下（意为向上，避免"倒下"一语不吉利），还要在杉木将倒下的地方垫些树叶之类东西，（意为喜梁杉木不受玷污）。砍伐时，木匠师傅要喝彩，其他人随和喝彩，木匠念：

"右边发斧千年发（好啊！）
左边发斧世代兴（好啊！）
发天长地久（好啊！）
村村兴发、户户荣昌（好啊！）
财丁两旺、富贵双全（好啊！）。"

取杉木树尾木权5～7盘，俗称"树缘"悬挂于喜梁当中，寓有头有尾，兴旺发达之意，并给喜梁披上红布，沿路鸣炮抬回。用三脚木撑将喜梁置于桥址旁空地，绝对不能将之置于地上，以免被玷污。喜梁树皮削好，不能乱丢。可将树皮置高处晒干，放锅中烧成灰作香炉灰用，也可倒溪中让水流走。作为喜梁的一根杉木，取好喜梁后，所剩之材要作为桥中神龛前边的左右两根柱子（图55）。

图55 露天制梁 （姚家飞摄）

喜梁的置办，表示造桥准备工作的开始。

（五）祭河动工

农历秋分后的枯水期，河水流量不大，雨水也不多，是适合造桥的好日子，一般会被选择作为造桥动工的时间。造桥工程开工之初，是必须先进行"祭河"仪式。仪式较复杂，但是比较固定：抬一头猪到溪边宰杀，然后将未死之猪放溪中，让猪血喷洒溪水里。染红溪水，溪水越红越好。而后摆好猪头、公鸡、香烛、茶酒、果点、斋菜祭奠河神。此后凡遇初一、十五要小祭，平时每日要焚香。建造桥梁的福礼酒席一般为四次（图56）。

清咸丰三年（1852年），邻省屏南县缘首张朝高等建造大岭桥，在桥合同中约定"唯祭河、竖柱、上梁、完桥

四次福礼。酒席并竹篾打铁系高（指缘首张朝高）办"。造桥还有月福的礼仪。清道光十七年（1837年）造古田汤寿桥时，签订的桥合同中有"外约月福三次给钱壹拾千文又付君（指造桥工匠张成君）前去自备"，这里的月福三次包括每月农历的初一、十五两日，还有一次具体日子不详。

图56 杀猪祭河 （姚家飞摄）

祭河仪式一结束，也就意味着整个造桥的准备工作业已完成，接下去就是正式造桥的开始。

（六）上梁仪式

在中国传统的营造活动中，无论是房屋还是桥梁建筑，在安上最后一根栋梁时，总有一个非常隆重的上梁仪式。这个仪式既是庆贺房屋和桥梁建筑在大木构架的完成，又是预祝整个建筑工程的顺利完满，乃至期望将来使用过程的完美以及给主事者、使用者带来好运和福气。在浙江省廊桥的营造过程中，因为有相当数量的廊桥直接委托福建省的木匠师傅建造，比如，泰顺县在旧时，就常常邀请寿宁桥匠参与建造廊桥。寿宁县与泰顺县虽仅是一山之隔，在营造活动中浙闽两省的工匠也经常交流往来甚至合作共事，但其营造习俗也不尽相同，因此上梁仪式的程序也不完全一样，其形式更是多种多样。

1. 上梁喝彩

木拱廊桥是泰顺县最为特殊的一类廊桥，从现存的廊桥来看，它的营造，尤其是主要的木拱构架部分，是由相邻的福建省寿宁县的木匠师傅主持的。寿宁师傅在木拱桥桥拱最后一根梁木合龙时有一个喝彩的仪式（图57）。

图57 上苗梁仪式 （姚家飞摄）

在通常的木拱桥建造过程中，第一步是立水柱架，其作用是架好第一系统的三排拱骨，亦即浙闽地区工匠常说的三节苗。第二步就是架好第一系统，即三节苗。在架好

三节苗的过程中，在安放平苗（亦即中间水平的拱骨）中间一根大梁时要举行祭梁仪式。2001年11月，中国中央电视台为拍摄《虹桥寻踪》，请寿宁造桥工匠郑多金建造木拱桥。郑师傅在上梁仪式前，还到溪边的社主（俗称大王）处祭拜。在溪中摆一供桌，供品有香烛、茶酒、果点、斋菜，以及木匠造桥工具墨斗、斧头、凿子等。

祭梁由主墨木匠主持。点烛焚香上茶酒后，主墨木匠念：

"一逢一、二逢一、三逢一，
吉日良辰天地开，阴阳相配大利此方。
谨请天皇銮驾到，谨请玉皇銮驾到，
太阳星君到，天智正马到，
传送正禄到，太阴星君到，
天乙星君到，鲁般师傅到，
贵人星君利，大吉星君到。
日子已定，时辰已到，鸣炮开发送上梁。"

然后边放鞭炮，边由主墨木匠喝梁（喝彩）。造桥木匠转动天门车（旧时造桥用于调动木料的工具，其工作原理类似今天工程上利用卷扬机牵动钢绳吊动重物之起重机械）抽紧天门车缆绳，大梁徐徐上升（图58）。

图58 开天门车运送木构件 （姚家飞摄）

主墨木匠喝梁，众人并同声喝彩：

"一来长命富贵（好啊！）
二来金玉满堂（好啊！）
三来三元及第（好啊！）
四来四季长春（好啊！）
五来五福长寿（好啊！）
六来积谷万仓（好啊！）
七来荣华富贵（好啊！）
八来承相同科（好啊！）
九来大发人丁千万口（好啊！）
十来十金大发永无疆（好啊！）
梁上金鸡来报晓，梁下玉鸡满千仓。华盖千秋火，富贵万年长（好啊！）"

也有另一种喝梁（喝彩）：

"一敬梁头一盏酒，财丁两旺家家有（好啊！）
二敬梁尾一杯茶，家家户户闹喧喧（好啊！）
三敬梁中一盏酒，荣华富贵满堂红（好啊！）
四敬各位缘首、董事年年生贵子，户户中状元（好啊！）"

在拱架上将三节苗平苗打入大牛头（浙闽山区的造桥工匠习惯将木拱桥两套结构系统中与纵向拱骨相垂直的横

向拱骨称为牛头）的榫头时喝彩：

"拜鲁般仙师下凡来，保佑弟子上金榜。

一要财丁两旺（好啊！）

二要金玉满堂（好啊！）

三要三元及第（好啊！）

四要四季吉祥（好啊！）

五要五福六寿（好啊！）

六要六国丞相（好啊！）

七要七财八宝（好啊！）

八要八仙聚会（好啊！）

九要九子登科（好啊！）

十要十全大发（好啊！）"

这些喝彩的语言形式虽然多种多样，但其核心内容无非是祈求各路神灵保佑造桥工程的顺利进行，以及保佑参与造桥人家的幸福吉祥。

2. 抛梁与取币赏众

闽浙山区在建造廊桥时，上梁的高潮是抬梁上柱架的时候。本篇以浙江省泰顺县境内泰福桥的营造为例，来谈谈颇为特别的"抛梁"仪式。

董直机师傅曾是泰顺县为数不多的造桥工匠之一，就是他当时以主墨的身份主持建造了泰福桥。上梁时，他带动副墨喊着诸如"国泰民安""五谷丰登"之类吉祥语，同时还要指挥大家将栋梁两端的梁头安放到准确的卯口位置。在上梁结束后，随即进行"抛梁"仪式。主墨师傅站在梁木上，一边念着吉祥语，一边将挂在栋梁上的七宝袋抛到铺在地上的布单上。传说抛梁习俗起源于姜太公，诸神都是姜太公所封，人们认为诸神地位都在姜太公之下，所以他的神位应在最高的梁木——栋梁上。这也是许多人家上梁时都写一张"姜太公在此"的红条幅贴在梁上，并通过抛梁方式，用七宝袋内之物敬奉姜太公，祈求得到他的护佑。正式抛梁后，建桥首事须将七宝袋在家里存放七天七夜，然后再将这些敬奉过神灵的七宝袋内的灵物：银、铜、铁、油酥、花生、枣、米等分给村内的各户人家。七宝袋内的物品各有吉祥的寓意。

在福建省寿宁县，"抛梁"则演变成取币赏众的仪式。

上梁时，主墨师傅须在梁中悬挂一小红布袋的铜币（约一千克）。上梁仪式结束后，主墨的木匠师傅就会挑选一个灵活且不惧危险的木匠，上梁取回铜币。取币的木匠，手提榔锤（竹柄石锤，用四片竹柄长米许，锤扁鼓形，木匠用来敲紧梁木的工具）走上三节苗梁头，说一些吉利的话，并走到栋梁中间将装铜币的布袋取下。此时桥下众人鼓掌称好，取币的木匠还要走到另一端梁头，再说些吉利的话。之后，木匠取回装铜币的布袋交给主墨师傅，由他将袋中的铜币赏给诸位造桥师傅以及助工者（图59）。

（七）圆桥与踏桥开走

建桥前有奠基破土仪式，桥成后则必定有"踏桥""踩桥""圆桥""初渡"等仪式。在中国的广东省、陕西省和四川省等地流行"踩桥"典礼，而在浙江省泰顺县的传统桥梁营造中，则通行"圆桥"仪式，可以说它是踩桥典礼的另一种地方类型（图60）。

图59 习俗——木匠授绶红带（龚健 摄）

图60 泰顺秀涧上村潇秀桥圆桥仪式中的舞龙（2013年1月28日，钟晓波 摄）

在当地乡民看来，举行圆桥仪式，为的是讨个好彩头，希望桥梁永恒长久。对于营造桥梁的工匠们来说，只有经过圆桥仪式之后，廊桥才算是完全和真正的竣工。不仅是泰顺，在浙江的其他地方，都会在新桥建成之后，还有摆一次"圆桥酒"的风俗。显然，圆桥仪式与婚俗中的圆房，具有类似的象征意义。在圆桥仪式中，桥梁被视为生灵之物，它的生命可以因仪式而延续永久[31]。

在福建省的宁德地区，却盛行的是"踩桥"典礼，或者叫"踏桥开走"仪式。何谓踏桥开走？其实很简单，桥梁建成后的第一次行走，就叫作踏桥开走。开走有两种情况，视桥行走人多寡而定。一是行走人少，待桥面板全部铺好开走；二是行走人多，上好桥苗板，仅钉上五六块板就开走。踏板开走前，桥董事、缘首选择乡村中出自三代同堂、夫妻双全，有一定名望且较殷实之家的二位男性长者（当地俗称"好命人"），好命人当众题缘若干后开走，开走之人可随意讲些吉利话，如：风调雨顺、五谷丰登、户户平安、村村兴旺、董事缘首添丁发财，造桥师傅名扬四海等等。

福建省周宁县楼下桥内梁上墨书："本境信士陈其榜室黄氏男长钧媳魏氏捐银壹佰两□□唯愿一树千枝者。"周宁县登龙桥内梁上墨书："水南境监生黄起洪室刘氏男监生道集媳叶氏孙庠生高捷媳叶氏曾孙监生祀昌媳周氏元（玄）孙旺漳媳刘氏旺粮媳刘氏旺畴媳刘氏喜捐银贰佰五拾两。""端源境监生叶际云室周氏李氏男监生逢清媳肖氏庠生永清室周氏秀清室郑氏灿清媳全清室周氏孙正莹媳吴氏正铨媳肖氏正铿媳李氏正煌正堂正柜乐捐壹佰贰拾两正。"像这些捐款数目较大，且三代或四代、五代同堂者，就是所谓的"好命人"，是踏桥开走的最佳人选。

（八）木拱廊桥建造的其他习俗与禁忌

在泰顺廊桥的营造活动中，包含着非常丰富的民俗文化。由于地处浙闽两省交界的山区，浙南、闽北的桥梁文化在这里得到了很好的交流和互济。除却上述提到的民俗活动外，还有如祭木工神、祭河神、祭梁神等。另外，还有一类民俗行为，那就是流传在泰顺民间的造桥禁忌。

据说，在泰顺建造木拱廊桥过程中，合龙木拱架这一工序，有一个专门的名称叫"接龙"。在接龙之前就需要祭祀，包括祭木工神和祭河神。木工神通常祭的是鲁班，工匠们希望他能保佑桥梁顺利接龙。祭河神则是工匠们祈求廊桥平安，免遭水患。

建造廊桥的桥屋也有很多讲究。比如安神龛要择吉，神龛必须对准来水的方向，才能镇住洪水；木拱桥廊屋两头的石阶步数要符合吉数；屋檐上的悬鱼要雕有"鱼""水"或"壬癸"，卷草做成后要洒水等。

做神龛时要择吉，据说因为只有吉日做的神龛，神灵才会归入座，否则，即使塑了神像供奉在神龛内，也不会显灵。建造廊桥与建造私宅对石阶步数的要求不同，私宅是按照生、老、病、苦、死五字来对应决定步数。廊屋属于公共建筑的一类，两头的石阶则按道、远、之、时、路、摇（遥）、通、达八字来演算。这个"法则"完整的内容，应为"道远之时路遥通达，何时返乡？"据说，当着众人的面工匠都要将整句话念出来，但心里却只是暗念前八个字，之所以要如此，目的是不让外人知道他们的独家"法则"。其中"遥"字公开念是"遥"，实际上是"摇"字，代表不稳定，属凶字。除"摇"字之外，不吉之字还有"路"字。八字之中，有"走之"偏旁的都被视为吉字，即"道、远、通、达"四字。"之"字属中，不凶亦不吉。根据这些吉凶文字来定台阶步数，如可以做成七、八、九、十步，分别与"通、达、道、远"相应，绝不能做成四、五、六步，因为与这些步数对应的分别是犯凶的"时、路、摇"三字。桥屋的宽度和高度的尺寸，也要按这吉凶八字来推算，如桥屋一般做成"丈八宽"（"丈八"是"鲁班尺"的尺寸，即5米），这个尺寸中带个"八"，与"达"相对应，常被视为吉利的尺度[32]。

这些造桥工匠们对于尺寸的习惯和禁忌，有些类似江浙一带木匠师傅常用的鲁班尺上的内容。普通的鲁班尺长44.8厘米，尺面平均分成八等份，每等份长约5.6厘米。鲁班尺的两面都被均分成了八格，每格对应三个字，各有吉凶。一面刻着"贵人星""天灾星""天祸星""天财星""官禄星""孤独星""天贼星"和"宰相星"等，另一面也对应刻着"财木星""病土星""离土星""义水星""官金星""劫火星""害火星"和"吉金星"等。用此尺来量取建筑物相关部件的尺寸，并根据尺面上对应的吉凶，来最终确定相关建筑物及其部件的长宽等尺度。

廊桥屋面的山花大多做有悬鱼，屋脊则做卷草或空花草龙，都是廊桥屋面最重要的装饰物。悬鱼的基本形式为直线和弧线两种，一般都雕刻成"鱼"的形象，也有的直接刻"壬""癸""水"等字。悬鱼的实用功能是为防止悬挑的檩条端头受潮。在乡民们的意愿中，这块小小的木牌还担当着镇火的重任。从这个意义上讲，它又是一个厌胜物。因为木构建筑极易遭火灾，而鱼为水中之物，壬、癸两字在五行方位中亦代表水，当地的乡民认为雕刻与水有关的图案或文字，可以起到镇火的作用。屋檐脊饰做卷草或空花草龙则有两种说法，一是认为无论卷草或是空花草龙，都是水中之物，所以可以克火；二是南方瓯越之民对龙的图腾崇拜。

五、木拱廊桥的营造世家与工匠

闽浙山区的木拱廊桥建造世家主要分布在福建省的周宁县、寿宁县和屏南县等地。普通的造桥工匠则散落在闽浙山区各地。

（一）周宁县秀坑村张姓造桥世家

秀坑村是福建省周宁县礼门乡后垅村属下的一个自然村，居民300余人，多为张姓。据张氏族谱记载，张氏先祖张圭公从河南迁来福建，历二十八世。嗣后张盈一公的长子张德茂由屏南寿山埔窑村迁徙至秀坑，又历十五世。据寿宁县原博物馆馆长龚迪发调查，秀坑村自张新祐等人于清乾隆三十二年（1767年）建造寿宁县城关鳌阳镇仙宫桥，至2006年张昌云重建屏南清爱桥的240多年中，张氏从新字辈至昌字辈的八代造桥匠师世代相承，其造桥事业从未间断。同样，据龚迪发统计，秀坑张氏一系先后新建、迁建共计56座木拱桥，至今尚存20座（图61）[33]。

图61 福建周宁廊桥匠师张昌智站在赴德国建德廊桥合龙的木拱架上（刘妍 提供）

秀坑张氏建造木拱桥技术精湛。据统计，张氏一系所建造的净跨度超过30米以上的木拱廊桥就不下6座，如：浙江景宁梅崇桥、福建屏南百祥桥、屏南千乘桥、周宁登龙桥、古田公心桥和寿宁张坑桥等。其张氏造桥世家八代建桥工匠群体中，又以从张新祐算起第三代匠师张茂秀最为杰出。从清代咸丰二年（1852年）至光绪二十年（1894年）的40多年中，他共主持建造了木拱廊桥15座，至今保存下来的有浙江省庆元县的后山桥[34]。

（二）寿宁县小东——东山楼村徐、郑氏造桥世家

小东村是福建省寿宁县坑底乡的一个行政村。小东村的造桥工匠徐兆裕于清嘉庆六年（1801年）建造小东上桥，传至第五代徐泽长。徐泽长又将木拱廊桥建造技术传至邻村东山楼村的表弟郑惠福，郑惠福再传至郑多金，小东—东山楼村徐郑世家一共传承七代，历时200余年[34]。在浙闽交界山区现存的木拱廊桥中，根据桥上栋梁题刻还能查到下落的工匠并不太多，年代也并不久远。而以徐元良为首的徐郑造桥世家的发现，可以说是调查浙闽木拱廊桥营造工匠的重要突破，也是了解清末、中华民国直至新中国成立初期的浙闽山区木拱廊桥营造详细情况的重要线索。至此，对木拱桥的考察和研究，可以从不能开口说话的文物建筑、家谱文献中转入到活生生的工匠群体本身。

笔者将徐兆裕、徐元良、郑惠福一系之造桥工匠个人档案罗列如下：

徐兆裕（生卒无考），福建省寿宁县坑底乡小东村人氏，师承何人待考证。清嘉庆六年（1801年）主持建造福建寿宁县小东村上桥，绳墨。

徐元良（生卒无考），福建省寿宁县坑底乡小东村人氏，师承何人待考证。清咸丰七年（1857年）主持建造浙江泰顺市三魁镇薛宅桥，绳墨。

徐斌桂（1828—？），徐元良长子，师徒关系。清咸丰七年（1857年）协助徐元良建造浙江泰顺三魁镇薛宅桥，现存，为副墨之首（副墨另有陈泽应、郑福寿、郑起鉴、薛思年四人）。清光绪四年（1878年）建寿宁县小东下桥，现存，绳墨。清光绪十四年（1888年）建浙江省景宁畲族自治县白鹤桥，现存。

徐世仁（1857—？），徐斌桂长子，师徒关系。清光绪十四年（1888年）建浙江省景宁畲族自治县白鹤桥，现存。

徐世礼（1863—？），徐斌桂三子，师徒关系。清光绪十四年（1888年）建浙江省景宁畲族自治县白鹤桥，现存。

徐世智（1869—？），徐斌桂四子，师徒关系。清光绪十四年（1888年）建浙江省景宁畲族自治县白鹤桥，现存；中华民国十二年（1923年）建浙江省景宁畲族自治县大赤坑桥，现存，主墨。

徐泽长（1892—1951年），又名择祥，徐世智长子，师徒关系。中华民国二十七年（1938年）建寿宁县飞云桥，现存；中华民国二十八年（1939年）建寿宁县单桥，现存，木匠；1950年建造寿宁县竹管垅乡刘坪桥，1999年拆。

郑惠福（1895—1978年），福建省寿宁县坑底乡东山楼村人氏，为徐泽长外甥，师从徐泽长。中华民国十二年（1923年）建浙江省景宁畲族自治县大赤坑桥，现存，木匠；中华民国二十八年（1939年）建寿宁杨梅州桥，现存。中华民国时期（1912—1949年）建浙江省庆元县南阳桥，已毁；1948年建浙江省泰顺县三滩桥，1950年毁于洪水；1950年建造寿宁县竹管垅乡刘坪桥，1999年拆；1952年建寿宁县凤阳乡弄桥，1981年拆除，改公路桥；1953年建浙江省泰顺县仕阳镇双神桥，已毁；1954年建红军桥，寿宁与泰顺交界的山溪之上，现存；1955年建寿宁县坑底乡前洋桥，已毁；1956年建浙江省文成县岭脚桥；1960年建寿宁县南阳镇布罗林桥，1998年毁于龙卷风；1963年建浙江省泰顺县富家垟桥；1963年建福安市棠溪桥，木匠，现存；1964年修缮寿宁县鸾峰桥，现存；1964年修缮寿宁县九岭溪桥，已毁；1966年建寿宁县溪南村普济桥，现存；1967年建寿宁杨溪头桥，木匠，现存。

郑多金（1929—），郑惠福长子，师徒关系，至今健在。1948年建浙江省泰顺县三滩桥，1950年毁于洪水；1950年建造寿宁县竹管垅乡刘坪桥，1999年拆；1952年建寿宁县凤阳乡弄桥，1981年拆除，改公路桥；1953年建浙江省泰顺县仕阳镇双神桥，已毁；1954年建红军桥，寿宁与泰顺交界的山溪之上，现存；1955年建寿宁县坑底乡前洋桥，已毁；1956年建浙江省文成县岭脚桥；1960年建寿宁县南阳镇布罗林桥，1998年毁于龙卷风；1963年建浙江省泰顺县富家垟桥；1963年建福安市棠溪桥，木匠，现存；1964年修缮寿宁县鸾峰桥，现存；1964年修缮寿宁县九岭溪桥，已毁；1966年建寿宁县溪南村普济桥，现存；1967年建寿宁县杨溪头桥，现存；2001年为央视摄《虹桥寻踪》建木拱桥架。

郑多雄（1953—）郑惠福三子，郑多金徒弟，至今健在。

2001年为中央电视台拍摄《虹桥寻踪》建木拱桥架。

另有：

郑福寿，清咸丰七年（1857年）建浙江省泰顺县薛宅桥，现存，副墨。

郑岩福（1919—1999年），徐泽长外甥，师徒关系。中华民国二十八年（1939年）建寿宁单桥，现存，木匠；1948年建浙江省泰顺县三滩桥，1950年毁于洪水；1950年建造寿宁县竹管垅乡刘坪桥，1999年拆。

郑多希（1943—），郑岩福子，师徒关系，至今健在。1967年参建寿宁县杨溪头桥，现存。

从上述的工匠资料中不难发现，徐郑世家从徐元良一代算起，已传了二姓六代共110年（如果算到2001年郑多金为中央电视台《虹桥寻踪》节目搭建木拱桥架，则为144年），培育出梁架工匠数十人，所造和维修的木拱桥梁不下20余座，地域横跨闽浙两省之寿宁县、福安市（闽）、泰顺县、庆元县、景宁县和文成县（浙）6个县市。当然，上述信息肯定不是完全的统计。再加上徐郑世家所造桥梁的名称、数量以及地点大多是郑多金、郑多希两兄弟根据回忆而来，除经过实地考察印证之外，其余或语焉不详，或不能证实，都不予以记录。实际上，徐郑氏家族数代工匠所营造的木拱廊桥，要远远超出上述数目。尤为可贵的是，他们建造了浙闽山区现存单孔跨度较大的几座木拱廊桥，比如浙江省泰顺县薛宅桥、景宁县白鹤桥、大赤坑桥，福建省福安市棠溪桥、寿宁县红军桥、鸾峰桥、杨溪头桥。其中，鸾峰桥和杨溪头桥的单孔跨度都达到了37.6米，是这一地区现存木拱廊桥拱跨之最。郑惠福、郑多金父子两人在浙闽山区共建造木拱桥18座，现在尚存8座，也是难能可贵。可以毫不夸张地说，从晚清至20世纪60年代以来，寿宁徐郑氏造桥世家俨然成为浙闽山区木拱廊桥营造活动中一支非常重要的家族力量，他们的建桥技术及团队合作特点都是值得很好研究和总结（图62）。

图62 寿宁廊桥营造工匠郑惠福三子之郑多雄、郑多金、郑多希（由左至右）（刘杰 摄）

（三）屏南县长桥村黄姓造桥世家

福建省屏南县长桥镇长桥村有一黄姓木拱廊桥建造世家，自清光绪年间（1815—1908年）黄金书师承长桥镇新乡村著名桥匠卓茂龙以来已历五代，至今仍有传人。150余年来，黄氏一脉造桥匠师主要活跃在福建省屏南、古田、建瓯、建阳、南平等县市，共计新建、迁建木拱廊桥20多座，现存8座，其中万安桥于2006年被公布为全国重点文物保护单位。黄氏造桥世家第三代（从黄金书算起）传人黄春财被公布为福建省第二批非物质文化遗产项目代表性传承人，原文化部第三批非物质文化遗产项目代表性传承人。黄氏世家是中国闽浙木拱廊桥传统营造技艺重要的传承世系之一（图63）。

图63 福建屏南廊桥匠师黄春财（引自刘杰、周芬芳《乡土屏南》）

其谱系如下：

卓茂龙，又称茂龙仙（生卒年不详）一生建造廊桥十余座，清道光年间（1821—1850年）复建万安桥，为屏南县清代中后期著名造桥工匠。

黄金书（生于清丰年间—1933年），师从长桥镇新乡村卓茂龙。中华民国时期造建瓯市龙仙恩桥、接龙桥、松岗尾桥。

黄生富（1900—1974年），黄金书长子。中华民国时期随其父黄金书参与建造建瓯市龙夏村桥，为副墨。1917年造南平市赤梅村桥、增丈桥，皆为主墨。1932年修复屏南县万安桥，为主墨。

黄象颜（1909—1984年），黄金书次子。1917年造建瓯市龙夏村桥为主墨。1917年造南平市赤梅村桥、增丈桥，皆为主墨。1932年、1954年两度修复屏南县万安桥，为主墨。1969年造古田县平湖唐宫村桥，为主墨。

黄春财（1936— ），黄象颜长子，现为屏南著名建桥师傅。1952年，洪水冲毁屏南县万安桥西北向2个拱架共计12间桥屋，1954年黄春财与其大伯、父亲重建此二拱。1956年造屏南县长桥镇上乾村桥，为主绳。2005年主持迁建棠口镇漈头村金造桥。2006年主持建造长66米、二墩三孔的白水洋双龙桥。2008年主持建造十锦桥。2009年重建百祥桥。

黄闽屏，1963年生，黄春财长子。

黄闽辉，1984年生，黄春财次子，两人均继承父业。2005年参与搬迁建造金造桥。2006年建造双龙桥，任副绳，2008年参与建造十锦桥，任副绳。

从黄金书到黄闽屏、黄闽辉共传承4代，达100余年。黄氏一系共建造和修复了建瓯市龙仙恩桥、接龙桥、松岗尾桥，古田县唐宫桥，屏南县万安桥、上墘村桥、金造桥、双龙桥、双虹桥、十锦桥等。

（四）屏南县忠洋村韦氏造桥世家

福建省屏南县黛溪镇忠洋村也有一廊桥建造世家，自第一代造桥传人韦学星始，至今已历60余年，前后共传承三代。韦氏家族并不是从事单纯的廊桥营造，其主要的经营范围是所有大木作建造，因此，从此意义上讲，韦氏世家并不是廊桥的专业建造者。

韦学星本是自学成才的大木匠师，后来有幸随古田县鹤塘路上村的木拱桥匠师黄玉云学习建造木拱廊桥。1948年，韦学星带领他的弟子建造了生平第一座木拱廊桥——屏南漈头金造桥。其时，尽管黄玉云年事已高，仍被韦学星延请到现场指导。因此，金造桥上廊屋内的梁书留下了主墨四人的名字：黄玉云、韦学星、韦万会、韦春霜。韦氏一系建造的木拱廊桥只限于屏南县当地，比较著名的如屏南县金造桥、龟潭桥、溪里桥和樟口桥等。具体建造工匠情况如下：

韦学星（1885—1955年），师承黄玉云，1948年建造屏南金造桥为主墨。

韦万会（1913—1971年），师承韦学星，1948年建造屏南金造桥为主墨，1955年建造樟口桥、1970年建造溪里桥皆为主墨。

韦春霜（1919—2008年），师承韦学星，1948年建造屏南金造桥为主墨，1968年建造龟潭桥为主墨。

韦泽衍（1923— ），韦学星之子，师承韦学星，1948年建造屏南金造桥为副墨。

韦忠承（1920—1992年），师承韦万会、韦春霜，1948年建造屏南金造桥为副墨。

韦孝款（1923—1980年），师承韦万会，1948年建造屏南金造桥为副墨。

韦顺托（1928— ），师承韦万会、韦春霜，1948年建造屏南金造桥为木匠，1968年建造龟潭桥时为木匠。

韦忠柘（1933— ），师承韦万会、韦春霜，1970年建造屏南溪里桥时为副墨。

韦忠枝（1945— ），师承韦春霜，1968年建造屏南龟潭桥为副墨，1970年建造溪里桥时为副墨。

韦顺岭（1949— ），韦万会之子，师承韦万会，1968年建造龟潭桥为副墨，1970年建造溪里桥时为木匠。

（五）闽浙地区的其他木拱廊桥建造工匠

除了上述的几个木构廊桥营造世家外，闽浙各地还散布着为数不少的建桥主墨、副墨或木匠。这些工匠虽然没有形成建造世家，但也有的形成了以某一地域为中心的建造群体。也有一些非常聪明、善于琢磨的匠人自学成才，虽无师傅亲传，通过对不少木拱廊桥的观摩和研究，独自也尝试着建造起木拱廊桥。当然，更多的是有师承，但并没有形成世家，也没有形成以某一地域为中心的群体，只是成为造桥工匠的一员。

1. 周宁县下荇造桥群体

前文已述，福建省周宁县秀坑村有张氏木拱廊桥建造世家。与秀坑村相邻的后垅、梅渡、洋坪三村，地理上都处在周宁县、宁德市蕉城区交界处的鸡角山山坳里，此地被当地人俗称为"下荇"。四个村子异姓相互间有通婚，除秀坑外其余三村也都有建造廊桥的工匠。据调查，后垅、梅渡、洋坪三村的廊桥建造工匠均是从秀坑村张氏处所学而来。因此，闽浙地区将这一特定区域的木拱廊桥建造师傅统称为"下荇师傅"。有的桥约书里也写成"荢荇"[34]。

2. 寿宁县小东村造桥群体

前文已述，福建省寿宁县小东村有徐郑木拱廊桥建造世家。由于徐家与郑家有姻亲关系，从而将木拱廊桥的建造技艺逐渐从徐氏一系转移到郑氏一系。事实上，在小东村及其附近的东山楼村、林山村、楼基坪村、地头村、半岭洋村、后坑村等地，都有不少木匠参与了徐郑世家的造桥活动。比如半岭洋村吴元明被郑惠福招为女婿后，就参与建造了6座廊桥。

3. 其他造桥工匠

除了上述的几个造桥世系和造桥群体之外，在福建省的福州、南平、宁德等市以及浙江省的泰顺县，也有建桥的工匠活跃在历史的舞台上。

根据龚迪发先生所作调查，福州就有闽侯县的方宗传（1930— ）、黄连妹（生卒年不详）建造了闽侯的塘里桥、蕉溪桥，陈齐老、陈水佃建造了塘里桥，方宗佃建造蕉溪桥；罗源县有周连寿（生卒年不详）曾于清道光二十五年（1845年）为主墨建造了闽侯三溪桥。南平一地就有卢木生（又名卢进荣，1932— ）曾参与1992年延平区八字桥以及月圆桥的修缮工作；政和县杨显华（1937— ）曾于1962年为主墨建造龙潭桥，吴守木（生卒年不详）曾于2007年修缮政和县洋后村厝桥，刘庭万（又名刘庭繁，生卒年不详）曾于2001年修缮政和后山村厝桥。顺昌县徐云双（1965— ）2011年建造顺昌合掌岩木拱桥。

宁德地区的木拱桥造桥工匠则数量更多，主要分布在周宁、寿宁和屏南三县。福安、古田以及蕉城等县（区）

也有造桥工匠。周宁县除了上文已介绍过的秀坑村张氏一系以及下荐造桥群体之外，纯池镇的禾溪村、纯池村和礼门乡梅渡村分别出过不少造桥工匠。比如道光年间在上禾溪村就有林仕柄、林廷怀、陈联进、陈景生、林廷寿等桥匠，他们都是建造政和县交龙桥的副墨。许顺全和许朝权则是分别参与周宁县纯池镇禾溪村三仙桥和周宁县纯池镇桃坑村七仙桥的建造工作。在礼门乡的梅渡村，清光绪年间以来有何常山、何艳帮、何开灏、何常献、何开城、何常荣等，曾担任木拱廊桥的桥下拱架副墨；在礼门乡达坪村，从清光绪以来有何常益、彭治统、彭伏党都曾从事过木拱廊桥的桥下拱架副墨；在礼门乡后垅村，从清道光（1821－1850年）以来有何圣泉、何圣前、何圣洪、何志昂、何天佗、何常云等为主墨、主拱木匠以及木匠等。

寿宁县除了坑底乡小东村徐郑世家及其关联的工匠外，在楼基坪村还有胡以文、胡灵发在清光绪年间活动，为建造寿宁县大宝桥的副墨。在地头村有魏正汉为清光绪年间建造寿宁县大宝桥的副墨，魏正有、魏正木于清光绪十四年（1888年）参与建造了浙江省景宁县白鹤桥。在半岭洋村，吴茂盛、吴元龙于中华民国二十八年（1939年）参与建造了寿宁县坑底乡单桥。在林山村，吴大清在中华民国二十八年（1939年）建造寿宁县坑底乡杨梅州桥为绳墨，叶若康于中华民国二十八年（1939年）建造寿宁县坑底乡单桥。在后坑村，在中华民国时期有徐长根、何廷发、叶秀苗参与了单桥的建造。在大安乡伏际村，有吴允灿参与了1967年建杨溪头桥。平溪乡有蔡光龙，芹洋乡有吴国才，南阳镇有龚若岩、龚阿生、龚生清、龚三弟、陈应生、龚明会、张启福等为副绳墨或木匠。犀溪乡有缪裕万参与寿宁县犀溪红军桥的建造，大安乡有项高尧参与浙江省庆元县莆田桥的建造。

屏南县除了长桥镇黄氏家族和黛溪镇韦氏家族造桥工匠外，在屏城乡有郑带涛、吴观赠、郑传春等工匠，在寿山乡有黄荣成、倪大火、张明生等造桥副绳墨，在棠口镇有张世伸，在熙岭乡有林振回等为造桥副绳墨。

宁德市的蕉城区有绳墨肖朱峰，曾于清道光十一年（1831年）建造芹洋乡尤溪里仁桥。福安市潭头镇有郑盛金曾于1963年建造福安市潭头镇棠溪桥，1966年建造寿宁县南阳镇溪南桥。古田县鹤塘镇有黄玉云于1948年建造屏南金脚桥，余添春、余根干分别参与建造了闽侯县泰山桥和屏南县茶溪桥。平湖镇有清宣统年间（1909－1912年）造桥匠师陈乃避、陈乃财，中华民国时期匠师李庆余、李庆能。在新城镇有丁秋香于1925年建古田县大桥镇百花桥[34]。

浙江省的泰顺县和庆元县也有造桥工匠，如泰顺的董直机（1924－2018年）曾于1948年主持建造了泰顺石拱木廊桥泰福桥，2004年主持建造了泰顺岭北同乐桥（图64）。

泰顺县另外一位造桥匠师是曾家快（1974－）也先后于2004年、2006年、2009年建造了南溪桥、衢州黄土岭廊桥和乌岩岭桥（图65）。庆元县桥匠吴复勇（1955－）曾先后参与了咏归桥、如龙桥、来凤桥的维修工作，主持建造了庆元县两墩三孔的木拱廊桥——濛州桥[35]。

图64 浙江泰顺董直机师傅在建造泰顺同乐桥过程中（2004年，钟晓波 摄）

图65 建造中的泰顺秀涧上村濛秀桥（图中人物为主墨曾家快师傅）（2012年，钟晓波 摄）

注释

1. 此论点源自笔者的国家自然科学基金资助项目"中国南方木作建筑技术源流研究"的结题报告，同时在《汉代阁道与廊桥考述》（发表于2011年建筑学报）中进行了详细的论述和总结。
2. 参见刘敦桢：《刘敦桢文集》，北京：中国建筑工业出版社，1987年，第3卷，第448-449页。
3. 参见刘杰：《江南木构》，上海：上海交通大学出版社，2009年，第131-135页。
4. 转引自水利部长江水利委员会、重庆市文化局、重庆市博物馆：《四川洪灾史料汇编》，北京：文物出版社，1993年，第195页。
5. [北魏]郦道元：《水经注》，长沙：岳麓书社，1995年。
6. [梁]萧统编，[唐]李善注：《文选》，北京：中华书局，1986年。
7. [汉]班固撰，[唐]颜师古注：《汉书》，北京：中华书局，2005年。
8. 参见刘敦桢：《刘敦桢文集》，北京：中国建筑工业出版社，1987年，第2卷，第23页。
9. 参见刘杰：《乡土中国——泰顺》，北京：生活·读书·新知三联书店，2001年，第42页。
10. 参见刘杰、沈为平：《泰顺廊桥》，上海：上海人民美术出版社，2005年，附录一。
11. [汉]许慎撰，[清]段玉裁：《说文解字注》，上海：上海古籍出版社，1988年。
12. 参考王玉、黄晓东：《重庆古代廊桥——兼论重庆廊桥与南方廊桥的关系》一文，载于重庆中国三峡博物馆编：《长江文明》第一辑，重庆：重庆出版社，2008年，第77-94页。
13. 参见于俊海：《中国广西三江风雨桥》，北京：中国旅游出版社，2002年，第10页。
14. 参见陈云峰、张俊：《云南古桥建筑》，昆明：云南美术出版社，2008年。
15. 参见杨大禹：《滇西南廊桥的建筑技艺特色分析》一文，载于《第一届中国廊桥国际学术研讨会论文集》，2005年，第44-51页。
16. 参考丽水市政协文史资料委员会编：《处州廊桥》，北京：中国民族摄影艺术出版社，2006年，第152-153页。
17. 参考福建省公路学会编：《福建古桥》，内部资料，2004年，第132-133页。
18. 参考福建省公路学会编：《福建古桥》，内部资料，2004年，第145页。
19. 参考福建省公路学会编：《福建古桥》，内部资料，2004年，第136页。
20. 参考福建省公路学会编：《福建古桥》，内部资料，2004年，第146页。
21. [宋]郭若虚：《图书见闻志》对范宽绘事的记录，转引自唐寰澄：《中国科学技术史·桥梁卷》，北京：科学出版社，2000年，第449页。
22. 参见唐寰澄：《中国木拱桥》，北京：中国建筑工业出版社，2010年，第3页。
23. 参见苏旭东、刘妍：《"双三节"苗木拱桥——木拱桥发展体系中的重要形式》，载于《华中建筑》，2010年第10期。
24. 详见刘杰、沈为平：《泰顺廊桥》，上海：上海人民美术出版社，2005年，第96-102页。另见刘杰：《江南木构》，上海：上海交通大学出版社，2009年，第200-206页。
25. 方拥在其《虹桥考》一文中认为浙闽虹桥更早，详见《建筑学报》，1995年第11期第56页。浙江省泰顺县文博馆夏碎香、张俊等人认为泰顺木拱廊桥有比虹桥更为悠久的历史，或者至少是一个独立发展的体系。
26. 详见刘杰2003年主持的国家自然科学基金（青年科

学基金）项目"中国南方古代木作建筑技术源流研究"的报告正文第13页。

27. 参见方拥：《虹桥考》，《建筑学报》，1995年第11期，第56页。

28. 详见龚迪发：《福建木拱桥调查报告》，北京：科学出版社，2013年，第223页。

29. 参考唐寰澄：《中国科学技术史·桥梁卷》，北京：科学出版社，2000年。

30. 参见薛一泉：《解读廊桥》，北京：中国民族摄影艺术出版社，2005年，第15页。

31. 参见周星：《境界与象征：桥和民俗》，上海：上海文艺出版社，1998年，第220页。

32. 据泰顺学者薛一泉介绍，他曾向泰顺董直机师傅请教木构营造的禁忌问题，以上内容为其口述整理。这些禁忌与规矩不仅适用于木拱廊桥的建造，也适用于普通建筑的营造。

33. 参见龚迪发《福建木拱桥调查报告》，北京：科学出版社，2013年，第15页。

34. 参见龚迪发：《福建木拱桥调查报告》北京：科学出版社，2013年，第2-7页。

35. 参见薛一泉、叶树生：《木拱桥传统营造技艺》，浙江：摄影出版社，2014年，第177-185页。

* 本节图文参见刘杰：《中国木拱廊桥建筑艺术》，上海：上海人民美术出版社，2016年，略有删减。

This research is supported by an initiative of the National Key R&D Program of China for Research and Demonstration Application of Green Ecological Wood Bamboo Structure Systems, which is named "Large-span timber structure system research and construction demonstration (No.2017 YFC0703506)".

This research is supported by an initiative of National Natural Science Foundation of China, which is named "Research on the evolution and development of China traditional timber structure bridges (No.51478259)".

Section I Origin of Covered Bridges: Types and Geographic Distribution

1.1 The Origin of Covered Bridges

Covered bridges originated very early. The roads that appeared in the Pre-Qin Dynasty palaces and courts, called *gedao* or *fudao* were built with the architectural technology used in covered bridges. Over the past ten years, the author has repeatedly emphasized in different occasions and publications that covered bridges, *gedao*, and *fudao* were all types or forms of pile architecture[1]. Essentially, the architectural genre of covered bridges was part of a series of pile architectural forms that spread widely since early Chinese history. To put it a different way, covered bridges share the same pulse as the architecture of residential structures, with both sharing a similar ancestry and origin. However, the compound noun for covered bridges (*langqiao*) came into usage extremely late.

In the 4th decade of the 20th century, the famous architectural historian Mr. Liu Dunzhen after researching the timber bridges in his hometown of Jingkou in Hunan's Xinning County authored an essay called "China's Covered Bridges." This was the first time the architectural form of a bridge with a gallery on-top was called *langqiao*, which more recently has been translated into English as "covered bridge." The choice of the name *langqiao*, a name with a particularly strong literary flavor, was also related to the *Records of the Renovation of Fragrant Mountain Temple*, by the great poet of the Tang Dynasty, Bai Juyi. A poetic verse from the record states "Resting before the temple is a bridge (*qiao*), and connected with the bridge are seven bays of a gallery (*lang*)." Liu Dunzhen either derived the name *langqiao* from this source, or because the structural form of covered bridges is closely approximated by this two-word description[2].

There are academics who, when relating covered bridges to the *gedao* common in the period from the Pre-Qin to Han Dynast, believe that the technology for covered bridges came from *gedao*. Actually, according to the author's research into the origin and development of southern China's ancient timber technology, there is not a question of a sequence "first and second" in terms of the development of covered bridges and *gedao*. They both originated out of the widespread use of pile construction technology that existed in the south. The term *gedao* in fact possibly comes from the term for "pile" (*ganlan*). The two Chinese characters that form the Chinese word *ganlan* only have significance for representing phonetic elements, as opposed to most Chinese characters which represent words and concepts. In the southern minority areas which call piles *gelan* (the same *ge* as used in *gedao*) or other names such as *malan* (as in "*ma*-railing"). As a result, it should be concluded that covered bridges and *gedao* are two forms of construction technology that developed together. They likely both arose from the relatively common long-house pile structures built in late neolithic period in Jiangnan (a region with great historical and cultural significance in China referred to as the area "South of the Yangtze River")[3].

Covered bridges and *gedao* were commonly jointly referred to in ancient documents as *qiaoge* (桥阁, combining the word *qiao* for "bridge" and *ge* for "*ge* roads"). For Instance, the *Song History: Chronicle of the Five Elements* records the matter of the flooding in Sichuan's Jialing River in 1191: "In the 60th day of the sexagenary cycle during the seventh month of the lunar calendar the Jialing River surged and overflowed. Xingzhou's seventeen sites, including the city gate, jail and governmental buildings were engulfed. Over 3,490 folk houses were swept away in the flood. Chongqing of Tongchuan, Mianzhou, Guozhou, Hezhou, Jinzhou, Longzhou, and Hanzhou together with Huai'an, Shiquan, Da'an Jun and Yuguan Pass were flooded. The water of the upper reaches along the boundary of east minority region of ancient Songzhou swelled and surged. Bridges and pavilions at over 500 sites in the ancient Longzhou were destroyed In Jiangyou County many people drowned." [4]

In fact, Liu Dunzhen early on not only recognized that *gedao* and covered bridges had a mutual relationship. He also affirmed that they arose simultaneously. In his work *China's Covered Bridges* he states, "Though galleries were installed on top of timber beams, we don't know when this practice started. Most probably, it developed around the same time as *gedao* ... In many palaces during the Western Han Dynasty, as recorded by Li Haowen in his work *Illustrations of Chang'an*... All cutting mountains as the base it seems as if these were dwelling for immortals. Elevated palaces were connected by *gedao*, refined and elegantly linked together, on a vast and endless scale, extending all the way to the boundary of Chang'an's western wall from Weiyang Palace to Jianzhang Palace. Furthermore, the *gedao* were entirely timber structures, with rooms and windows. Although covered bridges go by a different name, the structures they consist of seem to be the same. Hence the origin of covered bridges possibly dates to the time before the Western Han Dynasty, during the Spring and Autumn Period, or the Warring States Period." [1] There are three important components to this part of his thesis. Firstly, *gedao* and covered bridges both make use of covered gallery walkways. Secondly, the structure of both forms are highly similar. Thirdly, they both have a similar function as conduits for traffic. As a result, Mr. Liu concludes that although their names are different, in reality they seems to be one-of-a-kind.

In ancient written material from the Pre-Qin to Han Dynasty, the term *langqiao* does not exist. However, careful examination reveals that it is possible to discover several words that refer to covered bridges. For example, in such ancient material we can observe that in the Han Dynasty, both covered bridges and *gedao* used only the word *jian*, the number of modular bays, as a measuring unit. To put it another way, in this period it seems that all documents use the unit *jian* to measure the scale of bridges. This *jian* may very well refer to the number of bays in galleries on the top of bridges. All the way up to the present, in the areas of southwestern Zhejiang Province and northeastern Fujian Province where there are surviving examples of covered bridges, the number of *jian* in the galleries is used to indicate a bridge's scale. This has been confirmed by the author's ethnographic research in these areas.

The Baqiao Bridge of the Western Han originally was a covered bridge. According to the *Commentary on the Water Classic's section* on the Weihe River, "The waters of the Bahe River and the (capital's) north Zhidao Road meet 30 *li* from Chang'an County. The nine temple of Wang Mang lies to their south Passing through the Zhidao Road outside the capital's eastern gate, above the water is a bridge called the Baqiao Bridge." [5] From this it is clear that the Baqiao Bridge led to Chang'an's Zhidao Road. Of the famous *gedao* of the time it was said, "one travels several *li* on the road without being able to gaze at the sun." [6] So we can see that this bridge was covered with a gallery house. The bridge burned down at the time of Emperor Wang Mang according to *the History of Han Dynasty*, Biography of Wang Mang: "One night in the second month of the lunar year the bridge burned down. The fire raged from east to west all the way into the morning by which time the bridge was completely consumed by the flames. It's said the poor people who lived

under the bridge regarded the origin of the fire and disaster with suspicion."[7] Liu Dunzhen, in his *Description of Stone Columned Bridges* discussed the Baqiao fire. He stated, that there must have been a timber gallery above the stone structured bridge, and that was the reason for the day-long fire referred to in the historical record.[8]

On a surface level, the existence of a gallery above a bridge may be attributed to architectural style or artistic taste. But in fact, the existence of such structures had both structural significance as well as implications for a bridge's longevity. The later use was more important at a time when production methods and scientific technology were not so developed. The gallery houses on top of timber bridges had (and have) at least three uses:

Firstly, they helped provide shelter from the wind and rain for travelers, and also offered visitors a place to rest.

Secondly, they protected the timber structural body of the bridges.

Thirdly, and more importantly, they increased the weight of timber bridges. The use of bridge houses increases weight, and increases the resistance to impacts of floods and torrents as the *Record of Fujian Province* stated: "The bridges in Fujian are first rate, built across narrow mountain crevices. They are constructed by assembling large stone beams and installing buildings on top, and are all magnificent in appearance. In the beginning it was easy to simply assemble a bridge of stone and wood in mountains. But now we know this will not do. The waters that cover Fujian are furious and quick to rush forward. As a result the bridges must be weighed down with dozens of heavy loads of wood."[2]

1.2 The Categories of Covered Bridges

Owing to the barriers to more rapid social productive force's developments, China's bridges were primary composed of timber for a very long period of time. In the north, stone arched bridges appeared by the Eastern Han Dynasty at the latest, with additional archeological evidence and historical records documenting that such bridges were built during the Jin Dynasty. The earliest surviving example of such a bridge is the Sui Dynasty's Anji Bridge(also named Zhaozhou Bridge).In addition, in the south, bridges were once primarily built with timber structures. However in the Song and Yuan Dynasties, an overall substitution of timber by stone material occurred. The main reason for this transition was the development of social productive forces. During this period, new methods for transportation, and new equipment for lifting and construction were developed. It was precisely these technological innovations and developments that allowed for the substitution in bridge construction of the exclusive use of timber with the combined use of timber and stone, or with the exclusive use of stone material.

Since this time, except for a few mountainous areas that engaged in forestry and lumber production, most of the cities and towns in China's south area have relied primarily on stone for bridge building. Nowadays, we still can find the bridges built during Song and Yuan Dynasties and wood and stone materials were often used together. For example, in Jinze, a famous town for bridges in Shanghai's Qingpu District, there is just such a Yuan Dynasty stone bridge—the Yingxiang Bridge.

Yingxiang Bridge is a combined timber and stone structured bridge located at the south gate of Jinze Town. It is elegant and refined. The bridge's form, structure, and materials used all have distinctive characteristics. The bridge is a stone beam bridge. It is 34.25 meters long and 2.41 meters wide, supported by four piers, and with a maximum span between its center columns measuring 5.86 meters. It was constructed by installing densely laid round timber purlin beams on top of the stone piers, and by covering the bridge surface with narrow bricks. The bricks are placed in 1 meter segments, separated in between by an additional rows of bricks. Polished bricks are attached to the timber beams on both sides of the bridge's deck to protect the wood and to enhance the bridge's appearance. The bridge is replete with detailed craftwork. According to the *Jinze Town Gazetteer*, this bridge constitutes one of the town's eight most famous sites, which is described as presenting "a moon's impression in a flowing steam, where water and sky are of one hue." According to the *Jinze Town Gazetteer and Qingpu County Gazetteer*, the bridge was built in the Yuan Dynasty, rebuilt in 1462 as well as 1791. These renovations rebuilt the upper part of the bridge. However, the stone piers remain to this day.

Why would these sorts of mixed stone and timber beam bridge appear? From the perspective of current structural sciences this is easy to explain. When exposed to the elements, timber does not stay well preserved. However, it is a natural material that can excellently resist tension. While brick or stone materials, in particular granite, preserve well, and have a strong ability to withstand compression, their ability to resist the force of tension is inferior to that of timber. When used in beam bridges, the main beams are components that endure tension forces. As a result, stone piers serve as the compression enduring components of a bridge. And timber serves as the primary beams that serve as structural components for enduring tension. The bricks paved on the bridge's deck protect the entire bridge from the erosion of rain and wind, and abrasion from passing people, livestock, and vehicles. Each of these three materials thus used realizes the utmost potential of its mechanical properties. It can be said that this is the most brilliant example of bridge construction performed by China's ancient craftsmen.

Divided according to material, China's ancient covered bridges can be divided roughly into those made of timber, and those made of combined timber and stone. If we were to divide them according to structure, they would be divided into three types—beam bridges, bracing bridges and arch bridges. To be more specific, beam bridges can also be divided according to simply supported beam types and cantilever types; bracing bridges can be divided into *bazi* types that resemble the Chinese character "八", double *bazi*, and combined bracing types; arch bridges can be more finely categorized into woven timber arch bridges, and combined bracing with woven timber arch types. Generally speaking, simply supported beam bridges are structurally the most simple and convenient to manufacture. With developed technology they are relatively easy to make. They can be made of single-span beams or continuous multiple span beams. As a result, it is the most widely distributed type of covered bridge in China, with examples of it found in every part of the country's interior. Cantilever-beam type timber covered bridges developed on the foundation laid by non-covered type cantilever-beam timber bridges. The bridge represents a certain accumulation of skill and experience. The bridge requires significant material, it is relatively large in size, and its price of construction is relatively high. It is mostly found in the river basin of the Yangtze River, and southern regions, including Zhejiang, Fujian, Jiangxi, Anhui, Hunan, Hubei Provinces, Guangxi Zhuang Autonomous Region, Chongqing, Sichuan Province, and so on. In addition, in the parts of China's northwest, this sort of cantilever covered bridge has left historical traces. For example Xi'an's Baqiao Bridge and Shizhou Bridge are both examples of this form from an early period. Arch covered bridges also are divided into stone arch bridges and timber arch bridges. The most common region where stone arch covered bridges are found is also in the river basin of the Yangtze River, as well as the larger southern region of China. Timber arch covered bridges are found in Fujian and Zhejiang Provinces, as well as the southwestern region of China, such as Yunnan, Gansu Provinces, Chongqing, and so on.

Under normal circumstances, in order to concisely and completely describe the object of research, we will combine material and structures together, and hence divide China's ancient covered bridges into: Timber support covered bridges (simply supported timber beam covered bridges), stone support covered bridges (simply supported stone beam covered bridges), timber cantilever covered bridges, stone arch covered bridges, timber arch timber covered bridges, and more.

As the previous text has stated, a characteristic of covered bridges made of timber is that their construction is very similar to that used in residential dwellings. The artistic quality of their architecture is very high, but they require heavy use of labor and materials. They are not durable. From the time that stone material began to be used in bridge construction, the production of the distinctive form of the covered bridge began to gradually decrease. Through efforts of scholars in the fields of Chinese architecture history and the history of bridges over the past 20 years, China's covered bridges have received widespread admiration. In 2012, China proposed that the timber arch covered bridges of Fujian and Zhejiang be recognized as World Cultural Heritage Sites. The artistic craft of building China's covered bridges was included in UNESCO's 2009 list of the World's Top Intangible Cultural Heritage Sites. To satisfy the need to protect and pass on this form of intangible culture, Zhejiang, Fujian, as well as other places in China, together with Europe, America, and other countries invited traditional craftsmen to construct these characteristically Chinese timber arch covered bridges in their localities. Others reproduced the bridges by imitating the work of traditional craftsmen from afar.

According to their structural categories, covered bridges are divided into three types: Beam bridges, bracing bridges, and arch bridges. In the section below, we discuss the structural features, examples and distribution of these three types of bridges in detail.

1.2.1 Beam Bridges

The beam bridge refers to covered bridges whose lower bridge span structure is a beam structure. The beam used in the spanning structures of most old bridges were either cantilever beams or simply supported beam types. As a result of material distinctions, the number of timber beam covered bridges far exceeds that of stone beam covered bridges and more widespread. Today's stone beam covered bridges are most commonly found in royal and private gardens, or over narrow rivers that flow through the South of the Yangtze River region.

Cantilever beam bridges are a derivative of beam style bridges, and advanced from the foundational form of simply supported beam bridges. They consist of timber or stone beams layered on the abutments at either end of the bridge, or on the bridge piers. Timber beams are then supported on top of these structures. In this way, simply supported beams and cantilever beams extend from either side into the heart of a river, forming a spanning structure. The span of cantilever beam bridges tends to be larger than that of simply supported beam bridges, and the form also tends to be more long-lasting.

According to their structural characteristics, cantilever beam structures are divided into three types; one-way cantilever beam, two-way cantilever beam, and diagonal bracing cantilever beam. A common single-span cantilever beam bridge is usually a combination of two groups of one-way cantilever beams placed on each of the bridge abutments, while a multi-span cantilever beam bridge is composed of a combination of two groups of one-way cantilever beams placed on the two abutments, together with two-way cantilever beams located above the piers.

Timber cantilever beam bridges are frequently seen, whereas stone cantilever beam bridge are relatively rare. This is likely because the flexural properties of stone beams are inferior to those of timber beams. For example, the Nanyang Bridge in Sixi Town, Taishun County, Zhejiang Province is a special covered bridge. The bridge was built in the late Qing Dynasty with one pier and two spans. Its two-three level stone cantilever beam structure is built above the bridge's piers, which are made of stone. This in turn supports several timbers, on top of which rests a gallery house with over ten bays. This sort of method utilizing a combined stone cantilever beam and simply supported timber beam is relatively rare among known covered bridge structures.

Surviving cantilever covered bridges are common in areas of China where covered bridges are found, including Zhejiang, Fujian, Hunan, Hubei, Sichuan, Chongqing, Yunnan and other more. Their structural characteristics are similar, with their styles sometimes combined with local features resulting in slight alterations in form.

1.2.2 Bracing Bridges

A bracing bridge is a type of covered bridge whose bridge span structure is a bracing structure. The bracing in the bridge structure is a category that falls in between a beam and an arch structure. Its bracing is composed of a number of combined oblique and horizontal members. The bracing structure originated in the use of diagonal bracing components to reinforce or strengthen simply supported timber beam structures. When multiple diagonal braces under wooden beams jointly function to form a supporting structure, we call this sort of hybrid combination a bracing structure. The region of Fujian and Zhejiang Province has preserved almost all the types of bracing bridges currently known.

Similar to cantilever beam structures, the generation of bracing structures originated in the pursuit of a large span bridge structures, and hence represents another large-span solution. The bracing structures used are primarily composed of timber components. Stone bracing structures are relatively rare, and are only occasionally seen in Zhejiang and Fujian. The reason is probably also a reflection of material properties. Wood is more suitable for bracing structures than stone, and it is also more convenient to use, and also more economical. Therefore, existing bracing bridges are generally timber bracing bridges, and are mostly distributed in the southeast region.

1.2.3 Arch Bridges

Arch bridges refer to bridges that form an "arch" from a structural perspective. The arch structure originated very early, especially in Western European country. Arch and dome structures have a glorious history of more than 2,000 years. In China, the use of arch structures dates to the Han Dynasty at the latest. Its use in bridges is also verified in literature and archeological remains dating to the Wei, Jin, and Southern and Northern Dynasties.

However, the timber arch structure referred to here is not the commonly referred to arch. The construction principles of the timber arch structure in China are quite different from those overseas. The Chinese academic community's understanding of timber arch structure began with the awareness of the Bianshui Rainbow Bridge in the Song Dynasty's famous the Riverside Scene at Qingming Festival as well as later research into the timber arched bridge in mountainous area of Fujian and Zhejiang. The exact time of the origin of timber arch technology in Chinese history needs to be

further explored. However, based on the current literature, archaeological excavations, and physical remains, timber arch bridges are known to have existed extensively in the Central Plains area, and are one of the most important achievements of ancient Chinese bridge technology.

Based on covered bridges that remain at present, the distribution of timber arch bridges was concentrated in the southeast. In comparison, stone arch bridges were relatively widespread, and in addition to the southeastern regions, they are relatively commonly preserved in the southcentral and southwestern regions.

1.3 The Geographical Distribution of Covered Bridges

In ancient times, covered bridges in China were very common. They covered most all of China's interior. The special form of architecture spread all the way to snow-capped plateaus, as far as Lhasa, and reached the present day Korean Peninsula, Japan, Vietnam, and other Southeast Asian countries. The Himalayan region of Nepal, Bhutan, the island of Sri Lanka of the Indian Ocean, and even countries as far away as Turkey have examples of covered bridges that have been preserved up to the present era. The question of the technology used in their construction and a possible relation with China awaits further research.

As time has passed, existing examples of the once common covered bridges are now mostly found in China's southeast, southwest and northwest, as well as the central Chinese provinces of Hunan and Hubei. If we evaluate the existence of covered bridges according to provincial administrative units, the greatest occurrence of these bridges would be found in Fujian and Zhejiang. The southwest regions of Yunnan, as well as Sichuan, and Chongqing among other provinces and municipalities also have an abundance of covered bridge architecture. In communities of Yi and Miao Nationality, located at the intersections of Guizhou, Hunan, and Guangxi, covered bridges have been preserved to the present in the form of wind and rain bridges. The South of the Yangtze River Region has a certain number of surviving examples. Overall, if all over China dwellings evolved from pile structures, such as *chuandou* type structures (a form of traditional column-and-tie Chinese construction most common in the south of the country), then there is the basic possibility that timber covered bridges existed in such places as well. In fact we can infer the same for the great majority of places in Asia. In another perspective, this affirms that both covered bridges and *chuandou* architecture all developed from a common ancestor—pile based architecture.

Compared to other types of timber structural bridges, covered bridges are an architectural form possessing a higher degree of cultural uniqueness and architectural artistry. Their construction in respective locations is historically tied to local building traditions as well as local social economic conditions. Historical situations that led to their construction included government led construction of official roads, as well as the active participation by both government and the public in the construction of important commercial routes. Their production was also brought about by wealthy households or local elites who constructed *fengshui* bridges at the water-tails of their villages' rivers and streams to protect the fortunes of an entire clan or lineage. Covered bridges appeared in many places in China's earliest history and throughout much of the imperial period. Historically, there were many examples of covered bridges in Jiangsu Province. In ancient documents, the following sort of language can frequently be found:

Jianyuan Shiying, Volume Two, Part two records that "the Yinhong Bridge also known as the Xinqiao Bridge was formerly called the Wansui Bridge. It is located at Gufengtaifang. According to Records of Jiankang:

"The Xinqiao Bridge in southern Linhuai, was called the Wansui Bridge, though the name was later changed to the Yinhong Bridge, and today is called Xinqiao Bridge—even though it remains the same bridge as before. As recorded by Qiu Chong, in 1170 the bridge was rebuilt by governor Shi Zhengzhi, and covered with a gallery composed of tens of columns which was extraordinarily grand. Liu Shuxiang recorded that in 1208 Qiu Chong rebuilt the bridge. In 1256 Ma Guangzu rebuilt the bridge, as recorded by Liang Yi. During 1491 - 1521 the bridge was repaired."

Jianyuan Shiying, **Volume Two, Part Two** details the Yepu Bridge that: "The bridge is located on the Yepu River, five *li* east of Liuhe County. During the Five Dynasties Period in order to avoid the Emperor's name Yangpu, people called it Yeqing Bridge. It was built during 742-756 and 1207 - 1224. During 1425 - 1435, its scale was expanded by Shi Sigu, the county magistrate. It utilized thousands of Chinese mahogany trees to build. Stones were used to fill up voids, and its deck was formed from wood. It was covered with seventeen tiled houses, measuring 90 meters long. It created a glorious site, but later collapsed. In 1537 the county magistrate Zhou Wei rebuilt the bridge. During the ding chou [14th Day] Yepu Bridge Incident, bandits arrived from the west, and residents living to the bridge's east thought to burn the bridge down. As a result the bandits could not cross, and the people were protected. Later the official Li Zhenyue constructed a new bridge with a stone foundation and horizontal timbers, and constructed two pavilions on both sides of the bridge, with two houses in central bridge. It was far more spacious than the earlier structure."

While there are many old bridges preserved within the borders of Jiangsu, few of them are covered bridges, and most of them are stone beam bridges or stone arch bridges. A few covered bridges still exist there as well in traditional gardens and ancient towns. But their numbers pale in comparison to the great abundance of the structures that filled the landscape in times past. This is the case as well in the *Jiangnan* (South of the Yangtze River region) that falls within the economically vibrant northern and eastern parts of Zhejiang Province. Very few covered bridges can be found there. But in the southwestern region, where the economy is underdeveloped, there are quite a few relatively well preserved covered bridges. Why would this case occur?

This situation is closely related to the present level of economic development in a given location. If the economy develops relatively quickly, it will be relatively easy to use new technology to replace old technology. From this perspective, the, substitution of covered bridges made of timber with more long-lasting stone beam or stone arch bridges may represent a sort of evolution or step forward. This is the positive aspect of this development. However, from the perspective of preserving the legacy of architectural heritage, the accelerating disappearance of covered bridges may be a sort of helpless regret.

We cannot deny the fact that the previously common and age-old form of Chinese covered bridges are being destroyed tens or hundreds of times faster than they are being built. We can use the example of Zhejiang Province's Taishun County. In 1949, according to administrative statistics, there were hundreds of various forms of covered bridges that remained in the county. But half a century later, there were 26 that remained (this does not include new covered bridges that were built after 2000), a number that includes a bridge shared with the neighboring Shouning county in Fujian province. It is generally not known that Taishun County's historical timber arch covered bridges once included the following two titles: Firstly, the county's Yeshuyang Bridge, built in 1454, clarified the historical chronology of timber arch covered bridges. Secondly, the county's Santan Bridge is the largest spanning timber arch bridge—replete with a 42 meter wide arch. Unfortunately, the former was demolished in 1965 during road construction, and the latter was destroyed in a flood in 1950.[9] The same fate befell two other similarly timber arch bridges. These were the Jixia Bridge (also called the Fuqing) Bridge built in 1848, and the Shuangshen Bridge built in 1937. The former was swept away in a mountain flood in 1990, and the latter was demolished to make way for an electric power station in 1989.[10]

Overall, covered bridges in China are not evenly distributed. It is related to the local state of geographical resources, social economy, functional requirements, and technological abilities. These factors all affect the types and distribution of China's covered bridges.

According to current sources, China now has thousands of existing ancient covered bridges. Overall, both in terms of quantity and variety of bridges, China's south region exceeds north region. This is closely related to the differences between north and south in geography, climate, and natural resources. Based on geography, most of the covered bridges in China's north region are found in the northwest and northern central regions. Covered bridges found in China's south region are commonly located in eastern China, central China, southern China, as well as the southwest. Of course, within any specific region, the quantity and variety of covered bridges also varies.

Overall, if China's surviving covered bridges are divided according to territory, we can map out six covered bridge bands, namely in north, northwest, southwest, south central, southeast China, and the Jiangnan. Additional regions only contain sparse examples of covered bridges.

1.3.1 Existing Covered Bridges in China's North

The covered bridges in China's northern areas are generally preserved in the parks and temples of Beijing, Hebei, and Shanxi. They are primarily built with stone rafters, and composed of stone arches. Their numbers are few, but they are all generally very unique. We can take the Qing Dynasty's Summer Palace as a classic example of Qing Dynasty imperial parks. This large scale landscape pleasure garden was constructed by utilizing the artistic craft used in parks in the South of the Yangtze River Region, modified according to local environmental conditions. The park has a large number of pavilion bridges, which are in fact covered bridges. They include Liuqiao Bridge, Lianqiao Bridge, Jingqiao Bridge, Binfeng Bridge, Xingqiao Bridge, and more. These bridges are highly diverse, and are covered with galleries and pavilions. In the park they function as scenic elements. They all contribute to a glorious site to behold, whether one gazes at them from a distance or up close, or if one takes in the glimmer of the park's waters and colors of its hills from inside their pavilions.

Of course, there are also covered bridges located by temples in the region that are very unique. For instance, the Qiao loudian is a rare example of a stone arch covered bridge that is a combined palace and bridge. Its stone arch spans the gorge between the Cangyan Mountain's peaks. Above the bridge is a five bay palace hall with a double-eve xieshan roof. From a distance, it looks like pavilion suspended in space. The beauty of its construction rivals even that of nature.

1.3.2 Existing Covered Bridges in China's Northwest

Most covered bridges that remain in the northwest are found in the south central part of Gansu, the south part of Shaanxi, as well as the northwest part of Sichuan. In these areas there are examples of timber beam, timber arch, stone arch, and various other forms of covered bridges. Historically the northwest area has been home to many covered bridges, but not many remain today. In the past, Spring-Spreading of the Hongqiao Bridge was considered as one of the eight top sites to see in Lanzhou of Gansu. At that spot this Woqiao Bridge spanned the Leitan River and was a renowned covered bridge both near and far. Unfortunately, in the 1950s it was demolished because of roadway construction. Furthermore, Gansu's Weiyuan County in Dingxi Prefecture has an example built in Republic of China imitated Woqiao Bridge that spans Qingyuan River. This Baling Bridge has survived into the present. The bridge is a hybrid timber cantilever and timber arch covered bridge. It is extremely rare to find a bridge like this in the present. Many covered bridges in Gansu's southeast are constructed across gorges and river valleys, and served as important arteries for ancient Shaanxi and Gansu's Ancient Tea and Horse Road. Furthermore, Gansu's southwest and Sichuan's west are home to Zang, Qiang, and other minority nationalities. There are many special areas here that have timber cantilever beam covered bridges present reginal and ethnic features.

1.3.3 Existing Covered Bridges in China's Southwest

Covered bridges in China's southwest are mostly preserved in Sichuan's central-eastern region. In particular they exist in the western part of Chongqing, in Yunnan's west, and other regions. They are characterized by timber beam, stone beam, stone arch and other sorts of covered bridges. There are quite a few of them here. The central east of Sichuan and west of Chongqing occupies the Sichuan Basin and north of upper reaches of the Yangtze River whose main residents are Han Nationality. Yunnan's west is located in the southern part of the Hengduan mountain range, as well as within the watersheds of the Nu and Lancang Rivers. It has mostly been home to Bai, Yi, Hui, and other minority nationalities. The area's covered bridges are strongly influenced by minority national cultures and local characteristics. They also are closely related to the Ancient Tea and Horse Road of Yunnan-Tibet.

1.3.4 Existing Covered Bridges in China's South Central Region

The covered bridges in China's south central area mostly exist in the southwest part of Hubei, the southeast of Chongqing, the west of Hunan, the east of Guizhou, as well as the northeast of Guangdong. This area is located in the eastern Yunnan-Guizhou Plateau. It is a mountainous area dominated by hills. From ancient times to the present this has been an area populated mostly by minority nationalities who live in the Wuling Mountain area at the juncture of Hunan, Hubei, Chongqing, and Guizhou. Here Tujia, Miao, Dong, and other minorities have lived for generations. Furthermore, at the juncture of Hunan, Guizhou, and Guangxi, generations of Dong and Miao Nationalities have lived. The covered bridges here are primarily timber beam, stone beam, and stone arch types. There are many covered bridges here, with rich influences from the area and from minority nationalities.

1.3.5 Existing Covered Bridges in China's Southeast Region

China's southeast covered bridges primarily exist in the southern part of Zhejiang, the north of Fujian, and the east of Jiangxi, in the mountain area of these provinces where the terrain is dominated by hills. The areas have

mostly been home to generations of Han, She, and Hakka Nationalities. The southeast coastal areas also are covered with many small water basins, including those situated by the Oujiang, Feiyun, Changxi, and Minjiang Rivers. The existing covered bridges here are very numerous and diverse, seemingly including every type of covered bridge. This area also includes the most characteristic Chinese timber arch covered bridges, which have attracted attention from around the world.

1.3.6 Existing Covered Bridges in Jiangnan (The South of the Yangtze River Region)

The primary covered bridges in the South of the Yangtze River area are primarily preserved in the south of Jiangsu, the north of Zhejiang, the southeast of Anhui, and the west of Shanghai. The area is located in the Yangtze River Delta Plain, the Ningshao Plain, and the Huizhou Basin. The landform here is dominated by plains and basins, where belongs to the Taihu Lake, and the area of the Xin'an River basin. Here the environment is crisscrossed by waterways, and has many covered bridges, including timber beam, stone beam, stone arch, and other forms. They are generally located in villages and towns, or are hidden inside classical gardens. They all are exquisite and unique. From the time of the Sui and Tang Dynasties with the development of the Jiangnan area, the region has been of strategic importance in economy in every subsequent dynasty. It is known for its flourishing commerce and trade and as a central site for the prosperous culture. Subsequently, the construction there of covered bridges has generally been more advanced and spectacular than that in other areas.

1.3.7 Existing Covered Bridges in Other Areas

In addition to the areas described above, several covered bridges can be seen in the Tibet Autonomous Region as well as in Lingnan Area. As for those located in Lhasa—the "city of sunlight" of the Tibetan Plateau—outside of the city gates sits the Liuli Bridge, a stone beam covered bridge. According to local saying it was first built during 627—649 in Tang Dynasty and repaired during the Qing Dynasty. Originally it served as an essential road that connected the inside of the ancient city of Lhasa with the outside, but now the river it crossed has dried up.

Furthermore, the Guangji Bridge that lies at the entrance of Chaozhou in Guangdong Province is known as one of the top four famous bridges in China. It is also a solitary example of a combined beam, floating, and arch bridge. The bridge was built in 1171 during the Southern Song Dynasty. It was renovated during the Yuan, Ming, and Qing Dynasties and is also called Xiangzi Bridge. It is formed from east-west beams that are grouped together with a middle floating bridge segment. The east and western bridge segments are divided into twelve spans, with seven stone piers each forming a stone beam bridge, and a middle part composed of eighteen floating timber boats fastened together to form a "boat bridge." The beam bridge's stone piers are composed of slender stones stacked in a crisscross manner forming the shape of a boat, each of different sizes, and of different forms. They were all built following the past collapse of the bridge's piers. Every bridge pier when repaired was covered with a pavilion or chamber in the style of the Chaozhou and Shantou. Some of these are separate units and some are combined. The form is exquisite and very special.

Section 2 Simply Supported Beam Covered Bridges

2.1 The Origin and Characteristics of Simply Supported Beam Covered Bridges

Simply supported bridges are a primitive and simple form of beam bridges. According to *Notes on Deciphering Spoken Words and Characters* "The word for bridges (*qiao* 桥) comes from beams on the water. Beams refer to the connecting supports that run from south to north in buildings. The character for the word beam (*liang* 梁) comes from water. Hence the word for a building beam (*dongliang* 栋梁) was derived from the essential word for bridges (*qiaoliang* 桥梁). A single timber is called a bar (*gang* 杠). Parallel timbers are called a bridge. Large and sloping structures are also referred to as bridges. In ancient times, the device used for drawing water out of a well was referred to as a "well bridge" (*jingqiao* 井桥) as well."[11] and bridges (*qiao* 桥) are beams on top of water, and the essential meaning of beams (*liang* 梁) comes from bridges and later developed into the beams that are used in architecture. In ancient times, countless pieces of wood were used to cross rivers, ditches, or other sorts of obstructions, and served as bridges, and became the most simple simply supported bridge.

According to materials from archeological excavations, Neolithic era settlements were surrounded by a ditch 2-6 meters wide. The use of this ditch was to prevent unwanted intrusions by animals, and by people from other settlements. Furthermore, in the course of daily life, such ditches required similar bridges that could be installed or transported to allow for passage. Multiple archeological sites have confirmed this thesis. The bridges on top of such ditches were all simple parallel timber bridges, and these early simply supported beam bridges could be counted as timber bridges.

Simply supported beam bridges then referred to timber or stone beams that rested on a ramp or pier at either end. This sort of single-span bridge frequently was limited according to the length of a single length of stone or timber. Most of them were no longer than 10 meters. Except for temporary bridges, simply supported beam bridges that exist today often bear gallery houses on top with a certain number of bays. These are referred to as simply supported timber covered bridges. There are many forms of structures that emerge on top of their horizontal planes—which are also called timber support covered bridge. As they are relatively easy to construct, this type of covered bridge is frequently seen. Single spanned simply supported timber covered bridge are commonly installed on top of narrow rivers and creeks. Multiple spanned simply supported timber covered bridges are installed on wide rivers and creeks, where in their middle an addition pier or column is erected forming a "long bridge".

2.2 Types and Locations of Simply Supported Covered Bridges

The structure of single span simply supported covered bridges is relatively simple and common. In southern areas where covered bridges exist they are commonly seen. The inferior ability of stone beams to resist tension restricted the ability to expand the number of simply supported stone bridges bearing gallery houses on top. As a result, simply supported stone covered bridges that exist today are few. Most of them are seen in gardens or as small-form covered bridges or pavilion bridges on top of narrow rivers in the areas South of the Yangtze River.

Multiple spanned simply supported covered bridges are built with piers or columns. The material of these supports are often not the same as the bridges' corresponding beams. It is common to see stone columns or stone piers supporting a timber beam covered bridge, in addition to such bridges which contain beams and supports of the same material.

2.2.1 Stone Column Timber Beam Covered Bridges

Because microorganisms and water erodes wood over time, making wood columns as supports eventually rot away, later people gradually replaced wood columns in water with stone columns. This created the form of a timber beam covered bridge supported by stone columns.

A famous example of a timber beam covered bridge supported by stone columns is Shanghai's Yingxiang Bridge.

2.2.2 Timber Beam Bridges with Stone Piers

As can be told by its name, a stone pier bridge refers to the laying of stones to compose a bridge pier. In general it is made by laying down uniform lines of stones, and it is more durable, stable, long lasting, and water and erosion resistant than stone columns or wood columns. It is also generally better able to withstand deluges from flood waters, and collisions from boats or other floating materials. Therefore, stone piers became the primary middle structural form used to support bridges with multiple spans. The faces on the bases of stone piers include protruding rectangular forms.These include forms with rounded ends or with rounded edges, as well as the forms of boats. The forms used often is related to the volume of water flow in a river, its speed, and direction. Rectangle forms of piers are generally installed where there is not a large amount of water, and where the current in the middle of a river is slow. The boat form of a pier is installed where the water volume is large and rapid. The side of the boat-form pier that faces upstream is often shaped into the form of a point and called a water dividing point. By dividing the water flow, it lessens the direct impact from the water as well as the extent of erosion.

As a result of the above advantages, stone pier timber beam covered bridges became the primary type of ancient multiple spanned simply supported covered bridge. They are found in a vast number of places, and it seems that wherever one can find covered bridges, they can be found as well. Relatively well known examples include the Caihong Bridge in Wuyuan, Jiangxi. This bridge was built in the Song Dynasty before later being rebuilt. The bridge's name is derived from a poem that reads, "A bright mirror reflects both sides of the water, and rainbows descend from a pair of bridges." It is a stone pier timber beam covered bridge with four piers and five spans. The boat-form piers are very large, and the timber beams that they support create the frame for dozens of bays of a gallery house on top. There is also the example of the Bailiang Bridge which was built in the Song Dynasty, and repaired in the Yuan, Ming, and Qing Dynasties. The bridge is a stone pier timber beam covered bridge made up of five piers and six spans. Its piers are very narrow and contracted, and the side that faces oncoming water has a water dividing point. Between each set of piers are installed 14-16 beams of wood, altogether totaling about 100 beams(*liang*), hence the name Bailiang Bridge. It also has a gallery house with dozens of bays on the bridge. This type of covered bridge can easily be seen in China's southeast, southwest, central south, and other areas.

2.2.3 Timber Column and Timber Beam Covered Bridges

Early forms of timber column and timber beam bridges can be seen in portraits stone and brick, and from murals inside tombs Han Dynasty. For instance the Eastern Han Dynasty era portrait *Horse and Vehicle Cross a Bridge* excavated from Tiaodenghe Street in Sichuan's Chengdu shows horizontal timbers installed on top of columns. On top of the crossbeams in the direction of the bridge body beams are erected. On the deck above, boards alternating with triangular wedge shapes and rectangle shapes are alternatively installed. Horses with carriage are depicted traveling on top. The Weishui Bridge depicted in Eastern Han Dynasty cave murals found in the Inner Mongolian Autonomous Region's Horinger County is also an example of a timber column timber beam bridge. Related archeological excavations have showed that the bridges in such murals match those that were actually built. Examples surviving in the present include the Yuzhaofeiliang Bridge (Flying Beam Fish Pond) that can be seen in front of the Shengmu Palace of the Jinci in Shanxi's Taiyuan. Of course, there are also a few simpler forms of timber column and timber beam bridges, for instance the Bandeng Bridge found in ancient Huizhou area.

Furthermore, there are two timber column timber beam covered bridges hidden in the Museum of the Forbidden City in Beijing within the famous Song Dynasty *Painting of a Thousand Miles of Rivers and Mountains*. A long bridge is depicted in the painting with over thirty spans, and with a combined gallery and pavilion in the center. The other bridge is a covered (pavilion) bridge with three spans. Of course, there are many of these sorts of examples in ancient paintings. Timber column timber beam covered bridge was a primary type of surviving covered bridges. The examples are numerous.

Today the timber column timber beam covered bridges in China's center-southern areas are frequently found especially in mountainous regions, for example in the Dong Nationality settlements of northern Guangxi and southeastern Guizhou, as well as in Miao settlements, and in surrounding forest areas. Studying these structures and forms reveal that they are not dissimilar from traditional Dong and Miao's architectural construction, and share a common origin with the forms of pile architecture and lattice frame architecture commonly found in the south.

2.2.4 Stone Column Stone Beam Covered Bridges

There are many remaining ancient stone column stone beam bridges, especially in Jiangnan or in the areas of the southeast. To the present there are still many of these bridges that date to the Song Dynasty and later. The shorter ones have a total of two to three spans, and the longer ones reach as many as nine. They can be either level or curved. It is worth mentioning that the columns for such bridges in Jiangnan are straight and arranged close to one another. But in the southeastern areas, the columns in the center are straight, but the columns at the ends are tilted, and spread apart, forming the shape of the Chinese character *zhua* (爪) form causes the bridge column's foundational stones, vertical column, and capping stone beams to together create a more stable supporting structure. At the same time, it can be considered that in the southeastern areas there are many narrow rivers that pass through mountains which are frequently threatened by mountain floods. Constructing diagonal stone columns can lesson the force from impacting currents in order to ensure that during sudden rapid torrents the piers are not toppled over.

As has already been said, there are not many simply supported stone covered bridges that exist today, and those stone column stone beam bridges with multiple spans are even rarer. Today one of the only known that remains is the Xiaofeihong Bridge in the Zhuozheng Garden in Jiangsu's Suzhou. It is a covered bridge not commonly seen in Suzhou's gardens. The bridge has two columns and three spans, and is slightly curved. The bridge is formed by upright columns that support the capping stone beams above. Every span has five stone beams that form the bridge's surface. The bridge's upper

structure has a three bay gallery house which is connected with the surrounding galleries and corridors. It is extremely beautiful and elegant.

Section 3 Cantilever Beam Covered Bridges

3.1 The Original and Historical Locations of Cantilever Beam Bridges

The famed historian of science and technology Joseph T. M. Needham in his work *Science and Civilisation in China* that expressed the following opinions about cantilever beam bridges:

1-He stated that this type of bridge (cantilever beam bridges) possibly developed in the Himalayas, and at a very early time became familiar and widely used in China.

2-He believed that the origin of cantilever bridges possibly have had a relation with ladder bridges (*tiqiao*)in Han Dynasty.

3-He believed Chinese tamber cantilever bridges are related to the *dougong* bracket system used in roof bracket system of traditional Chinese architecture.

4-He believed that Chinese timber cantilever bridge technology spread to countries outside of China.

5-He believed there is a possibility that cantilever bridges made of stone existed in China.

These conclusions are not difficult to appreciate with the exception of Needham's conclusions about ladder bridges. So here we will first discuss *tiqiao*. A Chinese Han Dynasty portrait stone was excavated from Shandong Province's Liangcheng Mountain that depicts a *tiqiao*.

Dr. Needham explained that in China's Han Dynasty, in order to repair pavilions on lakes, it was necessary to install pavilions on top of a bracket which was very similar to a cantilever. This structure was called *tiqiao*. The question is whether this sort of *tiqiao* occurred at this time or if it was completely a product of Han Dynasty artists' imaginations. In 1971, a pavilion building was discovered named Yanyu Temple now called Duzhu Temple. It was built in Hanoi, Vietnam in 1049 (Hanoi was under the Han Dynasty's administrative control a millennium earlier). This pavilion was built on top of a stone column in the water, and its roof was supported by a timber cantilever beam and a horizontal supporting beam. In fact, in Chinese Han Dynasty's Portrait stone, there are multiple such pavilion buildings

and *tiqiao*. For instance, other examples can be seen in the murals *Painting of Watching Fish from the Pavilion* and *Painting of Fishing* excavated from Shandong's Weishan and Zaozhuang.

Needham's remarks about the structural similarities between timber cantilever bridges and the *dougong* system used in traditional Chinese architecture are likely correct. From the structural perspective, the two forms are clearly very much alike, and their origins must have been closely related. However today, Needham's categorization of the *Hongqiao Rainbow Bridge* depicted in the famous Northern Song Dynasty's *Painting of Riverside Scene at Qingming Festival* as a cantilever bridge clearly can be seen as a mistake.

The earliest known historical document that mentions a timber cantilever bridge dates to the early 4th century. The geographer Li Daoyuan who lived during the Northern Wei Dynasty quoted Duan Guo's *Shazhouji* (*Records of the Sandbars*) in the *Shuijingji* (Records of the Water Ways) stating that "Upstream of Tuyuhun a bridge was built over a mighty river that is over 500 meters long (author: it is doubtful if this is accurate. The measure unit used here of *zhang* may have been what is generally referred to as *chi*, in which case the bridge would have been 50 meters long). Stones serve as foundations at either side of the bank with successive ties and large timbers coming from either direction bearing most of the load. More timber thus accumulated adds more pressure, and the two sides hence gradually unite together, spanning a distance of about 10 meters." The *Shuijingji* has other records like this, for example referring to the Feiqiao Bridge that was built in Qinzhou's Qifo. It states this bridge very likely was a timber cantilever bridge. There are scholars believe that timber cantilever bridges were invented in Qinghai and Gansu Provinces in northwestern area. Furthermore, traces of such bridges can be found in many places, including Tibet, Shaanxi, Sichuan, Chongqing, Ningxia, Yunnan, Guizhou, Hunan, Hubei, Zhejiang, Anhui, Jiangxi, and Fujian. Such bridges required large amounts of wood. They were built and preserved in these areas because of the plentiful timber resources in these regions.

The Bahe Bridge and Shizhou Bridge in Shaanxi's Xi'an are all examples of timber cantilever bridges. From this we can understand that these bridges were once widespread in the north. However, along with the development of bridge construction technology and the disappearance of forest in northern area, they gradually decreased. Today it is already hard to

find more examples of such bridges in the broad expanses of the north. One can glimpse the scant traces of such timber cantilever bridges from old photographs from the 1920s to 1930s. And of course, this region still possesses examples of timber cantilever bridges, such as Weiyuan's Baling Bridge and the Lanzhou's Woqiao Bridge in Gansu Province.

3.2 Where Timber Cantilever Covered Bridges are Found and Their Characteristics

Overall, we can see from the perspective of the current geographic distribution of timber cantilever covered bridges that they occur mostly in China's south. Present scholars believe that timber cantilever covered bridges are mostly found in the following four large expanses of area: 1. In Fujian, Zhejiang, and Jiangxi, 2. In the upper reaches of the Yuanshui and Zishui Rivers, 3. In Hunan, Guangxi, and Guizhou 4. In western Yunnan. From a structural perspective, such bridges found in the upper reaches of the Yuanshui and Zishui Rivers are highly similar to those found the Hunan, Guangxi, and Guizhou. There is a historical relation between the origin and trends in development of bridges within these areas.

3.2.1 Timber Cantilever Covered Bridges in Fujian, Zhejiang, and Jiangxi

Most timber cantilever covered bridges in this larger region are located in Fujian. Those in Jiangxi are generally found in the south and east parts of the province where it shares a boarder with Fujian. Those in Zhejiang are general distributed in the province's southwest. And those in Fujian are primarily distributed in its western areas. In all of these areas, the bridges are generally distributed in the towering and steep mountains. The characteristic of bridges in these areas is that their cantilever components are made of fir trees, and are laid alternatively vertically and horizontally to bear the construction loads on top of the bridges. Their piers are primarily composed of a boat-shaped stone block or a boat-shaped pile of stones. Examples include the Yongzhen Bridge in Jiangxi's Anyuan, the Yong'an Bridge in Jiangxi's Nankang, as well as the Buyue Bridge in Fujian's Jianou. Another version of the bridge is the Dongguan Bridge built in 1145 during the Southern Song Dynasty in Fujian's Yongchun. Considering the volume of bridge piers, we can see that among the cantilever covered bridge piers in this area, regardless of whether they are in the form of common boat shapes or of distinct hexagonal shapes, the volumes of the piers are all very large. This is something common to them all, and is a particularly outstanding spatial characteristic.

The differences between timber cantilever covered bridges in the overall region primarily reside in the form of the gallery houses that sit on top of them. For instance, many of the gallery houses in Jiangxi are covered with overhanging gable roofs or bounded on either end by gables in which a doorway is installed to access the covered bridge. This form is common and it represents a relatively low level of construction. Bridges in this category such as the Chengbo Bridge in Qianshan, Jiangxi resemble simple residential dwellings. On the other hand, the gallery houses in Fujian and Zhejiang are comparatively diverse. Many of them bear hip and gable roofs or combined roofs representing a high level of architecture, comparable to those used in temples or palaces. Examples include the Zhiqing Bridge, the Buyue Bridge in Jianou, Fujian and the Yunlong Bridge in Liancheng, Fujian. Furthermore, the gallery houses in Jiangxi typically do not install a wall guard against wind and rain. Some have only a shallow eave installed on top of the bridge's railing. Examples of this include the Yongzhen Bridge built initially in 1652, and rebuilt in 1749. However in Fujian and Zhejiang, timber cantilever covered bridges use a suspended diagonal guard against wind and rain. For example the Yunlong Bridge, Buyue Bridge and Dongguan Bridge all hang a suspended diagonal guard from the eaves of the structure. According to historical analysis, Jiangxi's timber cantilever covered bridges were constructed from 627 during the Tang Dynasty to about 1644-1661 during the Qing Dynasty. The history of such bridge construction here started fairly early. In Zhejiang and Fujian, there are many forms of bridge construction dating back to ancient times, and there are many bridges dating from the Song and Ming Dynasties. The construction of cantilever timber covered bridges go as far back as the Song Dynasty. Some of these bridges were rebuilt fairly early, such as the Yunlong Bridge, which was first built during the end of the Ming Dynasty and rebuilt in the early Qing Dynasty. In the end though, while the gallery houses of such bridges in Jiangxi are different compared to those in Fujian and Zhejiang, the structure of their cantilever beams and boat-shaped piers are highly similar. Moreover, these timber cantilever covered bridges exist within a contiguous area in the borders of these three provinces.[12]

In this area, the cantilever timber covered bridges here originated in a fairly early period, and the scale of the bridges is relatively large. Their gallery houses are dominated by forms of temple architecture as well as types derived from vernacular residential dwellings.

3.2.2 Timber Cantilever Covered Bridges in the Upper Reaches of the Yuanshui and Zishui Rivers of Southern Hunan

The majority of the timber cantilever covered bridges in Hunan are located in the area of the Dongting Lake and the Yuanshui and Zishui Rivers. In particular they are found in Yiyang, Shaoyang, and other regions. The bridges are generally composed of piers made from layers of stones, timber cantilever beams, and in normal circumstances bear a bridge gallery house covered by a single-eave roof. They usually feature suspended roofs with a thin overhanging awning. Overall there are quite a few resplendent bridges in the area, but very few feature multiple story buildings or pavilions. Also they do not feature the sort of boards that carefully protect bridges from wind and rain in Zhejiang and Fujian. Instead, generally such shelter is restricted to the cantilever components of the bridge. Either end of the bridges generally use stone brick construction that closely resemble that used in Chinese decorated archways that serve as the bridges gates and entrances. Yiyang and Shaoxing's cantilever structures are overall similar to those in Zhejiang, Fujian, and Jiangxi. The development of the system for using overlapping logs follows the developmental principle of the Chinese *dougong* bracket structure. In Hunan, the logs used in the cantilevers are referred to as magpie wood, probably because the criss-cross manner of forming the structures resembles the way that magpies make their nests. An example of this is the Yongxi Bridge located in Hunan's Yiyang in the village of Xitan in Anhua county's Dongshi township. Its four spans stretch over the Maxi Creek, supported on three piers. It is 83 meters long, 12.8 meters high and 4.2 meters wide. The gallery house on top is composed of 34 bays. In April, 1876, Chen Wuzhi and other townspeople began contributing funds for the bridge's construction, and in October, 1881, it was completed. Three layers of crisscrossing fir logs rest on-top of the bridge's boat-shaped piers, and support the timber boards that make up the bridge's deck. Timber railing is installed on both sides of the bridge, on top of which is an overhanging eave. The cantilever beams have boards to protect them from the wind and the rain, and both entrances to the bridge are framed by decorated decorated archways.

The beam framework used in the cantilever timber covered bridges of Hunan Province's Yiyang and Shaoyang are of a similar sort to those in the Fujian and Zhejiang regions. The difference is that the Hunan bridges rarely use boards to protect the structures from wind and rain. Instead, these bridges use a shallow protective awning. In addition, it is common for bridges in these areas to install a decorative archway at both bridge entrances, made of timber or masonry architecture, creating a relative bold appearance. In Fujian and Zhejiang there is common use of gable walls at the entrances to the covered bridges, though ultimately the number of such examples are fewer than those found in Hunan. According to a survey, approximately 20 cantilever covered bridges in Yiyang and Shaoyang prefectures have stone brick or wooden decorated archway entrances, forming a unique architectural style in these areas.

A few of the timber cantilever covered bridges in Shaoyang and Yiyang were built in the Ming or in the middle of the Qing Dynasties. Those that were built fairly early include the Jiangdong Bridge, the Longtan Bridge, the Lishan Bridge, and more. Most of the bridges in the area were built in the late Qing Dynasty. Overall these bridges were built at a somewhat later time than their equivalents in Fujian and Zhejiang. As a result, there is the opinion that timber cantilever bridges possibly spread from Fujian and Zhejiang towards the north, and from the east to the west. It can also be surmised that carpenters in the upper regions of the Yuanshui and Zishui rivers made some modifications to the forms of these structures, and established the unique gallery bridge style of the bridges in these regions.

In the areas of Shaoyang and Yiyang, the beam framework of cantilever bridges were transformed in a way that had a large impact on the characteristics of the bridges to the west and north. An example of this is the Liangting Bridge built by the west Hunan Tujia and Miao nationality in the autonomous region of Xichehe Town's New Village in Longshan County. The bridge was built in 1780 during the Qing Dynasty, and it was rebuilt in 1887. It is a timber cantilever bridge built with two piers and three spans. It is 43.3 meters long and 4.9 meters wide. Its simply laid out hexagonal stone piers are 11.5 meters high, and the bridge overall has 12 bays, built with a suspended roof with a single eve. Another thin eve projects from below the bridge's railing. The entrance to the

bridge is formed by a decorative arch made of bricks. The cantilever component of the bridge connects with the bridge's piers. This sort of construction methodology is very similar to that used in the Nanyang Bridge and Wenzhong Bridge in Taishun, Zhejiang. The Taishun Nanyang Bridge was constructed in 1870, and the Wenzhong Bridge completed in 1921. As the Liangting Bridge was rebuilt in 1887, we can see that the practice of connecting the cantilever beams inside a bridge's pier was a relatively late technological development. As a result of this, these timber cantilever covered bridges only make use of lengthwise placed timbers and not horizontal ones. This is quite different from the cross-hatched method of layering lengthwise and horizontal "magpie timbers" in the southern areas of Hunan province. Furthermore it is a method with a high degree of similarity to construction practices in Chongqing, Yunnan, and other areas further to the west. Many of the remaining timber cantilever covered bridges of western Hunan demonstrate a tendency towards simplicity, and share characteristics of this later phase of bridge construction.

According to academic research, historically the Yuan and Zi Rivers were areas for Tujia, and Miao nationality, and also served as important sites for activities of the ancient Wuximan people. Hence by examining the location and historical period, we can see that these Ming and Qing dynasty timber cantilever covered bridges are bearers of the pile-based architectural heritage of the Tujia, Miao, and other southern national minorities. Interestingly, just like in the mountainous border region of Guizhou, Guangxi, and Hunan, the covered bridges in Shaoyang and Yiyang Hunan are called Fengyu Bridges)[12].

Covered bridges in west Hunan as well as in northeastern Guizhou, western Hubei, and southeast Chongqing are all referred to as Liangqiao Bridges. These bridges are primarily found in places where the Tujia nationality lives. The neighboring areas in Sichuan also call them Liangqiao or Liangting Bridges.

3.2.3 Cantilever Timber Covered Bridges in the Border Areas of Guizhou, Guangxi, and Hunan

There are scholars that believe that after the timber cantilever covered bridge entered this region from Zhejiang and Fujian, the form was influenced by the architectural practices of the Dong Nationality, and gained distinctive characteristics and relatively independent distribution area. This distinctive style of the bridges is primarily found in Guangxi's Sanjiang, Guizhou's Liping, and Hunan's Tongdao. The piers here often are built with protruding hexagonal bases, *shuifenjian* (points that separate the incoming water) and reinforcing walls. The exteriors of the piers are taller and thinner than boat-shaped piers. The piers' surface is composed by a crisscrossing method of laying down material, and a wooden cantilever in the shape of the Chinese character "井" lies on-top, formed of very thick material. Because of this, the gap between the lower and higher level logs is wider than those found in Fujian, Zhejiang, or southern Hunan. This, together with the height of these bridges makes for particularly inflexible structures. Just as in Hunan's south, in order to protect the bridge structure and railing, many are protected by a thin eave. Some bridges also have a large overhanging eave to protect such parts. The covered bridges in these areas often construct a structure in their centers or ends that resembles the *gulou* (drum tower pavilions) of Guizhou in Dong Nationality's Village. Many such pavilions are covered with roofs with multiple eaves, and with a *cuanjian* (pyramidal) top. They can be three, five, or seven stories tall. In contrast, the timber cantilever covered bridges of the Tongdao County in Hunan's south are supported by boat-shaped piers that show a common origin with those of similar bridges found in the Yuanshui and Zishui rivers. At the same time, the pavilion's structures on the surfaces of the bridges there resemble those in the Sanjiang's Dong Nationality areas, and feature similar drum towers. For instance the Guanyue Bridge is covered with pavilions that occupy two thirds of the total bridge's surface. The pavilion built above the central pier has a roof with five eaves, four corners, and a pyramidal top. Both ends of the bridge have a bridge pavilion built with a hip-and-gable roof, with three eaves.

The Chengyangfengyu Bridge located in Guangxi, Liuzhou prefecture's Ma'an Village is a classic example of this area's timber cantilever bridge. The structure combines a bridge, gallery, and pavilion. Its style is distinctive from all of China's other covered bridges. The Chengyang Bridge is also called the Yongji Bridge, and the Panlong Bridge. It was constructed in the end of the Qing Dynasty and the beginning of the Republic of China, and was completed in 1916 after 12 years of work. It spans the Linxi River, and is a timber covered bridge with four spans and three piers. The bridge's surface is covered with a gallery with nineteen bays, and five pavilions. It is a truly grand site to behold. The bridge's surface frame and deck are made of fir trees. It is 77.76 meters long, and its supporting frame is composed of two layers. The upper layer extends 4 meters, and the lower level 2.5 meters. Each is composed of seven logs of fir trees 40 centimeters in diameter closely bundled together, and on top of this is a beam structure gallery house composed of upright columns. The gallery house is 4 meters wide, and 10.8 meters tall. Each side of the bridge has a timber railing. The center has a hexagonal pavilion covered with a *cuanjian* roof with three eaves. The top of the roof is 7.3 meters from the bridge's deck. This structure is bordered on both ends with square shaped pavilions with a *cuanjian* roof rising 7 meters high, with three eaves. The opposite ends of the bridge have square shaped pavilions that rise 6.5 meters covered by *xieshan* roofs with three eaves. From a distance it seems like a cluster of pavilions are suspended in space above the Linxi River, and all of sudden a jade palace comes into focus.

In sanjiang county there also contains the Patuan fengyu Bridge on which people are seperate from animals. The scale of this bridge is smaller than that of the Chengyang Bridge. It spans the Miaojiang River, next to the Patuan Village in Dudong township. The bridge's two ramps are separated by a distance of 30.4 meters. Underneath it is supported by a stone brick pier. The bridge's surface extends 50 meters. Above it there are three pavilions. It was built in 1910. It is special for having a path for draft animals and livestock located next to the main bridge path, forming a double-decked bridge, each level separated by 1.5 meters. Separating people from animals allows for greater pedestrian safety, and makes for a cleaner bridge, constituting an innovation in the use of bridge space[13].

3.2.4 The Dianxi Area's Timber Cantilever Covered Bridges

Yunnan's timber cantilever covered bridges primarily are found in Yunlong County in of western Yunnan's Dali Prefecture, and Tengchong County of Baoshan. They are primarily represented by single spanned bridges. Yunnan's timber cantilever covered bridges have the following characteristics: 1) Their structures generally make use of diagonal bracing. 2) Their gallery houses generally have a single eave, and their beam structures mostly use shields to protect their components from the wind and rain. 3) The ends of the bridge generally construct four sided bridge gates made of rammed earth or bricks. 4) Their cantilevered components rarely show signs of crisscross-character "井" formed construction when viewed from the outside, and it is easy to observe laterally placed projecting timbers and harder to see those placed horizontally. This phenomenon is due to the smaller scale generally used on the horizontally placed timbers, or because of a special technique of concealing such structural elements in such construction. If one leaves out the bridge gates found on both sides of such bridges, the external appearance of Yunnan's covered bridges closely resemble to the timber arch covered bridges of Fujian and Zhejiang.

Typical examples of such bridges include the Tongjing Bridge and the Tongji Bridge. The former is located in Yunlong County, in the Dali Prefecture, and the latter in Tengchong County, with both bridges located in Yunnan Province. The Tongjing Bridge has the largest single span of all the timber cantilever covered bridges in Yunnan. It spans a clear distance of 30 meters. The Tongji Bridge's span is the second largest single span of such bridges in the province, covering a distance of 27.5 meters.

There are also many other bridges in Yunlong County that resemble the structure of cantilever covered bridges. These include the Jiancao Bridge in Jiancao Town, and the Caifeng Bridge in Baishi Township's Shundang Village. The Jiancao Bridge is 18 meters long, and clear distance of span is 10 meters. Its gallery house is 2.5 meters wide. The Caifeng Bridge crosses the Bijiang River. It is 33.3 meters long, and spans a clear distance of 27 meters. Its gallery house is 4.7 meters wide. Other than the Tongji Bridge, Tengchong County is also home to the Yongshun Bridge in Jietou Township, Shiqiao Village, and the Chengde Bridge, in Qushi Township, Qingqiao Village. The timber cantilever covered bridges in Tengchong County are all built over the Longchuan River. The Yongshun Bridge was built during 1522-1566 in the Ming Dynasty. Afterwards it was repaired many times. It is 20 meters long, and 3 meters wide, and about 10 meters tall. The Chengde Bridge is located deep in the mountains in a thick forest, where wild pigs frequently come and ago. As a result the bridge is also called the Yezhuqing Bridge. The bridge was built in an inauspicious era, in 1882, the official Chen Zonghai donated money to renovate it. During this subsequent work, four iron cables were added to the lower part of the bridge's deck. In 1942, it was demolished in order to halt the advance of Japanese invaders. In 1947, it was rebuilt by Li Genyuan according to its original form, using natural rot-resistant catalpa wood. The Chengde Bridge is 29 meters long, and spans a clear distance of 18.2 meters, and is 2.2 meters wide, and 10 meters tall. The Chengde Bridge connects an ancient courier route. Caravans coming from the Gaoligong Mountains to the east to the gorges of the Nujiang River would cross here and then arrive at Qushi Township in the northern part of Tengchong County.

The Tongji Bridge traverses the Longchuan River by Shunhe Village in Jietou Township, Tengchong County. It was first built during 1465-1487 and it was rebuilt in 1946. It is a beautiful timber cantilever covered bridge. The eroded railing which surrounds the bridge clearly reveals the wood material used. The bridge is 37.5 meters long, and 4.5 meters wide. The gallery on top has nine bays, and it spans a clear distance of 27.5 meters. It is about 9.3 meters tall. According to the *Tengchong County Gazetteer*, "The bridge was made of wood, and its lowest level rests on stone piers or on the pavilions located on either bank. The second level uses mortise and tenon technology to connect with the lower level, and so on with the third and fourth levels. The top level has long and thick timber beams that stabilize either end, thus forming the completed bridge. The bridge has the form of a bow shaped ladder. Both sides have pavilions, the main deck has buildings, and both lanes of the bridge have benches. Next to the benches are protective railings. The bridge's buildings keep out the rain and block the sun, and allow people to rest while also extending the life of the bridge. The bridge has an ingenious and unique structural logic. Gravity is transferred to the stone piers on either end by multiple levels of beam framework, adding to the bridge's stability and reflecting sound mechanical principles." [14]

Beneath the Tongji Bridge's exterior is a hidden and highly complex structure. The deck is created by layer upon layer of beam structures formed through cantilevered construction. The first layer is built on top of the stone piers and bridge pavilions on each bank, and gradually is layered upward, and advances forward, held in place through mortise and tenon fixtures. Then, according to the length of the bridge, further branches project outward. The greater the span, the greater the number of projecting layers. As building continues, the deck continuously expands, until both sides are linked together, at which point beams and boards are installed to reinforce the overall structure. In this way, a bridge resembling an arch grows[15].

Western Yunnan has an long history of timber cantilever covered bridges, with the heyday of such bridge construction occurring in the Ming and Qing Dynasties. According to structural and construction features, a regional form of such bridge building can be said to exist within Gansu, northeast Tibet, northwest Sichuan, and the Dali of Yunnan. In these areas, timber cantilever covered bridges are primarily single spanned, with cantilever beams projecting outward at sharp angles (to a greater extent than those found in other regions in the south) and with multiple buildings at the heads of the bridges together with other characteristic features[12].

3.3 The Historical Path of Timber Cantilevered Covered Bridges in China's Past

In regards to the historical origins and technological development of China's timber cantilever covered bridges, Wang Yu, a researcher at the Chongqing Three Gorges Dam Museum has the following opinion: the technology of such bridges originated in the east, in the provinces of Zhejiang and Fujian, and spread to the west, and it spread as far north as the southern area of Hunan, and to northern Jiangxi. It was only after this point that she speculates the technology spread to the mountainous border area of Guizhou, Guangxi, and Hunan—home to the Miao, Dong, and other minority nationality. The style of such bridges at this point blended with that of wind and rain bridges, and spread further west and north. Such influence reached the western part of Yunnan, the southern part of Chongqing, the northern part of Sichuan, as well as Gansu, Qinghai, and Tibet. In this way, such construction was transmitted to nearly the entire South of Yangtze River region, as well as to the Yangtze River's upper reaches. In the end it can be said that China's southern timber construction developed on the foundation of pile architecture from the South of Yangtze River region. From here it blended, developed, and evolved with the influence of northern civilizations and various indigenous civilizations. The geographical path for the transmission of pile construction technology is generally the same as that mapped out for timber cantilever covered bridges by Wang Yu. For a more detailed elaboration of this subject, refer to the text *Wooden Construction South of the Yangtze*[11].

However, from Wang Yu's general analysis of timber cantilever covered bridges it could be concluded that most important examples of bridges supporting the above theses were built during the Ming and Qing Dynasties. In fact, the ancient development and evolution of cantilever covered bridges was not limited to the Ming and Qing. Wang Yu established a path of development that placed cantilever covered bridges as the latest phase of bridge development. However as stated in the preface of this book, according to Joseph Needham's *Science and Civilisation in China*, the origin of cantilever covered bridge technology occurred during the Han Dynasty. And as the Northern Wei Dynasty geographer Li Daoyuan wrote in the "Records of the Sandbars" from his *Records of the Water Ways* the remains of the flying bridge that crossed the Yellow River built by the nomadic group named Tuyuhun was an example of a form that was already widespread. Why were the majority of timber covered bridges that exist today built during the Ming and Qing? The primary reasons for this is likely the limited lifespan of timber construction as well as the unceasing progress of bridge construction technology. The later reason seems to be more important.

In order to explain the complicated question of the historical development of architecture, the author will borrow an analogy from the process of wave transmission in physics. If an advance in technology occurs, its development and transmission can be compared to the effect of dropping a stone in a still lake. This will result in wave forms spreading out in all directions from the center, which overall explains the problem at hand. The technological advance can be said to occur at the center of the wave. And the ripples that spread out in all directions from the center represent the path and process of the transmission of technology. If the surface of the lake is not completely composed of water, but has islands or other objects, then the spread of the waves will be impacted, and the path of transmission will need to go around such obstructions. After the completion of an older phase of technological development, the site of origin of a newer phase of technological development may move. This site may be nearer or farther from the former location. But either way, the two phases of exchange and transmission of technology, just like ripples in water, will likely both experience similar interference and other overlapping phenomenon.

This theory can explain why the remotest regions preserve the most ancient examples of technology. Remote areas are relatively far from centers of civilization. In addition, new technology is not always transmitted with the same degree of momentum. As a result, successive waves of technological development do not always reach such regions. And the technology preserved in such areas is possibly technology transmitted during earlier periods. The overall technology there will tend towards

the old. Confucius discovered this principle during the Spring and Autumn(770-476 BC). He said, "When ceremonies become lost at the court, it is necessary to search for them in the countryside." The scholar Yang Hongxun's view should be cited, that the civilization of the South of the Yangtze River area arose from the Dongyi Nationality's coastal civilization. The Haidai region of ancient Shandong was the original territory of the Dongyi culture. After the crushing of the Huangdi's Yan-Huang alliance, they settled in the southeast coastal areas as well along the path of the Yangtze River. In the south of the Yangtze River area they became the latter day so-called "Baiyue". This area is approximately a part of today's territory of rice culture, as well as a segment of the region where pile architecture occurred. The source of this cultural area was the Haidai region, in the present day Shandong Peninsula. Consequently, the Han Dynasty stone relief drawings that Joseph Needham discovered that contained cantilever covered ladder bridges were mostly excavated from Shandong. Of course, this form of architecture followed the transmission of pile construction to the regions of the Baiyue, and continued to spread to the west and north, arriving at Gansu, Qinghai, and other northwest areas, before being recorded in Li Daoyuan's *Records of the Waterways* about the Flying Bridge.

3.4　China's Famous Timber Cantilever Bridge

In this section, the author offers brief introductions about a few relatively famous provincial and municipal timber cantilever covered bridges in order to allow readers to more clearly understand the bridges of this type that exist today.

3.4.1　Yonghe Bridge in Longquan, Zhejiang Province

The Yonghe Bridge crosses the Anren Creek in Anren Town in Longquan county, Zhejiang Province. The bridge is 125.7 meters long, 7.5 meters wide, and 13 meters tall. It is a cantilever covered bridge with three piers and four spans. The bridge was constructed in 1465 during the Ming Dynasty, and its original name was the Yongning Bridge. It burned down during 1638-1661 and was rebuilt in 1718 in Qing Dynasty at the cost of over 3,000 *liang* silver ingots. Subsequently, it was known as the Yonghe Bridge.

Its three supporting stone piers look like boats, with their sides facing incoming water

built in the form of a goose wing guardian wall. On top of the bridge piers are multiple levels of cantilever beams that maintain the load of the bridge's body. Above this is a gallery house with forty-two bays. At either end of the bridge is a five story decorative archway, with four columns and three bays which serves as a particularly grand entranceway. In front and behind the four columns are wooden drum-shaped bearing stones placed in order to strengthen the stability of the columns. In the central bay is a crossbeam in the shape of a crescent moon, and on top of this a dwarf-post and bracket were used to support the five-bay gallery of the outstretched bridge house. The bridge does not only have one protective awning, its beam structure also contains a shield against the wind and rain. The east and western ends also have a stone platform and two paths. The interior of the bridge house has a railing and a strip of benches for use for resting or sitting. In the Qing Dynasty, a poem was composed out of awe for the bridge, stating, "The wind sails through the leaves and sends ripples through the flowing water, the sparse trees on the two banks are painted in late autumn. Together it unites a rainbow and a jade mirror, a spectacle as good as that of old Chazhou." [16]

3.4.2　Zhiqing Bridge in Jian'ou, Fujian Province

Located in Huangcun Village, Dikou Town, Jian'ou, Fujian Province, the north-south Zhiqing Bridge was built in 1490 during the Ming Dynasty. The northern part is supported by piers made of layers of crushed stones while the southern part spans a stream. Its overhanging gable roof bears small grey tiles on top. The roof on top of the center of its three bay sis slightly higher than that covering the two adjacent ones, which forms the appearance of double-eaves. Awnings are installed below the eaves.

Zhiqing Bridge is an overhanging beam bridge with two layers of beams—an upper layer composed of nine fir logs and a lower one of seven. Wooden slats which form a joist are put on the beams, with another layer of planks placed at the top. The nine-bay gallery, composed of four Columns and nine purlins, is flanked by railings and benches. Shrines are erected in the middle and at the ends of the bridge and the middle roof is decorated with a caisson ceiling which consists of four layers of bracket sets. There is a crescent-shaped beam placed on a two-layer bracket set with the construction time of the bridge written on it, stating, "(the bridge was) completed in the third year of Hongzhi Emperor's reign of the

Ming Dynasty, corresponding to the 47th year of the sexagenary cycle on the first day, the *wushen* day, of the 12th month. On the morning of the fifth day of the month, the *renzi* day, many people took part in a celebration organized to celebrate the new construction". Bracket sets can also be found in the beam frame This has huge beams and columns connected with the *yueliang* crescent-shaped supporting beam through double bracket sets; components including *zhaqian*, *tatou* and *tuofeng* are delicately constructed. The main beam frame and *zaojing* have been painted but the colors are mottled now. The beam frame is built in the typical architectural style of the Song and Yuan Dynasties in Fujian. The bridge roof is composed of flat rafters with wood of the same size perpendicular to them on top, resembling today's roof battens—components used to fix tiles on top of a roof. Covered with blue-grey tiles, there is no obvious ridge or ridge decorations on the roof, which creates a simple but unique style.

3.4.3 Buyue Bridge in Jian'ou, Fujian Province

Buyue Bridge, spanning Yuxi River, is located at Yuxi Village, Jiyang Town, Jian'ou, Fujian Province. It is a cantilever timber bridge built with two piers and three spans. It is 127.5 meters long and 5 meters wide. The bridge was built in 1350 during the Yuan Dynasty and reconstructed in 1519 during the Ming. It was renovated three times during the Qing Dynasty. In 1998, Buyue Bridge underwent extensive reconstruction work. Steel truss beams were added to the timber structure. However, its archaic appearance was preserved. However, it has been burn up in 2019.

The bridge's boat-shaped stone piers under the bridge have *yanchijingangqiang* on the upstream side. Three groups of criss-crossing logs are placed on the piers, forming a cantilever beam structure in the shape of the character "井." Another three groups of criss-crossed logs are installed on top of this, constituting the main structure of the bridge. The gallery house set up on the bridge owns forty-two bays and the front consists of three bays and four columns. There are forty-three rows of column frames with one hundred and seventy-two columns in total. The bridge is a *tailiang* structure (a common form of column-and-beam construction used in traditional Chinese architecture) with *wudianding* (a hipped roof). Its beam frame and gateway columns are all coated with red paint. Multiple-eave hipped roofs protrude from both ends of the bridge. Underneath the eaves are layers of *ruyidougong*, which form upturned eaves that project at outstanding angles, forming a splendid gate tower. Long benches flanking the gallery are prepared for passers-by to have a rest and wooden awnings are erected under the eaves. In the middle of the bridge is a shrine dedicated to the Godness Guanyin. There are four characters 步月古桥 (Buyue Ancient Bridge) carved in lishu style (an ancient style of calligraphy from the Han Dynasty) on the left wall of the east gate tower. On top of the beam frame are tens of plaques recording the names and donations of the people who have contributed to the construction process and there is an octagonal caisson ceiling with drawings of the *Eight Immortals* and the *Entrepreneur*. There is also a plaque inscribed with Buyue Bridge hanging on the wall of the west gate tower, accompanied with a couplet, "Even at night the bridge projects an auspicious radiance / On the surface an auspicious atmosphere floats in return for the shielding peaks." [17]

3.4.4 Yunlong Bridge in Liancheng, Fujian Province

Yunlong Bridge is located at Xialuo Village, Luofang Township, Liancheng County, Fujian Province. It spans the Qingyan River from east to west. The four-pier and five-span cantilever beam covered bridge with a wooden gallery is 81 meters long, 5 meters wide and 6 meters high. Built in 1634 in Ming Dynasty, it was reconstructed in 1772 in Qing Dynasty and renovated several times with the latest renovation completed in 1984[18].

Four boat-shaped granite piers are put under the bridge, with *yanchijingangqiang* walls at the upstream side. There are three groups of criss-crossing logs on the piers, forming an overhanging beam structure in the shape of the character "井" and another three groups of criss-crossing timbers are placed on them to constitute the main structure of the bridge. The bridge deck is covered with cobblestones and the gallery-house on it consists of twenty-six bays. Two layers of awnings painted red are attached under the eaves at each side of the bridge. The basic frame is composed of a *tailiang* structure of four columns and nine purlins. The gallery house is composed of one hundred and eight primary columns. There are two pavilions: one has a six-corner pyramidal roof with double eaves, straight balustrades, and a pot-month window. The other is a pavilion with a single-eve hip and gable roof whose two slopes stretch in the same direction as the bridge roof. The former one is called the Wenchang Pavilion dedicated to *Wenchangdijun* (a Taoist deity, or literally King of Flourishing Culture). Wooden decorative gateways with three bays and four columns are erected at each end of the bridge, and its main building is equipped with a hip roof. There are layers of bracket sets under the eaves with *ang* in the shape of elephant trunks. A plaque bearing the words with "Yunlong Bridge" is hung above the alter in the central room.

It is said that the name Yunlong Bridge is derived from image created by the logs making up the bridge's cantilever system, which have turned brown from oxidation, and thus in the mist resembles a flying dragon in clouds (*yun* refers to clouds and *long* means dragon). In fact, many covered bridges are named Yunlong, such as the one mentioned above at the foot of Xinglong Mountain in Gansu Province. There may have been a cultural connotation in the name as well such as derived from the Tang Dynasty poet Du Mu's "A long bridge on the waves does lie, without clouds how could a dragon fly?"

3.4.5 Zhen'an Bridge in Pucheng, Fujian Province

Zhen'an Bridge, located at Linjiang Village, Linjiang Town, Pucheng County, Fujian Province, spans Linjiang Stream, a branch of Nanpu River. The two-pier and three-span cantilever beam bridge is 79 meters long and 3.5 meters wide. As it is recorded in the *General Annals of Fujian* and the *Record of Jianning*, Zhen'an Bridge, originally named Linjiang Bridge, was built in the Song Dynasty. It was rebuilt in the Ming Dynasty in 1368 and 1529, and was renovated several times in the Qing Dynasty. In 1925, however, the bridge was destroyed in a fire. It was reconstructed in 1933[19]. Zhen'an Bridge is supported by two boat-shaped granite piers upstream sides have *yanchijingangqiang*. There are three groups of criss-crossed logs on the piers, forming a cantilever beam structure in the shape of the character "井" and another group is built on top of them to constitute the main structure of the bridge. In addition, four diagonal beam bracings stretch out from each pier to the center of the bridge to support it. One end of these beams are connected with the stone piers or the rock face at the side of the bridge, and the opposite end is attached to the beam frame of the bridge's gallery house. In this way, Zhen'an Bridge is equipped with a combined cantilever beam structure and a diagonal beam bracing structural system. This method is rarely seen in China's early cantilever beam bridges, so the diagonal beams may have been added during a later reconstruction.

3.4.6 Yisheng Bridge in Ninghua, Fujian Province

Located in Huashi Village, Caofang Township, Ninghua County, Fujian Province, Yisheng Bridge is a four-pier and five-span cantilever beam bridge with a length of 58 meters and a width of 4.6 meters. It served as an important conduit connecting Ninghua to Changting and Liancheng. Originally called the Huashi Bridge, it was built in 1521 by the officials Chen Long, Mao Gongyi and Chen Zan using government funds. In 1542, the bridge was destroyed and in 1544 it was repaired by county magistrate Pan Shiyi together with local residents Lu Ruiyin and Zhang Hengxun. It was later repaired in 1611 by another county magistrate Tang Shiji, who renamed it the Jichuan Bridge. It was damaged again in 1636, and a third repair was organized by governor Tang Shihan and an assistant of county magistrate Huang Sezhong. This time the bridge was renamed Tanggong Bridge. In 1875, the chivalrous resident Cao Yi spent a large sum to reconstruct it as a timber cantilever covered bridge with stone piers, known as Shenxian Bridge. The bridge was given the name Jiefang Bridge in 1953 when it was renovated by the people's government of Ninghua County[20].

Four boat-shaped granite piers are established under the bridge whose upstream sides have *yanchijingangqiang*. There are three groups of criss-crossed logs on top of the piers, forming a cantilever beam structure in the shape of the character "#" and another group are built on top of them to constitute the main structure of the bridge. The rebuilt Yisheng Bridge consists of twenty-six beam frames and a twenty-five-bay gallery house with a walkway in the middle and long benches flanking it. There is a shrine in the middle of the house and a small awning under the eaves. At each entrance to the bridge is a three-bay gate tower with four columns and a plaque hanging over the arch.

Section 4 Bracing Covered Bridges

4.1 The Origin and Characteristics of Bracing Bridges

Bracing bridges structurally fall in between the categories of beam bridges and arch bridges. They can be divided into two types: ones with simple bracing and others with compound bracing. Early on they were also known as diagonal bracing bridges which developed from simply supported beam bridges. There are generally three situations in which bracing bridges are preferred: The span needed for a simply supported beam bridge approaches or surpasses that which wooden beams can achieve; piers or columns cannot be installed because of the dimensions of a deep valley or because of the force exerted by the fast moving waters of a river; or the stiffness, reliability and durability of a bridge needs to be reinforced.

Bracing bridges have a long history of development, and originated through the innovations of ancient people in the course of practice. They are usually built with common materials. Most such bridges have disappeared, but information can be found that document them, such as found in paintings from various dynasties.

Many kinds of bridges appeared as early as the Han Dynasty. Many images of arch and beam bridges have been illustrated on portrait bricks during this period. For example, there is an Eastern Han Dynasty portrait brick in Sichuan Museum depicting a carriage driving over a bridge. It was discovered in Pengzhou, Sichuan Province in 1984. An arched bridge is depicted, but below it no supporting columns or simple supports are shown. However, through points and lines, renzi bracing (in the shape of the Chinese character "人") is shown. In addition, an Azure Dragon and a White Tiger (two of the Four Symbols of the Chinese constellations) are carved in the space between the bracing and the deck. A carriage carrying two people is shown passing over it. There is no evidence of such a bridge, and it cannot be ruled out that it was imagined by the artist. However, the drawing does show characteristics of a bracing structure.

A bracing arch bridge is included in the painting *Waterfall in the Autumn Forest*, now part of the collection in the Taipei Palace Museum by Fan Kuan, a famous painter from the Northern Song Dynasty. It can be seen as representative of early bracing arch bridges. Putting emphasis on nature in painting, Fan Kuan was familiar with the natural and cultural landscape of Huashan Mountain where he resided[21], So the bridge, though presented in an artistic way, closely resembles a real structure. In the painting, a tall mountain is covered with a dense forest and with red autumn leaves; a partially concealed thatched hut is shown, and a waterfall descends out over the rocks; in the distance a gate tower is emerging from the void and in the foreground is a steep slope as well as a swift current. A timber bracing arch bridge is depicted at the bottom of the painting, connecting a *zhandao* (plank road) and a mountain road. Importantly, the painting clearly depicts the appropriate construction environment that would call for the construction of such arch bridges.

In the Shuishen Temple in Hongdong County, Linfen, Shanxi Province, one of China's few Yuan Dynasty murals on operas is painted named *Painting of Taizong Emperor's Journey for a Long Distance* with a scene on its southern wall: An elderly man holding a stick and an official document on an arch bridge looks back in surprise at the head of the bridge to see a public official grasping a *hu* (a ritual tablet made of bamboo or ivory used for note taking at court) in his hands and military officers with battle axes, seemingly sending him off. The bridge in the mural is composed of columns and *renzi* bracing with two rows of stone columns connected by horizontal wooden beams in the middle of the span. The floor beams at the middle span are supported by king posts placed on top of the block of the middle beam. At the same time the bridge consists of *renzi* bracing, with the diagonal members passing through two timber beams and the ends supporting the crossbeams of the bridge deck in the middle of the bridge's span. It is a small bridge but the structure is clear, simple and exquisite. It is estimated that the painting may be a direct copy of a real bridge because it is depicted in such detail.

There is also a bracing bridge over a river connecting a county road in the landscape painting *Boat on the Lotus Pond* by Shi Tao, a painter of the Qing Dynasty. Both ends of the bridge platform are supported by two rows of columns together with diagonal bracing, with one end supporting the bridge's floor beams while the other end is attached to the columns. The bridge deck is paved with planks and a four-bay gallery house is erected on each side of the bridge. Despite being a work of landscape painting, it manages to reflect the overall structural characteristics of this bridge.

4.2 The Types and Geographic Distribution of Timber Covered Bracing Bridges

Bracing bridges use the same principle of "accumulated timber forming beams" used in cantilever beam structures. Both make use of the mechanical properties of timber, but offer different methods for improving the ability of bridges to span space. Both types are derived from the foundational elements of simply supported beam structures but have evolved in different directions to develop two distinct structural system. In their latter phase of development they also developed types that integrated aspects of both systems. This demonstrates the diverse features that arise in the course of the practical implementation of bridge technology.

Timber bracing covered bridges are limited in number but are diverse in form and geographical distribution. Most of them are located in Zhejiang and Fujian Provinces with a few remaining in Yunnan, Hubei, Chongqing and Sichuan. Timber bracing covered bridges in different regions have distinct features reflecting the influence of local construction practices.

4.2.1 Simple Timber Bracing Covered Bridges

Bracing structures developed from early diagonal bracing, which at its earliest consisted of the addition of groups of diagonal bracing under the two sides of simply supported beams. This was done to reduce relying on horizontal timber beams to clear spans and to lesson associated deformation. Jubao Bridge in Jitou Village, Tangkou Township, Pingnan County, Fujian Province is a typical example. The bridge is supported by two sets of diagonal bracing. Each set consists of wood blocks, crosspieces, ties, and four diagonal timbers. The bracing is placed at a 60 degree angle, which efficiently reduces the net span covered by the floor beams. From the perspective of strength of materials and construction measures, the bracing used in the Jubao Bridge has the following two features: Firstly, the diagonal bracing supports and the bridge bearings—placed between the piers and the bridge deck—are relatively close together, which means the floor beams must still span a relatively large distance; and secondly, the diagonal bracing is placed at a steep angle, and can bear the load of the structure alone without auxiliary supports.

Generally speaking, diagonal bracing initially represented an independent trend in bridge structures from the main bridge forms. However, the progress in technology helped braces to evolve into a complete form of bracing frames, which can be divided into *bazi* bracing, *renzi* bracing and more. Timber bracing covered bridges are widespread throughout China, and have the following types:

4.2.1.1 *Bazi*-Shaped Timber Bracing Covered Bridges

A *bazi* bracing is composed of two sets of diagonal members, a set of horizontal timbers and two crosspieces. This results in the shape of the Chinese character "八".

Many *bazi* bracing covered bridges remain. They can be found in every area of China with covered bridges. There form also contains a large number of sub-categories, and the examples are as follows:

Bazi bracing covered bridges are usually constructed on top of the existent foundation of an existing simply supported bridge. This is done through the addition of a minimum of two *bazi*-shaped bracings below the structure. An example of this is the Yulin Bridge in Yushi Village, Meixian Town, Youxi County, Fujian Province. Most *bazi* bracing bridges are equipped with more than two sets of *bazi* bracing. Examples include Baiyun Bridge in Qingyuan County, Chiyuan Bridge in Taishun County, Zhejiang Province and Shangqiao Bridge, Xiaqiao Bridge and Gongqiao Bridge in Jianglu Village, Shouning County, Fujian Province.

Fujian Province also contains examples of more perfected versions of *bazi* bracing covered bridges, which combine *bazi* bracing with additional wooden blocks, *jiandaocheng* (cross bracing), bents (transverse rigid frames) and other components. It can be speculated that such bazi bracing combinations are possibly related to the construction of the more complicated woven timber arch bridge. For example, at Beikeng Village, Xiadang Township, Shouning County, Fujian Province, Guanyin Bridge has seven sets of *bazi* bracing constructed on top of cobblestone abutments. Two bents are put at the two ends to sustain the floor beams. In addition, there is a group to the right and the left of *jiandaocheng* that is used to reinforce the crosspieces of the *bazi* bracing. This construction strategy increases the structural strength and rigidity of the bracing, guaranteeing its durability. Similar examples include Shengxian Bridge in Xianfeng Village, Xixi Town, Shouning County and Yuanlin Bridge in Chunchi Town, Zhouning County, Fujian Province.

The types mentioned above combine the use of long wooden beams with *bazi* bracing. There are also various unique forms which are composed through a combination of *bazi* bracing and two short wooden beams. An example includes the Longfeng Bridge in Long'an Village, Zhangdun Town, Jianyang City, Fujian Province which consists of 11 sets of *bazi* bracing and two transverse timbers. A unique design element of the bridge is that the short horizontal wooden beams at each end of the deck are also connected with the crosspieces, so that the arch frame's horizontal members function as a part of the bridge's floor beams. This construction seems to be minimalist and suitable, but in fact, it results in an insufficient degree of structural redundancy. As a result, the bridge is prone to deformation.

There is another special *bazi* bracing covered bridge in Ankou Village, Shuiji Town, Jianyang City, Fujian Province. The Ankou Bridge uses a method of mortise and tenon joining different from that of the previous examples. Ankou Bridge uses a unique method for joining in order to distribute the bridge's pressure: the *bazi* bracing consists of a group on each side consisting of eight diagonal timbers, nine horizontal timbers and four crosspieces, all made of logs. The diagonal members intersect and attach with the horizontal ones, and the two horizontal timbers at the outside are slightly lower than the other seven. The upper section is composed of a timber block that is supported by two crosspieces in the middle. These crossbeams in turn are interspersed and attached with outer horizontal members on either side.

4.2.1.2 *Renzi*-Shaped Timber Bracing Covered Bridges

The *renzi* bracing consists of two sets of diagonal bracing and crossbeams which form the character "人" (meaning person). There are very few remains of timber covered bridges with *renzi* bracing left, the only existing one known at present is the Xiangxi Covered Bridge in Xibian Village, Caixi Township, Xianyou County, Putian City, Fujian Province. It is composed of three sets of two-layer *renzi* bracing. At one layer, the diagonal members are relatively wide, with their ends pressed into the bridge's supporting abutment, with a strip of stones installed on top forming a cantilever beam. Below this is another set of smaller members, almost parallel to the layer above, with crosspieces interspersed between them. The very ends of the two layers of diagonal timbers together support crossbeams, forming the structure of a *renzi* bracing. Strictly speaking, Xiangxi Covered Bridge is not entirely a *renzi* timber bracing covered bridge as part of its structure is made of cantilever beams. However because of its obvious use of *renzi* bracing construction, it can be classified as this type of bridge.

In addition, the author found another *renzi* bracing bridge in a historic photo by Samuel Marinus Zwemer (1867-1952), an American missionary in China. It was taken during his travels in China between 1932 and 1933. The photo depicts a timber covered bridge in Xunhua County, Qinghai Province, taken during his departure from the area. The bridge, spanning a valley, is a *renzi* timber bracing covered bridge. The five-bay gallery house has a single-bay memorial archway with *xuanshanding* (overhanging gable roofs) at each end. The gallery house's structure contains *bazi* bracing, with diagonal supports between the two columns to strengthen the structure. This forms a structural form similar to a modern day truss. The piers, made of cobblestones and earth, are equipped with cantilever beams that extend outward to support the floor beams. Two sets of *renzi* bracing at the middle of the bridge's span

extend diagonally at a 40-degree angle. This well-constructed bridge is elegantly designed, and is an exquisite example of timber arch covered bridge construction in the northwest China.

4.2.1.3 Other Simple Timber Bracing Covered Bridges

In addition to the *bazi* and *renzi* bracing bridges mentioned above from Fujian and Zhejiang Provinces, there are special types of timber bracing covered bridges in Yunnan Province. Modern bridge structures can be divided into three types according to the relative position of the spanning structural elements (including arch and truss structures): deck bridges, in which the deck is built on top of supporting arches or trusses, through bridges, in which the deck is located below the major arch and truss structures, and half-through bridges, in which the deck is located in the middle of arches and trusses.

Most of the ancient bridges in China, including stone arch bridges and timber bracing bridges are considered deck bridges. A few are half-through bridges, such as bamboo arch bridges and *gonggong* bridges (timber arch bridges, or literally, double-bow bridges). Most timber bracing covered bridges are also deck bridges, but more in Yunnan are half-through or through types. A few examples are listed below:

Yongji Bridge at Xunjian Village, Yongjian Township, Weishan Yi and Hui Autonomous County, Yunnan Province is a single-span timber bracing covered bridge. The main body of the bridge consists of five logs spanning a river with a set of short diagonal bracing under the beams at each end. Two long diagonal members project at 45-degree angle from under the short bracing, and rise one meter above the deck. A crossbeam is connected with the timbers by mortise and tenon joints and there is a vertical suspender linked with the floor beams hanging in the middle of the crossbeam. The bridge has a set of *bazi* bracing at both sides. There are many such half-through bracing bridges in Yunnan. Their construction methods are similar to one another. The main difference between them is the length and height of the crossbeam connected with the *bazi* bracing, as well as the number of vertical suspender, together with other aspects.

Qieye Bridge, located at Qieye Village, Liantie Township, Eryuan County, Yunnan Province, is similar to single-span timber bracing covered bridge, but unlike such bridges, the foothold of the *bazi* bracing and the support points of the horizontal wooden beams are located at the head of the bridge abutments. In addition, the position where the *bazi* bracing and crossbeams are connected is relatively high, and vertical suspenders are not used. As a result, the crossbeams are directly supported under the short one-step beams. This structure resembles modern truss through-bridge construction, and is a reasonable and reliable design.

There are also several multi-span timber bracing covered bridges in Yunnan which are all through bridges with *bazi* bracing or truss structures, including Yanjian Bridge in Dahui Village, Lijiao Township, Binchuan County, Dali Bai Autonomous Prefecture, a three-span timber covered bridge with *bazi* bracing; and Hetoufengyu Bridge in Longzhu Village, Songgui Town, Heqing County, Dali, a double-span timber covered bridge with timber bracing.

It should be noted that most of the timber bracing covered bridges in Yunnan are half-through or through bridges, categories which are hard to find outside of the province. And conversely, while deck-type timber bracing arch covered bridges are common in other regions, they are rarely seen in Yunnan. The development of bracing bridge technology shows that early bracing bridges were mainly deck bridges, which later developed into half-through and through bridges, and finally into truss structures. Tang Huancheng also writes in *Chinese Timber Arch-Bridge* that "bracing bridges are the origin of timber arch and timber truss structures."[22]

Looking at the modern course of bridge development, in this late period half-through and through bridges represent the dominant types. There are two major reasons for this: First, the emergence of large ships in modern times required more sailing space, and half-through and through bridges were able to fulfill that need, providing a solution safer for both bridges and ships; secondly, these two types reduced the workload required for construction on the water, which is replaced by land construction, making the bridge-building process safer and more convenient.

The upper part of the timber bracing covered bridge mentioned above at Xunhua County, Qinghai Province is a truss structure, but the construction time remains unknown; and Baoluan Bridge at Fengdu County, Chongqing, built in 1951, is a timber arch covered through-bridge with *bazi* bracing.

4.2.2 Compound Timber Bracing Covered Bridges

A compound bracing is usually composed of two types of bracing, and there are three classic combinations: *bazi* bracing and diagonal bracing, *renzi* bracing and *bazi* bracing, and double *bazi* bracing. Compound bracing, which developed from *bazi* bracing, improves the overall performance of the arch structure. Examples are listed below:

4.2.2.1 Combined *Bazi* Bracing and Diagonal Bracing

This kind of construction is rarely seen and there is only one example—Wodu Bridge—discovered in Yuanjiaao Village, Xiaowang Street, Fenghua District, Ningbo, Zhejiang Province. The arch of the bridge consists of four sets of *bazi* bracing, eight diagonal struts and two sets of diagonal bracing. The diagonal struts project out at a slight angle, and distribute pressure between the two crosspieces of the *bazi* bracing. The diagonal bracing supporting the crosspieces is clamped between the diagonal members of the *bazi* bracing and the diagonal struts, forming a structure similar to cross bracing. It is an ingenious design.

4.2.2.2 Combined *Renzi* Bracing and *Bazi* Bracing

Renzi bracing and *bazi* bracing structures are both independent structures, and the two are rarely combined in a bridge. There is one exception that has been found in Zhejiang, and one found in Fujian.

The one in Shangsankeng Village, Qiaoying Township, Xinchang County, Zhejiang Province is called Meishuban Bridge. Its arch consists of *bazi* bracing, *renzi* bracing and two crosspieces. The *bazi* bracing is composed of four diagonal members at each side and five horizontal timbers in the middle while the *renzi* bracing has three diagonal members on each side and a crosspiece. It is worth noting that the crosspieces of the *renzi* bracing are not connected together. Three sets of *renzi* bracing do not support the same crosspiece, but are bracketed within three small wood blocks, forming three separate braces. In addition, another two long crosspieces are put between the diagonal members of the *renzi* and *bazi* bracing.

The other example is Shangkeng Bridge, located in Shangkeng Village, Makeng Township, Zhouning County, Fujian Province. The arch of the bridge is made of *bazi* and *renzi* bracing, and cross bracing. The *renzi* bracing consists of four diagonal timbers at each side and a long crosspiece; the *bazi* bracing has nine diagonal members at each side, six horizontal timbers and two long crosspieces. There is two sets of cross bracing supporting the crosspieces of the *bazi* bracing.

4.2.2.3 Double *Bazi* Bracing

Namely, a double *bazi* bracing has two sets of *bazi* bracing which can be stacked or crossed. Examples are as follows.

The only known example of double stacked *bazi* bracing is found in the Xinglong Bridge, located in Kejian Village, Dikou Town, Jian'ou, Fujian Province. It is equipped with beam-columns, *bazi* bracing and stacked beams. The main part spanning the river is composed of two-layer *bazi* bracing. It includes five sets of bracing at the upper layer whose diagonal timbers project out at a 60-degree angle of inclination. Its bottom layer includes four sets of diagonal members that are set at a 45-degree angle. The *bazi* bracing is erected on timber blocks which are placed on top of cobblestone covered bridge abutments. Another form of combined double *bazi* bracing is a *bazi* "cross-combination" bracing. This form of bracing structure incorporates the classic characteristics of a timber woven beam-arch bridge. Recently, a few geographers in Nanping of northern Fujian Province discovered several timber covered bridges with double *bazi* bracing. Bazi Bridge in Xiayang Town, Yanping District, Nanping is constructed with three sets of *bazi* bracing, although the bottom set was added in 1979 to strengthen the bridge.[23] Overall, the double *bazi* bracing used in timber covered bridges in Nanping have two sets of *bazi* bracing crossed together with other components such as cross bracing and bents. Altogether this forms a relatively comprehensive structure. Each frame has a net span of 15-20 meters.

4.2.3 Special Types of Timber Bracing Covered Bridges

In addition to the simple and compound types above, there are also special kinds of bearing structures which are a combination of *bazi* bracing and cantilever beam structures. Examples are described below.

4.2.3.1 Huilong Bridge, Longdang Ditch, Youyang County, Chongqing

This bridge was originally built over a valley, but has now been moved. The bridge is a timber arch covered bridge with a horizontal cantilever beam and *bazi* bracing. It is a single-span deck bridge. The cantilever beam structure has six sets and three layers with each layer projecting out. There are *bazi* and diagonal bracings under the beams together with additional auxiliary shoring. All the components are connected in a complex but appropriate manner.

4.2.3.2 Yongshun Bridge, Maoba Township, Lichuan County, Hubei Province

Also named Qunceliang Bridge, this is a single-span through bridge with diagonal cantilever beams and *bazi* bracing. The beams are divided into three layers and six sets, and are covered with cobblestones at the ends to add stability. Different from the typical way in which cantilever beams project, the upper two layers of Yongshun Bridge stretch out at the same length in contrast to the layer below. An even more unusual feature is that the beams at the two ends are connected by two layers of horizontal tie bars, with each layer containing five members. The tie bars and cantilever beams are held together by interspersed crosspieces, forming a complete unit. Horizontal floor beams are installed on top of the arch frame and connected with the arch frame by means of upright columns.

4.2.3.3 Tongjing Bridge, Yunlong County, Yunnan Province

Tongjing Bridge is an important part of the Ancient Salt Horse Road and the Silver Transit Road. It is a single-span half-through timber arch covered bridge whose span is 30 meters long, with diagonal cantilever beams and *bazi* bracing. The cantilever beams consist of seven layers and five sets with each layer projecting outwards. The ends of the beams are inserted into the bridge abutment, and a gallery house is installed on top. Two sets of *bazi* bracing cross through the deck from under the cantilever beams and are connected by horizontal square wood through mortise and tenon joints. The wood is further connected with floor beams through upright tie bars, making the two sets a complete structure.

This is not the only example of such a structure. Similar ones include Yongzhen Bridge and Caifeng Bridge in Yunlong County. Yezhuqing Bridge in Tengchong County, Baoshan is also constructed in this way, but is unique in that in addition to cantilever beams and bracing, diagonal cables also strengthen the bridge. However, this addition has no influence on the bridge's classification as a combined cantilever beam and bracing bridge.

There are also other special timber bracing arch covered bridges. For example, Zhen'an Bridge in Pucheng County, Fujian Province is a half-through covered bridge with horizontal cantilever beams and *bazi* bracing. What is unique is that it is a two-pier and three-span bridge with *bazi* bracing at each span. Two sets of parallel bracing are established at each side with the bottom frame integrated into the balustrade and the upper one connected with the gallery house beams, improving the structural integrity of the bridge.

Types and Geographical Distribution of Bracing Covered Bridge (Partial List)

Table 1

Type	Characteristics		Examples	Notes
	Bracing and combination method	The position of the Bracing relative to the bridge deck		
Simple bracing bridge	*Bazi* bracing	Deck Bridges	Zhejiang Province: Guanyin Bridge, Jinghua Bridge, Puji Bridge (Liandu District, Lishui), Shuangxi Bridge (Longquan County), Baiyun Bridge, Baoguo Bridge (Qingyuan County), Huaisheng Bridge (Jingning She Autonomous County), Baxian Bridge (Songyang County), Chengshui Bridge, Xiazhuang Bridge, Naqing Bridge (Taishu County, Wenzhou), Waiying Bridge (Fenghua District, Ningbo) Fujian Province: Waiyangdang Bridge, Beikengguanyin Bridge, Guanyin Bridge, Jianglushang Bridge, Hulumen Bridge, Jiangluxia Bridge, Shengxian Bridge, Naidian Bridge (Shouning County, Ningde), Yuanlin Bridge (Zhouning County), Weiduan Bridge (Gutian County), Shuiwei Bridge (Jinshan Village, Fu'an), Longfeng Bridge, Ankou Bridge (Jianyang District, Nanping), Shuiwei Bridge (Xiaoju Village, Jian'ou City), Guanyin Bridge (Jinping Village, Zhenghe County), Yulin Bridge (Youxi County, Sanming) Sichuan Province: Hongjun Bridge (Pingwu County, Mianyang)	
		Half-through Bridges	Yunnan Province: Wuli Bridge, Jiancao Bridge, Xiaoling Bridge, Liandeng Bridge, Xiadideng Bridge (Yunlong County, Dali Bai Autonomous Prefecture), Yongji Bridge (Weishan She and Hui Autonomous County), Banghai Bridge (Eryuan County, Pu'er), Wen'e Bridge, Zhanniu Bridge (Jingdong Yi Autonomous County), Damulu Bridge (Guangnan County, Wenshan Zhuang and Miao Autonomous Prefecture)	Truss Structures
		Through Bridges	Yunnan Province: Qieye Bridge (Eryuan County, Dali Bai Autonomous Prefecture), Yanjian Bridge (Binchuan County), Hetou Bridge (Heqing County), Renhe Bridge (Yongsheng County, Lijiang) Qinghai Province: Covered bridges in Xunhua salar Autonomous County △	Truss Structures
	Renzi bracing	Deck Bridges	Fujian Province: Xiangxi Covered Bridge (Xianyou County, Putian) Qinghai Province: Covered Bridge in Xunhua (salar Autonomous) County △	
		Half-through Bridges	Yunnan Province: Wenxian Bridge (Jingdong County, Pu'er City)	
Compound bracing	Diagonal and *bazi* bracing	Deck Bridges	Zhejiang Province: Wodu Bridge (Fenghua District, Ningbo)	
	Renzi and *bazi* bracing	Deck Bridges	Zhejiang Province: Shangsankeng Bridge (Xinchang County) Fujian Province: Shangkeng Bridge (Zhouning County)	
	Double *bazi* bracing	Deck Bridges	Fujian Province: Bazi Bridge △, Yueyuan Bridge △, Luotuo Bridge △ (Yanping District, Nanping), Xinglong Bridge, Lanxiacuo Bridge (Shunchang County), Wentang Bridge (Minqing County), Jiaoxi Bridge (Minhou County), Xinglong Bridge (Jian'ou) Zhejiang Province: Gongqi Bridge, Fuxing Bridge (Liandu District, Lishui), Wohong Bridge, (Qingtian County)	
Special bracing	Horizontal cantilever beam and *bazi* bracing	Deck Bridges	Chongqing: Huilong Bridge (Longdang Ditch, Youyang County)	
		Half-through Bridges	Fujian Province: Zhen'an Bridge (Pucheng County, Nanping)	
	Diagonal cantilever beam and *bazi* bracing	Deck Bridges	Hubei Province: Yongshun Bridge (Lichuan County, Enshi Tujia and Miao Autonomous Prefecture)	
		Half-through Bridges	Yunnan Province: Tongjing Bridge, Yongzhen Bridge, Caifeng Bridge (Yunlong County, Dali Bai Autonomous Prefecture), Dahua Bridge (Fengqing County, Lincang), Yezhuqing Bridge (Tengchong County, Baishan City)	

Note: "△" indicates that the bridge has been destroyed or reconstructed using a different structural framework.

Section 5 Timber Arch Covered Bridges

5.1 The name, type and distribution of timber arch covered bridge

In southwest of Zhejiang Province, northeast of Fujian Province and areas around Fuzhou, over a hundred timber arch covered bridges remain dating to ancient times. The author calls these bridges "woven timber arch-beam covered bridges." The lower part of such bridges is a "woven timber arch-beam, combined with supported simply beam" a structure with characteristics of both an arch and a beam. It is different from the "rainbow bridge" in *Along the River side Scene at Qingming Festival* by Zhang Zeduan, the Song Dynasty artist, which the author calls a "woven timber arch bridge." There are a small number of timber arch bridges in the mountains along the borders of Zhejiang and Fujian Provinces having a structure similar to the "woven timber arch" of rainbow bridges.

In the academic world, awareness of Chinese timber arch bridge occurred relatively late. In *Science and Civilisation in China*, Joseph Needham mistakenly categorizes rainbow bridges as cantilever beam bridges. It was only in *Technology History of Ancient Bridges in China* published in 1986 and edited by Mao Yisheng that rainbow bridges were for the first time classified as timber arch bridges. The specification was made by Tang Huancheng, one of the writers of the book's section on "Bamboo Timber Arch Bridges." He also investigates and describes the newly discovered timber arch bridges in Zhejiang and Fujian, and names them "arch-type timber bridges" and "rainbow-type timber arch bridges" respectively. This is the first time that modern Chinese scholars have conducted systematic research and provided a preliminary categorization of rainbow bridges in such a notable work.

Tang further specifies in his later works the names of rainbow bridge and timber arch bridges in Zhejiang and Fujian. In the book *Ancient Chinese Bridges*, he groups their two structures together as *dielianggong* (combined beam arches) and calls the bridges with this structure *dielianggongqiao* (combined beam arch bridges). He also explains in the book that "timber bridges with a structure showing elements of both beam and arch construction can tentatively be called *dielianggongqiao* and the Bianshui Rainbow Bridge in *Riverside Scene at Qingming Festival* is a representative of such a bridge." This is the first time that modern Chinese scholars specified a name to categorize the lower part of rainbow bridges, evidence of progress in the research of the form.

Despite being an expert on bridges, Tang may not have known that *dieliang* had a well recognized meaning in ancient Chinese timber construction, referring to layers of criss-crossed beams. Many houses and bridges have *dieliang* with each layer of beams stretching out to expand the space of the structure or to lengthen the span. Such structures were used in very early architecture, and illustrations of such construction are etched on the bronze artifacts in the period before Qin Dynasty. If rainbow bridges were considered *dielianggong* because their lower parts are constructed with *dieliang*, then the cantilever beam bridge described earlier in this chapter would have to fall under this category too, as their cantilevers are composed using a *dieliang* method. Tang may have noticed the inappropriateness of such a categorization, as he writes that he only "tentatively is using the term *dielianggongqiao*." The article *An Investigation of Rainbow Bridges* published in Architectural Journal in November, 1995 by Fang Yong, a professor at Peking University, also quotes Tang's *dielianggong* categorization.

In January, 2000, *Science and Civilisation in China—Bridges* was published by Science Press. This time Tang Huancheng refers to the Bianshui Rainbow Bridge as a *guanmugongqiao* (intersecting timber arch bridge), which shows that he was not satisfied with the phrase *dieliang gong*. He explains in the book that the term *guanmu* comes from the Song Dynasty text named *A Record of Table Talk in Mianshui River*) which describes the rainbow bridge as constructed with "tens of huge intersecting logs." Objectively, *guanmu* is a more accurate term than *dieliang*, and support for use of the term can be found in historical literature. Still, such a term does not clearly reflect the particular method of construction being described, and hence is overly vague.

The author of this text originally proposed to use the term "woven timber beam arch bridge" to refer to the lower part of Bianshui Rainbow Bridge. Weaving was used relatively early in Chinese history for the creation of items used in the course of daily living, such as woven bamboo baskets and knapsacks. It was also used early only for a type of architectural structure, such as the woven bamboo wall. Use of the term woven timber beam arch bridge clarifies three features of such bridges:

(1) The feature:Woven beam, we should consider the three timber ribs and four timber ribs used in the two main arch systems as respectively constituting single continuous arcs. And we should also see their intersecting crosspieces as parallels. Hence the layered structure of rainbow bridges that distributes loads between these vertically interspersed arch ribs and crosspieces is similar to the technology that transforms intersecting lengthwise and transverse threads (often referred to as warp and weft threads) into fabric. Both methods utilize the friction between longitudinal and latitudinal elements to maintain the stability of the structure.

(2) The Material feature: Timber. This refers to the use of logs.

(3) The structure's mechanical feature: Arch. This is the primary structure that bears compression. The author used a finite elemental model to examine the structure, and deduced that the main internal force acting on the components is a vertical pressure. This is the characteristic of an arch strictly speaking from the perspective of mechanical science. As such it has a strong bearing capacity.

On June 14th, 2004, the author attended the 8th World Conference on Timber Engineering (WCTE2004) in Lahti, Finland and delivered a speech titled Chinese Rainbow Bridges in which he introduced the structural features of the Bianshui Rainbow Bridge and timber arch covered bridges in Zhejiang and Fujian. This was the first time that he used the term "woven timber beam arch bridge" to refer to the structure of the Bianshui Rainbow Bridge. In the structural mechanic analysis and computer stimulation of timber arch covered bridges in Zhejiang and Fujian, the first system analyzed a structure with five timber arch ribs, not a structure with four as is found in the Bianshui Rainbow Bridge. A structure with five such ribs relies on the central arch rib member to be the primary flexural component—the main part that bears tension. Because such a bridge has the characteristics of both an arch bridge and a beam bridge, the author named it a "woven timber beam arch-beam bridge". However, this term contains the term "beam" twice, a literary *taboo*, In addition, the two "beams" each respectively refer to different things: the first beam refers to woven logs, while the second refers to the flexural component in the structure.

Therefore, the author suggested that the name be changed into "woven timber arch bridge." This still indicates the three features of a rainbow bridge. The Song Dynasty text *the Chronicle of Sequel of Comprehensive Mirror for Aid Government* described rainbow bridges as being "woven with timbers." The lower part of timber arch covered bridges in Zhejiang and Fujian should correspondingly be called "woven timber arch-beam bridges." These two names reflect the similarities and differences of the two structures. These expressions have been stated in the English report of the 2004 World Conference on Timber Engineering (WCTE2004).

To sum up, the Bianshui Rainbow Bridge will be referred to as a woven timber arch bridge, and the remaining timber arch covered bridges in Zhejiang and Fujian will be referred to as woven timber arch-beam bridges[24].

In the summer of 2004, the author was invited to Pingnan County, Ningde, Fujian Province for the Baishuiyang Tourism Festival's cultural forum on covered bridges. Tang Huancheng also presented a speech at the event. During the seminar, both discussed the question of the correct nomenclature for timber arch bridges. After the discussion, Mr. Tang said he would think over which name to use in a soon to be published book on Chinese timber arch bridges. In January 2010, his book *Chinese Timber Arch-Bridge* was published by China Architecture & Building Press. On page 20, Mr. Tang writes, "the special timber arch bridge, unique to China, was invented in the 11th century, and is painted on a famous long scroll. In one of my previous articles, I referred to the structure as a *dieliganggong* bridge. After further investigation and research I decided to refer to such structures as *guanmugong* [intersecting timber arches] or *bianmugong* [woven timber arches] bridges, because it has been recorded in historical literature that such bridges are constructed with 'huge logs connected together.' In fact, they resembles parts of bamboo or reed woven baskets." The earliest scholar in modern China to study timber arch bridges, Mr. Tang finally published this research on timber arch bridges in his eighties after more than 50 years of hard work. He also accepted the author's suggestion and used the terms *guanmugong* and *bianmugong* to refer to these structures, the terminology of which has been a subject of debate in recent years. This can be considered as one of Mr. Tang's significant contributions as a Chinese senior scholar in the field of ancient bridges research.

As it is stated in both Mr. Tang's work and that of the author, woven timber arch bridges were widely distributed in the Yellow River Basin centered around Bianliang, the eastern capital of Northern Song Dynasty. In addition, similar structures still remain in parts of Gansu Province. Many of the woven timber arch bridges are maintained as covered bridges in the South of the Yangtze River area, especially in the mountains of southwestern Zhejiang and northeastern Fujian. Together with other team members, the author has investigated and studied these regions for over 20 years and has determined the following specific areas where such structures exist: Zhejiang Province—Jingning She Autonomous County, Qingtian County, Qingyuan County, Longquan County of Lishui; Taishun County of Wenzhou; Fujian Province—Shouning County, Pingnan County, Zhouning County, Gutian County, Fu'an County, Zherong County, Fuding County, Xiapu County of Ningde; Zhenghe County, Wuyishan County, Jian'ou County of Nanping; Jin'an District, Minqing County, Minhou County of Fuzhou. In general, there are more woven timber arch bridges in Fujian than in Zhejiang, but those in Zhejiang are better preserved, especially the timber arch covered bridges in Qingyuan and Taishun.

Except for newly built ones that were created to respond to the new popularity of covered bridges, over a hundred ancient timber arch bridges are preserved in these regions and most of them are woven timber arch-beam covered bridges. The table 2 is the number of remaining ancient woven timber arch-beam bridges in Fujian.

The Number of Ancient Woven Timber Arch-Beam Bridges in Fujian and Zhejiang

Table 2

Province	City	District/County	Name	Number
Fujian	Ningde	Shouning	Luanfeng Bridge, Yangmeizhou Bridge, Feiyun Bridge, Shengping Bridge, Xiangong Bridge, Dengyun Bridge, Yangxitou Bridge, Zhangkeng Bridge, Changlaixi Bridge, Liren Bridge, Wenming Bridge, Xiaodongshang Bridge, Dabao Bridge, Fushou Bridge, Danqiao Bridge, Shouchun Bridge, Hongjun Bridge, Huilan Bridge, Puji Bridge	19
		Pingnan	Wan'an Bridge, Qiansheng Bridge, Baixiang Bridge, Guangli Bridge, Guangfu Bridge, Longjing Bridge, Longjin Bridge, Jinzao Bridge, Qingyan Bridge, Huifeng Bridge, Jinxi Bridge, Zhangkou Bridge, Yingfeng Bridge	13
		Zhouning	Denglong Bridge, Houlong Bridge, Sanxian Bridge, Qixian Bridge, Louxia Bridge, Zhuling Bridge, Changfeng Bridge	7
		Gutian	Gongxin Bridge, Xuzhou Bridge, Tingxia Bridge, Lanxi Bridge, Shuyin Bridge	5
		Fu'an	Dengzhu Bridge, Yuting Bridge, Jigu Bridge, Yangkeng Bridge, Zhetou Bridge	5
		Zherong	Dongyuan Bridge, Guisi Bridge	2
		Fuding	Laoren Bridge	1
		Xiapu	Linqing Bridge	1
	Nanping	Zhenghe	Houshancuo Bridge, Yanghoucuo Bridge, Chixi Bridge, Longtan Bridge, Dalixi Bridge, Luoling Bridge, Xiaban Bridge	7
		Jian'ou	Jielong Bridge, Houjian Bridge, Desheng Bridge, Xian'en Bridge	4
		Wuyishan	Yuqing Bridge	1
	Fuzhou City	Minhou	Yuanji Bridge, Kengping Bridge, Taishan Bridge, Tangli Bridge	4
		Jin'an	Dianban Bridge	1
		Minqing	Helong Bridge	1
Zhejiang	Lishui	Jingning She Autonomous	Jielong Bridge, Dongkengxia Bridge, Dongkengshang Bridge, Dachikeng Bridge, Meiji Bridge, Lianchuandadi Bridge, Yongzhen Bridge, Xiongdailingjiao Bridge, Beixi Bridge, Changtan Bridge, Yongping Bridge, Shijiankeng bridge	2
		Qingyuan	Rulong Bridge, Lanxi Bridge, Houkeng Bridge, Yonggui Bridge, Luting Bridge, Niaoqiao Bridge, Banhuangshuichang Bridge, Futian Bridge, Zhuping Bridge, Shuangmen Bridge	10
		Longquan	Shunde Bridge, Hexing Bridge	2
		Qingtian	Huairen Bridge	1
	Wenzhou City	Taishun	Santiao Bridge, Beijian Bridge, Xidong Bridge, Xuezhai Bridge, Wenxing Bridge, Xianju Bridge	6

Note: the statistics in this table refer to the number of ancient woven timber arch-beam covered bridges in Fujian and Zhejiang as of May 2019.

5.2 The Development and Evolution of Timber Arch Covered Bridges

The author has compared the architectural and structural characteristics of the Bianshui Rainbow Bridge and the timber arch covered bridges in Zhejiang and Fujian in his work from over 20 years ago, and made a detailed analysis of their forms. This is the author's initial view on the matter:

The Bianshui Rainbow and Zhejiang-Fujian timber arch bridges are all bridges that demonstrate a complete timber structural system. Their structures are similar, sharing a characteristic that allows them all to be called (rainbow) arch bridges. However, there are many differences between them.

Firstly, the Bianshui Rainbow Bridge is a pure woven timber arch structure, while the subsequent ones are woven timber beam arch-beam structures which combines timber arches and beams.

Secondly, the rope lashing technology commonly used in the north is used in the woven timber arch of the Bianshui Rainbow Bridge, while the mortise and tenon technology commonly used in the south became more popular subsequently.

Thirdly, there is no gallery house on the timber arch of the Bianshui Rainbow Bridge, while later arch beam bridges sport structures with upturned eaves and grey tiled roofs.

Fourthly, the shape of the arch structure of Bianshui Rainbow Bridge forms a complete arch, while later arch-beam bridges form the shape of Chinese character "八".

Fifthly, the span of the Bianshui Rainbow Bridge is about 18 meters, while the length of later bridges extend from 9 to 42 meters. Comparatively speaking, the later ones are more adaptable to various river conditions and are more capable of spanning space.

Sixthly, because the Bianshui Rainbow Bridge structure was located in the Central Plain Region, it uses the woven timber arch structural system, while the later bridges were built in the mountains and dense forests of the Zhejiang and Fujian Mountains. There, to help cross deep gullies and high streams, in addition to the arch beam system, rigid scaffold frames were often used in lower structures near banks to enhance the mechanical performance of the bridge structure and to increase the span of the beam structure. Subsequently, if we compare the Bianshui Rainbow Bridge and these later bridges in detail, we will find additional differences. Faced with so many differences between the two kinds of structures, can the true relationship between the two be deduced? Can this be gleaned by examining research, historical documents, and field investigation of the more than 100 remaining wooden arch covered bridges in the Zhejiang and Fujian mountainous areas? From the point of view of architectural evolution, if the two forms are really related, which features were inherited and which ones developed later on?

Mr.Tang Huancheng believes that the timber arch bridges found in Zhejiang and Fujian Provinces are an improved bridge type that can trace their origins to the Bianshui Rainbow Bridge. Their form developed gradually with the introduction of bridge-building technology to the mountainous areas of Zhejiang and Fujian Provinces after the collapes of Northern Song Dynasty, combined with the influence of local wooden structure technology. This view is reflected in his two books, *The Technological History of China: Bridges* and *Ancient Bridges of China*. In Mao Yisheng's earlier book *The Technological History of Chinese Ancient Bridges*, the chapter about timber arch bridges was mainly written by Mr. Tang, so the views in both works are consistent. Later bridge and architecture experts also maintained this view. However, some experts have different opinions, including specialists in cultural relics in the Zhejiang and Fujian mountainous areas. Unfortunately, so far no more definitive evidence that can settle the question is available[25].

After many years of investigation and research, the author believes that the wooden arch bridges preserved in Zhejiang and Fujian mountain areas basically have the same arch beam structure, but due to regional differences, especially because of the practices of different carpenters (craftsmen lineages), there are differences in the construction process. However, these subtle differences cannot change the structural characteristics of the arch-beams of Zhejiang-Fujian timber arch bridges.

In the past, the author focused on the form of wooden arch bridges, through a relatively narrow scope focussing on the intersection between architecture and architectural history. After several years of research, he was unable to definitively resolve the technical origin of these wooden arch bridges. Since 2001, with expanded participation by relevant researchers, especially experts with profound backgrounds in engineering structural mechanics, the author has extended this research to all the timber-based bridges in the Zhejiang and Fujian areas, and used engineering technology and other disciplines to conduct comprehensive research. Because of its vast territory and expansive mountain chains and rivers, the total number of wooden bridges under this broader scope has exceeded 1,000.

Taking Taishun County of Zhejiang Province as an example, of all the wooden bridges that have been comparatively well investigated and studied, it can be seen that the main structures of these wooden bridges can be both simple and complicated, and there are many intermediate examples as well. This possibly corresponds to the developmental history of such bridges in the region.

Since ancient times, the construction of wooden bridges has belonged to the category of engineering technology. The author associates the historical development of engineering technology from conception to maturity with the law of evolution of organisms through heredity and mutation.

The principle is summarized as follows: When a technology can still meet existing needs, it will be "inherited," i.e. result in its generally stable replication; and when new needs arise and the original technology cannot suit such demands, it will lead to technological change and "mutation." What promotes technological progress is innovative change, i.e., mutation; mutation generally occurs locally, at the same time as most technology is produced by means of "heredity." Hence globally, there is a situation of "gradual change," together with local "mutation." "Mutation" will have multiple forms when it is nascent, coexisting and unstable during a certain period of time; and after some time, out of different forms of "mutation," "the fittest will survive," that is, the poorer ones will be eliminated, and the better ones will be retained. Finally, one or a few "mutated" forms will be perfected and steadily enter the "hereditary" stage. The above-mentioned process starts again and again, and occurs many times, forming a historical process of technological development[26].

Following the above principles, the author classified and sorted out the timber bridges in Taishun County, and basically outlined the following bridge development hierarchy: (1) simply supported timber beam bridges; (2) multi-span simply supported timber beam bridges; (3) multi-span simply supported timber bridges with diagonal bracing at both ends; (4) timber arch bridges transitioning into woven timber arch-beam structures; (5) woven timber arch-beam bridges in Zhejiang and Fujian; (6) the transition from woven timber arch-beam to large woven timber arch bridges; (7) woven timber arch bridges (such as the Bianshui Rainbow Bridge). In order to complete this course of development, it is necessary to go through seven stages. In these seven stages, the author initially made use of five found examples of bridges that corresponded to steps (1), (2), (3), (5), and (7). These bridges were studied in the course of field investigation. The author then inferred that there should be steps (4), and (6), two kinds of intermediate bridge types. This postulate informed the course of over two more years of on-the-ground research, leading the author to finally find actual examples of these two intermediate "missing-links" in the Zhejiang and Fujian mountainous areas.

Except for the case of bridge type (6) found in Qingyuan County, which is adjacent to Taishun, the other six cases are all located in Taishun. If the hypothesis of the evolution of timber bridges into timber arch bridges is established, then the view that timber woven arch-beam bridges developed independently in the mountainous areas of Zhejiang and Fujian can also be established. However, it is not easy to find thousands of timber bridges dating from the northern Song Dynasty in the area where the Bianshui Rainbow Bridge is located, even if the whole Central Plain Area is included in such a study area. This is because at that time, the central plains, which was an important economic and cultural center, had several types of advanced bridge construction to choose from, such as stone bridges and even stone arch bridges. Without an expansive foundation for the construction of timber bridges, the ability to produce advanced timber bridges in this local area would have withered away. Was this perhaps what happened to such a perfect woven timber arch structure as that found on the Bianshui Rainbow Bridge?

Let's take another look at the construction of timber arch bridges in the Zhejiang and Fujian mountainous areas.

When considering the history of the construction of Rainbow Bridge, researchers have paid close attention to a special case, the Santiao Bridge in Taishun County, Zhejiang Province. It is located on the Hengxi River between Zhouling and Yuanxi Townships, and shares a border with Shouning County, Fujian Province. Santiao Bridge is far away from the noisy highways and the built environments of modern civilization. It is situated in the silent creek and deep stream, along a winding mountain paths, by beautiful and elegant scenery. Strolling along this bridge makes it easy to forget historical time and to start to daydream. But then we are reminded that this bridge carries too many secrets about the history of construction of arched bridges in China.

According to Taishun's *Records of the Frontiers* from the Qing Dynasty, "Santiao Bridge is located in Qidu. It is very old, and is tens of feet long, with a rainbow-like roof overlooking the stream and gradually scrapped. In 1843, a villager whose family name is Su, carried out reconstruction work by himself, and removed the old tiles from the bridge." In 1982, the Taishun County Museum of Culture and Exposition made a special investigation of the bridge. On the roof of the bridge, an old tile inscribed with the words "In the 54th. year of the sexagenary cycle, in the seventh year of the Shaoxing period (year 1137 during the Song Dynasty), tiling started. That year the rice price was 50 *wen* for each *hu* (*wen* and *hu* respectively are units of monetary and measurement in ancient China)." It has been textually verified that this dates to the year 1137. The discovery of old tiles from the Tang and Song Dynasties on the bridge does not prove that the bridge body during this period was a wooden arch structure, but there should be little doubt that a wooden bridge structure existed then.

According to the *Taishun Traffic Record* published by China Ocean Press in 1991, and compiled by the Taishun County Traffic Bureau, it is recorded that "10 meters upstream from the current location of the bridge, on the west bank, on top of boulders, there are still the remains of the old bridge's pillar holes, with four square holes tilted towards the river's east bank, and two round holes facing the sky." Tang Huacheng and Zhang Jun, curators of the Taishun Cultural Museum, both have made restoration maps of timber bridges based on the remains of these bridges and apertures. Because of their different views, the style of the reconstructed bridge models they derived are different. Tang's reconstruction resembles the phase of bridge evolution described above between steps (3) and (4), while Zhang's reconstruction falls between steps (4) and (5). Either way, the old bridge upstream of the current bridge must be one of the seven intermediate phases. It is possible that these bridge holes do not belong to the same timber bridge, but instead are the remains of bridges of different styles that once sat in this area. Similarly, according to the *Records of the Frontiers*, the first Santiao Bridge was a simply supported beam bridge formed by three giant trees crossing the stream, i.e. a bridge that belongs to step (1) of the bridge evolution described above. It was because of these three trees used in this initial bridge that the name Santiao Bridge was derived.

Based on the study of Santiao Bridge, the author believes that the combination of it and the original surrounding bridges and apertures likely span the evolution included in steps (1), (2), (3), (4) and (5) in the development process described above. Of course, ultimately, the evolution of the site's bridge structure has not proceeded beyond the (5) type of bridge, that is, a timber woven arch bridge.

Relatedly, during his investigation of Qingyuan County, the author found that the Shuangmen Bridge of Daji Village is the earliest built bridge in the Lishui (although it was rebuilt at the end of 1992, the bridge type and beam frame basically did not change). On its gallery house, words are written in black ink on the beam of the central bay stating: "In 1025, in the 1th year of the sexagenary cycle, during the third year of the Tiansheng era of the Great Song Dynasty, brothers Wu Gu and Wu Hu established the Shuangmen Bridge." The *Qingyuan County Chronicle* compiled in 1877 during the Qing Dynasty also records: "Shuangmen Bridge, built by the joint efforts of the brothers Wu Gu and Wu Hu has double doors on each side of the bridge, which is how it gained its name." If Shuangmen Bridge was built in 1025, it would have been built at least 7 years earlier than Xia Zhi's construction of a Rainbow Bridge during 1032-1033, and 8 years later than Wei Huaji's abandonment of the effort to build the Wujiao Bridge in 1017.

Here, the story of Wei Huaji and his construction of the Wujiao Bridge should be described. In the early Northern Song Dynasty, there were many column and beam bridges along the Bianshui River by the capital, but ships often collided with bridges in times of floods or heavy traffic. The *Chronicle of Sequel of Comprehensive Mirror for Aid Government* states: "The court approved Wei Huaji's proposal. The Bianshui River is fierce, and many bridge columns have been ruined by ships. So a footless type of bridge was offered as a solution. The wood was to be woven together, and pegs ran through it. It was decreed that Wei Huaji and the *bazuosi* would carry out the construction. Later, the expense for the project was estimated by the sansi to exceed three times the original amount, and the project was halted." The *Compilation of State Regulations of Song Dynasty*, also states: "In the 1th month of the 1th year of the Tianxi era (1017), the work on the Wujiao Bridge was halted." What type of bridge was this footless bridge? Fang Yong believes that "this footless bridge, which was not constructed successfully because it required too much work, may have been a timber cantilever beam type." [27] How, the author believes the bridge was a woven timber arch-beam bridge. This is based on the phrase, "The wood was to be woven together, and pegs ran through it" from the record. The description of "woven timber" and "pegs" may refer to the southern use of mortise and tenon technology. In November 2001, the author participated in the TV documentary *Tracking the Hongqiao* produced by China Central Television (CCTV). In order to truly reproduce the actual construction of Zhejiang-Fujian timber arch bridges, the program invited master bridge builder Zheng Duojin, a member of a family lineage of bridge builders from Xiaodong Village, Shouning County, Fujian Province, to oversee the construction of a small-scale model of a bridge. And then with the help of Chinese-American Yu Min, the author got the TV documentary *Rainbow Bridge* filmed by NOVA TV in the United States, which recorded the whole process of restoring Bianshui Rainbow Bridge in Jinze Town, Qingpu District, Shanghai, with the supervision of Tang Huacheng and Professor Tom F. Peters. Comparatively speaking, the woven timber arch beam structures are more suitable for the construction of long-spanned bridges. The stone foundations on both sides of banks are very important to the construction. The cross sections at both ends of the structure are very large, and make use of rigid scaffold frames as well. Almost all joints are formed through the use of mortise and tenon technology. The method is much more complicated and costly than the timber-woven arch structure of Bianshui Rainbow Bridge. Hence it is unsurprising that costs for the Wujiao Bridge exceeded expectations by a factor of three.

Let's mention once again the Wu Gu and Wu Hu brothers and their Shuangmen Bridge. According to the *Qingyuan Chronicle* compiled in 1877 during the Qing Dynasty, "During the 2nd year of Tiansheng (i.e. a period during the Renzong reign), in the 1th year of the sexagenary cycle, Wu Gu was appointed as *taizizanshan* and *dianzhongcheng*, and this was recorded. During the first year of the Jingyou period of the Renzong reign (1034) in the *jiaxu* year of the sexagenary cycle, Wu Hu was appointed as *shoumicheng* and the magistrate of Haozhou Prefecture, and it was recorded." Wu Gu was the first resident of Qingyuan country in the Song Dynasty to become an official through the imperial examination, and he rose to the rank of *dianzhongcheng* (central palace

censor). According to the *Dictionary of Official Ranks in Dynastic China*, published by Shanghai Lexicographic Publishing House in 1992, "*Dianzhongcheng* was a title for a type of official and in 618, the office of internal palace censor was renamed as central palace director, which was responsible for the emperor's daily affairs, as well as six bureaus relating to food, medicine, clothing, housing, transportation and carriages. During the Song Dynasty, this office was a nominal position only for payment without any tasks, and the responsibilities of the office of the imperial commissary were transferred to another office." According to the above information, it is not impossible for Wu Gu to have participated in the construction of bridges in the imperial city. The existing Shuangmen Bridge has a span of 11.2 meters and a width of 4.6 meters. Its structure is very similar to the type (6) bridge mentioned above. Rather than the five arch ribs used in the second type of arch bridge structural systems, four are used here, as one has been omitted. Hence it can be considered to be a woven timber arch bridge type. Its span is also close to that of Bianshui Rainbow Bridge, (which was estimated to extend 16-18 meters). Therefore, it is very possible that given his background, Wu Gu brought this bridge to the Northern Song's capital before the Bianshui Rainbow Bridge was built. And hence it is possible that the technology of woven timber arch-beam bridges was then integrated with the existing wooden structural technology of the northern capital, and eventually formed the historically renowned wooden timber arch bridge, the Bianshui Rainbow Bridge.

Aside from the above two examples, the history of building timber arch bridges in Zhejiang and Fujian mountains can be traced back at least to the Ming Dynasty. According to the book *The Technological History of Chinese Ancient Bridges*, the oldest such bridge in the Zhejiang and Fujian mountains was the Shuyang Bridge in Taishun, which was built in 1454 during the Ming Dynasty. Unfortunately, it was demolished in 1965 during road construction. The well-preserved Rulong Bridge in Qingyuan County was built in 1625 during the Ming as well. According to the researcher of the Taishun Cultural Museum, the region also has several other timber arch bridges built during the Ming Dynasty. For example, the Xidong Bridge (also known as Dongxi Bridge) in Sixi Town was built in 1570. In addition, the Yonggui Bridge in Qingyuan County, which the author personally researched, was built in 1306 during the Yuan Dynasty, and rebuilt sometime between 1457-1464 during the Ming. Jigu Bridge in Kangcuo Township, Fu'an City, was also built between 1628-1644, during the Ming Dynasty. It is also possible that the Jinzao bridge in Pingnan County was built during the Ming Dynasty sometime during 1368-1644. [28] It can be seen that the history of timber arch bridge construction in the Zhejiang and Fujian mountainous areas likely extended from the Song Dynasty to the present, without an indication of discontinuity.

Later, the author found several timber bridges in Fujian Province which were built in the Song Dynasty. In Pingnan County, there are two woven timber arch-beam covered bridges, Qiansheng Bridge and Wan'an Bridge, which may have been built in the Song Dynasty. Another such bridge is the Helong Bridge in Minqing County, Fuzhou. Helong Bridge is located in Shenghuang Village, in Shenghuang Township. It was built in the Southern Song Dynasty sometime between 1165-1173, then destroyed during the Yuan Dynasty between 1314-1320, rebuilt during 1573-1619, 1699, and in 1927. Qiansheng Bridge is located in Tangkou Village, Pingnan County, Ningde, Fujian Province. *The Ancient Bridges of Pingnan County* (compiled and printed by the Cultural and Historical Committee of Pingnan County, 2003) records that: "(Qiansheng Bridge) was built during the years of Lizong Emperor of the Southern Song Dynasty (1201-1264). It burned down during the end of the Ming Dynasty. During the Qing Dynasty, it was rebuilt and reconstruction was completed in 1715 and 1729. In 1809 it was destroyed by a flood, and in 1821, the decision to rebuild it was made by the resident Zhou Daquan." Wan'an Bridge, commonly known as Changqiao Bridge by locals, is located in the east of Changqiao Village, Changqiao Township. It is a woven timber arch-beam covered bridge with five piers and six spans and is the longest existing timber arch bridge in China. According to the *Chronicle of Pingnan County* published in 1909, "The *Yutian County Chronicles* states that it was built where two mountain streams met, and resembles a long rainbow. A local saying was that it was built by immortals from heaven. In ancient times, it was also called Longjiang gongji Bridge. It was built in the Song dynasty, with piles of stones forming its five piers and pavilions on top. In the 25th year of sexagenary cycle it was destroyed by bandits with only one plank surviving. In the 7th year of the Qianlong reign (1718), the bridge was reconstructed." Later, personnel from the Cultural Museum discovered characters etched on the bridge's central pier, about 3 meters from the water, stating: "Son Jiangzhen who were living nearby the river raised money and grain, to form a stone pier. It was built in commemoration of their deceased parents, and in order to transmit their positive cause, as well as for the wish of the men and women off all families to preserve peace. Inscribed in the 5th year of Yuanyou reign (1090, during the Northern Song Dynasty), during the 9th month of the 7th year of the sexagenary cycle." This stone inscription is embedded in the stone pier. The inscription consists of fifty-four words in total. It is divided into nine vertical lines, with six words in each line.

Yuanyou was a period during the Zhezong Emperor of the Northern Song Dynasty, and its 5th year was 1090. If this bridge at the time of its initial construction was a woven timber arch-beam bridge, it would have been known as an ancient timber arch bridge only later than the time of the construction of Shuangmen Bridge in Qingyuan County. Mr. Tang Huancheng apparently also noticed this clue, explaining in his recently published book *China's Timber Arch Bridges*: "If the original Wan'an Bridge was an intersecting timber arch bridge, this record undoubtedly dispels the first hypothesis (i.e. the hypothesis that scholars, peasants, wokers and merchants brought timber arch bridge technology from the north to the south from the time of the Southern Song Dynasty). By 1090 (during the Northern Song, which preceded the Southern Song), 50 years had already past since the latest possible date of the invention of the intersecting arch bridge in 1041-1048, when the Bianjing [i.e. Bianshui] Rainbow Bridge was completed." In this way, Mr. Tang insisted that the technology of timber arch bridge was introduced from the Northern Song's capital Bianjing (present day Kaifeng) to Zhejiang and Fujian. However, in order for this to be logical, he thought that some people, such as Zhou Bangyan, a famous minister of the Northern Song Dynasty, might have been instrumental in the dissemination of this kind of bridge. It is written in the *History of the Song Dynasty* that Zhou Bangyan (1056-1121), a native of Qiantang, traveled to the capital at the beginning of Yuanfeng period of the Song Dynasty (about 1080), "offering more than ten thousand words of *Biandu Rhymes*, which delighted the Shenzong emperor." In the *Biandu Rhymes*, the busy water transportation on the Bianshui River is described meticulously. Therefore, Mr. Tang speculates that Zhou could not have avoided paying attention to the woven timber arch bridges on the Bianshui River. Moreover, the *History of the*

Song Dynasty also records that Zhou Bangyan first served as an official in the capital, then went to Longde as the magistrate, and from Mingzhou (today's Ningbo) ... went to Shunchang, Fujian Province, and then migrated to Chuzhou (today's Lishui), Zhejiang Province, where he died at 66 years of age. Zhou Bangyan, or those with experience similar to him probably brought this technology from Bianjing to Zhejiang and Fujian in the Northern Song Dynasty. In any case, Mr. Tang disagreed with the argument that this advanced timber arch technology in the southern provinces of Zhejiang and Fujian would have developed independently from the north. Therefore, in the book *Chinese Timber Arch Bridges*, Mr. Tang also raised a question from the opposite perspective: "If Fujian and Zhejiang in the Northern Song Dynasty had independently invented the intersecting timber arch bridge, why couldn't the equivalent in Fujian and Zhejiang to officials such as Xia Zhi and Chen Xiliang have submitted reports to the central government explaining how the capital could solve the problem of the bridges along the Bianshui River that were ruined by colliding ships?"

Of course, from the perspective of technological evolution, the author deduces that it is possible to independently develop the technology of woven timber arch-beam bridges in Zhejiang and Fujian Provinces. But it cannot be said for sure that such technology first developed in Zhejiang and Fujian and then spread elsewhere. At least three possibilities still exist until sufficient evidence resolves the question, namely:

The first possibility is that, as Mr. Tang Weicheng speculated, the technology of woven timber arch bridges spread from the Northern Song's eastern capital Bianliang.

The second is that Zhejiang and Fujian took the lead in developing the technology of woven timber arch-beam structures, and then examples of such technology were brought to the central government by local officials.

The third possibility is that the technology of woven timber arch-beam structures developed independently in Zhejiang and Fujian Provinces, and this has no definitive relationship with the woven timber arch structures of the Northern Song Dynasty.

Various sources suggest that the first two scenarios are far more likely than the third. Mr. Tang's speculation is not unreasonable either. If Mr. Tang's thesis is correct, then the key question for the author is: Why does this advanced wooden arch technology exist only in the mountains of Zhejiang and Fujian especially given these are economically underdeveloped areas? Further, what are the urgent practical needs that induced these underdeveloped regions to adopt such a state-of-the-art and sophisticated bridge-building technology? This will be an important issue that the author needs to continue to clarify in the future.

5.3 Types and Characteristics of Timber Arch Covered Bridges

The "Rainbow Bridge" in the painting *Riverside Scene at Qingming Festival* is called a woven timber arch structure by modern scholars. Its arch structure is mainly composed by the combination of two kinds of different arch systems arranged and combined. One is composed of three long members, one flat and two oblique, called System I; the other is composed of two long members and two short members, all oblique, called System II. The two systems are arranged by being placed together so they alternate along a horizontal axis. System I has 10 arch frames, System II has 11 arch frames. Four crosspieces are interspersed between them to distribute pressure, and these are connected by means of rope lashing. Together this forms an integral arch framework.[29] The Bianhe River's Rainbow Bridge has disappeared, and it is difficult to find traces of related bridge structures. Hence the only example of a woven timber arch bridge is the Rainbow Bridge.

In Fujian and Zhejiang, there are many existing examples of woven timber arch-beam bridges. They are widely distributed and diverse in forms. Among them, single span bridges are the most common type, and others have two, three, six spans, and more. In a typical single-span woven timber arch-beam covered bridge, the arch structure is mainly composed of two kinds of arch systems arranged and combined alongside one another. One is composed of three long members, one flat and two oblique, which is called system I; the other is composed of five members with different lengths, one flat and four oblique, which is called system II. The two types of arch systems are placed together so they alternate along a horizontal axis, in which the number of frames in system I is usually nine, and the number of frames in system II is usually eight. There are also combinations of eight and seven, and seven and six. Generally speaking, the number of system I arch frames exceeds the number of those in system II by one frame. The members in the arch frame of the same system are connected by mortise and tenon to crosspieces, arch timber blocks, arch stone blocks, vertical bents (transverse rigid frames) erected close to the abutment, and to cross bracing added to the upper part of the arch frame. In system II, a small bent is erected on the lower crosspiece to support the deck's timber beams. In addition, usually bracing is used to support the small bents. The combination of these two systems, including the auxiliary components such as the cross bracing, brace members, bents and deck beam forms the completed primary load-bearing structure of the woven timber arch-beam covered bridge. Of course, in the course of local construction, bridge builders in Fujian and Zhejiang use their own unique names for these components.

The woven timber arch-beam bridges in Fujian and Zhejiang share major similarities while differing in smaller details, with the examples too numerous to list. Two special examples will be listed here. One is Futian Bridge, located in Daji Village, Songyuan Town, Qingyuan County, Zhejiang Province. It is a single-span woven timber arch beam covered bridge. The span of the bridge is more than 9 meters. System I has nine arch frames and system II has eight arch frames. Especially, the horizontal members of system II's arch frames are very short in length and close to the width of the crosspieces. Similarly, the structure of the Shuangmen Bridge in the same village is the same, except that the span of the this bridge is slightly larger, reaching more than 11 meters. It contains seven arch frames in system I and six arch frames in system II.

The other special example is the Helong Bridge located in Shenghuang Village, Shenghaung Township, Minqing County, Fuzhou, Fujian Province. The bridge's historical background has been detailed above, and will not be repeated here. The bridge system is a two-span woven timber arch-beam covered bridge. The two spans are different in length. The short span is more than 12 meters long and the long span is more than 14 meters across. The two spans are composed of eight system I arch frames and seven system II arch frames. The difference is that the system II arch in the bridge's short span is composed of four diagonal members and is combined with the system I arch. This forms a structural system similar to the Rainbow Bridge, which is very rare in Fujian and Zhejiang Provinces.

The origin of the woven timber arch-beam structure has not been determined yet, but it is widely used in Fujian and Zhejiang. As an advanced timber bridge structural technology, timber woven beam covered bridge have a large elevation, spans of a minimum of 9 meters

and a maximum of more than 30 meters. Their constituent materials are easily obtained, and are very adaptable and flexible. They suit the construction requirements of various geological environments, including rural rivers and country canyons. From the perspective of the development of bridge technology, the maturity and development of woven timber arch-beam structures represents the peak of ancient timber bridge building technology in China.

5.4 The Artistry and Customs of Timber Arch Covered Bridge Construction

In traditional Chinese society, almost all construction activities were accompanied by important religious rituals and local folk customs. Bridge building, one of the important forms of built works, was no exception. Bridge building rituals are but an important part of a larger set of Chinese traditional architectural rituals. Ever since ancient times, erecting bridges and paving roads have been considered important public tasks in Chinese rural society. Such projects encompass large amounts of land, significant investments, and greatly impact the lives of villagers. Traditional geomantic theory is always invoked to provide many explanations for aspects of such bridge-building and roadwork. Many of these principles are quite contrived, such as that of locking in water outlets. Nonetheless, geomancy for a long period of history was a dominant theoretical framework in planning and construction, and its guiding role in traditional construction activities should be appreciated.

The basis for the occurrence and existence of bridge-building rituals is at least in small part due to the process of interrupting the realm of natural space with the creation of a realm of man-made space and of new culture. In Germany, for example, people think that there are gods or spirits living in rivers, and that building bridges offends the natural realm of such waterways. Therefore, they find it necessary to comfort the gods or spirits in the river through various offerings. In fact, there are similar examples in ancient Chinese history. The story of Ximen Bao's rule of Ye from the Warring States Period describes Ximen's opposition to the sacrifice of humans to *hebo* (god of the Yellow River). "When people in Sui Dynasty built a stone bridge, 280 sacrifices were offered," is a statement from Liu Chaoran's *Stone Bridge Renovation Record* inscribed on an octagonal stone pillar found in the riverbed under the Zhaozhou Bridge in Hebei Province.

The frequency of sacrificial activities performed during the building of bridges in ancient China can be glimpsed from this.

There are thousands of years of history of building bridges in the mountains along the Fujian and Zhejiang border. Timber arch covered bridges have been built there for at least 5-6 hundred years. Bridge builders have developed various bridge building customs during this long period of experience. Due to political, economic, and cultural reasons, the construction of timber arch bridges has gradually decreased since 1949, and since 1980 few timber arch bridges serve as major traffic arteries. Nowadays, there are fewer and fewer middle-aged and old bridge builders still alive, and there are only a few *zhumogongjiang* (master builders, or literally primary ink [setter] craftsmen, referring to the builders of arch bridges who "set out the lines" with ink for other workmen to follow in their endeavors) remain. The customs associated with building bridges that developed over the course of hundreds years are already hardly known. These customs include very reasonable elements as well as practices based in superstition and ignorance. But they were formed gradually over the long course of expended human labor. They are of great historical and academic value for understanding the traditional bridge building culture of China.

There are many customs and protocols observed in the construction of timber arch bridges. These arose for the purpose of supporting the building of such bridges. After bridges are successfully built, their use starts. A long period elapses between the use of a new bridge and its final abandonment. This often takes hundreds of years. During their use, ritual blessings of bridges or of one's fellow villagers are very solemn and are commonly made in a bridge's gallery house. Compared with the rituals that accompany the bridge building process, such practices are more free, diverse, and their form is not so fixed. The occurrence and development of these kinds of rituals and ceremonies are also very meaningful, but they are not elaborated on in this section.

On the basis of detailed investigation and research of many existing timber arch bridges in the Zhejiang and Fujian mountainous areas, the author summarizes the traditional rituals observed in the process of building timber arch bridges below. Such rituals were observed in the course of investigating and visiting veteran bridge builders and observing and participating in the construction and repair of these timber arch bridges.

5.4.1 The First Stage Bridge Builders and Establishing a "Bridge Approval" Document

In traditional Chinese rural society, repairing bridges and paving roads have always benefited local people. Moreover, they are engineering works for the public interest, and quickly earn the support of both officials and residents. The covered bridges in Zhejiang and Fujian were not only constructed through financing and organization by the government, as were the Dengyun Bridge in the south gate of Taishun County, and Xianju Bridge in Xianren Township, but also through the concerted efforts of lineages and clans (such organizations are dominant in villages in this region), such as the Xuezhai Bridge in Sankui Town, Santiao Bridge in Zhouling Township, Wenxing Bridge in Xiaocun Town, and Yongqing Bridge and Nanyang Bridge in Jianzhou Village. More bridges were built by local people than built by the government in Taishun County.

When a lineage or clan organization raised either an adequate amount of funds for bridge building, or at least a certain amount of funds, then it would be time to "find big trees, and to select a master builder." The tasks of raising funds and finding a master builder were heavy responsibilities and unusually difficult tasks. Those who could complete them were talented individuals, and this situation led to the creation of a speciality of "first stage bridge builders." Generally speaking, there were several people involved in the first stage of such bridge building projects, but in their ranks, one person was most essential. The first stage of bridge construction undertaken by the government was naturally completed by government administrators. Private bridges were usually organized by energetic and capable clan or lineage members who were highly respected and seen to possess great virtues. This was because overseeing bridge building was regarded as a painstaking task requiring a great deal of wisdom and energy. In Xiaocun Town, there is a touching story about the first stage of bridge construction:[30]

Wang Guangyi, one of the first stage bridge builders of Wenxing Bridge in Xiaocun Town, Taishun County, sold 12,000 square meters of good farmland and all his family's property in order to build this bridge. After its completion, Wang Guangyi, who had fulfilled this historic task, was penniless and had no other choice but to survive by begging. Upon hearing this, members of the Wang family lineage collected three loads of white rice for him. Unfortunately, Wang Guangyi had neglected eating and sleeping during the construction of the bridge, and had become ill. He died before he could finish eating the white rice given to him. Because they no longer had any property or land, Wang Guangyi's eight sons lived a very difficult life, and could not marry or have children. Finally, there was no way out. Several brothers learned of the She Nationality's practice of reclaiming wasteland for survival. One of the brothers agreed to live with a She family and to be their son-in-law expected to reproduce the She family's ancestral line rather than his own. It was lucky he did this, as he bore two grandsons for Wang Guangyi, and one took on the father's family name, finally preserving the Wang family's line.

Much time has passed since then, and the prosperity and honor of the former Wang family village has long disappeared and been reduced to dust. Only the slanted rays of the setting sun still illuminate several stone tablets daily on the Wenxing Bridge, including one engraved with the words "The first stage bridge builder: Wang Guangyi", which shines brightly…

Although the work of building bridges was hard and arduous, the cause of building bridges was generally supported by people. Because building a bridge is a good cause, often neighboring villages in addition to the project's sponsoring lineage organization, would gladly contribute to such a project. If the people of the lineage had money, they donated it, and if they could work, they worked. Some went up to their family's mountains, felled timber and donated the wood. Such is stated in *A Summary of the Reconstruction of Jinxi Bridge* from the Xue Lineage Genealogy of Sankui Town.

After the selection of "the first stage bridge builders", the building of a covered bridge can officially begin. The first step is to "chose a master builder". This is not only about choosing a bridge builder, but also about budgeting, and this information is set in a specific agreement. Some of these agreements are similar to today's commissioning contracts. In the mountainous areas of Zhejiang and Fujian, including Taishun County, the bridge construction contract signed by the bridge building director, captain and other bridge builders is called the "bridge approval document" "bridge agreement" or "invitation agreement". In later times, this was directly referred to as a contract.

Usually the bridge approval agreement was written on fine bamboo paper or Xuan Paper (rice paper, originating from Xuanzhou Prefecture in present day Anhui Province). The text of the document is written vertically with a brush. It mainly describes the director and captain who will build or repair a specified bridge in a specified place, and refers to the specific town and specific village that is inviting a specific bridge builder. The concrete contents are as follows: First, the commissioning party puts forward the length, height and width of the bridge, the number of the columns, whether it is necessary to erect benches and shrines inside the bridge; second, if an old bridge is to be demolished or rebuilt, then the members for the arch (serving as the arch's skeletal rib framework) needed to be removed or replaced are listed, as well as bridge deck beams, purlins, purlin-supporting beams and timber for railing; third, the height, width, thickness of the abutments are described, as well as their method of construction, and the dimensions of stones to be used; fourth, information related to material supplies and methods of transportation are listed including for arch components, bamboo used in the construction process, rope, nails, and even whether equipment such as the builders' *mudouxian* a carpenter's traditional straight-line ink marker tool will be provided by themselves or by the commissioning party; fifth, in addition to bridge builders, if there are additional craftsmen necessary such as stone masons, or other specialists needed for the building of gallery houses, then it is specified whether the commissioning party will be responsible for them or if the bridge builders will oversee them; sixth, the total cost for the project is listed together with a method of payment; seventh, expenditures are listed for religious rituals on the first and 15th of the lunar month involving the worship of gods and auspicious blessings, as well as expenditures for red envelope payments to the master bridge builder during the setting of the bridge beams; eighth, the penalty for breach of contract by either party is described. Lastly, the time of signing, names of signatories (certified by stamp or personal marker, such as a fingerprints), witnesses, transcriber, and the author are listed. After this, a character seal is added to the document, composed of auspicious words, and the phrase *daji* (the most favorable auspices) is added in the upper left corner of the document. If there are additional terms that had originally been omitted, they are later added together with prudently re-added signatures and personal markers.

After the signing of the agreement, the date of the start of construction can be chosen. Date selection also requires strict procedures and specific ceremonies. Detailed schedules for the whole bridge construction project are arranged. These schedules are set by an expert date-setting master, who selects appropriate times according to auspicious dates in a traditional almanac.

5.4.2 The Date-Setting Master and Setting the Date for Starting Work

After the bridge directors and captains have formally appointed bridge builders, they will begin to formally plan the construction of the bridge. In Taishun, Shouning, Pingnan, and other counties, the first thing to do in building a covered bridge is to determine the specific location for the bridge. The specific location and orientation of the bridge body are very important for the safety of the bridge after completion. This is especially the case for the construction of timber arch bridges. In order to choose the site of the bridge, a geomancy master must be invited.

After the geomancy master has determined the orientation of the abutments at both ends, the date setting master must be invited again to select the "beam setting date" and other auspicious days according to the traditional almanac. These proposed dates must be approved by the bridge builder according to his availability. Let's look at cultural relics from Fujian Province as an example of this process. In 1865, the Shuangguang Bridge in Zhusenhou Village, Longyan township was planned to built. Zhang Maoxui (of Xiukeng Village, Limen Township, Zhouning County, who probably lived between 1850-1920) and Zhang Maochao were invited to serve as the main bridge builders for the project. The program of setting auspicious dates for the project is still preserved. Its contents are as follows.

Choosing the time from 11 AM-1 PM of the 24th day (the 48th day of the sexagenary cycle) of the 6th month [months are according to the 12 months of the Chinese lunar calendar] for the carpenters to begin erecting the starting beam is auspicious.

Choosing the time from 7-9 PM of the 12th day (the 5th day of the sexagenary cycle) of the 7th month to set the pillars is auspicious.

Choosing the time from 5-7 AM on the 20th day (the 13th day of the sexagenary cycle) of the 7th month to demolish the old bridge is auspicious.

Choose the time from 5-7 AM on the 10th day (the 32nd day of the sexagenary cycle) of the 10th month to install the bridge's frame or to lay down the lower level of bridge boards.

Choosing the time from 7-9 AM on the 15th day (the 37th day of the sexagenary cycle) of the 10th month to lay down the horizontal bridge boards is auspicious.

Choose the time from 5-9 AM on the 21st day (the 43rd day of the sexagenary cycle) of the 10th month to find beams from the mountains.

Choosing the time from 7-9 AM on the 22nd day (44th day of the sexagenary cycle) to erect the columns, and 1-3 PM of that day to set the beams is auspicious.

In Sixi Town, Taishun County, there is also a story about bridge building captain Lin Zhengxu and a date setting master:

Xidong Bridge and Beijian Bridge in Sixi Town are the two most beautiful timber arch covered bridges in Taishun County. Because the two bridges are not far apart from each other and their respective streams unite downstream, local people call them the Shangqiao Bridge and Xiaqiao Bridge, and also as the Zimei Bridges. Lin Zhengxu was the first stage bridge builder for the construction of Xidong Bridge. After the completion of the bridge, according to local customs, a *yuanqiao* (completeness bridge) ceremony needed to be held. After choosing an auspicious day, the date setting master said to Lin Zhengxu: "Choosing this auspicious day will bring harm to one party, if [you], the first stage bridge builder is not harmed, then the master builder will be harmed. What will become of the two of you? A decision must be made." In order to let the bridge be used as soon as possible, Lin Zhengxu immediately decided to start the ceremony on the auspicious day established. But in order not to not imperil the master builder, Lin then decided that his own entire family must immediately leave their home in Sixi (hence enduring a hardship himself, and avoiding the risk of the master builder befalling some tragedy). In this story, the first stage bridge builder's selfless spirit and his willingness to sacrifice for the greater good, as well as the choice words of the date setting master are described incisively.

For choosing auspicious practices, there are statements such as "The pavilion should be situated to the southeast of the bridge (in the *xunzheng* direction corresponding to the Chinese eight trigrams). And the bridge is to be situated in a northeast orientation (corresponding to the wei direction corresponding to the eight trigrams). These are to be constructed during the period of the tenth month of this year, and with these two structures completed thus, it will be very auspicious." There are also more simple ones, such as "Having chosen 5-7 am of the sixth day (the 32nd day of the sexagenary cycle) of the tenth month of the lunar calendar for setting the top bridge beam and proceeding with construction is auspicious. And 5-7 am of the 18th of the month (the 44th day of the sexagenary cycle) is also an auspicious time for switching the columns, raising the beams and setting the rafters." Some bridges also write the names of the geomancy master, and the date-setting master on the bridge's inner beams.

The ritual date selection process carries with it a certain degree of superstition, but it plays an important role in the arrangement of scheduling and work planning and in the control of the entire project.

5.4.3 Geomancy Masters and the Selection of Sites

Geomancy masters, including those mentioned above, have always been both praised and criticized by society for their role. Geomancy proscriptions are too colored by superstition, which even received the scorn of ancient people. According to the *Yongjia County Chronicle* of the Guangxu era (1875-1908) in the Qing Dynasty, magistrates of the Wenzhou in Ming Dynasty, Wen Liu, He Wenyuan and other educated local gentry criticized and banned witchcraft temples, witches, and other such practices. They regarded this obsession as a phenomenon that weakened people's hearts and souls. Nevertheless, in the Qing Dynasty, Dong Yongfu of Taishun Country in *Records of the Renovation of Dengyun* Bridge recorded a passage about geomancy, which is also quite thought provoking: "A bridge is established for the purpose of people's journeys. Geomancy experts (*xingjia*, a form of fengshui master) use the harnessing of a water head (such as by symbolically locking in the positive qi there by crossing the water body with a bridge) as a source of propitiousness. It seems not believable, but some people believe in this."

With a compass in hand, a geomancy master would chant and point, and in this way determine the direction, orientation and place for the abutment of a large covered bridge. The name of Mr. Wang Shiyu, a geomancy master, is left on the beam of the gallery house on the Chengshui Bridge in Guihu Town, Taishun County. It is said that many bridges had been built here before the construction of the Chengshui Bridge. But they were all destroyed by floods. After they were swept away, villagers built temporary beam bridges with giant trees to facilitate traffic over the waterway. Eventually they invited the county's well-known geomancy master Wang Shiyu to survey the site. Wang Shiyu determined a location for a new bridge by examining the wind direction and the location of water hazards. And the Chengshui Bridge mapped out by Wang Shiyu has been in safe use until the present day.

Of course, it is not necessary for a geomancy master to determine the location of a covered bridge. People with relatively rich hydrological, geological and engineering experience can play this role too. For example, the reconstruction of Xuezhai Bridge in Sankui Town of Taishun County was overseen by Yang Bingchun, the newly appointed county magistrate. According to section of the Xue family genealogy's record on *Rebuilding the Jinxi Bridge*, Yang personally carried out an on-spot investigation of the site, and continued to plan and investigate throughout the whole process. He speculated that if the bridge was built over the bigger stream section, then "on the top the wind will threaten to damage it, and below there is a furious stream and the piles installed there will not be steady." But if it was build downstream by a smaller stream he speculated, "above it will be easier to withstand the wind, and the water below it is tranquil and still. So a bridge built there will last long. And the public agreed on this."

5.4.4 Finding Beams for Construction

In traditional Chinese buildings, purlins under the central roof ridge of the main structures are called *dongliang* (building beams), as they are called when used in the same position in the gallery houses of timber arch covered bridges in the mountains of Taishun County. In Ningde, Fujian, the same structures are called *xiliang* (happy beams). Because they occupy the tallest position in a roof frame, they are the focus of a good deal of respect and attention.

A lot of lumber is used in the construction of covered bridges. Except for *dongliang*, many other timber supplies can be donated by local villagers. As long as they meet the specifications and are of adequate strength, they can be used. *Dongliang* are different though, and the materials and selection requirements for them are much more stringent. In addition, a special ceremony exists for selecting these beams. First stage bridge builders organize the selection of the materials for such *dongliang* in the mountains and forests. The trees that can be selected as *dongliang* must satisfy the following conditions: They must grow in a "clean" place, which means that there are no graves, or latrines around them and no roads above them; the selected trees must be tall Chinese firs; in the Ningde of Fujian Province, three or two Chinese fir trees with common roots and flourishing branches should be selected, commonly known as "twin firewood" trees. In Taishun County, the trees selected to be *dongliang* should maintain their original appearance and retain their bark (as opposed to the normal practice in which bark is stripped after felling trees and before carrying them down the hillside). After being cut down, the trees cannot touch the ground. They must be supported by wooden supports, waiting for the village's renowned or distinguished members to symbolically lift them up as part of a lifting ceremony before being carried downhill by healthy strong men. Those whose own mountain forest areas are the source of *dongliang* are not upset to lose such specimens. Instead they are happy and subsequently donate more wood to the project. The reason is simple: since the wood from their own mountain forest land is strong *dongliang* material, how could they not but think that their own children will soon also become strong supports? This being the case, how could they not be happy?

In Ningde of Fujian Province that neighbors Taishun, felling timber also requires setting an auspicious day. This day in turn requires preparing a load of "mountain offerings" including a rooster, a piece of pork, five bowls of vegetable dishes, tea, and wine. Four (symbolizing the cardinal directions of north, south, east, and west) "boys with good fate" are selected to cut down the trees. These boys are to have two living parents, and three generations of ancestors who lived in the village as well. Before cutting down the trees, offerings are made to the mountain gods. The load of offerings are placed besides the Chinese fir trees, and sticks of incense are lit. The Chinese fir cut down should fall in the direction of the mountain's peak (signifying moving upward, to avoid "falling down," an inauspicious phrase). Foliage is placed on the place where the Chinese fir will fall (so that the timber would not be dirtied). When cutting down, the master carpenters cheer. They read:

The axe on the right - Prosperity for a thousands of years (Hooray!)

The axe on the left - generations will arise (Hooray!)

Prosperity as enduring as the universe is old (Hooray!)

Prosperity in every village, welfare for every family (Hooray!)

To be prosperous and multiply; rich and noble (Hooray!)

Five to seven forked branches from the end (tail) of the tree (called "tree sashes") are hung from the middle of the *xiliang*, to signify there is both a head and tail, indicative of prosperity. In addition, the beam is wrapped in red cloth. Along the road firecrackers are set off. Next the *xiliang* is rested on a three-legged wood support in an open space next to the bridge site. It must not be placed on the ground to avoid becoming dirty. The bark of the tree is then cut off, but is not thrown away. The bark can be dried at a high place, then burned and turned into ashes for use in an incense burner. It can also be poured into a stream to let the water take it away. After choosing the *xiliang*, remaining timber is used to serve as the left and right columns in front of the shrine inside the bridge.

The installment of a *xiliang* indicates the commencement of bridge construction.

5.4.5 Sacrifices for the River, Construction Starts for the Bridge

In the dry season after the autumnal equinox of the lunar calendar, river flows are generally reduced and rainfall is diminished. This is a good time for bridge construction, and the period has usually been chosen as the time for starting work. Before this begins, a ceremony for sacrifices to the river must be carried out. The ceremony is relatively complicated, but its content is relatively fixed. A pig is slaughtered by the riverbank, and before it dies it is placed in the river so that its blood sprays into the water. It is considered best for the water to become as red as possible in the process. After, a pig head, rooster, incense sticks, tea and wine, fruit and vegetarian food are offered up to one river god or another. Thereafter, on the first and fifteenth days of the lunar calendar, smaller sacrifices are prepared, with incense generally burned daily. In addition generally four bridge-building "blessing feasts" are organized.

In 1852, the Daqiao Bridge was first built by bridge building captain Zhang Chaogao in Pingnan County. In the contract, it was stipulated that "only four blessing ceremonies should be offered to cover the events of sacrificing to the river, erecting the columns, placing the beams, and completing the bridge. The banquet(s) as well as bamboo strips and forged iron will be organized by bridge building captain Zhang Chaogao." During bridge construction, moon blessing ceremonies were held as well. In 1837, when Tangshou Bridge was built in Gutian, Fujian Province, a bridge contract was signed, in which it stated "for moon blessing ceremonies, money in the amount of 1,000 *wen* should be given three times to you (referring to bridge builder Zhang Chengjun)." These three moon blessing ceremonies included the first and fifteenth days of the lunar calendar, as well as a certain inauspicious date.

The completion of the river sacrifice ceremony indicates that preparation work for bridge construction is finished, and the next step is the beginning of formal bridge construction.

5.4.6 The Beam Raising Ritual

In traditional Chinese construction, whether for houses or bridges, there would always be a grand beam raising ceremony when the last beam was put into place. This ceremony is not only to celebrate the completion of the timber frame of the building, but also to wish that the completed project will be used smoothly and successfully, and to wish good luck upon those who built it, and on those will use it. In the process of building covered bridges in Zhejiang Province, there were quite a number of master carpenters who were commissioned for such projects who came from Fujian Province. For example, in the old days, Taishun County in Zhejiang Province often invited bridge builders from Shouning in Fujian Province to participate in the construction of covered bridges. Shouning County and Taishun County are separated by only one mountain, and the craftsmen in Zhejiang and Fujian Province often worked together and shared ideas during the construction process. Still, the building practices of either region are not exactly the same, and as a result, the beam raising ceremonies in each place are not the same either. The form of the ceremony in fact has many variations.

5.4.6.1 Cheering the Raising of the Final Beam

The wooden arch bridge is the most special bridge in Taishun County. Based on the county's existing examples of such covered bridges, its construction, especially its primary arch frame, was produced through the support of master carpenters from Shouning, Fujian. Shouning masters have a cheering ceremony that is conducted when the last beam of the wooden arch bridge is put into place.

In the process of building timber arch bridges, the first step is to erect pillars that stand in the water. Their use is to support the first system of three rows of timber members that constitute the arch skeletal. This is what the builders in Zhejiang and Fujian refer to as the *sanjiemiao* (three sprout sections). The second step consists of putting together this first system. When installing the horizontally tending timber member, a sacrificial ceremony for the beam is held. In November 2001, CCTV asked Shouning bridge builder Zheng Duojin to build a timber arch bridge for the documentary *Tracing the Hongqiao Bridge*. Before the ceremony, Zheng went to the riverside shrine of a locally

worshipped deity to pray. He then set up a table in the stream with incense, tea, wine, fruit, vegetarian dishes, as well bridge building carpentry tools including the traditional straight-line ink (measuring) tool, axes, and chisels.

These offerings for the beam are overseen by the master bridge builder and carpenters. After lighting candles and incense and setting out tea and wine, the master builder and carpenters chant:

One to one, two to one, three to one,
On this auspicious and good time heaven and earth open up,
Yin and *yang* are balanced in this prosperous place.
We respectfully invite the Great Emperor of Heaven to arrive,
We respectfully invite the Jade Emperor to arrive,
The Sun God has arrived, The Horse of Heavenly Wisdom has arrived,
The *chuansongzhenglu* has arrived, The Lunar God has arrived,
The *tianyi* God has arrived, Master Lu Ban [renowned carpenter] has arrived,
The Honored Gods are Favorable, The God of Most Favorable Auspices has arrived,
The date has been set, the time has arrived.
Sound the cannons for the raising of the beam.

Then, while setting off firecrackers, the master bridge builder gives a cheer for the beam. The carpenters by his side then turn the *tianmenche* (heavenly gate vehicle, a device in old times used to move timber materials when building bridges, which uses a similar working principle to that of modern day machines that utilize hoists and cables to lift heavy objects) as the rope of the *tianmenche* is tightened this way, the large beam gradually rises. The master bridge builder, carpenters, and public then cheer the beam and chant:

"First is to wish for long life and riches (hooray!)
Second is for abundant wealth (hooray!)
Thirdly, for receiving first rank in the imperial exams (hooray!)
Fourth, for spring all year round (hooray!)
Fifth for the five kinds of good fortune (longevity, wealth, health, love of virtue, and natural death) and long life (hooray!)
Six is for thousands of storehouses filled with grain (hooray!)
Seven is for the glories and wealth (hooray!)
Eight become officials and pass the imperial examinations.
Ninth, may the population grow (hooray!)
And tenth, let all that be boundless! (hooray!)
Let the golden rooster on the top of the bridge herald the break of day, the jade rooster under the bridge fill the granaries, the royal canopy should extend throughout a thousand autumns, and prosperity last for thousands of years" (hooray!)

There was also another way of cheering:
First, a bowl of wine is offered for the head of the beam - may all families be prosperous and multiply (hooray!)
Second a cup of tea is offered for the beam's end - may the happy voices be heard in every family (hooray!)
Third, a bowl of wine is offered for the center of the beam, for honor, riches, splendor, and overall success (hooray!)
Fourth honor for the bridge building captains and directors, may they have sons every year, and may the members of their households get first rank in the imperial exams! (hooray!)

When the three sprouts sections on. the transverse skeletal timber members of the arch are combined with the tenons forming the *daniutou* large ox head, the bridge builders in Zhejiang and Fujian mountainous areas refer to the two structural arch systems together with the transverse skeletal timber members that run perpendicular to the horizontal skeletal structure as large ox heads, they cheer:

Pray that Lu Ban, the immortal master, descend to the world of ordinary men, and bless his pupils to enter the golden list (pass the imperial exam)
First, may all be prosperous and multiply (hooray!)
Second, for abundant wealth (hooray!)
Third, for receiving first rank in the imperial exams (hooray!)
Fourth, for luck all year round (hooray!)
Fifth, for the officials of the six kingdoms (hooray!)
Sixth, for happiness and prosperity for the Six Kingdoms (hooray!)
Seventh, for endless wealth (hooray!)
Eighth, let the eight immortals unite (hooray!)
Ninth, let all sons pass the exams (hooray!)
Tenth, let all the above be in abundance (hooray!)

Although the form and content of these cheers vary, they all are essentially prayers for the various gods to bless the smooth progress of the bridge construction and to bless all the people involved in the bridge building with happiness and good fortune.

5.4.6.2 The Beam Throwing Ceremony and Appreciating Public's Coin Giving Ceremony

In the construction of covered bridges in Fujian and Zhejiang mountainous areas, the culmination of the beam raising occurred when the beam was placed above the column frame. This article takes the construction of Taifu Bridge in Taishun County, Zhejiang Province as an example of the special *paoliang* (beam throwing) ceremony.

Dong Zhiji is one of the few bridge builders in Taishun County. At the time of the Taifu Bridge project, he served as master bridge during construction. When the beam was being raised, he instructed the assistant master builder to shout auspicious words such as "peace for the country and for the people," and "an abundant harvest of all the five grains". At the same time, he also directed people to place both ends of the beam in the precise position in the socket of the mortise. After this, the beam throwing ceremony was performed. The master bridge builder stood on the beams and read auspicious words while throwing seven treasure bags, that were hanging on the beam, onto a cloth sheet lying on the ground below. Legend has it that this custom originated with *Jiangtaigong* (Jiang Shang, who helped found the Zhou Dynasty, and is celebrated as a god) . Many gods are said to have been appointed by *Jiangtaigong*. As a result, people think the status of many gods is below that of *Jiangtaigong*, and that his "god position" should be on the highest beam, the *dongliang*. This is why many people write the words "*Jiangtaigong* is here" on a red banner and stick it on to the beam. People use the beam throwing ceremony's seven treasure bags to worship *Jiangtaigong* and to pray for his protection. After the official throwing of the treasure bags, the bridge building director stores them at home for seven days and seven nights. He then distributes the objects that have been used to honor the gods and spirits to the families of the villages. The bags contain silver, copper, iron, crisps, peanuts, dates, and rice. Each item contains an auspicious associated meaning.

In Shouning County, Fujian Province, the beam throwing ceremony has evolved into an appreciating public's coin giving ceremony.

There, when mounting the beam, the master builder must hang a small red cloth bag of copper coins (weighing about one kilogram) in the middle of the beam. After the ceremony, the head carpenter will choose a carpenter who is spry and not afraid of danger to retrieve the copper coins from the upper beam. The carpenter who retrieves the coins takes a hammer with him (a stone hammer with bamboo handles that could be extended with the use of additional handles, with a head shaped like a flat drum, used by carpenters to knock a beam tightly into place). This carpenter would walk onto the three sections of timbers forming the arch skeleton, say a few auspicious phrases, and then go to the middle of the *dongliang* beam to remove the cloth bag containing the copper coins. At this time, the people under the bridge would applaud and say "well done!" Then the carpenter would go to the other end of the beam and say some auspicious words. After that, the carpenter would give the cloth bag containing the copper coins to the master builder who in turn would distribute the coins out of appreciation to the other builders and assistants.

5.4.7 The Bridge Completing and Bridge Walking Ceremonies

Before bridge construction starts, various groundbreaking ceremonies are held, and so too after the bridge is completed there will be ceremonies such as "treading the bridge" "stepping on the bridge" "completing the bridge" and "first crossing". The "stepping on the bridge" ceremony prevails in provinces like Guangdong, Shaanxi, and Sichuan, while in Taishun County, Zhejiang Province, people prefer holding "completing the bridge" ceremonies, which could be considered a variation of the "stepping on the bridge" ceremony.

For local villagers, the bridge completing ceremony is held to express their wish that the bridge will forever remain solid. For bridge builders, the ceremony marks the completion of the bridge construction. In Taishun and many other places in Zhejiang Province, local people will have a custom of having "bridge completing wine". To some extent, bridge completing contains a similar symbolic meaning to consummation of marriage, called "completing the room". In the bridge completing ceremony, the bridge is regarded as a living thing, and its life is thought to be potentially lengthened in perpetuity through such a ceremony[31].

In Ningde of Fujian Province, the popular ceremony is called a "stepping on the bridge" or "beginning to tread on the bridge" ceremony. This allows people to take their first walk on the bridge. There are two types of "stepping on the bridge" ceremonies, depending on the number of participants. If few people do the walking, the event will start after the bridge road is fully paved. If more people join in, the event will start after five or six additional sprout boards are nailed into place. Before people walk along the bridge, the bridge building director and captain will choose two male elders, commonly known as "lucky people," coming from successful families with good reputations in which three-generations live together in the village. The two males and their wives should be in good health. Then, the lucky people will pledge donations, and then start walking on the bridge. As people cross, along the way they issue blessings, for instance for good weather, good harvests, peaceful households, village prosperity, wealth, and descendants for the director and captain, fame far and wide for the bridge building masters, and so on.

Black lettered calligraphy on the inner beam on the Louxia Bridge in Fujian Province, Zhouning County reads, "This records that in this area, the ancestral founder Chen Qibang's descendant surnamed Huang (male) named Longgou, husband of lady Wei have donated 100 tael of silver in but the hope that one tree will produce a thousand branches." Zhouning County's Denglong Bridge bears black calligraphy reading "In the Shuinan area, the ancestral founder Huang Qihong, graduate of the imperial academy, has a descendant Liu (male), graduate of the imperial academy, named Daoji, husband of lady Ye, and grandson, a graduate of the regional academy, named Gaojie, husband of lady Ye, as well as a great-grandson, graduate of the imperial academy, named Sichang, wife of lady Zhou, as well as great-great grandsons Wangzhang, married to lady Liu, Wangliang, married to lady Liu, and Wangchou, married to lady Liu. They have happily donated 250 tael of silver." "In the Duanjing area, ancestral founder and imperial academy graduate Ye Jiyun has a descendant Li (male), an imperial academy graduate, named Fengqing, husband of lady Xiao, a graduate of the regional academy named Yongqing, husband of lady Zhou, Xiuqing, husband of lady Zheng, Canqing, husband of lady Liu, and Quanqing, husband of lady Zhou, in addition to grandsons Zhengying, married to lady Wu, and Zhenggui, husband of lady Xiao, and Zhengkeng, husband of lady Li, as well as Zheng Huang, Zheng Tang, Zheng Gui. They have happily donated 120 tael of silver." If these donors who provide large amount of donation, come from a three, four, or even five generation family that lives together, they could be the best choice for lucky people to take the first walk on the bridge.

5.4.8 Other Timber Arch Covered Bridge Building Customs and Taboos

Bridge building activities for Taishun County's covered bridge incorporate extremely rich folk customs and cultural practices. Located along the mountainous border between southern Zhejiang and northern Fujian Provinces, the bridge culture here has benefited from rich geographical exchange and cooperation. Besides the folk cultural activities described above, these include sacrificial rituals for deities related to wood-working, rivers, and timber. There is also another sort of popular folk custom, Taishun's bridge building taboos.

The process of closing and hence completing the arches of Taishun's timber arch bridges is referred to as *jielong* (connecting the dragon). Before this is done, sacrificial rituals are performed. They are completed for deities including wood-working and river gods. The wood-working god is often said to be Lu Ban, and the bridge builders hope that he will protect the smooth completion of the *jielong* process. They also pray that the river deities will ensure the bridge's safety and prevent it from being overwhelmed by floods.

The construction of bridge houses on top of covered bridges also has many proscribed ritual elements. For example in order to be thought to be imbued with flood prevention properties, bridge shrines are required to face the direction that water flows from. In addition, the stone steps at both ends of the gallery houses must be of an auspicious number, and suspended fish sculptures that hang from the bridge house's eaves are carved that include the characters for fish, water, or *rengui* (the ninth and ten celestial stems that together represent water). When adjacent *juancao* (a traditional Chinese pattern composed of rolling flowers) are finished, they are to be sprinkled with water as well.

It is said that gods will only live in shrines if they are built on an auspicious day. Otherwise, even if the statues in shrines are worshipped, gods will not inhabit such places. In addition, the requirement of building stone steps in covered bridges is different from that in private houses. In residential construction, the number of stone steps is decided by numbers corresponding to the five characters 生 (living), 老 (aging), 病 (disease), 苦 (suffering), and 死 (death). But because bridge building is a type of public construction, the number of stone steps at both

ends of the covered bridge is based instead on numbers corresponding to the eight characters 道 (way), 远 (far), 之 (of), 时 (time), 路 (road), 摇 / 遥 (shaky, or remote), 通 (connected), 达 (attains). Bridge builders chant out the sentence corresponding to these characters of "道远之时路遥通达, 何时返乡" meaning: "When there is a long way to go the road stretches far, when can one return home?" However, the first eight characters in the phrase are read silently, and only "when can one return home" is read aloud, in order to protect the secrets of the bridge building craft. Although in the sentence the character read is 遥 (remote), what is actually meant is the character's homonym 摇 (shaky). But this is not stated out loud because 摇 (shaky) implies instability, and hence need to be disguised by another character. Besides 摇 (shaky), 路 (road) is considered an inauspicious character. The characters among the first eight with the traveling radical component "辶" are considered auspicious (道、远、通、达). The character "之" is neither auspicious nor ominous. The numbers corresponding to the auspicious characters are used to decide the number of the steps, which hence could be seven, eight, nine or ten, corresponding to 通、达、道、远 . The number of steps could never be four, five or six, since these correspond to the three inauspicious characters 时、路、摇 . The width and height of the bridge house should also be decided by the eight characters. Normally, they will reach the length of *zhangba*, which is about five meters, the *zhangba* here corresponding to the Lu Ban system of measurements, since eight corresponds to "达", an auspicious character[32].

The measuring practices and taboos used by bridge builders are similar to those used by carpenters in Jiangsu and Zhejiang. This can be demonstrated by their use of Lu Ban rulers. An ordinary Lu Ban ruler is 44.8 cm long, and both sides of the ruler are divided into eight equal parts of 5.6 cm. One side is inscribed with, Nobility Star, Heaven Calamity Star, Heavenly Disaster Star, Heavenly Wealth Star, Official Emolument Star, Lonely Star, Heavenly Thief Star, and Imperial Prime Minister Star. Another side is carved with, Wealth Tree Star, Sick Land Star, Leave Land Star, Righteous Water Star, Official Gold Star, Catastrophe Fire Star, Harm Fire Star, Golden Tripod Star, etc. The ruler is used to both measure units and to use the celestial terms to assess various dimensions to be used based on auspicious or inauspicious designations.

The suspended fish decoration on eaves and *juancao* or *konghuacaolong* (a pattern with dragon and flower decorations) on ridges are the most important decorative objects on the roofs of covered bridges. *Xuanyu* often include a carved fish design on top, and others include characters like *rengui*, or for *shui* (water). This *xuanyu* is used to protect the overhanging purlin from moisture. In addition, villagers hope this small wooden component will protect the bridge from fire. In this sense, it is a talismanic object. Since timber arch bridges are vulnerable to fires, and fish and *rengui* symbolize water among the five elements, local villagers think carving these patterns and characters relating to water can protect the bridge from fire. As for *juancao* and *konghuacaolong*, both are objects that emerge from water, thus they are thought to be able to extinguish fires. In addition, the *konghuacaolong* is sometimes explained by the ancient worship of the dragon totem by the Ou-Yue peoples (sometimes referred to as the Hundred Yue or Baiyue peoples) that lived this region.

5.5 Timber Arch Covered Bridge Builders and Building Lineages

The timber arch covered bridge building lineages in the Fujian and Zhejiang mountainous areas are mainly concentrated in the Zhouning, Shouning and Pingnan Counties of Fujian Province. Ordinary bridge builders are scattered throughout the mountainous areas of Fujian and Zhejiang Provinces.

5.5.1 Bridge Building Lineages Surnamed Zhang in Xiukeng Village, Zhouning County

Xiukeng Village is a natural village attached to the larger Houlong Village cluster in Limen Township, Zhouning County, Fujian Province. It has more than three hundred residents, mostly surnamed Zhang. According to the Zhang family's genealogy, Zhang Gui, ancestral founder of the lineage, moved from Henan to Fujian, where his descendants lived for twenty-eight generations. Later, Zhang Demao, the eldest son of Zhang Yingyi, moved from Haiyao Village in Shoushan Township, Pingnan County to Xiukeng Village, where the family has lived for fifteen generations. According to the research of Gong Difa (former curator of the Shouning Museum), Xiukeng's very own Zhang Xinyou built the Xiangong Bridge in Aoyang Town, Shouning county in 1767. In addition, in 2006, Zhang Changyun rebuilt the Qingyan Bridge in Pingnan County. During the 240 years that passed between the careers of Zhang Xinyou and that of Zhang Changyun, bridge building techniques were passed down for eight generations within the Zhang family. In addition, according to Gong Difa, fifty-six timber arch covered bridges were built, rebuilt, or relocated by the Zhang family in Xiukeng Village, of which twenty still remain[33].

The Zhangs in Xiukeng village have cultivated a tradition of superb and outstanding bridge building technology. Over six timber arch covered bridges with a net span of more than 30 meters were built by the Zhang lineage, including the Meichong Bridge in Jingning, Zhejiang Province, the Baixiang Bridge and Qiancheng Bridge in Pingnan, Fujian Province, Denglong Bridge in Zhouning, Gongxin Bridge in Gutian and Zhangkeng Bridge in Shouning. Among the eight generations of bridge builders from the Zhang family, Zhang Maoxiu, the third generation builder after Zhang Xinyou, was most outstanding. From 1852 to 1894, he directed the construction of fifteen timber arch covered bridges. Among these bridges, the Houshan Bridge in Qingyuan County, Zhejiang Province still exists today[34].

5.5.2 The Xu-Zheng Bridge Building Lineage in Xiaodong and Dongshanlou Villages in Shouning County

Xiaodong Village is an administrative village in Kengdi Township, Shouning County, Fujian Province. Xu Zhaoyu, a bridge builder in Xiaodong Village, built Xiaodongshang Bridge in 1801. His bridge building techniques had been passed down for five generations to Xu Zechang, who later handed down the construction techniques of timber arch covered bridge building to his cousin Zheng Huifu in Dongshanlou Village and then to Zheng Duojin. For over 200 years, bridge construction techniques have been passed down and inherited for seven generations in the Xu and Zheng families of Xiaodong and Dongshanlou villages.[34] Among the timber arch covered bridges in the mountainous areas of Zhejiang and Fujian, few have beam inscriptions confirming the names of their bridge builders. The era is really not faraway The discovery of the Xu and Zheng bridge building families by Xu Yuanliang represents a significant breakthrough in the study of timber arch covered bridge builders in Zhejiang and Fujian Province. In addition, the discovery has provided research material on the construction of timber arch bridge in the mountainous area of Zhejiang and Fujian from the late Qing Dynasty, the Republica of China and early years of the People's Republic of China. As a result the research of timber arch bridge building has begun to be transferred from historical construction and genealogical documents that "cannot talk," to the subject of living craftsmen.

Information about master bridge builders is listed below:

Xu Zhaoyu (birth and death unknown), a native of Xiaodong Village, Kengdi Township, Shouning County, Fujian Province, teacher unknown. He directed the construction of Shangqiao Bridge of Xiaodong Village, Shouning County, Fujian Province in 1801, master builder.

Xu Yuanliang (birth and death unknown), a native of Xiaodong Village, Kengdi Township, Shouning County, Fujian Province, teacher unknown. He directed the construction of Xuezhai Bridge in Sankui Town, Taishun County, Zhejiang Province in 1857, as the master builder.

Xu Bingui (1828-?), eldest son and student of Xu Yuanliang. He assisted Xu Yuanliang as chief assistant in building the Xuezhai Bridge in Sankui, Taishun County, Zhejiang Province, (Chen Zeying, Zheng Fushou, Zheng Qijian and Xue Sinian were the other four building assistants). The bridge still remains. built the Xiaodongxia Bridge in Xiaodong Village, Shouning County in 1878, as the master builder. The bridge still remains; built the Baihe Bridge in the Jingning She Autonomous County, Zhejiang Province in 1888. The bridge still remains.

Xu Shiren (1857-?), eldest son and student of Xu Bingui. He built the Baihe Bridge in the Jingning She Autonomous County, Zhejiang Province in 1888. The bridge still remains.

Xu Shili (1863-?), third son and student of. He built the Baihe Bridge in the Jingning She Autonomous County, Zhejiang Province in 1888. The bridge still remains.

Xu Shizhi (1869-?), forth son and student of Xu Bingui. He built the Baihe Bridge in the Jingning She Autonomous County, Zhejiang Province in 1888. The bridge still remains; built the Dachikeng Bridge in the Jingning She Autonomous County, Zhejiang Province in 1923 as the master builder. The bridge still remains.

Xu Zechang (1892-1951), also named Xu Zexiang, eldest son and student of Xu Shizhi. He built the Feiyun Bridge in Shouning County in 1938. The bridge still remains; built the Danqiao Bridge in Shouning County in 1939 serving as a builder. The bridge still remains. built the Liuping Bridge in Zhuguanlong Township, Shouning County in 1950. The bridge was demolished in 1999.

Zheng Huifu (1895-1978), born in Dongshanlou Village, Kengdi Township, Shouning County, Fujian Province, nephew and student of Xu Zechang. He built Dachikeng Bridge in the Jingning She Autonomous County, Zhejiang Province in 1923 serving as a carpenter. The bridge still remains; built Yangmeizhou Bridge in Shouning County in 1939. The bridge still remains; built Nanyang Bridge in Qingyuan County, Zhejiang Province during the Republic of China (1912-1949). The bridge was destroyed; built Santan Bridge in Taishun County, Zhejiang Province in 1948. The bridge was destroyed by floods in 1950; built Liuping Bridge in Zhuguanlong Township, Shouning County in 1950. The bridge was demolished in 1999; built Nongqiao Bridge in Fengyang Township, Shouning County in 1952. The bridge was demolished in 1981 and was rebuilt in the form of a bridge for a highway; built Shuangshen Bridge in Shiyang Town, Taishun County, Zhejiang Province in 1953. The bridge was damaged; built Hongjun Bridge across the mountain stream at the border of Shouning and Taishun County in 1954. The bridge still remains; built Qianyang Bridge in Kengdi Township, Shouning County in 1955. The bridge was damaged; built Lingjiao Bridge in Wencheng County, Zhejiang Province in 1956; built Buluolin Bridge in Nanyang Town, Shouning County in 1960. The bridge was destroyed by tornado in 1998; built Fujiayang Bridge in Taishun County, Zhejiang Province in 1963; built Tangxi Bridge in Fu'an County in 1963, as a carpenter. The bridge still remains; repaired Luanfeng Bridge in Shouning County in 1964. The bridge still remains; repaired Jiulingxi Bridge of Shouning County in 1964. The bridge was damaged; built Puji Bridge in Xinan Village, Shouning County in 1966. The bridge still remains; built Yangxitou Bridge in Shouning County in 1967, as a carpenter. The bridge still remains.

Zheng Duojin (1929-), eldest son and student of Zheng Huifu, alive and healthy. He built Santan Bridge in Taishun County, Zhejiang Province in 1948. The bridge was destroyed by floods in 1950; built Liuping Bridge in Zhuguanlong Township, Shouning County in 1950. The bridge was demolished in 1999; built Nongqiao Bridge in Fengyang Township, Shouning County in 1952. The bridge was demolished in 1981 and was rebuilt into a highway bridge; built Shuangshen Bridge in Shiyang Town, Taishun County, Zhejiang Province in 1953. The bridge was damaged; built Hongjun Bridge across the mountain stream at the border of Shouning and Taishun County in 1954. The bridge still remains; built Qianyang Bridge in Kengdi Township, Shouning County in 1955. The bridge was damaged; built Lingjiao Bridge in Wencheng County, Zhejiang Province in 1956; built Buluolin Bridge in Nanyang Town, Shouning County in 1960. The bridge was destroyed by a tornado in 1998; built Fujiayang Bridge in Taishun County, Zhejiang Province in 1963; built Tangxi Bridge in Fu'an County in 1963, as a carpenter. The bridge still remains; repaired Luanfeng Bridge in Shouning County in 1964. The bridge still remains; repaired Jiulingxi Bridge of Shouning County in 1964. The bridge was damaged; built Puji Bridge in Xinan Town, Shouning County in 1966. The bridge still remains; built Yangxitou Bridge in Shouning County in 1967. The bridge still remains; built a demonstration timber arch bridge frame for the documentary *Searching for the Rainbow Bridge* produced by CCTV in 2001.

Zheng Duoxiong (1953-), the third son of Zheng Huifu, the student of Zheng Duojin, alive and healthy. He built a timber arch bridge frame for the documentary *Searching for the Rainbow Bridge* produced by CCTV in 2001.

In addition:

Zheng Shoufu, assisted in building the Xuezhai Bridge in Taishun County, Zhejiang Province in 1857. The bridge still remains.

Zheng Yanfu (1919-1999), nephew and student of Xu Zechang. He built Danqiao Bridge in Shouning County in 1939, as a carpenter. The bridge still remains; built Santan Bridge in Taishun County, Zhejiang Province in 1948. The bridge was destroyed by flood in 1950; built Liuping Bridge in Zhuguanlong Township, Shouning County in 1950. The bridge was demolished in 1999.

Zheng Duoxi (1943-), son and disciple of master bridge builder Zheng Yanfu, alive and healthy. He participated in the construction of Yangxitou Bridge in Shouning County in 1967. The bridge still remains.

From the above information, it is not difficult to deduce that the Xu-Zheng bridge building lineage has lasted for six generations dating 110 years, starting with Xu Yuanliang. If we take into consideration Zheng Duojin's construction of the timber arch bridge frame for the CCTV documentary *Searching for the Rainbow Bridge* in 2001, the number will be 144 years. These families have cultivated over ten bridge builders,

who have constructed or repaired more than twenty timber arch bridges in the counties of Shouning, Fu'an, Taishun, Qingyuan, Jingning, and Wencheng in Fujian and Zhejiang Provinces. Of course, the above information is just a rough estimation. In addition, the names, numbers, and locations of bridges are mostly based on the memory of Zheng Duojin and Zheng Duoxi. Only some of this information has been confirmed by field investigation, and other is not quite clear or difficult to verify so we don't record them. In fact, the number of timber arch bridges built by craftsmen from the Xu-Zheng family far exceeds the number mentioned above. Furthermore, their builders constructed several long span timber arch covered bridges which still exist in Zhejiang and Fujian, such as Xuezhai Bridge in Taishun County, Baihe Bridge and Dachikeng Bridge in Jingning County, Tangxi Bridge in Fu'an County, Hongjun Bridge, Luanfeng Bridge, and Yangxitou Bridge in Shouning County. Among the bridges, Luanfeng Bridge and Yangxitou Bridge both have a span length of over 37.6 meters, representing the longest spans in the region. As father and son, Zheng Huifu and Zheng Duojin together built eighteen timber arch bridges in the mountainous area of Zhejiang and Fujian, and eight of them still survive. It is no exaggeration to say that since the late Qing Dynasty to the 1960s, the Xu-Zheng lineage in Shouning County has played a significant role in the construction of timber arch covered bridges in the mountainous areas of Zhejiang and Fujian. Their bridge building techniques and method of team work are worthy of careful study.

5.5.3 The Huang Bridge Building Lineage in Long Bridge Village, Pingnan County, Fujian

There is a bridge building lineage surnamed Huang in Changqiao Village, Changqiao Town, Pingnan County, Fujian Province. Five generations have continued the family tradition since the famous master bridge builder Zhuo Maolong from Xinxiang Village of Changqiao Town passed on the craft to Huang Jinshu during the reign of Guangxu Emperor during the Qing Dynasty (from 1875-1908). Since then, the tradition has been passed down within the family for almost 150 years, all the way into the present. The Huang family has worked on bridges in Fujian Province, including Pingnan, Gutian, Jianou, Jianyang, and Nanping. They have built or relocated over twenty timber arch covered bridges, with eight bridges still remaining, among which Wan'an Bridge has been listed as a Major Historical Cultural Site, Protected At The National Level since 2006. The third generation in the lineage that started with Huang Jinshu is Huang Chuncai who has been recognized as a "second level" Transmitter of Intangible Cultural Heritage within Fujian Province, and a "third level" Transmitter of Intangible Cultural Heritage by the Ministry of Culture. The Huang family is one of the most important lineages preserving the art of traditional timber arch covered bridge building in Fujian and Zhejiang Provinces.

Its notable members are listed below.

Zhuo Maolong, (year of birth unknown) also called Mao Longxian built over ten covered bridges, and rebuilt Wan'an Bridge during the reign of Daoguang Emperor of the Qing Dynasty (1821-1850). He is considered to be a highly renowned bridge builder of the late Qing Dynasty.

Huang Jinshu (born during the reign of the Xianfeng Emperor sometime between 1831-1861, and died in 1933) learned his craft from Zhuo Maolong of Xinxiang Village of Changqiao Town. During the Republican of China he built Jianou's Longxianen Bridge, Jielong Bridge, and Songgangwei Bridge.

Huang Shengfu (1900-1974), oldest son of Huang Jinshu, assisted his father by serving as the assistant master bridge builder of the Longxiacun Bridge in Jian'ou County in the Republic of China. In 1917 he served as the master bridge builder of both the ChimeicunBridge, and the Zengzhang Bridge. In 1932, he served as the main bridge builder during the reconstruction of the Wan'an Bridge in Pingnan County.

Huang Xiangyan (1909-1984), second son of Huang Jinshu. Master bridge builder of the Longxiacun Bridge in Jian'ou County. In 1917 he served as the master bridge builder of the Chimeicun Bridge, and the Zengzhang Bridge in Nanping County. He served as master builder in the reconstruction of the Wan'an Bridge in Pingnan County in 1932 and 1954. He was the master builder of the Tanghuancun Bridge constructed in Pinghu Town, Gutian County in 1969.

Huang Chucai (1936-), eldest son of Huang Xiangyan, and currently a well-known bridge builder in Pingnan County. In 1952, the two northwest arches of the Wan'an Bridge were destroyed along with twelve bays of its gallery house in a flood. In 1954, Huang Chuncai and his uncle and father rebuilt the two arches. In 1956, he served as the master builder of the Qiancun Village Bridge in Changqiao Town, Pingnan County. In 2005, he oversaw the relocation of the Jinzao Bridge in Jitou Village, Tangkou Town. In 2006, he directed the construction of the two column and three span Shuanglong Bridge totaling a length of 66 meters in the Baishuiyang River. He directed the construction of Shijin Bridge in 2008, and rebuilt Baixiang Bridge in 2009.

Huang Minping (1963-), eldest son of Huang Chuncai;

Huang Minhui (1984-), youngest son of Huang Chuncai. The brothers inherited their father's career. In 2005, they assisted in relocating the Jinzao Bridge. In 2006 they assisted in building Shuanglong Bridge. In 2008 they served as assistant master builders in building Shijin Bridge.

The Huang family has passed down its crafts for four generations over almost 100 years spanning the careers of Huang Jinshu, Huang Minping, and Huang Minhui. They built or reconstructed the Longxianen Bridge, Jielong Bridge, Songgangwei Bridge in Jian'ou County, Tanghuan Bridge in Gutian County, Wan'an Bridge, in Pingnan County, Shangqiancun Bridge, Jinzao Bridge, Shuanglong Bridge, Shuanghong Bridge, Shijin Bridge and more. [5]

5.5.4 The Wei Bridge Building Lineage in Zhongyang Village, Pingnan County

There is another covered bridge building family in Zhongyang Village, Daixi Town, located in Pingnan County, Fujian. Starting from Wei Xuexing, the family craft has been passed down for three generations spanning over sixty years. The Wei family does not only focus on covered bridge building, but also works on the construction of other timber structures. Thus, in this sense, the Wei family is not a building family that specializes in the construction of covered bridges.

Wei Xuexing was a self-taught expert timber master carpenter. Afterwards he happily studied how to build timber arch bridges from Huang Yuyun, a timber arch bridge master builder of Hetanglushang Village in Gutian County. In 1948, Wei Xuexing accompanied his apprentices in the building of his first timber arch bridge, the Jinzao Bridge in Jitou Village, Pingnan County. Actually, despite the old age of master builder Huang Yuyun at the time, he was still invited to the building site for guidance by Wei Xuexing. As a result, the upper beam in the gallery house of the Jinzao Bridge is inscribed with black calligraphy of four names: Huang Yuyun, Wei Xuexing, Wei Wanhui, and Wei Chunshuang. The series of timber arch covered bridges built by the Wei lineage are all enclosed within the limits of Pingnan County. Of them, the relatively well known include the Jinzao Bridge, the Guitan Bridge, the Xili Bridge and the Zhangkou Bridge.

The background of the master builders are as follows:

Wei Xuexing (1885-1955), student of Huang Yuyun, master builder of Jinzao Bridge in Pingnan County in 1948.

Wei Wanhui (1913-1971), student of Wei Xuexing, master builder of Jinzao Bridge in Pingnan County built in 1948. Master builder of Zhangkou Bridge built in 1955, and of Xili Bridge built in 1970.

Wei Chunshuang (1919-2008), student of Wei Xuexing, master builder of Jinzao Bridge of Pingnan County built in 1948, master builder of Guitan Bridge built in 1968.

Wei Zeyan (1923-), son and student of Wei Xuexing, assisted in building the Jinzao Bridge of Pingnan County in 1948.

Wei Zhongcheng (1920-1992), student of Wei Wanhui, Wei Chunshuang, assistant master builder of Jinzao Bridge of Pingnan County in 1948.

Wei Xiaokuan (1923-1980), student of Wei Wanhui, Wei Chunshuang, assistant master builder of Jinzao Bridge of Pingnan County in 1948.

Wei Shuntuo (1928-), student of Wei Wanhui, Wei Chunshuang, served as a carpenter in the construction of the Jinzao Bridge of Pingnan County in 1948, and in the construction of Guitan Bridge in 1968.

Wei Zhongtuo (1933-), student of Wei Wanhui, and Wei Chunshuang, assistant master builder of the Xili Bridge of Pingnan County in 1970.

Wei Zhongzhi (1945-), student of Wei Chunshuang, assistant master builder of the Guitan Bridge of Pingnan County in 1968, assistant master builder of the Xili Bridge of Pingnan County in 1970.

Wei Shunling (1949-), son and student of Wei Wanhui, assistant master builder of the Guitan Bridge in 1968, worked as a carpenter in the construction of the Xili Bridge in 1970.

5.5.5 Other Timber Arch Covered Bridge Builders in Fujian and Zhejiang Provinces

Besides the bridge building lineages above, there are many other skilled carpenters, and master and assistant master bridge builders in Fujian and Zhejiang Provinces. Although these craftsmen do not belong to bridge building family lineages, they have formed several bridge building groups in various locations. In addition, there are some clever craftsmen who became talented through self-study of the art. Of course, the majority of such bridge builders were apprentices or students of skilled craftsman despite not belonging to bridge building family lineages or regional professional bridge building groups.

5.5.5.1 The Regional Bridge Building Group in Xiajian, Zhouning County

As mentioned above, there is a family surnamed Zhang in Xiukeng Village, Zhouning County, Fujian Province, with a family tradition of building timber arch covered bridges. The neighboring village of Xiukeng, namely the Houlong, Meidu and Yangping Villages, are all located in Jijiao Hill at the junction of Jiaocheng District, Zhouning County and Ningde, an area people usually call Xiajian. People from these villages often intermarried. Besides Xiukeng Village, there are bridge builders in the other three villages. According to a survey, the covered bridge builders in Houlong, Meidu and Yangpig Village all learned the craft from the Zhang family in Xiukeng Village. Thus, timber arch covered bridge builders in this area share the same title—Xiajian master, also written as ejian in some books.[34]

5.5.5.2 The Regional Bridge Building Group in Xiaodong Village, Shouning County

As mentioned above, there is a Xu-Zheng timber arch covered bridge building family lineage in the Xiaodong Village of Shouning County, Fujian Province. Since the Xu and Zheng families are related by marriage, the bridge building craft was transferred from the Xu family to the Zheng family. As a matter of fact, many carpenters coming from Xiaodong Village or its neighboring villages such as Dongshanlou, Linshan, Loujiping, Ditou, Banlingyang and Houkeng Villages assisted in the bridge building activities directed by the Xu-Zheng family. For example, Wu Yuanming from Banlingyang Village assisted in building six covered bridges after becoming the son-in-law of Zheng Huifu.

5.5.5.3 Other Bridge Builders

Besides the bridge building families and regional groups mentioned above, there are some other famous bridge builders in Fujian's Fuzhou, Nanping, and Ningde as well as Zhejiang's Taishun County.

According to a survey conducted by Gong Difa, Fuzhou natives Fang Zongchuan (1930-), and Huang Lianmei (date of birth and death unknown) built Tangli Bridge and Jiaoxi Bridge in Minhou, Chen Qilao and Chen Shui built Tangli Bridge, Fang Zongdian built Jiaoxi Bridge; in Luoyuan County, native Zhou Lianshou (birth and death unknown) constructed Sanxi Bridge in Minhou in 1845 serving as master bridge builder. Nanping native Lu Musheng (also called Lu Jinrong, 1932-) participated in the repair of Bazi Bridge and Yueyuan Bridge in 1992 in Yanping District; Zhenghe native Yang Xianhua (1937-) constructed the Longtan Bridge in 1962 serving as master bridge builder, Wu Shoumu (birth and death unknown) repaired Cuoqiao Bridge in Yanghou Village, Zhenghe County in 2007, Liu Tingwan (also named Liu Tingfan, date of birth and death unknown) repaired Cuoqiao Bridge in Houshan Village, Zhenghe County in 2001. In 2011, Xu Yunshuang (1965-) from Shunchang County built a timber arch bridge in the Hezhang Rock scenic area.

There are even more timber arch bridge builders in the Ningde, mainly in Zhouning, Shouning and Pingnan Counties. Counties (Districts) like Fu'an, Gutian and Jiaocheng also have produced many bridge builders. Besides the Zhang family in Xiukeng Village and the Xiajian masters, Zhouning County is home to bridge builders from Hexi Village, Chunchi Village of Chunchi Town, and Meidu Village in Limen Township. During the reign of Daoguang Emperor of the Qing Dynasty (1820-1850) Hexi Village was home to Lin Shibing, Lin Tinghuai, Chen Lianjin, Chen Jingsheng and Lin Tingshou—who all served as assistant master builders of the Jiaolong Bridge in Zhenghe County. Xu Shunquan participated in the construction of Sanxian Bridge in Hexi Village, Chunchi Town, Zhouning County while in Taokeng Village, Xu Zhaoquan built the Qixian Bridge. Village in Limen Town, starting with the reign of Guangxu Emperor (1871-1908) during the Qing Dynasty, He Changshan, He Yanbang, He Kaihao, He Changxian, He Kaicheng and He Changrong have served as assistant master builders in the construction of the arches under timber arch bridges; in Yangping Village, He Changyi, Peng Zhitong, and Peng Fudang served as assistant master builders in the construction of such arches; in Houlong Village, He Shengquan, He Shengqian, He Shenghong, He Zhi'ang, He Tiantuo, and He Changyun all served as primary arch builders or as carpenters in other capacities.

Besides the Xu-Zheng family in Kengdi Township of Shouning County, Hu Yiwen and Hu Lingfa from Loujiping Village assisted in building Dabao Bridge in Shouning County during the reign of Guangxu Emperor of the Qing Dynasty. Wei Zhenghan from Ditou Village assisted in building the Dabao Bridge of Shouning County in the Qing Dynasty, Wei Zhengyou, Wei Zhengmu

participated in the construction of Baihe Bridge of Jingning County, Zhejiang Province in 1885. In Banlingyang Village, locals Wu Maosheng and Wu Yuanlong participated in the construction of Danqiao Bridge in Kengdi Township, Shouning County in 1939. In Linshan Village, local Wu Daqing assisted in building the Yangmeizhou Bridge and Ye Ruokang built Danqiao Bridge of Kengdi Township in Shouning County in 1939. In Houkeng Village, locals Xu Changgen, He Tingfa, Ye Xiumiao participated the construction of Danqiao Bridge in the Republic of China period (1911-1949). In Fuji Village of Da'an Township, local Wu Yuncan participated in the construction of Yangxitou Bridge in 1967. In Pingxi Township, Qinyang Township and Nanyang Town, locals Cai Guanglong, Wu Guocai, Gong Ruoyan, Gong Asheng, Gong Shengqing, Gong Sandi, Chen Yingsheng, Gong Minghui, Zhang Qifu all have served as carpenters or have served as assistant master bridge builders. In Xixi Township, Miu Yuwan participated in the construction of Hongjun Bridge, Shouning County. Xiang Gaoyao from Da'an Township participated in the construction of Putian Bridge in Qingyuan County, Zhejiang Province.

In Pingnan County, besides the Huang family in Changqiao Town and the Wei family in Daixi Town, Zheng Daitao, Wu Guanzeng, Zheng Chuanchun and other craftsmen have come from Pingcheng Township. In addition Huang Rongcheng, Ni Dahuo, and Zhang Mingsheng from Shoushan Township, Zhang Shizhuo from Tangkou Township, and Lin Zhenhui from Xiling Township have all served as assistant master bridge builders.

In the Jiaocheng District of Ningde, in 1831, Xiao Zhufeng, who came from the area, served as master bridge builder of the Liren Bridge in Youxi Village, Qinyang Township. In 1963, Zheng Shengjin built the Tangxi Bridge in Tantou Town, and in 1966 built Xinan Bridge in Shouning County's Nanyang Town. In Hetang Town, Gutian County, Huang Yuyun built the Pingnan County's Jinzao Bridge. In Pingnan in 1948, Yu Tianchun participated in the construction of Taishan Bridge in Minhou County and Yu Gengan participated in the construction of Chaxi Bridge. Pinghu Town was the home of bridge builders Chen Naibi Chen Naicai during the last years of the Qing Dynasty, and craftsmen Li Qingyu and Li Qingneng during the Republican of China. In Xincheng Town, native Ding Qiuxiang built the Baihua Bridge in Daqiao Town, Gutian County in 1925[34].

There are also bridge builders in Zhejiang's Taishun and Qingyuan Counties. These include Taishun's Dong Zhiji (1924-2018), who directed the construction of the county's Taifu Bridge, a stone-arch timber covered bridge—in 1948, and the Tongle Bridge in Lingbei Township, Taishun in 2004. Another bridge builder in Taishun County is Zeng Jiakuai (1974-), who built Nanxi Bridge in 2004, Huangtuling Covered Bridge in 2006 and Wuyanling Bridge in 2009. In Qingyuan County, a native builder called Wu Fuyong (1955-) participated in the repair of Yonggui Bridge, Rulong Bridge, and Laifeng Bridge and directed the construction of the Mengzhou Bridge, a two-pier and three-span timber arch covered bridge in Qingyuan County[35].

Reference

1. This argument comes from the author's summary report of *Research on the origin of timber building technology in South China* supported by the National Natural Science Foundation of China. At the same time, it is described and concluded in the paper of "Discussion on Flying corridor and Covered Bridge of the Han Dynasty", which is published on *Architectural Journal* in 2011.
2. See *Liu Dunzhen's Collected Works*, Beijing: China Architecture Industry Publishers, 1987, Volume 3, pp. 448-449.
3. See Liu Jie, *Wood Construction South of the Yangtze*, Shanghai: Shanghai Jiao Tong University Press, 2009, pp.131-135.
4. Quoted from the Yangtze River Committee of Ministry of Water Conservancy, Chongqing Municipal Bureau of Culture, Chongqing Museum, *Sichuan Flood Disaster Historical Materials*, Beijing: Cultural Relics Publishing House, 1993, p.195.
5. (Northern Wei Dynasty), Li Daoyuan, *Records of the Waterways*, Changsha: Yuelu Press, 1995.
6. (Liang Dynasty) Edited by Xiao Tong (Tang Dynasty) Commentary by Li Shan, *Selected Works*, Beijing: Zhonghua Book Company, 1986.
7. (Han Dynasty) Written by Ban Gu, (Tang Dynasty) Yan Shigu noted, *The History of Han Dynasty*, Beijing: Zhonghua Book Company, 2005.
8. See *Liu Dunzhen's Collected Works*, Beijing: China Architecture Industry Publishers, 1984, Volume 2, p. 23.
9. See Liu Jie, *Bucolic:Taishun*, Beijing: SDX Joint Publishing Company, 2001, p.42.
10. See Liu Jie, Shen Weiping, *Taishun Covered Bridge*, Shanghai: Shanghai People's Fine Arts Publishing House, 2005, Appendix I.
11. (Han Dynasty) Written by Xu Shen, (Qing Dynasty) Commentary by Duan yucai, *Shuowen Jiezi Zhu*, Shanghai: Shanghai Ancient Books Publishing House, 1988.
12. Reference to Wang Yu, Huang Xiaodong, *Ancient Bridges in Chongqing-Relationship between Chongqing Covered Bridge and Southern Covered Bridge*, Found in the work *Yangtze River Civilization*, edited by China's Chongqing Three Gorges Museum, First edition, Chongqing: Chongqing Press, 2008, pp. 77-94
13. See Yu Junhai *Sanjiangfengyu Bridge in Guangxi of China*, Beijing: China Travel and Tourism Press, 2002, p. 10.
14. Chen Yunfeng, Zhang Jun, *Ancient Bridges in Yunnan*, Kunming: Yunnan Fine-Art Publishing House, 2008.
15. See Yang Dayu's article "Analysis of the Architectural Skills of the South-West Yunnan's Covered Bridge", in the Proceedings of the First China Covered Bridge International Symposium, 2005, pp. 44-51.
16. Lishui CPPCC Cultural and Historical Information Committee. *Chuzhou Covered Bridge*, Beijing: China Ethnic Photographic Art Press, 2006, pp.152-153.
17. Reference to Fujian Provincial Highway Society, *Fujian Ancient Bridge*, internal information, 2004, pp. 132-133.
18. Reference to Fujian Provincial Highway Society, *Fujian Ancient Bridge*, internal information, 2004, p.145.
19. Reference to Fujian Provincial Highway Society, *Fujian Ancient Bridge*, internal information, 2004, p.136.
20. Reference to Fujian Provincial Highway Society, *Fujian Ancient Bridge*, internal information, 2004, p.146.
21. (Song Dynasty) Guo Ruoxu's *Books and Seeing Records* record of Fan Kuan's paintings, quoted from Tang Yucheng, *Chinese Science and Technology History, Bridge Volume*, Beijing: Science Press, 2000, p.449.
22. See Tang Huancheng, *China Wooden Arch Bridge*, Beijing: China Building Industry Press, 2010, p.3
23. See Su Xudong and Liu Yan, The Double-Three Sections of Seedling Arch Bridges - An Important Form in the Development System of Wooden Arch Bridges, *Huazhong Architecture*, 2010,10.
24. See Liu Jie, Shen Weiping, *Taishun Covered Bridge*, Shanghai: Shanghai People's Fine

Arts Publishing House, 2005, pp. 96-102. See also Liu Jie, Wood Construction South of the Yangtze, Shanghai: Shanghai Jiao Tong University Press, 2009, pp. 200-206.

25. In the article "Research of Rainbow Bridge", Fang Yong believed that rainbow bridge in Zhejiang and Fujian was earlier. For details, see *Journal of Architecture*, 1995, 11, p. 56. Xia Suixiang and Zhang Jun from the Museum of Taishun County, Zhejiang Province, believe that Taishun wood arcade bridge has a longer history than rainbow bridge, or at least an independent development system.

26. See the report of the National Natural Science Foundation of China (Youth Science Fund) project "Research on the Origin and Development of Ancient Wood Construction Technology in Southern China" by Liu Jie in 2003, p.13

27. Fang Yong, Research of Rainbow Bridge, *Journal of Architecture*, 1995, 11, p. 56.

28. See Gong Difa, *Fujian Wooden Arch Bridge Investigation Report*, Beijing: Science Press, 2013, p. 223.

29. Reference Tang Huancheng, *Chinese Science and Technology History, Bridge Volume*, Beijing: Science Press, 2000.

30. See Xue Yiquan, *Interpretation of the Covered Bridge*, Beijing: Chinese National Photography Art Publishing House, 2005, p.15.

31. See Zhou Xing, The Realm and Symbol: Bridge and Folklore, Shanghai: Shanghai Literature and Art Publishing House, 1998, p. 220.

32. According to Xue Yiquan, a scholar of Taishun, he asked the teacher Dong Zhiji of Taishun County about the taboo problem in creating the wooden structure. The above content is dictated by his oral content. These taboos and rules apply not only to the construction of wooden arcade bridges, but also to the construction of ordinary buildings.

33. See Gong Difa, *Fujian Wooden Arch Bridge Investigation Report*, Beijing: Science Press, 2013, p. 15.

34. See Gong Difa, *Fujian Wooden Arch Bridge Investigation Report*, Beijing: Science Press, 2013, pp. 2-7.

35. See Xue Yiquan, Ye Shusheng, *The Traditional Construction Techniques of Wooden Arch Bridges*, Hangzhou: Zhejiang Photography Press, 2014, pp. 177-185.

*The text of some sections and pictures refer to Liujie, *The Architectural Artistry of China's Timber Arch Covered Bridges*, Shanghai: Shanghai Fine Arts Publishing House. 2016, with slight deletion.

Chapter II Covered Bridge Belt in North China

In Shanxi, Hebei and Beijing, there are a small number of stone arch covered bridges or pavilion-style bridges with bridge houses of tailiang structure. The bridges in this area are mostly made of stones. Due to the arid climate, there is no need to build a corridor to protect the bridge from rain, thus in this region, there are only a few covered bridges distributed in different area. However, covered bridges in this area are distinctive with those in the other five covered bridge belts in style.

中国廊桥

第二章 华北廊桥遗存带

在山西、河北、北京等地仍存在少量石拱廊桥或亭阁桥，石桥上方有抬梁式的桥楼。这一地区目前仅存少量廊桥，且地域分散。因北方干旱少雨，桥梁多为石构，不需要建木屋来保护木结构的桥身，因此较少建造廊桥。从廊桥建筑风格上，同另外五个廊桥带存在明显的区别。

第一节 · 皇家苑囿中的亭桥与廊桥
Section I　Pavilion Bridges and Covered Bridges in Royal Gardens

01 — 柳桥

北京市颐和园西堤,清乾隆十五年(1750年)

乾隆皇帝下江南时,见到杭州西湖的玉带桥非常喜欢,即令随行画师绘图,添入自己创意在清漪园(清光绪十四年重建后改名颐和园)西堤建造四座、在万字河建造一座。五座廊桥形态各异美轮美奂。乾隆皇帝为柳桥赋诗"蓄眼云山影荡摇,玉峰矗矗翠林标。榜人曳使樯竿侧,却为比堤过柳桥"。

01.Liuqiao Bridge — Located at the west embarkment of the Summer Palace in Beijing, built in 1750.

During a visit in Hangzhou, Emperor Qianlong was attracted by the Yudai Bridge in the West Lake, so he asked painters to draw pictures of this bridge. Then based on the pictures and his own ideas, the emperor ordered craftsmen to build four covered bridges in the west embankment of Qingyi Garden (the former name of the Summer Palace after reconstructed in 1888) and one on the Wanzi River. The five covered bridges, of different shapes and structures, are exceedingly harmonious and beautiful. Emperor Qianlong once wrote a poem for the Willow Bridge: "Shadows of clouds and mountains are shaking, and Yufeng Pagoda in the green forest is shining. With a pole in hand, the boatman row to the Liuqiao Bridge to see the long dike."

中国廊桥

02—练桥

北京市颐和园西堤，清乾隆（1736—1795年）

方形独孔、石基石梁、石阶石栏、木柱瓦顶亭式廊桥。如法侵略军在1900年践踏焚烧，清光绪末年修整。

02.Lianqiao Bridge — Located at the west embarkment of the Summer Palace in Beijing, built during 1736-1795.

This bridge is a single-span pavilion-style covered bridge with wooden columns, grey tiles, and with steps, railings, beams and a base all made of stone. It was destroyed by British, French, and other foreign soldiers in the "eight-nation alliance" in 1900 and then rebuilt in the late Qing Dynasty.

03—镜桥

北京市颐和园西堤，清乾隆（1736—1795年）

清光绪年间（1875—1908年）修缮。桥墩采用黄色花岗岩石砌筑，台阶两侧、桥台四周的护栏采用青石、汉白玉。桥孔和桥台均为方形结构，亭桥上部由八根木柱支撑圆形双檐八角攒尖顶，寓意天圆地方。桥内绘有彩画。

03.Jingqiao Bridge — Located at the west embarkment of the Summer Palace in Beijing, built during 1736-1795.

This bridge was repaired during the Guangxu reign in Qing Dynasty 1875-1908. Its piers are built of yellow granite, and the guardrails on both sides of the steps or around the bridge abutments are made of green stones and white marble. The aperture and abutments are square in shape. The upper part of the pavilion bridge has a round double-eave pyramidal roof supported by eight wooden columns, symbolizing the concept that "the sky is round and the earth is square" (the ancient Chinese understanding of the universe). The bridge is decorated with colorful paintings.

04—豳风桥

北京市颐和园西堤，清乾隆（1736—1795年）

豳风桥是一座长方形的廊桥，乾隆皇帝命名为桑苎（泛指农桑种植事业）桥。清咸丰十年（1860年）桑苎桥被英法侵略者烧毁。清光绪十四年修整后改名豳风桥。

04.Binfeng Bridge — Located at the west embarkment of the Summer Palace in Beijing, built during 1736 -1795.

The Binfeng Bridge is a rectangular covered bridge. Emperor Qianlong named it the Mulberry Bridge (Sangning Bridge, in reference to the cultivation of mulberry trees, an important part of the sericulture silk farming industry). In 1860, the Sangning Bridge was burnt down by British and French invaders. It was rebuilt in 1888 and was renamed Binfeng Bridge.

第二章 华北廊桥遗存带

05—荇桥

北京市颐和园万字河，清乾隆二十三年（1758年）

清光绪十八年（1892年）按原样修缮。东西走向，长25米、宽4.8米、高2.5米，两侧各有25级台阶。黄色花岗石砌筑桥洞三孔，中孔过得小船。主桥孔两侧设立棱柱金刚䑳，上端斗拱表面站立镇水瑞兽两匹。荇桥从设计选材到施工装饰一丝不苟，美轮美奂无可挑剔。

05.Xingqiao Bridge – Wanzi River, Summer Palace, Beijing, built in 1758.

In 1892, the bridge was rebuilt according to its original form. Running from east to west, this bridge is 25 meters long, 4.8 meters wide and 2.5 meters high, with 25 steps on each side. The three bridge spans are built of yellow granite and the middle one is high enough to allow boats to pass through. The columns on either sides of the span incorporate "diamond" bases built in the form of the bows of a ship. On the columns' *dougong* bracket tops are figures of two auspicious beasts thought to protect the bridge from the flood. Built with meticulous design and decorations, the bridge is indeed very impressive and perfect.

06—水榭廊桥

河北省承德市避暑山庄热河湖，清康熙四十八年（1709年）

承德避暑山庄热河湖东侧界墙泄水闸，于清康熙四十八年（1709年）增辟荷花湖时改建水榭廊桥。由石条桥墩、平梁桥面、木柱木梁、歇山顶凉亭组成。中间大亭五墩六孔，南北小亭各有一孔。廊桥两端各有牌坊一座，横匾保存乾隆皇帝（1736—1795年）题词。南端为"远碧鲸横""晴宵虹亘"。北端为"古嵩碧霞""阆风涤碧"。

06.Shuixie Covered Bridge － Rehe Lake, Qing imperial summer residence at Chengde, Hebei Province, built in1709.

To the east from Emperor Kangxi's Summer Mountain Resort in Chengde there is a floodgate. In 1708 during the expansion of Lotus Lake, the Shuixie Covered Bridge was built. It consists of stone piers, a flat beam deck, timber columns and timber beams and has a pavilion with a hip-and-gable roof. The big pavillon on the middle of the bridge contains five piers and six spans. Small pavilions on the north and south ends of the bridge each have a span underneath them. Each end of the bridge has a memorial archway. Hanging plaque are inscribed with the words of Emperor Qianlong (1736-1795). On the southern end one reads, "the far moon is crossing the sky" and "making the night sky bright." One on the north end reads "the ancient Song Mountain's depth is magnificent" and "Lanfeng Mountain's emits a jasper light."

第二章　华北廊桥遗存带

第二节·庙宇祠观中的飞阁与楼殿桥
Section II Covered Bridges in Temples and Shrines

01—桥楼殿

河北省井陉县苍岩山断崖，唐代（618 — 907 年）

桥楼殿跨越苍岩山崖断裂之间，坐西向东长 15 米、宽 9 米、跨径 10.7 米，地势奇险。清康熙年间上部殿宇焚毁后复建。单跨敞肩拱桥石缝以蝶形铁箍加固，九脊重檐回廊楼殿歇山顶覆黄绿色琉璃瓦。其奇特的创意、精巧的构造、非凡的技艺，在世界古代桥梁史上是独一无二的，古人赞叹"千丈虹桥望入微，天光云影共楼飞"，被列为国家级重点文物保护单位。

01.Qiaolou Temple – Cangyanshan Mountain Cliff, Jingxing County, Hebei Province, built during 618-907.

It runs in an east-west direction between the perilously steep cliffs of the Cangyan Mountain. The bridge is 15 meters long, nine meters wide and spans 10.7 meters. During the reign of Kangxi (1661 – 1722) in the Qing Dynasty, the upper palace was reconstructed after burning down. It is a single-span open-shouldered stone arch bridge with butterfly-shaped iron fasteners for stone joints. Its gallery house is covered by a hip and gable roof with double eaves and nine roof ridges and yellow-green glazed tiles. The structure is exquisite and wonderful. This bridge is unique for its creativity and structure. There is no equivalent to it in the world's history of bridge building. In ancient times it was praised with the lines "The rainbow bridge reaches far into the distance and looks into the sky. It flies by the sun's rays and the clouds's shadows." It is listed as the Major Historical and Cultural Sites Protected at the National Level.

第二章 华北廊桥遗存带

中国廊桥

02—天桥

山西省介休市绵山绝壁，东晋（317－420年）

绵山天桥东西走向，长300余米，宽1米余至5米余不等，因修建在悬崖绝壁得名，为香客通道。天桥距峰顶近百米，距沟底300余米，是中国悬嵌于危岩上最长的栈道式廊桥。原为木柱木平梁结构，后改为木柱石平梁型制，1996年改建。天桥接通军事堡垒"石勒寨"，地势险峻易守难攻。

02.Tianqiao Bridge – Mianshan Mountain cliff in Jiexiu County, Shanxi Province, built during 317-420.

The Tianqiao Bridge in the Mianshan mountains is more than 300 meters long from east to west and is 1 to 5 meters wide at different sections. It earned its name because of its construction on steep cliffs. It was built to facilitate the passage of those on pilgrimages. It is located nearly 100 meters from the top of the mountain's peak and 300 meters from the bottom of a ditch. It is the longest *zhandao shi* (plank-road style) covered bridge suspended on rocky outposts in China. The original multi-span simply supported timber beam structure was changed to a multi-span simply supported stone beam structure with timber columns. It was rebuilt in 1996. The overpass connects a route to a military fortress Shi Le Outpost, and the steep terrain makes it exceedingly hard to attack.

03—二仙观廊桥

山西省泽州县金村乡东南村,宋大观元年(1107年)

始建于宋大观元年(1107年)至宋政和七年(1117年),被列为国家级重点文物保护单位。单孔木拱廊桥长5米、宽1米、高4米、拱跨3米,连同辅助设施全部为木质结构,构造精致、精彩夺目。与实际应用的木拱廊桥如出一辙。

03.Erxianguan Covered Bridge – Southeast Village of Jincun Township, Zezhou County, Shanxi Province, built in 1107.

It was built between 1107 and 1117 and has been listed as the Major Historical and Cultural Sites Protected at the National Level. It is a timber arch bridge with a single span, and is 5 meters long, 1 meter wide, 4 meters high and has a clear-span of 3 meters. The bridge and its associated structures are all made of wood. It is exquisite and gorgeous. Its structure is qualitatively the same as that of an actual timber arch covered bridge.

第二章 华北廊桥遗存带

04—峦桥

山西省沁源县五龙乡灵空山柏子河源头,明中期

峦桥纵横叠木八层为梁,在中国长江以北独此一座。长17米、宽4米、高7米,丹柱画廊,门首、立柱上端及两柱之间,安置彩绘圆雕"龙门雀替"(宋代《营造法式》称'绰幕'),悬山顶厚重朴素,顶脊两端有飞翘"鱼化龙"雕塑,造型优雅别致,装饰华丽美观。

04.Luanqiao Bridge – located over the origin of Bozi River at Lingkong Mountain in Wulong Township, Qinyuan County, Shanxi Province, built in the middle of Ming Dynasty.

The Luan qiao Bridge has eight layers of criss-crossing beams, and is the only one of its kind north of the Yangtze River. It is 17 meters long, 4 meters wide and 7 meters high, and sports an overhanging gable roof. Its gallery house is decorated with paintings and is supported by red columns. Colored decorated *longmen queti* (dragon-gate sparrow braces, also known as *chuomu* in the Song Dynasty construction manual *Yingzao-fashi*) were carved and installed on the gateways as well as between and on top of the columns, creating a simple but stately style. There are dragon fish (a fish that is in the process of becoming a dragon) sculptures at both ends of the roof ridge, the unique shape of which is beautiful and elegant.

第二章 华北廊桥遗存带

05—龙王庙桥

山西省武宁县芦芽山古栈道东端峭壁

木平梁全木结构，四重檐单脊单坡硬山顶，长5米、总高7米、宽1.5米，仅够行人交错通过，在悬崖上开凿洞穴建造廊桥异常罕见。

05.Longwangmiao Bridge – built over the cliff at the east of an ancient gallery road in Luya Mountain, Wuning County, Shanxi Province.

Longwangmiao Bridge is built entirely of wood and composed of timber beams. It has a quadruple-eave flush gable roof with a single ridge and slope. It is 5 meters long, 7 meters high and 1.5 meters wide, only wide enough to allow two people to walk side by side on the bridge at a time. A bridge such as this built through excavating a cave on-top of an overhanging cliff is truly a rare site.

06—仙桥

山西省沁源县五龙乡灵空山一线天绝壁

仙桥下有一块横亘在绝壁之间长约3米、宽1米的条石，即为最早的"仙桥"。仙桥之险天下称奇，绝壁双峡仅隔三尺，下方峡谷深达数十米，越高越窄几近弥合，自古人称"一线天"。单孔石拱上建敞棚式廊屋三间，长10米、宽3米、高9米，双檐悬山顶红柱青瓦。仙桥连同圣寿寺主体建筑被列为国家级重点文物保护单位。

06.Xianqiao Bridge – over the cliffs of a slot canyon at Wulong Township, Qinyuan County, Shangxi Province.

The original "Xianqiao Bridge" was a stone slab 3 meters long and 1 meter wide placed under the present structure. The current Xianqiao Bridge is located between precipitous cliffs of a canyon over a valley tens of meters below. It is known world wide as a fear-inducing bridge. The width of the canyon narrows as its height increases. The tops of the cliffs almost narrow to the point that they meet, and as a result it was referred to as the "single-line-sky" by ancient people. The present Xianqiao Bridge is a single-span stone arch covered bridge 10 meters long, 3 meters wide and 9 meters high. Its three-bay gallery house is decorated with a double-eave overhanging gable roof covered by grey tiles and supported by red columns. The Xianqiao Bridge was listed as the Major Historical and Cultural Sites Protected at the National Level together with the main body of the Shengshou Temple.

083

第三节·源泉景观和水利工程中的廊桥
Section III Covered Bridges in Water Projects and Spring Landscapes

01—分水廊桥

山西省洪洞县广胜寺霍泉口,清代(1636 — 1912 年)

霍泉甘洌醇美涓涓不息,是晋南平原小区域民生饮用和10余万亩粮田灌溉的重要水源,为共享水利,当地百姓在霍泉上建分水廊桥。桥下用铁柱分隔十孔,是早年洪洞、赵城两县分水始发处。南三北七,但实测水流量相近。桥长10.2米、宽3.7米、高2米、跨径8米。

01.Fenshui Covered Bridge – over Huo Spring at Guangsheng Temple, Hongdong County, Shanxi Province, built during 1636-1912.

Huo Spring is important for people in south Shanxi plain, providing them with water for drinking, and for irrigation of over 100,000 acres of cultivated land. In order share the resources of the spring, the local people built the Fenshui Covered Bridge. The bridge is separated by iron columns into ten openings which early on served as the point where water from the spring was divided between Hongdong and Zhaocheng counties. The ten openings are divided into three ones leading to south for Hongdong and seven to the north for Zhaocheng, but the amount of water flow in total diverted to the two counties is similar. The bridge is 10.2 meters long, 3.7 meters wide and 2 meters high, and spans a distance of 8 meters.

02—方亭桥

山西省太原市晋祠，清代（1636—1912年）

方亭桥为单孔石平廊桥，长4米，宽2.7米，高6米。石平梁、八柱抬梁式结构。檐下安置美人靠，卷棚翘角歇山顶。

02.Fangting Bridge – at Jinci Temple of Taiyuan, Shanxi Province, built during 1636-1912.

Fangting Bridge is a single-span covered bridge with stone beams, 4 meters long, 2.7 meters wide and 6 meters high. It is a *tailiang* structure with eight columns. Under the eaves is a *meirenkao* (a "rest for beauties", a traditional Chinese bench with back rests said to be a place where beautiful women would lean on in ancient times). The hip and gable roof is equipped with upturned eaves and a round ridge.

03—洪济桥

山西省襄汾县汾城古镇南关石坡下，金大定二十三年（1183年）

汾城镇是古太平县城。唐贞观七年（633年）创建。洪济桥东西走向，明嘉靖、明万历、明天启、清康熙、乾隆年间修缮。洪济桥原连通陕川两省重要驿道，西疙瘩城门楼尚存，是官道大路关口。中华民国九年（1920年）发大水将桥冲毁，县长纪泽蒲倡导集资重修。

03.Hongji Bridge – down the stone slope of the south gate of Fencheng Town in Xiangfen County, Shanxi Province, built in 1183.

Hongji Bridge, built in the 633, is located in Fencheng Town which was the former county seat of ancient Taiping County. The east-west bridge was renovated during the Jiajing, Wanli, and Tianqi periods of the Ming Dynasty and in the Kangxi and Qianlong periods of the Qing Dynasty. It connected the official courier route connecting Shaanxi and Sichuan provinces. The west gate tower of the town—which served as the entry point for the ancient state highway—has been preserved. A flood in 1921 destroyed the bridge after which county magistrate Ji Zepu organized fundraising efforts to rebuild it.

Chapter III Covered Bridge Belt in Northwest China

The northwest covered bridge belt covers the south-central Gansu and the southern Shaanxi Province. Now it is mainly inhabited by the Han Nationality, while the Qiang Nationality and Baima People are distributed in the southern mountainous areas. As for the extant covered bridges characteristics:
1. Diagonal bracing cantilevers are widely used on the covered bridges in Gansu Province.
2. Covered bridges in southern Shaanxi Province are mostly simply-supported timber-beam bridges

中国廊桥

第三章 西北廊桥遗存带

西北廊桥存在于甘肃省中南部及陕南一带。这里现在主要是汉族居住区，羌族、白马人则分布在南部山区。从现存廊桥特点上来看：一、甘肃廊桥结构上普遍使用斜撑伸臂；二、陕南廊桥普遍为简支木梁。

第一节·渭水流域的廊桥
Section I Covered Bridges in Weihe River Basin

01— 灞陵桥

甘肃渭源县城渭水河，中华民国（1912—1949年）

初为木平梁桥，清同治末年甘肃提督梅开泰重建。中华民国八年（1919年）县长黎之彦主持，乡绅白玉端、徐立朝出资督理，陇西木工名师莫如珍掌尺，建成纯木结构单梁悬臂廊桥。中华民国二十三年（1934年）改为叠梁木拱廊桥。南北走向长40米、宽4.8米、高16米、跨径30米、十三开间，是西北地区唯一大型木拱廊桥，被列为全国重点保护单位。

01.Baling Bridge － Weishui River, Weiyuan county, Gansu Province, built during 1912-1949.

Originally Baling Bridge was a timber beam bridge, and later it was rebuilt under the supervision of Mei Kaitai, provincial commander-in-chief of Gansu Province in the late Qing Dynasty. In 1919, under the direction of county magistrate Li Zhiyan, funded by local gentry Bai Yuduan, and Xu Lichao, and through the work of master carpenter Mo Ruzhen, the bridge was rebuilt as a single-beam timer cantilever covered bridge. In 1934, the bridge was reconstructed as a single-span timber combined beam-arch bridge (also referred to as a re-dundant beam-arch bridge). It has a gallery house with thirteen bays, and is 40 meters long, 4.8 meters wide, and 16 meters tall. It has a net span of 30 meters. An important timber arch covered bridge in the northwest region, it has been listed as the Major Historical and Cultural Sites Protected at the National Level.

第三章 西北廊桥遗存带

02—云龙桥

甘肃省榆中县马御山麓兴隆山，明代（1368—1644年

明末被洪水冲毁，清乾隆年间知县唐鸣钟重建取名唐公村清乾隆、嘉庆年间重建。清光绪二十六年（1900年）甘肃布政使岑春煊拨一千两白银复建后，更名云龙桥。这座桥的部现已替换为加固混凝土拱（梁）。整座桥长为155米，宽3米。桥上设廊七间，桥的两头各有一阁，是歇山顶四角飞的建筑。廊内雕梁画栋，廊顶覆盖琉璃瓦。它被列为省级文物保护单位。

02.Yunlong Bridge – Mayu Mountain and Luxinglong Mountain, Yuzhong County, Gansu Province, built during 1368-1644.

The bridge was destroyed by floods in the late Ming Dynasty. During the reign of Qianlong in the Qing Dynasty, Tang Mingzhong, the count magistrate, ordered craftsmen to rebuild it, and renamed it the Tanggong Bridge. The bridge was later reconstructed during the reigns of both Qianlong and Jiaqing in the Qing Dynasty. In 1900 Cen Chunxuan, the governor of Gansu Province allotted 1,000 tael silver to rebuild the bridge and renamed it as Yunlong Bridge. The lower part of the bridge was then replaced by a reinforced concrete arch. The bridge is 15.5 meters long and 3 meters wide. There are seven bays on the gallery house and each end of the bridge has a pavilion with a hip and gable roof, overhanging eaves and cornice. The gallery house's internal columns are covered with painted decorations and the house is covered by glazed tiles on top. The bridge has been listed as the Historical and Cultural Sites Protected at the Provincial Level.

03—小山门桥

甘肃省漳县贵清山中峰寺山门口，明嘉靖（1522—1566年）

石拱木屋廊桥坐南朝北，长22米、宽2.4米、自高3米。《漳县旧志》记，贵清山"在（县治）南七十里。山峰斗绝如削，中一桥通东西，下瞰云鸟。多产松柏，或大数人围、或十数围，皆突石出。涧底山巅，树皆平齐无参差，密若麻麦。庙宇古迹皆元明时故址，宽敞可容万家，居民每避乱其上，有一夫扼关之雄"。

03.Xiaoshanmen Bridge – Located at the entrance of Zhongfeng Temple, Guiqing Mountain, Zhangxian County, Gansu Province, built during 1522-1566.

is a stone arch covered bridge with a timber gallery ouse. The bridge is 22 meters long, 2.4 meters wide nd three meters high. According to *Zhangxian County ld Records*, "Guiqing Mountain is 22 miles south of the ounty seat. The hills are very precipitous and among the hills there is a bridge on which passengers can look out upon clouds and birds. There are many pine and cypress trees at the top and foot of the mountain which are as dense as hemp and wheat. The temples as well as other ancient sites, which were mostly built in the Yuan or Ming Dynasty, are all very spacious and can hold a large number of people. When faced with wars or other disasters, people will come to this impregnable place for shelter." It seems that easy to defend, but difficult to attack.

04—断涧仙桥

甘肃省漳县贵清山，明隆庆元年（1567年）

断涧仙桥跨越海拔 2340 米的中、西峰之间，是中国地势最险要的廊桥之一。顶峰遗存明隆庆年间（1567 — 1573 年）中峰寺，断涧仙桥、小山门桥是香客上香的唯一通道。有记载的大修、重建十八次，前十七次维持木平梁硬山顶廊桥形制，长 13.6 米、宽 1.8 米、自高 2.6 米，据悬崖谷底 600 余米。2013 年断涧仙桥因腐朽垮落深谷，2014 年重建。

04.Duanjianxian Bridge — Guiqing Mountain, Zhangxian County, Gansu Province, built in 1567.

Duanjianxian Bridge spans the mountain's middle and west peaks, which rise 2,340 meters above the sea level, and exists in one of the most perilous terrain where covered bridges were built in China. The Duanjianxian and Xiaoshanmen Bridges are the only channels through which pilgrims can use to travel to Zhongfeng Si Temple (Middle Peak Temple), built during the Ming Dynasty. According to records, this bridge was renovated or rebuilt 18 times, the first 17 times of which it maintained its timber beam covered bridge structure with a flush gable roof over its gallery house. This bridge is 13.6 meters long, 1.8 meters wide, 2.6 meters high, and rises more than 600 meters above the valley below. In 2013, the Duanjianshan Bridge collapsed due to rot and was rebuilt in 2014.

05 — 鹿仁廊桥

甘肃省宕昌县城关镇鹿仁藏族村口

鹿仁廊桥地处国家4A级景区官鹅沟。原为木拱廊桥，后改为混凝土斜梁支撑廊桥。长56米、宽4.2米、高8米、十四开间，具有汉、羌、藏族建筑相互融合的特征。绘画详尽描述了羌族的发祥、繁衍、生活，并与其他民族和睦相处的场景。

05. Luren Covered Bridge — Located at the entrance of Luren Village of Zan Nationality, Chengguan Township, Dangchang County, Gansu Province.

Luren Covered Bridge is located at Guan'e'gou National Forest Park, a national "4-A level" scenic area. It was originally a timber arch covered bridge and was later rebuilt as a concrete covered bridge with diagonal supporting beams. This bridge, which has embraced the construction techniques of Han, Qiang, as well as Zan Nationalities, is 56 meters long, 4.2 meters wide and 8 meters high. Its gallery house contain fourteen bays, and has decorated paintings tha vividly depict the life of the Qiang Nationality an their interactions with other nationalities.

第二节 · 白龙江流域的廊桥
Section II Covered Bridges in Bailong River Basin

01—中山桥

甘肃省康县云台镇，中华民国十六年（1927年）

曾名月风桥、永安桥。《白马关古城维修碑记》载："中华民国十六年（1927年）白马关警察分所所长王心永于东门外一十八丈处，马莲坝河上建一座穿斗式廊桥。名曰永安桥，后更名为中山桥。为省级文物保护单位。"

1.Zhongshan Bridge – Yuntai Township, Kangxian County, Gansu Province, built in 1927.

Zhongshan Bridge used be called Yuefeng Bridge and Yong'an Bridge. According to *Maintenance Record of Baimaguan Ancient City*, the bridge used a *chuandou* structure named Yong'an Bridge built in 1927 under the order of Wang Xinyong, the Director of the Baimaguan Police Station. The bridge crosses the Malianba River and is 60 meters from the east gate. Later, it was renamed Zhongshan Bridge. Currently, it is a Historical and Cultural Sites Protected at the Provincial Level.

02—康庄桥

甘肃省文县铁楼乡白马河，清光绪（1875—1908年）

白马河畔铁楼乡是白马人居住地。乡民讲述冬季大雪封山，会有大熊猫沿着山路过廊桥到村子里觅食，每家都会拿出最好的东西让大熊猫吃饱。全木结构平梁廊桥长20米、宽4米、高4米、五开间，顶覆小青瓦，两端建有矮泥墙凉亭式门楼。

2.Kangzhuang Bridge – Tielou Township, Wenxian County, Gansu Province, crosses Baima River, built during 1875-1908.

Tielou Township is where Baima People live. Villagers say that when snow seals the mountain pass in winter, pandas will walk along the mountain road to find food in villages, and whoever lives in a house that the pandas arrive at will always give them their best food until the pandas are full. The Kangzhuang Bridge is a timber beam bridge. The bridge's gallery house has five bays. The bridge is 20 meters long, 4 meters wide, and 4 meters high. It is covered on top with small grey tiles. On either end it has pavilion-style gatehouses built with low rammed-earth walls.

03—合作化桥

甘肃文县石坊乡石坊村白水江，明代（1368－1644年）

《文县志》记载"境内石坊古伸臂木桥亦称阴平桥。后改名合作化桥，是文县现存屈指可数的古桥建筑，有着极高的观赏保藏价值""古有阴平桥为铁链式吊桥，是通往蜀道咽喉，明代末年被匪寇焚毁后重建。清康熙四十一年(1702年)和清咸丰六年(1856年)重建木桥。1949年12月，国民党军队为阻止解放军南下，将桥焚毁"，1955年重建。2008年"5·12"汶川大地震后修缮。合作化桥长46米、宽5米、高9米。

03.Hezuohua Bridge — Baishui River, Shifang Village, Shifang Township, Wenxian County, Gansu Province, built during 1368-1644.

According to the *Wenxian County Annals*, this stone archway timber cantilever bridge inside the county was originally called the Yinping Bridge and was later was renamed the Hezuohua Bridge. As one of the few ancient bridges in Wenxian County that survive at present, this bridge is very valuable. During the Ming Dynasty, the Yingping Bridge was a suspended chain bridge which led to Sichuan Province. It was eventually destroyed by bandits. It was rebuilt in the end of the Ming Dynasty, and then again in 1702 and 1856 as wooden bridge. In December 1949, the Kuomintang army destroyed this bridge to stop the PLA from advancing south. It was then rebuilt in 1955. The bridge was repaired after being damaged in the May 12th, 2008 Wenchuan earthquake. Currently, the bridge is 46 meters long, 5 meters wide, and 9 meters high.

第三章 西北廊桥遗存带

第三节 · 茶马古道上的廊桥
Section III Covered Bridges along the Ancient Tea Horse Road

01—窑坪桥

甘肃省康县大南峪镇

《窑坪桥维修碑》记载，窑坪桥在大南峪镇，古称兰皋。唐景福元年（892 年）武州更名阶州后迁治所于此，至后唐长兴三年（932 年）凡四十余年。实秦蜀古道之名驿，属茶马交易之要镇。路始拓于秦汉，桥初架于唐宋，市兴盛于明清。最近一次维修于中华民国二年八月（1913 年）。长三丈三尺，宽一丈六尺，高一丈八尺，跨二长一尺，属廊房式风雨桥。

01.Yaoping Bridge – Dananyu Town, Kangxian County, Gansu Province.

According to the *Yaoping Bridge Maintenance Records*, the bridge originally was known as Langao Bridge and is located in Dananyu Town. In 892, Wuzhou was renamed Jiezhou and its government was relocated to this site for the next 40 years until 932. As an important stop along the ancient Qin-Shu Road, this town played a significant role in the tea and horse trade. In this town, the road was first laid in the time of the Qin and Han Dynasties, and the bridge was first constructed in the time of the Tang and Song Dynasties. Its market later thrived during the Ming and Qing Dynasties. The latest repair work on the bridge was performed in 1913. This wind and rain bridge with a gallery house on top is 10 meters long, 5.3 meters wide, six meters high, and has a span 7 meters long.

02—三功桥

甘肃省康县平洛镇药铺沟村，明洪武五年（1372年）

《三功桥维修碑》记载，三功桥规制沿袭（三公里外）团庄龙凤桥。中华民国八年（1919年）维修，乃茶马古道之遗迹，属省级文物保护单位。古道始于初汉，兴于隋唐，盛于宋明，衰于清末，康县段为捷径、为主线、为枢纽。在历史上曾为国家统一、民族融合、经济发展、文化繁荣发挥过重大作用。

02.Sangong Bridge — Yaopugou Village, Pingluo Town, Kangxian County, Gansu Province, built in 1372.

According to the *Sangong Bridge Maintance Stele*, this bridge imitated the size and structure of Longfeng Bridge in Tuanzhuang (which is 3 kilometers away). It was repaired in 1919, and as a surviving part of the Ancient Tea Horse Road, it is a Major Historical and Cultural Sites Protected at the Provincial Level. The ancient road was established in the early Han Dynasty and flourished in the Sui and Tang Dynasties, prospered in the Song and Ming, and declined in the Qing. The segment in Kangxian of which the Sangong Bridge is a part served as both a shortcut, a major artery, and a hub. In history, it played an important role in building national unity, nationality interactions, economic development, and cultural prosperity.

03—龙凤桥

甘肃省康县平洛镇团庄村，明洪武二年（1369 年）

陇南文物部门 2009 年在康县望关乡发现半块古石碑（存康县博物馆），只有 44 个阴刻楷体字可辨。其中"茶马贩通番捷路"证实陇南"北茶马古道"存在。龙凤桥为叠木平梁全木结构廊桥，长 16 米、宽 3.6 米、高 3.6 米、七开间，连接北茶马古道的"平乐古道"段。圆木纵横排列逐层叠伸，支撑粗长木梁组成基础架构。穿斗式廊屋，檩脚遗留四象、四龙、两凤木雕。被列为省级文物保护单位。

03.Longfeng Bridge － Tuanzhuang Village, Pingluo Town, Kangxian County, Gansu Province, built in 1369.

In 2009, the Longnan Cultural Relics Department found half of an ancient stone tablet (now part of the collection of the Kangxian Museum) in Wangguan Town, Kangxian County. On this tablet, only forty-four incised carving italic characters can be recognized, but among them is a phrase referring to horse and tea vendors to border areas proving the existing of a northern Ancient Tea Horse Road in southern Gansu. The Longfeng Bridge is part of the Pingle segment of this road. It is a combined-beam timber covered bridge. It is 16 meters long, 3.6 meters wide, 3.6 meters high, and has a gallery house on top with seven bays. Logs on the bridge overlap in a criss-crossing manner, and thick and long supporting timbers form a foundational structure. The gallery house is a *chuandou* style structure, and there are wood carvings of four elephants, four dragons, and two phoenixes on the purlin ends. It has been listed as the Major Historical and Cultural Sites Protected at the Provincial Level.

04—古松桥

四川省阿坝藏族羌族自治州松潘古镇中部偏南岷江

松潘古城形似半月形翡翠，岷江穿城而过，桥梁众多，古松桥和映月桥最负盛名。古松桥清宣统（1909—1911）年间焚毁，中华民国六年（1917年）重建为伸臂式木梁廊桥。连接南街与中街，北通镇羌门，南达延薰门。《松潘县志》记"松潘为蜀西北重镇，群山环绕纵贯大江，上接甘凉下通茂汶，其利戎事而便商旅者，实为古桥焉"。1953年修葺改名团结桥，1987年复名古松桥。

04.Gusong Bridge – Minjiang River in the south-central part of Songpan Ancient Town, Aba Zang and Qiang Autonomous Prefecture, Sichuan Province.

The ancient city of Songpan looks like a half-moon-shaped piece of jade. The Minjiang River passes under many bridges, and the most famous of them are the Gusong and Yingyue Bridges. The Gusong Bridge burned down sometime between 1909-1911, and was rebuilt in 1917 as a timber cantilever beam covered bridge. The bridge connects Nanjie Street with north to zhenqiang Gate and south to Yanxun Gate. The *Songpan County Chronicle* states that "Songpan is an important town in Northwest Sichuan, surrounded by mountains and with a river running through it, above is Ganzhou and Liangzhou and below is Maoxian and Wenchuan County, to facilitate military maneuvers and to accommodate merchant travelers, the ancient bridge was built." In 1953, it was renovated and renamed Tuanjie Bridge; in 1987 the old name Gusong Bridge was reused.

05—映月桥

四川省阿坝藏族羌族自治州松潘古镇，明永乐（1403—1424年）

松潘古称松州，初设于汉代。映月桥曾名蚂蝗桥，有岷江上游第一桥之誉。明永乐年间由官府倡导、大商户出资、百姓出力，在城西南修建一座木平梁殿阁式廊桥，跨越岷江将古城各村落与松潘草地连接起来。据说桥旁岩顶大悲寺佛头上一颗夜明珠，映照桥下水面犹如一轮明月，故称映月桥。

05.Yingyue Bridge – Songpan Ancient Town, Aba Zang and Qiang Autonomous Prefecture, Sichuan Province, built during 1403-1424.

Songpan, known as Songzhou in ancient times, was first set in the Han Dynasty. Yingyue Bridge was once known as the Mahuang Bridge. It was known as the first bridge in the upper reaches of the Minjiang River. During the Yongle period of the Ming Dynasty (1403-1424), the government advocated that a bridge be built in the area. Rich merchants invested in the project and common people contributed to its construction. The bridge is a timber beam palace and pavilion covered bridge. It is located in the southwest of the city, and connects the ancient city and its surrounding villages with the Songpan grassland across Minjiang River. It is said that a luminous stone on the head of the Buddha of Dabei Temple (that is located on a rock outcropping beside the bridge) casts light on the surface of the water under the bridge like a bright moon. As a result, the bridge is called the "Yingyue Bridge."

第三章 西北廊桥遗存带

105

第四节·陕南廊桥
Section IV Covered Bridges in South Shaanxi Province

01—东河桥

陕西省紫阳县高桥镇，清乾隆六十年（1795年）

《紫阳县志》载"高桥在县南内权河，一跨西河，一跨东河，清乾隆末杨道仁建。清嘉庆九年（1804年）周❏重建。清道光三年（1823年）周泰兴倡建石桥，清道光❏年（1827年）庞泰然捐修西河桥。清道光十二年（1832年❏周一刚捐修东河桥，清光绪乙己年（1905年）武生金玉堂❏左伦忠募资补修。"为全木结构平梁式廊桥，跨径15米，❏自高3米、宽3米。被列为省级文物保护单位。

01. Donghe Bridge — Gaoqiao Town, Ziyang County, Shaanxi Province, built in 1795.

According to the *Ziyang County Annals*, there were Gaoqiao Bridges that spanned over the Neiquan River in the southern part of the county, with one bridge crossing the Quanhe River's west river and another spanning its east river. The bridges were built in the late 18th Century by Yang Daoren, and reconstructed in 1804 by Zhou Gu. Later in 1823 Zhou Taixing proposed building a stone bridge. In 1827 Pang Tairan funded the Xihe Bridge's restoration. The Donghe Bridge was then renovated by Zhou Yigang in 1832. In 1905, the Donghe Bridge was overhauled with funding from Jin Yutang, and Zuo Lunzhong. It is a single-span simply-supported timber beam covered bridge. Its span is 15 meters, and it is ❏ meters high and 3 meters wide. It has been listed as the Historical and Cultural Sites Protected at the Provincial Level.

02—西河桥

陕西省紫阳县高桥镇，清乾隆六十年（1795年）

西河桥距东河桥150米，采用同样的结构、尺寸和建造形式。木平梁廊桥长10米、高3米、宽3米。古镇享有盛名，是由于遗存陕西全省仅有的2座双梁木平清代廊桥。修缮总监、帮办、经理、首仕、木匠及捐修人士的姓名，铭刻桥顶横梁。尽管被列为省级文物保护单位，廊桥依然是古镇河边居民日常通道。

02.Xihe Bridge – Gaoqiao Town, Ziyang County, Shaanxi Province, built in 1795.

Located 150 meters from the Donghe Bridge, the Xihe Bridge has almost the same structure, size and construction as its counterpart. It also is a single-span simply-supported timber beam bridge. It is 15 meters long, 3 meters high and 3 meters wide. This ancient town enjoys great fame for possessing the only 2 double set of covered bridges built in Qing Dynasty in Shaanxi Province. Names of the bridge's directors of renovations, assistants, managers, chief officials, carpenters, and donors are engraved on the bridge's top beams. Although the bridge has been listed as the Historical and Cultural Sites Protected at the Provincial Level, it still functions as a means for passage for the residents living by the ancient town's river.

Chapter IV   Covered Bridge Belt in Southwest China

Sichuan Province, western Chongqing, Tibet and Yunnan Province altogether form the southwest China covered bridge belt. The Tibetan-Burmese Groups live in the west of this area while the Han Nationality speaking mandarin gathers in the east.

The Hengduan Mountains stretch from the Minshan Mountains in north Gansu Province and move southward to the Gaoligong Mountains in west Yunnan Province, besides the border between China and Burma. These mountains ranges running from north to south form watersheds of great rivers, and also become the migration channel for some ethnic groups.

Migrated from the eastern part of the Qinghai-Tibet Plateau, the ancient Qiang and Di Nationality moved southward and westward along the Hengduan Mountains, forming the gathering region of Tibetan-Burmese groups in western China and its neighboring countries. Currently, there are about 60 million people who speak the Tibetan-Burmese language all over the world, and the vast majority of them live in this gathering region in western China. Furthermore, most of the extant covered bridges or timber bridges in southwest China are also located in this region.

After a massive migration from Hunan and Hubei to Sichuan, in early Qing Dynasty, people speaking southwestern mandarin started to gather in the eastern part of Sichuan Basin and the north part of Wuling Mountains. Southwestern mandarin also became the main dialect in Yunnan and Guizhou Province.

The bridges in these areas take on distinctive features. On the Qinghai-Tibet Plateau, bridges use the diagonal bracing cantilever beams; in Yunnan Province, the covered bridges use diagonal bracing cantilever beams or the arch bracing beams; in Sichuan Province, the bridges are mostly simply-supported timber-beam bridges.

中国廊桥

第四章 西南廊桥遗存带

包括四川、重庆西部、西藏、云南。西南廊桥带的西部是藏缅语群体聚集地，东部则是汉族西南官话群体生活地带。

横断山脉，起自甘南的岷山，自北向南一直绵延到滇西中缅边境的高黎贡山，形成了一系列南北走向的山脉，这些山脉成为一些大河的分水岭，也成为民族迁徙的通道。

古代羌族、氐族从青藏高原东部，沿着横断山脉不断南下和西进，形成了中国西部和临近国家的众多藏缅语群体。全世界使用藏缅语族语言的人口约有六千万人，绝大多数生活在这一区域内。现存西南廊桥或者木桥，多数都分布在上述西部的藏缅语族地区。

四川盆地东部和武陵山区以北的巴蜀地区，在清初湖广填四川后，形成了操西南官话的汉族聚集地。西南官话也是云贵地区的主要方言。

在结构特点方面，青藏高原现存木桥结构上都普遍使用斜撑伸臂，云南廊桥普遍使用斜撑伸臂和拱架，蜀地廊桥则通常采用简支木梁结构。

第一节·渝北渝西廊桥
Section I Covered Bridges in North and West Chongqing

01—五星桥

重庆合川区双槐镇双门村与四川华蓥市庆华镇宝马坎村流溪河，清道光二年（1822年）

一座廊桥跨越一省一市，在中国绝无仅有。五星桥以中线为界，桥南重庆市，桥北四川省。桥两岸几十户村民在农历初一、十五会餐，主食是稻米饭，主菜是豆花，配上辣椒酱，真是香喷喷的。桥上原有6户人家，四川省、重庆市各3家，2012年为恢复廊道，由文物部门劝离。五星桥又名火烧滩桥，长60米、宽6米、高5米、四墩五孔、每孔跨径8.8米，桥廊为穿斗式结构硬山顶。五星桥被列为四川省、重庆市文物保护单位。

01. Wuxing Bridge – over Liuxi River at Baomakan Village, Qinghua Town, Huaying, Sichuan Province and also in Shuangmen Village, Shuanghuai Town, Hechuan District, Chongqing, built in 1822.

It is the only bridge lies at the boundary between Sichuan Province and the Chongqing administrative region. The boundary between the two areas lies in the middle of the bridge, with Chongqing's territory covering the south of the bridge and Sichuan's the north. Villagers from the dozens of families on each side of the bridge dine together on the first and fifteenth days of every lunar month on the bridge. The main dishes are rice, tofu pudding, and chili sauce, which smell delicious. Three families from Sichuan and three from Chongqing lived on the bridge until 2012 when the cultural heritage department moved them away to restore the bridge's covered road. The bridge, also named Huoshaotan Bridge, is a *chuandou* structure with a flush gable roof. The five-span covered bridge with a stone arch is 60 meters long, 6 meters wide and 5 meters high. Each of its spans are 8.8 meters long. Wuxing Bridge has been listed as the Historical and Cultural Sites Protected by both Sichuan Province and by the Chongqing.

第四章 西南廊桥遗存带

02—锡福桥

重庆市丰都县汇南区新建场，清乾隆五十七年（1792年）十月初十

又名赐福桥、石佛桥，独孔木廊结构，古时候方圆几十里百姓出行就依靠这座桥。以前没有大桥，雨季常有行人过河落水与溺亡事故发生。当地乡绅倡导捐资、集资，请风水师勘察地形确定桥址，召集工匠建成。竣工典礼上，路过的新媳妇孙蒋氏文秀在桥心高喊一声"新人踩新桥，踩不断的铁板桥"。从此"媳妇桥"叫响开来。《丰都县志》记"新石桥建成后，一新媳脱簪珥足之，故名媳妇桥"。

02. Xifu Bridge — Xinjianchang, Huinan District, Fengdu County, Chongqing; built on the tenth of lunar October, built in 1792.

Also called the Cifu Bridge or Shifo Bridge, it is a single-span timber structure. In old times it was an indispensable passageway for people from tens of miles all around who relied on it for traveling back and forth. Before its construction there were often travelers who drowned in the river when trying to cross during the rainy season. As a result, the local gentry raised funds for a bridge's construction, and invited *fengshui* masters to investigate the land and determine the location for the bridge and convened craftsmen to build it. In a ceremony during its completion, the bride Sunjiang Wenxiu walked on the bridge, stood in the middle and called out, "The bride and groom tread on the new bridge, over its iron boards that will not be broken." Since then, that the name of the bridge has been also been Xifu Bridge (Xifu, meaning daughter-in-law, is used to refer one's wife in Chinese). As it is recorded in the *History of Fengdu County*, "When the new stone bridge was established, a bride walked on it without wearing her hairpin and earrings, hence its name is the Xifu Bridge."

第二节·渝东南阿蓬江、酉水流域的廊桥

Section II　Covered Bridges in Apeng River and Youshui River Basins in Southeast Chongqing

01—客寨桥

重庆市秀山县清溪镇客寨村平江河

又名中营桥，始终是清溪、龙凤、塘坳等乡的交通要道，兼乡民集会场所。清光绪年间（1875—1908年）增建重檐长廊。1982年水毁两座桥墩按原样修复，2010年维修。这座南北走向石墩木结构平梁廊桥，长58米、高8米。穿斗式梁架木檩结构硬山顶，西廊檐三重檐，东廊檐两重檐。两端建青砖山墙门洞，分别有七和十级台阶。被列为市级文物保护单位。

01.Kezhai Bridge － over Pingjiang River, Kezhai Village, Qingxi Town, Xiushan County, Chongqing.

It is also named the Zhongying Bridge, and serves a route linking Qingxi, Longfeng, and Tang'ao Townships. It serves as the site where market fairs for villagers are held as well. A multi-eave gallery house was added to the bridge sometime between 1875 and 1908. Two piers toppled in a flood were rebuilt in 1982, and the bridge was renovated in 2010. The timber beam covered bridge is supported by stone piers and runs from north to south. It is 58 meters long and 8 meters high. The gallery house is a *chuandou* style structure with a triple-eave flush gable roof on its west side and a double-eave roof on its east side. Either end of the bridge is bounded by an entrance that passes through a gable wall made of grey bricks. One of these entrances has seven steps leading up to it, and the other has ten. Kezhai Bridge is the Historical and Cultural Sites Protected at the Municipal Level.

中国廊桥

02—天生桥

重庆市秀山县溪口乡五龙村，清光绪二十九年（1903年）

　　秀丽山川的感染，铸就了当地人民"朴素至美"的审美观，那里的廊桥是大自然的一部分，连接着"桃花源"与现实世界。曾名板板桥，背靠五龙山横跨溪口河，石墩重檐木结构平梁廊桥长56米、宽7.5米、高8.5米，四墩五孔。两端桥头石墩建于岸畔。穿斗式廊架二十一开间，硬山顶覆小青瓦。两端建有高大砖墙石楼门，桥眉刻有"天生桥"三字。被列为市级文物保护单位。

02.Tiansheng Bridge – Wulong Village, Xikou Township, Xiushan County, Chongqing, built in 1903.

The astounding natural beauty in this area has influenced the aesthetic sense of people here, and there construction of covered bridges demonstrates the principle of natural simple beauty. Here, covered bridges are one part of nature, and serve to connect the "unworldly peach blossom garden" of nature with the real world. Tiansheng Bridge, originally called Banban Bridge, is built over the Xikou River with Wulong Mountain rising behind it. The five-span timber beam bridge with a double-eave roof and stone piers is 56 meters long, 7.5 meters wide and 8.5 meters high. Piers at its two ends rest on the banks. It is a *chuandou* structure with a gallery house containing twenty-one bays and topped with a double-eave flush gable roof covered by grey tiles. There is a stone archway supported by brick walls at each end of the bridge, engraved with the characters "天生桥" in a traditional style at the level of the bridge's brow. Tiansheng Bridge has been listed as Historical and Cultural Sites Protected at the Municipal Level.

第四章 西南廊桥遗存带

03—濯江桥

重庆市黔江区濯水镇阿蓬江

濯水镇商业联合会会长汪绍琪（1959年出生）介绍，"清初期阿蓬江上修建一座两米宽的石墩木梁桥，叫作唐岩桥，连通渝东、黔北、鄂西之间交流贸易。中华民国二十五年（1936年）中国军队为阻止侵华日军南下，派飞机将唐岩桥炸毁，1976年遭遇百年不遇洪水，桥墩了无踪影。2010年10月政府出资，建了这座廊桥。"桥长303米、宽6米、高12米，石质桥墩，全木结构廊道、廊塔。各结构榫头、卯目穿插衔接。2013年11月28日凌晨4时，因火灾焚毁。

03.Zhuojiang Bridge — Apeng River, Zhuoshui Town, Qianjiang District, Chongqing.

Wang Shaoqi (1959-), Native of the area and chairman of the Zhuoshui Town Commercial Association, stated that, "in the early Qing Dynasty, a bridge called Tangyan was built over the Apeng River. It was 2 meters wide and consisted of stone piers and wooden beams. The route it served connected east Chongqing, north Guizhou Province, and west Hubei Province, greatly facilitating trade and communication. In 1936, Chinese army blew up the bridge to stop the southern advance of the invading Japanese army. Then a once-in-a-hundred year flood in 1976 toppled the bridge's piers, leaving no trace of them. In October, 2010, the local government invested in rebuilding a bridge a the location." This Zhuojiang Bridge was timber structure with stone piers. It was 303 meters long, 6 meters wide and 12 meters high its timber members joined by mortise and tenor technology. This bridge was destroyed by fire a 4 a.m in November 28, 2013.

04—迴龙桥

重庆市酉阳县清泉乡龙溪河口，清同治十年（1871年）

单孔八字支撑穿斗式全木结构木拱廊桥，长29米、宽4.3米、高5米、十开间、距水面（非洪水期）40米。龙溪河口是风大水猛的险地，匠师在坚固的基台上以十数根粗大杉木做八字支撑，再用圆木横梁衔接支撑点，上铺木板桥面建廊屋，两端砖石垒砌拱门。各种规格材料铆扣衔固，未用铁钉铁箍，具备很强的抗风抗洪能力。2010年乌江洪水倒灌龙溪河，回龙桥在水中浸泡一个多月未受伤损。

04.Huilong Bridge — over Longxi River mouth, Qingquan Township, Youyang County, Chongqing, built in 1871.

Huilong Bridge is a single span timber arch bridge with *bazi*-shaped supports, and a *chuan-dou* style gallery house. It is built entirely of wood. Its gallery house consists of 10 bays, and the bridge is 29 meters long, 4.3 meters wide and 5 meters high. The river runs 40 meters below the bridge during the non-flood period. The mouth of the Longxi River is dangerous because of the high winds and swift current there. As a result, the master carpenters placed dozens of thick timbers of Chinese fir on top of the rigid foundation to form the *bazi*-shaped supporting members. Then they used log crossbeams to link together the nodes of the supporting members. Timber boards were laid on top of the deck, and a gallery house was built on top with archways composed of stone masonry at either end. All of the bridge's connections are constructed without the use of a a single iron nail or clamp, and it is extremely wind and flood resistant. Huilong Bridge was immersed in the flood from Wujiang River for more than a month in 2010, and even then was not damaged.

05—两河风雨桥

重庆市忠县白石镇中坪村，清嘉庆（1796 — 1820 年）

早期河道架有几条石板，供乡民往来，清嘉庆年间修建石拱桥。中华民国元年（1912 年），乡民集资在石拱桥面上加盖桥廊，从此成为四里八乡赶圩集市。桥长 37.7 米、宽 5 米、高 8.5 米，两墩三孔跨径均为 9 米。桥身使用当地山石砌就，是忠县最高、跨度最大的古桥。2017 年 11 月政府出资维修桥廊，被列为县级文物保护单位。

05.Lianghefengyu Bridge — Zhongping Village, Baishi Town, Zhongxian County, Chongqing, built during 1796-1820.

This bridge originally consisted of a few stone slabs that allowed villagers to travel back and forth. During Jiaqing reign of the Qing Dynasty (1796 — 1820), it was built as a stone arch bridge. In 1912, villagers raised funds to build a gallery house on top of the stone bridge to serve as a market place for nearby residents, and since then it has served as the site for market fairs for people in the surrounding villages. The three-span bridge is 37.7 meters long, 5 meters wide and 8.5 meters high. Each span is 9 meters long. It was built with rocks from the local mountains. It is the highest covered bridge with the longest span in Zhongxian County, and was renovated by the government in November 2017. It is listed as Historical and Cultural Sites Protected at the County Level.

第四章 西南廊桥遗存带

第三节·四川省域内的廊桥
Section III Covered Bridges in Sichuan Province

一、江河纵横 紫色盆地 夺目繁星
I. The Purple Basin with Crossing Rivers Shines Under the Twinkling Stars

01 — 姊妹桥

四川省绵阳市安州区晓坝镇五福村老脚岩晓茶河

清同治十一年（1873年）乡民公议出钱出力建成全木结构木平廊桥。又名双木桥、高桥、五福桥。两座廊桥高矮形制一致、宽窄长短相同，相隔6米，故称姊妹桥。河心岩石为桥墩自成两孔。桥高3.5米、宽4米、长11米。加墩台连阶总长29米。主梁由10根直径40厘米圆木并聚而成。桥面铺设厚木板坚固耐用。穿斗式结构各组构件扣榫工艺不见一钉一铆。单脊挑檐悬山顶。桥头建有牌楼

01.Zimei Bridges – Xiaocha River, Wufu Village, Xiaoba Town, Anxian District, Mianyang, Sichuan Province.

Also known as Shuangmu Bridges, Gaoqiao Bridges and Wufu Bridges, the two bridges were built in 1873 with funds collected by the local villagers. The two covered bridges jointly function to span the river below. They have the same shape and are separated by 6 meters. Because of this they are called Zimei Bridges. A rock outcropping in the middle of the river serves as a shared natural bridge pier for both of the bridges, hence creating two spans. The bridges are 3.5 meters in height, 4 meters in width, 11 meters in length and when including the rock pier in center of the bridges, the combined length of them is 29 meters. For each bridge, the main beam member is composed by combining together ten logs together that are 40-centimeters thick. The bridge's deck is covered with solid and thick timber boards. Every component of the *chuandou* style construction is completed using mortise and tenon technology so that not a single nail can be found in the joints. The bridges' gallery houses are topped with single-ridge roofs with upturned eaves.

02—合益桥

四川省江油市青林口镇，清乾隆（1736 — 1795 年）

合益桥位于江油市青林口镇新街、老街分界小河，原是"飞檐列栏、丹腹浩瀚"通车马的木制廊桥。清嘉庆五年（1800年）春山匪抢劫未得手，恼怒之下将合益桥烧毁。清嘉庆十四年（1809年）乡民募资集材，招募工匠民工建成两墩三孔的石拱廊桥。长 24 米、高 8 米、宽 6 米。清道光二十年（1840 年）多方资助修缮。

02.Heyi Bridge — Qinglinkou Town, Jiangyou County, Sichuan Province, built during 1736-1795.

Heyi Bridge crosses a river which serves as the boundary between the new street and the old street of Qinglinkou Town in Jiangyou County. It was originally a grand timber covered bridge with upturned eaves and railings over which carriages passed. In 1800, bandits from Chunshan Mountain failed to commit a heist, so they burned the bridge down in anger. In 1809, villagers raised funds and recruited craftsmen to rebuild the bridge as a three-span two pier stone arch covered bridge. The bridge is 24 meters long, 8 meters high and 6 meters wide. The bridge was repaired again in 1840 funded by contributions from many parties.

03—太平桥

四川省罗江县城纹江，清乾隆二十年（1755年）

初名启运桥，十一墩十二孔、三阁两坊四廊石拱廊桥，长180米、宽7.5米、高8.2米。清乾隆十八年（1753年）县令叶鉴集资千两白银在东门建桥，桥墩初成便被洪水冲毁。清乾隆十九年（1754年）百姓捐白银5884两，数百能工巧匠历时一年半建造。清乾隆二十八年（1763年）、清乾隆四十五年（1780年）水毁，清嘉庆年间"南北川陕必经之要桥"复建，为安享太平而面得名。太平廊桥一经落成，即被誉为"川西第一桥"。2007年保护性修缮，被列为县级文物保护单位。

03.Taiping Bridge – Wenjiang River, Luojiang County, Sichuan Province, built in 1755.

Originally named Qiyun Bridge, this twelve span stone arch bridge with eleven piers, four gallery houses, three pavilions and two archways. It is 180 meters long, 7.5 meters wide and 8.2 meters high. In 1753, Ye Jian, head of the county raised a large amount of funds to build this bridge at east gate. However, its piers were destroyed by flood right after the completion of construction. In 1754, the local common people donated 5,884 tael of silver for the project and hired hundreds of skilled craftsmen, who completed the bridge within a year-and-a-half. Unfortunately, the bridge was destroyed again by floods in 1763 and 1780. Since the location was of strategic importance between Sichuan and Shaanxi Provinces, it was reconstructed during the reign of Emperor Jiaqing (1796-1820), and was renamed Taiping Bridge, symbolizing peace and tranquility. Once completed, the Taiping Covered Bridge was acclaimed as "the first bridge in western Sichuan." In 2007, it was repaired and was listed as the Historical and Cultural Site Protected at the County Level.

04 — 南桥

四川省都江堰水利工程宝瓶口岷江内江宝瓶口，清晚期

元代称凌云桥。清光绪四年（1878年）县令陆葆德使用都江堰大修工程结余银两，建造一座木质廊桥取名普济桥。中华民国十五年（1926年）重建桥面加宽。中华民国二十二年（1933年）毗河之战爆发被拆毁，战后修复。1958年水毁后将木桩桥墩改为石拱桥墩，增建牌坊式桥厅，改名南桥。四墩五孔长45米、宽10米、高12米。2008年汶川特大地震殃及南桥，经川西能工巧匠整修，于2009年4月1日重新开放，四方百姓兴高采烈犹如过年。南桥有"天府第一桥"之誉，被列为国家级重点文物保护单位。

04.Nanqiao Bridge — Bottle-Neck Channel, Dujiangyan Project, Sichuan Province, built in late Qing Dynasty.

This bridge was named Lingyun Bridge in the Yuan Dynasty. In 1878, Lu Baode, the county magistrate used funds remaining from the Dujiangyan Irrigation System to build this timber covered bridge. He named it the Puji Bridge. In 1926, the bridge road was renovated and widened. In 1933, this bridge was destroyed due to the Battle of Pihe. It was reconstructed after the war. After suffering damage from a flood in 1958, the wooden piers of the timber pile bridge were replaced by stone piers for a stone arch bridge, and and a new pavilion and memorial archways were constructed on top as well. Afterwards, the bridge was renamed as the Nanqiao Bridge. This five span bridge with four piers is 45 meters long, 10 meters wide and 12 meters high. In 2008, it was destroyed by the Wenchuan Earthquake and was reopened on April 1, 2009, after being renovated by skilled craftsmen from western Sichuan. People from far and wide were overjoyed to witness its reopening, with spirits as high as during the celebration of the lunar new year. Nanqiao Bridge, known as the "First Bridge of Chengdu", the Major Historical and Cultural Sites Protected at the National Level.

05—安顺廊桥

四川省成都市滨江东路南河，元代（1271－1368年）

原名长虹桥，清乾隆十一年（1746年）华阳（成都县）县令安洪德重修，桥下是古码头。1947年、1981年两次发大水，古桥无存。2002年复建三孔廊桥。长81米、宽6米，叠檐歇山顶。作家鲁晓敏撰文称："公元1287年前后某日，受忽必烈派遣的马可·波罗由大都（北京）辗转来到成都。第二日清晨推开驿站窗户时，意大利人看到了一幅令他感到震撼的景象，一座叫'安顺廊桥'的桥梁，像长龙一样游荡在800米宽的锦江上，感慨道'世界之人无有能想象其甚者'。"

05.Anshun Covered Bridge – South River, Binjiang East Road, Chengdu, Sichuan Province, built during 1271-1368.

Initially named Changhong Bridge the Anshun Covered Bridge was rebuilt by An Hongde, the head of Huayang County in 1746. Under the bridge, there is an ancient wharf. The bridge was destroyed by floods in 1947 and 1981, leaving no trace of the original bridge. It was rebuilt in 2002 as a three span covered bridge. This bridge is 81 meters long and 6 meters wide, and boasts a hip and gable roof with stacked eaves. According to the author Lu Xiaomin, in 1287 Marco Polo was sent from Beijing to Chengdu by Kublai Khan. When he opened his window in the morning after his arrival, he saw this grand bridge which greatly impressed him. He remarked that the bridge resembled a dragon outstretched over the 800-meter wide Jinjiang River, a site he thought unimaginable to people throughout the world.

06—遍能桥

四川省乐山市大佛景区与尤乌寺之间分水渠，1976年

原名大濠桥。战国时代水利的工程专家李冰，修建都江堰到乐山，看到大渡河、青衣江、岷江汇流凌云山麓，水患甚大，遂开辟一条分水渠。自此往来凌云山与乌龙山就要过河，先修建了一座便桥，枯水季节尚可来往。清代改建铁索桥，行走时摇晃不定。1976年尤乌寺方丈遍能（1906—1999年，乐山人）大师筹资建成两墩三孔石拱廊桥。百姓为纪念遍能大师的功德，改桥名"遍能"。

06.Bianneng Bridge — Across the diversion channel between the Giant Stone-Buddha Scenic Spot and Youwu Temple, Leshan, Sichuan Province, built in 1976.

This bridge was originally named Dahao Bridge. Li Bing, an expert in water conservancy during the Warring States Period (475-221 B.C.), went to Leshan after finishing the Dujiangyan Irrigation Project. Here, he saw the Dadu River, Qingyi River and Minjiang River all combined as one at the foot of Lingyun Mountain, greatly increasing the risk of floods there. As a result he instructed that a water diversion channel be built there. After it was completed, a temporary bridge was built over it so that people could cross the channel. This bridge only allowed people to cross during the dry season. In the Qing Dynasty, it was rebuilt as a chain bridge which would shake from side to side when people walked over it. In 1976, Bianneng (1906-1999, born in Leshan), the abbot of Youwu Temple, raised money to build a three-span stone arch covered bridge here with two piers. In order to commemorate Bianneng, the bridge was named after him.

二、山泉终日伴佛灯——峨眉山伏虎寺

II. Fuhu Temple in Emei Mountain, Springs Murmur by the Buddha All Day Long

01—虎溪桥

四川省乐山市峨眉山伏虎寺山上端，清顺治八年（1651年）

　　明代胡世安撰《峨眉山道理纪》载："南宋绍兴三年（1133年）有虎为患，土性和尚特建'尊胜幢'于无量佛殿前溪边以镇之，虎患乃绝。"虎溪桥始建于清顺治八年（1651年），是伏虎寺三座廊桥中最小的，长5.6米、宽3米、高7.2米，一墩两孔平梁全木结构穿斗式廊桥。两侧设置木栏，两端建四角飞檐小阁，顶部满铺小青瓦。据虎溪精舍老年僧人介绍，虎溪桥、虎啸桥、虎浴桥自建成以来，从未损毁，一旦残旧即雇工修缮。

01.Huxi Bridge – Fuhu Temple, Emei Mountain, Leshan, Sichuan Province, built in 1651.

In the Ming Dynasty, Hu Shi'an wrote the *Emei Mountain Records* which states "in 1133, tigers posed a threat to local people. In order to solve this problem, a monk named Shixing erected a *zunshengzhuang*. He placed the stone tablet beside the river in front of the Amitabha Buddha Hall, resulting in the cessation of attacks by tigers." The construction of the Huxi Bridge started in 1651. It is the smallest of the three covered bridges by the Fuhu Temple, and consists of two spans and one pier. It is a timber beam bridge, 5.6 meters long, 3 meters wide, and 7.2 meters high. It is a *chuandou* structure, with wooden railings on both sides. It supports pavilions on either end with four cornices and upturned eaves and is covered with grey tiles. According to the older monks and nuns who reside by Huxi Monastery, the Huxi Bridge, Huxiao Bridge and Huyu Bridge have never been damaged, but as soon as any maintenance on the bridges is required, it is done immediately.

第四章　西南廊桥遗存带

中国廊桥

02—虎啸桥
四川省乐山市峨眉山伏虎寺山腰

　　虎啸桥长 9.9 米、宽 3.3 米、高 8.6 米，为独孔石拱全木结构、穿斗式廊桥。两侧设置木栏。廊桥两端建四角飞檐小阁，顶部铺满小青瓦。

02.Huxiao Bridge — Mountainside of Fuhu Temple, Emei Mountain, Leshan, Sichuan Province.

This is a stone arch timber frame covered bridge with a single span. It is 9.9 meters long, 3.3 meters wide, and 8.6 meters high. The bridge's gallery house is a *chuandou* structure with timber railing on both sides. Small pavilions stand either side of the bridge, topped with upturned eaves on all four corners and covered with small grey tiles.

03 — 虎浴桥

四川省乐山市峨眉山伏虎寺山脚

清顺治八年（1651年）伏虎寺重修一新，更名虎溪精舍。同时增建三座廊桥，自山门上行至寺门，分别为虎浴桥、虎啸桥、虎溪桥。虎浴桥长13.6米、宽3.6米、高9.6米，为一墩两孔平梁全木结构、穿斗式廊桥。桥廊两侧设置木栏，两端建双层四角飞檐小阁，顶部满铺小青瓦。石墩两端上水处设首，下水处设尾，有蛟龙镇制水患意味。

03. Huyu Bridge — Piedmont of Fuhu Temple in Emei Mountain, Leshan, Sichuan Province.

In 1651, Fuhu Temple was renovated and renamed as Huxi Monastery. At this time, three covered bridges were built from the path from the gate to the mountain to the entrance to the temple. These bridges were the Huyu Bridge, Huxiao Bridge, and Huxi Bridge. The Huyu Bridge is 13.6 meters long, 3.6 meters wide, and 9.6 meters high. It is a two-span timber beam bridge. The gallery house is a *chuandou* structure, with wooden railing on both sides. Two-story pavilions with four cornices and upturned eaves are found on either end of the bridge, covered by small grey tiles. At the ends where there is a stone pier, there is a dragon head above the water, and a dragon tail beneath the water, representing the idea that the scaly dragon is safeguarding against the threat of flooding.

三、龙溪畅流——宜宾龙华镇
III. Longxi River at Longhua Town, Yibin

龙华凉桥

四川省宜宾市屏山县龙华镇龙溪

龙华镇宋代始建，为国家级历史文化名镇。发源于大凉山的龙溪奔镇而过，凉桥跨龙溪建造。四墩五孔，木柱木梁，石平瓦顶廊桥。桥墩为石墙形制，上流墩首迎浪石柱上各蹲一只石狮。《龙华凉桥志》记："原名清虹桥，建于清代光绪年间。廊桥式样奇巧美观，为龙华古镇标志性建筑。逢年过节、赶场办事，镇上的人都要集在凉桥之畔，平常也为古镇人众纳凉休闲之胜地。1964 年、1974 年修葺。"

Longhualiang Bridge ~ Dragon Brook, Longhua Town, Pingshan County, Yibin, Sichuan Province.

Longhua Town was built in the Song Dynasty and is the National Famous Historical and Cultural Town in China. The Longxi Brook, which originates in the Daliang Mountains, passes through the town, and the bridge spans it. It is a covered bridge with four piers and five spans, with timber columns, timber beams and a roof covered with flat stone tiles. The piers are in the shape of stone walls with lions squatting on top, greeting the onooming waters. The *Chronicles of Longhualiang Bridge* records that "formerly known as Qinghong Bridge, the bridge was built during 1871-1908. The style of the covered bridge is interesting and appealing. It is the most famous architectural landmark in the ancient town of Longhua Ancient Town. During the Lunar New Year, or when going to the fair, people in the town gather besides the bridge, which is a famous scenic site and a place for the locals to enjoy and to cool down by. It was repaired in 1964 and 1974."

四、青衣江畔茶马古道东起点——雅安

IV. Ya'an by Qingyi River, the East Starting Point of the Ancient Tea Horse Road

雅州廊桥

四川省雅安市青衣江,清乾隆三十九年(1774年)

又名雅安廊桥,始建于清乾隆三十九年(1774年),依次为简易木桥、铁索桥、石拱桥。现桥于2005年8月建造,长240米、宽22米、三墩四孔、五殿四阁式大型廊桥。雅安市地处川藏、川滇公路交会处。素有川西咽喉、藏川门户、民族走廊之称。雅安边茶从唐代开始传入彝族地区和西藏,是中国南路茶马古道起点。

Yazhou Covered Bridge — Qingyi River, Ya'an, Sichuan Province, built in 1774.

Also known as the Ya'an Covered Bridge, it was built in 1774. It has gone through several transformations—from a simple timber bridge to a iron chain bridge, and finally becoming a stone arch bridge. The present bridge was built in August, 2005. It is 240 meters long, 22 meters wide, with three piers and four spans. On top it supports four pavilions and five halls. Ya'an is located at the intersection of the Sichuan-Tibet and Sichuan-Yunnan highways. It is known as "the strategic passage of western Sichuan Province" "the gate to Tibet" and "the pathway of nationalities." During the Tang Dynasty, the tea from the Ya'an border regions was introduced to the Yi Nationality area and to Tibet, and it served as the starting point of the southern Ancient Tea Horse Road.

第四节 · 云南省域内的廊桥
Section IV Covered Bridges in Yunnan Province

一、大理白族自治州云龙县廊桥
I. Covered Bridges in Yunlong County, Dali Bai Autonomous Prefecture

01—通京桥

云南省云龙县长新乡大包罗村沘江，清乾隆四十一年（1776年）

曾名通金桥，因附近"白羊厂"出产的白银运往北京，取"财通京城"之意。清乾隆四十九年（1784年）、清道光十九年（1839年）、1962年维修。1993年8月29日被百年不遇山洪冲毁，1994年6月依照古貌修复。独孔全木结构伸臂式廊桥，大小构件采用木桁扣榫连接。与浙南、闽北木拱廊桥有差别，但同属木拱廊桥。

01.Tongjing Bridge — Dabaoluo County, Changxin Township, Yunlong County, Yunnan Province, across the Bijiang River, built in 1776.

The bridge was originally known as Tongjin Bridge. Later, since the silver ore from the Baiyang Mine was transported from here to the capital Beijing, the bridge was renamed "Tongjing Bridge" (in Chinese, *tong* means transport, and *jing* means capital, which then, as now, was Beijing). Three major repairs on the bridge were conducted in 1784, 1839 and 1962. In August 1993, the bridge was damaged by a one-in-a-hundred-year flood and in June 1994, it was rebuilt in accordance with its old look. It is a single-span timber cantilever covered bridge. Both its large and small components are connected through the use of timber crosspieces and mortise and tenon joins. It is different from the timber arch bridges in southern Zhejiang Province and northern Fujian Province, but it still can be considered to be a timber arch bridge.

中国廊桥

02 — 检槽桥

云南省云龙县检槽乡

始建于清代晚期，斜梁支撑式全木结构廊桥，长 18.5 米、宽 2.5 米、净跨 10.5 米。廊屋内设立柱支撑廊顶，廊柱下设置木质长凳和护栏。廊桥两侧各建有一间亭屋，悬山顶覆小青瓦。

02.Jiancao Bridge — Jiancao Township, Yunlong County, Yunnan Province.

Built in the late Qing Dynasty, it is a timber covered bridge with diagonal supporting members. It is 18.5 meters long, 2.5 meters wide, and has a span of 10.5 meters. Its gallery house is supported by columns. Under the columns there are wooden benches and guardrails. There are pavilion houses on either end of the bridge, topped with overhanging gable roof covered by grey tiles.

03—双龙桥

云南省云龙县白石乡东侧山谷

山谷溪流汇入沘江犹如两条飞龙,双龙桥因此得名。木拱伸臂支撑式全木结构廊桥,长22米、宽2.6米、高4米。两侧有护栏木凳,桥亭歇山顶覆杂花瓦。《云龙县志》记:"清乾隆三十五年(1770年)白羊厂开采铜矿,年产黄铜10.8万两。清乾隆三十八年(1773年)开办银矿,年产白银41.72万两。双龙桥是白羊厂矿产重要通道之一。"被列为县级文物保护单位。

03.Shuanglong Bridge — Eastern valley of Baishi Township, Yunlong County, Yunnan Province.

The valley streams that flow into the Bijiang River here resemble the shape of two flying dragons, and this is how Shuanglong (in Chinese means double dragon) Bridge got its name. As a timber arch covered bridge, it is 22 meters long, 2.6 meters wide and 4 meters tall. There are guardrails on both sides and its bridge pavilion is covered with a hip and gable roof topped with a variety of tile types. According to *The Record of Yunlong County*, in 1770 the Baiyang Copper Mine here was producing about 5,400 kilograms of brass metal per year, and in 1773 started to mine silver, with an output of about 208,600 kilograms of silver per year. Shuanglong Bridge once served as an important road for the transport of resources from the Baiyang Mine. Currently it is listed as the Historical and Cultural Sites Protected at the County Level.

04—彩凤桥

云南省云龙县白石乡顺荡村，明崇祯（1628—1644年）

又名大花桥，始建于明崇祯年间（1628—1644年），是连通兰坪、鹤庆、丽江、剑川要津，也是顺荡五井盐产运往滇西北乃至西藏地区盐马古道的必经节点。木梁单跨伸臂式廊桥长33.3米、宽4.7米、跨径27米、高11.3米。桥架采用方木交错叠架逐层高拱，使用大木梁合龙，被列为县级文物保护单位。

04.Caifeng Bridge — Shundang Village, Baishi Towenship, Yunlong County, Yunan Province, built during 1628-1644.

It is also called Dahua Bridge. It was constructed sometime between 1628 and 1644. It connects Lanping, Heqing, Lijiang and Jianchuan. It also was an essential node on the Ancient Salt and Horse Road for the transportation of salt from Yunnan's historically renowned five salt wells (one of which was located in Shundang Village) to northwest Yunnan and even to Tibet. The covered bridge is a single-span timber cantilever arch-beam bridge. It has a total length of 33.3 meters, a width of 4.7 meters, a span of 27 meters and a height of 11.3 meters. The bridge has a high arch formed by stacking staggered square timbers. The arch is closed with the use of large timber beams. It is listed as the Historical and Cultural Sites Protected at the County Level.

第四章 西南廊桥遗存带

05—永镇桥

云南省云龙县长新乡大达河，清乾隆六年（1741 年）

建于清乾隆六年（1741 年），清光绪元年（1875 年）重修。1985 年毁于山洪，1987 年复修。长 26 米，宽 4.8 米，跨径 16 米。桥堍上部土砖砌筑凉亭门楼。桥口竖立粗大半圆顶方柱，外侧设挡雨板，内侧安放木凳。凉亭上设卷棚顶，门楼对角悬山顶覆花青瓦。永镇桥属伸臂式木拱廊桥，云龙县、腾冲市各遗存三座。与浙江、福建木拱廊桥的区别，是两侧各加装一组梯形方梁作为辅助支撑。

05.Yongzhen Bridge – Changchun Village over Dada River, Changxin Township, Yunlong County, Yunnan Province, built in 1741.

The bridge was constructed during 1741, was rebuilt in 1875 and restored in 1987 after being destroyed by a mountain flood in 1985. The bridge is 26 meters long, 4.8 meters wide, 11 meters heigh and has a span of 16 meters. Above its abutments are pavilion archways formed from adobe bricks. At the entrance, there is a large semi-circular column. Skirts run alongside the perimeter to protect the bridge from rain, and wooden benches are placed inside. The *juanpengding* (round ridge roofs) cover the pavilion, and the slopes of the gables on the gate building are topped with different types of grey tiles. Yongzhen Bridge is a timber cantilever arch covered bridge. Similar covered bridges can be found in Yunlong, Tengchong and Fengqing Counties. These bridges install trapezoidal assemblage of beams on each side to serve as auxiliary supports, making them unlike the timber arch beams in Zhejiang and Fujian.

06 — 龙潭桥

云南省巍山彝族回族自治县巍宝山文昌宫

龙潭桥又名文龙亭桥。文昌宫住持阎永仁道长（大理州道教协会副会长）介绍，"寺观建于三国时代（220—280年）"，龙潭桥也是那个时候建的。"由石台、木柱、飞檐翘角歇山顶组成水榭亭桥，具有云南大屋顶建筑风格。桥亭主脊较高，有朵梅、卷草装饰。四檐头各蹲"鱼化龙"兽吻一尊。桥亭顶部覆青色筒瓦，椽头置有图案各异的瓦当。柱头、横梁、斗拱、额枋均遗存精美华丽彩绘。

6. Longtan Bridge — Wenchang Palace, Weibao Mountain, Weishan Yi and Hui Autonomous County, Yunnan Province.

is also known as the Wenlongting Bridge. an Yongren, Vice President of the Dali aoist Association, who presides over the enchang Palace-Temple, explained that he temple was built in the Three Kingdoms eriod (220-280), and Longtan Bridge was uilt at the same time. This waterside pavilion bridge is composed of a stone platform, timber columns, and a hip and gable roof with upturned eaves at the corners. The large roof is characteristic of Yunnan style architecture. The main ridge of the bridge pavilion is high, decorated with assorted plum and scroll grass patterns. Each of the four eaves is decorated with fish-turning-into-dragon ornaments. The top of the bridge pavilion is covered with grey semi-circular tiles, and the ends of the rafters (called *wadang*) are carved with different patterns. The bridge's columns, crossbeams, *dougong* brackets, and remaining plaques are all beautifully painted.

二、龙川江流域的廊桥
II. Covered Bridges in Longchuan River Basin

01—高桥

云南省云龙县界头镇高桥村龙川江崖口，明成化二年（1466年）

两墩三孔木梁廊桥，长35米、宽2米、高25米，是桥墩最高的中国廊桥。龙川江发源于高黎贡山，在高桥峡谷骤然收拢，水流较大。界头镇副镇长杜福广（1963年出生、界头镇张家营村人）介绍，"雨季龙川江急流撞击高桥峡谷石壁，河谷沟崖壁表面伤痕累累。老辈人家讲是龙爪刨腾的痕迹，但是奈何高桥不得。"

01.Gaoqiao Bridge — Longchuan River, Gaoqiao Village, Jietou Town, Yunlong County, Yunnan Province, built in 1466.

This timber beam covered bridge has two piers and three spans. It is 35 meters long, 2 meters wide and 25 meters high. It has the highest piers of all covered bridges in China. Longchuan River has its source in Gaoligong Mountain and its large volume accumulates upon entering Gaoqiao Canyon. Du Fuguang, vice mayor of Jietou Town (born in 1963 in Jietou Town, Zhangjiaying Village), explained that during the rainy seasons, the rapid stream of the Longchuan River dashes against the cliffs of Gaoqiao Gorge, and as result the surface of the cliff walls are riddle with abrasions. Old people say this is a sign of dragon's paw, one though that is helpless whe met with the Gaoqiao Bridge.

02—太极桥

云南省腾冲市腾越镇大盈江瀑布顶峰峡谷

清光绪七年（1881年）重修。石墩石梁、石阶石柱、石栏石雀替、石斗拱石椽、石扁石顶筑成的亭式廊桥，南北对称单孔跨径5.5米，船艏型桥墩牢踞河心岩石高1.7米，两端叠梁悬臂支撑桥亭连接两岸。石亭高4.8米，宽3.5米，桥墩东西两侧有龟首蛇尾石雕。精妙独特秀丽至美，坚固耐久稳固无摧，业界誉之为建筑精品，被列为市级文物保护单位。

02.Taiji Bridge — Dayingjiang Waterfall Peak Canyon, Tengyue Town, Tengchong County, Yunnan Province.

It was rebuilt in 1881. This pavilion style covered bridge is composed of piers, beams, steps, columns, railings, sparrow braces (*queti*), dougong brackets, plaques, and a roof, all made of stone. Its symmetrical pair of north-south spans each cover a distance of 5.5 meters. The ship-bow shaped pier on the rock in the river's center is 1.7 meters tall. The two ends of the combined beam cantilevers supporting the bridge pavilion are attached to each of the respective banks. The stone pavilion is 4.8 meters high and 3.5 meters wide. On the east and west sides of the pier there are turtle heads and brittle stars (a species closely related to starfish), carved in the stone. Exquisite, unique, elegant, strong and unbroken, it is a renowned masterpiece. It is listed as the Historical and Cultural Sites Protected at the Municipal Level.

03—成德桥

云南省腾冲市曲石乡菁桥村龙川江，清乾隆三十年（1776年）

始建于明末清初，清末云南战乱时被烧毁，清光绪八年（1882年）重建为铁索桥，1942年当地驻军为了阻止日军将铁索桥炸毁，1947年重建为木拱廊桥，又名野猪箐桥。长29米、宽2.2米、高10米、跨径18米。桥身采用楸木建成，桥下部使用了伸臂和斜撑。桥身下的伸臂梁头，用铁索拴住，斜拉在两侧桥头石上，形成上有斜拉索，下有斜撑伸臂、桥廊上部密布剪刀撑的复合结构。该桥结构独特，是龙川江上最具代表性的木拱廊桥。

03.Chengde Bridge — Longchuan River, Qingqiao Village, Qushi Township, Tengchong County, Yunnan Province, built in 1776.

It was originally built at the end of Ming Dynasty and the beginning of Qing Dynasty. During the end of Qing Dynasty during rebellion in Yunnan Province, it was burned and destroyed. In 1882, it was rebuilt as a cable bridge. In 1942, a local garrison, in order to prevent the Japanese army from crossing the bridge, blew it up. It was rebuilt as a timber arch covered bridge in 1947. It is also known as the Yezhuqing Bridge. It is 29 meters long, 2.2 meters wide, 10 meters high, and has a clear span 18 meters long. The bridge was built using catalpa timber, and its lower structure is composed of cantilevers and diagonal bracing. On the rocks on both abutments, the ends of the cantilever beam are attached to iron chain fasteners and cable-stays. The structure is made of a composite of cables stays, with cantilevers and diagonal supports in the lower part of the bridge, together with dense cross-bracing on the upper part of the bridge's gallery house. The bridge has a very unique structure. Its characteristics are highly representative of the timber arch covered bridges on the Longchuan River.

三、滇东南廊桥
II. Covered Bridges in Southeast Yunnan Province

01 双龙桥

云南省建水县城西五公里泸江与塌冲河，清乾隆（1736—1795年）

又名十七孔桥，长148米、宽3米至5米、桥段高9米。两端双重檐攒尖顶望乡亭，东亭无存。正中砌筑长16米、宽9米、高10米墩台，主阁楼高29米，雕梁画栋雄伟挺拔，有"滇南大观楼"之誉。三重斗栱四脊飞檐均为歇山顶覆黄、褐、绿色琉璃瓦，檐头插如意龙首瓦当。双龙桥是著名古迹，在中国桥梁史上有重要地位，被列为省级重点文物保护单位。

1. Shuanglong Bridge — Lujiang River and Tachong River, 5 kilometers west of Jianshui County, Yunnan Province, built during 1736-1795.

Also known as the Shiqikong Bridge, it is 148 meters long, 3 to 5 meters wide and 9 meters high. Pavilions at both sides of the bridge with double eaves and pyramidal roofs were used to look out on the village from. However, the east pavilion no longer remains. A structure composed of masonry in the middle of the bridge is 16 meters long, 9 meters wide, and the bridge pier is 10 meters high. The bridge's main pavilion is 29 meters high; an imposing, richly ornamented and upright structure. It is known as the "great observatory of southern Yunnan". The building is replete with triple sets of *dougong* brackets, and a hip and gable roof with four ridges, and upturned eaves. The roof's glazed tiles are yellow, brown and grey. The *wadang* eave tiles are carved with auspicious dragon heads. Shuanglong Bridge is a famous historical site and it possesses an important position in the history of bridges in China. It has been listed as the Historical and Cultural Sites Protected at the Provincial Level.

02—保兴桥

云南省西畴县兴街镇畴阳河，清光绪三十二年（1906年）

横跨畴阳河（牛羊河），自古是滇东南地区与安南国（越南）商品贸易、走亲访友、物资交流的通道。又名牛羊太平桥。始建于清乾隆十三年（1748年），多次大修。桥全长27米，宽3.2米，高5米，桥廊进深九间。桥的两边设置长板椅，供路人避雨纳凉。桥的两端建有桥楼，桥楼石砌八字形防水墙，内侧立石碑五块。中孔上端建砖木结构双层风雨亭，重檐翘角悬山顶覆黄色琉璃瓦。两侧有1米高石栏，两端各有一迎门石狮。

02.Baoxing Bridge – Chouyang River, Xingjie Town, Xichou County, Yunnan Province, built in 1906.

Spanning the Chouyang River (also known as the Niuyang River), since ancient times the bridge has been a conduit for commercial and material trade—and for the travel of guests and relatives—between southeast Yunnan Province and Vietnam. It is also called the Niuyangtaiping Bridge. First built in 1748, it has since undergone many major repairs. The bridge is 27 meters long, 3.2 meters wide, 5 meters high and the gallery house on top is nine bays long. There are benches on both sides of the bridge for people to use to take shelter from rain, or to enjoy the cool temperature in the bridge. At both ends of the bridge, there are bridge houses, with stone *bazi*-shaped walls that provide protection from the rain. There are five stone steles inside the bridge houses as well. A brick and timber pavilion for shelter from the wind and rain stands in the middle span of the bridge. It has two stories, and is topped with a hip and gable roof with upturned eaves, covered with yellow glazed tiles. Each side of the bridge has a 1 meter high stone railing, and a pair of stone welcoming lions greet visitors at either end.

03—乡会桥

云南省建水县西庄镇新房村泸江河，清嘉庆十九年（1814年）

砖石结构两墩三孔石拱廊桥，主桥长18米，引桥长25米，宽7米，高6米。两层廊屋中的下层为通道，上层为魁星阁。

3.Xianghui Bridge — Lujiang River, Xinfang Village, Xizhuang Town, Jianshui County, Yunnan Province, built in 1814.

This is a masonry covered bridge with two piers and three stone arch spans. The main bridge structure is 18 meters long; the bridge approach is 25 meters long, it is 7 meters wide and 6 meters high. The first story of the two-story gallery house serves as a corridor for travel, and the second story forms the Kuixing Pavilion.

第四章 西南廊桥遗存带

04—天缘桥

建水县泸江河,清雍正六年(1728 年)

　　清嘉庆四年(1799 年)重修,三孔石拱亭桥长 121 米、宽 8 米、主桥跨河 43 米、南引桥长 36 米、北引桥长 42 米、宽 7.8 米,桥孔相隔 8 米。船舶型桥墩中孔高 10 米,侧孔高 9 米,南北引桥向东西方向延伸呈 S 型。双层重檐、四方八角、飞檐攒尖顶,亭阁高大雄伟。桥头石壁遗存一方清雍正八年(1730 年)残碑,依稀可见"游览斯桥者,只宜安静观望,不得损毁神像、阁亭砖瓦、墙壁、狮象等类。倘刁恶不羁,扭送官究决不宽贷"等文字,被列为省级文物保护单位。

04. Tianyuan Bridge — Lujiang River, Jianshui County, built in 1728.

The bridge was reconstructed in 1799. The stone arch pavilion bridge has three spans, and is 121 meters long and 8 meters wide. The main bridge is 43 meters long, the southern approach to it is 36 meters long, and the northern approach to it is 42 meters long, with a distance of 8 meters between the spans. The pier in the middle span is formed in the shape of a ship's bow, and is 10 meters tall. The adjacent piers are 9 meters tall. The north and south approaches extend first in an east and west direction respectively, forming an overall S-shaped bridge. The two-story pavilion building in the center of the bridge has two sets of eaves, the bottom set with four sides and the upper with eight edges and a pyramidal top. It is a tall and magnificent structure. The remnant of a stele, erected in 1730, is installed at the front of the bridge. It reads: "Visitors of the bridge should peacefully view it, and must not destroy its statues, pavilion tiles, walls, lion statues, and other objects. If one acts hatefully and unruly [towards it], they will be seized and delivered to the officials for judgement without mercy..." The bridge is listed as the Historical and Cultural Sites Protected at the Provincial Level.

第四章　西南廊桥遗存带

Chapter V Covered Bridge Belt in South Central China

The South-Central Covered Bridge Belt is one of areas in China, that is the most rich in covered bridges. It includes Western Hubei, southeastern Chongqing, Guizhou, Hunan, northern Guangxi and northwestern Guangdong regions.

This bridge belt contains from Qinling Mountains in the north to Lingnan Mountains in the south, from Wuling Mountains in the west to Wudang Mountains and Luoxiaoling Mountains in the east. It includes Zishui, Xiangjiang and Yuanjiang River Basins, Wuling and Eastern Sichuan regions and so on.

In terms of nationality groups, besides the Han nationality, it is also the place where Dong, Miao, Yao, Tujia, Gelao and other nationality groups live. It has strong regional and national architectural characteristics.

Sansheng slope of Dong nationality area, Wuling area and Zishui river basin have the biggest quantity of covered bridges.

Located in the northern part of this region, Wuling Mountain area boasts a large number of splaye bracing or simply-supported covered bridge of Tu nationality; In Dong nationality's residence with the three central provinces of this region, there a various timber bridges with horizontal overhangir beams; the Zishui River basin where the Ha Nationality lives in southwest Hunan is also famous f its timber bridges with horizontal overhanging beam These three areas together form the south-central Chir covered bridge belt.

中国廊桥

第五章 中南廊桥遗存带

中南廊桥带是中国廊桥最密集的区域之一。这里包括鄂西、渝东南、贵州、湖南、桂北和粤西北。中南廊桥带，北起秦岭，南抵岭南，西达武陵山区，东至武当山—罗霄岭。包括了三省坡侗族地区、资水流域、湘江流域、沅江流域、武陵地区、四川盆地东部地区等地。

在族群方面，除了汉族之外，这里也是侗族、苗族、瑶族、土家族、仡佬族等民族的世居之地，有着强烈的地域和民族建筑特色。

武陵地区、三省坡侗族地区和资水流域廊桥最为密集。

区域内北侧的武陵山区，现存大量八字撑或者简支梁型土家族凉亭桥；中部的三省坡侗族地区，拥有数量繁多的水平伸臂木梁花桥；资水流域，则是湘西南汉族聚集地，同样以水平伸臂的木梁桥为主。这三个地区彼此相连，构成了中南廊桥带无比精彩的篇章。

第一节 · 鄂东南廊桥
Section I Covered Bridges in Southeast Hubei Province

一、鄂南淦河流域廊桥
I. Covered Bridges in Ganhe River Basin, South Hubei Province

01—万寿桥

湖北省咸宁市咸安区桂花镇万寿桥村淦水河，清道光二十七年（1847年）

咸宁有"千桥之乡"美誉。令人奇异的是，石拱廊桥的桥孔均为单数，一孔、三孔或五孔。有的双孔石拱桥得体适度，工匠却着意在两孔之间墩台上凿筑一个附孔，千百年来一脉相承。三孔石拱全砖石结构，长34.4米、宽4.8米、高6米。廊亭青瓦覆顶，两侧有护栏，廊内置石椅、长凳。

01.Wanshou Bridge — Ganshui River, Wanshouqiao Village, Guihua Town, Xianan District, Xianning, Hubei Province, built in 1847.

Xianning in Hubei Province is famed for being a "countryside with a thousand bridges." Interestingly, stone arch bridges generally have an odd number of spans—one, three or five. Sometimes it is suitable for a stone arch bridge to be built with two spans, and subsequently carpenters will intentionally chisel a third hole in the pier between the two spans. This tradition has been kept for thousands of years. The Wanshou Bridge is a stone masonry arch bridge with three spans. It is 34.4 meters long, 4.8 meters wide and 6 meters high. A pavilion on its deck is covered with grey tiles, and has stone seats and long benches inside. There are protective railings on both sides of the bridge.

第五章 中南廊桥遗存带

02—刘家桥

湖北省咸宁市咸安区桂花镇刘家桥村，明代（1368－1644年）

为营造"小桥流水人家"的意境，刘氏先民在池塘水口建造了一座朴素雅致的廊桥。傍晚老人在廊桥相聚，常有"不求富贵命，但愿子孙贤"的谈论，路人多为老人们爽朗的笑声感染。单孔石拱廊桥长20米、宽5米、高6米、跨径10米。桥廊顶梁雕龙凤八卦图案，两端建牌坊式门厅，双坡顶覆小青瓦。桥侧2米高青砖方孔花格护墙，下设有长凳。

02.Liujia Bridge － Liujiaqiao Village, Guihua Town, Xianan District, Xianning, Hubei Province, built during 1368-1644.

In order to manifest the Chinese artistic and poetic trope of "family houses hidden past a narrow bridge under which a quiet creek flows", the ancestors of the Liu lineage built a simple and elegant covered bridge over the inlet that flows into their village pond. In the evening, the elders of the village often gather there, and can often be heard talking of "not desiring wealth, but wishing their children and grandchildren live virtuous lives". The laughter and nice words from such conversations are infectious to people passing by. The stone arch bridge is 20 meters long, 5 meters wide, 6 meters high and has a span of 10 meters. A dragon, phoenix, and the eight Taoist trigrams are carved into the top beam of the bridge's gallery house. Both ends of the structure have entrances built in the style of a memorial archway with a double-sloped roof covered with small grey tiles. Both sides of the bridge have a 2 meters. high grey brick lattice protective wall, and beside the wall are long benches.

03—白沙桥

湖北省咸宁市咸安区桂花镇白沙桥村,明正德二年(1507年)

两墩三孔石拱廊桥长34米、宽5米、高6米,3孔跨径10.3米,明正德二年(1507年)由白沙寺僧人四方募得桥资、桥材、粮食后,召集能工巧匠,并在附近乡民协助下建成白沙桥。清咸丰七年(1857年)大修。内侧安置木条凳供行人歇息。

03.Baisha Bridge － Baishaqiao Village, Guihua Town, Xian'an District, Xianning, Hubei Province, built in 1507.

This is a stone arch bridge with two piers and three spans. It is 34 meters long, 5 meters wide, and 6 meters high. Its three spans cover a distance of 10.3 meters. There are wooden benches inside the bridge allow travelers to take a rest. In 1517, after the monks of Baisha Temple collected funds, materials and grain for the bridge building from the surrounding area, they recruited skilled craftsmen for the project. Next, the bridge was built, together with the help of neighboring villagers. In 1857, the bridge underwent a significant overhaul.

第五章 中南廊桥遗存带

二、长江中游北岸鄂东门户——黄梅县

II. Huangmei County, a Portal to East Hubei Province on the North Bank of the Middle Reach of the Yangtze River

01—灵润桥

湖北省黄冈市黄梅县四祖寺山门水口,元顺帝至正元年(1341年)

又名花桥、四祖寺桥。单孔敞廊式廊桥,石墩木柱、木梁木檩、单脊双坡顶覆小青瓦。长20米、宽6米、高5米、跨径7.4米。两端使用青砖建高大卷顶式五花山门,门口石壁雕刻飞禽走兽。桥下岩石遗留古人书法刻字,据传"碧玉流"三个大字是唐代书法家柳公权题写。灵润桥被列为省级文物保护单位。

01.Lingrun Bridge – Shanmen Shuikou, Sizu Temple, Huangmei County, Huanggang, Hubei Province, built in 1341.

Also known as Huaqiao Bridge or Sizusi Bridge. This is an arch covered bridge with timber beams, columns, purlins, and with stone piers. It has a single span. Its roof has a single ridge and double slopes covered with small grey tiles. The bridge is 20 meters long, 6 meters wide, 5 meters high and its span is 7.4 meters. Grey bricks are used at both ends to build tall and large multicolored gates with arched roofs. Flying birds and walking beasts are carved on the gate walls. A stone under the bridge is inscribed with the phrase "the Green Jade Flows". It is said that these characters are inscribed by Liu Gongquan, a calligrapher of the Tang Dynasty. It is listed as the Historical and Cultural Sites Protected at the Provincial Level.

02—飞虹桥

湖北省黄冈市黄梅县五祖寺山门峡谷，元代（1271－1368年）

又名花桥。五祖寺由禅宗五祖大师弘忍（601－674年）于唐高宗永徽五年（654年）创建，初称东山寺，后称五祖寺。飞虹桥是通向五祖寺山门必经之桥，蕴涵普度众生之意。石拱独跨、砖木结构廊桥长33.65米、宽4.2米，距谷底8.45米，桥口建牌坊式门楼。

02.Feihong Bridge – Wuzu Temple Gate Canyon, Huangmei County, Huanggang, Hubei Province, built during 1271-1368.

Also known as Huaqiao Bridge. The Wuzu Temple was built in 654 by Hong Ren (601-674), the fifth master (*Wuzu*) the Chan school of Buddhism. It was initially called Dongshan Temple, and later called Wuzu Temple. The Bridge must be passed over to arrive at the mountain gate of the Wuzu Temple. This carries a symbolic Buddhist meaning of "delivering (or bridging the way across for) all living beings out of torment". It is a masonry and timber covered bridge, with a stone arch and a single span. It is 33.65 meters long, 4.2 meters wide, and passes 8.45 meters above the valley's bottom. It has a memorial arch styled gateway at its entrance.

第五章 中南廊桥遗存带

第二节·鄂西廊桥
Section II   Covered Bridges in West Hubei Province

鄂西南、湘北——山连水缠
Southwest Hubei Province and North Hunan Province, Rolling Mountains and Intertwined Rivers

01—永顺桥

湖北省恩施土家族苗族自治州利川市毛坝镇花板村三弯河峡谷，清嘉庆十二年（1807年）

永顺桥建在三弯河峡谷最窄处。由乡绅周正已、张启荣发起修建。独孔木拱伸臂平梁式全木结构廊桥，不用一钉一铆，以杉木凿榫衔接。长32.5米、宽3米、高40米。桥基依托坚固石壁，三排（组）圆木双方向斜伸支撑双排圆木横梁作为主体桥架，上部廊柱与桥架贯通形成坚固整体，再以两侧木栏加固。永顺桥被列为市级文物保护单位，于1880年、1952年、1967年、1991年修缮。

01.Yongshun Bridge — Sanwanhe Gorge, Huaban Village, Maoba Town, Lichuan, Enshi Tujia and Miao Autonomous Prefecture, Hubei Province, built in 1807.

Yongshun Bridge was built at the narrowest part of the Sanwanhe Gorge. Local gentry Zhou Zhengyi and Zhang Qirong called for the bridge's construction. It is a single span timber cantilever arch-beam covered bridge. Utilizing mortise-tenon technology, it doesn't use a single nail or rivet, instead tenons are chiseled out of Chinese fir wood to connect the structure together. It is 32.5 meters long, 3 meters wide and 40 meters high. Its foundation is formed from a solid stone wall. Three rows (assemblages) of logs extend diagonally in either direction to support two rows of crossbeams, forming the main bridge structure. The columns in the gallery house in the upper bridge structure pass through the main bridge structure, forming a solid overall unit, which is strengthened through the use of timber railings on either side of the bridge. It is listed as Historical and Cultural Sites Protected at the Municipal Level. The bridge has been repaired in 1880, 1952, 1967 and 1991.

02—深溪河桥

湖北省恩施土家族苗族自治州来凤县革勒车乡白果园村，清同治二年（1863年）

深溪河桥藏于山林田野之深处，发现十分不易。深溪河桥由张姓乡绅倡捐修建。一墩两孔凉亭式廊桥长25米、宽8米、高6.8米。1963年、1979年被山洪冲毁，于1964年、1981年修复。1981年修复时将桥墩升高1米，增强了抗洪能力。

02.Shenxihe Bridge — Baiguoyuan Village, Geleche Township, Laifeng County, Enshi Tujia and Miao Autonomous Prefecture, Hubei Province, built in 1863.

Shenxihe Bridge is hidden deep in the woods and fields, and it is quite difficult to get there. The Shenxihe Bridge was built at the initiative of a member of the local gentry surnamed Zhang who called for contributions for the effort. The "cool pavilion" covered bridge has one pier and two spans. It is 25 meters long, 8 meters wide and 6.8 meters high. In 1963 and 1979, it was destroyed by mountain floods, and restored in 1964 and 1981. During an overhaul in 1981, the pier was raised by 1 meter to enhance the ability to resist flood.

中国廊桥

03—龙家桥

湖北省恩施土家族苗族自治州来凤县旧司镇龙桥村打车河峡谷，清光绪四年（1878年）

又名楼房坝桥。一墩两孔全木结构平梁式廊桥，长28.5米、宽2.65米、高7.7米、跨径12.5米，九开间。龙家桥由楼房坝苗族首领龙通成主持，乡民捐资建成。而后每逢清明节雨季来临前，家族首领会召集族人讨论廊桥维护。1979年8月1日深夜，桥廊被特大洪水冲毁，百姓捐款捐粮于次年复建。龙家桥被列为省级文物保护单位。

03.Longjia Bridge — Dachehe Canyon, Longqiao Village, Jiusi Town, Laifeng County, Enshi Tujia and Miao Autonomous Prefecture, Hubei Province, built in 1878.

Also known as Loufangba Bridge. It is a timber beam bridge with one pier and two spans. It is 28.5 meters long, 2.65 meters wide, 7.7 meters high, and has a span of 12.5 meters. Its gallery house has nine bays. Long Tongcheng, the head representative of the village's Miao community, is in charge of the bridge. In addition, villagers contribute money to its maintenance. Before the rainy season around the time of the Qingming Festival (which occurs early April), the head will call on the clan to come together to discuss the maintenance of the covered bridge. On August 1, 1979, the bridge's gallery house was destroyed by a huge flood, and in the following year the common people of the village donated money and grain to support its rebuilding. It is listed as the Historical and Cultural Sites Protected at the Provincial Level.

04—龙山口桥

湖南省湘西土家族苗族自治州龙山县茅坪乡水沙坪村稻田小溪河

龙山口桥位于水沙坪村稻田小溪河,远离大路,是专为下田的乡亲避风躲雨建造的。每逢水稻、红薯、玉米快要成熟的季节,为防备野猪祸害、野禽啄食,家家都会有人到地里看守,面廊桥就是他们休息、吃饭的场所。

04.Longshankou Bridge – Xiaoxi River in Paddy Field, Shuishaping Village, Maoping Township, Longshan County, Xiangxi Tujia and Miao Autonomous Prefecture, Hunan Province.

Longshankou Bridge is located in the rice paddies of Shuishaping Village, far from the main road. It is built especially so the villagers in the fields can find shelter from the wind and rain. When rice, sweet potatoes and maize are almost ready to be harvested, villagers will come to the field to stand guard to prevent wild boars, birds, and beasts from stealing and ruining the crops. The covered bridge is also a place where they can rest and eat.

第五章 中南廊桥遗存带

05—凉亭桥

湖南省湘西土家族苗族自治州龙山县洗车河镇，清乾隆四十五年（1780年）

湘西名镇洗车河地处红岩溪河与猛西河交汇口，原有大小两座廊桥，现仅存大桥改名凉亭桥。逢圩设市，廊桥里货摊鳞次栉比，镇民对此桥十分珍爱。《龙山县志》记："大河桥系本埠乡绅肖家霖捐修，桥中廊柱、枋檩、坐凳、栏杆、檐板、桥板以榫卯合成，无铁钉铁铆。"四墩三孔，平梁全木结构，长75米，宽4米，高10.5米。2012年大修，新建两座双飞檐四角阁塔、两座单飞檐六角阁亭。

05.Liangting Bridge — Xichehe Town, Longshan County, Xiangxi Tujia and Miao Autonomous Prefecture, Hunan Province, built in 1780.

The town of Xichehe is situated at the confluence of the Hongyanxi River and Mengxi River. Originally, there were two bridges, one big, the other small, but now only the bigger one remains. This was renamed as the Liangting Bridge. During regular market fairs, the bridge is filled with stalls, making the bridge much beloved by the townspeople. The *Longshan County Chronicle* records that "Xiao Jialin, a member of the local gentry, donated money to build Dahe Bridge. Its pillars, purlins, benches, railings, eaves, and boards are made of mortise and tenons without the use of iron nails or rivets." The timber bridge has four piers and three spans. It is a timber beam bridge, 75 meters long, 4 meters wide, and 10.5 meters high. In 2012, four new pavilions were added to the site, including two with four cornered roofs with double upturned eaves, and two with six-cornered roofs with a single layer of upturned eaves.

第三节 · 黔北黔东廊桥
Section III Covered Bridges in North and East Guizhou Province

长寿桥

贵州省遵义市正安县小雅镇

长寿桥体现中国古人追求"大道至简"的境界。十八根圆木组成"双八字"木拱结构，开敞式廊屋简约明朗。《同结善缘》碑记："原名长寿桥。1947年当地名士倡导，在谷深水湍的雄塘岸上，集小雅、梨垭、教良等地乡民捐助和能工巧匠建成。其型制规模被称为黔北之最。"列为县级文物。原桥两侧各有宽80厘米封闭式廊道供牲畜通行，牛马只可前行不能调头。后来小雅镇城镇化没有人养牛马，廊道改建为整体桥面。

Changshou Bridge – Xiaoya Town, Zheng'an County, Zunyi, Guizhou Province.

Changshou Bridge, its design symbolizes the ancients' pursuit of simplicity. It is composed of a timber arch made of 18 logs grouped together to form two *bazi*-shaped arch structures. Its open-style gallery house is concise and bright. It is recorded in *All for Good Fortune Stele* that "the bridge, formerly named Changshou Bridge, spans the Xiongtang River. Its construction was advocated by a well known local gentleman in 1947, and craftsmen built it through the help of contributions from villagers from Xiaoya, Liya and Jiaoliang. It is the biggest bridge in north Guizhou and has been listed as the Historical and Cultural Sites Protected at the County Level." Previously, it included an 80 centimeter wide separate path for livestock on each side of the bridge, that required animals like cattle and horses to only walk forward and not turn around because of the narrow width. These two paths have been removed and connected with the overall bridge floor because Xiaoya Town has now been urbanized, and there are no longer horses and cattle there.

第四节·黔东南廊桥
Section IV Covered Bridges in Southeast Guizhou Province

01 地坪风雨桥

贵州省黔东南苗族侗族自治州黎平县地坪乡南江河，清光绪八年（1882年）

地坪风雨桥自古扼控贵东南通往湘西、桂北孔道。一座桥楼与桥廊不用一钉一铆，没有设计图纸，凭借侗族民间工匠的高超技艺建造。墩身长55.88米、宽3.85米、高11米，两孔净跨分别为13.77米和21.42米。1964年重建，1981年修复。2004年7月20日水毁，地坪乡乡民将28根大梁和73%的大构件找回，2009年按照古貌复建。

01 Dipingfengyu Bridge — over Nanjiang River, Diping Township, Liping County, Qiandongnan Miao and Dong Autonomous Prefecture, Guizhou Province, built in 1882.

Diping Fengyu Bridge has been a vital node connecting southeast Guizhou with west Hunan Province and north Guangxi Zhuang Autonomous Region. Its three pavilions and its gallery house were built by ethnic Dong craftsmen who, with their prodigious skills, completed the project without blueprints, and without use of a single iron nail or rivet. The double-span bridge is 55.88 meters long, 3.85 meters wide and 11 meters high. Its two spans are 13.77 meters and 21.42 meters respectively. It was rebuilt in 1964 and renovated in 1981. The bridge was knocked asunder by a flood on July 10, 2004, after which villagers were able to retrieve 28 of its displaced crossbeams and 73% of its large timber members. The bridge was rebuilt in 2009.

02—六约风雨桥

贵州省黔东南苗族侗族自治州黎平县龙额镇六约村，清同治三年（1864年）

桥廊门额上悬挂简介："六约风雨桥始建于清同治三年（1864年），长32米、宽2.4米，横跨六约河上，系悬臂式两孔木梁桥。桥面长廊中部为重檐悬山式桥顶，西端建三重檐歇山顶桥楼。桥（廊）两侧设坐凳和栏杆。该桥远观形如六甲'萨坛'，是纪念侗族一位名叫'萨岁'的女英雄而的风雨桥。"

02.Liuyuefengyu Bridge — Liuyue Village, Long'e Township, Liping County, Qiandongnan Miao and Don Autonomous Prefecture, Guizhou Province, built in 1864.

There is a plaque hanging from the bridge's gateway, with a description of the bridge. It states "the bridge spans the Liuyue River and is a cantilever beam bridge with two spans. It is 32 meters long, 2.4 meters wide and was first built in the third year of the Tongzhi reign of the Qing Dynasty (1864). The center of the gallery house is covered with a double-eave and overhanging gable roof, and its the western end is covered by a triple-eave and hip and gable roof. Long benches and railings run along the length of the bridge. From distance, the bridge looks like the (Goddes Sa Altars in the nearby villages. The bridg commemorates a heroine of the Don Nationality called Sa Sui, for whom th bridge was constructed."

03 — 仁团桥

贵州省黔东南苗族侗族自治州黎平县肇兴侗寨

肇兴侗寨发祥于汉代，是黎平县侗乡风景名胜核心景点，有"侗乡第一寨"之名。肇兴侗寨为陆姓分属五大族房，居住五区称为仁团、义团、礼团、智团、信团。"五团"各自建造鼓楼、风雨桥。在环寨河流、穿寨溪流上的风雨桥，也称花桥。花桥无论大小全部采用杉木横穿直套、榫卯相接，不用铁钉铁件。仁团桥依鼓楼建造独孔木平梁、木柱重檐瓦顶，朝天蛇形跷角有镇治水患意味。长6米、宽3米、高6米，三开间，设护栏木凳。

3. Rentuan Bridge – Zhaoxing Dong Stockade, Liping County, Qiandongnan Miao and Dong Autonomous Prefecture, Guizhou Province.

Zhaoxing Dong Stockade, dates back to the Han dynasty (202 BC - 220 AD), and is one of the foremost scenic areas in the region of Liping County inhabited by the Dong nationality. It is referred to as the best Dong village in the Dong region. The villagers there share the surname Lu, and live in five different large areas in the village, each situated in a separate area. The fives areas are called the *ren* (benevolence) group, *yi* (righteousness) group, *li* (propriety) group, *zhi* (wisdom) group, and *xin* (sincerity) group. Each group has its own drum towers and wind and rain bridges. These bridges, also named huaqiao bridges, are built on rivers and streams running around and across the village. Regardless of their size, they are all constructed with Chinese fir, and their components are joined by use of mortise and tenons. No nails or any other iron pieces are found in the structures. Rentuan Bridge is 6 meters long, 3 meters wide, and 6 meters high. Its gallery house consists of three bays. Rails and benches are installed inside, and it sits adjacent to a drum tower. The bridge has a single span, and is built with timber beams and columns. It has a double-eave roof, covered with tiles. Snake-figures on the upturned corners of the eaves that point towards the sky are thought to prevent flooding.

04—孟猫花桥

贵州省黔东南苗族侗族自治州黎平县肇兴侗寨

全木结构的孟猫花桥，木平梁独孔、敞廊穿斗式结构，护栏木凳，长8.2米、宽3米、高4米，三开间，硬山顶覆小青瓦，顶脊上二龙抢珠雕塑增加了美感。

04.Mengmaohua Bridge — Zhaoxin Dong Stockade, Liping County, Qiandongnan Miao and Dong Autonomous Prefecture, Guizhou Province.

Mengmaohua Bridge is a single-span timber beam covered bridge, with an open *chuandou* structure gallery house. Rails and benches are installed along the length of the bridge. The three bay design is 8.2 meters long, 3 meters wide and meters high. Its flush gable roof is covered with small grey tiles, and the sculpture on its roof ridge of two dragons vying for a pearl adds an element of beauty to the bridge.

5—牙双花桥

贵州省黔东南苗族侗族自治州黎平县雷洞乡牙双林区峡谷

牙双花桥连通贵州省南下广东、广西两省、自治区古通道，距广西壮族自治区三江侗族自治县独峒乡5公里。独孔全木穿斗式结构，长16米、宽3米、高7米，中部建四重檐歇山顶望楼。

5. Yashuanghua Bridge — located in a valley in the forest of Yashuang Village, Leidong Township, Liping County, Qiandongnan Miao and Dong Autonomous Prefecture, Guizhou Province.

Yashuanghua Bridge is a part of the ancient road that connected Guizhou with Guangdong and Guangxi. It is 5 kilometers away from Dudong Township in the Sanjiang Dong Autonomous County of Guangxi Zhuang Autonomous Region. The bridge is a single-span timber *chuandou* structure. It is 16 meters long, 3 meters wide, and 7 meters high. Its center has a viewing structure topped with a four-eave hip and gable roof.

06—守寨桥

贵州省黔东南苗族侗族自治州黎平县肇兴乡堂安寨

堂安寨是由中国与挪威政府联合兴建的"中国侗族生态博物馆"。不设固定场馆，村寨的整体文化遗存、寨门鼓楼、房舍亭阁、森林花草、廊桥古道、山泉田园、祭祀活动、语言图腾、乡民生活就是博物馆的全部内容。守寨桥全木结构，16根木柱支撑整座桥梁，既是承托横梁与桥面的墩柱，又是支撑桥顶的廊柱。

06.Shouzhai Bridge – Tang'an Stockade, Zhaoxing Township, Liping County, Qiandongnan Miao and Dong Autonomous Prefecture, Guizhou Province.

Tang'an Stockade has been recognized jointly by the Chinese and Norwegian governments as the "Chine Dong Nationality Ethnic Eco-Museum". The museum does not have a specific location, but includes the village's drum towers, houses, pavilions, forests, vegetation, covered bridges, ancient paths, springs, fields, sacrificial rituals, language, totems, and local people's ways of living. Shouzhai Bridge is a timber structure supported by 16 timber columns that support the entire bridge. On one hand, they serve as the bridge piers that support the crossbeams and bridge deck, and at the same time also support the roof of the bridge's gallery house.

第五章 中南廊桥遗存带

07—翠谷桥

贵州省黔东南苗族侗族自治州黎平县雷洞乡亚跨村山林崖口

屡有修缮,因坐落于叠翠山谷得名,位于黎平县雷洞乡亚跨村偏僻处。独孔双层平梁全木结构廊桥,长15.7米、宽2.8米、高5.2米,是连通桂北、贵南古通道的必经节点。

07.Cuigu Bridge – located at a cliff in Yakua Village, Leidong Township, Liping County, Qiandongnan Miao and Dong Autonomous Prefecture, Guizhou Province.

Cuigu Bridge gets its name from its location in the Diecui Valley. It has been renovated many times. It is located in a remote area of the village, it is a timber beam covered bridge with a single span and two layers of beams. It is 15.7 meters long, 2.8 meters wide and 5.2 meters high. It is an intersection of the ancient road that connected northern Guangxi to southern Guizhou.

08—岑管花桥

贵州省黔东南苗族侗族自治州黎平县雷洞乡岑管村，清代（1636 — 1912 年）

岑管花桥始建于清代，屡有毁建。桥长 35 米、宽 4 米。2004 年 7 月 20 日水毁，于 2005 年 8 月修复。

08.Cenguanhua Bridge — Cenguan Village, Leidong Township, Liping County, Qiandongnan Miao and Dong Autonomous Prefecture, Guizhou Province, built during 1636-1912.

Cenguanhua Bridge was first built in the Qing Dynasty, and has been damaged and repaired many times. It was swept away by a flood on July 20, 2004, and was rebuilt in August, 2005. The bridge is 35 meters long and 4 meters wide.

09—增盈桥

贵州省黔东南苗族侗族自治州从江县往洞镇增盈村大寨,清雍正五年(1727年)

始建于清雍正五年(1727年),一墩两孔木梁平廊桥,长22米、宽3米、高6米、八开间。中阁为六柱支撑六角攒尖顶,两端门楼为悬山顶,顶脊有游龙装饰。增盈桥被列为省级文物保护单位。1992年按原貌修复。

09.Zengying Bridge — Big Stockade, Zengying Village, Wangdong Town, Congjiang County, Qiandongnan Miao and Dong Autonomous Prefecture, Guizhou Province, built in 1727.

Zengying Bridge was first built in 1727. It is a timber beam bridge with two spans. It is 22 meters long, 3 meters wide, and 6 meters high. Its center pavilion has a six-corner pyramidal roof supported by six columns. On either end of the bridge are buildings with overhanging gable roofs and with a sculpture of a wandering dragon on the roof ridge. Zengying Bridge is listed as the Historical and Cultural Sites Protected at the Provincial Level. It was restored in 1992.

10—村尾花桥

贵州省黔东南苗族侗族自治州从江县往洞镇德桥村

独孔石拱加立柱石墩设置副孔，全木结构穿斗式廊桥，长28.2米、宽2.9米、高5.3米，十五开间，单脊双坡顶覆盖小青瓦，两端建有门厅。

10.Cunweihua Bridge – Deqiao Village, Wangdong Town, Congjiang County, Qiandongnan Miao and Dong Autonomous Prefecture, Guizhou Province.

Cunweihua Bridge is a stone arch covered bridge with a completely timber gallery house on top consisting of a *chuandou* structure. A secondary hole is carved into the bridge's stone pier. It is 28.2 meters long, 2.9 meters wide and 5.3 meters high. Its gallery house has fifteen bays. Its double-sloped roof is covered with small grey tiles, and entrance halls are erected at either end.

11—金勾风雨桥

贵州省黔东南苗族侗族自治州从江县往洞镇增盈村金勾寨，清顺治十二年（1655年）

金勾桥于清光绪九年（1883年）水毁后重建，石墩平梁全木结构廊桥长33.60米、宽4.75米。据碑记："金勾风雨桥位于金勾寨脚。原桥址建于村寨旁，多次毁于洪水。1992年村民集资重建迁至现址。穿斗式石墩廊桥建筑，一墩两孔结构。桥梁采用密布式简支梁，十七开间，中部为密檐四角攒尖顶结构。加装漏窗和斗拱，与两侧悬山顶桥楼遥相呼应，起到了突出冠冕的作用。其营造技艺精湛是研究侗族建筑工艺、科学文化的重要实物。"被列为全国重点文物保护单位。

11.Jingoufengyu Bridge – Jingou Stockade, Zengying Village, Wangdong Town, Congjiang County, Qiandongnan Miao and Dong Autonomous Prefecture, Guizhou Province, built in 1655.

This bridge was rebuilt in 1883 after being destroyed by a flood. The bridge has stone piers and a timber-bridge structure. It is 33.6 meters long and 4.75 meters wide. According to an inscription on a stele, "this bridge was original built at the foot of the village, but it was destroyed many times by floods. In 1992, villagers raised funds to relocate it to the present site. It is a *chuandou* timber covered bridge with stone piers. It has one pier and two spans, and uses closely arranged beams to support the structure. The central part of the bridge has a four-corner multiple-eave pyramidal roof structure. It is decorated with ornamental perforated windows and *dougong* bracket sets. It is bordered on either side by buildings with overhanging gable roofs. Due to its exquisite structure, this bridge is instrumental in research on the construction techniques and scientific culture of the Dong nationality (a minority nationality that lives primarily in the border regions between Guizhou, Hunan and Hubei Provinces in China)." It has been listed as the Major Historical and Cultural Sites Protected at the National Level.

第五章 中南廊桥遗存带

第五节 • 湖南省域内的廊桥
Section V Covered Bridges in Hunan Province

一、芷江县㵲水河——三楚第一桥
I. The Number One Bridge of Hunan Province over Wushui River at Zhijiang County

龙津桥

湖南省怀化市芷江侗族自治县㵲水河，明万历十九年（1591年）

明万历年间，宽云和尚募集白银一万五千两，粮食一万余石，建成十三墩十四孔、五层楼、七座塔，长246.7米、宽12.2米的巨型廊桥。抗战时期为通过载重卡车，撤除了桥廊、塔楼。冒着日军飞机的轮番轰炸，龙津桥承载抵抗的车轮滚滚向前。1945年8月21日16时，中国战区"受降仪式"在芷江七里村举行。龙津桥与亿万中国人民一起，见证了日本侵略者向正义的中华民族承认战败、低头认罪的历史时刻，"天下第一功勋桥"名扬天下。1999年龙津桥修复。

Longjin Bridge — Wushui River, Zhijiang Dong Autonomous County, Huaihua, Hunan Province, built in 1591.

In 1591, the monk Kuanyun raised 15,000 tael of silver and more than 10,000 dan (one dan is equivalent to about 100 liters) grains to build this large-scale covered bridge. It had a gallery house with five stories, resting on top of thirteen piers with fourteen spans. It was built together with seven pagodas. It is 246.7 meters long and 12.2 meters wide. During the War of Resistance Against Japan (1937-1945), the gallery house and pagodas were removed to facilitate the movement of heavy trucks along the bridge. The bridge braved multiple bombing raids by Japanese aircraft as the wheels of resistance advanced forward. On August 21, 1945, at 4 p.m., the surrender ceremony was held in Qili Village. Together with hundreds of millions of Chinese people, Longjin Bridge witnessed the historic moment when the Japanese aggressors admitted defeat to the Chinese nation and with heads bowed low confessed their guilt. The "world's most meritorious bridge" was hence well-known throughout the world. In 1999 the bridge was restored.

二、湘西沱江凤凰城
II. Fenghuang Ancient Town by the Tuojiang River, West Hunan Province

虹桥

湖南省湘西土家族苗族自治州凤凰城沱江，清康熙九年（1670年）

新西兰作家路易·艾黎把对凤凰城的感受归纳为"中国最美的小城"。虹桥为百姓提供晴雨两便、四季皆宜的通行便利，是凤凰城的标志。虹桥原名卧虹桥，长80米、宽8米、高12.3米，为两墩三孔石拱楼殿式廊桥，跨径11.8米。廊桥上部共三层，底层供行人过江，中层设茶楼店铺，上层为望远楼。

Hongqiao Bridge — Tuojiang River, Fenghuang, Xiangxi Tujia and Miao Autonomous Prefecture, Hunan Province, built in 1670.

New Zealand writer Rewi Alley summed up his feelings about Fenghuang by calling it "the most beautiful town in China". The Hongqiao Bridge is its most famed symbol. The bridge provides the common people of the town convenient transportation across the Tuojiang River in both rain and shine, and in all four seasons. It was formerly known as the Wohong Bridge and is an arch-palace style covered bridge. The bridge is 80 meters long, 8 meters wide and 12.3 meters high. It has two piers and three spans which have spans of 11.8 meters. The bridge has three levels. The bottom floor is for pedestrian crossing, the middle floor is for tea houses or shops, and the upper one is an observation tower.

三、湘西通道侗族自治县坪坦河风雨桥群

III. Fengyu Bridges at Pingtan River, Tongdao Dong Autonomous County, West Hunan Province

01—普修桥

湖南省怀化市通道侗族自治县皇都侗寨，清乾隆（1736—1795年）

侗族居住地古称"溪峒"，沟壑田畴四处是水。为"上避天水、下跨地水"，侗族人民创造了风雨廊桥，与鼓楼、萨坛合称侗族建筑三宝。四墩三孔宝塔式廊桥长57.7米、宽4.2米，二十一开间，桥墩上叠架双层枕木承托圆木平梁。重檐长廊上建三座宝塔，中塔顶尖设朱雀风向标。清嘉庆八年（1803年）山洪骤发被毁后重修。

01. Puxiu Bridge – Huangdu Dong Stockade, Tongdao Dong Autonomous County, Huaihua, Hunan Province, built during 1736-1795.

In old times, settlements of the Dong nationality were called *xidong*. This referred to the fact that their settlements are surrounded on all sides by water in gullies and fields. In order to shield themselves from the rain above, and to travel over rivers below, Dong nationality created fengyu bridges, one of their three treasured architectural structures, together with drum towers and (Goddess)Sa altars. This pagoda-style covered bridge has three spans, and is 57.7 meters long and 4.2 meters wide. Its gallery house has twenty-one bays. Double-layered cross-ties are piled on top of the bridge's piers to support the bridge's log beams. There are three pagodas on the bridge, and the middle one is decorated with a wind vane in the shape of the Chinese mythical vermillion bird of the south. The bridge was rebuilt after a flash flood in 1813.

02—迴龙桥

湖南省怀化市通道侗族自治县坪坦乡坪日村，清乾隆二十六年（1761年）

南北走向，桥体有较大弧度，如蛟龙摇尾富有动感，桥头难见桥尾。早称龙皇桥，中华民国二十年（1931年）复修，取"龙脉迂迴，环抱村寨"之意，改称迴龙桥。两墩三孔。主跨近30米。石墩叠梁木结构平梁廊桥，长63米、宽5.3米、高20米，二十二开间。双檐双坡顶，桥顶两端和中部建三重檐宝阁，具有鲜明的侗族建筑特征。

02.Huilong Bridge — Pingri Village, Pingtan Township, Tongdao Dong Autonomous County, Huaihua, Hunan Province, built in 1761.

The arch of the north-south orientated Huilong Bridge has a high degree of curvature, creating a dynamic effect resembling a dragon swinging its tail. Because of this shape, it is hard to see one end of the bridge from the other. The bridge formerly named Longhuang Bridge, it was renovated in 1931 and renamed Huilong Bridge, a reference to the notion that a dragon vein encircles and embraces the village. The timber beam covered bridge is formed of stone piers and a stacked beam structure. It has two piers and three spans. It is 63 meters long, 5.3 meters wide, and 20 meters high. Its gallery house has twenty-two bays and it main span is nearly 30 meters long. The bridge i covered with a double-eave roof with two slopes The center of the bridge and either side have three eave pagoda-style pavilions, reflecting the highl distinct characteristics of Dong architecture.

3—通坪桥

湖南省怀化市通道侗族自治县牙屯堡镇通坪村

独孔伸臂平梁全木穿斗式结构，长18米、宽3米、高5米。顶两端和中部建有四角挑檐飞阁，悬山顶满覆小青瓦。

3.Tongping Bridge — Tongping Village, Yatunbao Town, Tongdao Dong Autonomous County, Huaihua, Hunan Province.

Tongping Bridge is a cantilever beam covered bridge composed of a *chuandou* structure with all wood. It has a single span and is 18 meters long, 3 meters wide and 5 meters high. The middle and both ends have pavilions with four cornered overhanging gabled roofs with upturned eaves, covered with small grey tiles.

04—普济桥

湖南省怀化市通道侗族自治县坪坦乡坪坦村，清乾隆二十五年（1760年）清光绪二十一年（1895年）复修，中华民国三年（1914年）维修。单孔伸臂式木拱廊桥长31.5米、宽3.8米、跨径19.8米。伸臂木梁插在两端空心石墩内，压大卵石。被列为全国重点文物保护单位。

04.Puji Bridge — Pingtan Village, Pingtan Township, Tongdao Dong Autonomous County, Huaihua, Hunan Province, built in 1760.

The bridge was restored in 1895 and repaired in 1914. It is a cantilever arch covered bridge with a single-span. It is 31.5 meters long, 3.8 meters wide, and has a span of 19.8 meters. Its cantilevered timber beams are inserted in the hollow stone bridge piers at either end. The Puji Bridge has been listed as the Major Historical and Cultural Sites Protected at the National Level.

05—迴福桥

湖南省怀化市通道侗族自治县坪坦乡高升村，清道光二十年（1840年）

三墩两孔叠梁穿斗式木架廊桥，长42.5米、宽3.86米，十八开间。中部建五层攒尖顶亭阁，两侧建六角攒尖顶厅阁，清同治九年（1870年）和中华民国三十五年（1946年）修缮，1984年大修。杉板廊壁遗留民间画师花草虫鱼、民间传说、神话故事、民族英雄等题材绘画。被列为全国重点文物保护单位。

05.Huifu Bridge — Gaosheng Village, Pingtan Township, Tongdao Dong Autonomous County, Huaihua, Hunan Province, built in 1840.

This is a compound timber beam frame covered bridge with a *chuandou* structure. It has three columns and two spans. It is 42.5 meters long and 3.86 meters wide. Its gallery house has eighteen bays. In its middle, there is a five-story pagoda pavilion with a pyramidal roof. There are entrance pavilions on either end of the bridge with six-corner pyramidal roofs. The bridge was renovated twice in 1870 and 1964, and underwent extensive repairs in 1984. The walls of the bridge have been painted with folk art, including drawings of flowers, plants, insects, fish, and story illustrations of myths and of folk heroes. Huifu Bridge has been listed as the Major Historical and Cultural Sites Protected at the National Level.

6—永福桥

湖南省怀化市通道侗族自治县坪坦乡高上村，清乾隆五十年（1785年）

永福桥圆木平梁全木结构，不用一钉一铁，构件卯榫嵌合。孔叠木平梁、穿斗式木构架，长39米、宽3.8米、跨径16.2米，十一开间。东端建高大望楼，整桥为龙形。清嘉庆十年（1805年）、清道光十五年（1835年）、清同治三年（1864年）、清光绪二十年（1894年）、中华民国二十五年（1936年）复建。被列为全国重点文物保护单位。

6.Yongfu Bridge — Gaoshang Village, Pingtan Township, Tongdao Dong Autonomous County, Huaihua, Hunan province, built in 1785.

Yongfu Bridge is a combined timber beam frame bridge with a *chuandou* structure. Its beams are composed of logs and it has a single span. It is connected by mortise and tenon technology without the use of single iron nail. It is 39 meters long, 3.8 meters wide and has a span of 16.2 meters. Its gallery house has eleven bays. A tall building stands at the east end of the bridge. The whole bridge resembles a dragon. Yongfu Bridge has been restored and repaired in 1805, 1835, 1864, 1894, and 1936. It has been listed as the Major Historical and Cultural Sites Protected at the National Level.

07—大路桥

湖南省怀化市通道侗族自治县坪坦乡高升村

位于高升村田野，为村民下田劳作避雨使用。全木结构，独孔平梁廊桥长26米、宽3米、高6米，单脊双坡硬山顶覆盖小青瓦。

07.Dalu Bridge — Gaosheng Village, Pingtan Township, Tongdao Dong Autonomous County, Huaihua, Hunan Province.

Dalu Bridge is located near a paddy field in Gaosheng Village. It provides shelter to villagers who labor in the field from the rain. It is a timber frame covered bridge and has a single-span. It is 26 meters long, 3 meters wide, and 6 meters high. It has a single-ridge flush gable roof, covered with small grey tiles.

08 — 过路桥

湖南省怀化市通道侗族自治县桥在村

独孔叠木平梁全木结构廊桥，长 38 米、宽 3.5 米、高 6.5 米，顶部中段、东端建有双重檐阁楼，具有侗族建筑典型特征。桥堍建筑较大不设桥墩，桥面外侧设置一层木椽瓦顶雨披，专为保护底梁圆木免遭雨水侵蚀。廊道一侧与高脚屋相连，守桥人家居住。

08.Guolu Bridge — Qiaozai Village, Tongdao Dong Autonomous County, Huaihua, Hunan Province.

This is a compound timber beam covered bridge with a single span. It is 38 meters long, 3.5 meters wide, and 6.5 meters high. Both the center and east end of the bridge have a pavilion with a double-eave roof that shows the distinctive features of Dong architecture. There is a relatively large bridge approach at either end, and the bridge is not supported by piers. A skirt made of timber rafters and tiles runs along the outside of the deck and protects the beam logs below from rain erosion. One side of the bridge's pathway is connected to a pile-supported house where people guarding the bridge live.

09 — 黄土桥

湖南省怀化市会同县马鞍镇黄土村，清代（1636–1912 年）

黄土桥长 16 米、宽 3 米、高 5 米，七开间，为一墩两孔圆木平梁，穿斗式全木结构廊桥。

09.Huangtu Bridge — Huangtu Village, Ma'an Town, Huitong County, Huaihua, Hunan Province, built during 1636-1912.

The Huangtu Bridge is a timber log beam covered bridge composed of a *chuandou* structure. It is 16 meters long, 3 meters wide, and 5 meters high. Its gallery house consists of seven bays. It has one pier and two spans.

四、湘江、资水、沅水流域的廊桥
IV. Covered Bridges in Xiangjiang River, Zishui River, Yuanshui River Basins

01—马渡桥

湖南省益阳市安化县东坪镇马渡村槎溪河,中华民国六年(1917 年)

又名马仔桥,是连通益阳、常德、桃源、新化等县古道。长 47 米、宽 3.7 米、高 10 米,两墩三孔,二十二开间。蜈蚣号称"天龙",被古人雕刻在廊桥石墩表面,用以"镇水护桥"。安化县多座廊桥石墩迎水艏一侧雕刻蜈蚣,其他地区没有发现。

01.Madu Bridge — over Chaxi River at Madu Village, Dongping Town, Anhua County, Yiyang, Hunan Province, built in 1917.

Madu Bridge, also known as Mazai Bridge, helped connect the ancient road that passed through Yiyang, Changde, Taoyuan and Xinhua. The bridge has two piers and three spans, and is 47 meters long, 3.7 meters wide and 10 meters high. Its gallery house has twenty-two bays. The figure of a centipede, referred to as "a heavenly dragon" was carved into the face of the bridge's stone pier by the ancients, and is thought to protect the bridge and prevent flooding. There are many other bridges in Anhua county that have centipedes carved into the side of the bridge piers that point into the direction of oncoming water, this is a feature which is not found outside of the county.

02—红岩塘桥

湖南省益阳市安化县东坪镇新局村株溪，中华民国二十年（1931年）

    一墩两孔全木结构廊桥，长27米、高7米、宽3.8米，十三开间，叠木平梁附加六根两组木杆三角支撑。单脊悬山重檐顶，覆小青瓦。

02.Hongyantang Bridge — over Zhuxi Brook at Xinju Village, Dongpin Town, Anhua County, Yiyang, Hunan Province, built in 1931.

Hongyantang Bridge is a compound timber beam covered bridge with one pier and two spans. It is 27 meters long, 7 meters high, and 3.8 meters wide. The beams are supported by two timber assemblages composed of six logs. The bridg has a gallery house with thirteen bays. Its sing ridge overhanging gable roof with multiple-eave covered with small grey tiles.

03—永锡桥

湖南省益阳市安化县江南镇锡潭村麻溪河，清光绪四年（1878年）

永锡桥长83米、宽3.7米、高12.8米，三十四开间，三墩四孔南北走向，桥口建高大牌楼，是安化县规模最大、保存最完好的石墩平梁、全木结构廊桥。永锡桥的建造，从发起倡议、招聘匠师、购集物料到动工建造，直至大桥竣工前后耗时6年，耗资数十万两白银，牵动两县九乡数万百姓。北端桥厅与四合院内遗存石碑68块，详录建桥修桥捐资人姓名。

03.Yongxi Bridge — over Maxi River at Xitan Village, Jiangnan Town, Anhua County, Yiyang, Hunan Province, built in 1878.

The south-north orientated Yongxi Bridge is a timber beam stone pier bridge. It has three piers and four spans. It is 83 meters long, 3.7 meters wide, and 12.8 meters high. Its gallery house has thirty-four bays. It has a tall memorial arch at one end. It is the biggest and best-preserved timber beam covered bridge with stone piers in Anhua county. It took six years to finish the project. This period included the initial collection of funds, invitation of craftsmen, procurement of material, and the bridge's completion. One hundred of thousands of tael of silver were used for the project. Tens of thousands of common people participated in the construction, coming from nine townships spread throughout two counties. There are 68 steles in a hall in the north side of the bridge and in a courtyard, record the names of people who contributed funds towards the project.

04—思贤桥

湖南省益阳市安化县江南镇七一村麻溪河，清咸丰四年（1854年）

南北走向，长58米、宽4米、高9米，二十一开间，两墩三孔，歇山重檐小青瓦顶，悬臂挑梁木结构廊架。南、北桥亭加建装饰华丽的亭阁式牌楼，牌楼顶上安放青花瓷片拼成的"思贤桥"匾额。思贤桥防雨措施非常完善，上有厚实的房顶，中有瓦顶雨披，下设严实防护板，对廊桥持久使用有很大作用。

04.Sixian Bridge – over Maxi River at Qiyi Village, Jiangnan Town, Anhua County, Yiyang, Hunan Province, built in 1854.

Sixian Bridge, stretches from north to south, and is a cantilever beam bridge with two piers and three spans. Its gallery house has twenty-one bays. It is 58 meters long, 4 meters wide, and 9 meters high. It has a hip and gable roof covered by grey tiles. Pavilions on the north and south ends of the bridge have pavilion-style decorated archways. On the top of these archways are plaques with the words Sixian Bridge, decorated with pieces of blue-and-white style porcelain. Sixian Bridge is well protected from the rain. It has a thick roof on top, tile-covered awnings in the middle and well-designed skirts at the bottom, which contributes much to the longevity of the bridge.

05—燕子桥

湖南省益阳市安化县梅城镇启安村六组洢溪河，清乾隆（1736—1795 年）

清道光二年（1822 年）整修。一墩两孔圆木平梁全木结构廊，长38.5米、宽3.8米、高11米，十一开间，悬山重檐小青瓦顶，悬臂挑梁式木结构廊架。被列为全国重点文物保护单位。

05.Yanzi Bridge – over Yixi River at group six of Qi'an Village, Meicheng Town, Anhua County, Yiyang, Hunan Province, built during 1736-1795.

Yanzi Bridge is a timber log cantilever beam bridge with one pier and two spans. It was renovated in 1822. It is 38.5 meters long, 3.8 meters wide, and 11 meters high. Its gallery house has eleven bays. It has an overhanging gable roof with multiple-eave, covered with small grey tiles. It has been listed as the Major Historical and Cultural Sites Protected at the National Level.

06—复古双桥

湖南省益阳市安化县柘溪镇双桥村双桥溪，清光绪三十三年（1907年）

复古大桥长30.8米、高6米、宽3.8米，十三开间，两墩三孔重檐歇山顶、悬臂挑梁木结构廊架。大桥一侧的小型石拱廊桥长8米，宽约4米。双桥情似姊妹，远近闻名。被列为全国重点文物保护单位。

06. Fugushuang Bridge — on Shuangqiao River, Shuangqiao Village, Zhexi Town, Anhua County, Yiyang, Hunan Province, built in 1907.

The larger one of the Fugu bridges is a timber cantilever beam covered bridge with two piers and three spans, covered by a hip and gable roof with multiple-eaves. It is 30.8 meters long, 6 meters high and 3.8 meters wide. Its gallery house has thirteen bays. The smaller stone arch bridge beside the larger one is 8 meters long and approximately 4 meters wide. The sister-like relationship between the two bridges is known near and far. The two bridges are listed as the Major Historical and Cultural Sites Protected at the National Level.

第五章 中南廊桥遗存带

07—福星桥

湖南省益阳市安化县梅城镇道观村九组拦路河，清光绪十三年（1887年）

原名落马桥，南北走向，两墩两台，五层叠木悬臂平梁全木结构，长42米、宽3.6米、高7米，十五开间，中间为通道，两侧为歇亭。两座门亭歇山顶覆小青瓦，长廊为庑殿顶，中间的挑檐阁楼已不存。

07.Fuxing Bridge — Lanlu River, Nine Group, Daoguan Village, Meicheng Town, Anhua County, Hunan Province, built in 1887.

Originally known as the Luoma Bridge, it is a timber cantilever compound beam covered bridge. Its beam structure is built with five layers of timber members. It has two piers and two abutments. Running from north to south, the bridge is 42 meters long, 3.6 meters wide, and 7 meters high. Its gallery house has fifteen bays. The middle of the bridge serves as a passageway, and the adjacent sides serve as rest pavilions. There are gatehouses at both ends of the bridge, covered with hip and gable roofs and with small grey tiles. The gallery house is covered by a hipped roof. A pavilion once graced the middle of the bridge, covered by outstretched eaves, however it no longer exists.

08—晏家桥

湖南省益阳市安化县乐安镇横石村肖家组柳林溪，清乾隆（1736—1795年）

南北走向，长 35 米、宽 4 米、高 9 米，十一开间。一墩两孔、墩叠枕、平梁搭连、穿斗结构、歇山重檐、瓦顶廊桥。桥北建有住房、店铺、灶房，南端加建楼阁式廊厅。因风雨侵蚀重，清道光二十九年（1849 年）修缮。

08. Yanjia Bridge – Liulin River, Xiaojia Group, Hengshi Village, Le'an Town, Anhua County, Yiyang, Hunan Province, built during 1736-1795.

This is a timber beam *chuandou* structure covered bridge. It has stone piers and layered cross-ties which together with connected beams form its main structure. Running from north to south, it has one pier and two spans. Its gallery house has eleven bays and is topped by a multiple-eave and hip and gable roof covered with tiles. The bridge is 35 meters long, 4 meters wide and 9 meters high. There are dwellings, shops, and a kitchen on the north end of the bridge. On the south end, there is a pavilion-style hall. Due to severe erosion caused by wind and rain, the bridge was repaired in 1849.

09－肖家桥

湖南省益阳市安化县乐安镇横市村柳林溪，清乾隆四十九年（1784年）

全木结构廊桥，南北走向，长31米、宽3米、高9米，十四开间，一墩两孔叠木平梁，重檐小青瓦硬山顶。桥廊属穿斗式木架结构，南北桥厅上部加建小楼阁。被列为省级文物保护单位。

09. Xiaojia Bridge — Liulin River, Hengshi Village, Le'an Town, Anhua County, Yiyang, Hunan Province, built in 1784.

This is a timber combined beam covered bridge. It runs from north to south, and has one pier and two spans. It is 31 meters long, 3 meters wide and 9 meters high. With fourteen bays, the gallery house is a *chuandou* structure, replete with a double-eave and flush gable roof covered with small grey tiles. Small pavilions were built on top of the bridge halls at each end. The bridge has been listed as the Historical and Cultural Sites Protected at the Provincial Level.

第五章 中南廊桥遗存带

五、"入溆浦余儃徊兮，迷不知吾所如" ——《涉江》

V. "I Hesitated on Arriving at Xupu River, and not Know Where to Go." —*Shejiang*

01—万寿桥

湖南省怀化市溆浦县黄茅园镇万寿村龙潭河，明崇祯九年（1636年）

又名画桥。重檐阁楼式廊桥，东西走向，长60米、宽4米、高11米，二十四开间，四墩五孔。石砌桥墩、贯木叠拱、圆木平梁、木廊瓦顶。廊顶中部建造高4米的重檐六角攒尖顶塔阁。廊桥两端门厅建龙脊门枋，枋檐为四层如意斗拱式样。清乾隆八年（1743年）至中华民国三十四年（1945年）有七次大的修缮。2013年被列为县级文物保护单位。

01.Wanshou Bridge — Longtan River, Wanshou Village, Huangmaoyuan Town, Xupu County, Huaihua, Hunan Province, built in 1636.

Also known as Huaqiao Bridge, the bridge runs from east to west, and has four piers and five spans. It is 60 meters long, 4 meters wide and 11 meters high. Its gallery house has twenty-four bays, and is built in the style of a pavilion building with double-eave. The bridge's piers are made of stone work. Timbers are interconnected and piled to form the arch, and logs serve as the bridge deck's main supporting beams. The gallery house is topped with tiles. The middle of the gallery house has a four-meter tall pagoda building installed on top, with a six-corner multiple-eave pyramidal roof. Both ends of the bridge have memorial arch gateways with dragon-shaped ridges, and eaves made with four layers of *ruyi dougong* brackets. The bridge underwent extensive restoration work seven times between 1743 and 1945. In 2013, the bridge was listed as the Historical and Cultural Sites Protected at the County Level.

2.壶圆桥

湖南省怀化市溆浦县葛竹坪镇福江村，清同治四年（1865年）

又名双江桥、长亭子桥。两墩三孔，长45米，十四开间，墩上端三层井字枕木。原建有两座双层八角阁楼，现存一座。屈原在第二个放逐地溆浦县住过16年，"路漫漫其修远兮，吾将上下而求索"，不正是他对彼岸的遥想吗？溆浦我没有走全，只流连于几座廊桥，却已经感触到山水的神妙与屈原的呼吸。

2. Huyuan Bridge – Fujiang Village, Gezhuping Town, Xupu County, Huaihua, Hunan Province, built in 1865.

This bridge is also known as the Shuangjiang Bridge and Changtingzi Bridge. It has two piers and three spans, and is 45 meters long. The gallery house has fourteen bays. A criss-cross pattern of timber cross-ties consisting of three layers, forming the shape of the Chinese character for well（井）are played on the upper ends of the piers to support the bridge. The bridge formerly had a pair of two-layer pavilions with eight-corner roofs, but only one remains at present. The famed poet Qu Yuan spent 16 years in Xupu County, the second place where he was exiled. Qu Yuan once said "The road ahead is long and has no end; yet high and low I will search with my will unbending." This depicted his expectations about the future. Although I have not seen all of Xupu and have only been to a few of its covered bridges, I have experienced the charm of its landscape and the echoes of Qu Yuan.

第五章 中南廊桥遗存带

03—回龙桥

湖南省怀化市溆浦县葛竹坪镇福坪村,清咸丰五年(1855年)

桥旁曾建有五层鼓楼"回龙庵"而得名,又名鸳鸯风雨桥。呈八字形跨岚水江与卜鳌河(溆水支流)汇流处。双桥为湘西重要水陆通衢。桥中堡墩台用麻石砌筑在三角洲上,三墩四孔,两桥各长22.5米,中部建有三层六角的木塔阁楼,两端建叠拱门楼。总长45米、宽4米、高12米,十四开间。

03. Huilong Bridge — Fuping Village, Gezhuping Town, Xupu County, Huaihua, Hunan Province, built in 1855.

Also known as the Yuanyang Fengyu Bridge, Huilong Bridge was named after the Huilong nunnery which located in a five-story drum-tower building beside the bridge. This *bazi*-style bridge spans over the confluence of the Lanshui and Bu' ao (tributary of the Xushui River) rivers, and has served as an important passageway in Western Hunan. The bridge' s piers are built out of granite masonry placed on the delta below. The bridge has three piers and four spans. Each of the bridge' s two segments is 22.5 meters long, and in the middle where the segments meet there is a three-story six-corner timber pagoda. Hence the bridge is 45 meters long overall, and is 4 meters wide and 12 meters high.

第五章 中南廊桥遗存带

六、资江中游 湘中宝地

VI. The Middle Reaches of Zijiang River, Treasured Land of Hunan Province

01—余庆桥

湖南省娄底市新化县天门乡高田村六组

清水河余庆桥旁侧只有一户人家。户主老王奉养 83 岁父亲，携妻子、儿孙居住桥西。"一水、一桥、一人家"使人印象深刻。古称横板桥，长 38 米、宽 4.5 米、高 6 米，纵横叠木平梁、独孔全木结构。桥西端遗存清咸丰、清光绪与中华民国时期功德碑数方。其中清道光《奉宪示禁碑》记："从来规约不监则弊灾多生，贼盗不除则良善难靖，因故立此禁碑。永禁来往差役乘轿。"

01.Yuqing Bridge — Sixth Group of Gaotian Village, Tianmen Township, Xinhua County, Loudi, Hunan Province.

There is only one family who lives by the bridge. Mr Wang lives to its south together with his 83-year-old father, wife, children, and grandchildren. The phrase "one river, one bridge, one family" comes to mind. Such a scene is impressive. In the past, the bridge was known as Hengban Bridge. Spanning the Qingshui River, it has a single span. The deck's main supporting beams are arranged in a criss-cross pattern. It is 38 meters long, 4.5 meters wide and 6 meters high. At the west end of the bridge, there are several surviving steles dating from the Qing Dynasty and Republic of China period. Among them, the *Fengxian Warning Stele* records that "Without enforcement of rules, harm and misfortune will often occur. Without eradicating thieves and robbers, it will be difficult to spread goodness. Thus, this warning stele is placed here, eternally forbidding the yamen's runners (agents) from riding in sedan chairs" (i.e. servants of imperial officials riding in sedan chairs would be a sign of corruption).

中国廊桥

02—长丰桥

湖南省娄底市新化县长丰乡长丰村谷河，清咸丰八年（1858年）

长丰乡小学的学生上下学必过此廊桥，当地百姓称其为"学子桥"。逢圩日，廊桥成为交易中心，各种山货琳琅满目。独孔、叠梁伸臂式廊桥，长60米、宽4米、高14米。桥廊全木结构，各构件榫卯衔扣，牢固坚实抗风力强。重檐顶覆乌黑鱼鳞瓦，两端设牌楼厅。于中华民国二十三年（1934年）2005年修缮。

02.Changfeng Bridge — Guhe River, Changfeng Village, Changfeng Township, Xinhua County, Loudi, Hunan Province, built in 1858.

Elementary school students use the bridge to travel back and forth to school. Because of this, the bridge is also called the Xuezi Bridge. On market days, the eye is astounded by a wealth of mountain products arrayed on the covered bridge. The bridge has a single span, and is a timber cantilever compound beam bridge. Its joins are made with mortise and tenon technology, and it has a very high degree of stability and wind resistance. The bridge is 60 meters long, 4 meters wide, and 14 meters high. Its double-eave roof is covered with jet-gre "fish-scale" tiles, and memorial arch gateway stand at either end. The bridge was repaired 1934 and 2005.

3—广利桥

湖南省永州市东安县紫溪市镇塘复村印水河，清乾隆三十八年（1773年）

以"广济行人，利福万民"之意定桥名。两墩三孔，石墩木柱瓦顶廊桥，长36.8米、宽4.5米、高7米，十八开间。桥主拱顶部基石厚度仅一尺有余，故有"金鸡脚、豆腐腰"之称。桥面铺青砖，廊内两侧安置护栏、长条木凳。重檐桥廊另有一座悬山顶挑檐阁楼和两座门楼，上盖青瓦。1985年8月修缮。被列为省级文物保护单位。

3. Guangli Bridge — Yinshui River, Tangfu Village, Zixishi Town, Dong'an County, Yongzhou, Hunan Province, built in 1773.

The Guangli Bridge's name is derived from the saying that "It can widely help pedestrians through the bridge, fortune and happiness will accrue to multitudes." This stone arch covered bridge has two piers and three spans. It is 36.8 meters long, 4.5 meters wide, and 7 meters high. Its gallery house has eighteen bays. The capstone on top of its main arch is only a bit over one *chi* long (one *chi* equals about 0.33 meters), so people refer to the bridge as having a "golden chicken foot, and tofu waist". The bridge's deck is covered with grey bricks. Inside, timber protective railing and long benches run along both sides. The gallery house also has a pavilion on top covered by a overhanging gable roof with outstretched eaves. There also are memorial arches at either side of the bridge. These are also covered with grey tiles. This bridge has been repaired in August, 1985. It has been listed as the Historical and Cultural Sites Protected at the Provincial Level.

第五章 中南廊桥遗存带

04—木瓜桥

湖南省武冈市邓元泰镇木瓜村资水河

曾名红军桥。清康熙五十年（1711年）建桥亭，清同治八年（1869年）重建。东西走向，石墩，叠木平梁，木柱瓦顶廊桥，长44米、宽4.7米、高8米，四墩五孔，十二开间。桥廊两端入口高砌青砖马头墙式牌楼，门厅廊柱遗留楷书桥名藏头对联"木叶落亭前际资水秋深夜雨横飞圃树""瓜田连岸畔看平原草绿朝烟遥接板云"。

04.Mugua Bridge – Zishui River, Mugua Village, Dengyuantai Town, Wugang, Hunan Province.

This bridge was also known as Hongjun Bridge. The bridge pavilion was built in 1711 and rebuilt in 1869. Running from east to west, this four pier five span bridge has stone piers and compound beams that form the main support for the bridge's deck. It is 44 meters long, 4.7 meters wide, and 8 meters high. Its gallery house has twelve bays. On both ends of the covered bridge, there are tall horse-head wall (*matouqiang*) style memorial arches covered by grey tiles. In its entryway, there are two columns decorated with a poetic couplet that hides the name of the bridge within its words: "Tree leaves fall, and in front of the pavilion is a view of the Zishui River in autumn. In the dead of the night rains falls horizontally against the cultivated plants. Gourd fields on both sides reveal green plains. And smoke rises towards the board of a cloud." The characters that start each respective couplet line—"tree" and "gourd" together form the Chinese word for papaya.

第五章 中南廊桥遗存带

七、莽山长乐河——盐铁古道上的廊桥
VII. Changle River and Mangshan Mountain, Covered Bridges along the Ancient Salt Iron Road

01—观音阁桥

湖南省郴州市宜章县白沙圩乡才口村,北宋(960—1127年)

观音阁桥始建于北宋(960—1127年)时期。桥东端紧邻观音阁,为一墩两孔砖柱瓦顶三级宝塔式廊桥。三级宝塔用于纪念建寺的高僧和历代住持。观音阁桥保存完好,仍然造福于当地的百姓。

01.Guanyinge Bridge – Caikou Village, Baishaxu Township, Yizhang County, Chenzhou, Hunan Province, built during 960-1127.

Guanyinge Bridge was first built during the Northern Song Dynasty (960-1127). The Guanyin Pavilion is next to the east end of the covered bridge. The bridge forms the housing for a three-story pagoda. The bridge's internal columns are built of bricks and the gallery house is covered with tiles. The three-story pagoda is used to commemorate the eminent monks who built the temple and the abbots of past dynasties. The Guanyinge Bridge is well preserved and still benefits local people.

第五章 中南廊桥遗存带

02—广济桥

湖南省郴州市宜章县笆篱乡车田村大刘家村玉水河

清道光七年（1827年）重建。一墩两孔，叠木伸臂式砖石与木构混合形制廊桥，长30.6米、宽4.2米、高8.5米，桥墩上面方形碉楼宽9米。被列为省级文物保护单位。一副桥联闻名四方："真意焚香何须面朝南海，诚心拜佛此处就是西天。"

02. Guangji Bridge — Yushui River, Daliujia Village, Chetian Village, Bali Township, Yizhang County, Chenzhou, Hunan Province.

This bridge was rebuilt in 1827. The bridge has one pier and two spans. It is a timber cantilever covered bridge with a mixed stone and timber structure. Its cantilever assemblage is composed of combined timbers. It is 30.6 meters long, 4.2 meters wide, and 8.5 meters high. The square-shaped tower above the pier is 9 meters wide. The bridge has been listed as the Historical and Cultural Sites Protected at the Provincial Level. This bridge is decorated with a famous poem, "If incense is burned for a true motive, why must the southern seas be the direction faced. By sincerely worshipping Buddha, the Western Paradise is this very place."

第五章　中南廊桥遗存带

第六节·湘黔桂交界地及广西桂林的廊桥
Section VI　Covered Bridges on the Hunan, Guizhou and Guangxi Borders and in Guilin, Guangxi

一、大江三条——榕江、浔江、苗江廊桥群
I. Three Rivers, Covered Bridges on Rongjiang, Xunjiang and Miaojiang Rivers

01—程阳桥

广西壮族自治区柳州市三江侗族自治县古宜镇马安寨林溪河，中华民国二年（1913年）

又名永济桥、盘龙桥。是中国石木廊桥建筑艺术珍品，侗族文化标志性建筑，被收录于2003年版《中国桥谱》。长77.6米、宽3.75米、高20米，十九开间，三墩四孔。被列为全国重点文物保护单位。1965年郭沫若为程阳风雨桥赋诗："艳说林溪风雨桥，桥长廿丈四寻高。重瓴联阁怡神巧，列砥横流入望遥。竹木一身坚胜铁，茶林万载苗新苗。何时得上三江道，学把犁锄事体劳。"

01.Chengyang Bridge – on Linxi River at Ma'an Stockade, Guyi Town, Sanjiang Dong Autonomous County, Liuzhou, Guangxi Zhuang Autonomous Region, built in 1913.

Chengyang Bridge, also named Yongji Bridge or Panlong Bridge, is one of China's most precious stone and timber covered bridges. Representing distinct features of Dong architecture, it was included in *A Guide to Chinese Bridges* (*published in* 2003). It has three piers and four spans. It is 77.6 meters long, 3.75 meters wide, and 20 meters high. Its gallery house has nineteen bays. Chengyang Bridge has been listed as the Major Historical and Cultural Sites Protected at the National Level. In 1965, the famous writer Guo Moruo wrote a poem for the bridge: "Of Linxi River's Fengyu Bridge one speaks enthralled; A bridge twenty *zhang* long and four *xun* tall; On pleasing magical pavilions tiles lay; With stones that flow across into sites faraway. Bamboos stand as strong as iron; Tea groves' countless branches sprouting everyone; When the time comes go the way of Sanjiang; Study through plough and hoe to make the body labor strong."

第五章 中南廊桥遗存带

02—安济桥

广西壮族自治区柳州市三江侗族自治县林溪镇合华村

　　风雨桥是侗族人民的伟大创造，是侗族建筑的精华。安济桥的桥墩为石面柱体，上下游均为锐角，可减轻洪水冲击。桥面采用密布式悬臂托架简支梁体系，全木结构。桥廊采用榫卯衔扣的梁柱体系联成整体，三座桥塔高大雄伟，风雨檐板保护桥面并增加整体美感。

02.Anji Bridge – Hehua Village, Linxi Township, Sanjiang Dong Autonomous County, Liuzhou, Guangxi Zhuang Autonomous Region.

Fengyu bridges are a great architectural invention of the Dong nationality, and testament to the Dong nationality's glorious architectural achievements. Anji Bridge is supported by stone-faced piers which are tapered to become sharp at both ends to reduce the impact of flood waters. The bridge's deck is supported by closely and tightly arranged cantilever brackets and by a simply supported beam system. The gallery house's columns and beams are joined by mortises and tenons. There are three tall pagodas standing on the bridge, creating a magnificent site. Awnings are put up to protect the bridge deck from wind and rain, also adding to the bridge's overall charm.

03—赐福桥

广西壮族自治区柳州市三江侗族自治县独峒镇平流村，清咸丰十年（1860年）

《赐福桥序》碑记：" 赐福桥始建于清咸丰十年（1860年），至1947年正月二十七日因村民祭神不慎毁于一炬。我村父老民众立于当年五月十八日兴工重建，历时五载于1951年冬竣工。桥梁四层梁巨盈抱，横跨江岸坐两道山梁如双龙抢宝之势。桥长十一丈共二十间，宽丈一。三座重檐楼阁阔丈五、高五层。二丈余高的青料石桥墩砥柱中流，迎百年洪峰而岿然不动。"

3.Cifu Bridge — Pingliu Village, Dudong Town, Sanjiang Dong Autonomous County, Liuzhou, Guangxi Zhuang Autonomous Region, built in 1860.

is recorded on the stele *Preface to Cifu Bridge*, "Built in the tenth year of the Xianfeng reign of the Qing Dynasty (1861), Cifu Bridge was torched on the 27th of the first lunar month 1947 when villagers were not careful when conducting sacrifices to gods. The village's male elders then organized for reconstruction to start on the 18th of the following fifth lunar month, and work was completed five years later in the winter of 1951. Four layers of supporting beams enclose the bridge, which spans the two banks of the river. It passes over two mountain ridges in a way that makes it resemble two dragons vying for a treasure. It is 11 *zhang* long and 1.1 *zhang* wide. Its gallery house has twenty bays. The bridge has three five-story pavilions which are 1.5 *zhang* wide each with multiple-eave roofs. Its grey stone piers are over 2 *zhang* tall, and have not budged despite greeting over a hundred years of flood waters."

中国廊桥

04—华练培凤桥

广西壮族自治区柳州市三江侗族自治县独峒镇平流村，清咸丰七年（1857年）

《培凤桥修复志》碑记载："修桥铺路是侗民族的传统美德。依山傍水的侗寨，寨尾溪河下游都架设一座廊桥。一是方便过往行人，二是供人们纳凉歇息和避雨，三是作为寨尾一道屏障，其寓意锁住千年长流，村民纳财不流失。斯桥始建于1857年，桥为两墩两台四亭，17间桥廊，长65米、宽4米。"

04.Hualianpeifeng Bridge — Pingliu Village, Dudong Town, Sanjiang Dong Autonomous County, Liuzhou, Guangxi Zhuang Autonomous Region, built in 1857.

The bridge's stele, entitled *Restoration of Peifeng Bridge*, states, "Repairing bridges and building roads are aspects of the traditional moral excellence of the Dong Nationality. The Dong villages, which are built against mountainsides and alongside rivers, all have a covered bridge built downstream at the end of the settlement. This is done firstly to facilitate the passage of people, secondly to provide a cool place to rest and avoid the rain, and thirdly to serve as a sort of barrier to the channel, the significance of which is to symbolically lock in the flow of thousands of years so that the village's wealth and resources do not flow away. The bridge was built in 1857. It has two piers, two abutments and four pavilions. Its gallery house has 17 bays. It is 65 meters long and 4 meters wide."

95—巩福桥

广西壮族自治区柳州市三江侗族自治县独峒镇独峒乡八协村，清光绪三年（1877年）

《巩福桥修复志》碑记节录："我侗民族崇尚礼仪，热心公益。村寨中必设议事鼓楼，溪河上定架风雨花桥。构筑技艺超绝，美名饮誉中外。向者八协故有风雨桥一座，始建于清光绪三年（1877年）。是时建桥先人父老含辛茹苦，开凿山石筑基台双墩，斫伐良木造桥四楼重檐，经营十有三载精工细作。桥长二十四丈，雄伟壮观。桥之建成民安乐，故命名巩福桥。"

95.Gongfu Bridge — Baxie Village, Dudong Township, Dudong Town, Sanjiang Dong Autonomous County, Liuzhou, Guangxi Zhuang Autonomous Region, built in 1877.

It is recorded on the stele *Restoration of the Gongfu Bridge* that "We Dong Nationality strongly uphold propriety and deeply value the public welfare. As a result, the village had to install a drum tower in its center for public meetings, as well as erect a fengyu huaqiao bridge on the banks of the river. The structure was built with impeccable craftsmanship, and is famous both near and far. Since old times Baxie Village has had a fengyu bridge. It was first built in the third year of the Guangxu reign of the Qing Dynasty (1877). At that time, the villagers building the bridge endured bitter hardships, and chiseled two abutments and two piers out of the mountain rock for the bridge's foundation. They chopped down fine wood to construct the bridge's four buildings covered by roofs with multiple-eave. It was built through 13 years of excellent and careful work. The bridge is 24 *zhang* long, and is magnificent and grand. The bridge's construction brought peace and happiness to the people, and as a result its name is Gongfu Bridge."

二、中国罕见的立交式风雨桥
II. The Rare Flyover-Type Fengyu Bridge

岜团桥

广西壮族自治区柳州市三江侗族自治县独峒乡岜团寨苗江，清光绪二十四年（1898 年）

岜团桥连通湘西、桂北、黔南交通要道，三省、自治区往来官民甚多。为避免牲畜惊吓、误伤老少妇孺与过往行人，营造安全整洁的环境，乡民公议多捐银两，聘请侗族梓匠（建筑大师）石含章、吴金添设计建造了中国独一无二的"立交式"风雨桥。东西走向，一墩两孔平梁，楼殿式全木结构，上层人行道高 2.4 米、宽 4 米，下层畜行道高 1.9 米，宽 1.4 米，全长 50 米。人畜通道分为两层故称立交桥。三座楼阁五层重檐歇山顶，高 8 米。被列为全国重点文物保护单位。

Batuan Bridge — MiaoJiang River, Batuan Stockade, Dudong Township, Sanjiang Dong Autonomous County, Liuzhou, Guangxi Zhuang Autonomous Region, built in 1898.

Batuan Bridge was an important intersection connecting west Hunan, north Guangxi and south Guizhou. In the past, because a large number of people came and went on the bridge, villagers collected money and invited Shi Hanzhang and Wu Jintian, two Dong architects, to design a bridge that could lessen the number of people injured by livestock along the bridge while at the same time maintaining a more clean environment along its length. Hence, this unique interchange-type fengyu bridge was designed and built. The bridge runs from east to west. It has one pier and two spans, and beams support the main bridge structure. It is a palace-style bridge. The upper passage for people is 2.4 meters high and 4 meters wide, and the one below for livestock is 1.9 meters high and 1.4 meters wide. The separation of people and livestock into an upper and lower corridor led to calling the structure an interchange bridge. There are three five-story pavilions on the bridge which are each 8 meters high and sport multiple-eave and hip and gable roofs. Batuan Bridge has been listed as the Major Historical and Cultural Sites Protected at the National Level.

第五章 中南廊桥遗存带

三、万山环峙 五水分流——龙胜县

III. Longsheng County, Encompassed by Mountains with Five Rivers Flowing in It

孟滩桥

广西壮族自治区桂林市龙胜各族自治县平等镇，清光绪三年（1877年）

中华民国十二年（1923年）复建。两墩三跨伸臂木梁桥，桥长63.2米、宽4.1米，桥廊高3.94米，桥身到河面高度7.4米。桥中跨净跨23.2米，为现存侗族廊桥中跨度最大的廊桥。四座塔楼均为三重檐四方四脊攒尖顶。明清时期，湖南省城通往广西龙胜县的古道须翻越"八十里大南山"，必经孟滩桥。1949年后沿江修通公路，孟滩桥专为平等村官寨组村民出入通道。被列为县级文物保护单位。

Mengtan Bridge – Pingdeng Town, Longsheng Various Nationalities Autonomous County, Guilin, Guangxi Zhuang Autonomous Region, built in 1877.

The bridge was reconstructed in 1933. The covered bridge's main structure is supported by combined log beams. It has two piers and three spans. It is 63.2 meters long, 4.1 meters wide, gallery is 3.94 meters high, there are 7.4 meters high from the bridge body to river. The bridge has a middle span of 23.2 meters, it is the largest of all the surviving covered bridges in Guangxi. The bridge also has four pagoda towers, each with triple eaves, four faces, and pyramidal roofs with four ridges. During the Ming and Qing dynasties, the only way to get from Hunan Province to Longsheng County in Guangxi was to cross the "eighty-li Da'nan Mountain" and pass across the Mengtan Bridge. After 1949, public roads were built along the Yangtze River, and Mengtan Bridge became used mainly by (villagers) of Pingdeng Village's Guanzhai Group and officials to come and go. It is listed as the Historical and Cultural Sites Protected at the County Level.

第五章 中南廊桥遗存带

四、湘江上游 湘桂走廊——全州县

IV. Quanzhou County, in the Upstream of the Xiangjiang River along the Hunan-Guangxi Corridor

01—广福桥

广西壮族自治区桂林市全州县龙水镇光田村双车自然村，清嘉庆（1796 — 1820 年）

现桥建于清嘉庆（1796 — 1820 年）年间。一墩两孔石平梁廊桥，长 8 米、宽 3.6 米、高 5 米，两间半开间，双坡顶连接马头墙山字门，四根石柱支撑廊顶。被列为县级文物保护单位。

01.Guangfu Bridge — Shuangche Natural Village, Guangtian Village, Longshui Town, Quanzhou County, Guilin, Guangxi Zhuang Autonomous Region, built during 1796-1820.

The present bridge was built between 1796 and 1821. It has one pier and two spans, and is a timber beam supported bridge. It is 8 meters long, 3.6 meters wide, and 5 meters high. It has a gallery house with two and a half bays. Its double sloped roof is supported by four columns, and is connected to the gate's horse-head wall. The bridge is listed as the Historical and Cultural Sites Protected at the County Level.

02—虹饮桥

广西壮族自治区桂林市全州县龙水镇龙水村万乡河，清乾隆（1736—1795年）

《全州县志》记："全州县位于中原通岭南要道，系越楚尾之地，得楚、中原文化之先。境内有清乾隆年间修建的虹饮桥，系县内有名古建筑。县内工匠多为湖南、江西等省流寓客匠。"五墩六孔全木结构平梁、木瓦砖石结构廊桥，长72米、宽4.2米、高7米，中部设重檐挑角小阁。红廊碧瓦如"彩虹饮水"得名。1998年重修。

2.Hongyin Bridge — Wanxiang River, Longshui Village, Longshui Town, Quanzhou County, Guilin, Guangxi Zhuang Autonomous Region, built during 1736-1795.

The *Quanzhou County Chronicle* states that "Quanzhou County is located in the south of the Central Plains to the south of Five Ridges. It is where the ancient states of Yue and Chu share a border, and was the earliest region to acquire the culture of the state of Chu and of the Central Plains. In Quanzhou County, there is a bridge built during the reign of Qianlong of the Qing Dynasty, which is famous throughout the county. Many of the craftsmen in the county were guest laborers from Hunan and Jiangxi." It has five piers and six spans. It is a timber, tile, brick and stone structured covered bridge, with its main structure supported by timber beams. It is 72 meters long, 4.2 meters wide, and 7 meters high. There is a small pavilion with a multiple-eave roof with upturned corners in its center. The combination of the red gallery house and its jade colored tiles resembles "a rainbow drinking water", thus resulting in the bridge's name. In 1998, the bridge was rebuilt.

五、桂林山水甲天下
V. Guilin, the Most Excellent Landscape under the Heaven

花桥

广西壮族自治区桂林市七星岩，宋理宗嘉熙（1237－1240年）

始建于宋理宗嘉熙（1237－1240年）年间，原名嘉熙桥，明代改名为花桥，清代改名为天柱桥。石拱四墩五孔敞廊式廊桥，元末明初水毁。明景泰七年（1456年）知府何永全集资在原址建石墩木桥。明嘉靖十九年（1540年）重修并增建旱桥五墩六孔，自此该桥由东西两段组成。东段水桥长60米，建有单脊双坡顶廊屋，十五开间，西段旱桥长65.2米，宽均6.3米。1965年整修。

Huaqiao Bridge – Qixing Rock, Guilin, Guangxi Zhuang Autonomous Region, built during 1237-1240.

The bridge was built during the Jiaxi period of the Song Dynasty (1237-1240), it was originally called Jiaxi Bridge. Its name was then changed to Huaqiao Bridge in the Ming Dynasty and to Tianzhu Bridge in the Qing Dynasty. It is a stone arch covered bridge with four piers and five spans. Between the late Yuan and early Ming dynasties, it was destroyed by flood. In 1456, *Zhifu* (the prefectural magistrate) He Yongquan collected funds to construct a timber bridge with stone piers at the original site of the bridge. In 1540, the bridge was rebuilt, with the addition of a section over dry land with five piers and six spans, creating a complete bridge running from east to west with two sections. The east section passes over water and is 60 meters long. Its gallery house has fifteen bays covered by a double sloping single ridge roof. The west section passes over dry land and is 65.2 meters long, and the whole bridge is 6.3 meters wide. It was renovated in 1965.

六、三省、自治区交界处的潇贺廊桥群
VI. The Group of Xiaohe Covered Bridge along Three Provinces or Autonomous Regions' Borders

01—青龙桥

广西壮族自治区贺州市富川瑶族自治县油沐乡沐笼村，明代（1368 — 1644 年）

单孔砖石结构阁楼式廊桥，长 36 米、宽 4.6 米、高 9.8 米。中部顶端建歇山顶飞檐小阁，北端耸立一座三层阁楼。东、南、北三面有门。清道光《创修青龙亭题名记碑》载："其中以惟亭一座，路衢三通，创自有明。宅西宛若龙山之吐秀，故题其额曰青龙也。"

01.Qinglong Bridge — Mulong Village, Youmu Township, Fuchuan Yao Autonomous County, Hezhou, Guangxi Zhuang Autonomous Region, built during 1368-1644.

This is a stone arch bridge with a single span. It is 36 meters long, 4.6 meters wide and 9.8 meters high. Its center has a small pavilion with a hip and gable roof with upturned eaves. In its northern part, there is a three-story pavilion. There are gates to the east, south and north. A stele from the Qing Daoguang era (1821-1850) is titled *Memorial Stele for the Creation of the Green Dragon and its Naming*. The stele states, "In the middle sits a lone pavilion, that became well known because of the three roads there. The west house is just as beautiful as the Longshan Mountain, so it is titled Qinglong."

02—迴澜桥

广西壮族自治区贺州市富川瑶族自治县油沐乡沐笼村，明万历（1573—1620年）

明崇祯十四年（1641年）、清道光十九年（1839年）重修，1987年维修。三孔石拱、桥亭阁楼组合式廊桥，长38米、宽4.6米、高8米，跨径各6.22米。迴澜桥与青龙桥毗邻，被当地百姓称为鸳鸯风雨桥。同属全国重点文物保护单位序列。

02.Huilan Bridge – Mulong Village, Youmu Township, Fuchuan Yao Autonomous County, Hezhou, Guangxi Zhuang Autonomous Region, built during 1573-1620.

The bridge was rebuilt in 1641 and 1839, and repaired in 1987. It is a stone arch covered bridge with three spans. It is a combined covered bridge and pavilion structure. The bridge is 38 meters long, 4.6 meters wide, and 8 meters high. Each of its spans is 6.22 meters. Huilan Bridge is adjacent to the Qinglong Bridge. Local people refer to the two as the yuanyang fengyu bridge (*yuanyang* being a symbol in China of a loving couple). These two bridge are all listed as the Major Historical and Cultural Sites Protected the National Level.

3—集贤桥

广西壮族自治区贺州市富川瑶族自治县油沐乡沐村，清光绪十一年（1885年）

一墩两孔横木平梁、石墩砖墙廊桥，长17米、宽3.88米、高9米、深14米，五开间。桥面铺木板，穿斗式结构，桥廊桥亭覆盖小瓦，桥头建马头墙门厅。属全国重点文物保护单位。

3.Jixian Bridge — Mulong Village, Youmu Township, Fuchuan Yao Autonomous County, Hezhou, Guangxi Zhuang Autonomous Region, built in 1885.

The bridge has one pier and two spans, and is supported by timber beams and crosspieces. It stands on a stone pier and has a gallery house built with brick walls as well as a timber *chuandou* structure. It is 17 meters long, 3.88 meters wide, and 9 meters high. It has a gallery house with five bays. The deck is covered with timber boards, the gallery house and pavilion are covered with small grey tiles. A horse-head wall is erected at the bridge entrance. The bridge is listed as the Major Historical and Cultural Sites Protected at the National Level.

04—钟灵桥

广西壮族自治区贺州市富川瑶族自治县朝东镇福溪村，清光绪三十年（1904年）

两墩三孔、石墙木柱、平梁瓦顶、歇山顶阁楼式廊桥，长10.6米、宽4.35米、高10米、跨径9.10米，三开间。桥面铺木板，穿斗式结构。桥头三块高大狰狞的石头，当地百姓称为"扎根石"，为中国廊桥景观独有。据村老讲："是地下龙王三片鳞甲保佑村寨的。上下桥不那么方便但我们从不介意，老少妇孺皆视如珍宝。外乡人用力拍几下我们都心痛。"为全国重点文物保护单位。

04.Zhongling Bridge – Fuxi Village, Chaodong Town, Fuchuan Yao Autonomous County, Hezhou, Guangxi Zhuang Autonomous Region, built in 1904.

This is a timber beam supported bridge with two piers and three spans, its piers are made of stone. The bridge is built in the style of a pavilion building with a *xieshanding* hip and gable roof, covered with tiles. It is 10.6 meters long, 4.35 meters wide, 10 meters high and has a clear span of 9.10 meters. It has a gallery house with three bays. The bridge deck is covered with wooden boards and it is a *chuandou* structure. Three rugged natural giant stones have been preserved at the bridge entrance, which are called "root stones" by locals, something unique to covered bridges in China. According to the old people in village, these stones are "three pieces of the underground dragon king's scaled armor, which serve to protect the village. The villagers young and old regard the stones as a real treasure, how strangers treat them make us feel sad." The bridge is listed as the Major Historical and Cultural Sites Protected at the National Level.

05—东辕桥

广西壮族自治区贺州市富川瑶族自治县朝东镇白面寨村，清乾隆三十四年（1769年）

独孔石平梁、青砖桥面、穿斗式结构、殿宇式廊桥，长15.6米、宽5.5米、高9米，五开间。单脊双坡顶建敞阔歇山顶阁楼，覆盖小青瓦，马头墙桥头。属全国重点文物保护单位。

05.Dongyuan Bridge — Baimianzhai Village, Chaodong Town, Fuchuan Yao Autonomous County, Hezhou, Guangxi Zhuang Autonomous Region, built in 1769.

This is a single span stone beam palace-style covered bridge and it is a *chuandou* structure. Its deck is covered with grey bricks. The bridge is 15.6 meters long, 5.5 meters wide, and 9 meters high. The gallery house has five bays and has a single-ridge open hip and gable roof with double slopes, decorated with small grey tiles. At the entrance there is a horse-head wall. The bridge is listed as the Major Historical and Cultural Sites Protected at the National Level.

6 — 西门桥

广西壮族自治区贺州市富川瑶族自治县朝东镇儒村，清光绪十年（1884年）

砖石结构石平梁、青砖桥面、穿斗式结构廊桥，长7.3米、宽3.66米、高6米，三开间，桥廊桥亭覆盖小青瓦，马头墙桥头。西门桥没有建在村口，而是建在村子中央排水渠上，是半个村的村民进出的通道。

6.Ximen Bridge — Ruzi Village, Chaodong Town, Fuchuan Yao Autonomous County, Hezhou, Guangxi Zhuang Autonomous Region, built in 1884.

This single-span bridge is a masonry structure with stone supporting beams. Its deck is covered with grey bricks. Its gallery house is a *chuandou* structure with three bays. The bridge is 7.3 meters long, 3.66 meters wide, and 6 meters high. The gallery house and pavilion are covered with small grey tiles. There is also a horse-head wall at the entrance. The Ximen Bridge was not built at the entrance of the village, but instead over a canal in the center of the village. It serves as a passageway used by one half of the villagers.

7 — 双溪桥

广西壮族自治区贺州市富川瑶族自治县朝东镇东村，清光绪十一年（1885年）

位于山村水口，两墩三孔，圆木平梁亭阁式廊桥，长20.8米、宽4.40米、高8米、跨径17米，七开间。桥面铺木板，穿斗式结构，桥廊和桥阁覆盖小青瓦，马头墙桥头。属全国重点文物保护单位。

7.Shuangxi Bridge — Dongshui Village, Chaodong Town, Fuchuan Yao Autonomous County, Hezhou, Guangxi Zhuang Autonomous Region, built in 1885.

The bridge is located at the place where this mountain village meets the water, it has two piers and three spans. It is supported by log beams and is a pavilion style covered bridge, *chuandou* structure. It is 20.8 meters long, 4.40 meters wide, and 8 meters high. The bridge has a span of 17 meters, and its gallery house has seven bays. The deck is covered with wooden boards. The gallery house and pavilions are covered with small grey tiles, and the entranceways have horse-head walls. The bridge is listed as the Major Historical and Cultural Sites Protected at the National Level.

08—环涧桥

广西壮族自治区贺州市富川瑶族自治县朝东镇长塘村，清道光二十二年（1842年）

环涧桥位于长塘村田野小溪，用于村民下田耕种避雨。两墩三孔、平梁砖墙、木柱瓦顶、通天阁楼式廊桥，长9.8米、宽3.9米、高8.6米、跨径8.96米，三开间。穿斗式结构，歇山顶桥亭，马头墙桥头。属全国重点文物保护单位。

08.Huanjian Bridge – Changtang Village, Chaodong Town, Fuchuan Yao Autonomous County, Hezhou, Guangxi Zhuang Autonomous Region, built in 1842.

Huanjian Bridge spans a stream that runs through an open field in Changtang Village. Villagers use it when farming to find shelter from the rain. The bridge was built as a covered bridge with beam supports, and it had two piers and three spans. Its gallery house was covered with brick walls and timber columns. The *chuandou* structure gallery house has three bays, and is covered by tiles. It is connected to a pavilion building with a hip and gable roof. It is 9.8 meters long, 3.9 meters wide, 8.6 meters high, and has a span of 8.9 meters. The bridge entrances have horse-head walls. The bridge is listed as the Major Historical and Cultural Sites Protected at the National Level.

第五章 中南廊桥遗存带

Chapter VI Covered Bridge Belt in Southeast China

It mainly includes southern Zhejiang, Fujian, eastern and southern Jiangxi Provinces. This is the inhabited place of She Nationality, Hakka and Han Nationality of Zhejiang and Fujian Provinces. There are continuous mountains in these areas, which are the most developed timber beam bridges area in China. In addition to timber arch beams, the construction of cantilever timber beam bridges is also common, especially in the northwest Fujian and southern Jiangxi areas where Hakkas live.

On the appearance of architectures, in order protect the timber structure of the bridge body, t awnings are also in use on both sides of the bridge

中国廊桥

第六章 东南廊桥遗存带

主要包括浙南、福建、赣东和赣南。这里是畲族、客家人和浙闽汉族世居之地,群山连绵,是中国编木梁桥最发达的区域。除了编木拱梁之外,伸臂木梁桥也很常见,特别是在客家人生活的闽西北、赣南地区在建筑外观上,为了保护桥身木结构,桥身两侧还普遍使用风雨板。

第一节 · 瓯江流域的廊桥
Section I Covered Bridges in Oujiang River Basin

01—回龙桥

浙江省金华市武义县郭洞古村，元代（1206 — 1368 年）

一座古村因岭环如郭、幽深似洞而得名郭洞。世人有"郭外风光古，洞中日月长"的赞叹。回龙桥又名石虹桥，位于郭洞村水口要津。单孔石拱凉亭式廊桥，亭顶设龙脊飞檐，顶尖宝葫芦象征吉祥如意。明隆庆年间（1567 — 1572 年）、清康熙六十年（1721 年）整修。

01.Huilong Bridge — Guodong Ancient Village, Wuyi County, Jinhua, Zhejiang Province, built during 1206-1368.

The village's name Guodong derives from the high mountains that surround it like a high city wall (*guo*) and which are deep and cavernous like a cave (*dong*). Mortals have praised the village with the verse "the scenery outside Guo is ancient, days and nights in Dong are long." Huilong Bridge, also known as Shihong Bridge, is located by an important ferry landing located by the waterside of Guodong Village. It is a stone arch cool-pavilion-style covered bridge with one span. The pavilion roof has a dragon-shaped ridge with upturned eaves. On its top is the figure of a precious gourd that symbolizes good luck. The bridge was repaired sometime during 1567-1572 as well as in 1721.

第六章 东南廊桥遗存带

02—熟溪桥

浙江省金华市武义县熟溪，宋宁宗开禧三年（1207年）

原名石公桥，长140米、宽4.8米、高13.4米，八墩九孔，四十九开间，廊内设置木凳，中部建歇山顶亭阁。桥碑记："宋开禧三年（1207年），县主簿石宗玉发起修筑，称石公桥。700多年间桥屡建屡毁，每修必添其彩。明嘉靖二十五年（1546年）建六墩，明万历四年（1576年）增至十墩。桥长五十丈、宽一丈七尺，并建桥屋四十九间。清乾隆四十九年（1784年）重修桥屋至五十一间，两侧卫以护栏。"被列为省级文物保护单位。

02.Shuxi Bridge – Shuxi River, Wuyi County, Jinhua, Zhejiang Province, built in 1207.

Shuxi Bridge formerly known as Shigong Bridge, it is 140 meters long, 4.8 meters wide, and 13.4 meters high. It has eight piers and nine spans. Its gallery house has forty-nine bays, and timber benches run along its length. A pavilion with a hip and gable roof is built in its middle. A stele by the bridge states, "Shi Zongyu, the county's *Zhubu* (secretary of the magistrate) initiated the construction of Shigong Bridge in 1207. Over the past 700 years, the bridge has been built and destroyed repeatedly. Six pie were built in 1546, then four more piers in 157 at which time the bridge was 50 *zhang* long and *zhang* and 7 *chi* wide. During this time, a gallery hous with forty-nine bays was built on the bridge as we In 1784, the gallery house was rebuilt with fift one bays, and protective railing was added to bo sides." The bridge is listed as the Historical an Cultural Sites Protected at the Provincial Level.

3—西津桥

浙江省永康市永康江古渡口，清康熙五十七年（1718年）

僧人知和四方游募桥资，历尽艰辛建成西津桥。清雍正（1723—1735年）、清乾隆（1736—1795年）、清嘉庆（1796—1820年）年间大修或重建。1984年"永康台北同乡会"骆振韶先生等捐款10余万元，政府拨款60余万元聘请专家，召集能工巧匠，于1989年9月将西津桥按原样修复。因河道较初建时狭窄，长度由206米变为166.6米，宽4米，十四墩十三孔，五十八开间。被列为省级文物保护单位。茅以升先生（1896—1989年，江苏省镇江市人，桥梁专家）将西津桥编入《中国桥梁建筑史》。

3.Xijin Bridge – Ancient Ferry Landing on the Yongkang River, Yongkang County Zhejiang Province, built in 1718.

The monk Zhihe travelled near and far to raise funds for the bridge here, and endured many hardships to finally successfully construct it. The bridge was reconstructed during the Yongzheng, Qianlong and Jiaqing periods of the Qing Dynasty. In 1984, Mr. Luo Zhenshao, a member of the Yongkang regional association in Taipei, Taiwan, donated more than 100,000 yuan for the restoration of the bridge, and the local government allocated more than 600,000 yuan to the project. Many experts and skilled craftsmen were recruited for the effort. In September 1989, Xijin Bridge was successfully restored to its original condition. Because the river had become narrower in recent times, the bridge's length was shortened to 166.6 meters from its original 206 meters. The bridge is 4 meters wide and has fourteen piers, thirteen spans and a gallery house with fifty-eight bays. It has been listed as the Historical and Cultural Sites Protected at the Provincial Level. Mr. Mao Yisheng, a bridge expert and native of Zhenjiang, Jiangsu who lived from 1896 to 1989, entered the Xijin Bridge in his work *The Architectural History of Chinese Bridges* (*Zhongguo Qiaoliang Jianzhushi*).

04 — 仁安桥

浙江省丽水市松阳县玉岩镇周安村,清康熙
(1662—1722年)

单孔木平梁,全木结构廊桥,五开间,重檐歇山顶,铺小青瓦。长12米,宽3米,高4.2米。古为村民进出大山唯一通道,也是耕种时节人们躲避风雨、休息闲谈的场所。

04.Ren'an Bridge — Zhou'an Village, Yuyan Town, Songyang County, Lishui, Zhejiang Province, built during 1662-1722.

This is a timber beam bridge, supported with a timber structure. It has a single span. Its gallery house has five bays. This is covered with a hip and gable roof with multiple-eave, topped with small grey tiles. The bridge is 12 meters long, 3 meters wide and 4.2 meters high. In ancient times, it was the only way for villagers to go to and from the mountains. It was also a place for people to escape the wind and rain and to rest and have a chat during the farming season.

05—红军桥

浙江省丽水市松阳县安民乡安岱后村安民溪，光绪（1875—1908年）

原名善继桥，始建于清光绪（1875—1908年）年间。单木平梁廊桥，长27.8米、宽5.4米、跨径5.5米、九开间。碑记："岱后地处闽、浙、赣边界的浙江西南部，此处崇山峻岭，古木参天，万顷猴头杜鹃堪称华东一绝。1935年5月，中国工农红军挺进师在刘英、粟裕依托安岱后战略要地建立了浙西南革命根据地。"1997年3月，萧克将军题写的"红军桥"碑立于桥头西侧。

05. Hongjun Bridge — Anmin River, Andaihou Village, Anmin Township, Songyang County, Lishui, Zhejiang Province, built during 1875-1908.

The bridge formerly known as Shanji Bridge, it was built during the Guangxu reign of Qing Dynasty. It is a timber beam supported covered bridge. The bridge has one span, and is 27 meters long, 5.4 meters wide, and has a span of 5.5 meters. Its gallery house has nine bays. It stele states, "Andaihou is located in the southwestern part of Zhejiang Province on the border of Fujian, Zhejiang and Jiangxi, where the mountains are high and the ancient trees tower above, and ten thousand hectares rhododendron simiarum make it known as one of the best lands in East China. In May 1935, the advanced contingent of the Central Workers' and Peasants' Red Army under the command of Liu Ying and Su Yu created a revolutionary base area in Southwest Zhejiang Province on the basis of its strategic stronghold in Andaihou." In March 1997, General Xiao Ke's writing "Hongjun Bridge" was installed on the west side of the bridge entrance.

06—宏济桥

浙江省丽水市遂昌县王村口镇，明代（1368—1644年）

初名济川石桥，是王村口镇桥东村、桥西村近万人相互交往的唯一通道。跨乌溪江，连通衢州至闽北、赣东古驿道。圆木交叉支撑平梁廊桥，长35米、宽5.4米、高9米，九开间，桥堡两栋双檐翘角，单脊悬山顶覆小青瓦。清光绪初年改名宏济桥。清代（1636—1911年）、中华民国（1912—1949年）时期重建。1935年，中国工农红军挺进师师长粟裕在宏济桥上做过"北上抗日"讲演。

06.Hongji Bridge – Wangcunkou Town, Suichang County, Lishui, Zhejiang Province, built during 1368-1644.

The original name of the bridge is Jichuan Shiqiao Bridge, it was the only way for almost ten thousand villagers of Qiaodong Village and Qiaoxi Village in Wangcunkou Town to travel back and forth and communicate. Crossing the Wuxi River, it formed a part of the ancient courier road that connected Quzhou to northern Fujian and eastern Jiangxi. Logs are interspersed to support the bridge's supporting beams. The covered bridge is 31 meters long, 5.4 meters wide, and 9 meters high. Its gallery house has nine bays and is covered with an overhanging gable roof with a single ridge topped with small grey tiles. The bridge includes two structures bearing roofs with double-eave and upturned corners. The bridge was rebuilt during the Qing Dynasty and during the Republic of China period. In the early part of the Guangxu reign of the Qing Dynasty, the bridge was renamed to Hongji Bridge. In 1935, on the Hongji Bridge, Su Yu, division commander of the Red Army's advanced contingent, made his speech on "going north to resist Japan".

07—永和桥

浙江省丽水市龙泉市安仁镇，明成化元年（1465年）

丽水（古称处州）一市八县木拱廊桥群号称"处州九龙"，永和桥最长称"龙首"，原名永宁桥。《龙泉县志》记："长25.7米，宽7.5米，桥下用条石筑桥墩，桥墩上用巨松纵横相叠，层层挑出形成桥跨，上覆硬木板。桥屋四十二间，中有桥阁。"三墩四孔石墩全木结构廊桥高13米，两端建飞檐斗拱门楼。清顺治（1644—1661年）年间焚毁，清康熙五十七年（1718年）重建，改名永安桥。清咸丰五年（1855年）洪水冲塌两墩，复修改名永和桥。被列为全国重点文物保护单位。

07.Yonghe Bridge — Anren Town, Longquan County, Lishui, Zhejiang Province, built in 1465.

The timber arch covered bridges in the eight counties under the prefectural jurisdiction of Lishui (which was formerly known as Chuzhou) are called as a group "The Nine Dragons of Chuzhou". The Yonghe Bridge is the longest among them, and hence is called "the Dragon Head". Its original name was Yongning Bridge. It states in the *Longquan County Chronicle* that the bridge is "125.7 meters long, 7.5 meters wide, and 13 meters high. The bridge's piers are composed of strips of stones. On the piers, giant pines overlap vertically and horizontally, rising layer by layer to support the hardwood boards that cover the bridge span. The gallery house has forty-two bays, and includes a pavilion in its center." It has three piers and four spans. Its gate buildings at either side with *dougong* brackets and upturned eaves. Sometime during the reign of the Shunzhi of the Qing Dynasty (1644 — 1661) it burned down. And then, it was rebuilt in 1718 and renamed as the Yong'an Bridge. In 1855, two piers were destroyed by floods and its name was changed once again to the Yonghe Bridge upon being restored. It has been listed as the Major Historical and Cultural Sites Protected at the National Level.

08—双溪桥

浙江省丽水市龙泉市小梅镇孙坑村，清同治十年（1871年）

中华民国二十一年（1932年）重建。叠木平梁辅助八字支撑，全木结构廊桥，东南—西北走向，长32.6米、宽4.5米、矢高3.75米、跨径15.4米，十一开间。重檐单脊廊顶，中央建双檐翘角歇山顶小阁楼，内设神龛供奉观世音菩萨。被列为省级文物保护单位。

08.Shuangxi Bridge – Sunkeng Village, Xiaomei Town, Longquan County, Lishui, Zhejiang Province, built in 1871.

In 1932, the Shuangxi Bridge was rebuilt. It is a timber covered bridge supported by compound timber beams, together with auxiliary *bazi* bracing. It runs from the southeast to the northwest. It is 32.6 meters long, 4.5 meters wide, and 3.75 meters high. It has a span of 15.4 meters, and a gallery house with eleven bays. The gallery house has a multiple-eave single-ridge roof. In its center, there is a small pavilion with a hip and gable roof with double-eave and upturned corners. Inside it is a shrine built for the public's worship of Guan Yin, the Buddhist bodhisattva of compassion. It is listed as the Historical and Cultural Sites Protected at the Provincial Level.

第六章 东南廊桥遗存带

09—古溪桥

浙江省丽水市龙泉市小梅镇黄南村，明代（1368 — 1644 年）

清道光十八年（1838年）重建，单孔石拱木廊桥，东西走向，跨垟顺溪，长29.3米、宽5.6米、高5米，十六开间。两侧设置栏杆、长条凳，中间楼阁藻井下设神龛。重檐悬山顶两端建牌楼，多组老年木雕生动传神，具有较高艺术价值。

09.Guxi Bridge – Huangnan Village, Xiaomei Town, Longquan County, Lishui, Zhejiang Province, built during 1368-1644.

In 1838, the bridge was reconstructed. This single-span stone arch timber covered bridge runs in an east-west direction across the Yangshun River. It is 29.3 meters long, 5.6 meters wide, 5 meters high, and has a gallery house with sixteen bays. There are railings and benches on both sides; in the middle pavilion there are shrines. Memorial Archways are built at both ends of the overhanging gable roofs with multiple-eave, and many old wood carvings here have a high artistic value.

10—林坑桥

浙江省温州市永嘉县楠溪江畔林坑村

又名凉亭桥。据年长村民述说:"林坑村已有700年的历史,有村就有桥,修成廊桥还是中华民国的事情,可惜乡亲只知种田没有记载桥史。"全木结构独拱廊桥,长5.8米、高4.5米,穿斗式廊屋两侧设"美人靠"长条木凳供下田人避雨歇息,中高两端低,硬山顶覆青杂瓦。

10. Linkeng Bridge – Linkeng Village, Nanxi River, Yongjia County, Wenzhou, Zhejiang Province.

Linkeng Bridge also known as Liangting Bridge. According to village elders, "Linkeng Village has 700 years of history. As long as there has been a village, there has been a bridge. Bridge building and repair was still done during the Republic of China Period (1912-1949). Unfortunately, villagers only know farming and do not write down the history of the bridge." The timber covered bridge has a single arch, and is 5.8 meters long and 4.5 meters high. The gallery house is a *chuandou* structure. On both sides of the bridge, there are *meirenkao* benches with back rests for people to relax, and for people to sit while they take shelter from the rain. The lower flush gable roofs on the tall and central parts of the gallery house are covered with assorted grey tiles.

11—慕义桥

浙江省丽水市缙云县前路乡前路村，清道光十二年（1832年）

慕义桥长53米，宽3.4米，高7米，三孔跨径各8.7米，各方集资一万三千两白银历时一年建成。桥栏刻字"慕义桥，道光十二年，缙云县令张惟孝书"。西端桥亭高11.22米，北厢为庙、西厢为亭、六开间。慕义桥构造精湛，是缙云县有确切纪年并保存完好的石拱廊桥，具有较高的历史、文化、艺术及科学价值。被列为省级文物保护单位。

11.Muyi Bridge — Qianlu Village, Qianlu Township, Jinyun County, Lishui, Zhejiang Province, built in 1832.

The Muyi Bridge is 53 meters long, 3.4 meters wide, and 7 meters high. Each of its spans are 8.7 meters long. It was built through various contributions totaling 13,000 tael of silver, and was completed in one year's time. An engraving on the bridge's railing states, "Muyi Bridge, built in the 12th year of the Daoguang (1832), signed by *Xianling* (County Magistrate) Zhang Weixiao." The pavilion on the bridge's western end is 11.22 meters high. The bridge's northern chamber serves as a temple, and its western chamber is a pavilion, and its gallery house has six bays. Muyi Bridge has an exquisite structure, It is the best-preserved stone arch covered bridges in Jinyun County, whose built year was ascertained, with high historical, cultural, artistic and scientific value. The bridge has been listed as the Historical and Cultural Sites Protected at the Provincial Level.

第二节 • 钱塘江流域的廊桥
Section II Covered Bridges in Qiantang River Basin

01—通州桥

浙江省金华市兰溪市梅江镇塔山村梅溪，清康熙二十五年（1686年）

通州桥古为金华、兰溪、义乌、浦江、建德五县交通咽喉。初为木桥，清乾隆二十三年（1758年）改石桥。清嘉庆五年（1800年）水毁，清道光三年（1823年）重建石拱廊桥。长85米、宽4米、高9米，四墩五孔，单孔跨径9米，二十一开间，是浙江省最大的石拱廊桥。两端重檐歇山顶门楼，中部建重檐歇山顶阁楼。门梁木雕为清代匠师作品。

01.Tongzhou Bridge — Meixi Brook, Tashan Village, Meijiang Town, Lanxi County, Jinhua, Zhejiang Province, built in 1686.

In ancient times, Tongzhou Bridge served as a node for traffic from Jinhua, Lanxi, Yiwu, Pujiang and Jiande counties. At first, it was a timber bridge, and in 1758 it was converted into a stone bridge. In 1800, it was destroyed by floods, and in 1823 it was rebuilt as a stone arch bridge. It is 85 meters long, 4 meters wide and 9 meters high. It has four piers and five spans, with single span 9 meters long. Its gallery house has twenty-one bays. It is the largest stone arch bridge in Zhejiang Province. Both sides of the bridge have memorial arches covered by multiple-eave hip and gable roofs. In the center, there is a pavilion, also with a multiple-eave hip and gable roof. The wood carving on the beam by the bridge's entrance is the work of master craftsmen of Qing Dynasty.

第六章 东南廊桥遗存带

02—席场桥

浙江省金华市浦江县虞宅村壶源江，南宋理宗宝庆元年（1225年）

三墩四孔平梁式廊桥，长60米、宽3.9米，十七开间，栏栅下设置木凳，顶覆小青瓦。南宋理宗宝庆元年（1225年）正月，望耆毛日严择吉日置办酒席，召集贤达、族长商议建桥事宜。酒宴上将筹款份额、雇匠招工、买办桥材、主绳人选事项当场确定。同年桥成，毛老先生再次设办酒席，宴请有功人等并征议桥名。开工、竣工两场酒席令人印象颇深，一致将桥名定为"席场桥"。

02.Xichang Bridge – Huyuan River, Yuzhai Village, Pujiang County, Jinhua, Zhejiang Province, built in 1225.

The bridge has three piers and four spans and it is supported by timber beams. It is 60 meters long and 3.9 meters wide. Its gallery house has seventeen bays, and timber benches are installed under the bridge's railing. Its roof is covered by small grey tiles. In the first lunar month of the first year of the Baoqing period of the Southern Song Dynasty (1225), respected elder Mao Riyan, chose an auspicious day to host a banquet, during which prominent people and lineage heads came to an agreement about building a bridge. During the banquet, fundraising, material purchases, and the selection of the master bridge builder were all decided. That same year upon the completion of the bridge, Mr.Mao held yet another banquet. Worthy persons were invited to discuss and choose the name of the bridge. The banquet that started the work on the bridge, and the one that marked its completion left a strong impression, and as a result the bridge was named Xichang Bridge.

03—湖南亭桥

浙江省衢州市衢江区湖南镇湖南村,清乾隆(1736—1795年)

湖南亭桥受到村民珍惜呵护。一位避雨老人讲:"中华民早年,湖南亭桥办过私塾。其实有大房子用,教书的女先生喜欢这里,说这座桥'恰似家女绣花楼'。"叠梁单孔红柱花窗,平梁全木结构廊桥,长13.5米、宽2米,七开间,廊柱间花格窗棂工艺精细考究。清同治十二年(1873年)重建。

3. Hunanting Bridge – Hunan Village, Hunan Town, Qujiang District, Quzhou, Zhejiang Province, built during 1736-1795.

This bridge is cherished by villagers. An old man who took shelter from the rain here said, "In the early years of the Republic of China, the bridge was used as a private school. In fact, there was a large building for school use. The women who taught here liked this bridge a lot, saying that it was like a girl's embroidery." The bridge is formed from compound beams, and has a single span. Its gallery house has red columns and decorative windows. Its main structure is supported by beams. The bridge is 13.5 meters long and 2 meters wide. Its gallery house has seven bays. The lattice windows between the columns in the gallery house are exquisitely and delicately crafted. The bridge was reconstructed in 1871.

第三节 • 甬江流域的廊桥
Section III Covered Bridges in Yongjiang River Basin

01— 戈场桥

浙江省温州市平阳县吴垟乡戈场村，清康熙四十年（1701 年）

又名永安桥，初为全木结构木拱廊桥。清道光（1821—1850 年）年间改建为独孔石拱廊桥，长 23 米、宽 5 米。1961 年修缮。20 世纪 90 年代，上部木结构焚毁，1993 年重建。2007 年被强台风损毁，2010 年重建。桥北连通千步岭古道，现已荒芜难行。

01.Gechang Bridge — Gechang Village, Wuyang Township, Pingyang County, Wenzhou, Zhejiang Province, built in 1701.

Gechang Bridge also known as Yongan Bridge, it was a timber arch covered bridge originally. Sometime between 1821 and 1850, it was rebuilt as a stone arch bridge with a single span. It is 23 meters long and 5 meters wide. In 1961, it was repaired. In the early 1990s the bridge's upper timber structure burned down, and was rebuilt in 1993. The bridge was destroyed by a strong typhoon in 2007, and was rebuilt in 2010. The ancient Qianbuling Road that connects to the north side of the bridge has become overgrown, and now is difficult to access.

02—镇东桥

浙江省宁波市宁海县西店镇铁江村紫江入海口，清乾隆八年（1743年）

镇东桥紧靠海岸牡蛎滩，内廊烛火是引导渔民回家的灯标。清嘉庆（1796—1820年）时期宁海县令程煜作《镇东桥记》："或捐资或输力莫不踊跃争先，路已告竣桥又成，时在乾隆八年（1743年）岁次癸亥冬吉旦。咸丰辛酉（1861年）秋洪水冲圮，同治壬申年（1872年）修复仍名镇东。"镇东桥是中国距海岸最近的廊桥，长23.5米、宽5.4米、高6.5米。民间传说一户编打草鞋的邬氏母子，不顾三餐无继、娶媳无着，倾囊捐助修桥为铁江村世代教典。1953年加筑桥墩一座，1983年大修。

02.Zhendong Bridge — Zijiang Estuary, Tiejiang Village, Xidian Town, Ninghai County, Ningbo, Zhejiang Province, built in 1743.

Zhendong Bridge is close to Muli Beach, it is very close to the coast, in fact it is the nearest to the ocean of all known covered bridges in China. A lantern in the bridge's inner gallery serves as a beacon to guide fishermen home. According to the *Records of the Zhendong Bridge*, "After funds were collected and labor contributed, a road was established, and a bridge built too, completed on an auspicious day in the winter during the eighth year of the Qianlong reign (1743). During the autumn of Xianfeng reign in 1861, floods damaged the bridge. During the Tongzhi reign in 1872, it was restored, and was named Zhendong." It is 23.5 meters long, 5.4 meters wide and 6.5 meters high. There is a story passed down in the village that there was a mother and son in the Wu family who knitted straw shoes. Despite being destitute and not being able to afford for the son to be married, they donated everything they had to the bridge, thus setting an example for the future generations of Tiejiang Village. In 1953 an additional pier was added to the bridge, and the whole bridge was renovated in 1983.

03—中山桥

浙江省台州市天台县南屏乡下汤村大淡溪，1950年

中山桥因汤氏祖先居"中山郡"得名。村民汤毓礼（道南乡长）1950年初提出"全木质结构廊桥"建桥方案，村民惊异好奇。按照这个方案，木料、石料就地取材，各类工匠不外聘。主梁由五株合粗大柏树并排铺成，棚屋两侧两根斜柱形成拱架支撑棚顶。桥长13米、宽3.2米，木栏两侧安置长椅，最受老年人欢迎。中山桥成为村民避雨遮阳、闲谈休憩、集市贸易的"活动中心"。

3. Zhongshan Bridge — Dadan Brook, Xiatang Township, Nanping County, Tiantai County, Taizhou, Zhejiang province, built in 1950.

Zhongshan Bridge was named after the residence of the ancestral founder of the Tang lineage in Zhongshan County. It is a timber covered bridge and it was built in early 1950 according to a proposal by villager Tang Yuli (the township head of Daonan Township), to build "a covered bridge entirely out of wood". This made the villagers excited and curious. According to the plan, timber and stone were all acquired locally, craftsmen were also local people. The main beam is composed of five thick cypress trees arranged side by side, and two slanting columns on both sides of the gallery structure form a support for the roof. Benches are placed on both sides of the timber railings, which are especially appreciated by older villagers. The bridge is 13 meters long and 3.2 meters wide. It has become a center for activity, a place can provide shelter from the sun and the rain, rest and chat, and hold market fairs.

04 金朱桥

福建省宁德市福鼎市管阳镇金钗溪村

清乾隆（1736—1795年）、清咸丰（1851—1861年）年间重修。石拱木结构廊桥，东西走向，长28.24米，宽4.27米，高4.2米，十一开间，竖柱46根。桥东端遇有"大清乾隆二十年（1755年）""大清咸丰五年（1855年）"重修金朱桥纪事碑各一方。原为木梁廊桥，清乾隆二十年（1755年）族首朱肇衍公等筹资改建为石拱廊桥，取金钗溪与朱姓合二之意，取名"金朱桥"。

4.Jinzhu Bridge — Jinchaixi Village, Guanyang Town, Fuding County, Ningde, Fujian Province.

The bridge was rebuilt sometime between 1736 and 1795 as well as sometime between 1851 and 1861. It is a timber covered bridge with a stone arch, with a single span. It is 28.24 meters long, 4.27 meters wide and 4.2 meters high. Its gallery house has eleven bays and is orientated in an east-west direction. At the eastern end of the bridge, steles dedicated to the bridge dating from the "The Second Decade of Emperor Qianlong of the Qing Dynasty" (1755) and the "The Fifth Year of the Emperor Xianfeng of the Qing Dynasty" (1855) are installed. Originally it was a wooden bridge. Later, in 1755, Zhu Zhaoyan, the lineage head, raised funds to rebuild it as a stone arch bridge, and named it the Jinzhu Bridge, based on the shared relationship between the Jinchai Brook and the Zhu lineage.

05—老人桥

福建省宁德市福鼎市管阳镇西阳村桥头冈，明正德（1506—1521年）

清光绪《乡土志》记："邱阜，瓦洋人，有齿德，为遐迩排难纠纷者数十年。有某妇悍甚，小忿涉讼。（邱）阜劝谕弗听，自耻德薄，赴水死。闾里感其诚，建桥设主以祀。至今呼为老人桥云。"伸臂式木拱廊桥，长30.8米、宽4.8米、高8米。由135根贯木设置上中下三层分为五组，形成互为依托、衔紧密、稳固支撑的梁架结构。

05.Laoren Bridge — Qiaotougang, Xiyang Village, Guanyang Town, Fuding County, Ningde, Fujian Province, built during 1506-1521.

A *Local Chronicle* from the Qing Dynasty's Guangxu era (1875-1908) records that "Qiu Fu, a man of Wayang, was a person of venerable age and eminent virtue. For over ten years he had presided over difficult cases from near and far. There was a shrewish woman who then pursued a lawsuit over a small dispute. Qiu Fu did not succeed in admonishing her, so he was ashamed of his limited virtue, drowned himself. The people in the area were moved by his virtue, and built the bridge as a tribute to him, and up to the present it has been known as Laoren Bridge." The timber cantilever arch covere bridge is 30.4 meters long, 4.8 meters wide, a 8 meters high. Three stories composed of 13 timbers are divided into five groups, formir an interdependent, tight and stable supportir beam-frame structure.

06—多亭桥

福建省福州市晋安区日溪乡店坂村，清嘉庆十六年（1811年）

又名状元桥、店坂桥。南北走向，单孔全木结构，长32米、宽4.7米、跨径20米、十一开间。木拱架采用三节苗和五节苗组合穿插连贯，抬梁式木构架歇山顶。被列为市级文物保护单位。

06.Duoting Bridge — Dianban Village, Rixi Township, Jin'an District, Fuzhou, Fujian Province, built in 1811.

Duoting Bridge also known as Zhuangyuan Bridge and Dianban Bridge. The bridge is orientated in a north-south direction. This timber arch bridge has a single span. It is 32 meters long, 4.7 meters wide, and has a span of 20 meters. It has a gallery house with eleven bays. The arch is composed of a combination of a frame composed of three timber members, and a frame with five members. The bridge's gallery house is a timber *tailiang* structure, with a hip and gable roof. It has been listed as the historical and cultural Sites Protected at the Municipal Level.

第四节·长溪流域及其边缘地区的廊桥
Section IV Covered Bridges in Changxi River Basin and Surrounding Areas

一、瓯江发源地庆元县廊桥
I. Covered Bridges in Qingyuan County, the Origin of Oujiang River

01—兰溪桥

浙江省丽水市庆元县五大堡乡西洋村松源溪,明万历二年(1574年)

原址位于兰溪村,谢子隆、吴丰募资建造。清乾隆四十八年(1783年)水毁,清乾隆五十九年(1794年)吴星海募资重建。因兰溪桥处在新修水库蓄水区,政府拨款5.45万元,桐樟村捐杉木19立方米,黄皮村捐杉木18立方米,桥阳村捐杉木15立方米,1984年将兰溪桥整体搬迁至现址,伸臂式木拱廊桥,长48米,宽5米,高9.8米,跨径37米,十九开间,被列为省级文物保护单位。

01. Lanxi Bridge — Songyuan River, Xiyang Village, Wudabao Township, Qingyuan County, Lishui, Zhejiang Province, built in 1574.

Lanxi Bridge formerly located in Lanxi Village, and built with initial funds raised by Xie Zilong and Wu Feng. In 1783, during the reign of Emperor Qianlong, the bridge was destroyed by flood, and in 1794, Wu Xinghai raised funds for its restoration. In 1984, the bridge was relocated to its present site because its former location was to be covered by a new reservoir. The government allotted 51,500 yuan for the relocation and rebuilding. In addition, Tongzi Village donated 19 fir trees, Huangpi Village donated 18 fir trees, and Qiaoyang Village donated 15 fir trees for the project. It is a timber cantilever arch covered bridge, 48 meters long, 5 meters wide, 9.8 meters high, and has a span of 37 meters. Its gallery house has nineteen bays. In 1997, it was listed as the Historical and Cultural Sites Protected at the Provincial Level.

中国廊桥

02—白云桥

浙江省丽水市庆元县举水乡月山村，明代（1368—1644年）

始建于明代，桥位于月山村半山腰，是月山村五座廊桥中位置最高的，桥下飞瀑直泻状若白云，故得此名。叠梁木拱廊桥南北走向，长8米、宽3米、跨径7.5米，双飞檐歇山顶满覆小青瓦。

02.Baiyun Bridge – Yueshan Village, Jushui Township, Qingyuan County, Lishui, Zhejiang Province, built during 1368-1644.

Baiyun Bridge was built in the middle of the mountain in Yueshan Village. As the highest among the five covered bridges in Yueshan Village, it gets its name from the cloud-like spray that rises from the waterfall under the bridge. The bridge is a woven timber arch-beam bridge, and runs in a north-south direction. It is 8 meters long, 3 meters wide, and has a span of 7.5 meters. The bridge has a hip and gable roof with upturned double-eave, covered with small grey tiles.

03—步蟾桥

浙江省丽水市庆元县举水乡月山村，明永乐（1403 — 1424 年）

中华民国六年（1917年）重建。独孔石拱廊桥，长50米、宽5米、高8米、跨径16.6米，十八开间。桥面铺条石块石，两侧设木制鳞叠护板，桥顶五脊四角挑檐，三间阁楼中间略大。正中八角藻井和雕花垂柱。步蟾桥上游30米溪水中一块巨石似蟾蜍，古人以此石为趣，为廊桥取名"步蟾"。被列为全国重点文物保护单位。

3.Buchan Bridge — Yueshan Village, Jushui Township, Qingyuan County, Lishui, Zhejiang Province, built during 1403-1424.

The present Buchan Bridge was rebuilt in 1917. The single-span covered bridge has a stone arch that is 50 meters long, 5 meters wide and meters high, with a span of 16.6 meters. Its gallery house has eighteen bays. The deck bridge covered by stones with multi-layer wooden awnings at each side. Its roof has five ridges, four corners, and overhanging eaves. Of its pavilion's three bays, the middle one is slightly larger than the others. Inside, there is an eight-panel sunken caisson ceiling, as well as columns decorated with carved flowers. There is a stone resembling a toad (*chanchu* in Chinese) in the stream 30 meters upstream of the bridge, so the ancient people named the bridge Buchan Bridge as a result. The bridge has been listed as the Major Historical and Cultural Sites Protected at the National Level.

04—如龙桥

浙江省丽水市庆元县举水乡月山村，明天启五年（1625年）

宋元王朝更替，"延陵望族，三让世家"的吴氏一支迁至月山村后，修祠堂、建庙宇、竖佛塔，同时营造了"二里十桥的廊桥峡谷"。其中，如龙桥是中国第一座被列为全国重点文物保护单位的廊桥（2001年）。长28米、宽5.4米、跨径21米，圆木支撑拱架与全木结构廊屋组合。桥楼北高南低似蛟龙首尾，古称"蜈蚣桥"。"如龙桥"匾牌系吴子球（清）书写。

04.Rulong Bridge — Yueshan Village, Jushui Township, Qingyuan County, Lishui, Zhejiang Province, built in 1625.

The bridge is located in "Covered Bridges Valley", and built by the Wu family, which was an influential lineage from the time spanning the Song to the Yuan dynasties. They built shrines, temples, and pagodas after moving to Yueshan Village. They also organized the building of the "Two *Li* Ten Covered Bridges Valley". Rulong Bridge is located there, and is the first covered bridge in China listed as the Major Historical and Cultural Sites Protected at the National Level (2001). It is 28 meters long, 5.4 meters wide, and has a span of 21 meters. It is a woven timber arch-beam bridge. The bridge's northern structures are higher than those in the south, resembling the head and tail of a dragon. In the past, it was called Wugong Bridge. The name Rulong Bridge was written on a plaque in the bridge by Wu Ziqiu of Qing Dynasty.

第六章 东南廊桥遗存带

05—五步桥

浙江省丽水市庆元县举水乡月山村，清乾隆二十六年（1761年）

又名秆坑桥。位于月山村稻田小溪，长4.6米、宽3米、高4.2米、跨径2米，五步可过。五步桥夹在步蟾桥、如龙桥之间，就像两座大廊桥的孩子。

05.Wubu Bridge — Yueshan Village, Jushui Township, Qingyuan County, Lishui, Zhejiang Province, built in 1761.

Wubu Bridge also named Gankeng Bridge, It is built over a stream in the fields of Yueshan Village. It is 4.6 meters long, 3 meters wide, and 4.2 meters high. It has a span of 2 meters. It can be passed with five steps, from which its name is derived. The bridge is located between Buchan Bridge and Rulong Bridge, like the child of them.

6—来凤桥

浙江省丽水市庆元县举水乡月山村

焚毁后于清道光十八年（1838年）重建，形成独孔石拱廊结构。长30米、宽5.5米、高于河床10米，十一开间。据吴懋修（1603—1674年，浙江省庆元县人）所著《举溪记》载："由下溯上又见一桥，若飞若舞，与如龙等者，即新造来凤桥。"来凤桥倒映清溪呈圆月形，桥柱对联"水从璧玉怀中出，人在莲花瓣上行"是对其恰到好处的描写。

6.Laifeng Bridge – Yueshan Village, Jushui Township, Qingyuan County, Lishui, Zhejiang Province.

Laifeng Bridge was destroyed in a fire, in 1838, it was rebuilt as a single-span stone arch bridge with a timber gallery house. It is 30 meters long, 5.5 meters wide, and sits 10 meters above the river bed. Its gallery house has eleven bays. As stated in the *History of Juxi Stream* by Wu Maoxiu (a native of Qingyuan County, Zhejiang Province who lived from 1603 to 1674), "Walking upstream, another bridge came into my sight. It was like a bird, as if at flight, as if in a dance, similar to the Rulong Bridge. It was the newly constructed Laifeng Bridge." The bridge form reflects the round moon that appears in the pure waters of the creek. A couplet on the bridge columns provides an apt description: "From the body of a jade disc water flows. On top of lotus petals the traveler goes."

07—护龙桥

浙江省丽水市庆元县岭头乡杨家庄村，清代晚期

木平梁全木结构廊桥，长27.8米，宽5.2米，跨径7米，十一开间，双层木质雨披，悬山顶覆小青瓦，被列为省级文物保护单位。

07.Hulong Bridge — Yangjiazhuang Village, Lingtou Township, Qingyuan County, Lishui, Zhejiang Province, built in the late Qing Dynasty.

Hulong Bridge is a covered bridge supported by timber beams with a wooden gallery house. It is 27.8 meters long, 5.2 meters wide and has a span of 7 meters. It has a gallery house with eleven bays. A double-layer wooden awning protects the bridge from rain. The bridge is covered by a overhanging gable roof topped by small grey tiles. It has been listed as the Historical and Cultural Sites Protected at the Provincial Level.

08—查洋桥

浙江省丽水市庆元县黄田镇陈边村，元顺帝至元（1335—1340年）

又名半路亭桥、云岩桥。伸臂式木拱廊桥，东西走向，长28.65米、宽5米、高5.75米、跨径21.25米，九开间，双檐悬山顶，中设双层飞檐阁楼铺小青瓦，两侧安置三叠遮雨板。清嘉庆二十三年（1818年）、中华民国六年（1917年）整修。被列为省级文物保护单位。

08.Zhayang Bridge — Chenbian Village, Huangtian Town, Qingyuan County, Lishui, Zhejiang Province, built during 1335-1340.

Zhayang Bridge, also known as Banluting Bridge or Yunyan Bridge, it is a timber cantilever arch bridge runs in a east-west direction. It is 28.65 meters long, 5 meters wide, and 5.75 meters high, with a span of 21.25 meters. It has a gallery house with nine bays. It is covered by a double-eave, overhanging gable roof with upturned eaves, and topped with small grey tiles. Three-layer awnings is installed at either side of the bridge to protect it from rain. The bridge was rebuilt in 1818 and 1917. It has been listed as the Historical and Cultural Sites Protected at the Provincial Level.

09—双门桥

浙江省丽水市庆元县松源镇大济村，宋景德元年（1004年）

东西走向，长 11.15 米、宽 4.5 米、高 5.2 米、跨径 10.24 米，开间，未用一钉一铆。宋景德元年（1004年），吴崇熙举家迁来，"大济"为村名，企盼辈辈出济世大才。他倾尽家资聘请名师教授嗣。宋天圣二年（1024年），长子吴毂得中进士官至大理寺评事、子赞善改殿中丞。宋景佑元年（1034年），次子吴毅中进士；兄双登金榜。村民将临清桥改名双门桥。

09.Shuangmen Bridge – Daji Village, Songyuan Town, Qingyuan County, Lishui, Zhejiang Province, built in 1004.

The east-west woven timber arch bridge uses mortise and tenon technology and is not joined by not a single nail. It is 11.15 meters long, 4.5 meters wide, and 5.2 meters high. It has a span of 10.24 meters, and its gallery house has five bays. In 1004, Wu Chongxi moved to the village with his family group. The Village was named Daji ("great abundance") signifying a hope for prosperous and talented future generations to come forth from the village. Wu Chongxi devoted all of his wealth to hiring scholars to teach the young. In 1024, his eldest son was awarded the *Jinshi* degree (the highest degree awarded for passing the imperial examination), and then served as an official at Dali Temple. In 1034, his second son also obtained a Jinshi title, and the villagers changed the name of Linqing Bridge to Shuangmen Bridge, referring to the double-success accrued by the brothers.

10.一垅桥

浙江省丽水市庆元县龙溪乡鱼川村，清乾隆四年（1739 年）

石拱单孔木柱瓦顶廊桥，长 22 米、宽 4 米，距谷底高 12 米，跨径 12 米，九开间。桥廊正中设置神龛供奉观世音菩萨。垅桥所在河谷崖壁狭窄，岩石狰狞古怪。旱季水流不大，游人可下到谷底观赏。

10.Longqiao Bridge – Yuchuan Village, Longxi Township, Qingyuan County, Lishui, Zhejiang Province, built in 1739.

Longqiao Bridge is a single-span covered bridge with a stone arch, timber columns and a tile roof. It is 22 meters long, 4 meters wide and has a span of 12 meters. It sits 12 meters above the river below. Its gallery house has nine bays. A shrine in its middle is dedicated to Guanshiyin (Guanyin), the Buddhist bodhisattva of compassion. The rocks in the narrow valley are highly unusual. Visitors can enjoy them from the bottom of the valley during the dry season. .

第六章 东南廊桥遗存带

11 — 后坑桥

浙江省丽水市庆元县竹口镇枫堂村，清康熙十年（1671年）

又名普济桥、红军桥。伸臂式木拱廊桥，东西走向，长36.2米、宽5.45米、高6.05米、跨径28.5米，十五开间。清光绪十一年（1885年）乡民集资重建。廊桥主梁上遗有"大清光绪乙酉拾壹年桂月拾壹日旦时鼎新重建"墨迹。2005年获得联合国亚太地区文化遗产保护卓越奖，被列为省级文物保护单位。

11. Houkeng Bridge – Fengtang Village, Zhukou Town, Qingyuan County, Lishui, Zhejiang Province, built in 1671.

Houkeng Bridge also named Puji Bridge or Hongjun Bridge, it is a timber cantilever arch bridge that stretches from east to west. It is 36.2 meters long, 5.45 meters wide, 6.05 meters high and has a span of 28.5 meters. Its gallery house has fifteen bays. In 1885, local villagers united to rebuild it. Its main beam is engraved with the words "rebuilt on the eleventh day of the eighth lunar month in the eleventh year of the Guangxu period of the Qing Dynasty". In 2005, the bridge was awarded the UNESCO Asia-Pacific Award for Excellence in Cultural Heritage Protection. The bridge is listed as the Historical and Cultural Site Protected at the Provincial Level.

2—包果桥

浙江省丽水市庆元县岭头乡包果村，清乾隆十一年（1746年）

包果桥跨越排水渠，水流来自一片稻田。此桥专供下田劳作农夫歇凉避雨。长18.2米、宽4.3米、跨径11.3米，为八字斜支撑平梁全木结构廊桥。被列为县级文物保护单位。

12. Baoguo Bridge — Baoguo Village, Lingtou Township, Qingyuan County, Lishui, Zhejiang Province, built in 1746.

Baoguo Bridge spans a channel where water flows from an expanse of rice paddies. It serves the needs of farmers who can use the bridge to cool off and to escape from the rain. The timber structure is supported by *bazi* bracing. The bridge is 18.2 meters long, 4.3 meters wide, and has a span of 11.3 meters. It has been listed as the Historical and Cultural Sites Protected at the County Level.

13—黄水长桥

浙江省丽水市庆元县合湖乡黄水村，清乾隆十九年（1754年）

又名飞阁桥。清同治十一年（1872年）迁建到现址。2003年因修建水电站整体抬升1.7米，单孔全木结构伸臂式廊桥，南北走向，长55米、宽4.90米、高8.70米、跨径17.45米，二十一开间。桥拱依托石砌桥堍，粗大贯木穿插别压组接拱架，上建廊屋，弧形硬山顶覆青杂瓦，两侧三叠木质雨披，引桥占整座廊桥三分之二。被列为省级文物保护单位。

13. Huangshuichang Bridge — Huangshui Village, Hehu Township, Qingyuan County, Lishui, Zhejiang Province, built in 1754.

The bridge also called Feige Bribge, it was moved to the present location in 1872. The bridge was raised by an additional 1.7 meters when a hydroelectric power station was built at its location in 2003. The single-span cantilever beam bridge stretches from north to south, and it is 55 meters long, 4.9 meters wide and 8.7 meters high. Its gallery house has twenty-one bays and it has a span of 17.45 meters. Its timber arch is supported by stone abutments. The thick wood is inserted to form the arch frame, on which there is a gallery house. The gallery house is covered by an arched flush gable roof with grey tiles, replete with three-layer awnings at each side. The approaches to the bridge occupy two thirds of the whole bridge. It has been listed as the Historical and Cultural Sites Protected at the Provincial Level.

第六章 东南廊桥遗存带

二、众壑闹飞流——景宁县廊桥

II. Covered Bridges in Jingning County, Stream Fallen Down in the Valley of the Mountains

01 — 大赤坑桥

浙江省丽水市景宁畲族自治县大均乡大赤坑村，清嘉庆十五年（1810年）

又名大赤坑楼桥、成名桥。清道光二年（1822年）、清同治三年（1864年）、中华民国十二年（1923年）整修。单孔伸臂式木拱廊桥，长50米，宽6米，高10米，十四开间，两侧安置遮雨护板，全木穿斗式构造，梁、柱、檩卯榫衔接，单脊双坡顶，中部置挑角飞檐小阁，覆小青瓦。大赤坑桥昔为景宁县至沙湾、英川、庆元县等地驿道津梁。被列为全国重点文物保护单位。

01.Dachikeng Bridge — Dachikeng Village, Dajun Township, Jingning She Autonomous County, Lishui, Zhejiang Province, built in 1810.

Dachikeng Bridge, also known as Dachikenglou Bridge or Chengming Bridge. It was renovated in 1822, 1864 and 1923. The single-span timber cantilever arch covered bridge is 50 meters long, 6 meters wide, and 10 meters high. It has a gallery house with 14 bays. Baffles run along both sides of the bridge to protect it from rain. The gallery house is a *Chuandou* structure, and its beams, columns and purlins are joined by mortise and tenon technology. The single-ridge roof has two slopes, and there is a small pavilion in its center which is decorated with upturned eaves and small grey tiles. The bridge connects the ancient courier road that ran from Jingning County to Shawan, Yingchuan and Qingyuan counties. Dachikeng Bridge has been listed as the Major Historical and Cultural Sites Protected at the National Level.

02—清风桥

浙江省丽水市景宁畲族自治县梧桐乡高演村，清乾隆（1736—1795年）

又名清风楼桥、中间桥。位于高演村水稻田园溪流。清风桥是高演村第二道风水屏障，长21米、宽5.5米，与上游环胜桥、下游回龙桥形成"三桥并连"的独特景观。

02.Qingfeng Bridge – Gaoyan Village, Wutong Township, Jingning She Autonomous County, Lishui, Zhejiang Province, built during 1736-1795.

It is also named Qingfeng Louqiao Bridge and Zhongjian Bridge. It crosses over a stream in a paddy field in Gaoyan Village. The bridge is the second *fengshui* barrier of Gaoyan Village that is thought to protect the village. It forms a special scenic view, together with Huansheng Bridge in the upstream and Huilong Bridge in the downstream. Qingfeng Bridge is 21 meters long and 5.5 meters wide.

03—回龙桥

浙江省丽水市景宁畲族自治县梧桐乡高演村，清乾隆（1736—1795年）

又名末尾桥。长21米、宽6米，为高演村口第三道风水屏障。永乐（1403—1424年）年间，山村任家热心推崇勤耕苦读，族规"诗礼传家，书香踵接"。清乾隆至清光绪一百七十年中数十户家庭的高演村，出贡生34人。某年村塾十名学子赴温州科考，九名考取，以"十学九贡"的声誉震惊朝野。之后历届知县均到高演村连过三桥，以体味其中奥妙。

03. Huilong Bridge — Gaoyan Village, Wutong Township, Jingning She Autonomous County, Lishui, Zhejiang Province, built during 1736-1795.

Huilong Bridge is also known as the Mowei Bridge. It is 21 meters long, and 6 meters wide. It serves as the third *fengshui* barrier to Gaoyan Village. People in the village were known as industrious farmers and scholars, with a lineage principle that "culture should be passed through the generations and reading should be an unceasing practice." between 1403 and 1424. During the 170 years from the Qianlong to the Guangxu periods in the Qing Dynasty, 34 people in this small village of only several dozen households became *gongsheng* who were then eligible to sit for the provincial or national exams. Once ten students from the village attended the state exams in Wenzhou, and nine of them passed it, astounding people near and far. After this, every magistrate of the county would walk over the three bridges in Gaoyan Village to experience this place's tradition and success.

04—环胜桥

浙江省丽水市景宁畲族自治县梧桐乡高演村，清乾隆（1736 — 1795 年）

又名顶头桥，长 35 米、宽 5 米、高 10 米，跨径 3.6 米，数根粗大杉木承载桥体，属独孔平梁全木结构楼阁式廊桥。桥楼三层，一层阔大廊屋为村学课堂，二层设文星阁兼师爷住所，三层是四角挑檐悬山顶魁星楼。两端各有通道走廊，连接龙泉市通往温州的沿海古道。被列为全国重点文物保护单位。

04. Huansheng Bridge — Gaoyan Village, Wutong Township, Jingning She Autonomous County, Lishui, Zhejiang Province, built during 1736-1795.

Also named Dingtou Bridge, Huansheng Bridge is 35 meters long, 5 meters wide, and 10 meters high. It has a span of 3.6 meters. It is a single-span covered bridge with its main structure supported by timber beams. Its gallery house includes a three-story pavilion. The first floor served as classroom for villagers; the second one as a room for teachers as well as a shrine dedicated to *wenquxing* (the Taoist god of art and literature); and the third floor is a pavilion for *kuixing* (the Taoist god of examinations). The structure is covered by a overhanging gable roof with four-corner upturned eaves. There are covered passageways at both ends which served the ancient road that connected to Longquan County and to the coastal areas of Wenzhou. Huansheng Bridge has been listed as the Major Historical and Cultural Sites Protected at the National Level.

第六章 东南廊桥遗存带

中国廊桥

05—怀胜桥

浙江省丽水市景宁畲族自治县章坑乡章坑村，清光绪元年（1875年）

在景宁畲族自治县，被称作"坑"的乡村较多，意为偏僻难寻。怀胜桥长18米、宽3.6米、高4米，为独孔木拱廊桥。由本村名士吕品端自荐桥董，捐款并广募桥资所建。被列为县级文物保护单位。

05.Huaisheng Bridge – Zhangkeng Village, Zhangkeng Township, Jingning She Autonomous County, Lishui, Zhejiang Province, built in 1875.

There are many villages in the Jingning She Autonomous County called *keng* which means they are located in a remote place and are difficult to find. Huaisheng Bridge, a single-span timber arch bridge, is 18 meters long, 3.6 meters wide, and 4 meters high. It was built by Lü Pinduan, a man well known in the village for his literary talents, and who donated and collected money for the construction of the bridge. It has been listed as the Historical and Cultural Sites Protected at the County Level.

06—护关桥

浙江省丽水市景宁畲族自治县大漈乡境内，清乾隆四十六年（1782年）

长28米、宽7米、高8.5米，为悬山顶三层重檐，一墩两孔梁廊桥。桥屋一层关帝庙、二层文昌阁、三层魁星楼，通道宽不足2米。桥侧古色古香的时思寺，建于宋绍兴十年（1140年）。

06.Huguan Bridge — Daji Village, Dongkeng Township, Jingning She Autonomous County, Lishui, Zhejiang Province, built in 1782.

The bridge has one pier and two spans, and its main structure is supported by timber beams. It is 28 meters long, 7 meters wide, and 8.5 meters high. The bridge is covered by a overhanging gable roof with triple-eave. The first floor of the pavilion serves as a shrine for Emperor Guanyu (a general during the Three Kindoms period), the second for *wenquxing*, and the third for *kuixing*. The passageway of the pavilion is less than 2 meters wide. There is a temple named Shisi besides the bridge which was built in 1140.

07—畲桥

浙江省丽水市景宁畲族自治县东坑乡平桥村，清康熙三十一年（1692年）

古官名永安桥。长37.5米、宽5米、跨径29.2米、东西走向，为全木结构独孔木拱廊桥。畲桥横跨疾水厉石的白鹤溪，英姿挺拔，深受畲族人民喜爱，故改名为畲桥，以代表民族气质。清道光十二年（1832年）、清光绪二十年（1894年）整修。《景宁县志》描述畲桥"依壁如虹"。桥头遗存清道光（1821—1851）功德碑、记事碑八方。

07.Sheqiao Bridge – Pingqiao Village, Dongkeng Township, Jingning She Autonomous County, Lishui, Zhejiang Province, built in 1692.

Its ancient official name was the Yong'an Bridge. It is 37.5 meters long, 5 meters wide, and has a span of 29 meters. It is a single-span timber woven arch-beam bridge, stretching from east to west. Crossing the White Crane River, its appearance is bold and heroic. Much beloved by the She nationality, its name was changed to the She Bridge to represent the attributes of their people. It was renovated in 1832 and 1894. As stated in the *History of Jingning County*, She Bridge is "like a rainbow." Eight stone steles built during the Daoguang period of the Qing Dynasty (1821-1851) are installed at the gateway to the bridge, recording good deeds and history related to the bridge.

中国廊桥

08—苳岱上桥

浙江省丽水市景宁畲族自治县家地乡苳岱村，清同治九年（1870年）

唐懿宗咸通十一年（870年）始建，初为简易木桥，后改建为伸臂式木拱廊桥。南北走向，跨石壁溪，长38米，被列为县级文物保护单位。

08.Xiongdaishang Bridge － Xiongdai Village, Jiadi Township, Jingning She Autonomous County, Lishui, Zhejiang Province, built in 1870.

It was at first a simple timber bridge built in 870 and was later developed into a covered bridge with an overhanging wooden arch. The north-south bridge spanning Shibi Stream is 38 meters long. It has been listed as the Historical and Cultural Sites Protected at the County Level.

09 — 芎岱下桥

浙江省丽水市景宁畲族自治县家地乡芎岱村

过芎岱上桥沿蜿蜒山崖公路穿越狭窄山谷一直到山顶尽头，一个小山村静卧在幽静盆谷里，迎接你的是几株参天古树和一座古朴廊桥。穿斗式全木结构，石砌独孔、廊屋硬山顶、重檐小阁歇山顶，九开间。

9.Xiongdaixia Bridge — Xiongdai Village, Jiadi Township, Jingning She Autonomous County, Lishui, Zhejiang Province.

Passing the Upper Xiongdai Bridge, one walks along a highway and through a narrow valley, until one arrives at the mountain top where a tranquil village comes into site. There several tall ancient trees greet the visitor, together with a covered bridge. It has a *chuandou* structure, with stone abutments. It has a single span, and its gallery house has nine bays, covered by an flush gable roof. It also has a small pavilion decorated with multiple eaves and a hip and gable roof.

第六章 东南廊桥遗存带

10—接龙桥

浙江省丽水市景宁畲族自治县东坑镇章坑村龙潭,中华民国六年(1917年)

又名庆安桥,位于章坑村森林峡谷飞云江。长38.5米、宽4.6米、据水面高20米、跨径30.7米、十七开间,歇山顶四柱九檩,五架抬梁,为经典大跨度木拱廊桥。接龙桥是景宁县临水最高、地势最险、保存最好的廊桥,古为文成至景宁交通要道。被列为全国重点保护单位文物。

10.Jielong Bridge — Longtan Pond, Zhangkeng Village, Dongkeng Town, Jingning She Autonomous County, Lishui, Zhejiang Province, built in 1917.

Also known as the Qing' an Bridge the Jielong Dragon Bridge spanning Feiyun River is located at the canyon in Zhangkeng Village. It is 38.5 meters long, 4.6 meters wide, and 20 meters above the water. Its gallery house has 17 bays. It has a span of 30.7 meters. This bridge is a classic long-spanned timber arch covered bridge. Its gallery house has a hip and gable roof, and is supported by four columns, five beams, and nine purlins. Jielong Bridge is the best preserved, and highest bridge in Jingning county. It is also built in the most dangerous of terrain. In ancient times, it served as a major passageway linking Wencheng and Jingning counties. It has been listed as the Major Historical and Cultural Site Protected at the National Level.

第六章 东南廊桥遗存带

三、浙江屋脊——泰顺县廊桥

III. Covered Bridges in Taishun County, Roof Ridge of Zhejiang Province

01—仙居桥

浙江省泰顺县仙稔乡仙居村，明景泰四年（1453年）

贯木叠插别压式木拱廊桥，由泰顺知县郭显宗倡建，连通府衙至温州的要道。明成化十九年（1483年）水毁，明弘治四年（1491年）知县范勉筹资重建。明嘉靖三十年（1550年）仙居桥倒塌，明嘉靖四十二年（1563年）知县区益多方募捐在原址重建。清康熙十二年（1673年）正月，村众集资重建。长43米、宽4.9米、高12.6米，跨径35.5米、十八开间。被列为全国重点文物保护单位。

01.Xianju Bridge – Xianju Village, Xianren Township, Taishun County, Zhejiang Province, built in 1453.

This woven timber arch-beam covered bridge was built by Guo Xianzong, the magistrate of Taishun County, to connect the government office to Wenzhou. The bridge was destroyed by a flood in 1483. In 1491 county magistrate Fan Mian raised money to rebuild it. Then, the bridge collapsed in 1550 and was rebuilt in 1563 with the money raised by Ou Yi, the county magistrate. In 1673, villagers raised funds to reconstruct this bridge. Now the bridge is 43 meters long, 4.9 meters wide, 12 meters high, and has a span of 35.5 meters. Its gallery house has 18 bays. This bridge has been listed as the Major Historical and Cultural Sites Protected at the National Level.

02—永庆桥

浙江省泰顺县三魁镇战州下溪坪村，清嘉庆二年（1797年）

清道光二十二年（1843年）重建。独墩两孔伸臂式木拱桥，长33米、宽4.5米，十二开间。桥墩青石叠砌，上置两层长梁圆木支托桥体，桥面铺有宽木板，内有扶梯可供上下，两侧设置防雨木板，歇山顶覆小青瓦，正中建双层飞檐阁楼，被列为全国重点文物保护单位。

2. Yongqing Bridge – Xiaxiping Village, Zhanzhou, Sankui Town, Taishun County, Zhejiang Province, built in 1797.

The bridge was rebuilt in 1843. It is a cantilever timber arch covered bridge. It has one pier with two spans. The bridge is 33 meters long, and 4.5 meters wide. It has a gallery house with 12 bays. The bridge pier is made of stacked grey stones. Two long log beams are placed on the piers to support the bridge structure. The bridge deck is covered with timber planks. Stairs are installed on the bridge allowing people to go up and down. Skirts run along both sides to protect the bridge from rain. The bridge has a hip and gable roof covered by small grey tiles and in the middle of the bridge there is a two-story pavilion topped by a roof with upturned-eaves. It has been listed as the Major Historical and Cultural Sites Protected at the National Level.

03—薛宅桥

浙江省泰顺县三魁镇薛宅村锦溪，明正德七年（1512 年）

古称锦溪桥。叠梁木拱廊桥，长51米、跨径29米、高10.5米、十五开间，桥面拱矢斜度较大。明万历七年（1579年）突发山洪将薛宅桥冲毁，清咸丰七年（1857年）复建。2016年9月15日受台风"莫兰蒂"影响，薛宅桥被完全冲毁，次年复建。被列为全国重点文物保护单位。

03.Xuezhai Bridge – Jinxi River, Xuezhai Village, Sankui Town, Taishun County, Zhejiang Province, built in 1512.

It was named Jinxi Bridge in ancient times. It is a woven timber arch-beam covered bridge. It is 51 meters long, 10.5 meters high, and has a span of 29 meters. It has a gallery house with 15 bays. The bridge arch rises at a steep angle. In 1579, the bridge was destroyed by a flood and it was reconstructed in 1857. Affected by Typhoon Meranti on September 15, 2016, Xuezhai Bridge was damaged, and it was repaired the following year. It has been listed as the Major Historical and Cultural Sites Protected at the National Level.

第六章 东南廊桥遗存带

04—北涧桥

浙江省泰顺县泗溪镇下桥村，清康熙十二年（1674年）

北涧桥，"身红装如彩蝶舞翅"，在古桥研究界，众多中外游客中有"中国最美的廊桥"的评价。长51.7米，宽5.37米，径29米，二十九开间，歇山顶正中建重檐楼阁，被列为国重点文物保护单位。

04.Beijian Bridge – Xiaqiao Village, Sixi Town, Taishun County, Zhejiang Province, built in 1674.

Beijian Bridge, which looks like a butterfly flapping its wings from a distance, is acclaimed as the most beautiful covered bridge in China by scholars of ancient bridges and by tourists from home and abroad. It is a woven arch-beam covered bridge. It is 51.7 meters long, 5.37 meters wide, with a span of 29 meters. Its gallery house has 29 bays. The bridge has a hip and gable roof. In the middle of the bridge, there is a pavilion with multiple eaves. It has been listed as the Major Historical and Cultural Sites Protected at the National Level.

05—溪东桥

浙江省泰顺县泗溪镇溪东村，明隆庆四年（1570年）

溪东桥与北涧桥相隔一里，互称姐妹桥。清乾隆十年（1745年）重建，清道光十年（1830年）修缮。长 41.7 米、宽 4.86 米、高 10.35 米、跨径 25.7 米、十五开间。被列为全国重点文物保护单位。

05.Xidong Bridge – Xidong Village, Sixi Town, Taishun County, Zhejiang Province, built in 1570.

Xidong Bridge and Beijian Bridge are one mile apart, and they are called sister bridges. The bridge was reconstructed in 1745 and repaired in 1830. A woven timber arch-beam bridge, it is 41.7 meters long, 4.86 meters wide, 10.35 meters high, and has a span of 25.7 meters. Its gallery house has 15 bays. It has been listed as the Major Historical and Cultural Sites Protected at the National Level.

06—南阳桥

浙江省泰顺县泗溪镇岩头村，清同治九年（1870年）

伸臂式平梁廊桥，长41.7米、宽4.6米、高5.9米。农历七月初七，是晋朝以来中国民间传说由喜鹊搭桥，牛郎相会织女的日子。这一天村民会拿出各家做的圆锥形米粉蒸糕作祭品，摆放到廊桥内廊祈祷五谷丰登，祝福后生幸福美满。列为全国重点文物保护单位。

06.Nanyang Bridge – Yantou Village, Sixi Town, Taishun County, Zhejiang Province, built in 1870.

This timber cantilever beam covered bridge is 41.7 meters long, 4.6 meters wide and 5.9 meters high. According to Chinese folklore, on the 7th day of the seventh month of the lunar calendar, the star-crossed lovers of the Cowherd and the Weaver Girl are able to see each other by crossing heaven on a bridge formed by magpies. On this day, villagers present steamed cone shaped rice flower cakes and other food as offerings, and place them in the gallery house of the Nanyang Bridge to pray for a healthy harvest and happiness. The bridge is listed as the Major Historical and Cultural Sites Protected at the National Level.

第六章 东南廊桥遗存带

07—文兴桥

浙江省泰顺县筱村镇坑边村玉溪，清咸丰七年（1857年）

木拱廊桥长 46.2 米、宽 5 米、跨径 29.6 米、十六开间。北侧略高的桥屋供奉三座神像，上挂"灯火千秋"古匾。逢初一、十五乡民前来祭祀。被列为全国重点文物保护单位。有"守桥女神"之名的钟篮玉（畲族，1926 年生），在老伴去世后，在桥北小屋住下。白天清扫轰赶畜禽，晚上掐灭香头烛火。涨大水前一定会召集乡亲抬来重物将桥身压稳。

07.Wenxing Bridge — Yuxi River, Kengbian Village, Xiaocun Town, Taishun County, Zhejiang Province, built in 1857.

It is a timber arch covered bridge, and It's 46.2 meters long, 5 meters wide, with a span of 29.6 meters. Its gallery house has 16 bays. Three statues of gods are enshrined in the north end of the bridge's gallery house (which is slightly higher than the others). An ancient plaque hangs from the bridge that reads "To Last for a Thousand Years." On the first and fifteenth day of the lunar new year, villagers come here to offer sacrifices. The bridge is listed as the Major Historical and Cultural Sites Protected at the National Level. The bridge's guardian is Zhong Lanyu (of the She nationality, born in 1926). She has lived in the house to the north of the bridge since her husband passed away. During the daytime, she sweeps the bridge and rids it of pests and animals. Before night, she extinguishes lit candles and incense on the bridge to prevent fires. During times of the flood, she will organize the villagers to place heavy objects on the bridge to stabilize it.

第六章 东南廊桥遗存带

中国廊桥

08—文重桥

浙江省泰顺县筱村镇东洋村，清乾隆十年（1745年）

又名板桥。伸臂式木平廊桥，长26.4米、宽4.6米、跨径22.4米、十一开间，船舷型桥墩抗洪能力增强，重檐歇山顶覆小青瓦。2016年9月15日受台风"莫兰蒂"影响，文重桥被完全冲毁，次年复建，被列为全国重点文物保护单位。

08.Wenchong Bridge — Dongyang Village, Xiaocun Town, Taishun County, Zhejiang Province, built in 1745.

Also known as Banqiao Bridge, this timber cantilever beam bridge is 26.4 meters long, 4.6 meters wide, and has a span of 22.4 meters. Its gallery house has 11 bays. Its piers are designed in the shape of the bows of a ship to increase flood resistance. Its multiple-eave hip and gable roof is covered by small grey tiles. On September 15, 2016, Wenzhong Bridge was damaged by Typhoon Meranti. It was repaired the following year. The bridge is listed as the Major Historical and Cultural Sites Protected at the National Level.

09—登云桥

浙江省泰顺县罗阳镇南门外，明正德（1506—1521年）

原名镇南桥。始建于明正德（1506—1521年）年间，由县刘桐使用官银主持修建。位于泰顺罗阳镇南门外泰寿溪，连通西南进出古道，也是往返福建省寿宁县要道。明万历（1573—1620年）年间重建更名登云桥。一墩两孔伸臂式木拱廊桥，长40米、宽5.5米、两孔跨径共25米、十二开间。被列为省级文物保护单位。

09.Dengyun Bridge — South Gate of Luoyang Town, Taishun County, Zhejiang Province, built during 1506-1521.

Originally known as Zhennan Bridge, it was built by the decree of county magistrate Liu Tong, with government funding. Crossing the Taishou Creek outside the south gate of Taishun County's Luoyang Town, the Dengyun bridge not only connected the county with the ancient roads that led to southwest China, it also served as an important passageway to Fujian's Shouning County. During the reign of Wanli in the Ming Dynasty (from 1573 to 1620), it was renamed the Dengyun Bridge. The bridge has one pier and two spans, and is a timber cantilever arch bridge. It is 40 meters long, 5.5 meters wide, and has a span of 25 meters. Its gallery house has 12 bays. It has been listed as the Historical and Cultural Sites Protected at the Provincial Level.

中国廊桥

10—三条桥

浙江省泰顺县洲岭乡和洋溪乡的界河

三条桥最初用三根粗大圆木搭建得名。据泰顺县志记述，修缮三条桥时发现顶瓦中尚存刻有唐"贞观"文字的旧瓦。专家据此推断三条桥建于唐代贞观年间。伸臂式全木结构廊桥，长32米、宽4.9米、高12.6米、跨径21.3米、十一开间。宋绍兴七年（1137年）、清道光二十三年（1843年）重建。被列为全国重点文物保护单位。

10. Santiao Bridge — the Boundary River between Zhouling Community and Yangxi Township, Taishun County, Zhejiang Province.

The bridge was initially built out of three thick logs, from which its name is derived. Now it is a timber cantilever beam covered bridge. According to the Taishun County Annals written in the late Qing dynasty, tiles engraved with the characters for "Zhenguan" were found while repairing the Three Strip Bridge. As a result, experts inferred that the Santiao Bridge was built in the Zhenguan period of the Tang Dynasty. The bridge is 32 meters long, 4.9 meters wide, 12.6 meters high, and has a span of 21.3 meters. Its gallery house has 11 bays. The bridge was reconstructed in 1137 and in 1843. It is listed as the Major Historical and Cultural Sites Protected at the National Level.

第六章　东南廊桥遗存带

1—刘宅桥

江省泰顺县三魁镇刘宅村，明永乐三年（1405年）古名仙洞虹桥，清康熙、清乾隆及清代晚期整修，殿宇式木廊桥，长25米，宽8.2米，跨径9.2米。廊屋正脊两龙对视夹舌宝珠有镇宅求财寓意，两层阁楼扶梯连通，下层供通行，上层皆庙观。"魁跨高阳刘氏洞下桥记"，修建仙洞虹桥"一为高阳本境风水之系，二为往来负担荷之便，三为经商歇客休息之所，四为秋七迎福康乐之会"，被列为全国重点文物保护单位。

1.Liuzhai Bridge – Liuzhai Village, Sankui Town, Taishun County, Zhejiang Province, built in 1405.

riginally known as the Xiandonghong idge, it was renovated during the reigns f Emperor Kangxi, Emperor Qianlong and the late Qing Dynasty. The palace-style mber beam covered bridge is 25 meters ng, 8.2 meters wide, and has a span of 9.2 eters. There are carvings of two dragons eying a flaming jewel on the ridge of the gallery house's roof, with the associated significance of protecting the bridge from flooding. The gallery house has two levels: the first for people to walk through, and the upper level serves as a shrine. According to a travel journal, this bridge has four primary functions, firstly to promote positive *fengshui*, secondly to serve as a passageway for porters, thirdly as a place for travelers and merchants to rest, and fourthly as the site for autumnal festival gatherings. The bridge is listed as the Major Historical and Cultural Sites Protected at the National Level.

12—泰福桥

浙江省泰顺县岭北乡上洋村，中华民国（1912—1949年）

又名坑口桥，因连接泰顺县城通往福建省福安县驿道得名。独孔石拱木结构廊桥，长27米、宽4米、高11米、跨径11米。

12. Taifu Bridge — Shangyang Village, Lingbei Town, Taishun County, Zhejiang Province, built during 1912-1949.

Also known as Kengkou Bridge, the Taifu Bridge was named because of its function as a segment of the ancient courier road connecting Taishun County to Fu'an County in Fujian Province. This single-span stone arch covered bridge has timber frame and is 27 meters long, 4 meters wide, 11 meters high, and has a span of 11 meters.

3—霞光桥

浙江省泰顺县横坑乡华洋村，清雍正元年（1723年）

又名下洋桥。单孔石拱木屋廊桥，长17米、宽4.5米、券高7.3米、跨径13米、七开间，二重檐悬山顶覆薄灰瓦。初为木拱廊桥，因乡民用火不慎多次焚毁。清雍正、清咸丰年间多次重建。清代晚期村社望耆召集村众"议者不利于木思易以石，虽计费倍之，然木不如石之安且久也"。四方百姓广捐资财，最终"砌以石，而仍屋之"，改建为独孔石拱木屋廊桥。

3.Xiaguang Bridge — Huayang Village, Hengkeng Town, Taishun County, Zhejiang Province, built in 1723.

Also known as Xiayang Bridge, this single-span one arch covered bridge with a timber gallery house is 17 meters long, 4.5 meters wide, with an arch height of 7.3 meters, and a span of 13 meters. Its gallery house has seven bays. Its double-eave overhanging gable roof is covered by thin grey tiles. The bridge burned down several times due to accidents by villagers. It was reconstructed many times during the Yongzheng and Xianfeng period of the Qing Dynasty. In the late Qing Dynasty, after a discussion called for by the elders in the village, it was decided that despite representing an extra expense, stone would be safer to use than timber. Donations for the project came from near and far. In the end stone was used for the masonry of the bridge, forming a single-span stone arch covered bridge. However, its roof was still built with timber.

14—毓文桥

浙江省泰顺县洲岭乡洲边村,清道光十九年(1839年)

1986年村民自筹资金修缮,桥长23米、宽4米、跨径7.6米、七开间、内设扶梯,为独孔石拱木结构廊桥。拱券式桥墩由青石筑砌,呈半月状横跨小山之间。上部结构为三层楼阁式,屋顶为重檐歇山顶式样,屋脊正中有宝葫芦装饰,四翼飞檐翘角,桥屋二楼设立文昌阁。被列为全国重点文物保护单位。

14.Yuwen Bridge – Zhoubian Village, Zhouling Town, Taishun County, Zhejiang Province, built in 1839.

The bridge is 23 meters long, 4 meters wide, and has a span of 7.6 meters. It has single span, and has a stone arch and a timber structure. Its gallery house has seven bays. A ladder is installed inside the bridge. It was rebuilt in 1986 with funds collected by villagers. Its rolling-arch style bridge piers are composed of grey stone masonry, forming the shape of a crescent moon spanning the space between the hills. The upper part of the bridge has a three-story pavilion covered with a multiple-eave hip and gable roof with four-wings and upturned eaves and winged corners. On the roof ridge sits a long-melon jewel decoration. The second story serves as a pavilion dedicated to wenchang, the Taoist god of art and literature. The bridge has been listed as the Major Historical and Cultural Sites Protected at the National Level.

第六章 东南廊桥遗存带

15 旗峰桥

浙江省泰顺县筱村镇翁山外洋村,中华民国十三年(1924年)

石拱单孔木屋廊桥,长22.58米、宽4.35米、高4.4米、跨径14.2米。桥内设置佛龛,村民常来瞻仰膜拜。旗峰桥四面环山、三面邻水,山峰满眼青翠,溪水甘甜清冽,环境优美空气好。

15.Qifeng Bridge — Waiyang Village, Wengshan Community, Xiaocun Town, Taishun County, Zhejiang Province, built in 1924.

This single-span stone arch covered bridge has a timber gallery house. It is 22.58 meters long, 4.35 meters wide, 4.4 meters high and has a span of 14.2 meters. Buddhist shrines are installed in the bridge for villagers to worship. Surrounded by verdant hills on four sides and bordered by sweet and clear water on three sides, this bridge and its surroundings together form a picturesque site.

16—普宾桥

浙江省泰顺县雅阳镇新久村，清道光元年（1821年）

双木支柱平梁式全木结构廊桥，长13.6米、宽4.25米、高3.75米、跨径8.55米，是泰顺县通往东部邻县和福建省北部各县的重要津梁。当年建桥信息一经传播，得到泰顺县、平阳县、寿宁县、柘荣县、桐山等地百姓捐助。工程告竣后的节余银两在廊桥西端修建茶亭，供行人免费饮茶直到余款用尽。以"普天下皆宾客"之意取名普宾桥。

16.Pubin Bridge — Xinjiu Village, Yayang Town, Taishun County, built in 1821.

This timber beam covered bridge supported by two wooden columns is 13.6 meters long, 4.25 meters wide, 3.75 meters high, and has a span of 8.55 meters. It serves as an important passageway running from Taishun County to the eastern adjacent counties and to the northern counties of Fujian Province. The construction of this bridge was funded by common people from Taishun County, Pingyang County, Shouning County, Zherong County, Tongshan County, and other places, who donated to the project as soon as news of the construction was received. After finishing the project, remaining funds were spen on building a tea-pagoda at the west end of th bridge to provide free tea to travelers until fund were exhausted. The bridge is named Pubi Bridge to signify that all people are welcom guests at this place.

7—道均洋桥

江省泰顺县岭北乡道均洋村

又名水尾桥。毁于清道光二十一年（1841年）、中华民国〔年（1919年）重建。石拱廊桥，长34.25米、宽4.7米、高5米、径8米、十二开间，木柱木梁穿斗式结构，悬山顶阁楼。

17.Daojunyang Bridge — Daojunyang Village, Lingbei Town, Taishun County, Zhejiang Province.

Also known as Shuiwei Bridge, this bridge was destroyed by floods in 1841 and was reconstructed in 1919. The stone arch covered bridge is 34.25 meters long, 4.7 meters wide, 5 meters high, and has a span of 8 meters. It has a gallery house with twelve bays. Its gallery house is a *chuandou* structure with timber columns and beams, and its pavilion building has a overhanging gable roof.

18 城水桥

浙江省泰顺县龟湖镇后章岗村,中华民国三十一年(1942年)

独孔全木结构廊桥,长15米,宽4.2米,跨径8米。城水桥边可欣赏到最完好的绿色宝库,整座峡谷树茂花繁进发无尽生机。

18.Chengshui Bridge – Houzhanggang Village, Guihu Town, Taishun County, Zhejiang Province, built in 1942.

This single-span timber frame covered bridge is 15 meters long, 4.2 meters wide and has a span of 8 meters. One can enjoy the pleasant view of trees, grass, and flowers on the valley from the bridge.

第五节·闽江流域的廊桥
Section V　Covered Bridges in Minjiang River Basin

一、山深溪流十八曲——寿宁县廊桥
I. Covered Bridges in Shouning County, Eighteen Bends of Hills and Streams

01—飞云桥

福建省寿宁县鳌阳镇，明天顺七年（1463年）

曾名步云桥、后墩桥，县丞（副县长）李贞、乡绅吴永忠募建。清嘉庆二十三年（1818年），清光绪二年（1876年）重修。中华民国二十七年（1938）修葺，1995年修缮。两端桥堍用条石砌筑，长29.2米、宽5.3米、跨径18.8米，十三开间。东南与西北走向，双坡顶中间升出歇山顶小阁楼。

01.Feiyun Bridge – Aoyang Town, Shouning County, Fujian Province, built in 1463.

The present bridge was built in 1938. The bridge is also known as Buyun Bridge and Houdun Bridge. Li Zheng, the assistant county head and Wu Yongzhong, a member of the local gentry, raised money for the construction of the bridge. In 1818 and 1876, the bridge was renovated. It was also renovated in 1995. The two ends of the bridge are made of stone. Its length is 29.2 meters, and its width is 5.3 meters. Its span is 18.8 meters and its gallery house has thirteen bays. The bridge is oriented from the southeast to the northwest. Its roof has two slopes. In the middle there is a small pavilion with a hip and gable roof.

2—仙宫桥

福建省寿宁县鳌阳镇

又名玉带桥，始建于明代（1368—1644年）。清乾隆十四年（1749年）水毁，清乾隆三十二年（1767年）重建，1992年修缮。两端桥堍块石砌筑，南北走向，全木结构独拱廊桥，长27米、宽5米、跨径24.5米、十三开间。四柱九檩抬梁式构架廊屋，中心如意斗拱叠梁八角藻井，两边设木凳、风雨挡板。双坡顶中心与两端建八角攒尖阁。

2. Xiangong Bridge – Ao'yang Town, Shouning County, Fujian Province, built during 1368-1644.

Also known as the Yudai Qiao, it was destroyed by a flood in 1749, rebuilt in 1767, and repaired in 1992. The two ends of the bridge are composed of stone masonry. The bridge has a north-south orientation. It is a single-span covered bridge with a timber frame, and is 27 meters long, 5 meters wide, and has a span of 24.5 meters. Its gallery house has 13 bays. It is a *tailiang* structure, with four columns, and nine purlins. Its center has an octagonal caisson *zaojing* ceiling with *ruyi dougong* brackets. Inside the gallery house are wooden benches on either side, and skirts to protect the bridge from wind and rain run alongside both ends as well. At the center of the double-slope roof as well as at both ends of the bridge are octagonal pyramidal-shaped pavilions.

3—升平桥

福建省寿宁县鳌阳镇东门，明天顺元年（1457年）

曾名横溪桥。此桥曾于1545年毁于火灾。明隆庆五年（1571年）、清乾隆四十三年（1778年）重建。1997年修缮。南北走向，单孔全木结构廊桥，长25.5米、宽5.6米、跨径23.5米、十一开间。独脊双坡顶中央建蝶翅斗拱翘角望阁，廊内正中斗拱层叠承托八角藻井，雀替雕刻卷草纹。被列为全国重点文物保护单位。

3. Shengping Bridge – East Gate of Ao'yang Town, Shouning County, Fujian Province, built in 1457.

Also known as the Hengxi Bridge, in 1545 the bridge was destroyed by fire. It was rebuilt in 1571 and 1778, and was repaired in 1997. Stretching from the north to the south, it has a single span, and is a timber frame covered bridge. It is 25.5 meters long, 5.6 meters wide, and has a span of 23.5 meters. Its gallery house has 11 bays. In the middle of the gallery house's single-ridge two-sloped roof is a scenic pavilion with butterfly-wing *dougong* brackets and upturned roof corners. In the center, *dougong* brackets are layered so as to support an octagonal caisson *zaojing* ceiling, and *queti* braces are decorated with rolling grass patterns. The bridge is listed as the Major Historical and Cultural Sites Protected at the National Level.

04 — 小东下桥

福建省寿宁县坑底乡小东村,清光绪四年(1878年)

又名大宝桥。清光绪四年(1878年)重建,东南与西北走向,全木结构单孔木拱廊桥。长44.3米、宽4.6米、跨径33.1米,十九开间。悬山顶鹊尾脊覆小青瓦。桥头檐下至梁上部的粉墙有彩绘。神龛供奉临水夫人。桥中梁上墨书建桥时间、捐助贤达、工匠姓名。小东廊桥是省级名胜"杨梅州生态长廊"暑重要景观。

04. Xiaodongxia Bridge — Xiaodong Village, Kengdi Town, Shouning County, Fujian Province, built in 1878.

First built in the Ming Dynasty, rebuilt in 1878. It is 44.3 meters long, 4.6 meters wide, and has a span of 33.1 meters. Its gallery house has 19 bays. The overhanging roof has two slopes and is covered by small grey tiles. There are colored illustrations on the whitewashed wall, running from the eaves to the bridge's supporting beams. The bridge houses a shrine dedicated to a goddess believed to watch over the river. The middle beam of the bridge is engraved in black ink with the date of the bridge construction, the names of those who contributed funds for the project, and the names of the bridge's craftsmen. Xiaodongxia Bridge is listed as a provincial-level scenic area within the Yangmeizhou Ecological Corridor.

05—小东上桥

福建省寿宁县坑底乡小东村上水口，清嘉庆六年（1801年）

全木结构单跨木拱廊桥，长 21.5 米、宽 4.6 米、高 7.6 米、跨径 16.6 米、八开间。桥台采用大块鹅卵石砌筑，双坡单脊顶满覆小青瓦。廊屋正梁墨书建桥修桥时间及工匠姓名。

05.Xiaodongshang Bridge – Xiaodong Village, Kengdi Town, Shouning County, Fujian Province, built in 1801.

This single-span timber arch bridge is 21.4 meters long, 4.6 meters wide, 7.6 meters high, and has a span of 16.4 meters. Its gallery house has 8 bays. The abutment is built of large stones, and its roof has two slopes and a single ridge. It is covered by small grey tiles. The date of construction and the names of participating craftsman are written on the gallery house's main beam in black ink.

06 — 福寿桥

福建省寿宁县犀湾乡犀湾村南水口，清嘉庆十九年（1814年）

又名坝头溪桥。中华民国十九年（1930年）修缮。南北走向，木结构、独孔伸臂式木拱廊桥，长40.8米、宽5米、拱跨33米、十八开间，双坡顶上覆青杂瓦。南桥堍接河岸岩壁，北桥堍大块条石砌筑。桥廊穿斗式结构正中设置神龛，正中供奉观世音菩萨，右侧供奉土地神公，左侧供奉临水仙姑。桥廊内两旁设置木制条凳，两侧檐下有遮挡风雨的护板。

6.Fushou Bridge — Nanshuikou in Xiwan Village, Xiwan Township, Shouning County, Fujian Province. built in 1814.

Also known as Batouxi Bridge. In 1930 it was repaired. It is a timber-frame cantilever arch covered bridge that stretches in a north-south direction. It has a single span, and is 40.8 meters long, 5 meters wide, and has an arch that spans 33 meters. Its gallery house has 18 bays and its two-slope roof is covered by assorted grey tiles. The south end of the bridge is connected with the rock wall of the river bank and the north end is built with large blocks of stone. In the middle of the gallery house a shrine is set up to worship Guanyin, the bodhisattva of compassion, on the right is a shrine for a village god, and to the left is a shrine for the immortal aunt river goddess. There are wooden benches on both sides of the gallery house, and protective boards under the eaves on both sides protect the bridge from wind and rain.

中国廊桥

07—大宝桥

福建省寿宁县坑底乡小东村，明代（1368—1644年）

曾名小东桥，长44.5米、宽4.6米、跨径33米、十九开间，挑檐悬山顶覆小青瓦。因洪水期水面高流速快，大宝桥拱跨弧度很大，两端桥堍用大块坚石砌筑，并在河水主峰头一侧桥堍建造一座船舶型石墩。廊内设木凳、木板床。清光绪四年（1878年）重建。被列为省级文物保护单位。

07.Dabao Bridge – Xiaodong Village, Kengdi Township, Shouning County, Fujian Province, built during 1368-1644.

Also known as Xiaodong Bridge, it was rebuilt in 1878. It is 44.5 meters long, 4.6 meters wide, and has a span of 33 meters. Its gallery house has 19 bays. Its two-slope overhanging gable roof has extended eaves, and is covered with small grey tiles. Because of the speed and force of sudden floods here, the bridge's arch is built with a steep angle of incline, the two sides of the bridge use large stone blocks, and the bridge pier is shaped as the bow of a ship. The bridge is listed as the Historical and Cultural Sites Protected at the Provincial Level.

第六章 东南廊桥遗存带

08—鸾峰桥

福建省寿宁县下党乡下党村，清嘉庆五年（1800年）

又名下党桥。南北走向木拱廊桥，长47.6米、宽4.9米，跨径37.6米、十七开间。南北桥堍依托岩石砌筑。桥廊神龛供奉临水夫人。列入世界文化遗产备份名录，被列为全国重点文物保护单位。

08.Luanfeng Bridge — Xiadang Village, Xiadang township, Shouning County, Fujian Province, built in 1800.

Also known as Xiadang Bridge, this timber arch covered bridge is 47.6 meters long and 4.9 meters wide, with a span of 37.6 meters. Its gallery house has 17 bays. The north and south ends of the bridge are built with stone masonry. A shrine in the gallery house is dedicated to a river goddess. The bridge was included in a preparatory list of China's world cultural heritage sites. It is also listed as the Major Historical and Cultural Sites Protected at the National Level.

09—杨溪头桥

福建省寿宁县下党乡杨溪头村，清道光二十年（1840 年）

清道光二十年（1840 年）重建。单孔全木结构经典式木拱廊桥，长 50.5 米、宽 4.96 米、跨径 36.6 米，十七开间，东西走向，双坡顶覆小青瓦。1961 年水毁，1967 年按照原型制重建。

09.Yangxitou Bridge — Yangxitou Village, Xiadang Township, Shouning County, Fujian Province, rebuilt in 1840.

It was rebuilt in 1840. This classical timber arch covered bridge has a single span and a timber frame. It is 50.5 meters long, 4.96 meters wide, with a 36.6 meter span and a gallery house with 17 bays. It stretches from east to west with small grey tiles covering its roof. It was destroyed by floods in 1961 and was rebuilt according to its original form in 1967.

10—升仙桥

福建省寿宁县犀湾乡先锋村，清道光十九年（1839年）

东西走向，全木结构，独孔三重檐阁楼式廊桥，长26.8米、宽4米、跨径14.5米、九开间。建于清康熙四十一年（1702年）的永乐宫处水尾，与升仙桥结为一体，村民称为"水尾宫""宫桥头"。

10. Shengxian Bridge – Xianfeng Village, Xiwan Township, Shouning County, Fujian Province, built in 1839.

The bridge has an east to west orientation and has a full timber structure. It has a single span and is a triple-eave-style pavilion. It is 26.8 meters long, 4 meters wide, and has a span of 14.5 meters. Its gallery house has 9 bays. The Yongle Gong temple, built in 1702 at the village's shuiwei "water-tail," is integrated into the Shengxian Bridge as one unit. The villagers call the structures the "water-tail temple" and the "temple's bridge-head" respectively.

第六章 东南廊桥遗存带

11—岭兜桥

福建省寿宁县犀湾乡岭兜村，清乾隆十九年（1754年）

清咸丰七年（1857年）重建。南北走向，独孔木平梁廊桥，长30米、宽4米、跨径6.5米，十一开间。两端桥堍大块青石砌筑，桥南端墙壁嵌石碑四方。岭兜桥一侧连通两间客栈。清代早期闽浙两省往来热络，桥旁大小客栈36家。桥头客栈造饭锅灶已塌毁，灶王爷神像还在。

11.Lingdou Bridge — Lingdou Village, Xiwan Township, Shouning County, Fujian Province, built in 1754.

The bridge was rebuilt in 1857. This timber beam covered bridge has a single span and runs in a north-south direction. It is 30 meters long, 4 meters wide, with a span of 6.5 meters and has a gallery house with 11 bays. Both sides of the bridge are built with large grey stone masonry. The walls at the south end of the bridge have 4 steles encased within. Lingdou Bridge is connected with two inns. In the early Qing Dynasty, the bridge served a much trafficked artery connecting Fujian and Zhejiang provinces. It previously had 36 large and small inns beside it. While the large kitchen stove for the bridge's inns has been destroyed, a statue of the god of the kitchen remains.

第六章 东南廊桥遗存带

二、山涧清泉鲤鱼溪——周宁县廊桥

II. Covered Bridges in Zhouning County, Liyu Brook Flowed in the Mountains

01—观音桥

福建省周宁县浦源镇鲤鱼村鲤鱼溪,宋代（960 — 1279 年）

圆木平梁木结构廊桥，长8米、宽4米、高5米，东西走向，两侧设置木墙南面开窗，双层挑檐悬山顶覆小青瓦，顶脊有两条奔龙和鱼化龙雕像，西端紧靠郑氏祠堂。桥梁与寺庙合一供奉观世音菩萨。浦源村逢年过节、逢喜庆大事往溪中放生鲤鱼，久而久之蜿蜒一华里鲤鱼满溪。村民爱鱼、护鱼、敬鱼，迷恋于鲤鱼的美丽与自由、健康与优雅，而他们自己又何尝不是如此呢。

01.Guanyin Bridge — Liyu River, Liyu Village, Puyuan Town, Zhouning County, Fujian Province, built during 960-1279.

This timber log beam covered bridge stretches from east to west, and is 8 meters long, 4 meters wide, and 5 meters high. A timber wall is built on both of its sides, and a window faces out from its south. The gallery house is covered by a overhanging gable roof, covered by small grey tiles. The roof ridge is decorated by figures of a decorative succulent plant, and of a fish transforming into a dragon. The west end is close to the ancestral hall of the Zheng family.

This combined bridge and temple is used to worship Guan Shiyin (Guanyin) the Buddhist bodhisattva of compassion. Villagers from throughout Puyuan release carp in the stream on festivals, wishing the river to be full of carp long into the future. Residents here love, protect, and respect fish. They are fascinated by the beauty and freedom, health and elegance of carp, attributes which probably can be ascribed to themselves as well.

第六章 东南廊桥遗存带

02—赤岩虹桥

福建省周宁县泗桥镇赤岩村，清康熙四十一年（1702年）

原为木拱廊桥通古驿道。清嘉庆十六年（1811年），生员谢联元、吕振茂募资重建，仍为木拱廊桥。清光绪三十三年（1907年），乡绅谢春荣捐家财改建为石拱廊桥，坚牢稳固百余年无损。长27米、宽5米、九开间，高于河床30米。36根朱漆大柱支撑双层挑檐八角阁楼。

02.Chiyanhong Bridge — Chiyan Village, Siqiao Town, Zhouning County, Fujian Province, built in 1702.

Originally, this was a timber arch covered bridge, leading to an ancient courier road. In 1811 two members of the local literati who had passed the first level official examinations, Xie Lianyuan and Lu Zhenmao, raised funds to reconstruct the bridge, and it was still a timber arch covered bridge. In 1908, Xie Chunrong, a member of the local gentry, donated his family's wealth to rebuild it as a stone arch bridge, which ha remained firm and stable for over a hundre years without suffering any damage. It is 2 meters long, 5 meters wide, and has a galler house with 9 bays. The bridge spans 30 meter above the riverbed. Thirty-six large column covered in red lacquer support the two-stor pavilion's octagonal roof and overhanging eaves

03—金凤桥

福建省周宁县七步镇溪头村

石拱独孔，全遮挡廊屋，四排木柱，穿斗式结构卯榫衔扣（无铁钉）。廊内设神龛供奉观世音菩萨，两侧设木凳，双脊翘角悬山顶，顶脊正中安置"小灯塔"式宝顶。长9米、宽4.2米、高6.4米、五开间。

03.Jinfeng Bridge — Xitou Village, Qibu Town, Zhouning County, Fujian Province.

This is a stone arch bridge with a single span. Skirts protect the entire bridge from wind and rain. Its gallery house has 4 rows of timber columns. Its gallery house is a *chuandou* structure with 5 bays, built with mortise and tenon technology without the use of a single iron nail. Inside the bridge is a shrine for the worship of Guanyin, the Buddhist bodhisattva of compassion. Timber benches run along both sides of the bridge. It is covered by a two-ridge overhanging gable roof with outstretched corners. A "small lighthouse" is installed in the center of the roof ridge. It is 9 meters long, 4.2 meters wide, and 6.4 meters high, with 5 bays.

中国廊桥

04—三仙桥

福建省周宁县纯池镇禾溪村，明成化三年 (1467 年)

曾名澄明桥、三顶桥，因供奉杨、柳、倪三位仙姑而改名。穿斗式架构，单孔亭阁式木拱廊桥，长 18.4 米、宽 5.4 米、跨径 19 米、七开间。桥面铺木板，桥端建门亭，桥顶建中大侧小四角挑檐阁楼。中华民国六年(1917年)建桥匠师许顺金主持重建。1949 年后两次大修。三仙桥是村民沟通往来、议事休闲、粘贴布告、物品买卖场所。被列为县级文物保护单位。民间说书艺人常在廊桥内为村民表演。

04.Sanxian Bridge — Hexi Village, Chunchi Town, Zhouning County, Fujian Province, built in 1467.

Previously, it was called the Chengming Bridge and Sanding Bridge, but its name was changed to honor the three female immortals Yang, Liu, and Ni. It is a timber frame arch covered bridge. Its gallery house is a *chuandou* structure and has seven bays. It is 18.4 meters long, 5.4 meters wide, and has a span of 19 meters. Its deck is covered with timber boards. Pagodas are installed at the end of the bridge. The gallery house is tall in the center and smaller at the sides, and is covered by a four cornered roof with overhanging eaves. Xu Shunjin, a master bridge builder, presided over the reconstruction of the bridge in 1917. After 1949, the bridge underwent two major renovations. Sanxian Bridge is a place for villagers to communicate and relax, post announcements, and buy and sell goods. It is listed as the Historical and Cultural Sites Protected at the County Level. A traditional storyteller often performs for villagers on the covered bridge.

第六章 东南廊桥遗存带

05—观音桥

福建省周宁县纯池镇前溪村，清康熙七年（1668年）

又名前溪桥，全木结构木拱廊桥，长22米、九开间。曾多次重修，2005年维修。观音桥连接村落两岸，也是闽东与闽北古驿道重要节点。

05.Guanyin Bridge – Qianxi Village, Chunchi Town, Zhouning County, Fujian Province, built in 1668.

It is also known as Qianxi Bridge. this bridge is a timber framed arch bridge with a length of 22 meters and with a gallery house of 9 bays. It has been repaired many times, most recently in 2005. Guanyin Bridge connects the two sides of Qianxi Village. It also served as an important node of the ancient courier road that connected eastern and northern Fujian.

06—院林桥

福建省周宁县纯池镇纯池村

位于般若寺旁侧。清早期、中华民国九年（1920年）重新修建。通纯池到莲地、周宁、宁德古官道。院林桥还曾是科举晋级考场，被纯池读书人奉为圣地。院林桥为全木结构木拱廊桥，背后新建一座同名砖石结构廊桥。

06.Yuanlin Bridge — Chunchi Village, Chunchi Town, Zhouning County, Fujian Province.

Located beside the Panruo Temple, the bridge was rebuilt in the early Qing Dynasty and in 1919. The bridge was part of the old official road that connected Chunchi to Liandi Village, and to Zhouning and Ningde counties. The Yuanlin Bridge once served as the examination hall for the first-level official examinations, and was regarded as a holy place by the scholars of Chunchi Village. Yuanlin Bridge is a timber frame arch covered bridge. A new covered bridge made of bricks now sits behind it.

7 — 登龙桥

福建省周宁县七步镇八蒲村，清代（1636 — 1912 年）

登龙桥是闽西与闽东古道相连的重要节点。清康熙、乾隆、光绪年间重建。独拱全木结构廊桥，长 38 米、宽 5 米、跨径 23.5 米、高 9 米、十五开间。被列为省级保护单位文物。周宁县廊桥匠师张昌智，其祖张新佑自清乾隆三十二年（1767 年）建造鳌阳镇仙宫桥开始，经新、成、茂、学、明、世、必、到昌宇辈，前后八代建造木拱廊桥 46 座。2015 年张昌智受邀在德国雷根斯堡建造木拱廊桥，引起轰动。

7.Denglong Bridge — Bapu Village, Qibu Town, Zhouning County, Fujian Province, built during 1636-1912.

Denglong Bridge is an important node that connected the ancient road that ran from western to eastern Fujian. It was rebuilt during the reigns of Emperor Kangxi, Emperor Qianlong, and Emperor Daoguang of the Qing Dynasty. It is a timber frame covered bridge with a single span, and is 38 meters long, and 5 meters wide. It has a span of 23.5 meters. It is 9 meters high and has a gallery house with 15 bays. It is listed as the Historical and Cultural Sites Protected at the Provincial Level. Zhang Changzhi, a bridge builder in Zhouning County, is the descendant of Zhang Xinyou who built the Xiangong Bridge in Aoyang Town in 1757. Subsequent bridge builders were found in eight subsequent generations of the Zhang family, who participated in the construction of 46 timber covered bridges. In 2015, Zhang Changzhi was invited to build a timber arch bridge in Regensburg, Germany, and was the subject of much acclaim.

三、溪涧纵横交错——柘荣县廊桥

III. Covered Bridges in Zherong County, Stream Flowed between the Hills Crisscrossing

01—东源桥

福建省柘荣县东源乡东源村，元至元元年（1335 年）

又名水浒桥，明嘉靖十三年（1534 年）、清乾隆十六年（1751 年）重建。贯木拱廊屋桥，南北走向，长 43.2 米，单孔、跨径 25 米、十八开间，108 根立柱象征梁山一百零八条好汉。被列为全国重点文物保护单位。

01.Dongyuan Bridge — Dongyuan Village, Dongyuan Township, Zherong County, Fujian Province, built in 1335.

Also known as the Shuihu Bridge, it was rebuilt in 1534 and 1751. The woven timber arch-beam covered bridge runs from north to south, and has a gallery house with 18 bays. It is 43.2 meters long and has a single span of 25 meters. Its 108 internal columns symbolize the 108 heroes of Liangshan (referred to in the Chinese classic *Water Margin*). is listed as the Major Historical and Cultural Site Protected at the National Level.

02—登云桥

福建省柘荣县楮坪乡洪坑村水口，元至正二十四年（1364年）

现桥建于元至正二十四年（1364年）。西南、东北走向，孔石拱廊屋桥，长19.2米、拱跨5.2米，距离水面5.3米，廊屋七扇六开间，共28根立柱，抬梁式单檐双坡顶，现存桥廊为清代建筑。桥东北端北侧岩壁保留有元至正二十四年摩崖石刻一处，字幅高1.35米、宽1.1米，内容为登云桥记。桥廊滴水线四周各向外延伸20米为文物保护范围。

2. Dengyun Bridge — Shuikou, Hongkeng Village, Zhuping Township, Zherong County, Fujian Province, built in 1364.

The present bridge was built in 1364. The bridge runs from the southwest to the northeast. It is a stone arch bridge with a single span. It is 19.2 meters long, has a span of 5.2 meters, and rises 5.3 meters above the water. Its gallery house has 6 bays and a total of 28 columns. It is a *tailiang* structure, with a double sloping roof with a single eave. The current gallery house is a Qing Dynasty structure. On the north side of the northeastern end of the bridge, there is an inscription on a rock face dating to 1364. The inscription is 1.35 meters high and 1.1 meters wide, and describes the background of the Dengyun Bridge. The drip line around the bridge corridor extends 20 meters to the outside for the protection of historical and cultural sites.

四、丘陵溪流交汇——政和县廊桥
IV. Covered Bridges in Zhenghe County, intersection of Hills and Streams

第六章 东南廊桥遗存带

01—花桥

福建省政和县杨源乡坂头村，明正德六年（1511年）

南北走向，单孔石拱楼阁式廊桥，长 38 米、跨径 12.2 米、十三开间、宽 8 米。抬梁穿斗式结构，三重檐歇山顶五层飞檐翘角，中亭和两端建阁楼，犹如盛开的莲花，由此得名。清康熙、清道光、清咸丰年间、中华民国三年（1914年）、1982 年重修。常来上香的妇女祈祷远在他乡打工的晚辈健康平安、财进事成。古代专供女人行走的狭窄通道，今天有些年老妇女仍在行走。

01.Huaqiao Bridge – Bantou Village, Yangyuan Township, Zhenghe County, Fujian Province, built in 1511.

Running from north to south, this stone arch pavilion covered bridge has a single span. It is 38 meters long, 8 meters wide, and has a span of 12.2 meters. The gallery house has 13 bays, and is a combined *tailiang* and *chuandou* structure. It has a five story gallery house with a triple-eave hip and gable roof with upturned eaves and winged corners. There is a pagoda in the center and pavilions built on each side. This bridge appears like a blooming lotus flower, and its name refers to this resemblance. The bridge was rebuilt several times during the reigns of Emperor Kangxi, Emperor Daoguang, and Emperor Xianfeng of the Qing Dynasty, as well as in 1924 and 1982. Women often come here to burn incense and pray for health, safety, prosperity, and success. A narrow passageway on the bridge was once provided for the exclusive use of women, and it is still used by a few of the elderly women in the village today.

02—水尾桥

福建省政和县岭腰乡后山村乐溪河,明代（1368 — 1644 年）

又名后山桥、安溪桥,传说为庆元县吴姓造桥师傅所建,全长 41.50 米,净跨 32 米,矢高 11.15 米,面阔 5 米,廊屋 15 间,是闽北单孔跨度最长的木拱廊桥。清朝嘉庆四年（1799 年）重建,2001 年重修。至今已有 210 余年历史,现已被列入世界文化遗产保护预备名单。

02.Shuiwei Bridge — Lexi River, Houshan Village, Lingyao Township, Zhenghe County, Fujian Province, built during 1368-1644.

Also known as the Houshan Bridge, and as the Anxi Bridge. Locals say that the bridge was built by a master bridge builder surnamed Wu from Qingyuan County. It has a total length of 41.50 meters, a net span of 32 meters, and a height of 11.15 meters. It is 5 meters wide, and has a 15 bay gallery house. The bridge was rebuilt in 1799 and 2001. It has a history of more than 210 years and was included in list submitted by China for recognition of sites to be celebrated as examples of world cultural heritage.

03—雾中桥

福建省政和县杨源乡洞宫村

村老讲述："雾中桥距山村一里，跨山谷溪流常有云雾缠绕，故名。武夷山至福安、霞浦之间东西六百里古代大通道上，雾中桥恰居其中，是西部山货、东部海货贸易运输走廊中的转运交易站。村里人招待来往客商赚了些银两，各家拿出一些在桥头烧茶水免费给行人喝。"全木结构木拱廊桥，长19米、宽3米、高8.2米、十开间、单脊硬山顶，内设护栏木凳。

3. Wuzhong Bridge – Donggong Village, Yangyuan Township, Zhenghe County, Fujian Province.

An old villager explained that "The Wuzhong Bridge is about one *li* from the mountain village, and as fog and clouds often envelop the mountain river valley, it has this name. In ancient times the road from the Wuyi Mountains to Fu'an and Xiapu counties was about a 600 *li* east to west passage. The Wuzhong Bridge was located right in its center. It served as an important transfer station for goods shipped from the sea to the east, and for goods carried from the mountains from the west. Villagers were able to earn money by hosting the travelers and merchants. Every family would provide hot tea to travelers on the bridge for free." The timber arch bridge has a length of 19 meters, a width of 3 meters, and a height of 8.2 meters. Its gallery house has 10 bays, and is covered by a single ridge flush gable roof. Protective timber railings and benches are installed in the bridge.

04—矮殿桥

福建省政和县杨源乡杨源村,北宋崇宁(1102—1106年)

又名杨源水尾桥、朝阳桥。南北走向,单孔平梁全木廊桥,长19.5米、宽6.5米、跨径10.8米、高8.3米、七开间。飞檐翘角重檐歇山顶覆小青瓦,八角覆斗藻井描绘《西游记》《三国演义》故事。廊屋穿斗式结构榫卯连接,中部神龛供奉观世音菩萨,北端设三层塔式香纸炉,两侧铺钉双层风雨板下置木凳。中华民国十八年(1929年)重修。

04.Aidian Bridge – Yangyuan Village, Yangyuan Township, Zhenghe County, Fujian Province, built during 1102-1106.

Also known as the Yangyuan Shuiwei Bridge or as the Chaoyang Bridge. The bridge runs from north to south and is a timber frame covered bridge with a single span. It is 19.5 meters long, 6.5 meters wide, and has a span of 10.8 meters. It sits 8.3 meters above the water and has a gallery house with seven bays. The eaves and cornices on the top of the hip and gable roof are covered with small grey tiles, and its eight-panel caisson *zaojing* ceiling depicts scenes from the Chinese classics *Journey to the West* and *Romance of the Three Kingdoms*. The gallery house is a *chuandou* structure and is connected by mortise and tenon technology. The central shrine is dedicated to Guanyin, the Buddhist bodhisattva of compassion. At the north side of the bridge is a three-story pagoda-style oven for burning incense and paper. There are timber benches under the double-layer wind and rain awnings on both sides of the bridge. The bridge was rebuilt in 1929.

第六章 东南廊桥遗存带

05－文泰桥

福建省政和县杨源乡和平村，明成化（1465 — 1487 年）

又名上车桥，为石拱木屋廊桥。《上车桥重修简记》载："石拱桥始建于明成化（1465 — 1487 年）年间。始建桥屋不知何时，据梁上文字记载'大清道光三十年岁次庚戌壬午月庚戌日壬午时重新建造'。自古以来乃进出洞宫山必经之路。古代刘鹗、祝仕奇曾经在路旁刻石。今重建，既保留历史文化古迹，又供行人避风雨。"

05.Wentai Bridge – Heping Village, Yangyuan Township, Zhenghe County, Fujian Province, built during 1465-1487.

Also known as the Shangche Bridge, it is a covered bridge with a stone arch and a timber gallery house. According to the *Brief Notes on the Restoration of the Shangche Bridge*, "the stone arch bridge was built in the Chenghua Period of the Ming Dynasty. There is no information about when the bridge house was initially built. According to words recorded on the bridge's beam, 'In the 30th year of the Daoguang period of the Qing Dynasty the bridge was rebuilt.' Since ancient times, this has been the only way to get in and out of Donggong Mountain. Ancient masters Liu E and Zhu Shi carved inscriptions on the rock face beside the bridge. Today's restoration of the bridge not only preserves a historical and cultural site, also provides shelter for pedestrians from the wind and the rain."

06 — 洋后桥
福建省政和县外屯乡外屯村洋后自然村

又称洋后厝桥。桥碑记载:"清道光三十年(1850年)重建。木拱廊桥,西南—东北走向,跨七星溪。长34米、宽4.86米、跨径27.7米、高5.5米。桥体由9组三节苗、8组五节苗及剪刀苗拱骨相贯面成。置廊屋十四间,抬梁穿斗式木构架,歇山顶檐下施风雨挡板。桥面以条板横铺,两侧设木凳、栏杆。是研究古代廊桥建筑艺术珍贵的实物资料。"被列为省级文物保护单位。

06. Yanghou Bridge — Yanghou Ziran Village, Waitun Village, Waitun Township, Zhenghe County, Fujian Province.

It is also known as the Yanghoucuo Bridge. An inscription on the bridge's stele reads, "The bridge was reconstructed during the 30th year of the reign of Daoguang of the Qing Dynasty. It is a timber arch covered bridge, that has a southwest to northeast orientation, crossing the Qixing River. It is 34 meters long, 4.86 meters wide, has a span of 27.7 meters, and is 5.5 meters high. The bridge body's arch skeleton is formed by the intersection of a three-segment system formed by 9 groups of timbers, a five-segment system composed of 8 groups of timbers, and cross-bracing. The gallery house has 14 bays, and is a combined *tailiang* and *chuandou* structure. Awnings to keep out the wind and rain are installed underneath the hip and gable roof eaves. The bridge deck is covered with timber horizontal strips, and timber benches and railings are installed on both of its sides. The bridge is a precious resource for the study of the art of ancient covered bridge architecture." It is listed as the Historical and Cultural Sites Protected at the Provincial Level.

五、白水洋鸳鸯溪——屏南县廊桥
V. Covered Bridges in Pingnan County, with Baishui River and Yuanyang Brook

01—百祥桥

福建省屏南县棠口乡下坑尾村与寿山乡白洋村交界白洋溪，南宋咸淳（1265 — 1275 年）

又名松柏桥、白洋桥。史为闽北地区贯通西部山区与东部沿海"茶盐古道"重要节点。独孔全木结构伸臂式木拱廊桥，长 38 米、宽 4.5 米、跨径 35 米、桥面距谷底 27 米。四柱九檩穿斗式桥廊。清道光、清咸丰年间重建。清光绪年间重修后漂头、旺坑村十余人合资买下桥西一片山坡，植杉树 480 余株作为修桥专用林。同时捐谷放贷，收取薄利作为每年立冬村民锄草扫桥午餐。屏南县的百祥桥、千乘桥、万安桥，均被列为全国重点文物保护单位，有"百千万"之名。

01.Baixiang Bridge – Baiyang Creek at the junction of Baiyang Village in Shoushan Township and Xiakenwei Village in Tangkou Township, Pingnan County, Fujian Province, built during 1265-1275.

Also known as the Songbai Bridge and the Baiyang Bridge. Historically, this was an important node on the ancient "Tea and Salt Road" that linked the western mountainous areas to the eastern coastal areas in northern Fujian. It is a timber cantilever arch bridge with a single span. It is 38 meters long, 4.5 meters wide, and has a span of 35 meters. It sits 27 meters above the valley below. It has a *chuandou* structure gallery house with four columns and nine purlins. It was reconstructed twice during the Qing Dynasty. During its reconstruction during the Guangxu period in the Qing Dynasty, more than ten people from Jitou and Wangkeng villages jointly bought a hillside to the west of the Baixiang Bridge and planted more than 480 fir trees there to supply timber for the bridge's reconstruction. At the same time they donated grain and funds, and what was left was used annually for a lunch that villagers eat together on the bridge after completing weeding during the *lidong* period of the lunar calendar. Pingnan County's Baixiang, Qiancheng, and Wan'an bridges are listed as the Major Historical and Cultural Sites Protected at the National Level, and are referred to collectively by the first characters in their names—Bai Qian Wan, a homonym for "millions and millions."

第六章 东南廊桥遗存带

02—千乘桥

福建省屏南县棠口村，宋代（960—1279年）

又名祥峰桥。南北走向，石墩木拱廊桥，长62.8米、宽5米、二十二开间、一墩两孔跨径各27.5米。灰色花岗岩砌筑船形桥墩上首雀喙形状。九檩穿斗式构架两侧安置木凳，飞檐翘角悬山顶覆小青瓦。桥南端遗存三方功德碑，一方《千乘桥志》记载："棠溪有桥颜曰千乘，双峰其对峙也，双涧汇其流也。虽居僻壤而北抵县城，南通省郡实往来之通衢。自宋以来重建三次矣。"

02.Qiansheng Bridge – Tangkou Village, Pingnan County, Fujian Province, built during 960-1279.

Also known as Xiangfeng Bridge. This is a timber arch covered bridge with stone piers. It runs from north to south, and is 62.8 meters long, 5 meters wide, and has a span of 27.5 meters. Its gallery house has 22 bays. The heads of its grey granite piers are shaped like the beak of a sparrow. Timber benches are placed on both sides of the bridge house, which has nine purlins and is a *chuandou* structure. Small grey tiles cover the roof. At the southern end of the bridge, there is a three-sided stele extolling acts of merit and virtue. On one side, the *Record of Qiansheng Bridge* states that The Tang Creek's bridge was also called the Qiansheng Bridge, its two peaks confronted each other, and two streams converge into one another. Although situated in a remote area to the north of which is the county seat, the south is connected with neighboring provinces and hence it is a thoroughfare for coming and going. It has been rebuilt three times since the Song Dynasty.

03 — 金造桥

福建省屏南县棠口乡漈头村，明代（1368—1644年）

清乾隆十四年（1749年）重建。清嘉庆十年（1805年）焚毁，清嘉庆十五年（1810年）贡生张永衢募捐重建。中华民国三十七年（1948年）孟夏倡资重建。全木结构伸臂式独孔廊桥，长41.7米、宽4.8米、跨径32.5米。廊屋十五开间，悬山挑檐顶覆小青瓦。金造桥处在新修水电站淹没区，遂于2005年被迁建距原址数公里外国家级森林保护区。

03. Jinzao Bridge — Jitou Village, Tangkou Township, Pingnan County, Fujian Province, built during 1368-1644.

The bridge was rebuilt in 1749. In 1805 the bridge burned down, and later, in 1811, it was restored, with the help of Zhang Yongqu, who raised funds for the project. In 1948, Meng Xia organized donations for the bridge's reconstruction. It is a timber frame single-span cantilever covered bridge. It is 41.7 meters long, 4.8 meters wide and has a span of 32.5 meters. Its gallery house has 15 bays, and its overhanging eaves are covered with small grey tiles. In 2005, the bridge was relocated to a national forest reserve several kilometers away from its original site due to the construction of a hydropower station.

第六章 东南廊桥遗存带

中国廊桥

04 — 万安桥

福建省屏南县长桥镇，宋元祐五年（1090年）

又名长桥、龙江公桥。五墩六孔不等跨木拱廊桥，长98.2米、宽4.7米、高8.5米、三十七开间，九檩穿斗式构架，双坡单檐悬山顶。明万历二年（1574年）山贼为阻断追剿将万安桥烧毁，清乾隆七年（1743年）重建。清道光二十五年（1845年）乡绅筹资重建。中华民国初年流民取暖失火焚毁，1932年重建。被列为全国重点文物保护单位。

04. Wan'an Bridge — Changqiao Town, Pingnan County, Fujian Province, built in 1090.

It is also known as the Changqiao Bridge and as the Longjianggong Bridge. It is a timber arch covered bridge with five piers. Its six spans are of different respective lengths. It is 98.2 meters long, 4.7 meters wide, and 8.5 meters high. Its gallery house is a *chuandou* structure with 37 bays and nine purlins. It is covered by a two-sloped overhanging gable roof with a single eave. In 1574, bandits burned the Wan'an Bridge down in order to avoid their pursuers. The bridge was rebuilt in 1743. In 1845, local gentry raised funds for its reconstruction. In the early years of the Republic of China, refugees burned it down accidentally while trying to stay warm from the cold. The bridge was rebuilt again in 1932. It is listed as the Major Historical and Cultural Sites Protected at the National Level.

第六章 东南廊桥遗存带

05 — 庵前桥

福建省屏南县长桥镇官洋村

清咸丰元年（1851年）重修。独孔石拱廊屋桥，飞檐翘脚，山顶。桥碑记："庵前桥乃我村亘古及今之唯一名胜古迹，凡全村男女老幼都应遵守护桥禁约，保护好庵前桥不受任何破坏。"

05. Anqian Bridge — Guanyang Village, Changqiao Town, Pingnan County, Fujian Province.

Rebuilt in 1851, this is a stone arch bridge with single span. Its gallery house has a overhanging gable roof with upturned eaves and extended corners. The bridge's stele states "Anqian Bridge is the only historical wonder that remains in our village up to the present. All men and women, and old and young, should adhere to the bridge's prohibitions and protect the bridge so it doesn't experience any damage."

06 — 龙井桥

福建省屏南县寿山乡白玉村金造溪峡口

清乾隆（1736—1795年）年间焚毁，清嘉庆二十五年（1820年）重建。清光绪十四年（1888年）修缮。全木结构伸臂式木拱廊桥，长27.5米、宽4.9米、跨径22.2米、十三开间，九檩穿斗式构架，单脊挑檐悬山顶。被列为县级文物保护单位。

06. Longjing Bridge — Jinzaoxi Gap, Baiyu Village, Shoushan Township, Pingnan County, Fujian Province.

It burned during the reign of Qianlong in the Qing Dynasty and was rebuilt during the reign of Jiaqing in the Qing Dynasty in 1820. It was repaired in 1888. It is a timber frame cantilever arch bridge, 27.5 meters long, 4.9 meters wide, and with a span of 22.2 meters. Its gallery house has 13 bays, and is a *chuandoushi* structure with nine purlins supporting a overhanging gable roof with a single ridge and extended eaves. It is listed as the Historical and Cultural Sites Protected at the County Level.

07—迎风桥

福建省屏南县陆地村峡谷，清咸丰四年（1854年）

曾名陆地桥。清光绪三十年（1904年）重建。东西走向，单孔贯木伸臂式廊桥，长29米、宽4.25米、跨径13.8米、八开间。穿斗式构架两侧设双层雨披，为全木质构造。被列为县级文物保护单位。

07.Yingfeng Bridge — in a valley at Ludi Village, Pingnan County, Fujian Province, built in 1854.

Originally named Ludi Bridge, Welcome Wind Bridge was rebuilt in 1905. It is a timber cantilever covered bridge formed by intersecting timbers. It stretches from east to west, and is 29 meters long, 4.25 meters wide, and has a span of 13.8 meters. The gallery house is a *chuandou* structure and has 8 bays. Double-layer awnings protect the bridge from the wind and rain on both sides of the bridge. The bridge is listed as the Historical and Cultural Sites Protected at the County Level.

08—龙津桥

福建省屏南县后垅村，清顺治（1644 — 1661 年）

曾名玉锁桥、溪尾桥。东西走向，全木结构伸臂式木拱廊桥，长 33.5 米、宽 4.5 米、跨度 23 米、十三开间，九檩穿斗式构架支撑悬山顶式廊顶。桥东《龙津桥碑记》载："子孙万世之业，永世原于实有功德，而功德莫大于造桥实济之为一也。余水尾厝桥水坏百余年重建，难再观矣。"

08.Longjin Bridge — Houlong Village, Pingnan County, Fujian Province, built during 1644-1661.

Once known as the Yusuo Bridge and the Xiwei Bridge, this timber cantilever arch bridge runs in an east to west direction. It is 33.5 meters long, 4.5 meters wide, and has a span of 23 meters. Its gallery house has 13 bays, and is a *chuandou* structure with nine purlins that support a flush gable roof. An inscription on the stele to the west of the bridge authored by Zhang Fang in 1847 states that "the deeds of many generation originate from merit, and what merit is greater than that of building a bridge and striving together for this one purpose? After one hundred years of water damage, it was difficult to reconstruct the bridge."

六、岩茶故乡——武夷山九曲溪廊桥
VI. Covered Bridges on Jiuqu Stream in Wuyi Mountain, Home of the Rock Tea

01 扣冰桥
01 Koubing Bridge – built at the gate of Ruiyan Temple, Wutun Town, Fujian Province.

扣冰桥是古寺时代建筑。据法悟《南吕人》师父介绍，瑞岩寺是千年古寺，扣冰桥为千年古桥。扣冰桥始建于唐广明元年（880年），古代扣冰桥建有百米长廊，廊顶铺满黄色琉璃瓦。远远望去就像隐伏在翠林中的一条黄龙。今天的扣冰桥长30余米，廊顶上的琉璃瓦已被小青瓦取代。瑞岩寺及附属扣冰桥均为市级文物保护单位。

Koubing Bridge was built around the same time as the Ruiyan Temple. According to Monk Fawu, "Ruiyan Temple has a history of about one thousand years, and so does the bridge. Koubing Bridge was built in the eighth year of the Xizong period in the Tang Dynasty (880 A.D.). It was one hundred meters long and was decorated with yellow glazed tiles, resembling a yellow dragon cloaked by the surrounding green woods." Koubing Bridge is now 30 meters long and is covered by small grey tiles. Ruiyan Temple and the bridge are both listed as Historical and Cultural Sites Protected at the Municipal Level.

02—遇仙桥

福建省南平市武夷山市上梅乡茶景村，明嘉靖（1522—1566 年）

又名步仙桥。（明代）夏玉鳞、王佃版《嘉靖建宁府志一卷之九"津梁"》部分有记载。现桥为清代（1636—1912 年）重建。1979 年重修，主绳师傅王魁林。1994 年修葺时增建东西廊亭。木结构桥廊，长 50 米、宽 4.5 米、高 4.3 米、跨径 10.3 米，桥梁部分长 17.4 米，五开间悬山顶覆小青瓦。农历三月初三，乡民相聚遇仙桥办村酒。

02. Yuxian Bridge — Chajing Village, Shangmei Township, Wuyishan County, Nanping, Fujian Province, built during 1522-1566.

Also named the Buxian Bridge, Yuxian Bridge was recorded in volume nine of the *Jinliang* of *History of Jianningfu in the Jiajing Period* by Xia Yulin and Wang Dian. The present bridge was rebuilt in the Qing Dynasty. It was renovated in 1979, in a project directed by Wan Kuilin. Two pavilions were then added in the east and west ends of the bridge in 1994. The timber frame covered bridge is 50 meters long, 4.5 meters wide, and 4.3 meters high. It has a span of 10.3 meters, and the bridge's beam structure is 17.4 meters long. Its gallery house has 5 bays and is covered by a overhanging gable roof covered by small grey tiles. Every year villagers will gather for a lunch banquet at Yuxian Bridge on the third day of the third lunar month.

03 — 馀庆桥

福建省武夷山市区南郊崇阳溪沙古洲，清光绪（1875 — 1908 年）

《崇安县新志》记载："崇安（武夷山市）南郊阳大行者病涉，（缙绅）朱敬熙（1852-1917 年）秉母命以三万金创馀庆、垂裕二桥，雄伟为闽北冠。"抗日战争中垂裕桥毁于战火。馀庆桥西北东南走向，长 79 米、宽近 7 米、高 9 米，由长廊、亭阁、门楼、台阶、桥拱、桥墩组成。四座石墩艒顶安置长颈鸢，后放"压惊石"。2011 年 5 月 28 日下午馀庆桥失火倒塌。2014 年 7 月复建。被列为全国重点文物保护单位。

3.Yuqing Bridge — Shagu Shoal along Chongyangxi River in the southern suburb of Wuyishan Downtown, Fujian Province, built during 1875-1908.

As it is recorded in the *New History of Chong'an County*, "people had a difficult time crossing the river in the southern suburb of Chong'an (now Wuyishan City), so an official named Zhu Jingxi (1852-1917), under the guidance of his mother, built two bridges named Yuqing and Chuiyu there with thirty thousand taels of silver. The magnificence of the bridges is known all around north Fujian Province." Chuiyu Bridge, however, was destroyed during the Chinese People's War of Resistance Against Japanese Aggression. Yuqing Bridge though remains, and stretches from northwest to southeast. It is 79 meters long, and nearly 7 meters wide, and 9 meters high. It consists of a long gallery that includes pavilions, gateways, steps, arches, and piers. Sculptures of kite birds are installed on the four stone bow-shaped bridge piers. Yuqing Bridge collapsed in a fire in the afternoon of May 28, 2011. It was rebuilt in July 2014, and has been listed as the Major Historical and Cultural Sites Protected at the National Level.

七、钱塘江水系与闽江分水岭——浦城县廊桥

VII. Covered Bridges in Pucheng County, the Divide between Qiantang River System and Minjiang River

01—镇安桥

福建省浦城县临江镇，明洪武十二年（1379 年）

《镇安桥修复记》载："古有'川无梁，政不修'之说。古贤者云'余邑之胜以山，山之胜以浦，浦之胜以桥'。闽中桥梁巨丽，桥上架屋翼翼楚楚，无处不堪图画，镇安桥如是矣。"原名临江桥，明正统十一年（1446 年）更名镇安桥。桥堡式廊桥横跨临江溪，东西走向，四墩三孔，叠木平梁辅以贯木八字支撑。桥屋二十间庑殿顶。长 96.5 米、宽 3.6 米，两端石砌台阶 21 级引道 5 米，旁立石栏，东西桥头砖砌拱门，眉刻"镇安保障"。2009 年焚毁，2012 年重建。

01. Zhen'an Bridge – Linjiang Town, Pucheng County, Fujian Province, built in 1379.

As it states in the *Restoration of Zhen'an Bridge*, "In the past there was the saying 'A creek not crossed (by a bridge) shows that rule has not been achieved.' Ancient sages remarked that 'mountains are the pride of our area; rivers are the pride of mountains, and bridges are the pride of rivers.' Bridges of Fujian are magnificent and everywhere boast distinctive pavilions, with no place less wondrous than a painting. Zhen'an Bridge is one such a place." Formerly named Linjiang Bridge, it was renamed Zhen'an Bridge in 1446. This covered bridge spans the Linjiang River from east to west, and has four piers and three spans. Its woven timber beams are supported by *bazi* bracing. Its gallery house has twenty bays, and is 96.5 meters long, and 3.6 meters wide. It is covered by a hipped roof. At both ends are 21 stone steps and a 5 meter approach flanked by a stone wall. There are also archways at both ends inscribed with the words "Zhen'an Bridge Protector." The bridge was destroyed in a fire in 2009, and was rebuilt in 2012.

02—乐丰桥

福建省浦城县临江镇水西村田畈，清嘉庆十四年（1809年）

四根木柱支撑圆木平梁，全木结构廊桥，重檐悬山顶，双层雨披。朱漆木柱，两端稍窄中部两侧加宽。

02.Lefeng Bridge — in a field of Shuixi Village, Linjiang Town, Pucheng County, Fujian Province, built in 1809.

This is a timber frame covered bridge, its log beams supported by four timber columns. It is covered by a multiple-eave overhanging gable roof. Two layers of skirts run along the bridge protecting it from the rain. Its columns are painted with red lacquer, and their top and bottom portions are narrower than their middles.

03—青龙桥

福建省浦城县古楼乡洋元村，清光绪（1875—1909年）

据照片中三位村民毛先孙（左、76岁）、张荣汉（中、70岁）、毛可惜（右、80岁）介绍，是他们的三世祖大公（曾祖父）毛如兴、张德荣、毛如高建造了青龙桥，连通了当地乡镇通往武夷山的官路。

03.Qinglong Bridge – Yangyuan Village, Gulou Township, Pucheng County, Fujian Province, built during 1875-1909.

As explained by the three villagers in the photograph Mao Xiansun (left, 76 years old), Zhang Ronghan (middle, 70 years old) and Mao Kexi (right, 80 years old), the Qinglong Bridge was built by their grandfathers Mao Ruxing, Zhang Derong, and Mao Rugao. It connected the village town's "Big Official Road" at the time to Wuyi Mountain.

04—观音桥

福建省浦城县古楼乡洋溪村,明代(1368—1644年)

观音桥为浦城通往崇安(武夷山)和江西广丰之津梁。桥口通道两旁店铺林立,皆为二层挑廊木构建筑。原名洋溪桥,清乾隆五十二年(1787)乡绅募资重建。单孔石拱廊桥,长11.3米、宽5.2米、跨径9.8米、三开间。两端均有十三级台阶引道。廊屋宽阔神龛供奉观世音菩萨,桥头两端各出一廊间,四柱九檩抬梁屋架歇山顶桥厅。

04.Guanyin Bridge – Yangxi Village, Gulou Township, Pucheng County, Fujian Province, built during 1368-1644.

Guanyin Bridge serves as the intersection leading Pucheng to Chong'an (now Wuyishan) and Guangfeng in Jiangxi Province. Stores flanking the entrances of the bridge are all two-floor timber structures with overhanging roofs. Originally named Yangxi bridge, it was rebuilt in 1787 by the local gentry. It is an arch bridge with a single span, and has a 13-step approach at each end. It is 11.3 meters long, 5.2 meters wide, and has a span of 9.8 meters. Its gallery house has 3 bays. The bridge's large wide shrine is dedicated to Guanyin, the Buddhist bodhisattva of compassion. There are *tailiang* structure pavilions at each end of the bridge covered by hip and gable roofs supported by four columns and nine purlins.

八、百里松荫碧长溪——松溪县廊桥

VIII. Covered Bridges in Songxi County, Green Streams with the Shadow of Pine-trees on Bath Sides

01 花桥

福建省松溪县花桥乡花桥村，清雍正（1723—1736年）

初为石墩杉木夹板桥水毁。清光绪三十一年（1903年），水北街镇乡绅吴观星倾其所有建造了两墩三孔廊桥。村民张明浪介绍"修建花桥倾尽吴观星一家数代勤俭度日所余积蓄。以后每逢浦城人到花桥赶集卖东西，花桥乡民都会把路边最好的摊位让出来。"东西走向，石拱廊屋桥，长36米、十一开间、重檐歇山顶辅以单脊双坡顶马头墙桥口。桥孔、桥面使用长方形条石砌造，正中建造桥阁内置四角藻井。

01.Huaqiao Bridge – Huaqiao Village, Huaqiao Township, Songxi County, Fujian Province, built during 1723-1736.

Hua Bridge was initially built with fir planks and stone piers, and then was destroyed in a flood. In 1903, Wu Guanxing, a member of the local gentry from Shuibeijie Town, contributed all he had to the construction of a two pier three span covered bridge. The villager Zhang Minglang said, "Wu Guanxing spent all the money collected through generations for the construction of Huaqiao Bridge, so every time people from Pucheng (where Wu came from) came and sold goods on the bridge during market days, villagers of Huaqiao would give the best roadside stalls to them." The bridge's gallery house has 11 bays. It is 36 meters long, and extends from east to west. It consists of a stone arch and is covered by a multiple-eave hip and gable roof. Its gateway also has a two-slope single ridge horse-head gable wall. The bridge's span and its deck are constructed with rectangular stones. In the bridge's center is a four-panel sunken *zaojing* caisson window.

第六章 东南廊桥遗存带

02—马登桥

福建省松溪县渭田镇株林村吴村溪峡谷，明洪武十二年（1379年）

原名官门桥。以后桥门口安放了上马石磴改称马登桥。桥头一幅古联"官箴整肃簪缨三代显赫门第冠盖九州""马跃鸾峰鹏程万里登临吴水德泽千秋"。渭田镇竹贤村、溪尾村相继发现两块南宋开禧元年（1206年）的《交通法规碑》，规定交通法规"少避长，轻避重，去避来"。

02. Madeng Bridge – over Wucun Stream at Zhulin Village, Weitian Town, Songxi County, Fujian Province, built in 1379.

Formerly called the Guanmen Bridge, its name was changed when a stone was put at its entrance on which people could step on to mount horses. There is also a couplet at the entrance that reads, "Rulers of righteousness, three generations in the robes of statesmen, glory to the household, officials of rank throughout the land. The horse leaps to *luan* (a mythical bird) peak, winged ambition soars fa visiting the Wu river, virtue spreads through on thousand years." In addition, the nearby village of Zhuxian and Xiwei both discovered Souther Song Dynasty *Traffic Rule Steles* dating to 1206 tha stated "the young should yield to the elderly light loads yield to heavy loads, those leavin yield to those arriving."

03—家坛桥

福建省松溪县渭田镇董坑村家坛自然村,清嘉庆（1796—1820年）

单孔石拱木质廊桥，双坡顶覆小青瓦。家坛桥的石拱末处于中央，如此不对称的方式在其他地方不多见。家坛桥与同一乡镇的马登桥、大旺桥型制类同，应为一个门派的师徒建造。

03.Jiatan Bridge — Jiatan Natural Village, Dongkeng Village, Weitian Town, Songxi County, Fujian Province, built during 1796-1820.

Jiatan Bridge is a single-span stone arch timber structure covered bridge. Its double-slope roof is covered with small grey tiles. The bridge's arch is not in the center of the bridge, an asymmetric style rarely seen in other places. Jiatan Bridge, together with Madeng Bridge and Dawang Bridge are located in the same area, have a similar style, and were built by the same group of craftsmen.

04—五福桥

福建省松溪县渭田镇渭田溪，明永乐（1403—1424年）

曾名八岭桥，长108米、宽5.2米、高12米，四墩五孔，东西走向，横跨渭田溪。据《书经》"长寿、宝贵、康宁、好德、善终"为五福定前名。《重修五福桥记》载："清光绪二十七年（1901年）端午，狂涛怒吼冲圮两墩。逾二年各界人士募捐重建，清光绪三十四年（1908年）竣工。桥如旧制。"墩尖雕琢鹰鸦头嘴，桥北两端桥门为牌坊式三层挑角结构。正中建重檐翘角亭阁，题曰"赛濠观"。枋板绘《三国演义》《东周列国》故事。

04. Wufu Bridge — over Weitian Stream at Weitian Town, Songxi County, Fujian Province, built during 1403-1424.

Originally named Baling Bridge, it is 108 meters long, 5.2 meters wide and 12 meters high, and spans the Weitian Creek from east to west. It has four piers and five spans. Its present name comes from *The Book of Documents* (one of the five classics of ancient Chinese literature) which lists five blessings for "longevity, affluence, health, benevolence, and a natural death." As *The Reconstruction of Five Blessing Bridge* states, "During the Dragon Boat Festival in the 27th year of the Guangxu period of the Qing Dynasty (1901), the roaring river toppled down two bridge piers. Two years later, people from all walks of life collected money to rebuild the bridge, which was restored in the 34th year of Daoguang (1908)." The tip of the pier is carved in the shape of the beak of an eagle or crow. At the bridge's north and at its gateways are decorative three-story archways with projecting corners. In the center of the bridge there is a pavilion with multiple eaves and upturned corners, called the Saihao Temple. Beams in the bridge are painted with scenes from *Romance of the Three Kingdoms* and *Chronicles of the Eastern Zhou Dynasty's Kingdoms*.

第六章　东南廊桥遗存带

九、武夷山北段、富屯溪上游——光泽县廊桥

IX. Covered Bridges in Guangze County, North of Wuyi Mountain, Upstream of Futun stream

承安桥

福建省光泽县鸾凤乡油溪村，明万历（1573－1619年）

农历七月初六日子夜，方圆数十里乡众会聚集承安桥，祈求有情人终成眷属，夫妻恩爱。又名七星桥、夫妻桥。中华民国三十一年（1942年）毁于大火，次年重建。三墩四孔木结构廊桥，长60米、宽6.5米、高7米。桥面铺石板和鹅卵石，两侧安置挡雨板。村里妇女逢修桥开工，会聚到桥旁祈祷顺利圆满。

Cheng' an Bridge — Youxi Village, Luanfeng Township, Guangze County, Fujian Province, built during 1573-1619.

Every year during the night of the sixth day of the seventh lunar month, villagers from surrounding villagers congregate at the Cheng' an Bridge to pray that lovers will form honorable households, and that husbands and wives will find love and comfort. Also named Qixing Bridge and Fuqi Bridge, it was destroyed in 1943 by a fire accidentally. It was rebuilt the following year. The bridge has three piers and four spans. It is a timber frame bridge that is 60 meters long, 6.5 meters wide, and 7 meters heigh. The bridge deck is covered by stone slabs and cobblestones. Both sides are protected by awnings to keep out the rain. Traditionally when repairs are made on the bridge, the village' s women gather to pray that the project be smooth and successful.

第六章 东南廊桥遗存带

十、闽北—闽江建溪水系全域发育——建瓯市廊桥

X. Covered Bridges in Jian'ou, along Jianxi River System of Minjiang River Basin in North Fujian Province

01—腾云桥

福建省建瓯市玉山镇下寨村

曾名敷锡桥,石砌叠木桥墩、单拱圆木双层平搭伸梁式廊桥,长54米、宽5米、高7.6米、跨径16米。《腾云桥记》载:"据《八闽通志》、清《建宁府志》记载,敷锡桥明洪武二年(1369年)由里人黄任波筹建。清嘉庆十七年(1812年)敷锡詹氏子孙42人为首筹资重建为单拱木架伸臂廊桥,改名腾云桥。因桥屋瓦片、桥面、雨披等多处破损,2008年整修。"桥头遗留雍正三年(1725年)《严禁砍伐树木碑》一方。

01. Tengyun Bridge – Xiazhai Village, Yushan Town, Jian'ou, Fujian Province.

Originally named Fuxi Bridge, Tengyun Bridge has piers composed of stone masonry and stacked timbers. It is formed with logs, and is a two-story cantilever covered bridge with a single arch. It is 54 meters long, 5 meters wide and 7.6 meters high. It has a span of 16 meters. It is recorded in *Records of the Tengyun Bridge* that, "As it is stated in the *History of Fujian* and the Qing Dynasty *History of Jianning*, Fuxi Bridge, a timber arch covered bridge, was built by Huang Renbo and other villagers in the second year of the Hongwu period in the Ming Dynasty (1369). It was reconstructed as a timber cantilever covered bridge with a single span in the 17th year of Jiaqing period in the Qing Dynasty (1812) by 42 members of the Zhan lineage, at which time it was renamed the Tengyun Bridge. The bridge was renovated in 2008 because its tiles, deck and awnings had been worn out." A *Prohibition of Logging stele* erected in 1752 stands at the entrance to the bridge.

第六章 东南廊桥遗存带

02—普通桥
福建省建瓯市小桥镇普通村，南宋（1127—1279年）

一墩两孔木拱廊桥，长60米、宽5米、高9米。桥墩由当地山石料砌筑，两端建有门亭。双层挡雨木板之间设置木栅廊窗，鱼脊双坡顶覆小青瓦。

02.Putong Bridge – Putong Village, Xiaoqiao Town, Jian'ou, Fujian Province, built during 1127-1279.

The bridge has one pier and two spans. It is a timber arch covered bridge that is 60 meters long, 5 meters wide, and 9 meters high. The piers are made of stones from local mountains and there is a gateway pavilion at each end of the bridge. Timber lattices between the two layers of rain awnings at the sides of the bridge serve as windows for the gallery house. The single ridge two-slope roof is covered with small grey tiles.

03—后建桥

福建省建瓯市迪口镇深溪村，清光绪三十二年（1906年）

全木结构伸臂式独拱廊桥，长30米、宽4米、高5米、十二开间。正梁遗存"大清光绪丙午叁十二年季冬月十三日巳时生梁"墨迹。1976年各界人士捐资修缮。后建桥连接的古道已废弃，廊桥以及周围山谷有野猪、猕猴、山鸡出没。2006年不法商贩盗走廊架十多根金丝楠木主梁，乡民使用竹竿、木柱支撑整座廊屋，后修缮。

03.Houjian Bridge – Shenxi Village, Dikou Town, Jian'ou, Fujian Province, built in 1906.

Houjian Bridge is a timber cantilever bridge with a single arch. Its gallery house has twelve bays. It is 30 meters long, 4 meters wide, and 5 meters high. Characters written on its main beam state that "the beam was placed during the time period between nine and eleven o'clock in the morning on the thirteenth day of the eleventh lunar month in the 32nd year of the Guangxu period in the Qing Dynasty." The bridge was renovated in 1976 with funds collected by people from all walks of life. The ancient road that once connected to the Houjian Bridge has become overgrown, and wild boars, macaques, and pheasants now occupy the valley around the bridge. In 2006, a dozen or so bridge beams made of nanmu wood were stolen by criminal peddlers. Villagers then used bamboo poles and timber columns to support the entire gallery house. Repairs were subsequently made on the bridge.

第六章 东南廊桥遗存带

04—上桥

福建省建瓯市小桥镇尤慕村

　　独孔石拱廊屋桥，是一座综合性建筑，桥南是村庙，桥下是洗菜房，桥北是祠堂。村民介绍："紧挨着北桥口一棵二百多年的樟树与廊桥同龄。"一条小河是划分村舍与田园的分野。从早到晚脚步匆匆的过桥人很多。

04.Shangqiao Bridge – Youmu Village, Xiaoqiao Town, Jian'ou, Fujian Province

This single-span stone arch covered bridge is a combined structure with various functions. Its southern part serves as a village temple, under it is a room for cleaning vegetables, and an ancestral shrine is located to its north. In the words of a local villager, "the covered bridge is the same age as the over 200 year-old camphor tree near its northern entrance." The small river under the bridge separates the homes of villagers from their fields, and from dawn to dusk people hurry to and fro along the bridge.

05 — 登云桥

福建省建瓯市迪口镇阳泽村南才溪

原名矮桥，连通古田县至南平市古道。四墩五孔木平梁廊桥，长60余米、宽5米。鹰嘴墩舶减轻水流冲击力，优质杉木层叠梁，桥面铺木板、细沙、方砖。廊屋青瓦覆顶，两边安置栏杆、条凳。

05. Dengyun Bridge — Nancai Creek, Yangze Village, Dikou Town, Jian'ou, Fujian Province.

Dengyun Bridge, originally called the Aiqiao Bridge, was part of the ancient road that connected Gutian County to Nanping City. The bridge has four piers and five spans. It is a multi-span simply supported timber beam covered bridge. It is over 60 meters long and 5 meters wide. Its piers are shaped in the form of an eagle's beak to reduce the force of impact from incoming water. The bridge beams are formed by stacked high-quality timber made of Chinese fir. The bridge deck is covered by timber planks, fine sand, and square bricks. The gallery house is covered by grey tiles, and its two sides have a long strip of benches, as well as railings.

06 — 钱仓桥

福建省建瓯市迪口镇霞抱村清泉禅寺山脚下南溪

《清泉禅寺碑记》载："寺下是南溪，有明建古桥一座，横跨南北，建筑极其精工巧雅，具有福建桥梁之特色，名曰钱仓桥。"1993年重建。

06. Qiancang Bridge — over South Creek below Qingquan Temple, Xiabao Village, Dikou Town, Jian'ou, Fujian Province.

It is recorded on the *Stele for Qingquan Temple*, "Below the temple flows the South Creek. A famous ancient bridge is there, which spans from north to south, with construction both exquisite and elegant, possessing the distinctive features of bridges from Fujian. It is called the Qiancang Bridge." The bridge was reconstructed in 1993.

07—值庆桥

福建省建瓯市迪口镇黄村路口小溪河，明弘治三年（1490年）

曾名集庆桥。廊屋正中方形斗拱藻井，主梁遗留"大明弘治叁年（1490年）岁次庚戌月建"墨迹。南北走向，穿斗式构造，卯榫穿插连接式全木结构廊桥，长32米、宽4米、高5米、十二开间。桥北端处在因河道萎缩而形成的陆地上。桥面铺木板两侧安置防护栅栏和长条木凳，两端一侧夯筑土墙。

07. Zhiqing Bridge — over a Xiaoxi River in Huangcun Village, Dikou Town, Jian'ou County, Fujian Province, built in 1490.

Formerly named Jiqing Bridge, the middle of Zhiqing Bridge's gallery house has a square sunken caisson *zaojing* ceiling, composed of dougong brackets. Characters on the bridge's main beam state that it was built in the third year of the Hongzhi period of the Ming Dynasty (1490). The bridge runs from south to north and is a *chuandou* structure. It is connected through the use of mortise and tenon technology. It is 32 meters long, 4 meters wide, and 5 meters high. Its gallery house has twelve bays. Because the river has shrunk, the north end of the bridge is now located over dry land. The bridge deck is covered by timber boards, and its two sides have protective railings and long benches. A rammed earth wall is located at either side of the bridge.

08—接龙桥

福建省建瓯市迪口镇龙北溪村，中华民国六年（1917年）

长46米、宽4米、高11.5米、跨径31米。廊屋为弧月形抬梁穿斗式结构，两端建筑马鞍型山墙，桥面铺河卵石，廊屋内设置神龛。单脊硬山顶铺小青瓦，中央设置翘角小飞檐攒尖宝塔。桥墩采用方青石筑砌，两侧安设挡雨木板。

08.Jielong Bridge – Longbeixi Village, Dikou Town, Jian'ou, Fujian Province, built in 1917.

Jielong Bridge is 46 meters long, 4 meters wide, and 11.5 meters high. It has a span of 31 meters. The gallery house has a curved moon shape, and combines *tailiang* and *chuandou* construction. Both ends of the bridge have saddle-shaped gable walls. The bridge deck is covered by cobblestones. A shrine is placed inside the gallery house. On top is an flush gable roof, covered by small grey tiles. There is a small pagoda in the middle of the bridge, with an upright pyramidal top, surrounded by a roof with small upturned eaves and upturned corners. The bridge is supported by piers made of square bluestones. The bridge's two sides have skirts to protect the structure from rain.

09—德胜桥

福建省建瓯市迪口镇郑魏村吉溪，清光绪二十五年（1899年）

又名胜桥。全木结构单拱廊桥，长36米、宽4.2米、高7.5米、跨径23米、十五开间。神龛供奉真武大帝神像。五脊悬山顶铺小青瓦。被列为市级文物保护单位。

09.Desheng Bridge – over Jixi Creek, Zhengwei Village, Dikou Town, Jian'ou, Fujian Province, built in 1899.

Also named Shengqiao Bridge, Desheng Bridge is a timber arch covered bridge. It has a gallery house with fifteen bays. It is 36 meters long, 4.2 meters wide, and 7.5 meters high. It has a span of 23 meters. There is a shrine dedicated to the Zhenwu Emperor (a Taoist deity). It is covered by a five-ridge overhanging gable roof covered with small grey tiles. It is listed as the Historical and Cultural Sites Protected at the Municipal Level.

10—仙恩桥

福建省建瓯市迪口镇郑魏村，清光绪三十年（1904年）

又名马桥。穿斗式全木结构独拱廊桥，长44米、宽4米、高7.5米、跨径26米。桥架、桥廊防护木板遮盖有较强的保护作用，一百多年来未做大修，状态完好。仙恩桥是村民上山砍柴伐竹、采药挖笋的可靠通道。

10.Xian'en Bridge – Zhengwei Village, Dikou Town, Jian'ou, Fujian Province, built in 1904.

Xian'en Bridge, also named Maqiao Bridge, is a single-arch timber covered bridge with a *chuandou* structure. It is 44 meters long, 4 meters wide, and 7.5 meters high. It has a span of 26 meters. The sheltering timber skirts that run along the gallery house and the bridge frame have a strong protective function, and delightfully the bridge has not required any extensive repair work in the past one hundred years. The bridge is relied on by villagers who use it to reach the neighboring mountain where they chop wood, cut bamboo, pick medicinal herbs, and dig bamboo shoots.

11－集瑞桥

福建省建瓯市南雅镇集瑞村

"母子廊桥"大小合成一体为中国孤本。《嘉靖建宁府志》记载:"集瑞桥成化二年（1466年）重建，木梁，构亭七楹。"清咸丰三年（1853年）整修。大桥建于明早期，长27米、宽5米、跨径8米、九开间，四柱九檩抬梁式全木结构，硬山顶下置遮雨板。小桥建于清中期，长18.5米、宽1.2米、四开间、单坡顶覆小青瓦。歇凉老人家说:"老年人、牵牛扛犁耙、赶猪赶羊、生病怀孕的人过大桥很吃力气。秋天家家往回挑稻谷，两三百斤重一趟趟上桥太辛苦，饭多吃、酒多喝，婆姨愁。后来合倡银子建造了这座小桥，过河如踏青云。"

11. Jirui Bridge — Jirui Village, Nanya Town, Jian'ou, Fujian Province.

As the *History of Jianning in the Jiajing Period* states, "Jirui Bridge, was reconstructed in 1466, and is made of timber beams and a pavilion with seven columns." It was rebuilt in 1853. The larger of the two bridges was built in the early Ming Dynasty. It is 27 meters long, 5 meters wide, and has a span of 8 meters. Its gallery house has 9 bays. It is a *tailiangshi* structure with four columns and nine purlins. It is covered by an flush gable roof, with awnings installed to keep off the rain. The smaller bridge was built in the mid Qing Dynasty. It is 18.5 meters long, 1.2 meters wide, and has a gallery house with 4 bays. Its single-slope roof is covered by small grey tiles. An elder sitting in the shadow of a tree explained, "It took a serious amount of energy for the elders, the sick, pregnant women, and those traveling with cows, pigs, sheep, and carrying heavy equipment to go over the big bridge. Every autumn in the harvest season, villagers had to carry hundreds of kilograms of grain back across the bridge, an enormous burden. Wives had to work harder to prepare more food and drinks for them as a result, and this made them upset. So the villagers raised money to build the small bridge, and now crossing the river feels like walking on a cloud".

12—兴龙桥

福建省建瓯市迪口镇李溪村

又名李溪厝桥。廊架正梁遗留"大明崇祯柒年（1634年）运甲戌孟冬玖月十八旦辛未寅时良辰重新建造""时维大清道光肆年（1824年）甲申岁拾月二辛未日午时升梁重建"墨迹。兴龙桥构成实用简洁八字木拱居中、石台复合支撑木平梁。全木结构廊桥，南北走向，长35米、宽4米、高9.6米、单孔跨径12.7米、十二开间，穿斗式结构，单脊双坡硬山顶覆小青瓦。被列为市级文物保护单位。

12. Xinglong Bridge – Lixi Village, Dikou Town, Jian'ou, Fujian Province.

Xinglong Bridge is also named the Lixicuo Bridge. Characters written on its main beam state, "Rebuilt during *yinshi* (three a.m. to five a.m.) on the eighteenth day of the ninth lunar month in the seventh year of the Chongzhen period in the Ming Dynasty (1634)" and "Rebuilt during *wushi* (11 a.m. to one p.m.) on the twelfth day of the tenth lunar month in the year *jiashen*, the fourth year of the Daoguang period in the Qing Dynasty (1824)." The structure of Xinglong Bridge is practical and concise—it has an arch formed by succinct *bazi* bracing in its center, and its compound stone abutments support the bridge's horizontal timber beams. The north-south timber frame covered bridge is 35 meters long, 4 meters wide, 9.6 meters high, and has a span of 12.7 meters. Its gallery house has twelve bays, and is a *chuandou* structure covered by a single-ridge two-slope flush gable roof topped by small grey tiles. The bridge is listed as the Historical and Cultural Sites Protected at the Municipal Level.

13—步月桥

福建省建瓯市吉阳镇玉溪村,明正德十四年(1519 年)

乡民在中秋灯笼节将象征"吉祥、添丁"的红、白灯笼挂在步月桥廊,看上别家灯笼可摘走,"摘一"次年须"还六"民俗延续至今。一墩两孔复合叠梁木平梁廊桥,长128 米、宽6 米、高7 米、四十二开间。清乾隆二十六年(1761 年)商户张士华雇工在玉溪河放木失控将步月桥撞塌,赔偿铜钱七百万修复。清道光五年(1825 年)士绅葛军操捐钱粮修缮。清光绪十九年(1893 年)黄声遏出资大修。1998 年洪水淘空墩基桥体倾斜。妇女耕山队长葛兰妹带头捐款百姓响应,政府筹资 90 万元重建。2019 年 1 月 31 日步月桥因失火焚毁,复建筹备中。

13. Buyue Bridge — Yuxi Village, Jiyang Town, Jian'ou, Fujian Province, built in 1519.

During the Mid-Autumn Lantern Festival, there are always red and white lanterns placed in the Buyue Bridge's gallery house, used to pray for happiness and for the birth of sons. Anyone can take his or her favorite lantern back home. The next year, however, one has to hang six times the number of lanterns that were taken the previous year. This tradition has been passed on to the present day. Buyue Bridge has one pier and two spans. It is a compound woven timber beam and multi-span simply supported timber beam covered bridge. Its gallery house has 42 bays, and it is 128 meters long, 6 meters wide, and 7 meters high. In 1761, an employee of the merchant Zhang Shihua lost control of the timber he was transporting along the Yuxi River, destroying Buyue Bridge. Zhang then paid seven million copper coins to restore the bridge. In 1786, a member of the local gentry, Ge Juncao, donated money and food to repair the bridge. Major repairs were completed again on the bridge in 1893 with the use of a large donation by Huang Sheng'e. The pier foundations were knocked at an angle by flooding in 1998. In response, Ge Lanmei, who led the formation of a renowned all-female ploughing team in 1963, set an example again by donating to rebuild the bridge, and many local villagers followed in kind. This, together with 900,000 yuan in government funding, allowed the bridge to be rebuilt. On January 31, 2019, the bridge caught fire and burned down. Preparation for its reconstruction are currently underway.

十一、源短流急暴涨暴落——南平市廊桥

XI. Covered Bridges in Nanping, Turbulent River with Rising and Falling

01 一种善桥

福建省南平市延茫荡镇盖头行政村高地自然村，清光绪二十九年（1903年）

清《闽小记》"闽中桥梁最为巨丽，桥上建屋翼翼楚楚，无处不堪图画。"石块平梁、独跨全木结构楼阁式廊桥，长 19 米、宽 4.4 米、高 8 米、跨径 7.2 米。一说始建唐代，但未见史据。被列为县级文物保护单位。

01.Zhongshan Bridge — Gaodi Natutal Village, Gaitou Village, Yanmangdang Town, Nanping, Fujian Province, built in 1903.

It is stated in *A Brief Record of Fujian* written in the Qing Dynasty: "the Bridges of Fujian are magnificent and everywhere boast distinctive pavilions, with no place less wondrous than a painting." The approach to the bridge is made of stone, and it is supported by crossbeams. It has a single span, and a timber frame, built as a pavilion style covered bridge. It is 19 meters long, 4.4 meters wide, and 8 meters high. It has a span of 7.2 meters. It has been said that the bridge was initially built in the Tang Dynasty, but there is no proof of this. It has been listed as the Historical and Cultural Sites Protected at the County Level.

第六章 东南廊桥遗存带

02—高地桥

福建省南平市延平区高地村，清代（1636—1912年）

又名接龙桥。中华民国三十一年（1942年）重建，全木质结构，悬山顶覆小青瓦。茫荡山至黄石山距宝珠岭约有三十米间隔。

02.Gaodi Bridge — Gaodi Village, Yanping District, Nanping, Fujian Province, built during 1636-1912.

Also named Jielong Bridge, Gaodi Bridge is a timber frame covered bridge, rebuilt in 1942. Its overhanging gable roof is covered by small grey tiles. The area that extends from the Mangdang to Huangshi mountains is separated by a gap of about 3 meters from Baozhu Mountain ("Jewel Hill").

03—瑞龙桥

福建省南平市延平区芒荡镇茂地村，清乾隆十八年（1753年）

瑞龙桥连接明代修建的"三千八百坎"闽中往来赣东商道。始为简易木桥，后由乡民捐资改建。独孔石拱木结构廊桥，长18米、宽6米、径跨7米、八开间。石拱由山石砌筑拱券较为坚实牢固，遭多次大洪水冲击依然完好。全木质穿斗式结构，木立柱支撑木檩青瓦顶。桥面遍铺厚实青砖，两侧安装防雨板、长木凳。

03.Ruilong Bridge — Maodi Village, Mangdang Town, Yanping District, Nanping, Fujian Provicne, built in 1753.

Ruilong Bridge is connected with the scenic "3,800 step ridge" located on the ancient trade route that connected Fujian to east Jiangxi province. It was initially a simple timber bridge which was reconstructed with money donated by local villagers. The single-span stone arch covered bridge is 18 meters long, 6 meters wide, and has a span of 7 meters. Its gallery house has eight bays. The arch is formed from stones from the surrounding mountains, and is very stable, in perfect condition after having weathered many floods. The gallery house is a *chuandou* structure, with logs supporting the roof's timber purlins. It is covered by grey tiles. The bridge deck is covered by thick grey bricks and both sides of the bridge have long benches, as well as awnings that protect the bridge from the rain.

十二、鳌江不犯闽江——古田县廊桥

XII. Covered Bridges in Gutian County, Where Aojiang River doesn't Inflooded into Minjiang River

01 — 沉字桥

福建省古田县鹤塘镇西洋村,南宋德祐元年（1275 年）

民谚传说,"宋中期溪岭十岁男孩'谢神童'路过新建廊桥,在桥柱题写对联'中国有至仁书同文车同轨,圣人必得寿月重轮星重晖'。人们琢磨之际墨迹已入木三分,定名沉字桥。"四墩五孔石墩木梁廊桥,船艄型石墩,抬梁式全木结构,内设木凳、木栏,单檐庑殿顶覆青杂瓦。长 54 米、宽 3.8 米、高 5.8 米、十七开间。连接古田与宁德驿道。被列为县级文物保护单

01. Chenzi Bridge — Xiyang Village, Hetang Town, Gutian County, Fujian Province, built in 1275.

As a local folk tale goes, "In the middle of the Song Dynasty, there was a ten-year-old boy known in the neighborhood as Prodigy Xie. He came across a newly built bridge and wrote a couplet on its columns. The ink words penetrated deep into the logs before anyone could figure out its meaning, so the bridge was named Chenzi Bridge." The bridge has four piers and five spans. Its piers are made of stone, and its beams of wood. Its piers are shaped in the forms of the bows of ships. The gallery house is a *tailiangshi* structure with seventeen bays. The bridge is 54 meters long, 3.8 meters wide, and 5.8 meters high. Inside the bridge there are timber benches an railings. It is covered by a single-eave hip roof an topped with assorted grey tiles. The bridge is locate along the ancient courier road that connected Gutia to Ningde. It is listed as the Historical and Cultur Sites Protected at the County Level.

02—田地桥

福建省古田县鹤塘镇田地村峡谷绝壁，清嘉庆十一年（1806年）

曾名公心桥，中华民国二十四年（1935年）重修。全木结构伸臂式廊桥，长41米、宽6米、拱跨33米、十六开间，桥体为弧形桥面铺青砖。单脊双坡飞檐式顶覆青杂瓦。桥东61级石阶，桥西111级石阶。被列为全国重点文物保护单位。

02.Tiandi Bridge — Tiandi Village, Hetang Town, Gutian County, Fujian Province, built in 1806.

Originally named Gongxin Bridge, Tiandi Bridge was rebuilt in 1935. It is a timber frame cantilever covered bridge, 41 meters long, 6 meters wide, and with an arch span of 33 meters. Its gallery house has sixteen bays. The bridge has a curved form and its deck is covered by grey bricks. Its single-ridge two-slope roof has upturned eaves and is topped by assorted grey tiles. There are 61 steps at the east end of the bridge and 111 at its west end. Tiandi Bridge is listed as the Major Historical and Cultural Sites Protected at the National Level.

十三、降雨分四季——闽东闽侯县廊桥
XIII. Covered Bridges in Minhou County, East Fujian Province, Rain Fallen in Four Seasons

01 塘里桥

福建省闽侯县廷坪乡塘里村，1951年。

单孔伸臂式木拱廊桥长28.8米，宽4.4米，高3.9米，跨径24.8米。桥魂砌于岩壁，多组贯木斜撑交错搭架成拱，顶部铺设贯木为梁；桥面铺木板；穿斗式结构廊屋；桥廊神龛供奉玄天大帝神像；两侧设置安全护栏；上面安装两层风雨板。两侧山岗森林茂密，生态环境完好，野生动物自由繁衍。

01 Tangli Bridge — Tangli Village, Yanping Township, Minhou County, Fujian Province, built in 1951.

The single-span cantilever arch bridge is 28.8 meters long, 4.4 meters wide, 3.9 meters high, and has a span of 24.8 meters. The approaches of the bridge are built along a rock face, and its arch is formed from multiple assemblages of interspersed and intersecting timber diagonal bracing. There are intersecting timbers placed on top functioning as beams as well. The bridge deck is covered by timber boards, and its gallery house is a *chuandou* structure. Inside there is a shrine dedicated to Emperor Xuanwu (a Taoist deity). Protective railings run alongside, and a double-layer awning for the rain is installed on top. There is a dense and verdant forest in the mountains on both sides of the bridge and the ecological environment is superb. As a result, wild animals prosper and multiply here.

02—坑坪桥

福建省闽侯县延坪乡石洋村坑坪自然村，清乾隆十三年（1748年）

伸臂式木拱廊桥，长26米、宽6.4米、高3.6米。两岸桥堍用条石砌筑，托承贯木穿插支撑拱架。廊屋为全木穿斗式结构，两侧设长木板凳，外置遮雨木板。桥廊内东侧悬挂一块募捐芳名匾。两侧山岗森林茂密，峡谷云聚霞蒸，清幽气象感染着匆匆而过的行人。

02. Kengping Bridge – Kengping Natural Village, Shiyang Village, Yanping Township, Minhou County, Fujian Province, built in 1748.

This timber cantilever arch bridge is 26 meters long, 6.4 meters wide, and 3.6 meters high. Both approaches to the bridge are built with slabs of stone which support the arch's interspersed and interconnecting timber bracing. The gallery house is a *chuandou* structure equipped with long benches. Awnings are installed at the outside to protect the bridge from rain. A plaque hangs from the east end of the bridge that displays the names of donors that contributed to the bridge's construction. The views of the mountains and rich forests on both sides, and of the glow of clouds in the valley, cannot but affect even those who cross the bridge in a hurry.

03—岭下桥

福建省闽侯县大湖乡六锦村岭下自然村，清代（1636 — 1912 年）

岭下桥是村庄交通要道。单跨八字木架支撑式廊桥，长 9.6 米、宽 4.6 米、跨径 6.8 米。支架上方另架贯木平梁，再上是桥面板。由 8 根砖柱、8 根木柱支撑起廊顶，五脊悬山顶覆小青瓦，另覆压瓦锭。桥廊无墙只设护栏开敞式结构。

03.Lingxia Bridge – Lingxia Natural Village, Liujin Village, Dahu Township, Minhou County, Fujian Province, built during 1636-1912.

Lingxia Bridge serves as an important node for traffic. The single-span covered bridge is supported by bazi bracing. On top of this support is another frame of interconnecting horizontal timber beams. On top of this are the floor boards of the bridge deck. The bridge is 9.6 meters long, 4.6 meters wide, and has a span of 6.8 meters. The gallery house is covered by a five-ridge overhanging gable roof topped with small grey tiles. The roof is supported by eight brick columns and by eight timber columns. The gallery house is an open structure without walls, and has only a protective railing on either side.

04—三溪桥

福建省闽侯县大湖乡六锦村与坂头村交界山谷，清道光二十四年（1845年）

雪溪、乌溪、凌云溪汇流桥下，故名三溪桥。又名蔡峰桥，自古是进出大山的唯一通道。距村六公里连通闽县、侯官、罗源、闽清、古田五县交通。三溪桥建在火山岩形成的悬崖绝壁之间，长32米、宽5.4米、高3.7米、十二开间，距河床10数米。2016年台风"莫兰蒂"裹挟狂风暴雨，特大洪水冲毁闽侯县四座木拱廊桥，其中有三溪桥。

04.Sanxi Bridge — in a valley between Liujin Village and Bantou Village, Dahu Township, Minhou County, Fujian Province, built in 1845.

Sanxi Bridge gets its name from the three streams flowing under it—the Xue, Wu, and Lingyun Streams. Also named Caifeng Bridge, since ancient times it has served as the only path allowing people to come and go from the mountains. The bridge is located six kilometers away from the village, serving as an intersection of five counties including Minxian, Houguan, Luoyuan, Minqing and Gutian. It spans between cliff precipices formed out of volcanic rock. It is 32 meters long, 5.4 meters wide, 3.7 meters high, and sits 10 meters above the river bed below. Its gallery house contains twelve bays. In 2016, Typhoon Meranti struck Fujian. Especially large flood waters struck and destroyed four covered bridges in Minhou County. Included in their number was the Sanxi Bridge.

第六章 东南廊桥遗存带

05 — 泰山桥

福建省闽侯县延坪乡后溪村，中华民国二十二年（1933年）。

"原桥窄小车马难通，后乡众捐资、聘请匠师在原址建造木拱廊桥，祈望稳如泰山，故名。始建年代待考，桥廊脊檩遗有"中华民国贰拾贰年岁在癸酉葭月吉旦日重建，木司古邑路上乡余添春建造"字迹。单孔伸臂式木拱廊桥，长28米、宽4.5米、七开间，跨径22米。九檩四柱穿斗式构架，双坡顶覆青杂瓦。

05. Taishan Bridge — Houxi Village, Yanping Township, Minhou County, Fujian Province, built in 1933.

The initial bridge at this location was narrow, which made it difficult for horses and carriages to pass. As a result, villagers donated money and invited craftsmen to build a timber arch covered bridge at the same location. It was named Taishan to express the hope that the bridge would prove as solid as Mount Tai (which is to what Taishan refers). The year it was built is unknown, but it is written on the highest purlin in the gallery house that the bridge was "reconstructed on the first of the eleventh lunar month in the twenty-second year of the Republic of China (1933) by craftsman Yu Tiancun from Lushang Village." The timber arch bridge is 28 meters long, 4.5 meters wide, and spanned 22 meters. Its gallery house has seven bays and is a *chuandou* structure with nine purlins and four columns. Its double-slope roof is covered with assorted grey tiles.

十四、串珠状河谷盆地——连城县廊桥

XIV. Covered Bridges in Liancheng County, Where Basin Valleys Linked like a String of Beads

01—玉沙桥

福建省连城县四堡古镇花溪河，清康熙二十三年（1684 年）

河床沙石晶如白玉故名。发祥于南宋（1127 — 1279 年）时期的四堡镇有四件宝"古书坊""古雕版""古民居""古廊桥"。石墩木梁瓦屋廊桥，长30米、宽5米、高10米，桥面铺鹅卵石，两旁建有木栅栏和木凳，桥侧桥头安置木制雨篷。廊顶三座双层飞檐阁楼高低错落精致美观。船艄式桥墩上架七层交叉重叠圆木承托桥身安稳牢固。

01. Yusha Bridge — Huaxi River, Sibao Ancient Town, Liancheng County, Fujian Province, built in 1684.

The sand on the riverbed here shines like white jade from which the bridge's name is derived. Sibao Town's history dates to the Southern Song Dynasty. It is famous for its "four treasures"—its ancient bookstore, ancient woodblocks, ancient residences, and its ancient covered bridge. This stone-pier timber-beam tiled-roof covered bridge is 30 meters long, 5 meters wide, and 10 meters high. The bridge deck is covered with cobblestones. It has timber railings and benches on both sides. Awnings to protect the bridge from the rain are installed at both sides of the bridge and at the bridge heads. Three two-story pavilions of different sizes with upturned eaves are both exquisite and well arranged. On top of the ship bow shaped bridge piers are seven layers of overlapping logs, which support and stabilize the bridge body.

02—永隆桥

福建省连城县莒溪乡璧洲村，明洪武二十年（1387年）

南北走向、四孔五跨、石墩平梁木结构廊桥，长85米、宽6米、高7.5米。桥北端建有重檐歇山顶阁楼，桥中、桥尾南端建有歇山顶矮阁。穿斗架构，花岗岩桥墩上纵横叠木七层组成主体支撑，桥面铺满由河床捞取的鹅卵石，硬山式覆小青瓦，桥侧设置双层挡风薄木护板。六百余年未受损毁，是闽西极具文物价值的古代建筑标本，被列为省级文物保护单位。

02. Yonglong Bridge – Bizhou Village, Juxi Township, Liancheng County, Fujian Province, built in 1387.

Running from south to north, the bridge has four piers and five spans. It is a multi-span simply supported timber beam covered bridge with stone piers. It is 85 meters long, 6 meters wide, 7.5 meters high, and is a *chuandou* structure. On the north side of the bridge is a pavilion building with a multiple-eave hip and gable roof. In the center and southern end of the bridge are small pavilions also covered with hip and gable roofs. Seven layers of criss-crossed logs form the main bracing structure, placed upon the bridge's granite piers. The bridge deck is covered with cobblestones gathered from the river bed. The gallery house is covered by an flush gable roof, topped with small grey tiles. The bridge has a flush gable roof covered by grey tiles and double-layer protective skirts made of thin wood run alongside the bridge, blocking the wind. For over 600 years the bridge has not become damaged or worn down. It is a true specimen of valuable architectural cultural in western Fujian. The bridge is listed as the Historical and Cultural Sites Protected at the Provincial Level.

03—云龙桥

福建省连城县罗坊镇下罗村口青岩河，明崇祯七年（1634年）

东西走向，石墩圆木叠梁、全木结构亭阁式廊桥，长81米、宽5米、高20米。廊桥正中偏西建有双层六角攒尖顶魁星楼，两端安设高挑檐牌楼。桥型巍峨雄奇犹如蛟龙，故名。被列为省级文物保护单位。每年正月十五下午一点半，罗坊镇云龙桥下青岩河会准时上演客家人呼啸"走古事"数万人助威的盛大狂欢。七族各选勇敢男童上扮主官，下扮护将。

03.Yunlong Bridge — Qingyan River at Xialuo Village, Luofang Town, Liancheng County, Fujian Province, built in 1634.

Running from east to west, it is a pavilion-style combined log beam covered bridge with stone piers. It is 81 meters long, 5 meters wide, and 20 meters high. Just to the west of the center of the bridge is a two-story six-sided pyramidal kuixing Tower (named after the Taoist god) with a pyramidal roof. Both ends of the bridge have decorative archways with tall protruding eaves. The bridge's form is towering and bold, like a dragon, and it is named because of this resemblance. It is listed as the Historical and Cultural Sites Protected at the Provincial Level. Every year at 1:30 p.m. on the 15th day of the first lunar month, villagers will follow the Hakka Nationality's tradition of hosting a large scale festival and performing a pageant which is conducted through the participation of thousands of people. Seven lineages each select brave boys who are costumed as main characters who stand on the upper part of a platform, and as guards in the lower part of the platform.

十五、源溪流呈树枝状分布——上杭县廊桥

XV. Covered Bridges in Shanghang County, Where Streams Distribute as Branches

01—振兴桥

福建省上杭县步云乡古炉村水尾，明嘉靖（1522 — 1566 年）

全木结构独孔平梁廊桥，主梁、立柱、横檩、檐椽、棋枋、札牵等木质构件之间全部卯榫衔扣，未用一钉一铆。长 17 米、宽 7 米、高 4.5 米、跨径 9.4 米、五开间。石砌桥块上纵横排列垫木，支托十八根粗大圆木组成两层平梁，桥面铺木板。抬梁穿斗式构架，两侧安置雨披（上覆压瓦石）、护板、窗栏、长凳。双脊双坡歇山顶中间建小阁楼。

01.Zhenxing Bridge — Gulu Village, Buyun Township, Shanghang County, Fujian Province, built during 1522-1566.

This is a simply supported timber beam covered bridge with a single span. All of its components are joined by mortise and tenon technology without the use of a single nail. The bridge is 17 meters long, 7 meters wide, 4.5 meters high, and has a span of 9.4 meters. It gallery house has five bays. On the stone bridge bases are rows of criss-crossing timber blocks that support the 18 thick logs that form two layers of simply supported timber beams. The bridge deck in turn is covered with timber boards. The bridge is a *tailiang* and *chuandou* structure, and its two sides have skirts to protect the bridge from rain, as well as guard board-railings, window slats, and long benches. Its two-ridge two-slope hip and gable roof has a small pavilion building installed in its center.

02—天后宫桥

福建省上杭县步云乡梨岭村

桥头"前言"记："为纪念妈祖，梨岭村民于清乾隆二十五年（1760年）在村尾水口石拱桥上建起'林姑婆庙'即'天后宫'。三层牌楼全木结构庙顶飞檐翘角，飞禽走兽，人均百态镂空浮雕栩栩如生，宫内龙柱凤栋，金碧辉煌。村民林桥扬、林立芳等五人于桥竣当年三月赴莆田湄洲岛'天妃庙'迎回'圣母神驾'并割香火。三月二十三日入'天后宫'受香祀奉。近期重建"。

02.Tianhougong Bridge – Liling Village, Buyun Township, Shanghang County, Fujian Province.

A "preface" displayed at the head of the bridge states, "In commemoration of Mazu, in the 23rd year of the sexagenary cycle during the era of Qianlong (1760) the villagers of Liling built an Auntie Lin Temple (Lin being the surname of Mazu), also known as Tianhou Palace on the stone arch bridge at the waterfront at the tail end of their village. The structure is entirely made of timber and has a three story decorative arch with upturned eaves and corners. This is decorated with hundreds of life-like figures of flying birds and walking beasts. Inside the temple are gilded renderings of dragons on columns and phoenixes on beams, all radiantly depicted. After the construction of the bridge, in the March of that year, Lin Qiaoyang, Lin Lifang, and three other villagers went to the 'Heavenly Princess Palace' in Meizhou Island, Putian City (a journey of several hundred kilometers) to 'invite' the heavenly mother's heavenly carriage to return. A fire cutting ceremony (gehuo, a practice involving lighting incense, associated with the return of a spirit to its ancestral temple) was then conducted. On the 23rd of the month, 'Mazu' was enshrined in the Tianhou Palace (in Liling Village), greeted with offers of incense. The bridge was recently rebuilt."

03—镇隆桥

福建省上杭县步云乡梨岭村口

清光绪十四年（1888年）重建。单孔平梁木廊桥坐东向西，长12米、宽3.5米、高3.7米、跨径3米、五开间。石砌桥堍上圆木纵横相间架二层过梁，抬梁穿斗式全木构架，单脊中部隆高悬山顶满铺小青瓦，叠檐下木板封闭留窗棂。木制构件衔接榫卯紧密牢固。廊道两侧摆放古旧稻谷脱粒风车、米斗等农用器物。

03.Zhenlong Bridge — Entrance of Liling Village, Buyun Township, Shanghang County, Fujian Province.

The bridge was reconstructed in 1888. This is a single-span simply supported timber beam covered bridge that runs from east to west. It is 12 meters long, 3.5 meters wide, 3.7 meters high, and has a span of 3 meters. Its gallery house has five bays. The bridge has stone bases on which are placed criss-crossing and interconnecting logs, which support two layers of simply supported timber beams. The bridge has a combined *tailiang* and *chuandou* structure, and tall overhanging gables extends from both sides of its single roof ridge. The roof is covered by small grey tiles. There is a window lattice that peaks through the sealed boards beneath the stacked eaves. The mortise and tenon timber connecting components hold the structure together tightly and firmly. On both sides of the gallery, there are ancient agricultural implements, including a rich threshing machine, and grain buckets.

XVI. Covered Bridges in Ninghua County, with Short and Turbulent Streams

01 — 神仙桥

福建省宁化县曹坊镇滑石村，明景泰元年（1450年）至明天顺四年（1460年）

又名温孙桥、解放桥。四墩五孔全木结构廊桥，长80余米、宽6米、高6.2米、二十一开间。船艄型石筑桥墩迎水面呈雀啄状，墩台上圆木纵横交错七层或十层承托木梁。桥廊中间安设神龛，遮雨板下侧做护栏、长凳。单脊双坡顶桥头建悬山顶重檐小望阁。神仙桥为明代始建原物，是宁化县遗存最久远的大型廊桥。为泰宁、建宁、宁化等县通往汀州府"盐米古道"的重要津

01. Shenxian Bridge – Huashi Village, Caofang Town, Ninghua County, Fujian Province, built during 1450-1460.

Also known as Wensun Bridge and Jiefang Bridge, the bridge has four piers and five spans. It is a timber frame covered bridge that is 80 meters long, 6 meters wide, and 6.2 meters high. Its gallery house has twenty-one bays. The side of its stone pier facing upstream is shaped in the form of a sparrow's beak. On top of the stone pier are seven to ten layers of of criss-crossing logs that support the bridge's beams. The middle of the bridge has a shrine, with an awning to block the rain above, and a protective railing below. The bridge has a single-ridge double-slope roof, and at its ends there are small viewing pavilions with multiple-eaves and overhanging gables. As a well-preserve bridge built in the Ming Dynasty, Shenxian Bridg is the oldest large-scale covered bridge i Ninghua County. In ancient times, it served th important "Ancient Salt Grain Passageway" that connected Taining, Jianning, and Ninghu counties to Tingzhou Prefecture.

02—万荷桥

福建省宁化县安远镇吴家际村

万荷桥连通闽赣古驿道。因是广昌县唐坊镇盛产的白莲运往福建沿海地区的重要通道而得名。斜木支撑平梁全木结构廊桥，长12米、高5米、宽4米。

02.Wanhe Bridge — Wujiaji Village, Anyuan Town, Ninghua County, Fujian Province.

Wanhe Bridge served the ancient courier road that connected Fujian and Jiangxi provinces. Since this was an important corridor for the transport of white lotus from Tangfang Town in Guangchang County to the coastal areas in Fujian Province, the bridge earned its present name. The bridge is a timber frame covered bridge supported by diagonal bracing and simply supported timber beams. It is 12 meters long, 5 meters high, and 4 meters wide.

03—蛟潭桥

福建省宁化县水茜镇安寨村水口，清早期

独孔石拱廊桥，长 10.5 米、宽 3.2 米、高 4 米、跨径 3.2 米、七开间。全木穿斗式结构，顶梁、立柱、木枋等构件全部以榫卯形式扣合，坚固且便于维修。木质雨披下设置护栏、长凳。桥下碧潭水深数十米，是闽江八大发源地之一。赶场乡亲回家途中会在廊桥中歇脚。

03. Jiaotan Bridge — Anzhai Village, Shuixi Town, Ninghua County, Fujian Province, built in early Qing Dynasty.

This is a stone arch covered bridge with a single span. It is 10.5 meters long, 3.2 meters wide, 4 meters high, and has a span of 3.2 meters. Its gallery house has seven bays, and is a *chuandou* structure. Its columns, beams, and other timber components are joined by mortise and tenons, which makes the bridge solid, stable, and easy to maintain. There are guardrails and benches under the wooden awnings. The Bitan River that flows under the bridge is dozens of meters deep, and is one of the eight headwaters that flow into the Minjiang River. Villagers on their way home will often rest on the bridge.

第六章 东南廊桥遗存带

十七、山地切割强烈——永安市廊桥
XVII. Covered Bridges in Yong'an, with Intensely Cutting Mountain Area

01—安仁桥

福建省永安市青水畲族自治乡三房村，清雍正二年（1724 年）

原为独墩两孔平梁全木结构廊桥，后因河道变窄，桥墩逐渐靠附河岸，现为单孔只有一半桥段跨小河。长 55 米、宽 5 米、高 6 米。两侧安置遮雨护板，有供行人歇息的长凳。两端桥头建造歇山顶门庭，廊顶中部建三面双飞檐挑角阁楼。廊屋中央藻井为卯榫拱劵式样。

01.An'ren Bridge – Sanfang Village, Qingshui Autonomous Township of She Nationality, Yong'an, Fujian Province, built in 1724.

This bridge was originally a multi-span simply supported timber beam covered bridge with one pier and two spans. Later, the river narrowed, and the bridge pier gradually approached the riverbank. Thus the bridge became a single-span bridge with only half of the structure spanning the river. The bridge is 55 meters long, 5 meters wide, and 6 meters high. Awnings are installed on both sides and benches are placed inside on which pedestrians can rest. Both ends of the bridge have a gatehouse with hip and gable roofs. In the middle of the bridge there is a three-sided pavilion with double-upturned-eaves and protruding corners. Mortise and tenon joins are used to build the arch-style caisson *zaojing* ceiling in the center of the gallery house.

02—福兴桥

福建省永安市贡川镇张荆村底洋自然村水尾悬崖口，元代（1206－1368年）

福兴桥连接进出山谷的古驿道。村民进山采药、挖笋、耕作、砍柴、植树仍然常走福兴桥，并按时令在廊桥社交集会、膜拜祭祀。明清两代先后进行修缮，1993年修缮。单孔石拱廊桥，长20.5米、宽6.4米、高5米，海拔970米。是永安市历史最悠久、海拔最高的廊桥，有"永安第一桥"之誉。被列为市级文物保护单位。

02.Fuxing Bridge – Diyang Natural Village, Zhangjing Village, Gongchuan Town, Yong' an, Fujian Province, built during 1206-1368.

Fuxing Bridge connects the ancient courier road that led in and out of the mountain valley. When villagers enter the mountains to collect herbs, dig bamboo shoots, chop woods or plant trees, they still will cross this bridge. In addition, villagers will congregate on the bridge for seasonal social gatherings, and for religious ceremonies and sacrifices. The bridge was repaired in the Ming Dynasty, and during the Qianlong and Xianfeng periods of the Qing Dynasty, and in 1993. It is a stone arch covered bridge with a single span. It is 20.5 meters long, 6.4 meters wide, and 5 meters high. It is the oldest covered bridge in Yong' an and the covered bridge at the highest altitude in Yong' an. It is honored as the "Number One Bridge in Yong' an." It is listed as the Historical and Cultural Sites Protected at the Municipal Level.

03—永宁桥

福建省永安市青水乡澄江水口，清雍正二年（1724 年）

2014 年 7 月 27 日（农历七月初一），永宁桥戏台从上午到夜晚唱大戏，夜半散戏后失火将上部廊屋烧毁。当年 10 月，政府出资、乡民集资按照原样式复建。石拱独孔木屋廊桥，长 22 米、宽 5 米，双坡悬山顶正中建飞檐翘角挑阁，正脊鸱吻向内高翘，两条火尾龙昂首相对一只宝葫芦。桥廊两侧安置木板雨披，下设护栏长凳。桥东建有一座大戏台，逢年过节当地的"大腔"戏班子就会开场唱大戏，廊内可容纳七百余人观看。被列为省级文物保护单位。

03.Yongning Bridge — Chengjiang River, Qingshui Township, Yong'an, Fujian Province, built in 1724.

On July 27, 2014 (the first day of the seventh month of the lunar calendar), the upper part of bridge house burned down after the completion of an opera that ran from the morning into the night. In October of that year, with funding provided by the government as well as from donations by villagers, the bridge was rebuilt according to its original form. This is a covered bridge with a timber gallery house and a stone arch. It has a single span. It is 22 meters long and 5 meters wide. Its roof has two sloops and overhanging gables. In its center is a pavilion with upturned eaves and upturned corners. Its main ridge is decorated with *chiwen* dragons that reach up towards the center, together with two dragons whose heads face each-other, stretching out towards a gourd-shaped treasure. Awnings are set on both sides of the gallery house, under which are guardrails and benches. On the bridge's eastern section there is a stage where local Daqiang Opera troupes perform during traditional festivals. The covered bridge can hold more than 700 audience members. The bridge is listed as the Historical and Cultural Sites Protected at the Provincial Level.

04—会清桥

福建省永安市贡川镇集凤村,明天启六年（1626 年）

沙溪、胡贡溪在廊桥下交汇清浊分明,浊水多被清流融会,因此得名会清桥。清道光二十年（1840 年）大修。南北走向、两墩三孔,长 41 米、宽 7 米、高 8 米,十一开间。两端建门楼、歇山顶桥亭。农历三月三,乡民祭拜水神,祈盼风调雨顺。屋檐下有泥塑彩绘,正脊"鱼吻"寓意防火镇水。被列为省级文物保护单位。

04.Huiqing Bridge — Jifeng Village, Gongchuan Town, Yong'an, Fujian Province, built in 1626.

The Shaxi and Hugong creeks converge under this covered bridge, during which muddy water is purified by the larger-volume clean current. This is how the bridge got its name. The bridge was overhauled in 1840. Running from north to south, it has two piers and three spans. It is 41 meters long, 7 meters wide, and 8 meters high. Its gallery house has 11 bays. Pavilions with hip and gable roofs, together with gateway arches are built on both ends. On the third day of the third lunar month, villagers gather at the bridge to worship the god of the water, and pray for good weather. There are clay sculptures and colorful paintings inside the bridge and on the ridge, there is a sculpture of a fish, thought to offer protection against flooding and fires. The bridge is listed as the Historical and Cultural Sites Protected at the Provincial Level.

第六章 东南廊桥遗存带

十八、闽江支流沙溪贯穿——沙县、大田县、泰宁县廊桥

XVIII. Covered Bridges in Shaxian County, Datian County and Taining County, with Shaxi Brook, Tributaries of Minjiang River Flowing through

01 进谷桥

福建省沙县夏茂镇大布村彭邦自然村，明代（1368 — 1644 年）

曾名坡角桥。单孔石拱廊桥，长 47 米、宽 7 米、高 8 米、十一开间。清雍正末年（1735 年）、清嘉庆六年（1801 年）重建。2000 年乡民集资修缮。进谷桥飞檐翘角，精致美观。廊中厅高筑一层，桥厅悬挂进谷桥牌匾传为夏茂镇秀才罗永藻题写。被列为县级文物保护单位。

01. Jingu Bridge – Pengbang Natural Village, Dabu Village, Xiamao Town, Shaxian County, Fujian Province, built during 1368-1644.

Formerly called the Pojiao Bridge, this stone arch covered bridge has a single span and is 47 meters long, 7 meters wide, and 8 meters high. Its gallery house has eleven bays. It was rebuilt in 1735, and 1801. In 2000 it was repaired after donations were collected by local villagers. The bridge roof has upturned eaves and corners, and is elegant and beautiful. An extra floor is added to the pavilion in the center of the gallery house. A plaque that hangs at the entrance to the bridge is graced with the writing of Luo Yongzao, a member of the literati from Xiamao Town. The bridge is listed as the Historical and Cultural Sites Protected at the County Level.

02—流泗桥

福建省大田县桃源镇兰玉村，明成化（1465—1487年）

清康熙年间、中华民国时期整修。一墩两孔全木结构廊桥，东西走向，长42.2米、宽4.5米、高5米，两门厅十开间，两旁设有鹅颈椅，外搭遮雨篷。船艏形条石桥墩迎水面呈鸟喙状，其上六层圆木交叉支托横木平梁，桥面使用长条木板铺设。单脊三重檐悬山顶，中脊安置翘尾龙抢宝葫芦，各檐角安放"水花"雕塑。

02.Liusi Bridge – Lanyu Village, Taoyuan Town, Datian County, Fujian Province, built during 1465-1487.

This bridge was overhauled in the Kangxi period of the Qing Dynasty and during the Republic of China period. It has one pier and two spans, and runs from east to west. The bridge is 42.2 meters long, 4.5 meters wide, and 5 meters high. It has two halls and its gallery house has ten bays. There are benches on both sides and awnings that protect the bridge. The side of the stone pier facing upstream is shaped in the form of a sparrow beak, and above this are six intersecting layers of logs which support the horizontal bridge beams. The bridge deck is covered with long timber boards. The bridge is covered by a single-ridge overhanging gable roof with three-eaves. In the center of the ridge is a dragon with an upturned tail, grabbing a gourd-shaped treasure. The ends of all the eaves are decorated by carvings of splashing water.

03—仁寿桥

福建省大田县桃源镇兰玉村仁寿溪，元延祐元年（1314年）

明弘治元年（1488年）、清嘉庆十六年（1811年）、1969年大修。仁寿桥为客家传统建筑（坚固安全、封闭、融于自然）风格，双桥堍、独墩两孔、全木结构廊桥，东西走向，长27米、宽4.65米、高7米，九开间，船艏形石砌桥墩与两座桥堍上叠搭十层交叉（俗称喜鹊窝）伸臂圆木，将粗大平梁平稳托起，桥面夯土平实便于车马通过。单脊悬山顶满铺小青瓦，中间建飞檐翘角小阁楼，两端建对角翘檐牌坊。木质雨披内则安置护栏、长条凳。

03.Renshou Bridge－Renshou Creek, Lanyu Village, Taoyuan Town, Datian County, Fujian Province, built in 1314.

This bridge was overhauled in 1488, 1811, and 1969. An example of traditional architecture of the Hakka Nationality (known for structural stability and safety, closed-forms, and integration with nature), this is a timber frame bridge with one pier and two spans. It runs from east to west and is 27 meters long, 4.65 meters wide, and 7 meters high. Its gallery house has 9 bays. The ship-bow shaped stone piers as well as structures on both ends of the bridge hold ten layers of intersecting cantilevered logs (referred to locally as a magpie nest) which steadily support the bridge's thick horizontal log beams. The bridge deck's tamped earth allows carts and horses to travel across smoothly. The bridge's single-ridge overhanging gable roof is covered by small grey tiles, and in the center there is a small pavilion with upturned eaves and upturned corners. Both ends of the bridge are framed with memorial arches. Under the wooden awnings are guardrails and long benches.

第六章　东南廊桥遗存带

十九、山多水足，闽中宝库——德化、安溪、仙游、永定、永春县廊桥
XIX. Covered Bridges in Dehua County, Anxi County, Xianyou County, Yongding County and Yongchun County, Fujian's Treasury with Abundant Mountains and Water

01—铭新桥

福建省德化县大铭乡大铭村，清雍正八年（1730年）

　　原名大铭桥，乡绅林君宝出资募集桥材，乡民捐物捐劳建造。木架结构平梁独孔廊桥长30.8米，宽4米，八耳间小廊阁居中歇山顶双重翘角飞檐，正中安置七级宝塔，两边各有奔腾彩龙。廊道两侧双重木制雨披下面安置长凳。铭新桥多次被山洪冲毁又多次复建，最近一次大修是中华民国二十七年（1938年）。目前保护完好，仍然是大铭村通往外界的要道。铭新桥坐北朝南东西各依山岗，满目翠绿掩衬抹桥红。

01. Mingxin Bridge – Daming Village, Daming Township, Dehua County, Fujian Province, built in 1730.

Originally known as Daming Bridge, this bridge was funded by Lin Junbao, a member of the local gentry, with material and labor provided by local villagers. It is a simply supported timber beam covered bridge with a single span. It is 30.8 meters long, 4 meters wide, and has a gallery house with 8 bays. It has a hip and gable roof with double-upturned corners and upturned eaves. In the center there is a seven story pagoda, decorated on either side with sculptures of a dragon. Under the two-layer wooden awnings are benches. Mingxin Bridge was rebuilt several times after being destroyed by floods. It was most recently overhauled in 1938. Now this well-preserved bridge still serves as an important passageway between the village and the outside world. Looking out north from the bridge one can enjoy a view of hills from east to west, filling one's vision with verdant green together with a splash of red from the bridge.

02—济美桥

福建省德化县水口镇承泽村石牛山北坡山腰

又名承泽桥。明万历、清乾隆年间修缮加固，中华民国时期、1955年、1962年整修。承泽村黄氏族谱记载："亭桥建于南宋，位于乡之关键，悬崖飞瀑潆尾也。"圆木平梁廊桥长22.5米、宽3.6米、高6米。桥基紧附山岩，基座由四层圆木分两组纵横叠搭支撑桥身。主梁中段有两根木柱作为辅助支撑，两侧安装木质雨披护板。

02.Jimei Bridge — Shiniu Mountain, Chengze Village, Shuikou Town, Dehua County, Fujian Province.

Also known as Chengze Bridge, this bridge was overhauled in the Wanli period of the Ming Dynasty, and during the Qianlong Period of the Qing Dynasty. It was also repaired in the Republic of China period, and in 1955 and 1962. The Huang lineage genealogy in Chengze Village states that a pavilion bridge was built in the Southern Song Dynasty that served as a key connection for the area, and that it spanned over a waterfall. The current bridge is a timber horizontal log beam covered bridge. It is 22.5 meters long, 3.6 meters wide, and 6 meters high. The bridge foundation sits adjacent to the mountain's rock face. It uses four layers of logs, divided into two criss-crossing groups, to support the bridge body. There are two timber columns attached to the middle of the bridge's main beam that serve as a source of auxiliary support. Skirts to keep away the rain run along the length of the bridge.

03—湖山桥

福建省德化县水口镇淳湖村，北宋（960—1127年）

又名风水桥，始建于北宋（960—1127年）时期。石拱涵洞桥墩可将积水迅速排出。全杉木结构阁楼总面积600余平方米，是德化县建筑面积最大的宋代廊桥。长36米、宽6米，五层楼阁高13.5米。翘角飞檐歇山顶正中竖立宝葫芦。

03.Hushan Bridge — Chunhu Village, Shuikou Town, Dehua County, Fujian Province, built during 960-1127.

Also known as the Fengshui Bridge, a culvert that passes through this stone arch bridge's piers allows excess water to rapidly drain from the opposite side. The bridge's pagoda is made entirely of Chinese fir, and has a square area of over 600 meters. It is the largest Song Dynasty covered bridge that exists in Dehua County. The bridge is 36 meters long, and 6 meters wide. Its five-story pagoda is 13.5 meters high. There is a gourd-shaped treasure that decorates the top of the bridge's upturned-corner and upturned-eave hip and gable roof.

04—广济桥

福建省德化县春美乡双翰村水尾，明嘉靖元年（1522年）

又名双翰下桥。联通永春县经德化县到大田县古官道。清顺治十四年（1657年）、清乾隆九年（1744年）水毁重建。1972年旅居马来西亚华侨苏重仁、苏苜相等人回乡祭祖，发起海外华侨同乡募捐集资，于1974年重修。被列为县级文物保护单位。石墩叠木伸臂式廊桥。长24米、宽5.5米、高6.5米，七开间。

04.Guangji Bridge – Shuanghan Village, Chunmei Township, Dehua County, Fujian Province, built in 1522.

Also known as Shuanghanxia Bridge, Guangji Bridge connected a major ancient courier road that linked Yongchun County to Datian County via Dehua County. The bridge is a timber cantilever covered bridge built with timbers stacked on top of its stone foundation. It is 24 meters long, 5.5 meters wide, and 6.5 meters high. Its gallery house has 7 bays. The bridge was damaged by floods and then rebuilt in both 1657 and 1744. In 1972, overseas Chinese residents of Malaysia Su Chongren, Su Shouxiang, and others returned to the village to pay respects to their ancestors. They then organized their fellow landsmen abroad to raise money to repair the bridge, leading to its renovation in 1974. The bridge has been listed as the Historical and Cultural Sites Protected at the County Level.

05—登龙桥

福建省德化县浔中镇蒲坂村，宋代（960 — 1279 年）

曾名惠政桥、观音桥。连通德化县城通往大田县、尤溪官道。两墩三孔杉木搭跨为梁，全木结构，廊桥长 62.5 米、宽 4.1 米、高 6.6 米，十四开间。船舲式桥墩，桥面铺杉木板，廊屋两侧安置条凳，外侧设木质双层雨披。硬山顶覆小青瓦。清顺治、清康熙、清雍正、清乾隆、清光绪年间整修。中华民国十二年（1923 年）当地归国华侨陈簪发、李书植出资并发动海外华侨捐资 9500 银元，按古貌重建。被列为县级文物保护单位。

05.Denglong Bridge — Puban Village, Xunzhong Town, Dehua County, Fujian Province, built during 960-1279.

Formerly called Huizheng Bridge and Guanyin Bridge, this bridge once connected the official state built road that linked Dehua's county seat to Datian and Youxi counties. The bridge has two piers and three spans. It is a timber beam covered bridge built with Chinese fir. It is 62.5 meters long, 4.1 meters wide, 6.6 meters high and rests on piers shaped in the form of ship bows. Its gallery house has 14 bays. The bridge road is covered with timber planks and benches are set on both of its sides. It has a flush gable roof and the surfaces below are protected from the rain by two-layer awnings. The bridge was renovated during the Shunzhi, Kangxi, Yongzheng, Qianlong, and Guangxu periods of the Qing Dynasty. In 1923, Chen Zanfa and Li Shuzhi, overseas Chinese residents originally from the area, returned home and organized other members of the overseas Chinese community to raise money for the bridge. They raised 9,500 silver dollars with which the bridge was restored according to its original appearance. The bridge is listed as the Historical Cultural Sites Protected at the County Level.

06—宴林口桥

福建省德化县盖德乡林地村

唐代至中华民国，德化县二百余座瓷窑分布在偏僻山村，以北宋盖德镇"碗坪仑窑"为代表烧制各种白瓷。林地村又称宴林口为德化五口之一，是山地窑场制品东运泉州港外销的重要通道。宋代建简易木桥，清乾隆四十七年（1782年）改建廊桥。一墩两孔木平廊桥，长27.3米、宽3.4米、高3.95米。两侧设长板坐凳，外侧敷设双层雨披板，直脊对称三叠悬山顶覆青杂瓦。清光绪三十年（1904年）水毁，乡绅林仁礼捐家财重建。1959年修缮加固。

06. Yanlinkou Bridge — Lindi Village, Gaide Township, Dehua County, Fujian Province.

From the time of the Tang Dynasty to the Republic of China period, over 200 kilns for producing porcelain operated in remote mountain villages throughout Dehua County. During the Northern Song Dynasty, the "Wanpenglun Kiln" in Gaide Town was renowned for its production of all sorts of white porcelain. Lindi Village (also known as Yanlin Port), was one of the five key ports in Dehua County, and served as an important node for the goods of the mountain kilns along their way to export from the port of Quanzhou. At this village, a simply supported timber bridge was constructed during the Song Dynasty. It was rebuilt as a covered bridge in 1782. It has one pier and two spans, and is a timber frame covered bridge. It is 27.3 meters long, 3.4 meters wide, and 3.95 meters high. On both sides of the bridge are benches and outside the bridge is a double-level awning. The bridge is covered by a three-layered symmetrical overhanging gable roof, and is topped with assorted grey tiles. The bridge was destroyed by a flood in 1904, after which Lin Renli, a member of the local gentry, donated his family's wealth to rebuild it. In 1959, the bridge was completely repaired and reinforced.

07—天竺桥

福建省安溪县蓝田乡后清村与进德村之间小溪，宋代（960 — 1279 年）

木平梁亭阁式廊桥，长 6 米、宽 3 米，小巧古朴，玲珑可人。依托两岸花岗岩石基座，11 根贯木平架为梁，上铺木板为桥面。双檐燕尾翘角歇山顶主脊安放双龙巡游、宝葫芦雕塑，活泼灵动。两侧及桥口安置双层雨披木板为行人遮风挡雨。20 世纪 60 年代初，天竺桥水毁，乡民到下游数公里外将大部分木梁、木板捞回，不足部分捐资捐物补充，半年后复建。

07.Tianzhu Bridge – Across creek between Houqing Village and Jinde Village, Lantian Township, Anxi County Fujian Province, built during 960-1279.

Built in a classic and elegant style, this is a simply supported timber beam pagoda style covered bridge. It is 6 meters long, and 3 meters wide. It uses granite stones on both banks to serve as its foundation. Its beams are composed of 11 linked timbers. The deck bridge is covered with timber planks. The bridge is covered with a hip and gable roof with double-eaves and upturned "swallow-tail" corners. The roof ridge is decorated with live carvings of two roaming dragons and a gourd-shaped treasure. In the early 1960s, Tianzhu Bridge was destroyed by a flood. However villagers were able to recover beams, columns, and timber planks that had been carried kilometers away downstream. They industriously carried the material back, and collected funds for the material that was still needed. Within half-a-year, the bridge was rebuilt.

08—瑞云桥

福建省安溪县蓝田乡进德村进德溪，南宋咸淳元年（1265 年）

始建后二百年间两次水毁皆重建。明永乐三年（1405 年）第三次水毁，当年秋按照高僧选定的吉日吉时，秉承九为尊祖制，精选 9 根长 16 米的粗壮杉木，砌筑桥堍，架木为梁，重建瑞云桥。明崇祯三年（1630 年）整修。2007 年焚毁，2008 年重建。长 14.7 米、宽 5 米，桥廊内木雕精美。被列为县级文物保护单位。明代书法家张瑞图（1570－1641 年，福建省晋江人）为瑞云桥书写"津梁大千"题匾。

08.Ruiyun Bridge – Jinde Creek, Jinde Village, Lantian Township, Anxi County, Fujian Province, built in 1265.

In its first 200 years of existence, the bridge was rebuilt twice after being destroyed by floods. In the autumn of 1405, after suffering damage caused by floods for a third time, the bridge was reconstructed with nine thick 16-meter-long Chinese firs on an auspicious date picked by a monk. It was renovated in 1630. In 2007 it burnt down and was rebuilt the following year. The bridge is 14.7 meters long and 5 meters wide, with exquisite wooden carvings inside its gallery house. It is listed as the Historical and Cultural Sites Protected at the County Level. The words "Beams of Boundless Strength," written in the calligraphy of Zhang Ruitu, a native of Pujiang, Fujian, who lived from 1570-1641, grace a plaque that hangs from the bridge.

09—济行桥

福建省龙岩市永定区湖坑镇新南村南溪，明嘉靖二十年（1541年）

地处永定土楼沟核心带，是南溪两岸480户农家唯一通道，也是永定通往漳州、厦门的重要节点。两墩三孔木廊平桥，长26米、宽3米、高15米、跨径15米。粗大杉木托架全木桥体，各构件采用榫卯形式连接未见一钉一铆。两座桥墩使用鹅卵石与三合土垒砌，迎水面锐利，背水面厚实。1996年，百年一遇的洪灾突发，急流漫过桥面安然无恙。1992年旅美华侨苏汝台等贤达捐资修整。廊道里常有乡民聚会。

09. Jixing Bridge — Nanxi Creek, Xinnan Village, Hukeng Town, Yongding District, Longyan, Fujian Province, built in 1541.

Situated in the central area of Yongding County, this bridge is the only passageway that links the 480 families that live on both sides of the Nanxi Creek, and also is an important node that links Yongding County to Zhangzhou and Xiamen. It is a timber frame covered bridge with two piers and three spans. It is 26 meters long, 3 meters wide, 15 meters high, and has a span of 15 meters. A frame composed of thick Chinese fir supports the bridge body. Since the bridge uses mortises and tenons for connections, there is not a single nail in the entire structure. The two bridge piers are formed of cobblestones and concrete. The side that faces upstream comes to a sharp point, while the side downstream is thick and wide. In 1996, the bridge suffered a once-in-100-year flood. Fortunately, despite flood waters surging over the bridge deck, the bridge was not damaged. In 1992, Su Rutai, a member of the overseas Chinese community living in America and others donated money for the bridge's renovation. The bridge's gallery house is often the site of village meet-ups.

第六章 东南廊桥遗存带

10—通仙桥

福建省永春县东关镇东美村湖洋溪，南宋绍兴十五年（1145年）

原名东关桥，是闽南大型石墩木梁廊桥。长85米、宽5米，四墩五孔。清末遭暴雨重创破损，清光绪元年（1875年）复建。中华民国十八年（1929年）李俊承（1888—1966年，永春县人，实业家、爱国华侨）出资，选良材并招募能工巧匠，按宋代原貌重修。被列为省级文物保护单位，载入《中国名胜词典》。

10. Tongxian Bridge — Huyang Creek. Dongmei Village, Dongguan Town, Yongchun County, Fujian Province, built in 1145

Originally known as Dongguan Bridge, it is an example of a large-scale southern Fujian style stone pier timber beam covered bridge. It has four piers and five spans, and is 85 meters long, and 5 meters wide. It was damaged during the late Qing Dynasty, and was rebuilt in 1875. In 1929, Li Juncheng (1888-1966), an overseas Chinese businessman and patriot, originally from Yongchun County donated funds, found good quality material, and recruited talented craftsmen to renovate the bridge to its original Song Dynasty look. It is listed as the Historical and Cultural Site Protected at the Provincial Level. It also is listed in the *Chinese Dictionary of Scenic Spots*.

中国廊橋

二十、闽江源头——尤溪县廊桥
XX. Covered Bridges in Youxi County, the Origin of Minjiang River

01—新坑桥

福建省尤溪县西城镇新坑村,清同治元年（1862年）

又称水尾桥。石砌单孔木廊桥,长21米,宽5米,八开间,穿斗式结构悬山顶,屋檐壁画工艺精美,梁上木雕古朴细致。村老陈家叶用笔记的形式记录家乡历史民俗:"新坑村百十户家庭均为陈姓。祖先自宋高宗绍兴二十一年（1151年）四月,由河南省颖川郡（禹州市）迁徙到四面环山,一条清流穿流谷底的好地方,"被列为县级文物保护单位。

01.Xinkeng Bridge – Xinkeng Village, Xicheng Town, Youxi County, Fujian Province, built in 1862.

Also known as Shuiwei Bridge, the bridge is built with stone masonry and timber. It has a single span and is 21 meters long, 5 meters wide, and has a gallery house with eight bays. It has a *chuandou* structure, and an overhanging gable roof. The murals on its eaves are exquisite, and carvings on its timber beams are elegant and meticulous. A villager named Chen Jiaye used a pen to write down the area's history, writing that "the families in Xinkeng Village are all surnamed Chen, and In April 1151, their ancestors migrated from Yingchuan County (currently called Yuzhou) in Henan Province to this place, surrounded by mountains, with a winding river flowing through it." The bridge is listed as the Historical and Cultural Sites Protected at the County Level.

02—水尾桥

福建省尤溪县新阳镇上地村下洋自然村水口，清道光（1821 — 1850 年）

又名栖鸾桥。小村四面环山显得天狭地窄，甘泉终日里流淌。多处泉眼汇聚峡谷溪流，在村口形成瀑布，水尾桥架临其上。全木结构廊桥长 17.5 米、宽 4.2 米、高 4.6 米，七开间，穿斗式构造，重檐瓦顶中间设立飞檐挑阁。巨石垒砌的桥堍上架设木梁，厚木板铺设桥面，雨披下安置护栏、长条凳。

02.Shuiwei Bridge – Xiayang Natural Village, Shangdi Village, Xinyang Town, Youxi County, Fujian Province, built during 1821-1850.

It's also known as the Qiluan Bridge. Surrounded by mountains, the sky and land in the village appear narrow, and its sweet springs gurgle from morning to night. At the entrance of the village, several rivers intersect and form a waterfall, above which the Shuiwei Bridge spans. This timber frame covered bridge is 17.5 meters long, 4.2 meters wide, and 4.6 meters high. It has a gallery house with seven bays. It is a *chuandou* structure with a multiple-eave tiled roof, at the center of which is a protruding pavilion with upturned eaves. Piled stone construction on both ends of the bridge support the bridge's timber beams. The bridge deck is covered with thick planks, and under its awnings are protective railings and long strips of benches.

03—岐坑桥

福建省尤溪县汤川乡黄林村

黄姓祖先捐资始建，清道光六年（1826年）重建。单孔石拱廊桥，长10米、宽3米、高6米，七开间。桥墩使用河床溪石砌筑，桥孔跨径2.8米，由古人根据常年最大水量设定。桥屋用杉木搭建，抬梁穿斗式结构是中国传统建筑中最节省木材、最便于维修的组合形式。单脊双坡悬山顶上三座挑阁亦为悬山顶。岐坑桥至今仍在为上山砍竹挖笋、种地采药的乡民遮风挡雨。被列为县级文物保护单位。

03.Qikeng Bridge — Huanglin Village, Tangchuan Township, Youxi County, Fujian Province.

The ancestors of the Huang lineage funded the original construction of this bridge. Later, it was rebuilt in 1826. This is a stone arch covered bridge with one span. It is 10 meters long, 3 meters wide, 6 meters high, and has seven bays. The stone piers are made of stones from the riverbed. The bridge spans a distance of only 2.8 meters, which was determined by villagers in the distant past according to the maximum annual water volume that passes through the river. The gallery house is built of Chinese fir, and is a combined *tailiang* and *chuandou* structure. The structure is one of the most materially efficient examples of traditional Chinese architecture, and is also very easily maintained. It is covered by a single-ridge double-slope overhanging gable roof. And above this are three protruding pavilions, which are also covered with overhanging gable roofs. This bridge provides shelter from the wind and rain for villagers who go into the mountains to cut bamboo, dig up bamboo shoots, do farmwork, or collect herbs. It is listed as the Historical and Cultural Sites Protected at the County Level.

第六章 东南廊桥遗存带

04—见龙桥

福建省尤溪县新阳镇双鲤村，明正统元年（1436年）

双鲤村因见龙桥下两块巨石形如鲤鱼得名。全木结构单孔廊桥，东西走向，长30米、宽5米、高4米、单孔跨径14米，八开间，悬山顶。桥面由圆木三层纵横叠架，两侧安置遮阳板、栏杆、长条凳。中华民国十三年（1924年）里人卢兴邦为造福桑梓出资重修。

04. Jianlong Bridge — Shuangli Village, Xinyang Town, Youxi County, Fujian Province, built in 1436.

Under the Jianlong Bridge, there are two giant stones that resemble two carp fish, and this is what the village is named after. Running from east to west, this single-span timber frame covered bridge is 30 meters long, 5 meters wide, 4 meters high, and has a span of 14 meters. Its gallery house has 8 bays, and has an overhanging gable roof. The bridge deck is supported by three levels of stacked crisscrossed logs. Railing and benches are installed on both sides of the bridge. In 1924, Lu Xingbang contributed funds for the bridge's reconstruction.

Chapter VII   Covered Bridges in Jiangnan

It includes the areas like southeastern Hubei, southern Anhui, northern Jiangxi, Jiangsu, Shanghai and northern and eastern Zhejiang in the middle and lower reaches of the Yangtze River.

Located in the interlaced zone between the hills in the south of the Yangtze River and the plains in the middle and lower reaches of the Yangtze River, it is a fertile region with flat terrains and many rivers and lakes. Since ancient times, it has been densely populated, culturally prosperous and economically developed region. It has long been the living region of Han Nationality who use the Wu, Hui and Southwest Mandarin (Hubei) dialect.

Xianning, a prefecture level city in southeast Hubei province, and Wannan, a place in southern Anhui province, are the areas with the biggest quantity of gallery bridges in the south of the Yangtze River.

Covered bridges in southeastern Hubei are mainly distributed in Xianning. Xianning is located in the mountainous area. It is a place where ancient houses and villages are well preserved and there are many existing covered bridges.

The covered bridges in Jiangsu and Shanghai mainly exist in some private gardens and ancient towns.

The main representatives of this belt are stone arch covered bridge, stone slab covered bridge and a small number of simply supported wooden beam Covered bridges.

中国廊桥

第七章 江南廊桥遗存带

包括长江中下游的鄂东南、皖南、赣北、苏沪和浙北浙东。这里地处江南丘陵和长江中下游平原交错地带，地势平坦，河湖密布，为鱼米之乡，自古人口密集、文化昌盛、经济发达。这里长期为使用吴语、徽语和西南官话（湖北方言）的汉族族群生活区域。鄂东南的咸宁和皖南的徽州是江南廊桥最集中的地带。

鄂东南廊桥主要分布在咸宁。咸宁地处鄂南山区，是湖北古代村落、民居保存比较好的区域，也是现存廊桥较多的地方。苏沪的廊桥则主要存于一些"私家园林和古镇里。

主要桥型有石拱廊桥、石板廊桥，兼有少量简支木梁廊桥。

第一节·皖赣廊桥
Section I Covered Bridges in Anhui Province and Jiangxi Province

一、新安江水系徽派廊桥群
I. Anhui-style Covered Bridges in Xin'an River System

01—北岸桥

安徽省歙县南部的北岸镇北溪河，清代（1636—1912年）

长33米、宽4.7米、高6米、二十二开间，为两墩三孔石墩砖墙、木柱瓦顶廊桥，被列为省级文物保护单位。桥头上端马头墙与古民居同为徽派风格。桥墙两侧正中"西流毓秀""北岸桥"刻字醒目。西侧廊墙花窗，满月一扇，古瓶、桂叶、葫芦、书卷各两扇。西墙朱漆外窗青瓦挑檐，窗下扶手靠背木椅。

01. Bei'an Bridge — Beixi River, Bei'an Town, Southern Shexian County, Anhui Province, built during 1636-1912.

It was built by 33m long, 4.7m wide, and 6m high. This bridge has two piers and three spans, and has stone piers, brick walls, timber columns and a tiled roof. Its gallery house has twenty-two bays. The bridge is listed as a cultural relic protected at the provincial level. At the head of the bridge, a horse-head wall and ancient residence are both constructed in the distinctive style of the Huizhou region. On the sides of the bridge walls are eye-catching inscriptions stating "Beauty of the Western Current," and "North Bank Bridge." The west side of the gallery house is decorated by windows in the shape of a full moon, ancient bottle, osmanthus leaf, gourd, and scroll. There are grey tiles and protruding eaves outside the red lacquered west bridge wall. Under the windows, there are wooden chairs with armrests and backrests.

第七章 江南廊桥遗存带

02—拱北桥

安徽省休宁县蓝田镇岭下村夹溪河，宋代（960—1279年）

拱北桥始建于宋代(960—1279年)，明万历（1573—1620年）、清乾隆（1736—1796年）年间重建，桥上建有遮风避雨的砖木结构长廊，廊屋内设有靠背长条凳，是安徽省最长的古廊桥。拱北桥属徽派建筑风格的石墩木平廊桥，长75米、宽5米、高7.6米、四墩五孔，被列为省级文物保护单位。

02.Gongbei Bridge — Jiaxi River, Lingxia Village, Lantian Town, Xiuning County, Anhui Province, built during 960-1279.

The Gongbei Bridge was built in the Song Dynasty, and was rebuilt in the Wanli period of the Ming Dynasty and the Qianlong period of the Qing Dynasty. Its gallery house is made of brick and wood. It has awnings on top to protect against the rain, and benches with backrests installed inside. It is Anhui's longest ancient covered bridge. The bridge is also known as the Lingxia Bridge. It has stone piers and timber beams, and is built in the Huizhou architectural style. The bridge has four piers, five spans, and is 75 meters long, 5 meters wide, and 7.6 meters high. It is listed as the Historical Cultural Sites Protected at the Provincial Level.

03—三棵树桥

安徽省休宁县兰田镇隆光村，明代（1368－1644年）

三棵树桥，因旁侧三株近三百年树龄苦楮树得名。早名淙潭桥，两墩三孔、石拱单面敞轩式廊桥。清雍正、清咸丰年间整修。桥头立有清乾隆四十五年（1780年）徽州府正堂颁布"严禁砍伐树木，严禁在夹溪河药鱼"石碑。

03.Sankeshu Bridge － Longguang Village, Lantian Town, Xiuning County, Anhui Province, built during 1368-1644.

The Three Tree Bridge is named after three castanopsis evergreen trees that are adjacent to the bridge and which are almost 300 years old. Originally Called Congtan Bridge, this bridge has two piers and three spans. It is a stone arch bridge with one side of its pavilion structure exposed. It was renovated during the Yongzheng and Xianfeng periods in the Qing Dynasty. In 1780, the Huizhou prefectural government inscribed a stone stele at the entrance of the bridge warning that "Fishing and cutting down trees is prohibited."

中国廊桥

04 — 高阳桥

安徽省歙县许村，元代（1271 — 1368 年）

诗人李白称赞许村"十里沙滩水中流，东西石壁秀而幽"，王安石、文天祥、朱熹、董其昌也留有诗文。高阳桥又名离合桥，乡绅许友山捐资募款建造。被列为国家级重点文物保护单位。桥右侧是古渡口，左侧是明代石牌坊。

04.Gaoyang Bridge – Xucun Village, Shexian County, Anhui Province, built during 1271-1368.

Xucun Village was acclaimed by the renowned poet Li Bai who stated it was a place where, "ten *li* of beach the current flows between, and east and west rock walls are exquisite and faraway seen." Poems about the village were also penned by historically noted literati including Wang Anshi, Wen Tianxiang, Zhu Xi, and Dong Qichang. Also known as the Lihe Bridge, the construction of the bridge was funded by member of the local gentry Xu Youshan. It is listed as a cultural relic protected at the national level. On the right side of the bridge there is an ancient ferry landing, and on the left stands a Ming Dynasty stone memorial arch.

第七章 江南廊桥遗存带

05—桃源桥

安徽省祁门县闪里镇桃源村，明成化九年（1473年）

单拱砖石结构廊桥，长22米、宽4米、高6米。桥西两方石碑，一为禁丐碑，一为禁赌碑，均为清代遗物。

05.Taoyuan Bridge – Taoyuan Village, Shanli Town, Qimen County, Anhui Province, built in 1473.

It is built of bricks and is an arch covered bridge with a single arch. It is 22 meters long, 4 meters wide and 6 meters high. Two stone steles in the west of bridge are relics of the Qing Dynasty, one prohibiting gambling and the other banning aggressive panhandling.

06—乐寿桥

安徽省黄山市屯溪区奕棋镇占川村，明万历（1573—1620年）

又名关爷桥、关阳桥。按《论语》"智者乐，仁者寿"的寓意定桥名。木廊穿斗式廊桥，一墩两孔，长30米、宽5.6米，七开间。粗大圆木为梁，上面逐层铺木板、薄砖、细沙，桥面用麻石板铺设。亭阁式桥顶，中间高、两侧低，覆青杂瓦。桥廊靠溪水上游一面置木凳，供乡民交谈聚会歇息。清光绪三十二年（1906年）、中华民国三十七年（1948年）重修。被列为区级文物保护单位。

06.Leshou Bridge – Zhanchuan Village, Yiqi Town, Tunxi District, Huangshan, Anhui Province, built during 1573-1620.

Also known as Guanye Bridge and Guanyang Bridge, the Leshou Bridge was named after a saying from the *Analects of Confucius*— "The wise are joyful; the virtuous are long-lived." The one pier two span timber *chuandou* pavilion-style covered bridge is 30 meters long, 5.6 meters wide, and has a gallery house with seven bays. Its beams are made of thick logs. On top of them are layers of timber boards, thin bricks, and fine sand. Its deck is covered by granite stone. It is taller in the middle and lower on either end. It is covered with assorted grey tiles. On the side of the bridge facing upstream. There are wooden benches that allow villagers to talk together and rest. The bridge was rebuilt in 1906 and 1948. It is listed as the Historical and Cultural Sites Protected at the Distict Level.

07—唐模高阳桥

安徽省歙县唐模古村水街入口，清雍正（1723－1735年）

又名观音桥。一墩两孔石拱砖瓦结构廊桥，由唐模村许氏家族出资，始建于清雍正年间（1723－1735年）。中华民国刻印版《歙县志》载，高阳桥由许克云所建。长7米、高3米，面积60平方米。木梁、立柱、挑檐、斗拱均按明式风格建造。

07.Tangmogaoyang Bridge – Entrance of Shuijie Street, Tangmo Ancient Village, Shexian County, Anhui Province, built during 1723-1735.

Also known as Guanyin Bridge, the construction of this one pier two span stone arch covered bridge was funded by the Xu family of Tangmo Village and built in between 1723 and 1735. According to the *Shexian County Annals* published during the Republic of China period, the Gaoyang Bridge was built by Xu Keyun. The bridge is 7 meters long, 3 meters high and has an area of 60 square meters. Its timber beams, columns, protruding eaves and *dougong* are all designed in the style of the Ming Dynasty.

08—环秀桥

安徽省歙县呈坎村，元代（1271－1368年）

曾名黑桥、红旗桥，始建于元代（1271－1368年），是溪东街和前后街的通道，并连接休宁县通往许村、歙县县城要道。两墩三孔石桥，长26.6米、宽3.8米、高4.5米，廊屋占整桥三分之一。

08.Huanxiu Bridge – Chengkan Village, Shexian County, Anhui Province, built during 1271-1368.

Formerly known as Heiqiao Bridge and Hongqiao Bridge, the Huanxiu Bridge connects Xidong Street with Qianhou Street, and also links Xiuning County to both the Shexian County county and to Xucun Vitlage. It has two piers and three spans, and is a stone arch covered bridge. It is 26.6 meters long, 3.8 meters wide, and 4.5 meters high. Its gallery house occupies one third of the bridge's total length.

09—虹桥

安徽省黄山市岩寺镇后街丰乐河，明成化五年（1469年）

又名洪福桥。两墩三孔、七开间、砖石结构、木椽瓦顶廊桥。清雍正年间（1723—1736年）郑为翰捐资重新修建。中华民国元年（1912年）再次重修。红色花岗岩砌筑桥墩，平架石板作为桥面，桥梁上部竖红漆木柱24根，廊顶为单脊硬山顶形制，顶覆青薄瓦。桥的两端出入口上部为马头墙式样。桥东建一间小屋，取名"香积"，供修桥和打扫卫生的劳工暂住。

09.Hongqiao Bridge — Fengle River, Houjie Street, Yansi Town, Huangshan County, Anhui Province, built in 1469.

Also known as Hongfu Bridge, this bridge was rebuilt during the Yongzheng period in the Qing Dynasty, with funds donated by Zheng Weihan. It was reconstructed in the early Republic of China period as well. It has two piers and three spans, seven bays, and is built with bricks. Its roof is covered with timber rafters and tiles. The piers are formed of red granite and the bridge's deck is covered with flat slabs of stone. There are 24 red-lacquer timber columns on the upper part of the bridge, and the gallery has a single-ridge flush gable roof covered with thin grey tiles. Both entrances to the bridge are framed on top with horse-head walls. In the east of the bridge, a cabin called Xiangji provides for repairmen and upkeep workers with a temporary place to live.

10—云溪桥

安徽省休宁县岭南乡三溪村,明代（1368—1644年）

独孔石拱砖石结构亭阁式廊桥,长25米、宽3米、高12米、拱跨6米。

10. Yunxi Bridge — Sanxi Village, Lingnan Township, Xiuning County, Anhui Province, built during 1368-1644.

This single-span bridge has an arch made of stone and a structure built of bricks. It is a pavilion style covered bridge, and is 25 meters long, 3 meters wide, and 12 meters high. It has a span of 6 meters.

二、龙山湖水之侧——太湖县廊桥
II. Covered Bridge in Taihu County by Longshan Mountain and Taihu Lake

龙门桥

安徽省太湖县北中镇马嘶村望天河,清道光二十五年（1845）年。平梁木结构廊桥,长14米、宽4.6米、高3.5米,五开间东西走向。内侧置美人靠坐凳和木制栏杆,桥身外侧安置防雨裙板。桥面由方木条榫卯铺砌。西端各建一小园青砖小瓦龙脊桥头堡,石头垒筑,石缝批桐油石灰浆砌。皖西南仅存的古代廊桥,受到百姓珍爱,被列为县级文物保护单位。

Longmen Bridge — Wangtian River, Masi Village, Beizhong Town, Taihu County, Anhui Province, built in 1845.

This single-span simply supported timber beam bridge is 14 meters long, 4.6 meters wide and 3.5 meters high. Its gallery house has five bays. Benches with chair back (rest of beauty) and timber railings are set inside the bridge and rain-proof boards are installed outside the bridge. The deck is covered with timber boards fastened together with mortise and tenons. At both ends of the bridge, there are small bridgeheads built with grey bricks and small tiles, with mortar formed of tung oil and calcium hydroxide. The Dragon Gate Bridge is the only ancient covered bridge that remains in Southwest Anhui Province, and it is cherished by the people here. It is listed as a cultural relic protected at the provincial level.

三、婺江之源泛徽派廊桥群

III. The Group of Anhui-style Covered Bridges at the Origin of Wujiang River

01—通济桥

江西省婺源县思溪延村，明代（1368 — 1644 年）

一墩两孔平梁木结构廊桥，长 20 余米，桥墩前端尖锐如锋当地俗称燕嘴。墩台立六角如来石刻尊柱，寓意镇水保民。桥廊奉大禹神，村民崇敬他为民生社稷操劳、一心治水的仁心善举。思溪延村俞氏一族数百年前加入徽商行列并自成一脉，常有经商致富的人携资归乡兴建书院祠堂、建桥修路等。

01.Tongji Bridge — Sixiyan Village, Wuyuan County, Jiangxi Province, built during 1368-1644.

This multi-span simply supported timber beam bridge has one pier and two spans, and is more than 20 meters long. The sides of the bridge piers that face upstream come to a sharp point, and local people call them "swallow beaks". The hexagonal piers are carved with status of buddhas, thought to protect local people from floods. The gallery house is dedicated to god Yu the Great, in honor of his benevolent achievements in flood control. Hundreds of years ago, the Yu lineage (not surnamed the same Yu as "Yu the Great") from Sixiyan Village joined the legendary Huizhou merchants, and formed their own network. Wealthy merchants returned home with funds that they contributed to the construction of academies, ancestral halls, bridges, and roads.

第七章 江南廊桥遗存带

02 — 韩家庄桥

江西省婺源县紫阳镇韩家庄自然村

一条无名小河丝带一般缠绕着韩家庄村，偶尔有打鱼的小船悄悄划过水面。河岸两侧森林茂密，从远处看似朵朵绿色的云，韩家庄桥是一座两孔廊桥，坐落在村子小河出口上。

02.Hanjiazhuang Bridge — Hanjiazhuang Natural Village, Ziyang Town, Wuyuan County, Jiangxi Province.

An unnamed river winds around much of Hanjiazhuang Village like a silk ribbon. One can occasionally see fishing boats quietly paddle across the waters here. On either riverbank one can see dense forests which look like green clouds from a distance. At the point where the river exits the village there is a covered bridge with two spans.

03—上庙桥

江西省婺源县江岭镇庆源村

庆源村又名"小源""小桃源",山峦紧紧围抱,只有一条小路进出。双层石拱上庙桥在众多村桥中最具特色,二层桥楼高16米,四门进出,日月形墙窗。正门两侧古代对联"描来新月半弓封成石磴,添得闲云一片锁住花村"。

03.Shangmiao Bridge — Qingyuan Village, Jiangling Town, Wuyuan County, Jiangxi Province.

Qingyuan Village, also known as Xiaoyuan or Xiaotaoyuan, is surrounded by dense hills, with only one path in and out. The stone arch bridge here stands out among all rural bridges. Its two-story gallery house is 16 meters high, and the bridge has four gates from which to go in and out. Windows in the walls are shaped in the form of the sun and the moon. The main gate has a couplet written on it stating, "Resembling a new moon's crescent bow sealed in stone With the addition of a flower village locked in by a cloud alone."

04 — 上大夫桥

江西省婺源县坨川篁村，南宋（1127 — 1279 年）

篁村原有两座南宋（1127 — 1279 年）时期的廊桥，"上大夫双桥"为纪念宋代出了"双进士"，都是木平梁结构仅存一座。

上大夫桥地处水口长 20 米。桥面、桥柱、桥顶均为木质结构，廊屋两侧设靠背木椅，青瓦素墙木栏杆，马头墙桥口。

04.Shangdafu Bridge — Tuochuanhuang Village, Wuyuan County, Jiangxi Province, built during 1127-1279.

This village originally had two covered bridges built in the Southern Song Dynasty (1127-1279) to commemorate two scholars who earned top rank in the imperial exams. They both were simply supported timber beam bridges, but only one remains. It is located at the village's waterfront. It is 20 meters long, and its deck, columns, and roof are all made of wood material. Both sides of the bridge have wooden chairs, timber railings, and the gallery house is covered by grey tiles. There are horse-head walls at both ends of the bridge.

05—水口虹桥

江西省婺源县障山乡菊径村，明代（1368－1644年）

一墩两孔，上部廊道全木结构。改建为廊桥始于明代，未曾遭受大的伤损，是全村百姓共爱之桥。

05.Shuikouhong Bridge – Jujing Village, Zhangshan Township, Wuyuan County, Jiangxi Province, was built during 1368-1644.

This bridge has one pier and two spans. The gallery house on the top of the bridge is entirely a timber structure. The bridge was rebuilt as a covered bridge in the Ming Dynasty. It has not suffered any serious damage, and it is deeply beloved by all villagers here.

06—题注桥

江西省婺源县镇头镇游山村，北宋太宗朝（976—997年）

原名函谷亭桥，始建年代与村庄同，独孔石拱廊桥。因曾有"彩凤"飞落，自古婚嫁以桥为发端，迎亲家人在桥外等候，送亲家人鸣炮三通，迎娶仪式方可进行。"走完桥，喜酒才可以喝起来。"农历正月十五，游山村户户连龙闹元宵，祈庆丰年，游龙沿水街热烈奔腾，以穿桥为莫大吉祥。

06.Tizhu Bridge — Youshan Village, Zhentou Town, Wuyuan County, Jiangxi Province, built during 976-997.

Originally known as Hanguting Bridge, it was built at the same time as the founding of the village. The stone arch bridge has a single span. Since ancient times, marriage ceremonies have started at this bridge. This is because a colorful phoenix is said to have descended here. The party receiving relatives would wait outside the bridge, while those sending relatives off would fire a cannon three times, allowing the wedding ceremony to proceed. As the saying would go "Walk over the bridge before the wedding wine can be drunk." In addition, on the fifteenth day of the first lunar month, households from Youshan Village and from the surrounding mountain villages participate in the Lantern Festival here. At that time, Youlong Yanshui Street becomes bustling with excitement, and it is considered highly auspicious then to cross the bridge.

第七章 江南廊桥遗存带

07—霞港桥

江西省婺源县中云镇霞港村

整座廊桥平稳匀称、古意依然。长25米、宽3米、高4米、十二开间,硬山顶满铺小青瓦。各地的游客喜欢霞港村的幽静,青山绿水间的廊桥令其流连忘返。

07.Xiagang Bridge – Xiagang Village, Zhongyun Town, Wuyuan County, Jiangxi Province.

Two piers formed out of red granite support the body of this bridge, and the whole structure is smooth and symmetrical and has an old air to it. The bridge is 25 meters long, 3 meters wide, 4 meters high, and has a gallery bay with twelve bays. Its flush gable roof is covered with small grey tiles.

08—贾耕桥
江西省婺源县镇头乡朱村

古驿道交叉纵横遍布婺源全县，是徽商外出必经之路。许多廊桥位于驿道与河流的节点，是徽商获得喘息、回望故乡的地方。徽商"以贾代耕"，"贾"是出路，"耕"是根本，此廊桥因而得名。独孔石拱、木柱瓦顶敞廊式廊桥，长12米、宽2.6米、高4.2米。

08.Gugeng Bridge – Zhucun Village, Zhentou Township, Wuyuan County, Jiangxi Province.

Ancient courier roads intersect all over Wuyuan County, forming the essential roads which Huizhou merchants used to set out from. Many covered bridges are located at the nodal points of roads and rivers. Huizhou merchants "replaced farming with trade." "Trade" was said to be their way out, and "farming" served as their foundation. The bridge was named after this concept. This is a stone arch bridge with a single span. It has timber columns, a tiled roof, and is an open gallery house covered bridge. It is 12 meters long, 2.6 meters wide, and 4.2 meters high.

09—麟清桥

江西省婺源县浙原乡十堡村水口，清道光二十三年（1843年）

桥下河水清澈，一群鱼儿悠然自得，鳞片的幽光清晰可见，故桥名为"麟清"。原为木平梁全木结构廊桥，后因村人维修时珍惜树木，将木梁改为水泥梁，保留敞廊式穿斗结构、木柱瓦顶的古貌。桥长22米、宽3米、高4.2米。

09.Linqing Bridge – Shuikou, Shibao Village, Zheyuan Township, Wuyuan County, Jiangxi Province, built in 1843.

The water below Linqing Bridge is clear, and fish leisurely swim there, the light green shade of their scales clearly visible. As a result, the bridge was named Linqing Bridge. Originally this was a simply supported timber beam covered bridge. Later because villagers highly valued timber during repairs, they replaced the timber beams with cement ones, and retained the bridge's open gallery house *chuandou* structure, as well as its ancient appearance through the use of tiles and timber columns. The bridge is 22 meters long, 3 meters wide, and 4.2 meters high.

10 — 彩虹桥

江西省婺源县清华镇,南宋(1127—1279年)

南宋僧人胡济祥三年募集桥资,四年建成廊桥。覆盖最后几片青瓦时天空惊现彩虹,借"两水夹明镜,双桥落彩虹"之意定桥名。石墩木梁,长140米、宽3米、六亭五廊桥体。桥墩不等距,船艏船舯船艉形制,廊亭、桥墩一体建造构成抗击洪水冲压的独立体系。部分桥体毁损,整桥不必大拆大建。构件不用昂贵木料,梁栋不作雕刻彩绘只为降低修复成本。维修不必聘请高级匠师,村里木匠能够胜任。

10. Caihong Bridge — Qinghua Town, Wuyuan County, Jiangxi Province, built during 1127-1279.

Hu Jixiang, a Southern Song Dynasty abbot raised funds for the construction of the bridge in three years. The bridge was then constructed in four years. As the last few grey tiles were being installed, a rainbow suddenly appeared in the sky. Master bridge builder Hu Yongban used a verse from the poet Li Bai "two clear mirror rivers encircle, two bridges arched like rainbows above them" to give the bridge its name. The bridge has stone piers and timber beams. It has four piers and five spans and is 140 meters long and 3 meters wide. It has six pavilions and five gallery structures. The bridge piers are separated by varying distances, and they are shaped like the bow and stern of a ship. The bridge pavilions and piers are built according to an independent flood resistant system. If a portion is destroyed, the entire bridge does not have to collapse. The components do not use expensive wood material, and beams are not carved or painted in order to reduce repair costs. As a result there is no need to hire a senior craftsman for repairs, and village carpenters can complete any necessary work.

11—庆远桥

江西省婺源县秋口镇田湾村

又名情缘桥。一墩两孔、条石平梁、木柱瓦顶、穿斗式结构，长11米、宽3米、高5米、九开间。石墩迎水面因洪水挟裹石块撞击，久而久之如同钝口刀锋。廊桥一侧紧靠的"水月宫"村庙同为明代建筑。

11.Qingyuan Bridge – Tianwan Village, Qiukou Town, Wuyuan County, Jiangxi Province.

Also known as the Qingyuan Bridge. The bridge is a stone simply supported beam covered bridge. It has one pier and two spans, as well as timber columns and tiled roof. It is a *chuandou* structure bridge that is 11 meters long, 3 meters wide, and 5 meters tall. Its gallery house has nine bays. The sides of the stone piers facing oncoming water have become blunted overtime because of the impact of waters and floods. On one side of the bridge there is a village temple called Shuiyuegong that was built in the Ming Dynasty as well.

12—龙岗桥

江西省婺源县秋口镇龙岗村

一墩两孔、圆木平梁、垒石桥墩、木柱瓦顶、穿斗式结构榫卯衔扣，长21米、宽2.8米、高5米、十一开间，两侧设护栏长凳。龙岗桥距离庆远桥2.5公里，同为驿马大道与深山村庄群落的连接点，是山地优质粮食、竹笋、茶叶、药材、林菌家畜、家禽外运的唯一通道和乡民休息站。

12.Longgang Bridge – Longgang Village, Qiukou Town, Wuyuan County, Jiangxi Province.

It was built by the one-pier two-span timber beam *chuandou* structure with stone piles, timber columns and tiled roof. And the component are connected by mortise and tenon joint. It is 21 meters long, 2.8 meters wide, 5 meters high, with balusters and benches on both sides. Longgang Bridge is located not far from Qingyuan Bridge in 2.5 kilometres. It is also the connecting point between Yima Avenue and the community of deep mountain villages. It is the only channel for the transportation of high-quality grain, bamboo shoots, tea, medicals, forest fungi, livestock and poultry, and the rest station for villagers in mountainous areas.

13—罗溪桥

江西省婺源县思口乡河山坦村

穿斗式全木结构廊桥，长36米，宽3米，高5米，两墩三孔平梁，单脊硬山顶，上覆小青瓦，桥廊十一开间。

13.Luoxi Bridge — Heshantan Village, Sikou Township, Wuyuan County, Jiangxi Province.

The bridge is a timber *chuandou* style covered bridge. It is 36 meters long, 3 meters wide, and 5 meters high. It has two piers, three spans, and simply supported timber beams. It has a single-ridge flush gable roof. It is covered with small grey tiles and has an 11-bay gallery house.

14—护禾桥

江西省婺源县中云镇中云村

又名亭桥，单孔石拱砖石瓦顶半敞式廊桥。长7.6米、宽3米、高5.2米，位于古时连通景德镇至婺源的通商故道。

14.Huhe Bridge — Zhongyun Village, Zhongyun Town, Wuyuan County, Jiangxi Province.

Also known as the Tingqiao Bridge, it has a single span, a stone arch and a brick-tile roof. It is a semi-open covered bridge, 7.6 meters long, 3 meters wide, and 5.2 meters high. In ancient times, the bridge served an important trade route that connected Jingdezhen to Wuyuan.

15—梅岭桥

江西省浮梁县瑶里镇梅岭村，宋代（960—1279 年）

桥长 9 米、宽 4 米、高 6 米，为独孔石拱全砖石结构半阙型廊桥。廊桥连通的徽饶古道百余公里，山路皆由大块厚实花岗岩铺砌。桥两侧断断续续保留着几百米遗存的古道。徽饶古道已废弃，桥已无人行走。到瑶里古镇游览的人，知道梅岭桥的会到桥边春赏梅花、秋赏桂花。

15.Meiling Bridge — Meiling Village, Yaoli Town, Fuliang County, Jiangxi Province, built during 960-1279.

The bridge is located along the ancient Huirao Road, where more than 100 kilometers of mountain roads are paved by massive pieces of thick granite. The Meiling Bridge served as an important node, and the two ends of the bridge are still connected to several hundred meters of old road. This stone arch bridge is 9 meters long, 4 meters wide, and 6 meters high. The ancient Huirao Road has become overgrown, and Meiling Bridge is no longer crossed. Still, people will go to the bridge to enjoy plum blossoms in spring and osmanthus in the autumn.

第七章 江南廊桥遗存带

16—登云桥

江西省浮梁县江村乡柏川村,清同治七年(1868年)

单孔石拱穿斗式廊桥,长9米、宽3.5米、高6米、五开间,拱券、台阶、门厅全部用规整青石、青砖砌筑,上部的木柱、横梁以榫卯形式连接,牢固稳定。建成后未有大的损坏,只做过局部修缮。

16.Dengyun Bridge – Baichuan Village, Jiangcun Township, Fuliang County, Jiangxi Province, built in 1868.

This stone arch covered bridge has one span, and is 9 meters long, 3.5 meters wide, and 6 meters high. It is a *chuandou* structure with a gallery house with five bays. Its arch, steps, and halls are all built with authentic bluestone and blue-bricks. The upper portion of the bridge has timber columns and simply supported timber beams joined by mortise and tenon technology, making them firm and stable. After completion, there has been no major damage on the bridge, and only partial repairs have been required.

17—富春桥

江西省浮梁县江村乡严台村，明弘治十五年（1502年）

独孔石拱、砖柱、木梁、瓦顶，开敞式凉亭类廊桥。桥长9米、宽3米、高4米，是古代乡民进出村庄的必经要道。

17. Fuchun Bridge — Yantai Village, Jiangcun Township, Fuliang County, Jiangxi Province, built in 1502.

This open style cool-pavilion type stone arch covered bridge has a single span. It has brick columns, timber beams, and a tile roof. It is 9 meters long, 3 meters wide, and 4 meters high. In old times, it was the only way people could enter or leave the village.

四、赣江水系廊桥群
IV. Covered Bridges in Ganjiang River System

01—花桥

江西省靖安县中源乡茶坪村白云峰峡谷，宋代（960—1279年）

中国唯一铭文"文身"的廊桥。花桥如商周青铜器表面布满铭文、图案。数百字铭文，以正楷为主，间杂行楷工整遒劲，字体美、字数多、凿刻深、字形大，图文并茂，古风昭昭。曾名洞桥，清乾隆五十七年（1792年）重建。连接靖安、奉新两县古道。独孔石拱凉亭式廊桥，长20.6米、宽4米、高10米。被列为省级文物保护单位。

01. Huaqiao Bridge – Baiyunfeng Canyon, Chaping Village, Zhongyuan Township, Jing'an County, Jiangxi Province, built during 960-1279.

This is the only covered bridge in China inscribed with "tattoos." This bridge is inscribed with many characters and designs, similar to the inscriptions on Shang and Zhou Dynasty era bronze artifacts. Hundreds of character inscriptions primarily in standard scripts are placed on the bridge, which are well-organized and vigorous. The style of calligraphy is beautiful, with deeply chiseled large-form characters, rendered brilliantly as in ancient times. Huaqiao Bridge, once known as Dongqiao Bridge, was rebuilt in 1792. It connects the ancient road that linked Jing'an and Fengxin counties. The stone arch pavilion-style covered bridge has a single span, and is 20.6 meters long, 4 meters wide, and 10 meters high. It is listed as a Cultural Relic Sites Protected at the Provincial Level.

02—善述桥

江西省修水县新湾乡回坑村回溪，清光绪二十九年（1903年）

又称郎桥。石墩木平梁廊桥，东南至西北走向，长31米，宽5米。桥碑记载："回溪车生咏堂为贯通回溪与外之往来，独出资千余银两，于清光绪二十九年修建善述桥。"桥廊所用木料取自当地山林优质柏木。平梁圆木经桐油数月浸泡，坚硬耐水，抗虫蚁蛀蚀。

02. Shanshu Bridge – Huixi Brook at Huikeng Village, Xinwan Township, Xiushui County, Jiangxi Province, built in 1903.

Also known as Langqiao Bridge, this is a stone pier and timber simply supported timber beam covered bridge that runs from the southeast to the northwest. It is 31 meters long and 5 meters wide. A stele on the bridge states that "In order to connect the Huixi Brook with the outside world, more than 1,000 tael silver were contributed to rebuild Shanshu Bridge in the 29th year of the Guangxu period in the Qing Dynasty (1900)." The timber, used for the bridge gallery construction, came from high-quality cypress forests in the nearby mountains. The simply supported beam-logs were soaked in tung oil for several months to become hard, and to improve resistance to damage from water, termites, and erosion.

中国廊桥

03—三川桥

江西省崇仁县许坊乡三川桥村 清乾隆（1736—1795年）

石拱独孔木结构廊桥，长12米、宽3.8米、高4米、跨径4米、七开间。桥面坡度较大，台阶由独轮车道隔为左右，上下往来两侧不相干扰。桥廊支柱、横梁、檐枋等构件的衔接采用榫卯结构，清末大修一次。三川桥是崇仁县仅存的古代廊桥，整体构造为国内廊桥罕见，对于研究古代桥梁技术、建筑工艺、区域文化具有重要价值。

03.Sanchuan Bridge－Sanchuanqiao Village, Xufang Township, Chongren County, Jiangxi Province, built during 1736-1795.

This single-span stone arch covered bridge is 12 meters long, 3.8 meters wide and 4 meters high. It has a gallery house with seven bays and a span of four meters. The bridge deck has a steep slope, and its steps have two grooves for wheelbarrows on the right and on the left, so that people going up the bridge will not be disturbed by those going down. The gallery house uses supportive columns, transverse beams, architraves, and other parts, which are all joined by mortise and tenon technology. The bridge was once overhauled during the end of the Qing Dynasty. Sanchuan Bridge is the only ancient covered bridge that survives in Chongren County, and it demonstrates unique construction which is rarely seen elsewhere in China. As a result, it is of great value in the research of ancient bridge construction techniques, craftsmanship, and reginal culture.

第七章 江南廊桥遗存带

04—横港桥

江西省黎川县日峰镇篁竹村，宋代（960—1279年）

桥址原为渡口，初建为木结构便桥，水毁后建石墩木梁桥，清乾隆二年（1737年）改建为石拱廊桥。两墩三孔石拱廊桥，长42米、宽5米、高8米。砖石结构廊道长16米，石门石窗、木梁砖墙、单脊双坡顶满覆小青瓦。两端门楣清光绪十六年（1890年）整修。被列为市级文物保护单位。

04. Henggang Bridge – Huangzhu Village, Rifeng Town, Lichuan County, Jiangxi Province, built during 960-1279.

Henggang Bridge is located at the site of a former ferry terminal. Originally a simple timber bridge, it was destroyed by a flood and rebuilt with stone piers and timber beams. Then in 1737, the bridge was converted into a stone arch covered bridge. It has two piers and three arches, and is 42 meters long, 5 meters wide, and 8 meters high. Its brick gallery house is 16 meters long, and has stone gates, stone windows, and timber beams and brick walls. Its double-slope single-ridge roof is covered with small grey tiles. The top of the gate frames at the two ends of the bridge are artifacts of the bridge's renovation in 1890. The bridge is listed as a Historical and Cultural Relic Sites Protected at the Municipal Level.

05—新丰桥

江西省黎川县城南津街

明弘治九年（1496年）由士绅、商贾出资改建为石墩叠木平梁木结构廊桥，长92米、宽4.3米、高8米、二十四开间、五墩六孔，桥面铺砌花岗岩条石。明清时期位于连通黎川县城往福建省邵武、建宁、泰宁等县商道，商旅马帮摩肩接踵。新丰桥与横港桥近在咫尺，有"黎川双虹"之誉。历经水火灾害、兵匪战乱六次塌毁，后均修复。

05.Xinfeng Bridge — Nanjin Street, Lichuan County, Jiangxi Province.

In 1496, local gentry and merchants funded the transformation of the Xinfeng Bridge into a covered bridge with stone piers and combined simply supported timber beams. The bridge has five piers and six spans, and has a gallery house with twenty-four bays. It is 92 meters long, 4.3 meters wide and 8 meters high. Its deck is covered by slabs of granite stone. During the Ming and Qing dynasties, it was a busy and crowed intersection along the trade route that connected Lichuan County with Shaowu, Jianning, and Taining counties in Fujian. It has been destroyed and repaired six times after floods, fires, and warfare. Xinfeng Bridge, and the nearby Henggang Bridge are known as the "Two Rainbows of Lichuan."

06—澄波桥

江西省铅山县湖坊镇陈坊河，唐贞观四年（630年）

唐代澄波和尚募捐，百姓协助兴建。石墩木平廊桥，长60余米、宽4米。桥头建砖石门庭。门额镌刻"河清海晏""风静浪恬"，传为澄波和尚墨迹。桥墩尖锐船艏型，墩尾平直，工匠称为"分水金刚墙"。石墩上纵横堆叠七层方形木枕俗称"喜鹊窝"。两墩之间架设长大贯木主梁，全木结构。被列为省级文物保护单位。

06.Chengbo Bridge — over Chenfang River, Hufang Town, Qianshan County, Jiangxi Province, built in 630.

During the Tang Dynasty, the monk Cheng Bo raised money to build this bridge with the help of local people. It is a timber simply supported covered bridge with stone piers. It has a length of more than 60 meters and a width of 4 meters. A gateway at the bridge head has a plaque inscribed with the words, "A Clear River and Tranquil Seas" and "Calm Winds and Still Waters" said to be written by monk Chengbo. One side of the pier is sharp like a ship bow while the other side is flat. It is called a water-separating *jingang* wall by carpenters. On top of the stone piers are seven criss-crossed layers of timber known as a "magpie nest". In between the piers is the large timber main beam connecting with the complete timber structure. It is listed as a Historical and Cultural Relic Sites Protected at the Provincial Level.

07—登仙桥

江西省乐安县谷岗乡登仙村，北宋开宝（968—976年）

所处地势险要，自古兵家必争。桥身弹痕累累。细长峡谷常有大雾，埋伏千军万马不易察觉。1933年红一方面军在登仙桥反击第四次"围剿"，激战数小时活捉敌军师长、参谋长、旅长各一名，缴获武器一批、大洋数万元。史称"黄陂大捷"。硝烟散去，小桥流水人家的景致再现峡谷。登仙桥麻石砌筑，墩台嵌入岩石。长19米、宽6米、高6米、跨径17米。中华民国元年（1912年）山洪暴发桥毁，中华民国十一年（1922年）重建。被列为市级文物保护单位。

07.Dengxian Bridge – Dengxian Village, Gugang Township, Le'an County, Jiangxi Province, built during 968-976.

Since ancient times, Dengxian Bridge has serves as a heavily contested battleground, and the bridge body has many scars from bullets. It is located in a long and narrow valley that is often wrapped by fog, and has been the site of many well concealed ambushes. In 1933, the First Front Red Army fight against the forth "encirclement and suppression" campaign organized by Chang Kai-shek at the Dengxian Bridge. Through hours of fierce battle, Chang Kaishek's division commander, chief-of-staff, and brigade commander were all taken captive. A batch of weapons and silver coins were subsequently seized. This was known as "the Victory of Huangpi". The valley, however, regained its tranquility after the war. The bridge is built with granite masonry, with its abutments embedded in the surrounding stone. The bridge is 19 meters long, 6 meters wide, 6 meters high, and has a span of 17 meters. The bridge was once destroyed in 1912 by a flash flood and was rebuilt in 1922. Dengxian Bridge is listed as a Historical Cultural Relic Sites Protected at the Municipal Level.

08—永宁桥

江西省石城县延岭乡上柏村，清乾隆三年（1738年）

单孔石拱楼阁式廊桥，长34米、宽5.2米、高4.4米、跨径10.6米、十二开间。永宁桥坚实牢固，古朴大方。中部亭阁设神龛，供奉关公神像。桥基由麻石砌筑，穿斗式全木结构外侧设置木板可遮风雨，歇山顶覆小青瓦。被列为省级文物保护单位。

08. Yongning Bridge – Shangbai Village, Yanling Township, Shicheng County, Jiangxi Province, built in 1738.

This single-span stone arch pavilion covered bridge is 34 meters long, 5.2 meters wide, and 4.4 meters high. It has a span of 10.6 meters. Its gallery house is a timber *chuandou* structure with twelve bays. The structure is strong, simple, and elegant. The pavilion in the middle of the bridge has a shrine dedicated to Guan Yu, a general from the three kingdoms period, worshipped as a deity. The bridge has a hip and gable roof covered with small grey tiles, and the bridge's foundation is made of granite. It has been listed as a Historical Cultural Relic Sites Protected at the Provincial Level.

09—万寿桥

江西省广昌县塘坊镇村里村，清道光元年（1821年）

《广昌县志》记："万寿桥始建于一八二一年（清道光元年），广昌十景之一。初为纯木构造鸦雀薮桥，后因屡遭水患历时三年，耗银九千余元改为石墩拱桥。"三孔联拱砖石廊桥长66米、宽5米、高7米、三孔各跨径13米。桥墩使用长方体石块砌筑，迎水面为舰艏型，顶尖鹰喙用于分解洪水。砖石廊道两端门厅装饰马头墙飞檐，中部顶端建四角挑檐小阁。

09.Wanshou Bridge － Cunli Village, Tangfang Town, Guangchang County, Jiangxi Province, built in 1821.

It is recorded in *The History of Guangchang County* that "Wanshou Bridge, one of the ten scenic spots in Guangchang, was built in 1821. It was at first a pure timber Yaquesou bridge but was reconstructed into a stone arch bridge after repeated floods. The construction took three years at a cost of more than 9,000 silver dollars." The bridge is 66 meters long, 5 meters wide, and 7 meters high. Its three spans are 13 meters long each. The piers are made of rectangular stones, and their sides that face upstream are shaped in the form of a ship bow, with "eagle beak" points used to lessen the impact of flood waters. Both ends of the brick gallery house are decorated with horse-head walls with upturned eaves. In the center there is a small pavilion with a four-corner roof sporting upturned eaves.

第七章 江南廊桥遗存带

10—玉带桥

江西省信丰县虎山乡中心村虎山河谷，清乾隆五年（1740年）

玉带桥以"一弯澄水镜，半璧佩玉带"的弧状桥形得名。连通赣南客家聚集区通往粤北、闽西、湘南商贸古驿道。两墩三孔石拱楼阁式廊桥。桥墩青石砌筑状如船舰，跨径14.3米。桥体弧长88.15米、弦长74.44米、弧弦最大距离10.84米，宽3.8米、三十二开间。两端各建4.2米高砖瓦桥头堡。被列为省级文物保护单位。

10. Yudai Bridge – Hushan River Valley, Zhongxin Village, Hushan Township, Xinfeng County, Jiangxi Province, built in 1740.

Jade Belt Bridge gets its name from its curved bridge shape which is like "a round mirror reflecting clear water, the form of half of a jade belt". The bridge was part of the ancient trade and courier route that connected Hakka settlements in southern Jiangxi Province with north Guangdong, west Fujian, and south Hunan. The stone arch pavilion style covered bridge has two piers and three spans. It is supported by bluestone piers that have the shape of ship bows. The bridge has an arch length of 88.15 meters, and a chord length of 74.44 meters, with a maximum distance between the arch and chord of 10.84 meters. It is 3.8 meters wide and has clear spans of 14.3 meters. Its gallery house has thirty-two bays. Each end of the bridge has a 4.2 meter brick-tile bridge tower. The bridge is listed as a Historical and Cultural Relic Sites Protected at the Provincial Level.

11 — 永镇桥

江西省安远县新龙乡江头村甲江河，清顺治九年（1652 年）

又名五渡水瓦桥，清顺治九年（1652 年）僧人欧阳融募化桥资建造，后遭水毁，清乾隆十四年（1749 年）乡民广捐木石予以重建。长 38.5 米、宽 4.33 米、高 8 米，两墩三孔木平廊桥。船舶形桥墩，顶似鸟喙，客家人称为"鹅胸"。被列为省级文物保护单位。

11. Yongzhen Bridge — over Jiajiang River, Jiangtou Village, Xinlong Township, Anyuan County, Jiangxi Province, built in 1652.

Yongzhen Bridge, also named the Wudushuiwa Bridge, built with alms collected by a monk named Ouyang Rong in 1652. The bridge was destroyed by a flood and was rebuilt in 1749 with wood and stone donated by local villagers. The bridge has two piers and three spans. It is a timber beam covered bridge that is 38.5 meters long, 4.33 meters wide, and 8 meters high. Its piers have the shape of a ship bow with the point resembling a beak, and which Hakka people call a goose breast. It is listed as a Historical and Cultural Relic Sites Protected at the Provincial Level.

12—永安桥

江西省赣州市南康区莲花河，清光绪（1871—1908年）

据《钟氏族谱》记载，以"永以为好既安且吉"确定桥名。永安桥由石墩、石梁、石柱、砖门、木枋、瓦顶组成，为一墩两孔叠梁式平梁廊桥。叠梁承载上部构造，长13.2米、宽4米。桥廊两侧安置长条木凳护栏，4根方石柱挺拔坚固。廊柱遗留两副古联"永留司马题斯柱，安得重阳卧此桥""永怀冀免褰裳者，安坐何须纳履人"。对联将"永安"两字藏嵌其中。

12. Yong'an Bridge – over the Lianhua River, Nankang District, Ganzhou, Jiangxi Province, built during 1871-1908.

As recorded in *The Genealogy of the Zhong Lineage*, the name Yong'an (enternal peace in Chinese) Bridge comes from the statement "for eternal peace and auspiciousness." The bridge is composed of stone piers, stone beams, stone columns, a brick gate, timber architraves, and tiles. It has one pier and two spans, and is a combined beam style simply supported beam covered bridge. The combined beams support the upper structure. It is 13.2 meters long, and 4 meters wide. It is equipped with long benches and guardrails on both sides. Its four rectangular stone columns are strong and steady. There is a couplet on the columns which includes the characters "eternal" and "peace" hidden within the verse.

13—初石桥

江西省定南县鹅公镇石柱村，清同治十二年（1873年）

双坡顶八角灯塔式廊桥，连通赣南至粤东古驿道，辐射赣粤两省十余县。又名柱石桥。桥长16米、宽5米、高16米。桥基、桥面使用桐油拌合石灰浆黏合条石坚固如磐，二层阁楼设置神龛供奉真武大帝。《重修初石桥序》碑记："清光绪乙酉年（1885年）、民国十五年（1926年）、1987年重修。初石桥是本地最早建造的单拱石桥，故称初石桥。是我县仅存的桥亭结构建筑物。"

13.Chushi Bridge – Shizhu Village, E'gong Town, Dingnan County, Jiangxi Province, built in 1873.

Chushi Bridge is a double-slope eight-corner lighthouse-style covered bridge. It connected the ancient courier route that linked southern Jiangxi to eastern Guangdong province, serving ten counties in the two provinces. Also known as Zhushi Bridge, the bridge is 16 meters long, 5 meters wide, and 16 meters high. Its foundation and deck are held together with a mixture of tung oil and lime, which makes the structure solid and strong. A shrine in the pavilion on the second floor is dedicated to Zhenwu (a Taoist deity). As stated in the *Preface for the Reconstruction of First Stone Bridge*, "the bridge was the first single-span stone arch bridge built in this area. It was thus called Chushi Bridge. It was rebuilt in 1885, 1926, and 1987. It is also the only pavilion bridge left in our county."

14—太平桥

江西省龙南县杨村镇车田村峡谷太平江，明正德（1506－1521年）

桥长50米、宽4米、高17米、两孔跨径11.9米、12.9米，拱高6.2米。花岗石一墩两块，桐油、石灰、红糖、糯米浆为灰浆砌筑。砖石结构大跨度拱形四通桥亭，长30米、高10米，跨径8.4米。亭顶有三对翘角飞檐，顶覆小青瓦。被列为国家级重点文物保护单位。

14.Taiping Bridge — over Taiping River in Chetian Village, Yangcun Town, Longnan County, Jiangxi Province, built during 1506-1521.

The bridge is 50 meters long, 4 meters wide, and 17 meters high. Its two spans are 11.9 meters and 12.9 meters long. The height of its arch is 6.2 meters. The bridge is built with granite and has one pier and two approaches, and uses tung oil, lime, brown sugar and glutinous rice to serve as mortar. On the bridge deck, there is a pavilion built with bricks and stones and composed of a large-span arch. The pavilion is 30 meters long, 10 meters high, and has a span of 8.4 meters. The pavilion roof has three pairs of protruding corners with upturned eaves, and is covered by small grey tiles. The bridge has been listed as a Historical and Cultural Relic Sites Protected at the National Level.

第七章　江南廊桥遗存带

中国
廊橋

第二节·江苏省、上海市、浙江省北部廊桥
Section II Covered Bridges in Jiangsu Province, Shanghai, and North Zhejiang Province

一、大运河水系廊桥群
I. Covered Bridges in Grand Canal River System

01—五亭桥

江苏省扬州市瘦西湖莲花堤,清乾隆二十二年(1757年)

为恭迎圣驾,巡盐御史高恒主持盐商襄赞,于乾隆皇帝第二次南巡前夕将此桥建成。又名莲花桥,长55米,跨度7.13米的中心桥洞与12座桥洞相通。桥阶下另设两孔扇形桥洞。桥面中亭为重檐四角攒尖式宝亭,亭顶坡度较陡,向上呈尖锥状,四条垂脊交会于宝顶。翼亭为单檐攒尖式,置中亭周围。

01.Wuting Bridge – Lianhua dam of Shouxihu Lake, Yangzhou, Jiangsu Province, built in 1757.

In order to greet the "sacred throne," Shi Gaoheng, a salt merchant, presided over the construction of Wuting Bridge on the eve of Emperor Qianlong's second Southern Tour. Another name of the bridge is Lianhua Bridge, and it is 55 meters long. Its central archway is 7.13 meters long, and is connected with another 12 archways. There are another two fan-shaped archways set underneath the bridge steps. The pavilion in the center of the bridge deck is slightly higher than the other pavilions that have multiple-eave four-corner roofs and protruding tops.

中国廊桥

02—小飞虹桥

江苏省苏州市拙政园，明正德四年（1509年）

拙政园为明代御史王献臣归隐苏州营建。小飞虹桥取意南朝宋人鲍照《白云》诗句"飞虹跨秦河，泛雾青轻弦"而名。红色桥栏倒映小湖，波影潋滟宛如飞虹，婷婷怡似琉玉。桥体为一跨石梁，微微拱起呈八字形。桥面两侧设有万字护栏，三间八柱，廊屋檐枋下饰以倒挂楣子，两端与曲廊相通。

02.Xiaofeihong Bridge – Zhuozheng Park, Suzhou, Jiangsu Province, built in 1509.

The Zhuozheng Garden was built for the retirement of imperial envoy Wang Xianchen of the Ming Dynasty to his residence in Suzhou. The bridge's name is derived from the poem "White Cloud" by Bao Zhao (who lived from 412-466 AD) that states, "A flying rainbow overlooks the Qin River, and overflowing mist is made into light strings." The red bridge railing is reflected in the lake, sparkling like a rainbow, and graceful as rare jade. The bridge is a three-span stone-beam bridge with a slight *bazi* shaped arch. On both sides of the bridge are guardrails. The gallery house has three bays and eight columns. The eaves of the gallery buildings are decorated with suspended railings, and the bridge buildings are connected with a winding pathway.

03—永丰桥

江苏省苏州市锦溪古镇溪河，清代（1636－1912年）

晨晖夕照、东风徐来时分，金辉、花英尽洒，碧采充溢水面，璀璨恍如流动的锦绸，故面古镇得名锦溪。永丰桥长8米，宽4米，高4米，桥堍、主梁均采用红灰色花岗岩石料，8根红色立柱支撑着庑殿式廊顶。

03.Yongfeng Bridge – Xihe River, Jinxi Ancient Town, Suzhou, Jiangsu Province, built during 1636-1912.

In the morning and evening, when the east wind slowly blows, the sun's rays and flowers sparkle in the water, appearing like a flow of brocaded silk. For this reason the town is named Jinxi, "brocaded creek." The ancient Yongfeng Bridge is 8 meters long, 4 meters wide, and 4 meters high. Its footings and main beams are made of red-grey granite. Eight red pillars support its *youdian* style roof.

04—三亭桥

江苏省吴江市同里古镇，清代（1636—1912年）

同里位于古运河东，由5个淡水湖分离为7个小岛，49座古桥连为一体，三亭桥是唯一的廊桥，为"小桥、流水、人家"典型景致。因水隔桥连成就了共同的乡里，故名同里。桥垛由河岸伸展进入河中数米，上架条石为梁，两侧有护栏。4根直立、斜立木柱支撑3个青瓦廊亭。两边廊亭略小，为歇山顶。中亭较大攒尖顶竖立宝珠钮。桥坡石阶高5.8米、宽2.6米、长13米。

04. Santing Bridge – Tongli Ancient Town, Wujiang County, Jiangsu Province, built during 1636-1912.

Tongli is located to the east of an ancient canal. It is separated by five freshwater lakes into seven islands. Forty-nine ancient bridges are connected together here. The Three Pavilion Bridge is the only covered bridge among them. The bridge projects several meters into the water from its base on the shore, and stones are rested on top to serve as beams. Protective guardrails are placed on both sides of the bridge. Four upright and four oblique timber columns are used to support three tiled pavilions. The pavilions on either side of the bridge are slightly smaller than that at the center, and are covered by hip and gable roofs. The central pavilion is relatively big, and has a cone shaped roof. The stone steps on the bridge slope are 5.8 meters high, 2.6 meters wide and 13 meters long.

05 — 古荷桥

江苏省昆山市锦溪古镇

据传宋孝宗赵昚（1163－1190年）皇帝与爱妃陈氏一同到锦溪品尝湖鲜，流连山水。陈妃不幸早逝，令宋孝宗难以释怀，就将她安葬在锦溪小湖岛，并钦赐建造庙宇、楼阁亭台、水榭画舫。古莲桥是莲池禅院的附属建筑。古莲桥残损毁塌。1996年苏州市文物部门出资将陈妃水墓、莲池禅院、古莲桥一并复建。

05.Guhe Bridge — Jinxi Ancient Town, Kunshan, Jiangsu Province.

According to legend, Emperor Zhao Shen of the Song Dynasty (1163-1190) and his beloved concubine Chen went to Jinxi to taste fresh delicacies and to linger among the mountains and waters. Concubine Chen's subsequent unfortunate and early death was hard on Zhao Shen. He buried her in a small lake island in Jinxi, and built a temple, pavilion-pagoda, and a pleasure boat structure there in her honor. The Ancient Lotus Bridge is a component of the Lianchi Chan Temple. Previously the bridge was damaged and collapsed. In 1996, the cultural relics department of Suzhou invested in the reconstruction of Concubine Chens water tomb, Lianchi Temple and the Gulian Bridge.

第七章 江南廊桥遗存带

中国廊桥

06—怀古桥

浙江省湖州市南浔古镇古运河，清代（1636－1912年）

南浔古镇清代建有一座百余米的三亭廊桥，名故乡桥。镇里70岁以上的老人都走过，1960年以后因碍航拆除。古镇乡民怀念那座长长的"故乡桥"，2006年依照原样在古运河上建造了一座曲廊式全木结构廊桥，为纪念先民功德，定名"怀古桥"。

06.Huaigu Bridge － Ancient Canal of Nanxun Ancient Town, Huzhou, Zhejiang Province, built during 1636-1912.

During the Qing Dynasty, a three-pavilion covered bridge was built in Nanxun Ancient Town that was over 100 meters long. It was called Guxiang Bridge. Local people over seventy-years-old recall walking over it. However in the 1960s it was demolished because it impeded river transport. In memory of the long "Guxiang Bridge" villagers built a timber-structure covered bridge with a winding corridor on the ancient canal imitating the look and structure of the old bridge. In order to commemorate the achievements of their predecessors, they named it "Huaigu Bridge".

07—镇东桥

浙江省余姚市四明山镇庙下村梨洲溪，明代中期

镇东桥为村口上洋庙僧人募资建造。目前由村民王东平、唐凤彩夫妇守护。单孔石拱廊桥，长 13.2 米、宽 4.6 米、高 4.7 米、跨径 7.5 米，五开间。桥面卵石平铺，桥墩石块砌筑。溪流至镇东桥前有 90°急转弯，转弯处山岩突兀，急流受山体阻挡锐势大减。

07.Zhendong Bridge — Lizhou Creek, Miaoxia Village, Simingshan Town, Yuyao, Zhejiang Province, built in the mid-Ming Dynasty.

The construction of Eastern Village Bridge was funded by donations raised by the monks at Shangyang Temple, which is located at the entrance of the village. The couple Wang Dongping and Tang Fengcai are the guardians of the bridge. This single-span stone arch bridge is 13.2 meters long, 4.6 meters wide, 4.7 meters high, and has a span of 7.5 meters. Its gallery house has five bays. The bridge's deck is covered with cobblestones, and its piers are built of stones. The stream makes a sudden 90-degree turn before approaching the Eastern Village Bridge. However the speed of the water decreases sharply due to being impeded by mountain rocks at this point.

第七章 江南廊桥遗存带

08—镇西桥

浙江省余姚市四明山镇棠溪村

单孔石拱、木柱瓦顶廊桥。棠溪村位于四明山镇的西端，廊桥自落成取名镇西桥。棠溪村四面环山，东溪、南溪分别从东面、南面流入汇合形如一朵海棠，村庄因此得名棠溪。桥南百余株数百年树龄的金钱松、香枫树、香樟树，被视为风水林，历代受到保护。

08.Zhenxi Bridge – Tangxi Village, Simingshan Town, Yuyao, Zhejiang Province.

This is a single span stone arch covered bridge with timber columns and tiles. Tangxi Village is located at the west end of Simingshan Town. Consequently, the bridge is named the "West Town Bridge". Tangxi Village is surrounded by mountains, and is located at the site of the confluence of streams coming from the east and south, forming the appearance of a Chinese flowering crabapple. Thus the village gets its name. There are hundreds of trees planted to the south of the bridge which are over a hundred years old, such as golden larches, maple trees, and camphor trees. The area is regarded as a "*fengshui* forest", and as a result the trees here have been protected by people generation after generation.

中国
廊橋

09—惠民桥

上海市青浦区朱家角古镇北大街，清代（1636—1912年）

惠民桥搭盖草棚，全木结构，中华民国元年（1912年）重建。20世纪60年代被拆除，1996年镇民陈先生捐资10万元复建。朱家角河上桥多，但廊桥仅此一座。长9米、宽1.5米、高4米、四开间。

09.Huimin Bridge — Beidajie Street, Zhujiajiao Ancient Town, Qingpu District, Shanghai, built during 1636-1912.

The Huimin Bridge is covered with a thatched roof, and its structure is made of timber. It was rebuilt in the first years of the Republic of China. It was demolished in the 1960s. In 1996, Mr. Chen, a townsman, donated 100,000 yuan for its reconstruction. There are many bridges that span the Zhujiajiao River but this is the only covered bridge. It is a timber structure, 9 meters long, 1.5 meters wide, 4 meters high and has a gallery house with four bays.

10—坝子桥

浙江省杭州市艮山门东河，北宋（960—1127年）

又名顺应桥，始建于北宋（960—1127年）时期。廊桥下筑有东河与京杭大运河交汇的滚水坝，故名坝子桥。据《西湖游览志馀》记载"坝子桥北宋时居民甚盛，碧瓦红檐，歌管不绝"。古称"凤凰亭"，清咸丰八年（1858年）被焚毁，清光绪九年（1883年）重建。1980年市政府出资，整修桥面石阶和凤凰亭。

10.Bazi Bridge – East River of Genshan Gate, Hangzhou, Zhejiang Province, built during 960-1127.

Also known as Shunying Bridge. It was first built in the period of the Northern Song Dynasty (960-1127). Under the covered bridge, there is a dam where the East River converges with the water of the Beijing-Hangzhou Grand Canal. As a result, the bridge is called the Dam Bridge. According to *Xihu Tour Records*, "the residents of the Dam Bridge were very prosperous during the Northern Song Dynasty, and they constantly sang under the grey tiles and red eaves." In ancient times, it was known as the Fenghuang Pavilion. In 1858, it burned down, and was reconstructed in 1883. In 1980, the municipal government funded the renovation of the bridge deck and stone steps.

11—晴雨亭桥

浙江省杭州市河坊街胡雪岩故居，清同治十一年（1872年）

处在巅峰之际的胡雪岩，历时3年建造一座占地11亩的宅院，被称为江南第一豪宅。晴雨亭桥是整个院落的点睛之作。四周楼榭假山环绕，将西湖"花港观鱼"演绎成"花桥观鱼"，为三孔石拱重檐八角攒尖顶亭桥。1999年由杭州市政府投资按照原模样、原结构、原营造，用时16个月修缮。被列为国家级重点文物保护单位。

11.Qingyuting Bridge – Hu Xueyan's former residence in Hefang Street, Hangzhou, Zhejiang Province, built in 1872.

When in power, Hu Xueyan ordered the construction of a villa with an area of 11 *mu*, which took three years to build and was acclaimed as the most luxurious house in the South of the Yangtze River area. The Qingyu Pavilion Bridge is the most impressive part of the garden, surrounded on four sides by pavilions and rock gardens. This bridge is like the famed West Lake scenery "Observing Fish at the Flower Pond," but here instead people observe fish by the bridge instead of by a pond. This is a three span stone arch pavilion bridge with multiple-eaves and an octagonal pointed roof. In 1999, the bridge was renovated according to its original form in 16 months, with funding from the Hangzhou municipal government. It is listed as the Major Historical and Cultural Sites Protected at the National Level.

12—玉带桥

浙江省杭州市西湖曲院风荷湖堤，清雍正九年（1731年）

桥碑记载，浙江总督李卫建玉带桥，为亭式廊桥，石墩石台木柱歇山顶，两墩三孔上斜石阶，重檐翘角廊亭覆小青瓦，汉白玉栏杆雕刻龙凤波涛、莲叶荷花。中华民国期间损毁，1983年文物部门按照原桥尺度式样修复。"玉带晴虹"是清代西湖十八景之一。

12.Yudai Bridge – Fenghe Lake Embankment, Quyuan, West Lake, Hangzhou, Zhejiang Province, built in 1731.

According to the bridge's stele, Zhejiang governor Li Weijun built the Yudai Bridge. It is a pavilion type covered bridge with stone piers and stone abutments, together with timber columns and a hip and gable roof. It has two piers and three spans, as well as slanted stone steps. Its multiple-eave pavilion roof has upturned corners and is covered with small grey tiles. Its "Han White Jade" (*hanbaiyu*) protective wall is carved with dragons, phoenixes, waves, lotus flowers, and lotus leaves. It was damaged during the Republic of China period. In 1983, the department of cultural relics restored the bridge according to its original scale and design. The "Jade Belt and Sunny Rainbow" is one of the eighteen scenic spots of the West Lake dating to the Qing Dynasty.

第七章 江南廊桥遗存带

中国廊桥

13—云溪桥

浙江省淳安县瑶山乡何家村云溪河

又名花桥，是浙西山区河网地带百姓往来重要通道。长32.6米、宽3.4米、桥墩间跨距9.2米。两墩三孔穿斗式平梁木结构廊桥，硬山顶覆小青瓦。桥北石碑刻有"清道光六年（1826年）拾壹月"等文字。为避免廊桥被洪水整体损毁，分为各自独立的四段体系整合衔接建造。

13.Yunxi Bridge — Yunxi River, Hejia Village, Yaoshan Township, Chun'an County, Zhejiang Province.

Also known as Huaqiao Bridge, the Yunxi Bridge is an important passageway for people living in the mountainous area in western Zhejiang Province criss-crossed by rivers. It is 32.6 meters long, 3.4 meters wide with spans of 9.2 meters between piers. It is covered by a flush gable roof, and topped by small grey tiles. At the north end of the bridge, there is a stone stele inscribed with the words "built in the 11th month of lunar calendar in the 6th year of the Daoguang reign of the Qing Dynasty." The bridge is constructed with four separate sections, designed so as to avoid total destruction of the bridge in the case of flooding.

14—逢源双桥

浙江省桐乡市乌镇

　　两墩三孔石梁石阶、木柱木梁六开间穿斗式廊桥，长16米、宽4米、高6米。桥下铁栅是水流关卡，左右两桥合并故称双桥。桥廊中央筑1.5米高青砖隔墙，上部由通顶木质花窗分隔，两桥下部各有两道石栏。传说男女并行难免滋生尴尬，故有男左女右过桥的习俗。另有来走左边、往走右边、左右逢源升官发财之说。

14.Fengyuanshuang Bridge — Wuzhen Town, Tongxiang County, Zhejiang Province.

This is a two pier three span bridge with stone beams and stone steps, as well as a six-bay *chuandou* gallery house with timber columns and timber beams. It is 16 meters long, 4 meters wide, and 6 meters high. Under the bridge there is an iron grid used to stem the flow of water. Since the bridge is formed by two adjacent bridges, it is called a double bridge. In the center of the gallery house, a 1.5-meter-high grey brick partition wall is built, with its upper part separated by a wooden window. There are two stone fences at the lower part of the two bridges. It is said that on this bridge, men would pass left while women would pass right to avoid causing embarrassment by walking together.

15-送子来凤桥

浙江省嘉善县西塘古镇小桐街东侧，明崇祯十年（1637年）

俗称来凤桥、晴雨桥、情侣桥、鹊桥，小桐街东端连接千米廊棚。三孔石板廊桥，清康熙、清道光年间大修。千年古镇经纬弄堂分布小河两岸，送子来凤桥宽7米，正中有花墙相隔，行人各走一边。老人讲述"新婚夫妇走走桥，南边送子，北边来凤"。

15.Songzilaifeng Bridge – East of Xiaotong Street, Xitang Ancient Town, Jiashan County, Zhejiang Province, built in 1637.

Also known as the Laifeng Bridge, Qingyu Bridge, Qinglv Bridge and Queqiao Bridge, this bridge is next to the east end of the Xiaotong Street. It has three spans and is a stone covered bridge. It was renovated during the Kangxi and Daoguang periods in the Qing Dynasty. Alleys passing through this ancient town are situated on both sides of the river. The Songzi Laifeng Bridge is 7 meters wide, and is divided into two walkways by a lattice wall in the middle. According to local elders, it is said that if a newlywed couple walk on the bridge's south end they will have a son, and on the north end they will have a daughter. Songzi in the bridge name refers to "delivering sons", and Laifeng to "arriving phoenixes", which in this case signifies the birth of daughter's.

16—雨读桥

浙江省嘉兴市乌镇西栅昭明书院西入口

东西走向，单孔石平梁廊桥，长 10.25 米、宽 3.72 米、跨径 4.25 米。桥亭北侧筑墙开有三扇木窗，南侧安置美人靠（木背靠椅）供游人休憩，观赏水乡风景。

16.Yudu Bridge — west entrance of Zhaoming Academy, Xizha, Wuzhen Town, Jiaxing, Zhejiang Province.

The single-span stone beam covered bridge running from east to west, is 10.25 meters long and 3.72 meters wide, with a span of 4.25 meters. The north side of the bridge pavilion is walled in which there are three wooden windows, and a beauty bench (wooden backchair) is set in the south side for visitors to have a rest and enjoy the scenery of the watery countryside.

二、甬江水系廊桥群
II. Covered Bridges in Yongjiang River System

01—普济桥

浙江省新昌县巧英乡三坑村，清嘉庆十九年（1814 年）

又名棚桥，桥廊梁檩留有"时嘉庆拾玖年拾月总理国学生俞熠、刘正辉督造"墨书。普济桥连接通往宁海的驿道，长16.8 米、宽 4.8 米、高 8 米，木柱 36 根，单脊双坡顶，两侧设木板桥栏，桥面铺木板。桥架由 20 余根圆木按双八字形组合支撑，其中 14 根圆木嵌入岸壁石槽。

01.Puji Bridge — Sankeng Village, Qiaoying Township, Xinchang County, Zhejiang Province, built in 1814.

Also known as the Pengqiao Bridge, the gallery house's purlin beam still bears the black-ink characters "built under the supervision of Yu Yi and Liu Zhenghui in the 10th month of the lunar year during the 19th year of the reign of Jiaqing in the Qing Dynasty (1814)." The Puji Bridge connected the courier road that led to Ninghai. It is 16.8 meters long, 4.8 meters wide and 8 meters high. Its has 36 timber columns, and a single-ridge double-slope roof. Timber railings are installed on both sides and its deck is covered by timber boards. The bridge is supported by a combined double *bazi* brace consisting of more than 20 logs. Of these, 14 logs are embedded directly into the stone groves on the walls of the riverbank.

02—洞桥

浙江省宁波市洞桥乡洞桥村，宋太祖建隆元年（960年）

古称光溪洞桥，长26.8米、宽8米、九开间，两侧设置木制挡雨板，是浙东最古老的石墩、伸臂式木梁廊桥。廊桥两端遗留对联"巩固舆梁广通过客，苍茫瑞水频泛来船"，"舟楫频摇波依月，楼台倒影水中天"。

02.Dongqiao Bridge — Dongqiao Village, Dongqiao Township, Ningbo, Zhejiang Province, built in 960.

Dong Bridge, formerly called Guangxidong Bridge, is 26.8 meters long, and 8 meters wide. Its gallery house consists of nine bays. Timber awnings are put up on both side of the bridge. It is the oldest timber cantilever beam covered bridge with stone piers in Zhejiang Province. Couplets are displayed on both entrances to the bridge. One reads "Across a bridge made firm with beams do travelers pass. On vast auspicious waters do many ships arrive." The other reads "A paddle shakes the moon that lingers in the wave. A pavilion is reflected inversely in the river's sky."

中国廊桥

03—百梁桥

浙江省宁波市宁峰乡百梁村鄞江，宋代（960—1279年）

使用一百余根杉木架设横梁故名，号称"浙东第一桥"。唐中宗神龙元年（705年）建起木船连板的"浮梁桥"。宋神宗熙宁元年（1068年），邑首朱文伟筹谋建桥，惜未动工病逝。其子朱用谥继承父志捐资，百姓协助于宋神宗元丰元年（1078年）建成长百米、宽7米、高10米、六墩七孔石墩木梁廊桥。后廊桥北端焚毁，朱老太公孙子朱世则、朱世弥重建。朱氏三代善举千年流芳。元顺帝、明成化、清嘉庆、清咸丰、清光绪年间修缮。

03.Bailiang Bridge — over Yinjiang River in Bailiang Village, Ningfeng Township, Ningbo, Zhejiang Province, built during 960-1279.

The lower part of the bridge's lookout structure uses 100 horizontal beams made of Chinese fir, and this is where its name comes from. It is known as the "Number One Bridge in East Zhejiang". It was built in 705 as a "floating beam bridge", a pontoon bridge consisting of connected timber boats. In 1068, Zhu Wenwei, the head of the region, prepared plans for the construction of a bridge, but he died before the work started. His son Zhu Yongmi then carried out his father's wish by donating funds for a bridge, and was aided by the efforts of local people. As a result, in 1078 they completed a covered bridge 100 meters long, 7 meters wide, and 10 meters high. It has six piers and seven spans, and is composed of stone piers and timber beams. The northern part was later destroyed in a fire which was rebuilt by the grandsons of great-grandfather Zhu—Zhu Shize and Zhu Shimi. The kindness of these three generations has been passed down for a long time. Hundred Beam Bridge was restored in the Shundi period of the Yuan Dynasty, the Chenghua period of the Ming, and the Jiaqing, Xianfeng and Guangxu periods of the Qing Dynasty.

第七章 江南廊桥遗存带

04－万安桥

浙江省宁波市横街镇林村

又名洞桥。长 16 米、宽 3.2 米、跨径各 5 米、三开间，二孔石拱木廊桥，南北向横跨浣花溪。16 根木柱支撑硬山顶，南北桥堍设踏阶十三级，抬梁穿斗式结构。清早期重建后一直未有改建、添建。桥孔高度大于桃源溪最大洪峰高程，有足够的泄洪空间。村民喜欢桥的清雅俏丽，对其呵护有加。

04.Wan'an Bridge — Lincun Village, Hengjie Town, Ningbo, Zhejiang Province.

Also named Dongqiao Bridge, Wan'an Bridge is 16 meters long, 3.2 meters wide, and has a span of 5 meters. Its gallery house has three bays. It spans the Huanhua Stream from north to south. Its approaches have 13 steps at each end, and it has a *tailiang* structure with a flush gable roof supported by 16 timber columns. Since the early Qing Dynasty, there have been no additions or renovations on the bridge. Its span is higher than the peak flood elevation of the Taoyuan Stream, and adequate room for the discharge of flood water is provided. Villagers admire the bridge's elegance and good looks, and it has been well protected by them.

05—广济桥

浙江省宁波市南浦乡南渡村，宋代（960—1279年）

又名南渡桥。宋哲宗绍圣三年（1096年）奉化主簿李肃主持募捐，百姓相助重建。宋光宗绍熙元年（1190年）建成两墩三孔木石砖瓦结构廊桥，长51.68米，宽6.6米。元至元二十三年（1286年）主簿卢振龙主持复建，两侧加建石亭一座。明洪武、明天启、清雍正、清乾隆、清嘉庆年间和1986年大修。被列为省级文物保护单位。

05.Guangji Bridge – Nandu Village, Nanpu Township, Ningbo, Zhejiang Province, built during 960-1279.

Guangji Bridge, also known as Nandu Bridge, was rebuilt in 1096 when Li Su, the secretary of Fenghua County raised donations for it, together with additional assistance from local people. In 1190, it was retrofitted as a timber stone and brick covered bridge with tiles. It contains two piers and three spans. It includes four groups of stone supports, each group containing six column-style stone pier supports. A timber pavilion is constructed on the bridge deck as well. It is 51.68 meters long, and 6.6 meters wide. In 1286, the county secretary Lu Zhenlong oversaw the restoration of the bridge, and added a stone pavilion at each of its sides. The bridge underwent extensive repairs in the Hongwu and Tianqi periods of the Ming Dynasty, the Yongzheng and Jiaqing periods of the Qing Dynasty, and also in 1986. It is listed as a Historical and Cultural Relic Sites Protected at the Provincial Level.

06 毓秀桥

浙江省青田县阜山镇陈宅村,明万历四年(1576年)

单孔石拱砖石结构廊桥,依山傍溪古树环绕,小巧秀丽精致,原村埂梁村民喜爱。桥北侧有"毓秀桥"和"万历四年创建"的题记,数百年来几度修缮增建,安然保留着初建时的模样。长13.8米,宽3.3米,高3米,拱径5米,廊屋五间,外侧设置12根方形砖柱,当中两侧设廊栅靠背椅,四角攒尖阁楼顶,小青瓦,桥面鹅卵石铺道。被列为省级文物保护单位。

06 Yuxiu Bridge — Chenzhai Village, Fushan Town, Qingtian County, Zhejiang Province, built in 1576.

Surrounded by ancient trees, this single-span stone arch covered bridge has a brick structure and is situated beside mountains and rivers. It is much beloved by villagers because of its delicate, graceful, beautiful, and refined look. There are inscriptions of "Yuxiu Bridge" and "built in the fourth year of the Wanli reign (1576)" at the north part of the bridge. It has been overhauled several times over the past several hundred years, but still remains true to its original look. The bridge is 13.8 meters long, 3.3 meters wide, 3 meters high, and has an arch that spans five meters. Its gallery house has five bays. There are 12 rectangular brick columns on the outer side of the gallery house, and in its center are chairs with backrests. The bridge has a pavilion with a four-corner pyramidal roof covered by small grey tiles. The bridge deck is covered with cobblestones. It is listed as the Historical and Cultural Sites Protected at the Provincial Level.

07—长安桥

浙江省宁波市溪口镇栖霞坑村,清同治元年（1862年）

单孔石拱桥，长 18.7 米，宽 17 米，拱高 5 米，横跨于南培岭水。桥面由鹅卵石与碎石砌成，连接紧密美观，形成简单大方的图案。桥上木屋自古为村民遮阳避雨，桥南两株香樟四季碧绿。

07.Chang' an Bridge – Qixiakeng Village, Xikou Town, Ningbo, Zhejiang Province, built in 1862.

This is a single-span stone arch bridge that is 18.7 meters long and 17 meters wide. Its arch is 5 meters high, and spans the Nanpeiling River. The compact and beautiful bridge deck is made of cobblestones and gravel arranged in simple large-scale patterns. The timber gallery house on the bridge has been used to shelter villagers from sunshine and rain. There are two camphor trees at the southern end of the bridge that are green all year round.

08—关爷殿桥

浙江省宁波市溪口镇敏坑村敏溪

早名镇难桥，后因桥头建了一座关爷庙改名。始建年代无考，据乡民介绍："与桥侧一株550年树龄的香樟同期，大致为明成化时期（1465－1487年）。"石拱独孔木柱瓦顶廊桥，至今仍在为乡民上山砍柴、采药、挖笋提供便利。敏坑村地处凤凰山东麓，村老讲"这里上有一线天，下有小溪源，故称敏坑"。关爷殿桥连接山谷十来个自然村的"孟沿岭古道"，是当下生态旅游热线。

08.Guanyedian Bridge — Minxi Stream, Minkeng Village, Xikou Town, Ningbo, Zhejiang Province.

Originally called the Zhennan Bridge it was renamed Guanye Temple Bridge because a Guanye Temple (dedicated to Guan Yu, a general during the Three Kingdoms Period in China) was installed on one of its ends. It is not clear when the bridge was built, but according to a villager "it is as old as the camphor tree besides the bridge, which is over 550 years old, so it was probably erected during the Chenghua period of the Ming Dynasty (1465-1487)." This single-span stone arch covered bridge has timber columns and a tile roof. It is still is used by villagers who cross it on their way to chop wood, collect herbs and dig bamboo shoots in the mountains. Minkeng Village is located on the east side of Phoenix Mountain. Guanye Temple Bridge connected the old Mengyanling Road that linked together dozens of villages in the valley, and which is now a popular scenic path of ecotourism.

09—卧波桥
浙江省宁波市袁家岙村龙溪，清乾隆二十四年（1759年）

袁家岙村《袁氏宗谱》记，清乾隆二十四年（1759年）族人"叠木为梁，架分七进"，建造了一座楼阁式木梁廊桥，长24米，宽6.4米。

09.Wobo Bridge – over Longxi Stream at Yuanjia' ao Village, Ningbo, Zhejiang Province, built in 1759.

The Genealogy of the Yuan Family records that in 1759, lineage members built a pavilion style timber beam covered bridge, with combined timbers serving as beams. It is 24 meters long and 6.4 meters wide.

Chapter VIII   Covered Bridges in Other Areas

In addition to the above areas, several unique bridges can be seen in the Tibet Autonomous Region and the Lingnan area. For example, the "Sunlight City" located above the Qinghai-Tibet Plateau-there is a "Liuli Bridge" located in the city gate of Lhasa. The bridge is a stone-beamed covered bridge. It was built during 627-649 in the Tang Dynasty and was rebuilt in the Qing Dynasty. It was originally the traffic pass way of the ancient city of Lhasa, but now the river has dried up.

The Guangji Bridge in Chaozhou, Guangdong Province of the Lingnan area also known as the "Xiangzi Bridge", is one of the "four famous bridges" in China. It is also an "an isolated case" of the ancient bridges combining the beam bridges, pontoons and arch bridges. It was built in 1171 of the Southern Song Dynasty, and was rebuilt in the Yuan, Ming and Qing Dynasties. Guangji Bridge is composed of the east and west beam bridge sections and the middle pontoon section. The east and west bridge sections are twelve-span and seven-span stone pier covered bridges, and the middle bridge section is a floating bridge connected by 18 bridge wooden ships. The stone piers of the beam bridge section are mostly ship-shaped piers formed by criss-crossing of thin strips of stone. They vary in size and shape, and are mostly caused by multiple damages of the pier. Each pier is built with pavilions or pavilions in the style of Chaozhou and Shantou area, either individually or in combination, with various shapes and features.

中国廊桥

第八章 其他地区遗存的廊桥

除上述地区外，在西藏自治区以及岭南地区尚能见到数座独特的廊桥。如位于青藏高原之上的『日光城』——拉萨的城关就有座『琉璃桥』。该桥是座石梁廊桥，相传始建于唐贞观年间（六二七至六四九年），重修于清代，原为拉萨古城内外的交通要道，但现在河已干涸。

而岭南地区的如广东潮州的广济桥，又名『湘子桥』，是中国『四大名桥』之一，也是国内集梁桥、浮桥、拱桥于一体的古桥『孤例』，始建于南宋乾道七年（一一七一年），元、明、清三代均有重修。广济桥由东、西梁桥段与中间浮桥段组合而成。东、西桥段分别为十二孔、七孔石墩石梁桥，中桥段为十八艘木船连接而成的浮桥。梁桥段的石墩多为细条石纵横交错叠砌而成的船形墩，大小不一，形态各异，多因桥墩屡次损毁修复所致。每个桥墩上都修建有潮汕地域风格的亭或阁，或单个或组合，形态各异，极具特色。

中国廊桥

第一节 · 雪域高原廊桥遗存
Section I Covered Bridges on the Tibetan Plateau

01—波日桥

四川省甘孜藏族自治州新龙县乐安乡雅砻江，清代（1636 — 1912 年）

波日桥连接云南丽江、四川稻城、理塘、甘孜，直至青海甘德南北大通道。藏族建筑大师设计指挥构筑。叠木伸臂式拱梁，长125米、宽3米、跨径60米。有"康巴第一桥"盛誉，被列为国家级重点文物。中华民国十九年（1930年）噶厦政府军队进驻新龙，烧毁6座藏式伸臂桥，唯有波日桥幸存。中华民国二十二年（1933年）民间建筑师率领藏族工匠维修一新。

01. Bori Bridge — Yalong River, Le'an Township, Xinlong County, Ganzi Tibetan Antonomous Prefecture, Sichuan Province, built during 1636-1912.

Bori Bridge connects Lijiang, Daocheng, and Litang counties and Garze prefecture in Sichuan Province to the Gande North-South Passage in Qinghai. A Tibetan architectural master completed the design of the structure. It is a timber cantilever arch-beam bridge composed of combined wooden beams. It is 125 meters long, 3 meters wide, and has a span of 60 meters. It is called "The Tibetan Khampa Area's Number One Bridge" and is listed as a Historical and Cultural Relic Sites Protected at the National Level. In 1930, the army of the Tibetan Kashag government council stationed in Xinlong burned down six Tibetan-style cantilever bridges. Only the Bori Bridge survived. In 1933, a vernacular architect, led Tibetan craftsmen in restoring the bridge.

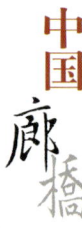

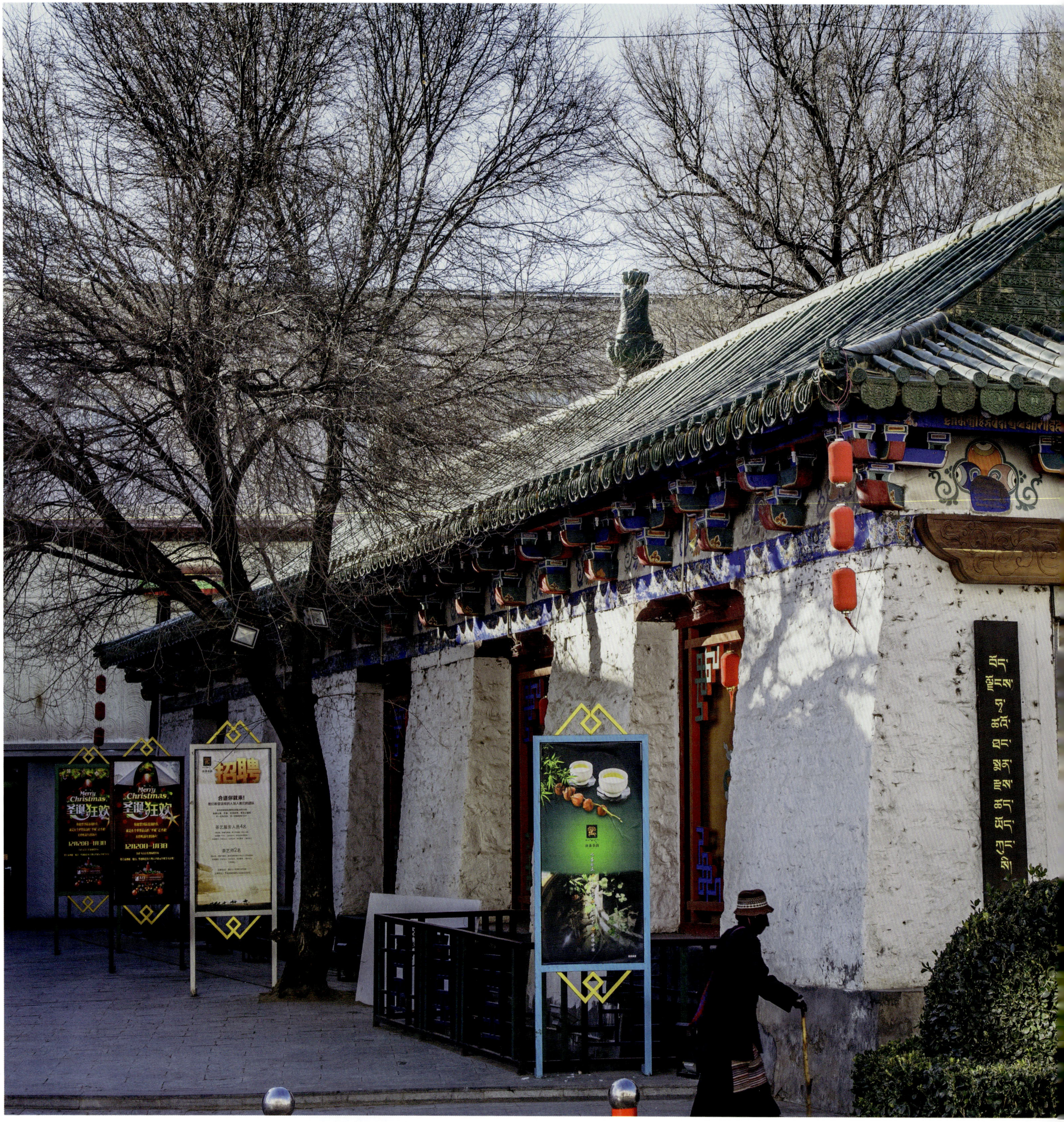
Merry Christmas
圣诞狂欢
Merry Christmas
圣诞狂欢
招聘

02—琉璃桥

西藏自治区拉萨市大昭寺西街，唐贞观十九年（645年）

中国海拔最高的廊桥。藏语称"宇妥桑巴"，意为绿松石桥，被列为自治区重点文物保护单位。石木结构跨径28.5米、宽6.8米，甬堂式桥廊石墙厚1米无立柱。5个宽2.3—2.5米孔洞间距2.6米、高3.2米，属汉藏结合建筑。四檐翘角安置琉璃龙首，屋脊中央竖立高1米琉璃宝顶，两端设琉璃供果脊幢。河流上游被改道后已见不到"琉璃桥下琉璃水"。

02.Liuli Bridge — West Street of Jokhang Temple, Lhasa, Tibet, built in 645.

This is the highest covered bridge in China. The Glazed Bridge is called "Yutuo Sangba" in Tibetan, meaning that it is a turquoise stone bridge. It is listed as the Major Historical and Cultural Sites Protected at the Level of the Autonomous District. The bridge is built of stone and timber. It is 28.5 meters long, 6.8 meters wide, the gallery walls are 1 meter thick, and there are no internal supporting columns. The five arches under the bridge are 2.3 to 2.5 meters wide, 3.2 meters high, and are set 2.6 meters apart. The structure reflects the influence of both Han and Tibetan architecture. There are glazed dragon heads on the upturned corners of the four eaves, and in the center of the roof ridge is a one meter tall glazed treasure top. There are also glazed designs of fruit on both ends of the ridge. It is said that after the upper reaches of the river were diverted, "one no longer sees glazed water underneath the glazed bridge".

第二节 · 岭南地区廊桥遗存
Section II Covered Bridges in the Lingnan Region

一、潮州市母亲河，韩江上的巨星——世界首座开合式、国内最长廊桥
I. The First Folding Bridge in the World and the Longest Covered Bridge in China, as the Superstar across Hanjiang River, the Mother River of Chaozhou

广济桥

广东省潮州市东门外韩江，明正德八年（1513年）建成。

宋乾道七年（1171年）始建，明正德八年（1513年）建成。长515米石墩、石梁廊桥亭屋126间，西端十墩长165米，东端十三墩长286米，之间由18只小船托载浮桥连接。每日上午10时浮桥连接百姓通行，下午5时浮桥撤走船只航行。清雍正二年（1724年）放置在西桥八墩、东桥十二墩上的两尊硕大铁牛，于清道光二十二年（1842年）被洪水冲走一尊。民谣传咏"潮州湘桥好风流，十八梭船二十四洲，二十四楼台二十四样，二只牲牛一只溜"。广济桥与赵州桥、洛阳桥、卢沟桥并称中国古代四大名桥，同列国家级重点文物保护单位。

Guangji Bridge — on Hanjiang River outside of the East Gate of Chaozhou, Guangdong Province, built in 1513.

Guangji Bridge was first built in 1171, and further additions were completed in 1513. The bridge is 515 meters long and is supported by stone piers and stone beams. Its gallery house pavilion structure has 126 bays. It is composed of three parts: the west end has ten piers and is 165 meters long; the east end has 13 piers and is 286 meters long; and its pontoon bridge in the middle is spanned by 18 small floating boats. At 10 o'clock in the morning, the pontoon bridge is linked with the other two segments, allowing people to travel along it. After 5 p.m. the middle section is opened, and only boats can pass. In 1724, two huge ox statues made of iron were cast, one placed on the eighth pier of the west bridge segment, and the other on the 12th pier of the east bridge segment. In 1842, however, one of the statues was lost to a flood. As a folksong describes, "the bridge scene is so great, 18 ships, 24 lands, 24 pavilions and 24 shapes, two cattle, and one that escapes!" The bridge is renowned as one of China's four famous ancient bridges, the other three being Zhaozhou Bridge, Lugou Bridge, and Luoyang Bridge. All four are listed as the Major Historical and Cultural Relic Sites Protected at the National Level.

二、余荫山房廊桥
II. Covered Bridge in Yuyin Ancestral Garden

余荫桥

广东省广州市番禺区南村镇东南角北大街，清代（1636 — 1912 年）

余荫山房是清代举人邬彬（刑部主事）于清同治三年（1864 年）历时五载建成的一座两亩多的养老花园。其中独孔石拱飞檐翘脚亭式廊桥中"虹桥印月"的景观，深得游人喜爱。

Yuyin Bridge — North Street at southeast Nancun Town, Fanyu District, Guangzhou, Guangdong Province, built during 1636-1912.

Yuyin Garden was built in 1864 by Wu Bin (a secretary in the Ministry of Justice during the Qing Dynasty) for his retirement. It took him five years to complete the garden which covers more than 1,200 square meters. This single-span stone arch covered bridge has a pavilion with upturned eaves. At night when the sky is clear, the moon and rainbow-like bridge are reflected in the river here to the delight of visitors.

三、"石头、木头、水头"资源大县——封开
III. Covered Bridge in Fengkai County, with Rich Stone, Wood and Water Resources

泰新桥

广东省封开县平凤镇平岗村,明嘉靖十二年(1533年)

据《封川县志》记载,此桥"嘉靖十二年(1533年)邑人陈时用等募缘修建,长十余丈,阔一丈,上覆以亭"。桥廊正梁存"大清嘉庆十六年(1811年)岁次辛未十一月十七日壬辰日癸卯时东西社众缘信等重建"墨迹。长10.9米、宽3.4米,方形石柱桥墩,四根石柱一组共四排上托石梁。1987年冬修缮。

Taixin Bridge — Pinggang Village, Pingfeng Town, Fengkai County, Guangdong Province, built in 1533.

As it is recorded in *The History of Fengchuan County*, "In 1533, Chen Shiyong and other villagers collected donations to build the bridge which was over 10 *zhang* long (about 33.3 meters) and 1 *zhang* wide (about 3.3 meters) with a pavilion on top." On the bridge's main beam it is written that the bridge was rebuilt at *guimao* (5 a.m. to 7 a.m.) in the 16th year of the Jiaqing reign in the Qing Dynasty (1811). Taixin Bridge is 10.9 meters long and 3.4 meters wide with square stone piers and four rows with four stone columns each supporting the bridge's stone beams. The bridge was renovated in the winter of 1987.

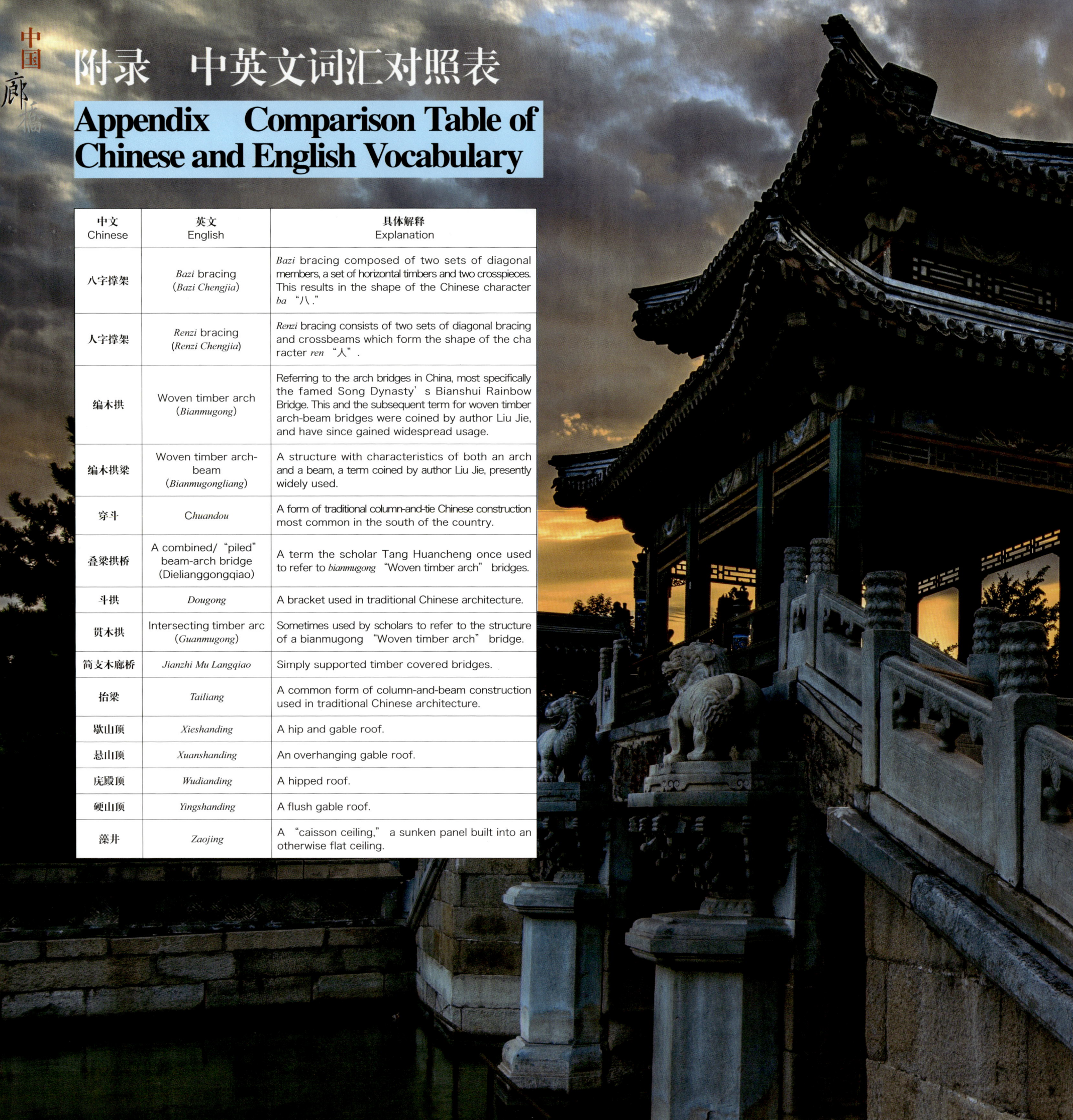

附录　中英文词汇对照表
Appendix　Comparison Table of Chinese and English Vocabulary

中文 Chinese	英文 English	具体解释 Explanation
八字撑架	*Bazi* bracing (*Bazi Chengjia*)	*Bazi* bracing composed of two sets of diagonal members, a set of horizontal timbers and two crosspieces. This results in the shape of the Chinese character *ba* "八."
人字撑架	*Renzi* bracing (*Renzi Chengjia*)	*Renzi* bracing consists of two sets of diagonal bracing and crossbeams which form the shape of the character *ren* "人".
编木拱	Woven timber arch (*Bianmugong*)	Referring to the arch bridges in China, most specifically the famed Song Dynasty's Bianshui Rainbow Bridge. This and the subsequent term for woven timber arch-beam bridges were coined by author Liu Jie, and have since gained widespread usage.
编木拱梁	Woven timber arch-beam (*Bianmugongliang*)	A structure with characteristics of both an arch and a beam, a term coined by author Liu Jie, presently widely used.
穿斗	*Chuandou*	A form of traditional column-and-tie Chinese construction most common in the south of the country.
叠梁拱桥	A combined/ "piled" beam-arch bridge (*Dielianggongqiao*)	A term the scholar Tang Huancheng once used to refer to *bianmugong* "Woven timber arch" bridges.
斗拱	*Dougong*	A bracket used in traditional Chinese architecture.
贯木拱	Intersecting timber arc (*Guanmugong*)	Sometimes used by scholars to refer to the structure of a *bianmugong* "Woven timber arch" bridge.
简支木廊桥	*Jianzhi Mu Langqiao*	Simply supported timber covered bridges.
抬梁	*Tailiang*	A common form of column-and-beam construction used in traditional Chinese architecture.
歇山顶	*Xieshanding*	A hip and gable roof.
悬山顶	*Xuanshanding*	An overhanging gable roof.
庑殿顶	*Wudianding*	A hipped roof.
硬山顶	*Yingshanding*	A flush gable roof.
藻井	*Zaojing*	A "caisson ceiling," a sunken panel built into an otherwise flat ceiling.

附 录
中英文词汇对照表

后记

中国具有丰富多元的自然地理景观与悠久灿烂的历史文化，廊桥作为古老的建筑艺术存在，也是中华各民族历史文化的重要组成。为了总结和回顾中国廊桥的发展历程、技术水平、艺术风格和建设成就，发掘桥梁发展的珍贵历史文化遗产，2018年3月，中国公路学会组织编纂大型文献类科普图书《中国廊桥》，经过一年半时间的努力，2019年9月最终定稿。值此新中国成立70周年之际，正式出版。

本书主创兼摄影吴卫平先生，经过长达20年的实地拍摄，考察记录520余座廊桥，拍摄图片5万余幅，踏访数不清的高山大川，足迹遍及大江南北，涉及国土面积450余万平方公里。吴卫平先生独创性的探索，为我国廊桥遗存的整体面貌，勾勒出一个清晰的轮廓。

本书总撰稿人上海交通大学教授、廊桥研究专家刘杰先生，对中国现存的廊桥进行归纳梳理，并为本书撰写绪论、各廊桥遗存带概述共计10万余字，使本书具有了宝贵的学术研究价值。此外，他领导的廊桥研究团队承担了全书的英文翻译工作。

奉献给读者的《中国廊桥》共收录了中国不同地区、不同历史时期最具代表性的廊桥360余座，涵盖华北廊桥遗存带、西北廊桥遗存带、西南廊桥遗存带、中南廊桥遗存带、东南廊桥遗存带、江南廊桥遗存带，集中展现了中国廊桥遗存的整体面貌。

受资料所限，本书收录的廊桥不包括香港、澳门和台湾地区。

由于《中国廊桥》涉及的桥梁范围广、历史跨度大，遗漏和偏颇之处难免，敬请各界人士指正。

在本书的编辑和出版过程中，得到交通运输部、国家新闻出版广电总局等有关部门和桥梁专家、学者、国际友人的鼎力帮助，在此谨致以诚挚的谢意。

《中国廊桥》编委会
2019年9月

Postscript

There are abundant geographical landscape and long history in China. The covered bridge as art of ancient architecture is an integral part of the Chinese history and culture. China Highway and Transportation Society started the compilation of the literature book, China's Covered Bridges, in March 2018 and finished it in September 2019 in order to sum up the development process, the technology, the artistic style and the construction achievements of the covered bridge and to explore its historical and cultural heritage. The book is officially published on the occasion of 70th anniversary of the founding of the People's Republic of China.

Mr. Wu Weiping, the chief editor and photographer of this book, has visited over 520 covered bridge scattered in 4.5 million sqm all over China and taken over 50,000 photos in the past twenty years. His original investigation outlined the status of the covered bridge remains in China.

Prof. Liu Jie at Shanghai Jiao Tong University, the chief writer of the book, summarized the existing covered bridges and wrote more than 100,000 words of the introduction and the chapters' preface of each area of the covered bridge, which remains and adds academic values to the book. Besides, his team has taken on the English translation of this book.

China's Covered Bridges contains over 360 covered bridges in various regions in various historical periods, including the covered bridge remains belts of the north, the northwest, the southwest, the central south and the southeast China, as well as the south of Yangtze River. It reflects the overall status of the covered bridge remains in China.

The materials collected are within certain limits, and this book's compilation of covered bridges does not include those in Hong Kong, Macau and Taiwan.

Due to the large historical span and the wide range of the covered bridge involved in the book of China's Covered Bridges, the omissions and biases are inevitable. Welcome to correct us.

Sincere thanks are given to the Ministry of Transport, the State Administration of Press, Publication, Radio, Film and Television, and all the experts, scholars, foreign friends who provided great support.

China's Covered Bridges Committee
September 2019

中国廊桥
CHINA'S COVERED BRIDGES